Ex Libris

William Kraus

Triumph and Turmoil

Triumph

A Personal

New York

and Turmoil

History of Our Time by

EDGAR ANSEL MOWRER

Weybright and Talley

To Lilian, muse, critic and gentle reader

Contents

I shall hold my own

MOTTO OF THE ROYAL HOUSE OF ORANGE

The
Beginnings

*By his neesings a light doth shine and his
eyes are like the eyelids of the morning.*
JOB 41:18

1

Son of the Pioneers

*La vallée du Mississippi est, à tout prendre,
la plus magnifique demeure que Dieu ait jamais
preparée pour l'habitation de l'homme.*
ALEXIS DE TOCQUEVILLE

UNTIL I WAS ABOUT TEN, the most influential person in my life was unquestionably my brother Paul. He embodied all that seemed most desirable. In the first place he was there.

My mother, a country girl from Illinois, was anything but permissive, something for which I have always been thankful. I loved her
dearly. But she was bedridden for years and unable to give me more
than partial attention.

To my fair-skinned, red-haired father I gave love and total respect.
He inspired self-confidence, a quality which, as a petted infant facing
a midwestern male world, I needed badly. As a traveling salesman,
however, he was absent much of the time. But I recognized behind his
deep-set, steel-blue eyes, an unconquerable yet tender spirit upon which
I could depend.

Paul's four years and eight months' seniority made him an apt
substitute as protector and model. What a difference between the games
he and his friends played and the insipid amusements of boys of my
own age!

Accordingly, I made myself a nuisance by stubbornly trying to
enforce my less developed presence upon him and his companions.

Success here was due to two circumstances for which I was in no
way responsible. At the time I was three, Paul decided that by proper
training and discipline I could be made a distance runner. Thereafter,
whenever we went on an errand together, he compelled his whimpering
kid brother to run all the way by switching his legs.

Again, alone in our neighborhood, I was uniquely qualified for

3

essential roles in two important games. Why thick curls falling to the shoulders were considered essential to a Texas steer I cannot now imagine. But they were. Playing the part of the steer meant being lassoed and thrown to the ground while in full gallop. Yet I so relished the society of the bigger boys that I willingly accepted the bumps and bruises.

My other privileged role was that of Indian chief. On the subject of Indians, the Mowrer boys were experts. How could it be otherwise when my father's close friend was none other than the famous Pawnee Bill, Buffalo Bill's only real rival in the Wild West field? When his show came to Bloomington, we always attended the first performance as his guests and he often dined at our house. Sometimes he even told us stories of his beloved Pawnees!

Foremost among the Indian lore he imparted was insistence upon feathered headdresses. Obviously, when they were not cowboys or soldiers, most of my brother's friends would have preferred to be Indian chiefs. Yet, properly, they could not—their hair was too short. Only little Edgar had enough hair to support the essential turkey feathers. Therefore, from the age of four or five, he was indispensable as Sitting Bull.

Such an Indian role had its inconveniences. Sitting Bull may have killed General Custer, but on East Grove Street in Bloomington, Illinois, the U.S. Army or the intrepid cowboys took care of Sitting Bull. At the least, he was scalped; at the most, shot and left for dead on the ground, after which, trembling but exalted, he could go home. On one All-Indian occasion, Sitting Bull, curls and all, was captured, roped to a tree, burned at the stake, symbolically, of course, and entirely forgotten until well after supper time.

On July 4 we regularly waged war by throwing firecrackers at each other's sand fortresses. For since my fifth year, my otherwise rigid father had extended to his younger son the privilege of shooting off fireworks. My sixth and last July in Bloomington was the best.

Then in the autumn of 1898 we moved from Bloomington to the South Side in Chicago. Still reluctant to accept the handicap of age difference, I continued to seek my brother's company. In most games I was incurably inferior to boys four or five years older. So I fell back on a little-boy game, namely, marbles. There nothing counted but skill and the strength of knuckle to knock an agate or carnelian out of a large ring. This strength I set about developing.

At first I lost heavily to almost anyone, and wore out my mother's patience with ever renewed requests for money for more marbles. But by the end of the second marble season I was regularly coming home with full pockets. This ability to provide marbles of almost any size and color became a new key to my brother's company. Paul had invented a way of using marbles for varied and fascinating floor games, beside which those described by H. G. Wells would have seemed tame. Marbles became anything one wanted, from Wild West combatants to medieval knights in stories taken straight from books.

Meanwhile I discovered still another method of gaining acceptance by older companions. In a contest of courage, nothing prevented a little boy from equaling bigger boys. All he needed was never to refuse a dare. To be sure, confronted with a thirty-foot drop, my legs literally shook, even though I knew from experience that the sandpile below would cushion the landing. The price of paradise was not inconsiderable, and twice before the age of ten, I was carried home senseless.

Unconsciously, I now believe, I was trying to overcome an inherent timidity which made me reluctant to stand up to hostile challengers. Father had warned me of the consequences of not doing so, and three times I failed him. At the age of five, I watched weeping while a neighbor boy of eight, to show his contempt of my long curls ("little girl"), urinated in my new straw hat. At eight, I acknowledged publicly that I was "licked" by the superior pugilism of a smaller boy whom I could easily have thrown to the ground. And at fifteen I shrank from a confrontation with a grocery boy who had stolen my bicycle. Father properly refused to buy me another and I promised myself never again to refuse a human challenge.

In the long run, of course, in seeking acceptance by my elders, I was waging a losing fight. Paul, up to twelve or thirteen years, might, when better company was not available, still enjoy floor games with a precocious little brother who furnished the marbles. But with the onslaught of puberty, this changed. He developed an interest not only in girls (in my eyes, unworthy of his attention), but in other fields, social, intellectual, and artistic, which I could not share with him. At fourteen or fifteen he wrote his first poem.

Less and less he went to play on the vacant lot. More and more he resented my attempts to be with him. My grief at neglect became resentment. When he rebuffed my wistful requests that he "play with me" or take me along, disappointment sometimes turned to fury.

One day out by the woodshed on Shady Island in Lake Minnetonka, I bitterly reproached him for his neglect. He, in turn, sharply enlarged upon my tender years and small size. Suddenly, in the worst rage I can ever remember having felt in all my life, I grabbed a nearby hatchet and hurled it at his head. Fortunately he had started running in time. But the miss was close.

Then with awful suddenness I realized that I had almost killed him! Better my own death than that! Twice in subsequent years I was tempted to take a human life. But never again did I allow anger to rise to the point of madness.

Thereafter, my attitude toward Paul became ambiguous. On the one hand, I continued to try to keep up with him. When he swam half a mile, I plunged in the very next day and did the same thing, with him accompanying me the whole distance in a rowboat, almost with a certain pride. On the other hand, his new activities failed to interest me.

Thus I found my brother's "alienation" from our former common pursuits easier to accept than I had imagined. Though I still resented his "abandonment," I turned wholeheartedly to the society of boys, and eventually of girls, of my own age group and inclinations. It was high time.

Now what I dreamed of most was travel and high adventure.

Chaucer had called March "the month in which the earth was born." To interpreters of omens, I might note that on March 8, 1892, at the hour of my birth, the planet Saturn was in the ascendant. This meant a great deal to two German "astrologers" whom I was to meet thirty-three years later.

Or, to continue the game, one can assume that mine was a case of atavism. Genealogy buffs have, on both sides of our family, unearthed an almost unbroken series of adventurous forebears. From that John Scott of Long Island who reached back to King Malcolm of Scotland; from the wayward daughter of the House of Orange, Anneke Bogardus; from the Christian Maurer who sailed from Rotterdam for America on the good ship *Polly* back in 1735, all known ancestors had been restless. Father's immediate forebears had pushed across the Appalachians, first into "dark and bloody" Kentucky, then into Ohio, where they had helped runaway slaves escape to Canada, and finally to Illinois.

Great Grandfather Sellman, at the age of seventy, went "west" to fight Indians, successfully if one could trust the evidence of the notches on his gunstock.

Mother's direct ancestors, the Scotts and Shoudys, drove no farther west than Illinois. But a great uncle Scott found gold in the Black Hills, lost it in a single night at a gaming table, and settled down in Fargo. Mother's youngest brother, Edgar, for whom I was named, died in California after a stormy life. Only rarely have I hankered for roots, and never for long. I had the pioneer spirit "in my blood," and the only stability I sought lay inside.

For Christmas when I was eight, I asked for and received a large atlas. Thereafter I spent uncounted hours "traveling." Flat on the floor with legs up, the huge book spread out before me, I greedily mopped up descriptions of the great world. Reinforced by simple accounts of strange peoples, this preoccupation with maps not only made subsequent school geography easy, but developed a sense of topography which never failed me in later years.

Father had been a country boy and saw to it that we early acquired "what boys ought to know." He taught me to have no fear of woods or water, to sleep out anywhere, and, at twelve, to shoot a rifle and a revolver. Once when my mother protested that one escapade or another was too risky, Father put her right: "Nell, if a boy has not learned to look out for himself by the time he is ten, he never will."

A little later, Mother allowed me to join the new Hyde Park Y.M.C.A. Life thereafter became fuller by a weekly gym class: setting up exercises, "apparatus," competitive games and swimming.

Almost the first day at the "Y," a dark-haired boy about my size challenged me to a wrestling match. He was well muscled, but I had sworn never again to refuse a challenge. For a good half hour we struggled without either scoring a fall. Then, exhausted, we decided to call it a draw.

Gradually we became inseparable. Albert Green was an indifferent golfer but already so adept at tennis that he later became one of the ten best players in the United States. All our other tastes were similar, from books to chess and poker.

I brought Al together with another close friend, Samuel Austin Pope. Austin's was one of the few families in our neighborhood to own a motorcar, and he managed to communicate to us an enthusiasm for "horseless carriages." We learned to distinguish one make of automobile from another, not only by its appearance but by its mechanical characteristics. Austin, who shared his father's mechanical ability, even induced me to help mount a toy hot-air engine on a toy wagon to produce our own car! The "Pope-Hotty," as we called it, had neither driver nor steering gear and was difficult to manage. But it ran for blocks along the sidewalk and that was all that mattered.

This association with Austin served me well when my father brought to Crystal Lake, Michigan, where we were spending the summer, a twenty-two-foot motorboat, slim and graceful with an eight horsepower, two cylinder engine. With it came a mechanic to show the fifteen-year-old son how to run and keep it in order.

We named it the *Wistik* (from the Dutch, "if I knew"), because we were never sure if it would start or not. Once I had to take the whole thing apart and then, without help, get it together and running again. This I found a bore.

Yet an adventure in the *Wistik* taught me how legends start. One moonlit night, I took my mother and two or three guests for a cruise. Half a mile from shore, we ran out of gas. The lake was dead calm and we might have stayed there tranquilly until daylight brought rescue. Instead, I stripped to my underwear and swam for the nearest cottage. I knocked at the door and explained our plight. The occupant generously lent me a can of gas and the use of his boat.

I rowed back, filled the tank, rowed ashore again, swam back to Mother and the guests, and we continued our moonlit cruise.

Half a century later, old people at Crystal Lake were still telling how the Mowrer boy had swum out half a mile holding a can of gasoline between his teeth like a St. Bernard dog carrying a keg of brandy to a snowbound traveler!

Girls exploded into my life when I was sixteen. Twice I met rebuffs. One red-haired, popular, and studious girl, after accepting my invitation to the Junior Prom (one of the few school dances I deigned to attend), left me stranded at the last moment. A second girl called Ruth first accepted my attentions and then revealed a preference for a handsome football hero. The conclusion was obvious: athletic prowess was the key to a girl's heart.

I determined to excel in sports. My rival had his H.P. (school letters for Hyde Park) in football only. I would win them in three! The football team was clearly beyond the reach of a one hundred and thirty pounder. But there were alternatives less dependent on poundage. Early in the autumn I persuaded Albert and two other Hyde Park students who happened to be in the same group at the "Y," to try out for the school basketball team with me. All four of us made the first team.

Since we were notably lighter than most rival players, we had to pit against their brawn our superior skill, speed, and brains. We managed to reach the zonal semifinals. The school voted us the coveted letters.

Ruth remained unimpressed, but I was no longer trying to convince her but to show myself what I could do if I tried. The number three spot on the tennis team was good for a second set of letters. Playing number two on a successful golf team brought me a third H.P. Thereafter, I regularly appeared in classes wearing the blue and white blazer of the successful athlete.

Just before I left high school, Father encouraged me to take boxing lessons from a retired heavyweight prizefighter named Joe Choynski, who had once fought the great Jeffries to a draw! Joe did not spare his pupils. Once, after he had sent me crashing into a corner, he dropped his hands, stuck out his chin, and hissed: "Now you're mad: come on, hit me, hit me."

So, with blood streaming from my nose, I hit him as hard as I could, a right straight to the point of his chin. Horror! Joe's great body slumped to the floor. Surely, no punch of mine could have jarred that sturdy frame; he must have had a heart attack! Should I call a doctor?

A moment later he arose, grinning cheerfully. "Edgar," he explained, "you have just learned all you need to know for self-protection. Hit any man, no matter how big, square on the button as you hit me, and he'll black out and drop, just as I did."

Later circumstances never compelled me to follow Joe's advice, but it gave me confidence.

The summer after graduating, thanks to Albert Green's superb playing, he and I won the tennis doubles championship against university players at the annual tournament of the Congregational Church Assembly at Crystal Lake. Thereafter, I was far too busy with other matters ever again to compete in organized sport.

Long before entering school, I was reading books. By the age of nine, when Mother took me out of school because of headaches, books had become, with the outdoors, the major influence in my life.

What books? Anything and everything. As a younger son I had access to three libraries—the family's, my older brother's, and my own growing stock. Once kindly relatives and older friends discovered my mania for reading, they relied on gifts of books to solve both the Christmas and birthday problems of little Edgar.

How list the hundreds I read before, say, the age of eleven, when I again returned to school full time, even if I could remember them all?

Among the earliest were the rhymed adventure of one *Miltiades Peterkin Paul*; the *Prince and the Pin Elves*; the *Wizard of Oz*; *Tommy Ann and the Three Hearts* and *Wabeno the Magician*; the Jack Harkaway series; uncounted volumes by G. A. Henty; Howard Pyle's incomparable *Robin Hood* with its unforgettable illustrations; fairy tales; *Treasure Island*; the *Jungle Books*; *Uncle Tom's Cabin*; *Gulliver's Travels*; Slocum's *Sailing Alone Around the World*; Bulfinch's *Age of Fable*; that haunting study of death, *At the Back of the North Wind*; and, above all, *The Quest*, by the Dutch writer, Frederik Van Eeden. The latter was a fantastic account of the inner development of Little Johannes, at first, in sand dunes not unlike those I knew in Michigan and, later, in a city. For years I literally lived with him.

Bookishness drew me to like-minded companions. Yet it was not primarily love of reading that, in high school, led to the coalescence of five of us to the exclusion of "outsiders." For in temperament we differed sharply.

Albert and I relished ideas, particularly the logic of geometry. So did Austin, although he was by nature a technician. Other friends, Harold Kernan and Ralph Harvey, were more practical than intellectual. What brought us together was the fact that we were all, to use an expression of later times, "inner directed." We were not the best students, or the most intelligent, but such as it was, we did our own thinking.

Though we served on several school committees, none of us had been tapped for a Greek letter fraternity, or would have accepted if he had been.

Yet alas for "inner direction"! Even while we looked down on "brainless" fraternity youths, we felt constrained to imitate them by organizing our own Greek letter society. This we called modestly *The Mighty Five*, and went to the expense of obtaining gold pins to identify members.

Meanwhile I had been finding high-school studies interesting. For my attractive, red-haired English teacher, Miss Elizabeth Buchanan, I turned out a prose variant of *John Gilpin's Ride* as John might have told it to friends, which drew her praise. Next Miss Alice Beardsley, who loved literature, took me to task for not reading more selectively. ("Why do you read such trash when there are so many good things available?") I had read some good books, including most of Shakespeare, but simply for their narrative value. Miss Beardsley awakened a feeling for style and verbal beauty.

A further appreciation of style was encouraged by Uncle Albert, in some ways the most interesting member of the Scott family. Like his brother Ansel, Albert Scott had studied law, and had gone to work for James J. Hill as advance agent of the Great Northern Railroad.

Hill later criticized Albert for not enriching himself at the railroad's expense! But while living in Anaconda, Montana, my uncle had written a number of poems, some of which he still quoted with pride. Since they were lacking in lyricism, they drew no praise from Brother Paul. But I enjoyed philosophic aphorisms. After Albert came to live with us in Chicago, we became the closest of friends. To this day I have never met a more fascinating conversationalist.

The Scotts considered a knowledge of Latin essential to the good education of young men. Yet at that time Latin in Hyde Park High School remained incredibly remote from our lives. Presented as reporting by the first war correspondent rather than as an exercise in grammar, *De Bello Gallico* might possibly have meant more.

Half-learned Latin contrasted conspicuously with my real knowledge of French. My French teacher, Bertha des Combes Favard, was an educational genius. Never before or since have I met a teacher who could evoke as much interest in a subject, or who used such unique methods.

Most teachers addressed Hyde Park High School students as *Mr.* or *Miss*. Not Mademoiselle Favard. To her I was, and remained to the age of forty-five when I last saw her, "mon petit Edgar." She would slide around the classroom, perch familiarly on somebody's desk, crack jokes with her pupils, and indulge in puns and rhymes. Yet at the same time she maintained total discipline! Making trouble for Mademoiselle was unthinkable.

One day in her senior class she asked us to translate a French poem. As poetry, my translation was merely competent, but it made a small sensation. Mademoiselle read it aloud to the class. The editor of the school magazine, the *Aitchpe*, asked permission to publish it.

The piece must have impressed the English faculty, too, for shortly thereafter I was asked to become an editor of the school yearbook. What with so much sport and the imminence of final examinations, I had plenty to do in that spring of 1909, without taking on the annual. But, after all, the school had sought me, and not I the school. So I graciously consented. Our annual was no worse than others.

Some years before, I had gone through a religious crisis. Mother rarely went to church. But she brought up her sons to believe in an approachable God, and sent them to Protestant Sunday School.

Even today, "Now I lay me down to sleep" brings back Mother's grey eyes and black hair, and the lovely songs she always sang after she heard my prayers.

To the search for identity, Sunday School contributed relatively little. By high-school days, difficulties had arisen. Genesis and geology were obviously incompatible accounts of Creation. The dichotomy of Christian fundamentalism and science really worried me, as it did many others. Yet a fascinating alternative had come my way. This was something called "theosophy."

The father of one of my brother's closest friends was an uncanny physician, Dr. Julius C. Hoffman. Professionally, he specialized in curing drug addicts. But he was also a mystic, if theosophists can rightly be called mystics. His passion was Indian Vedanta, in all its aspects.

To my brother he lent the books of Annie Besant and Leadbeater, and I too read them avidly. Ineffable Brahma and Ishvara seemed more convincing than the God of Christianity. Also, the theory of reincarnation satisfied my innate thirst for justice. Why should the best suffer agonies while the worst went unscathed? The doctrine of karma gave an answer: only after many lives would the perfected being, in full knowledge of them all, return to that One from which it originally came. To young Edgar this pilgrim's progress was immeasurably more attractive than the harp-singing heaven of the fundamentalists.

Theosophy, moreover, added magic to the human adventure in the form of occultism: to each man it attributed, in addition to his physical body, an etheric (formal), an astral, a mental and a spiritual body— all of which he might hope to know. As my brother described it, Dr. Hoffman's physical body regularly lay on his couch at the top of his house while his consciousness sallied forth for contacts with others' astral and mental bodies. He used this faculty as a means of helping his patients! Yet anyone less suggestive of a madman or a faker than Dr. Hoffman could not be found.

I soon concluded that extrasensory experience was both real and possible. And this conviction was to stand the test of years.

My first year at the University of Michigan was a disappointment. Ann Arbor was unquestionably charming: a small town dominated by a big university, situated in pleasant rolling country on the Huron River ("Urine" to us) which in spring and autumn swarmed with canoes. But I had not anticipated that the life of a freshman would be distressingly like that of a senior in high school, minus the prestige. My brother's former friends were courtesy itself, and in the course of nine months I made a few new ones: Arnold Eggerth, the son of a German immigrant, who intended to become a physician; William W. Welsh, a sophomore in the same German class, who persuaded me to take up cross country running—six and a quarter miles through the February snows; and a small shapely girl with mischievous eyes and a sense of humor, Maude Edwards, who adored Poe and Oscar Wilde.

I also came under the influence of another great teacher, Professor James A. Craig, who lectured on Biblical studies. He quoted the classics in half a dozen languages, and by treating interested students as intellectual equals, involved them inextricably in whatever he was lecturing about. By the end of the first term he had me in intellectual bondage. After studying the Wisdom literature of the Old Testament, I signed up for a course on the Hebrew prophets. Here Craig demonstrated to my satisfaction not only that the Book of Job was a turning point in Judeo-Western thought but that, in the King James original version, it contains the noblest prose in the English language.

For the rest, my courses bored me. At the end of that first year, I informed the family that I wanted to shift to the University of Chicago, where I could again enjoy the comradeship of my friend Albert Green. In spite of the larger tuition fee, Father consented.

In the autumn of 1910, I entered the University on the Midway as a sophomore. What did I study? The records indicate German, Shakespeare, *The Problem of Suffering in the Old Testament* (a disappointment after Craig's lectures), and a breathtaking philosophy course with Professor James H. Tufts, an inspiring teacher. This was something I had always unconsciously craved. Yet aside from endless discussions with Albert, I found the Midway even less intellectually exciting than Michigan.

Moreover, I could not readjust to living at home. Mother had been deeply hurt by Paul's early marriage a couple of years before and seemed determined to hold on to her younger son. At the least, she felt he should be punctual at meals and explain why and where he sometimes stayed out late. Her demands, after a year of independence, he found irksome—and said so to his ever-understanding father. Reminding me of Mother's ill health, Dad begged me to "go slow" and let her get used gradually to my changed status.

Then, out of the winter sky, came an invitation from Paul, now a foreign correspondent, to visit him in Paris, perfect my French, and attend lectures at the famous Sorbonne. This experience would, he argued, be "broadening" beyond anything I could get in America.

Father saw the point: if I wanted to go, I could. Wanted to go? The idea was fabulous. In mid-January, 1911, after a stormy Atlantic crossing, I landed in Boulogne-sur-Mer.

Paris was civilization, the first I had ever seen. For two months I lived near the Bois de Boulogne with Paul, Winifred his wife, and my twenty-five-year-old cousin, Mildred Scott.

My brother and I were again on excellent terms. I liked my sister-in-law even while I mischievously recorded her "prejudices" and, for my handsome cousin, I had a deep affection. With her I started attending lectures at the Sorbonne.

Within a week I realized that this was the education of which I had dreamed. Here ideas were the center of life—and I sharpened my mental teeth on metaphysics as an ancient armorer might have honed a sword blade.

Gabriel Séailles, a little man whose head barely appeared over his desk, convulsed us students by seeming to pull his ideas about pluralism one by one out of his long beard. But we listened spellbound to his exposition of the doctrine of Renouvier, namely, that the earth is alive and our souls are part of its soul.

Over at the Collège de France, another professor, a handsome bearded man called Henri Bergson, was restoring flow and direction to philosophy. Bergson had gone back to Heraclitus: the "real reality" is *pure duration*, with all the changed conceptions that this implies.

True time, as the failures of past philosophers had demonstrated, could be grasped only through that memory which gives continuity to existence. What pleased me most was Bergson's insistence on the validity of intuition as a method, indeed, the only method, of grasping the "creation evolution" of which we are a part. Indeed, "creative evolution" validated the method, if not the finding, of theosophy.

Stimulated by Bergson, I tackled Berkeley. Yet the theory that the permanence of anything indicated by sensations can never be demonstrated, struck me as preposterous. To refute it, I wrote a long essay based on the *a priori* validity of geometric space, hence, that of the objective reality of everything which fills space. Since I totally misunderstood Berkeley's argument, my refutation was worthless. And my insistence on reading it aloud to Mildred and Winifred drove them into nervous exhaustion. I was growing up the hard way and had become difficult to live with.

So when Paul's household stubbornly turned a deaf ear to Anatole France and Verlaine, which I also insisted on reading aloud, I gladly accepted my brother's suggestion to take a room in the Latin Quarter and really taste student life. On May 3, 1911, I moved into a front room in Montparnasse, high up in a building in the Rue Vavin. Here at last was *la vie de Bohème*—and how I loved it!

What with exploring the Quarter; taking lessons on the flute (always my favorite instrument); translating Huneker's *Iconoclasts* into French at the Bibliothèque Nationale; attending lectures at the Sorbonne and enjoying an occasional concert, opera, or classical play; browsing through the bookstores of the Boulevards and the Odéon; sitting at cafés and staring at the girls; from time to time going to Passy (usually on foot) for a real bath and dinner at Paul's; and writing furiously in my new room—each day was too short.

What did I write? Poetry, including a rondel to a Chicago girl, which began, "A crowd is ever the same age,/But Minnie, you and I grow old," and occasional short stories—one in French. But chiefly I filled notebooks with quotations and a large copy book with short studies, half essay, half confession.

Practice in writing was having its effect. And a new friend helped. This was a young Frenchman, Gabriel Marie Charles de la Garde, who earned a living in my brother's office in order to write poetry like Henri de Régnier. Charles had taught French in Ireland and at once concentrated on perfecting mine. He made me not only dig into French prosody but converse in improvised French hexameters. He also introduced me to Baudelaire and to J. K. Huysmans, whose des Esseintes of *A Rebours* had been the model for Oscar Wilde's Dorian Gray.

Huysmans' symbolic description of the great church at Chartres, *La Cathédrale*, was de la Garde's aesthetic bible. Until I knew Chartres I could, he insisted, understand nothing of architectural sublimity. So when, in June, de la Garde took a vacation, we spent two days exploring that greatest of Gothic churches.

It was so beautiful and impressive that I almost wished I were a Catholic. But on the third morning, Charles and I, drowsy with the dim religious light, decided to visit the adjacent, and empty, archbishop's residence. The concierge said, no admittance. He did not know us. Below the house the bishop's garden was supported by a forty-foot wall whose alternate corner bricks, protruding an inch or two, offered an easy footing.

In five minutes we were in the abandoned garden and had slipped into the house through a broken window. What a disappointment! It was empty of everything, with tattered paper and torn brocades clinging to the walls of the once noble chambers. Seeking our way out, however, we took a wrong turn, missed the broken window, and emerged in the courtyard under the eyes of the surly concierge.

He took one look and yelled, "Police!" Before we could slip away, two gendarmes appeared, seized us by the collars, and began shaking us. When as a free-born American, I jerked myself loose and warned my captor to be polite, the two led us handcuffed to jail. Ten minutes later, stripped of our belongings, we found ourselves in a filthy cell with no plumbing and no beds—just a single inclined wooden shelf and blankets that stank.

Nonetheless, fortified by good meals brought in from a nearby café, we spent the next forty-eight hours enjoying the situation, singing improvised grand opera at the top of our voices. Appealing for help to my brother in Paris was the last thing we had in mind.

For a few hours we were temporarily put in another cell with a thief caught stealing cast iron. I was uneasy until I found that for some inexplicable reason, he stood in awe of us. Then, once more handcuffed, we were led through the streets to the law courts. The chief of the three robed judges confronted us for the first time with the charge: burglary. Since we had no lawyer, he told somebody to appoint one, and remanded the case for two weeks. Before we knew it, we passed through an enormous gate in high walls with armed guards perched on them—the State prison.

Shades of François Villon! The adventure was turning sour. We were booked, our fingerprints taken, and ordered to take a hot bath before having our heads shaved and being shown into our new cell. While we were arguing the point with the ferocious looking warden, the director called us downstairs to the visitors' parlor. There we faced a youngish individual who introduced himself as our "court-appointed advocate."

"Come on now, tell me what you were doing in the archbishop's palace."

In classical French, rich with imperfect subjunctives, Charles expressed our indignation. We had done nothing worse than trespass upon an empty premise, yet *les flics* had treated us like common criminals. Were the Chartres authorities all mad—*"tour fous"*?

His manner of speech impressed the lawyer: "Tell the truth—who are you?"

"Students from Paris."

"Why didn't you say so."

"We did. They paid no attention."

"Parbleu! I might have known it. Gentlemen, I too was a Paris student, and would give ten years of my life to be back there. You cannot imagine—life in this provincial hole! I'll have you out of here and the burglary charge dropped immediately. But I must hurry, for nobody leaves the prison after six P.M."

He just made it. I still remember the snarl on the skeptical warden's face as he freed us.

Filthy but free, we went straight back to the *boulangerie* where we had originally eaten our meals—and found ourselves heroes. The baker and his daughters embraced us. The clerk of the court and two friends dropped in to drink a toast to the "pretty trick" we played on the "stupid police." Seeing our bewilderment, the baker brought us a newspaper. "Read that."

The story went something like this:

"Chartres. Our zealous police have finally managed to lay hands on the leaders of a band of brigands who have long been preying upon our peaceful countryside. One of them, a sinister individual, claims to be an American. But we know that he is an American from Montmartre and a *joueur de pantomime.*"

That evening Monsieur outdid himself at dinner, pressed free wine upon us, and suggested we stay another day at his expense. It was tempting, but we had had enough of Chartres, and after warm farewells, left for Paris.

Months before Charles had introduced me to some Russian friends: Maroussia Archangelsky, her sister Sonya, and the latter's fiancé, Vladimir Nikolaitch Michailov, a painter from St. Petersburg. Within a week I had warmed to Maroussia, Maroussia had shifted her interest from Charles to me, and I was spending several evenings a week with the three Russians, while Charles dined on the Boul' Mich' with a new favorite called Alice.

From these Slavs I learned something later proved indispensable: what makes Russians behave like Russians. Vladimir, Maroussia, and Sonya preserved me from the dangerous assumption that "at bottom" Russians are very like Americans. "Life," I had just written in my copybook, "is a great roaring decomposition." Vladimir and Maroussia were sure of it, each in a different way.

Vladimir combined a real artistic gift and training at the Petersburg Academy with a passion for Indian philosophy, great physical strength, and a delight in Greco-Roman wrestling. At our first meeting, he confided that to hasten his way to Nirvana he was learning English, since more translations from Sanskrit were available in that language. How was he learning? In true Russian style—by copying out a stanza of Poe's *Raven* in large letters on a huge sheet of paper, and affixing the paper to the wall where he could memorize the lines while lying flat on his bed!

Like most Russians, he could, on occasion, be uproariously inconsistent. Once, after he had wrestled with a fellow Russian, a peasant turned painter, at a group of studios called *La Ruche*, and the three of us had consumed several bottles of good red wine on top of the inevitable glasses of tea, while the peasant played the balalaika, he and Vladimir shook the studio with their songs, first melancholy, then wild. Then they paraded before the studio of a Russian Jewish artist, shouting the traditional Russian call to a pogrom: "Beat the Jews."

I was seeing ever more of Maroussia. Eighteen years old, rather large, with a good figure, the face of a Botticelli Madonna and a rich voice I learned to identify as Russian, and "like no one I had ever met." Our favorite rendezvous was the Marie de Medicis fountain in the Luxembourg Garden, which includes two naked lovers being spied upon by an envious god.

In her voice and in her amazing variability lay much of Maroussia's charm. She was never twice alike. She seemed an introvert, yet blurted out her most intimate thoughts and emotions like a child. Sometimes she laughed an entire evening, poked fun at Vladimir and me, and confessed her own vanities with glee. Again she was sentimentality personified. On the stroke of midnight before Easter, in the Russian church near l'Etoile, when everyone broke into the glad cry, "Christ is risen," she flung herself on my neck and kissed me passionately, an appropriate religious ritual, so she said.

Yet a week later, on an evening which we had set aside for dinner and the *Bal Bullier*, I found her still in her peignoir, her yellow hair falling far down her back, her head thrown back, tears streaming. No, she could not go out and I should leave her forever. What was wrong? Nothing. No bad news, no troubles. Just a bad attack of *Weltschmerz* beyond my *"grossière"* comprehension. And she continued to pace the room with long strides, weeping as though heartbroken.

To understand her and her baffling, fascinating countrymen, I made a stab at learning Russian. I memorized the alphabet and a few pet phrases of Vladimir's. In fact, for a time I caressed the idea of following Maroussia to Russia and settling down in that strange world.

Yet as the weeks went on, I began to suspect that she was less fond of Edgar than of a romantic game into which the American in Paris fitted. Moreover, perhaps I really was too *grossier* for her. Or was I simply too different? My problem was to eliminate self-pity. By the end of the summer I was convinced that, fascinating as she was, Maroussia was too temperamental for me.

Yet it was another Archangelsky who shaped my work during my last weeks in Paris, namely, the girls' elder brother. Intense, as dark as his sisters were blonde, Alexei was a musical composer and a Bohemian. One day he told me he was looking for an unusual libretto for an opera he would like to compose. I suggested that he might take as the basis for it a short story by Théophile Gautier, "*La Morte Amoureuse*," called by George Saintsbury, "a gem of the most perfect workmanship." It is the story of a monk bewitched by a vampire courtesan alternately dead and alive.

"Wonderful," Alexei said. "Won't you write it for me?"

Me, who had never published anything, write a libretto for a known composer? Would I not!

My writing schedule for the next forty days already included short stories, two essays, one poem, and translations of others. These I swept aside in favor of Alexei's libretto.

Before leaving for America in the middle of September, I had completed *Clarimonde, an Opera in Four Acts*, almost a thousand lines of blank verse, plus some lyrics. Alexei never composed the opera, but for the next two years, the thought that he might nourished my self-confidence.

From Paris the cheapest way to Chicago I could discover led through London, Liverpool, and Montreal. London, where I remained three days, was a disappointment. I liked the street and place names, familiar from a hundred books. My boarding house in Bloomsbury was Dickens-like, quaint if dilapidated. I found the National Gallery superb. But most of the city, as observed from the back of a motorcycle of a young American friend, was depressingly drab.

As a city, Liverpool was worse. Due to misinformation, I missed the transatlantic liner and during the next seven days got an indelible impression of Britain's industrial slums. Yet that week was magically brightened by an English girl whom I had met in the train and almost miraculously remet by chance so many times that she finally consented to take walks and an occasional meal with me. Tallish, well-made, handsome, with brown eyes, clean-cut features, and quiet self-assurance, Lilian Thomson was a superb musician, an actress, as well-read and interested in books and the fine arts as I was, and even more so in the theater. After our first encounter, I sent my brother in Paris not only an urgent request for funds to tide me over, but the news that I had met the girl I intended to marry.

2

The Nonconformist

I am sorry for anyone who has not been an anarchist at twenty.

—GEORGES CLEMENCEAU

OCTOBER, 1911, saw me back at the University of Michigan, determined to become a philosopher, that is, a professor of philosophy.

Externally, things were much as before: the same pleasant town, the same atmosphere, the same professors. Actually, everything seemed different because I was different. And thenceforth, like Job, I intended to "maintain my own ways."

The outward symbols of this attitude were a brown corduroy suit and a black windsor necktie. The suit, bought in Chicago before I left for Europe, had attracted no attention on the Boul' Mich' in Paris. In fact, I had frequently walked in my bathrobe to the *bureau de tabac* without causing a flutter.

On State Street in Ann Arbor, however, the windsor tie gave rise to some legitimate misunderstanding. American socialists and IWW-ers sometimes affected such ties and black slouch hats as manifestations of their convictions.

I had warmed to Oscar Wilde's *Soul of Man under Socialism*. If more economic security and equality would leave more people free for higher purposes, then I had no objection to them. Since I had no interest in any form of politics, why should I be disturbed by the fact that the outstanding student socialist on the campus who had done public speaking for Eugene Debs, Peter Fagan, also wore a windsor tie? If the Michigan campus wished to misinterpret my Paris attire, well, that need not worry me.

The effect of this attitude on some of the faculty was easy to foresee. In those days the University of Michigan shared the vigor and breeziness of the Middle West, but also its conservatism. The faculty was there to inculcate established learning and sound Americanism, not to encourage dissent.

Moreover, from its founding in 1837, the University had been academically under German influence. To many professors, Paris was less the home of the most famous university in the world than of frivolity and loose living. Only one member of the faculty, C. B. Vibbert, had studied in Paris. He had returned with the mustache and airs of a spruce young *boulevardier*. His colleagues sarcastically called him "Monsieur Vibbert" (pronounced French fashion) and looked upon him as something of a freak. If they felt this of a competent colleague and philosopher (his course, *Modern French Philosophy since 1860,* included that of my favorite Renouvier), one can imagine their attitude toward a bumptious nineteen-year-old who emphasized "French" habits.

Professor Clarence Meader, a remarkable scholar, with whom I took several courses, including a year of Russian language, a study of Russian novelists in English, and a semester of French versification, never understood my choice for my term paper of the formally perfect Turgenev instead of the profound Dostoievsky. French superficiality, no doubt.

Another who disapproved of my interior life as well as of my exterior one was the head of the philosophy faculty, Professor Robert Mark Wenley, a Scot from Edinburgh who had come to Ann Arbor with British honors and a certain contempt for Americans (and Frenchmen) which he made no effort to conceal. Wenley, a neo-Hegelian, had a fine mind. But he had little use for students who resisted his intellectual influence especially if, like me, they were able to win a reluctant *A* from him. Specifically, he reproached me for not "getting" the Hegelian dialectic. The truth was that British Neo-Hegelians like Bradley and Bosanquet, with their abstract Absolute resolving all contradictions, struck me as hopelessly arid.

On the other hand, Professor Alfred Henry Lloyd inspired Peter Fagan and me to the point where we considered writing his original philosophy of history for him, since he seemed unable to express it in anything but an obscure jargon.

Another close friend was DeWitt Parker, a superb teacher, with whom I studied aesthetics, metaphysics, and Neoplatonism.

Professor Craig, looking more like Elijah than ever, greeted me like a younger brother and persuaded me to take his course in Hebrew. Fred Newton Scott, a typical scholar in appearance, the head of the department of rhetoric, and a teacher who inspired generations of students, admitted the returning junior to his senior courses and advanced seminars. After an exhausting examination, the French faculty gave me enough credits to make up for those credits I missed while in Europe.

The university librarian accorded me "stack privileges"—with a desk among the shelves and the right to help myself to any number of volumes.

Finally, the Quadrangle Club elected me to membership almost immediately. This was a limited association of faculty and a sprinkling of students. The members met about once a month in rooms over a store on State Street. Somebody would read a paper, which was then hotly discussed, with the full participation of the students.

My first essay dealt with what I apodictically called the "failure of our education." The second, submitted first to Professor Scott's seminar in rhetoric and criticism, and then at his suggestion read aloud to Quadrangle, bore the provocative title: "Literature—A Vanished Study." In it I deplored the current analytical, pseudoscientific, and biographical, rather than the aesthetic, approach to literary masterpieces, thus anticipating the "new criticism" of the Thirties.

Why this paper should have stirred up so much controversy among the faculty members present I cannot now say, unless it was the bluntness of my language. But it did. When we student members finally slipped out to go home, the professors were still arguing about it.

Equally significant were the contacts with fellow students, some of them old friends, some new. Arnold Eggerth, already specializing in the bacteriology (or was it histology?) which was to become his life's work, and Maude Edwards, who, for financial reasons, was teaching school in nearby Detroit, remained close associates. So close that on one occasion the three of us nearly created a scandal. One day during that winter of 1911–1912, Arnold and I met Maude in Detroit and together made an aesthetic pilgrimage to the opening of the Toledo Art Gallery. After much art, and a sumptuous luncheon with my father, who happened to be in that city on business, we took the evening train back and ran full into a midwestern blizzard. When at 6:00 A.M. the train finally reached Ann Arbor, Maude was exhausted. Since she had no place to stay there (a hotel room would have cost too much), I offered her the bed in mine and gallantly betook myself to a lunch counter for a leisurely breakfast. When, some hours later, the landlady found Maude asleep, she threatened to eject me for immorality. "What provincialism!" I thought. In Paris, a man brought whomever he liked into his room.

Another close friend was a Hindu from Calcutta, Dhirendra Kumar Sarkar, who was majoring in chemistry, and like all dark-skinned exotics in America, suffering from a largely unplanned racial discrimination. Finding in me not only no prejudice against, but a real admiration for, the people and civilization which had produced what I considered the greatest "life philosophy" in the world, Dhirendra poured out both his nation's hopes and his personal disappointments.

But with Maude living in Detroit and Arnold and Dhiren deep in scientific studies, I turned for comradeship primarily to students whose interests were similar to mine. One was a highly gifted senior named George Oliver Spaulding with whom I shared Hebrew with Craig, Russian with Meader, and Advanced English Composition with Fred Newton Scott. Oliver was a sensitive writer, and learned foreign languages more quickly than anyone else I have ever met. He and I joined forces in what was to be the most exciting adventure of my university life: the publication of a student monthly. The previous Michigan magazine, the *Inlander*, of which my brother had been an editor, had suspended publication five years before and we wanted something less "newsy." The existing humorous magazine, the *Gargoyle*, we hardly bothered to read. Our review was to be jealously independent and frankly highbrow with no concessions to athletes, to social leaders, to orthodox "grinds," or indeed to the tastes of the bulk of the students and faculty.

To emphasize our unorthodoxy, we deliberately chose a title and a format calculated to repel, or at least not to attract, any but *aficionados* of the true faith. We called it *The Painted Window* after the cover design—a Gothic window such as might have been taken from Chartres Cathedral, designed by the budding architect, Joseph Hudnut.

Where the original money came from escapes me. Yet by midwinter, with some advice from Professor Scott and Instructor Tompkins, eleven of us, including three co-eds, met in my room and took the plunge.

The choice of meeting place had meant nothing to me. In Paris, Sonya and Maroussia on the one hand, Vladimir and I on the other, had used each other's rooms virtually as our own. But this was Michigan in January, 1912. The choice seemed scandalous, not only to my already indignant landlady but to the three lady editors. One of them, Maud Robertson, later described their embarrassment: "We three girls went together. Not one of us had ever before been in a man's room unchaperoned. We did not want to appear to be three little maids straight from a ladies' seminary, but that is how we felt inside. Afterwards, we agreed future meetings should be in the library or some other public place."

At that first meeting it suddenly became shockingly apparent that we had no one to look after the business side. Who was going to obtain even that minimum of advertising which seemed the indispensable midwife? Oliver and I had planned to do most of the editing. But as a senior, he outranked me by a year. *Faute de mieux*, I reluctantly accepted the position of business manager and found myself stuck with it for the rest of the term. Selling advertising was as alien to me as lion taming. Since I was carrying over twenty hours of courses, and writing on the side, the result was inevitable: financially the magazine languished. There was almost no paid promotion. Successive monthly numbers appeared when they could, and after a first small burst, circulation stagnated at about two hundred copies monthly.

The lack of buyers did not particularly depress us. How many Americans had bought the first edition of Whitman's *Leaves of Grass*? Rather let our magazine perish in beauty than live on in shabby compromise.

The editors liked their monthly. The suggestive Gothic window on the cover, the solid etchings and unpretentious presentation—these made up for occasional misprints.

Above all, we were proud of our poetry. For the first number (March, 1912) a student named Harold P. Scott provided a superb "apology" in rhyming couplets, with a mastery of rhythm and word magic which many recognized poets could envy. Here is an example which we published later.

Croon of the Sea

Swiftly the dark waters slide to the salt deep,
Silently follow the tide with a long sweep,
Trailing their moonlit foam where the dead sleep
Under the watery dome of the salt deep.

Sweetly the night sea croons, as the surf rolls,
Ancient unsyllabled tunes to her lost souls;
Quiets the restless hearts 'neath her wave knolls,
Soothing the dreamer who starts, as the surf rolls.

Sweet is your crooning to me of the long rest;
Soft is the sleeping, O sea, where your waves crest;
Mother, make end of my pain on your cool breast;
There I shall seek not in vain for the long rest.

Sentimentally adolescent if you like—but what virtuosity, with inside rhymes and terminal spondees worthy of Swinburne!

To the third issue Editor Spaulding contributed his prize-winning poem, *The Death of Judas*, in which Jesus' betrayer expresses what was to become the Manichaean heresy. Howard Devree and Martin Feinstein also contributed talented verse, as no less stern a critic than Professor Scott acknowledged.

Not surprisingly, the romantic pose that went well enough in poetry, gave a false or pretentious ring in prose. For instance: "For each must see the glimmer of truth through the chrysoprase of his convictions. Verily, the mind of man is a many-paned window of stained glass." (Chrysoprase, indeed—and I suspect I wrote it! Small wonder that the campus snorted and kept its money.)

October, 1912, found Harold Scott and me co-editors. I had, after electing it, renounced Astronomy One because of my deficient mathematics. Owing to a lack of available students, Professor Meader canceled the only course in second-year Russian. And toward the end of the month, Professor Craig, at the susceptible age of fifty-five, eloped to Canada with his children's governess, never to return. These cancellations left me free to give my best efforts to the magazine.

During the previous year, I had, in addition to a couple of brash editorials, contributed material composed in Paris: satirical verse, an anonymous sonnet to my brother, a short story with a French background, and, above all, a description of a memorable walk from Chartres to Orleans. Called "Unshaded Ways," it was filled with stilted inversions like "very old they were" and "all day long had I walked"; and gems such as "the pure hemisphere above smiled, replete with loveliness"; "in great Gothic cathedrals throng dark shades of forgotten crimes"; etc.

Now I wrote a novelette: *While There's Life*. This was an account of the destruction by noxious gases from a passing comet of the entire human race, except for one group which had providentially constructed a shelter. As science fiction, it was inspired by Poe and H. G. Wells, two favorites. But the anticipation of humanity's situation after the Second World War, thirty years later, remains startling.

Like many a better writer, I wrote the story month by month. The last installment, with the climactic denouement, was scheduled for the April, 1913, issue. Since *The Painted Window* expired in March, how the human race preserved itself will never be known.

From the beginning, our editorials, of which I wrote more than half, were indiscriminately critical. Our task, as we saw it, was to challenge the assumptions and practices of a humdrum state university.

"Here at Michigan we have never recognized the place of scholarship in the undergraduate course."

"The prevailing attitude of a large portion of the faculty is indirectly opposed to independent thought on the part of the student. . . ." Instead "recitations that are but unreal images of the hackneyed thoughts of which the professor himself is only the dispenser . . . ideas fit for the upper shelves of forgotten mental pantries. . . . Better a university of differentiated faculty, undignified seekers for truth, and students who would rather be wrong than insignificant . . . than the single abortive type prevailing now."

"Worst of all is the negative character of the universe. . . ."

Only on one occasion did the editors deign to admit their hope of a "new America . . . (which) will have made a complete diremption (!) of the merely useful and the essential. The new America will permit each to diverge that he may the better conform . . . will demand a better economic structure upon which a culture may be raised and a sense of fellowship in the community of the mind. . . . Poet and statesman must proclaim the spiritual necessity of work and man the machine must become man the creator."

On this one cheerful note, *The Painted Window* suspended publication, leaving its debts to be paid by the members of the editorial board (or by their fathers—much to the latters' discomfiture).

Ours was essentially an old story. Maude Edwards later described it: "From time to time, on campuses as elsewhere a talented, self-conscious group, searching for excellence of expression in form and content, of whatsoever things are true, not so much for society as for the individual, is born in hope and travail, has its brief day and fades." So it was with *The Painted Window*.

Its fading was a foregone conclusion. Harvard or Oxford might possibly have been receptive to this overly "literary" writing. Michigan was not. Americans still took pride in being a new and better world, and had little sense of continuity with the past. But were American citizens fiddling with their machines really happier than medieval Europeans toiling at their crafts? Having known Paris and written a paper on William Morris, I had my doubts.

We of *The Painted Window* were among the forerunners of the writers' revolt against American anti-intellectualism of the nineteen twenties. To us the American scene looked like John Donne's famous lines:

> 'Tis all in pieces, all coherence gone,
> All just supply and all relation.

As individuals, however, most of our contributors did anything but fade. One or two became teachers or professors. Among them was Scotty. Perhaps he was too diversely gifted: he painted and played several musical instruments. In any case, after graduating he wrote little verse except a curious set of *101 Biographettes*. Conceivably, as he was to write of Leonardo da Vinci, Harold "never knew, just what it was he best could do."

Howard Devree had a long career as art critic of the *New York Times*. Martin Feinstein and Leonard Cline subsequently published volumes of verse. Both died prematurely, Leonard by his own hand—after murdering a companion.

Peter Fagan, after an unsuccessful courtship of Helen Keller, settled down as a radical newspaper editor in Michigan. His daughter Ruth married the poet Maxwell Bodenheim and perished with him at the hands of a lunatic.

One studious girl, Marjorie Nicholson, became a renowned scholar and educator. Several contributors drifted to newspapers and stayed there.

By the time *The Painted Window* folded, I had realized once more what I did *not* want to do in life. Just as I had decided years before that, much as I loved an argument, the practice of law was not for me, I now realized that teaching philosophy would offer me small satisfaction. For although I enjoyed metaphysics as I enjoyed chess, the Hegelians' Absolute, the Positivists' "First Cause" or—worse—the pragmatic definition of truth as "what works"—these repelled a young man thirsty to know the "real" nature of being, transcendance and free will.

I talked so much about philosophic questions that on one occasion Scotty lampooned my incomprehensible (to him) addiction in these terms:

> Philosophy, philosophy,
> A holy hymn of praise to thee!
> Beloved mistress, thou dost know
> That all thy knowing is not so.
> And so thou knowest that the so
> Is that the so thou canst not know
> And that thy knowing is not so.

By the spring of 1913, I had come almost to agree with him. Actually, another book had strengthened the growing suspicion that the truth in the matters that interested me could only be individual and "subjective." This was Max Stirner's *Der Einzige und Sein Eigentum*. Impossible logically to escape this anarchist's rigid demonstration that, try as he will, no human being can be other than what he is. Without a transrational standard, a society can not legitimately pass moral judgment even on those delinquents whom it finds necessary to eliminate. For they too are only expressing their own natures.

The conclusion, to a nonconformist just turned twenty-one, was clear: reason could only rehash the known. Why stop there? Plato and Bergson had legitimized intuition. Beyond reason lay such fascinating fields as those described by William James in *Varieties of Religious Experience* and Evelyn Underhill's *Mysticism*, both of which I devoured.

How then could I conscientiously devote my life to teaching a mere intellectual discipline? The attractive alternative was a life of letters: I would, with Father's permission (and monthly allowance), return to Europe for another year, during which I might hope to write a book that would launch me as an author. If he refused, I could continue studying and then teach philosophy and try to save enough money within a few years to turn to free-lance writing.

Generous as ever, Father agreed to continue for one year the meager but adequate allowance on which I could live in Paris and test my worth as a writer. He insisted, however, that I pay my fare to France.

Pay with what? I had just made a contribution to settling *The Painted Window's* liabilities. A year earlier I had almost had to ask Father to pay a considerable gambling debt I had rashly contracted at poker with three Chinese students. But for my undeserved luck in holding the only straight flush of my life, I should have had to seek a side job, as many Michigan students did. At this moment I lacked funds to pay for a ticket to Chicago, much less to Europe. What should I do?

One night at dinner, somebody asked Scotty who was going to win the annual Nelson C. Field poetry prize, which Oliver had won the year before. And suddenly I saw a vision of a possible one hundred dollars.

Easier envisaged than earned! The deadline for entering a poem was April 21—just six days ahead. And several of the presumed contenders, Scotty himself, Devree, Feinstein, Cline, were first-class versifiers.

I decided to appeal to the professors who would make the choice much as an unsure lawyer appeals to the prejudices of the judge. Since I could never surpass my rivals in quality, I must do so in quantity. What about a rousing narrative poem like those of John Masefield with a plot contrived to please?

For the next five days, I did nothing but work on *Barnaby*. Nearly a thousand lines of rhymed verse (more impressive than blank) told the tragic tale of a village girl driven insane by disappointed love. Half way through, I began to be absorbed by my own story and finished the first draft in a burst, a day and a half before the deadline. Another half day of revision, a final day at the typewriter copying the manuscript, and *Barnaby* was complete. Whereupon I went to bed supperless and slept fourteen hours.

Two weeks later, after class, Professor Scott turned to me. "I hope you aren't disappointed. We have split the hundred dollars between you and Martin Feinstein. Congratulations."

3

La Belle Epoque

Oh, that my words were now written! Oh that they were printed in a book!

JOB

FOR BOTH FINANCIAL and sentimental reasons, my way from Chicago to Paris led through New York, Montreal, Glasgow, Edinburgh, and Liverpool, where I planned to visit Lilian Thomson, the girl I had met almost two years before in the English train. Since that time, we had been in regular correspondence, and she meant more to me than anyone I had met before—or since. After two days with her, I left for France even more certain than before that this was the wife for me—provided she was willing, and my pen would provide the necessary income.

Paris was at the end of its June glory. Father and Mother were already there visiting my brother, and by luck I found a room overlooking the Rue de Seine on the Left Bank, near the bookstalls on the Quais and only a short walk from my brother's office on the Grands Boulevards and his apartment in the Rue du Bac.

At the former I could read the current magazines without charge, and in the latter luxuriate in the bathtub and the occasional "better dinner" which neither my landlady nor my finances would provide. A coal grate supplied the only heat in my room, and the toilette was off the main stairs outside the flat. Yet nowhere have I felt more in my element than *chez* Madame Hostiou.

There, in the shadow of the Institut de France (and the Ecole des Beaux Arts) I settled down to a writer's career, but what should I write? Past experience seemed to indicate that I had more ideas than imagination, hence was better equipped for essays and criticism than for fiction or poetry. My subject ought logically to be modern French literature, in which I was already deeply immersed. But which authors?

26

Accident decided. Almost under my window was a small, "modern" picture gallery. During my previous stay in Paris, lectures at the Sorbonne and miscellaneous writing had left me little time for *les beaux arts*. In Ann Arbor I had seen some examples of new European painting that left me wondering. But those in the gallery window on the Rue de Seine were downright baffling. This, remember, was 1913, the year of the Armory Show in New York, when the famous *Nude Descending a Staircase* discombobulated America. During the previous two centuries, French painting had dominated the West. But some of the pictures I saw in the Rue de Seine gallery hardly seemed art at all. What were these painters (some of whose work was twenty-five years old, though I did not know it) really up to? After a day or two of hesitation, I went inside the gallery to try to find out.

The owner, a woman with a heartening smile, introduced herself as Rose Vildrac, and set about enlightening the young American. Modern French artists, she explained, were weary of the banal, classical, "Bouguereau-Sargent" style of painting. It had reached a degree of perfection that excluded further development. Besides, the world had changed and as usual, artists had been the first to reflect the dissolution of past cultural patterns and to embark upon the search for new ones. With a little application one could understand and even enjoy these experiments which, though preponderantly French, were being made by artists from all over Europe and even from America.

At my next visit, Rose introduced me to her husband, Charles, "*un poète très distingué*." Furthermore she was, she added, the sister of another poet, by profession a physician, called Georges Duhamel. Vildrac and Duhamel had, along with several other young writers, been members of a group they called the *Abbaye*, from an abandoned monastery near Paris where they had for a time lived together and "got away from the vulgarity and commercialism" of most contemporary French literature. Their patron was no less than the great Romain Rolland, of whose novel, *Jean-Christophe*, I had heard, indeed had read the first two volumes. When Rose learned that I had come to France to write about French literature, she insisted I meet her husband's colleagues.

Within a week or two, having done so, I realized with a glow that it was my immense fortune to be adopted almost as one of their own by what was perhaps the most gifted group of young writers in France.

All because I happened to find a bedroom above a picture gallery in the hands of people with whom I could immediately communicate. Charles Vildrac, a slight man with a dreamy look and a dreamier dark beard, was a poet of rare sensitivity and iron convictions. As a pacifist, he had refused to become a reserve officer in the French army on the ground that he disliked the "officer mentality."

Duhamel, the physician, was tall and blond in a Germanic way. His handsome actress wife, Blanche Albane, played, I believe, with Copeau at the recently opened *Vieux Colombier* theater. Jules Romains, a product of that supreme mandarin factory, the Ecole Normale

Supérieure, was a dark sturdy Auvergnat of tremendous energy. Out of a combination of Whitman and Gustave Le Bon, he had produced his own "crowd theory," which he called *unanimisme*.

Léon Bazalgette, slightly older than the others, and an outdoor type, was chiefly known as the translator of Whitman, whose humanity and implied internationalism had stirred all the *Abbaye* authors. "Bazal" soon invited me to his apartment, a gesture which, I learned, was in France a sign of particular esteem.

Unlike Vildrac, Romains, and Duhamel, René Arcos was a bachelor with free time on his hands, and a small income to which he added by giving French lessons. It happened that my mother, who had stayed on in Paris after Father returned to America, decided to learn French Before I knew it, Mother was reading Mérimée aloud with Arcos, and her teacher, from the eminence of his published books and thirty years, was advising the son of his pupil.

A small man with tiny hands and feet, Arcos was accomplished at any craft from painting to carpentry. At his little apartment, high above the Boulevard Montparnasse, formerly a maid's quarters but now beautifully furnished, he lectured to me long and learnedly on all aspects of French literature. There I even met a grave, severely dressed man, the "great European," Romain Rolland. Since Rolland was from Burgundy, and Burgundians are traditionally an easy-laughing, self-indulgent lot, his reserve surprised me.

From Arcos I learned that Walt Whitman had not invented free verse. One "Aloysius" Bertrand had, somewhat earlier, written, in *vers libres*, a book called *Gaspard de la Nuit*. And in language and subject, Jules Laforgue had been the great innovator, transforming the spirit of French poetry. Régnier and Viélé-Griffin (*un Américain!*) founded symbolism, which Mallarmé brought to perfection (and, sometimes, I found, to unintelligibility).

After Mallarmé, French poetry split into separate schools, some of them merely farcical, some serious, of which the *Abbaye* group was one.

I soon came to realize that although *vers libres* might be poetry, it was not, in any true sense, verse. Verse, whether rhymed or blank, requires regularity of length and meter, in short, discernible rhythm. Anything that could be printed as prose without revealing itself as verse was not verse. Baudelaire had recognized this in entitling one of his books *Petits Poemes en Prose*. In the hands of modern innovators, one of whom, a minor figure called Francis Berbouard, was the first to omit all punctuation, *vers libres* remained prose, however poetic.

Patiently, Arcos steered me away from the authoritative but stodgy *Revue des Deux Mondes* through the thicket of lesser-known literary magazines, introducing me to the editors he favored. On certain Sundays, we dropped in at noon at the *Closerie des Lilas* to hear the director of *Vers et Proses* magazine, the "prince of poets," Paul Fort, read aloud from his dramatic *Odes et Ballades* or from his verse novel about *Louis XI—Curious Man*—to the applause of adoring bluestockings.

Fort had a peculiarity: while many others were writing prose as *vers libres*, he wrote stanzas of perfectly regular verses printed as prose paragraphs.

Most of the young writers I met were anticlerical as well as anticommercial. But though my friends mocked priests, they had great respect for certain Catholic writers. Péguy and Francis Jammes they approved, and for Paul Claudel their feeling approached veneration. Arcos insisted that I read not only Claudel's *Odes*, but all his plays. (I liked *Tête d'Or* best.)

Many contemporary French novelists my friends brushed off impatiently, notably the popular Paul Bourget. One exception was Anatole France. Though deploring his "nihilism," they thoroughly approved the satirical *Ile des Pengouins* and the fiercely irreligious story, *Les Dieux Ont Soif*. Arcos also lent me *The Adventures of Tyl Ulenspiegel* by Charles de Coster, a marvelous legend embodying the unconquerable spirit of Flanders.

Two new novels that made a great impression on them, and through them on me, were *Du Côté de Chez Swann*, by an unknown writer, Marcel Proust, and *Barnabooth* by Valéry Larbaud. I found the former unusually competent but overprecious.

My friends also steered me to the *Théâtre Libre* of Antoine and Lugné-Poe, and to the *Vieux Colombier* (whose manager occasionally gave me free tickets), and indicated their favorite playwrights. These were few in number: Claudel, Maeterlinck, Verhaeren, Rolland, a man called François de Curel of whom I had never heard; to a lesser extent, the Rostand of *Cyrano*, Emile Fabre, Courteline, and even Porto-Riche and Maurice Donnay. All others, including the popular Brieux, were written off as "boulevard writers." I had no money for unnecessary books, but during this period the *L'Illustration* magazine published a whole play every week. These I borrowed from Paul's office as fast as they appeared and came to understand why cultured people then looked upon "boulevard theater" as they were later to look on Hollywood.

From Arcos I further learned that in France the word author meant nothing in particular. One could be the *author* of anything, from a new washing machine to an astronomical theory. And a *writer* was merely one who wrote. He might turn out copy for Cadum soap or Michelin tires or even—God help him—for a "boulevard" newspaper. People devoted by profession or avocation to the creation of literature called themselves *men* (or *women*) *of letters*. As such, no matter how poor or unknown they might be, they were accepted by all classes. In fact, their social eminence resembled that of *Herr* Professors in Germany and of corporation presidents in the United States. Leading politicians increased their stature by producing novels or *belles lettres*.

As an illustration of status, Arcos told me that on one occasion he had, after an exchange of sharp words, been challenged to a duel by his own publisher. "With swords or pistols?" I gasped.

"Naturally, I answered that according to the code of honor, a man of letters could not accept a challenge from a tradesman. That settled him."

My immediate reaction was to grow a mustache, to make myself, at twenty-one, more plausible as an *homme de lettres*.

Painting was important to René Arcos. No mean painter himself, he was universally regarded as a sharp connoisseur of contemporary art. In consequence he took particular pains to acquaint me with his favorite modern artists. Of them I preferred Van Gogh, and admired, while not liking, Cézanne. I also took great delight in the fantastic paintings of Gustave Moreau and the Englishman, James Ensor. And I became an admirer of Arcos' friend, Frans Masereel, whose woodcuts were to reveal him as one of the great craftsmen of our century.

Incidentally, Arcos also introduced me to the first modern primitive, Customs Inspector (*Douanier*) Rousseau, a couple of whose pictures my friend had bought for five francs each. The *Douanier* was the spiritual forerunner of Grandma Moses. At the Vildracs', I occasionally met other revolutionary painters whose capacity for taking themselves seriously contrasted comically with the funny (to me) things they produced.

One aspect of the new painting was revealed at one of several dinners to which I was invited by a group calling themselves the "Artists of Passy."

On this occasion, leading cubists expounded the theories behind their odd geometry. (Frenchmen, I had discovered, needed a theory much as Americans needed to be loved.) Prominent cubists explained, each in turn, the motives that had led them to desert traditional curves for the angles of cubism. One explained that just as Emile Verhaeren wrote of "tentacular cities," so sensitive artists felt the need to *paint* the angularity of modern life. The last speaker, Albert Gleize, had another theory. He argued that cubists, instead of painting objects as they exist in nature "side by side," "superimposed" one object upon another. This, he insisted, amounted "to the same thing."

At this point, a fellow cubist, Delaunay, exploded. "It is not the same thing, it is not the same thing," he shouted. "You, Gleize, are *beside* Madame. You are not superimposed on Madame, so far as I know."

The dinner broke up in terrific laughter.

Although I listened eagerly to everything writers and artists had to say, I had certain misgivings. For one thing, without being in any oppressive sense nationalist, the literary Paris of 1913, unlike that after the First World War, was too narrowly French.

My particular friends had read the great Russians, Shakespeare, Dickens, Shaw, and Kipling. Among Americans, Edgar Poe (pronounced Po-ay) was revered as having inspired Baudelaire and French writers of detective stories. Emerson and Mark Twain were respected. Vildrac admired Stephen Crane's *Red Badge of Courage*. Whitman they considered the symbol of the new age.

Yet, though the *Abbaye* group traveled, they wrote about other countries with all the wonder of Herodotus portraying the Ethiopians, or Marco Polo the Mongols. Most of their countrymen spoke no foreign language, saw life in strictly French terms, and looked upon all other peoples as the Athenians had envisaged the Scythians.

At the end of the first performance of the French translation of Synge's *Playboy of the Western World*, the Frenchman next to me exclaimed: "So he killed his father? What's so funny about that?"

Twenty-five years later a Paris surgeon reacted to my suggestion that he accompany me to China with candid amazement. "Me? Go to China? When everything is better here?"

Actually, in many cultural matters, Paris in 1913 *was* Athens. In consequence, cultured Frenchmen took it for granted that foreign writers like Stefan Zweig the Austrian, Christian Rimestadt the Dane, and young Edgar Mowrer should focus their attention on French literature and only natural that Moreas the Greek, Apollinaire the Pole, and two other Americans, Francis Viélé-Griffin and Stuart Merrill, had adopted French as their chosen vehicle of expression. That Joseph Conrad had abandoned his native Polish for English was beyond their understanding. Were not Frenchman leading in all the arts?

In music, Claude Debussy, whom I was to meet and admire, had stretched classical forms in accordance with his belief that "melody is . . . almost anti-lyrical and powerless to express the constant change of emotion and life."

Yet in Moscow, Alexander Scriabine claimed to have broken old molds with new chords. And, in addition, improving on Rimbaud, he had proclaimed what he called the "chromatic value of tone": C—rose; G—rosy orange; D—yellow; A—green; E and B—pearl blue (?) with a shade of midnight; F—dark red; F-sharp—bright blue; D-flat—violet; A-flat—purple; E and B-flat—steely with a glint of metal. This in turn encouraged a French woman named Valentine de Saint-Point to stage, in December, 1913, something she called "Mélanchorie," a fusion of all the arts, in which geometry and color, poetry, music, and even smell were supposed to blend with her dancing in one supreme harmony.

Unhappily the unique Paris performance, which I attended, was interrupted by an eruption of smoke from the incense pots causing such paroxysms of coughing and laughing that there never was a second.

The new music inspired one sardonic traditionalist to urge that it always be played on the newly invented reversible gramophone since "it is not certain that the composers themselves would be capable of telling which way the disk was revolving."

In painting, the impressionists were being pushed aside by post-impressionists, primitivists, "fauves," expressionists, and cubists, whose productions occasionally confused one in Vildrac's gallery. Some young writers found Rodin "plaster-casty" and preferred Epstein, Gaudier-Brzyska, and a Serb called Mestrovic. In literature, young men like my new friends were consciously creating a "new poetry" that was to predominate for a long time.

This, decidedly, was the age of the little literary magazine. New ones blossomed regularly. When it became known in Paris that a young American was writing on French literature, editors put my name on their respective free lists.

The French theater was less touched by revolution. With the exception of the national playhouses (where I was twice fortunate enough to see Sarah Bernhardt act), it was pretty much cluttered with "bourgeois" dramas, all very much alike. Only at the *Vieux Colombier* was the talented Jacques Copeau exploring new directions.

To me the greatest thrill of an exciting year was the Russian Ballet at the Châtelet Theater. As a young opera buff in Chicago, I had become familiar with classical ballet. I had also witnessed a superb performance by Pavlova and Mordkin and been fascinated by the dances of Jacques Dalcroze. Fokine's *Ballets Russes* were something different, a marvelous mixture of "nature" (revived by Isidora Duncan) and of primitive Russian romanticism embodied in those two living miracles, Vaslav Nijinsky and Tamara Karsavina. These I had seen in 1911. Fokine, who succeeded Nijinsky, had less to offer, but the ensembles were incomparable. By economizing on meals for a couple of months I managed to see each ballet in Fokine's Paris repertoire at least once.

Isidora Duncan's beauty, vitality, and "Hellenistic" abandon had fascinated artists like Gordon Craig. But her major interest, it seemed to me, lay in her intense personal life. Her dancing, though admittedly "seminal," interested me far less than the formal Greek patterns revived and being taught in Paris by her brother, Raymond.

This strange American son of Scotch-Irish parents, who looked like a Sioux Indian, went around Paris, rain or shine, summer or winter, in a knee-length, hand-woven Greek peplum, bare feet in sandals, with no hat on his black, shoulder-length hair.

Shortly after arriving in France, I visited his school-colony, a place called the "Froggery" at Montfermeil just outside of Paris, in order to write an article about it. I could not sell the article, but Raymond's disciples "sold" me and my sister-in-law, Winifred.

Raymond aimed at a complete reeducation of the human being through handicraft and beauty. Every true Duncanite was not only classical dancer but carpenter, mason, potter, weaver, gardener, and cook.

For some months Winifred and I frequented the Duncan studio in Rue Campagne-Première, dancing with Jacques (a medical student), Bertrand (a shoemaker), Marguérite (a stenographer), Aïa (a pretty student who sold me a peplum she had woven), and other young people. Raymond, unfortunately, soon departed for Albania (assisted, incredibly, by the American Minister at Athens) in order to save the Epirotes, mostly Albanians, from a Greek government that wished to annex the area. In his absence, handsome young Bertrand led the dancers.

Although there were a number of American artists and writers in Paris, they were anything but conspicuous at the *Dôme*, the *Closerie des Lilas*, or the *Deux Magots*, which I usually patronized. Most of them had come to France "to sit at the first table, not the second," and like most of the other foreigners tried to appear, act, and even feel "French."

One or two, such as the sculptor, Paul Bartlett and the pianist, Walter Rummel, both of whom I met through Brother Paul, were already famous. One heard of Louis Ritman and Abel Warshavsky and we had known sculptor John Storrs since Chicago days. Paul introduced me to still another American sculptor, Hendrick Christian Andersen of Rome, who was peddling the idea of a fabulous world city and to the writer, Francis Grierson, whose study of Lincoln, *The Valley of the Shadow*, impressed me more than subsequent biographies of that great President.

Still another American, Horace Holley, kept a small bookshop where I occasionally went for a literary chat.

Holley wrote pious verse which inspired James Stephens, a marvelously mad Irish writer whom I met at Paul's dinner table, to produce for the *Dublin Review* one of the shortest book reviews on record: "Holley! Holley! Holley! Lord God Almighty!"

I considered Stephens to be one of the great prose writers of our time.

Shortly before my twenty-second birthday I decided to write not one but two books, one on contemporary French poetry, a sort of sequel to Arthur Symons' *Symbolist Movement in Literature*, another on the plays of François de Curel, a powerful dramatist almost unknown to Americans. As preparation I steeped myself in modern criticism, beginning with Taine (whose descriptions of certain past societies delighted me) and including Brandes, Emile Faguet, and Jules Lemaître.

So equipped, I made my choice of contemporary poets writing in French, beginning with Emile Verhaeren. This Belgian had made the shift from "traditional" poetic subjects to utmost modernity, notably, to the industrial cities that were mushrooming on both sides of the Atlantic. Verhaeren, I wrote, had been able "to sing in great rough chants the significant beauty of modernity." Twice I visited him at his apartment in Saint-Cloud and actually obtained both verbal encouragement and a couple of explanatory letters, parts of which I incorporated into my study of his work.

Imagine a small intense man with droopy mustache, who had overcome an original pathological introspection that brought on a nervous breakdown and, with the aid of his greatly devoted wife, remade himself into something like an extrovert. His chief talent, for me, lay in his ability to extract the last ounce of romance from a rapidly industrializing world: the interminable rain in Flanders, the monotonous Belgian plains (so diminutive compared with those I knew in the Middle West), and the new "tentacled cities" with their sporadic popular riots.

Among other recognized "greats," I included Henri de Régnier, the idol of my friend, Charles de la Garde; the towering Claudel, whose latest play, *l'Otage*, I saw produced; gentle Francis Jammes; the Comtesse de Noailles, typical of French women poets; the two American-born symbolists, Stuart Merrill and Francis Viélé-Griffin; and Paul Fort (for his spontaneity, so different from so much labored "modern" verse).

I planned to add the unique writing couple, Georges and Cécile Perrin, and devote a short chapter to that notorious freak, Guillaume Apollinaire, whose masterpiece, *Alcoöls*, was said by some to express his sorrow at being abandoned by Marie Laurençin, whose noseless portraits I found charming.

Finally, I expected to describe fully the works of the *Abbaye* poets, whom I considered the most promising in all France.

My book grew slowly, for I was desperately eager to achieve status (and money) by writing articles, and regularly interrupted my major task to treat any subjects that might sell: a study of the late French novelist, Jules Renard, whose *Poil de Carotte* I admired; another of Britain's new poet laureates, Robert Bridges; an adverse criticism of Anatole France's *Le Génie Latin*; translations of a short story by Arcos and an essay of Bazalgette, and a critical study of *The French Today and Their Drama*.

All were rejected. During thirteen months as a youthful freelancer, I earned just forty-six dollars. Nonetheless my confidence never lagged. For shortly after my arrival, either Francis Grierson or Horace Holley, I forget which, had directed my attention to *The New Free Woman*. This was, I was told, a magazine put out in England by Dora Marsden, devoted to "individualism, anarchy, and experimentalism." To be sure, it did not pay anything.

What did I care? Just to be published would be heaven.

The New Free Woman was both free and feminist. Its discussions of eroticism were as uninhibited, though far less vulgarly expressed, than the Henry Miller–Durrell–Burroughs type decades later. As for its feminism, well . . . marriage, a contributor pontificated, "is dead among refined women . . . the vast majority of refined women have left marriage behind them forever."

The magazine was also dedicated to the kind of artistic disorder which a few months in Paris had led me to distrust. Therefore it was with no great hope that, around the end of September, 1913, I sent the editor *Discipline and the New Beauty*, a short attack upon irresponsible aesthetic experimentation. While recognizing that the modern world had "gone too far along the road of individualism to return to fixed artistic rules," I wrote optimistically: "Happily it appears that individual thought will gradually become more and more general and that it will not be long until each man will feel the need for disciplining himself. . . . Meanwhile chaos reigns—an amusing and fascinating, fermenting chaos that juggles with the great ideas of the past with a sort of feverish grace—but still a chaos."

Yet this "reactionary" outburst Dora Marsden accepted. She even asked for further contributions! My delight was total. Without waiting a day I went to work on *The Dearth of Genius,* which further criticized those who wanted "thrills in the way of painted or musical monstrosities." Their unnatural thirst would, I predicted, end when "the motion picture sifts those from the reading public who do not find it worth while to read . . . and a better social adjustment gives sensitive intellectuality time to catch up with the other faculties of the race."

The Dearth appeared December 1, 1913, one month after *Discipline.* Thus I found myself among an unusual group of writers, most of them young. Britishers included Richard Aldington, F. S. Flint, D. H. Lawrence, a Ford Maddox Hueffer (not yet Ford), and Rebecca West. Many were Americans: Robert Frost, Amy Lowell, Ezra Pound, H. D., and that pair of experimental *vers libristes,* William Carlos Williams and John Gould Fletcher. I admired Lawrence, Frost, H. D., and some Aldington; the others did not impress me. In fact, *Imagistes* and Futurists compared with my favorite contemporary poets, Francis Thompson and Yeats, as the *Graeculi* of the Greek anthology with Sophocles. Iconoclasm I could appreciate, but not the kind that replaced a broken Buddha with a Billikin.

The New Free Woman had been founded on the avowed assumption that "scientifically speaking, woman is the human type of which man is an eccentric abnormal development." But on January 1, 1914, Dora and her friends, perhaps to attract male "abnormals," changed the magazine's name to the *Egoist,* a classification in which neither sex had a monopoly.

The first *Egoist* carried my contribution, *France Today, A Group of Modern Thinkers,* in which I defended the French against the perennial Anglo-Saxon charge of being decadent. Succeeding issues contained two more of my pieces—a chapter from my coming book, about the young poet suicide, Léon Deubel; and a mocking study of a French eccentric, Georges Politi, who claimed to have reduced all possible literary characters to exactly 154,980, and all possible plots to a number I have forgotten. Of both only so many remained to be created.

The *Egoist* was simultaneously publishing a serial, *Portrait of the Artist as a Young Man,* by a not-so-young, erudite, decidedly offbeat Irishman named James Joyce, whose previous manuscript, *Dubliners,* was about to appear as a book.

Thanks to the hospitality of the *Egoist,* I had already decided to remain in France until Father suspended my allowance or I became able to support myself by writing.

France was becoming a second home. Parisians worked hard but idled a great deal. The Grands Boulevards at carnival time were often so packed with young people, laughing, talking, that traffic was stalled for as much as twenty minutes. On Sundays and holidays those who could went to the country. Others strolled along the Champs Elysées. A population stabilized at under forty million appalled the nationalists, who saw the Germans increasing steadily in numbers and power. But it made for a spacious life.

We *Rive-Gauche*-ers had little love for the city west of the Invalides, north of the Palais Royal, or east of the Place des Vosges. Our own quarter offered bookstores, picture galleries, cheap restaurants, attractive cafés and parks. What more could we want?

Living where I did, my usual walks were along the Seine. In particular, the Pont des Arts, the foot bridge facing the Institut, became a great magnet to me as it had been half a century earlier to Little Billee of Du Maurier's *Trilby*. Sometimes I stared for hours at the smooth, sliding waters, the caravans of tug-drawn barges, the Louvre, the Institut, the statue of Henry IV against the sky, workmen in purple corduroy pants and berets, passing girls, nothing at all, thinking of my coming book, my future as an author, planning this and that, and always enjoying myself. Whenever I could, I traveled by river boat (*bateau mouche*) instead of by bus.

Better to know the city, I made a practice of setting out from the Rue de Seine at 6:00 P.M. every free evening and walking in one direction for sixty minutes, and then returned home by bus or metro. Thus I became familiar with most of the town, from Saint-Ouen to the Porte d'Orleans and from La Villette to the Pointe du Jour.

Sometimes, as late as midnight, I prowled the distant Bois de Boulogne in the company of an American girl, Mary Heitkamp, an excellent pianist. It did not occur to Mary or me to be afraid. Compared with American cities of the nineteen sixties, "wicked" Paris was a law-abiding place.

Early in 1914, I began supplementing walks through Paris with weekend tramps in the countryside. Each Friday afternoon I bought a third-class railroad ticket to wherever five francs would take me—toward Rouen, Amiens, or Chartres. Leaving the train at an unknown and generally obscure destination, I sought dinner and cheap lodging. Saturday and most of Sunday I walked, ending at another railroad station, and back to Paris. In the process I learned to know the rural French, so different from the Parisians. When, after hearing me speak, these country people sometimes concluded that I was a Frenchman from "another part of the land," I was flattered.

Repeatedly I visited Notre Dame and even more often the Sainte Chapelle. Letting the light pour in upon me through the latter's stained glass windows, which I preferred even to those of Chartres Cathedral, I became ever more certain that great art requires a great subject. And of all subjects, religion is the greatest. This explained why those whose art served religion—the Hindus, the Greeks, the best Byzantines, Gothic builders and glass makers, the earliest Renaissance artists—surpassed the others. They simply had more to say. This, I now think, is what Henry Adams had in mind in describing the role of the Virgin of Chartres.

In the early spring of 1914, Mother invited me to take her on an "art trip" through Belgium and Holland. There I came really to know Rubens, Breughel, Vermeer, Hals, and Rembrandt. The chimes of Antwerp Cathedral still echo in my dreams.

During the winter, Lilian had twice visited me in Paris, and we agreed to marry. Around Easter, I visited her at Hastings and met her mother.

Never have I been happier. In retrospect, Winston Churchill described these years as the "sunset of the old world." And truly, a world was dying. But to many who were young then, it seemed a glorious sunrise.

Yet by the time Mother and I returned to Paris from the Low Countries, before the chestnut trees bloomed along the boulevards, I began to sense a new and disturbing spirit, part sheer irrationality, part national belligerence. Some two years before a syndicalist named Georges Sorel had published a book, *Réflexions sur la Violence*, which was an appeal to labor for "direct action." I could not know that Sorel had found a disciple in a revolutionary refugee from Italy called Mussolini and, through him, would inspire an Austrian called Schicklgruber to set the world aflame. But another Italian, a vociferous poet called Marinetti, who had glorified Italy's unprovoked invasion of Turkish Libya in 1911, advocated destroying all of Italy's past art works and historical monuments.

And in staid England, of all places, young Richard Aldington hailed Marinetti as "a fearless experimenter . . . a great deal better than the bourgeois and women who grin at him when he reads. He must be very good for Italy."

Certain French newspapers were becoming more and more truculent concerning the need for France to recover from Germany the lost provinces of Alsace and Lorraine, whose symbolic statues on the Place de la Concorde were permanently draped in black. Déroulède and Barrès fanned the flame of nationalism. Even the admirable Péguy added fuel.

An Englishwoman, a Miss Richardson, had deliberately cut up Velasquez's incomparable painting of Venus in the Louvre. And in March, 1914, the wife of the French Minister of Finance, Joseph Caillaux by name, had shot dead the editor of *Le Figaro*, Gaston Calmette, for attacking her husband's integrity. Calmette was a nationalist, a champion of the recently voted increase in French military service.

Obviously, too, the rivalry between the Triple Alliance and the Triple Entente was sharpening, although I could not see just why. In April, Britain had had "naval talks" with Russia in Paris.

Even in America chauvinism seemed to be rising. Our troops in Mexico were fighting a usurper called Huerta. But was it not high time, as Bazalgette had argued in the essay I translated, that civilized peoples limited their rivalry to economic and cultural matters?

My friends felt almost sure that major war was a thing of the past. Small Balkan peoples might still fight or a larger power invade a colonial territory. But Norman Angell had demonstrated in the *Great Illusion* that large countries could not wage war against each other for more than three months and avoid bankruptcy. What country could be sure of winning in so short a period?

Yet war or no war, I could not expect Father to continue supporting an able-bodied son. Unless I had a book accepted by the end of the summer, thus acquiring at least the prospect of a regular income, I would find myself going home with no hope of an early marriage with Lilian.

All through May and June I worked harder and harder, generally not even taking time to read the newspaper headlines. Then at dinner one night, the wife of Gelett Burgess, of "Purple Cow" fame, gave me a shock. The previous evening the papers had reported that a half-crazy young Serb, Gavrilo Princip, had deliberately murdered the Archduke Francis Ferdinand of Austria. Mrs. Burgess related that she had found the hotel chambermaid, Marie, weeping while she made the bed. Asked why, Marie had muttered something about the dead Archduke and her husband, Alphonse. What, Mrs. Burgess wanted to know, was the possible connection between Francis Ferdinand of Austria and Marie's Alphonse?

I saw the connection only too well. Marie expected war. Just at this point Paul unexpectedly returned alone from America, explaining that he anticipated trouble.

Next, I overheard my landlady, Madame Hostiou, talking of war with her brother, a handsome young Breton drayman. Yvon might have to go. The gentle Vildrac suddenly became taciturn. Arcos, the ever serene, was irritable. Among friends only Charles de la Garde, strangely enough, seemed unmoved by the prospect of a fight with Germany. Looking coldly at the French people for perhaps the first time, I had to admit that there were a good many like Charles. By July, I was finding it increasingly hard to concentrate on my work.

For a few weeks nothing conclusive happened. The weather became wet and stuffy. The newspapers spoke of constant diplomatic negotiations to arrange matters. Father had, I believe, wired Mother to come home and she had refused. For the first time in her life she was in the middle of big events and she intended to see all she could. So did I. Instead of working, I roamed the streets, often dropping into Paul's office for the latest news.

When the Serbs accepted almost *in toto* an Austrian ultimatum, I told myself: "Now we shall have peace."

But the following day, Austria rejected the Serbian answer. Russia began growling. Germany followed. And Madame Hostiou's other lodger, a young German bookstore clerk, suddenly disappeared, ordered home by the German Consulate General in Paris. Britain expressed concern over Belgium.

Next Austria declared war on Serbia. The gold and silver money hitherto in universal use swiftly disappeared into the stockings of hoarders. The Banque de France put out paper five and twenty franc notes.

On July 31, bands of young men marched through the streets singing the *Marseillaise,* and shouting "To Berlin," "Death to the Kaiser!" and "Long live the Army." The same evening a young French nationalist, Raoul Villain, assassinated the socialist leader, Jean Jaurès. Jaurès, like Caillaux, stood for an understanding with the Germans and had advised inviting President Wilson to mediate the current dispute.

On the following morning, when Madame Hostiou brought in my breakfast, she announced: "The young men are beginning to leave. The stations are full of them. Oh Monsieur Mowrer, this is it."

In the middle of the afternoon, after hours at my table unable to write a sentence, I went out to see what I could see. By sheer coincidence, as I approached the Préfecture de Police on the Ile de la Cité, I noticed a policeman pasting a huge announcement on the official bulletin board. At the top, in big letters, I read: *Land and Sea Armies* . . . and just below: *Order of General Mobilization.*

This was it, all right. *La Belle Epoque* was over. Things would never be the same again—nor would I.

PART TWO

War

Witness

Howbeit every nation made gods of their own and put them in the high places.

II KINGS 17–29

4

Journalist Pro Tem

*Ce qui n'a pas été perçu, et est en même temps
simple, est nécessairement imprévisible.*

HENRI BERGSON

BY AUGUST 5, Europe, including Britain, was at war. Most French
people were confident of a fairly rapid victory. Nothing had so helped
France's morale as to have both Belgium and Britain as allies. Reliance
on the Russian "steamroller" was general. Only Reginald Kann, a
veteran French war correspondent, anticipated a drawn-out conflict.

One thing puzzled me. The bulk of the French and British peoples
had not wanted to fight. Yet on both sides of the Channel the outbreak
of hostilities had released a deep something that varied from quiet
satisfaction to wild enthusiasm. That two rival novelists, Thomas
Mann in Germany and Maurice Barrès in France, should exalt combat
was perhaps natural. Their respective countries had been enemies for
two thousand years. But why did France's anything but belligerent
Premier, René Viviani, who had withdrawn French troops six miles
behind the frontier to avoid incidents, echo Barrès?

Many Englishmen had, according to the *Egoist's* editor, Dora
Marsden, anticipated the chance to fight with "silent hope." Could it
be that, to quote Miss Marsden, in all countries arguments against war
broke down whenever an "opportunity presented itself to wage a good
one"? Admittedly, most of the history one studied centered around
armed conflict. And I was reminded that my brother Paul, who until
1912 had considered war obsolescent, returned from covering the Balkan
conflict convinced that he had misjudged human nature.

"I was an eater of tea-cake," he wrote in a poem that slightly
shocked me. Now the outbreak of war fever in so many unexpected
places seemed to show that he was right.

43

Actually, I had a slight touch of that fever myself. Not that I thought of enlisting in the French Army, the way many other foreigners in France were doing. Just as French recruits went to the railroad stations singing, "*C'est l'Alsace et la Lorraine qu'il nous faut*," so in those first war days hundreds of young Scandinavians, Rumanians, Luxembourgers, Spaniards, Latin Americans, Britishers, and even Russians paraded through Paris streets, some of them with drums, carrying banners and singing the *Marseillaise*, of all war songs the most exciting. Over a hundred young U.S. Americans enlisted in the French Army or air force. I watched them with interest but felt no urge to imitate them, if only because I felt sure that the war would be over before anyone with no previous military training would be ready for active combat. Spending the war in a French barracks was the last thing I wanted.

Nonetheless, those August days produced within me a flush of excitement and curiosity that made literary work impossible. During my brother's absence in America in early summer, I had, at his request, left the Rue de Seine and moved into his apartment in order to keep Mother company. There I brought my baskets of papers and my many cases of books. But how concentrate on French poetry or drama when all around me was the raw stuff of supreme poetry and the most heroic drama in a hundred years? More often than not, instead of working, I found myself reading those single sheets to which Paris newspapers had shrunk or listening for the sound of a demonstration outside. The first hint of one of these brought me into the street determined to miss nothing.

During the week of general mobilization, thousands of young men poured out of Paris through the North and East Stations, where poignant partings brought tears to my eyes as well as to theirs. Troop trains frequently bore the inscription, "To Berlin." Some French might eventually reach the German capital, but many, I thought sadly, were going on their last journey.

As the young soldiers left, thousands more poured in from the South and West, only to leave in turn for some unknown battlefield. To fill the empty places, all over France old men and women took over.

In the capital many shops closed altogether. So did the museums, theaters, and big hotels like the Ritz, some of them reopening as hospitals. The Government put a curfew on wineshops and restaurants, 8:00 and 9:00 P.M. respectively. On August 8, it began locking the old-fashioned city gates from 6:00 P.M. to 6:00 A.M. Since the nearest German troops were still hundreds of miles away, nobody understood just whom the authorities were keeping out. A week later somebody rescinded the order.

In the days immediately following the outbreak of war, some Parisians molested a few German-speaking people, and asked young foreigners like me why they were not in uniform. "Patriotic" mobs broke into shops with Germanic names like Appenrodt and Rumpelmayer, and smashed everything they could not carry away, unmindful of the occupants' frantic protests when they happened to be neither German nor Austrian. That the Maggi milk chain was indubitably Swiss did not save it.

Yet I could not but notice that even as the rioting abated, popular hatred of Germany increased. Rumors and eyewitness stories of German atrocities in Belgium and northern France increased from day to day. Obviously the German Army was trying to make the war "short, sharp, and decisive" by adopting the terrorism recommended by Clausewitz. German commanders were permitting wholesale looting. Let but one Belgian or French civilian open fire and the invaders burned and destroyed the nearest community and shot scores of hostages. Conspicuous examples were the deliberate burning of the great Belgian library of Louvain and the senseless bombardment of Rheims Cathedral three weeks later. A Luxembourg girl whom I met in the subway on the way to the Gare du Nord, and persuaded to have a drink with me before her train left, had received a letter from home via Switzerland. Its description of the treatment of her countrymen and nearby Belgians by the German soldiery shocked me almost to the point of nausea. How was this possible? The Germans I knew in America were no worse than the rest of us.

Yet no physical atrocities so hurt the German cause the world over as Chancellor Bethmann-Hollweg's reference to the treaty guaranteeing Belgian neutrality as a "scrap of paper."

Once the mobilization was complete, a great silence crept over Paris. The poorer quarters had, in contrast with the cheering crowds in the center, from the beginning accepted the war with silent resignation. Many French workmen had adored the murdered Jaurès. The Latin Quarter, once alive with students and Bohemians, took on a dreamlike emptiness. Once the stillness had spread to the center, the "entrenched camp" was, as I wrote, "like a city plague-stricken on a holiday, its flags flying, its fountains playing, its women sad-faced and waiting." Others compared it to a "summer hotel out of season." Yet there were no draft-dodgers and few defeatists. In 1914, as Barbara Tuchman later put it, "glory was a word spoken without embarrassment and honor a familiar concept that people believed in."

How was the war going? We waited in vain to know. Both sides seemed to have launched what would now be called a *Blitz*. Although some Germans were held up by the forts of Liège, the German right wing was clearly planning to sweep into France from Belgium. The French, following their current doctrine of "extreme offensive," had stormed into Mulhouse in Alsace and then been forced to retreat. According to rumors and scraps of information that got back, bayonet charges were proving ineffective against massed German machine guns.

As the novelty of wartime began to wear off, I became even more restless. Within a few weeks at most, I feared, Father would expect me to return to America.

Unexpectedly a letter came from Lilian inviting me to join her at the annual Shakespeare festival in Stratford-on-Avon. Here was a chance to observe England at war. Fortunately, a limited number of trains for civilians were again running, subject to military delay.

Then a happy surprise: at Amiens, where I had to change trains, the station and several waiting trains were full of a medley of foreign soldiers—Scots in kilts, Indians in turbans, and wild-looking Moroccans. They had come! In Paris we had not known that any foreigners had landed. Boulogne was also full of them. The Tommies' relations with the French population, especially with the girls, were obviously excellent. And one of three tall kilted Scots, with whom I took an evening walk along the beach, informed me that Britain was sending no less than half a million men to France.

At Stratford, Lilian and I went boating on the gentle Avon, where a friendly boatman urged us to rent, instead of a rowboat, a broad, flat-bottomed punt . . . "more convenient for the likes of you." Truly a kind thought, though we stuck to the rowboat.

Each evening we saw a different play by Shakespeare. Almost as if it had foreseen the coming of war, Stratford was producing the historical dramas. And Frank Benson, both producer and leading actor, electrified his audiences with lines like, "O God of Battles, steel my soldiers' hearts."

Yet so far as most Britishers were concerned, the God of Battles was still asleep.

If their relaxation was noticeable in charming rural Stratford, it was overwhelming in London. All shops were open. Men were busy at their weekend golf. Even in a people sheltered behind an invincible fleet, the total absence of urgency was perplexing. Here was Britain involved in a war of uncertain cost and duration. Yet any number of citizens were advocating business as usual. Still, I told myself, the war could not last very long and "our side" (Lilian's side was obviously mine) could not lose. (Think of those millions of Russians!) So sure were we that we parted with a promise to spend the coming Christmas holiday together skating in Holland.

Yet I found the Chicago *Daily News* correspondent in London, Edward Price Bell, tense enough to satisfy anyone, passionately pro-British, and as bitter against the Germans as any Frenchman. President Wilson's recent appeal to Americans to be "neutral" in word as in deed had outraged him. He saw the war less as a German attempt to conquer France (incidental) than as the culmination of a long-term policy to oust Britain from the European leadership it had exercised since it defeated Bonaparte. When I described the contrast between London and Paris, Ed begged me to write my impressions for the *News*. With great care I produced my first story for a real newspaper.

Thirty-six hours later, at Paul's apartment in the Rue du Bac, my brother came into the room where I was working perfunctorily on my study of François de Curel.

"I need an assistant to look after the office when I travel. De la

Garde cannot write proper English. Nor can Arcos, whom I am thinking of hiring if he is relieved of military service. But you know France and can both write your own pieces and translate theirs. What about taking a job in my office? You could not have a better place from which to see the war. And when it is over, you can go back to the work you like. I'll give you fifteen dollars a week to start on."

"That's not much," I objected, concealing a wild desire to shout.

"It's as much as I got when I started. Let's agree that after two weeks I'll either fire you or raise you to twenty-five. Either way you won't be disappointed."

Here was the independent income I so badly needed. Sixty dollars a month was more than Father was giving me.

The end of August found the erstwhile "man of letters" seated at an imposing desk in the Chicago *Daily News* office at 10, Boulevard des Capucines, summing up the morning newspapers for the chief correspondent. And just at the right time. The previous day, I had watched a German warplane, a *Taube*, dropping over Paris three small bombs and leaflets calling on the French to surrender. (General Foch considered the military value of airplanes to be "zero.") As a result, the French Government ordered a nocturnal blackout of the capital. Instead of panicking, the Parisians started collecting in boulevard cafés at 6:00 P.M., called "dove time" (*l'heure des Taubes*), in order not to miss what became regular appearances over the city.

The French Cabinet, after long debates, had decided to defend Paris "to the last man" and, in consequence, to betake itself to Bordeaux lest it be captured if the city fell.

Clearly a showdown was approaching. Excitement mounted. Women lined up for food supplies before the larger groceries. Rumor insisted that the English were at Compiègne, only fifty-two miles from Paris, then that the Germans were there. When the French Government decamped to Bordeaux, thousands of nervous citizens went along, clogging the stations in their eagerness to escape. Many who stayed behind ridiculed the fugitives by singing a parody of the *Marseillaise*: "*Aux gares, citoyens!! Montez dans vos wagons!*" Once again Mother refused to budge.

The place of those who fled was taken by thousands of incoming refugees from the North, some on foot, a few in motorcars, a good many in horse-drawn wagons. Some came in barges all the way from Belgium.

And all this, mind you, was occurring in Paul's absence. Exactly twenty-four hours after installing me in his office, he had set out to cover the fighting in Belgium.

This left his inexperienced brother in what seemed likely to become a beleaguered city, cut off from all communications or instructions, yet responsible for reporting what he could learn of a coming battle that might decide the outcome of the entire war!

I did what I could. I read everything available, including occasional London newspapers, which were less heavily censored. I consulted anyone who might possibly have something to tell. I interviewed selected refugees from among the many thousands. Above all, I relied on my brother's friend and colleague, Phil Simms of the United Press, an experienced correspondent who took pity on my lack of experience. But mostly, like the Parisians, I just waited.

After Paul left, my first dispatch, on whose composition I spent many hours, evoked a cabled protest from the Chicago editor: he objected to the Latin quotation with which I led off, and suggested that "in deference to our readers," I stick to English. But since he printed it (without the Latin) and thereafter front-paged what few bulletins and descriptions the French censors grudgingly passed, what did I care?

Traditional newspaper leads—first the gist in one sentence, then the substance in one paragraph, and only then the detailed account— these violated all those rules of literary suspense which I had carefully cultivated. However, I was on probation and thereafter almost always wrote as Chicago would have it. Nonetheless, a few weeks later, the paper featured my story of a cavalry combat between British hussars and German uhlans which began with a quatrain of William Morris:

"Swerve to the left, young Roger," he said,
"When you catch his eye through the helmet slit,"
"Swerve to the left, then out at his head,
"And the good God give you joy of it!"

Though far from the battlefields, our editor recognized how beautifully these lines introduced my story, and front-paged them once again.

Before September, Paris had seen only isolated Frenchmen in uniform—their red pants made them conspicuous anywhere. Suddenly thousands began pouring into the city.

One morning, the Rue du Quatre Septembre outside the office was filled with marching French *fantassins*. Onlookers started to cheer, then suddenly stopped. Were these men or zombies? Rank on rank they filed by, in perfect order, heavy packs on back, rifles on shoulder, but with faces the color of putty, and eyes shut tight. They were asleep!

A policeman explained: "They have covered fifty miles in the last twenty-four hours!" The weather was stiflingly hot, the men's uniforms of heavy wool. (General Franchet d'Esperay, one of France's finest, had cut short a subordinate who complained that his men could walk no further by shouting: "You will march or drop dead." Thereby he saved his army.)

For the endless marches in the sweltering heat were as exhausting for the pursuing Germans. Moreover, their commanders, arrogantly confident of a speedy victory (their plan of battle called for the defeat of France by the thirty-ninth day) were permitting their pursuing columns to refresh themselves with whatever spirits and wine they could steal. A good many young invaders became drunk and had to be left behind, while the rest pressed on, reviving their courage from time to time by singing *Die Wacht am Rhein* and *Heil Dir im Siegerkranz*.

Fortunately for France, not all the soldiers who made up Maunoury's new Sixth Army were exhausted.

Paris wildly cheered a regiment of Zouaves fresh from Africa, as they swaggered through town from the Gare Montparnasse to their barracks. A first British warplane that circled over the waiting city became an omen of victory. Two separate stories that spread like forest fires silenced the doubters. The first was the true report of a great Russian victory over the Austrians at Lemberg (the Russians' defeat by the Germans at Tannenberg was still unknown). The second, the source of which nobody seemed to know, was startling: a large force of Russian Cossacks had been seen passing through Britain on their way to France. They could not be long in arriving. This highly successful canard was a fine example of that "psy-war" which was to become so important in later years.

Obviously, a decisive battle was imminent. On September 4, the censors passed my bulletin to the effect that French preparations to defend Paris were complete. On September 7, they let through another bulletin: the right flank of the oncoming Germans had swerved away from Paris to the southeast. Implication: no siege of Paris, at least not until after a lost battle. On the other hand, the censors adamantly stopped all references to the Parisian taxicabs which transported from the city to the Ourcq Canal several thousand French troops who were to prove a decisive factor in the Battle of the Marne. On September 10, four days after the event, I was allowed to mention that the fighting was "moving farther to the East."

Only on September 15 did the *Daily News* receive my story of the French victory (definite three days earlier) and my prediction that, as a result of the French offensive on the River Aisne (actually launched on that same day), the German retreat might become a rout.

Instinctively (and how rashly!) we in Paris felt that with the failure of the German *Blitz*, the *Entente* was bound to win. Yet at the same time, I was conscious of a certain letdown. Mother seemed almost disappointed that Paris was not going to be besieged.

By this time Paul had returned from Belgium after fascinating experiences under German occupation, though somewhat chagrined at having missed the main show. Phil Simms consoled him by insisting how little he would have been able to know, still less publish, had he remained in Paris.

To me, the important thing was his coming reaction to my cable file. Like Nebuchadnezzar, I had been tried in the balances. Would I too be found wanting?

"Not too bad. I am raising your salary to twenty-five a week, and expect you to stay to the end of the war. It can't be long now."

I had made it.

Thereafter, greatly to my relief, Paul wrote most of the big stories while I switched to features: a description of a military hospital; another of a canteen for needy Bohemians from Montparnasse and Montmartre;

an aviator's report that, in all, two million German soldiers (the largest army yet recorded) had crossed the Rhine bridges and entered Belgium and France; eyewitness accounts of battle incidents and a gruesome thriller about the River Marne becoming so polluted by blood and corpses as to be undrinkable.

All through these stirring days American correspondents in France were unwelcome anywhere near the fighting. Like other newsmen, I was crazy to see all I could. Unlike most of them, I had a passport dating from 1913 (when I had half-expected to visit Russia), spoke fluent French, and was familiar with French habits. So when, at Paul's suggestion, Gelett Burgess and I finally wangled from the Prefecture of Police credentials permitting us to leave the entrenched camp, we piled ourselves and two rented bicycles into a northbound train and left it at Senlis, fourteen miles short of the front on the Aisne. A sentry discouraged any further advance in that direction. We could, however, as newsmen go anywhere else. And after lunch we pedaled eastward, disappointed but eager to see what we could of the recent battlefields.

The road was dense with civilians. Some were refugees returning to their homes on foot or in carts, now that the Germans had gone. Inhabitants who had remained behind mocked those who had fled.

About five o'clock Burgess, who was uncomfortable on a bicycle, demanded that we stop for a drink. The Germans had taken everything from the café except syrups and flavoring extracts, but the proprietor actually scraped up some bread and tea. Instead of relishing his good fortune, Burgess demanded napkins and when told there were none, complained, "Personally, I'd rather have the napkins than the tea."

Long before we reached Villers Cotterets, the sun had set. In the dark, we were twice nearly run over by detachments of French dragoons going to the front, who asked if *we* had seen *their* regiment! When we finally arrived, I realized with delight that we were at the headquarters of the French Fifth Army. To the north we heard the faint roar of guns.

Directed by a passing soldier, we headed for the Café de Paris, where we hoped to spend the night. Failing to find it, I approached a sentry standing before a large building.

"Be sure and ask him for the best hotel," Burgess insisted.

But when I did so, the sentry grinned. "Have you just arrived? Come in. Somebody here wants to see you."

Before we knew it, we were under arrest as spies. In answer to my insistence that we were free-born Americans with papers from the Paris police, the captain cursed me roundly. Next a major led us to the courtyard and locked us up in separate sheds. An hour later gendarmes arrived, and searched us, admitting their surprise to find that our papers were in order. Thereafter, chilled and unable to sleep either on half a sofa or on the wet muddy floor, I had plenty of time during the night to develop righteous resentment at such treatment.

The next morning a friendly corporal led us to the police station, where the *commissaire* apologized and explained that we had been "lacking in respect" to the captain. Back at headquarters, the major of the night before returned our bicycles and said we were free to go anywhere we liked except toward the front.

My pent-up resentment exploded. "As a favor, give me the name of that captain," I begged.

"Why do you want that?"

"When this war is over, I shall seek him out and break his nose!"

The major smiled indulgently.

"I understand your feelings, young man. But get over them. Not the captain, the entire French army is responsible for shutting you up, and remember that he may be dead tomorrow."

The last sentence hit home. I said nothing more.

Soon we were riding southward along the east bank of the Ourcq where the battle had raged two weeks before.

A few signs of the fighting still remained, mostly empty German, French, and British uniforms stripped of their buttons by the peasants. The latter seemed not to have suffered greatly. But they were indignant against the Germans for the financial levies on towns and for their posters proclaiming that in the case of shooting by civilian *francs-tireurs,* hostages would be hanged and towns burned.

"Nice people, the Germans!" Burgess commented.

"Remember the 'water cure' we gave to certain Filipinos," I countered. Yet I could not forget those posters. Did they really express the German people?

At Meaux, a strayed British hussar leading a limping horse gave us a marvelous description of his encounter with a German uhlan, which gave me the later description of cavalry combat. We returned to Paris by train.

In the absence of better material, the *News* in Chicago welcomed feature stories. At Paul's suggestion, I next wrote a long account of the propaganda war, concluding that intellectuals, particularly neutral Americans, should reserve their judgment on the responsibility for the conflict until all the facts were available.

Neither he nor I knew at the time we wrote that Chancellor Beth-mann-Hollweg, reputed to be a "moderate," had, as early as September 2, 1914, drawn up a plan for the German domination of Europe, which became the chief obstacle to a negotiated settlement.

Meanwhile the fighting was spreading rapidly. What Gelett and I had witnessed on the trip to Villers Cotterets had whetted my ambition to see and report as much of it as Paul and the military authorities would permit.

5

Death in Flanders Field

If we are to be crushed, let us be crushed gloriously.

BARON DE BASSOMPIERRE
*Belgian Under Secretary of
Foreign Affairs*

EARLY IN THE afternoon of October 16, 1914, I emerged from a building on the handsome Grand' Place in the little Belgian town of Furnes, with a paper in my hand that gave me such joy that on the steps I stopped to read it again: "Permit the bearer to circulate freely if he does not disturb operations; if he does, send him to the rear. He may not cross over to the enemy.

"Hénon, Major, General Headquarters."

I was a full-fledged war correspondent at last. Aged twenty-two, almost as young as Winston Churchill when he started covering the Cubans' revolt against Spain. Moreover, I was equipped with everything else the job required: a good pair of legs, comfortable shoes, field glasses, nearly a thousand dollars in British gold sovereigns in a money belt. That very morning I had walked the sixteen miles from Dunkerque to Furnes.

At the Hotel Royal, the glimpse of the sovereign in my hand had caused the *patronne* to decide that she could, after all, find me something to eat and even give me the front bedroom overlooking the square. Obviously, "St. George's Cavalry" worked magic.

While I hesitated on the steps of the headquarters in the Hôtel de Ville, a motorcar containing three British soldiers drove up. I asked them where the German armies were.

"Good Lord," one answered, "have they let you come this far? Well, since you are here, it can do no harm to tell you where they are. Here." On his map he pointed to the Belgian village of Middelkerke,

half way between Nieuport and Ostend. "Our line extends along the
Yser River from Nieuport to Dixmude."

Thanking him, I immediately set out on foot through the fields
—no poppies in October—toward Nieuport, some six miles distant. In
vain. At Wulpen, about half way, a dull-witted Belgian sergeant, after
looking at my new pass, turned me back, insisting that he had orders
to pass no civilians. My protests were no more potent than they had
been with the French officers at Villers Cotterets. It was too late to try
another road that day. With my spirits dashed but my dander mounting,
I returned to Furnes, determined to try another sector of the front and
then, if necessary, to appeal to Major Hénon. Surely he could not allow
his order to be flouted. . . .

That evening, as I sat in the crowded hotel dining room over a
three-franc meal and good Belgian beer, a tall civilian of perhaps twenty-
five approached.

"My name is Lumby. London *Times*. I'm staying here too. They
tell me you are an American journalist from Paris. May I sit down and
talk with you?"

Gladly I told him what I knew: how Joffre and the French had
decided to outflank the Germans on the Aisne and around Péronne,
and win the race to the sea; how, when we learned of this, my brother
had ordered me to go to Belgium; how, unable to get a hotel room in
Calais, I had spent the night in a private house with twenty-one refugees,
sharing a narrow bed with a wounded and bleeding Belgian soldier
who moaned continually for water which I fetched; how, with the
help of the American Consul in Calais, I got permission to proceed to
Dunkerque and thence to Furnes; how, learning that all such permissions were about to be revoked, I had evaded the French frontier police
by walking along the unguarded beach from Dunkerque until well into
Belgium.

In turn, Lumby informed me that one million out of eight million
Belgians had preferred exile to military occupation. Now the situation
was critical. The German divisions that had taken Lille and Antwerp,
heavily reinforced by new army corps from Germany, were advancing
rapidly. Only the Belgian troops stood between the Germans and the
vital Channel ports through which the British were coming into France.
London and Paris had asked King Albert who was living on the coast
at La Panne, just a few miles away, to hold a ten-mile front until they
could send reinforcements. If he failed, the next few weeks would be
disastrous.

"Could we not cover the story together?" he asked.

Readily I agreed. Why not start out early the following morning
so as to see the show before other competing newsmen arrived?

"We don't have to hurry," Lumby grinned. "This whole area is now
closed to journalists. You were lucky. And anyhow, there are no
facilities for getting news out. I went once to Dunkerque and wired

from there, but if I go again I cannot get back. Perhaps we can persuade some officer to see that our dispatches get to London."

So, that was it. In Paris one could cable but not see. In Furnes one could see but not communicate. Still, the first thing was to see something worth communicating.

That very night, I awoke to find the windows of the Hotel Royal rattling under a terrific cannonading. The German offensive had begun. Too excited to sleep further, I rose early and, not finding Lumby, started on foot for Dixmude, from which the noise had come. Two hours later, I had covered the eight miles and reached the edge of the town without seeing a single soldier. Abruptly, about twenty-five yards away, an unseen Belgian gun emitted a roar followed by something between the whir of a high-speed electric motor and the scream of a wild animal. I must have jumped two feet. Then I heard laughter. A Belgian lieutenant appeared out of the ground, grinning at my discomfiture. When he had examined my papers, he asked: "Is this your first taste of war?"

When I said it was, he suggested I cross the Yser River, go about a kilometer further, and see something "really interesting." Still stunned by the noise, which had become continuous, I pushed on.

Fortunately for me, a French Marine captain stopped me in the middle of town and turned me back, explaining that the destination indicated by the Belgian would have left me halfway between the opposing lines.

"If the Belgians choose to let you pass their line of fire, I cannot object. But I refuse to let you get killed because of any negligence of mine." When he had described in full detail the opening German attack in the night, I retraced my steps and then, carefully stepping around three fresh corpses, the first I had ever seen, cut northward across the fields, to a tiny village called Oud-Stuyvenskerke, close to the river. There I got my next shock: out of nowhere came a whir that grew louder until it burst above me with a bang, scattering lead slugs at my feet—German shrapnel. So this was how it felt to be under fire.

I should have been afraid. Yet in some incomprehensible manner I had convinced myself that, as a "neutral," I ran no danger. . . .

My immediate goal was the belfry of the abandoned church. Climbing up a rickety ladder to a couple of planks stretched out over nothing, I suddenly found a revolver poked into my stomach and a stern voice demanding to know who I was. Yet once the Belgian artillery observer saw my pass, he offered me champagne from a bottle in a bucket, and kindly pointed out spots of interest along the front that stretched for miles on both sides of us.

"There, beyond the river, the French Marines have their bridgehead. Just beyond are the German front lines, and beyond those burning buildings in the distance, the German batteries. Here below us is our second line with our guns. See how the Yser River cuts the landscape into a chessboard as it approaches the sea. Ours is a strong position."

When the artillery duel died away, I thanked the lieutenant and returned to Furnes by way of Pervyse, a village with a leaning church tower. To witness my first battle, I had walked twenty miles.

Thereafter, for the next few days, with one brief interruption, Lumby and I registered every turn in the battle.

And we saw plenty. Two days later, we poked our heads through the skylight of a building in Nieuport Bains, at the mouth of the Yser, while thirteen French and British warships poured shells on the Germans attacking the Belgian bridgehead across the river at Lombaertzyde. They had set fire to the German-held village of Westend two miles up the coast. Nearest the shore and firing continually were four monitors originally built in Britain for the Brazilian Navy. When they suddenly made off in the direction of Dover, seven destroyers raced toward Westend with bow guns blazing, turning aside only at the last moment. Then it was the turn of two cruisers farther out, whose six-inch shells struck well inland with dull roars.

Meanwhile, the German guns along a two-mile stretch were concentrating their fire on the Belgian infantry outposts behind the river and the Belgian second line right at our feet. Some shells knocked stones from the nearby lighthouse, and some fell into the Yser, sending up clouds of water and shaking our building until I felt sure it would fall.

At the very height of the artillery duel, Lumby handed me his field glasses and pointed upstream. There, creeping over what looked like a shining thread was a stream of ants. Further examination identified them as Belgians going forward over a bridge of boats to reinforce their comrades beyond Lombaertzyde. The men seemed to spring from the ground, indicating the presence of a large Belgian force which we had not noticed. Even as we watched, the fire came nearer, the continuous tat-tat-tat of the Belgian machine guns contrasting with the regular one-two, one-two of the Germans.

Almost immediately clusters of other Belgians came running back across the sand dunes toward the bridge of boats. And suddenly the German gunners found the range and their shrapnel started making hits. Only when the mist thickened and the cannonading died away did the result of the fighting become apparent. The Belgians had lost Lombaertzyde but saved the bridgehead. The last figures to disappear were stretcher bearers painfully working their way back across the darkening dunes, carrying their precious burdens.

Once about a mile north of ruined Pervyse I stopped at a field hospital in a battered cellar to try to exchange a good cigar for a lunch. Just then a soldier came out, and when he saw me, ran forward holding the bandaged remains of what had been a hand.

"Just look at that! Just look at that! It happened just fifteen minutes ago right here."

His distress was so poignant that I winced. Yet all too soon, as I discovered, one ceased to be moved by such sights.

Lumby and I were seeing them regularly. But what good was this to our respective newspapers? During my first eight days in Furnes I had been able to transmit to London just one brief bulletin. Lumby had done no better. Finally, one night over dinner he informed me that he had decided to try to join the British Army which had, he was told, taken a position in front of Ypres.

This made sense for him. But I was one of those neutrals for whose news-needs neither the British nor the French were showing any understanding. Obviously, I must find some other way to get my battle stuff out. And in the middle of the night I awoke with a possible solution. Eight o'clock found me in Major Hénon's office.

After thanking him for permitting me to witness the valor of the Belgian soldiers, I voiced regret that Americans were learning so little about it. Moreover, German agents in America were insisting that Belgium was trying to use the German invasion as a means of later territorial aggrandizement. Would it not be useful if King Albert stated exactly what Belgium's position was?

Major Hénon thought it would. Two hours later I received, from the King's aide-de-camp, Major Gallet, at La Panne, a declaration to the American people:

"His Majesty King Albert desires it be made known that the one condition on which terms of peace can be discussed is the complete independence of the Belgian people, for which he is determined to struggle so long as a single man remains."

With this in hand, I returned to headquarters and told Hénon that in view of the political importance of the message, I felt I should take it personally to London and cable it from there. But with the battle still going on, I must be assured of the right to return to Furnes and report the rest of it. Within a few minutes I was in possession of a two-way pass marked "Important." That same evening, in a dilapidated ambulance, I set out for Dunkerque and London.

Ed Bell of the Chicago *Daily News* received me like a member of the family—and almost chained me to a typewriter.

"How many words?" I asked.

"All you can think of, Edgar; yours is the best story of the war so far."

For two full days I poured out an account of the Battle of the Yser—strategy, description, personal experiences, human interest—a four- or five-column story. Next, at Bell's request I completed three or four long mailers: eyewitness accounts by others, and picturesque anecdotes.

Ed not only rushed these to Chicago, but turned the cables over to the London *Daily Telegraph* which played them up in competition with Lumby's dispatches to *The Times*.

By this time I was back in Furnes—but not without further adventure. In Calais, the station master had told me: "There are no passenger trains from Dunkerque to Furnes. And I am not sure the French police will be impressed by your Belgian *laissez-passer*. They don't like newsmen."

What was I to do? At the station café, I was soon in conversation with an English chief surgeon at the next table, who seemed fascinated by my tales of the Belgian front.

"When are you going back?" he asked.

"As soon as I find a train for Furnes."

"Do you speak French?"

"Yes."

"Look here: we have a load of Belgian wounded coming in fresh from Furnes late tonight. If you will stand by and interpret while we give them first aid, I'll put you in the empty hospital train for Furnes."

"It's a bargain." That night for hours I stood by in the evacuation hospital and acted as an interpreter for the English doctors and nurses, while orderlies unloaded wounded Belgians fresh from the battlefields.

My instructions were to say something nice to each wounded man and then ask those who needed it if they consented to be operated on, as British law required, war or no war.

Simple enough. And for a while I had no difficulty. Then a bedraggled boy of about eighteen in a torn uniform limped into the operating room on a mangled foot in which shoe and flesh were inextricably mingled. When, following precise instructions, I asked him if the surgeon might amputate, he collapsed. And after a second wounded soldier, this time carrying half of his intestines in his hat pressed to his belly, fainted at the mention of an operation, I stopped asking the sinister question and let the British doctors think that the patients had specifically consented.

By 4:00 A.M., after the last wounded soldiers had gone through the hell of what was called "first aid," and moved on, I found myself in an empty third-class railroad car headed for Furnes, immeasurably relieved.

In fact, to a young man who had never seen a surgical operation without feeling sick, those two hours in the Calais station had been anguish. Twice I had to go outside for air. This, then, was the essence of war, of which battle spectacles were merely the glittering façade!

As the hospital train slowed down at Dunkerque, I had a moment's panic. What if the French perceived me through the window and ordered me out in spite of my royal Belgian authorization to return? Down I flopped under the seat into a puddle of blood, coming out only when the ambulance train had cleared this last French station.

It was high time to be back in Belgium. What might be called the second wave of the German offensive had started two days before, to the dismay of the defenders. Twenty thousand Germans had established a bridgehead on this side of the Yser. The Belgians had retreated to strong positions behind the railway embankment parallel to the river.

The very next day the Germans launched a new offensive at Ramscappelle, southeast of Nieuport. By walking along the railroad embankment in front of the Belgian lines I managed to reach the leaning church belfry at Pervyse.

Hardly had I climbed to the observation post when the Germans attacked again across the soggy fields. Through my glasses I could faintly see them advancing in mass formation, singing as they came, though just what I was too far away to determine. Then as the fire became hotter, I climbed down, made my way northward—and was sent to the rear by a French artillery lieutenant whose "seventy-fives" were "pouring it on" Ramscappelle. That night the Germans reached the embankment.

The situation looked desperate. Yet the next day a regiment of French black troops ("Turcos"), assisted by tough French Zouaves, and, I believe, by French foot *chasseurs*, drove the Germans back five hundred yards, as I observed when I arrived on the spot late that afternoon. The same day I had the fun of lunching with three goumiers (volunteer African cavalry in native dress), a Negro and two Arabs, who shared their rations with me. We could not converse, their French was too primitive. But I think I conveyed my thanks for their food and pleased them by the warmth of my admiration for their beautiful Arab horses tethered not far away.

That evening, again by sheer good luck, I ran into a Belgian acquaintance, Lieutenant Burney of the Armored Cars.

"How many Germans did you kill today?" I asked.

"None. You know, for me, it's all over here. The bridges are down and the roads will soon be under water."

"You mean flooded?"

"Sure. We opened the sluices three days ago and the water is rising. The Germans have called off their offensive. Ypres is where the next battle is going to be. In fact, it has already started."

Naturally, Burney would want to be in it, I thought. For this English-born Belgian volunteer, who spoke no English, was a dare-devil. Starting as a mechanic in Charleroi, he had, in just three months, by sheer daring worked his way up from private to command four armored cars—"motorized machine guns," he called them. Each car, a "bulletproof, topless tin can on a chassis," carried a machine gunner and two men with rifles to guard the flanks. Their principal function was covering retreats and raiding advancing German detachments while avoiding artillery fire. Burney claimed to have been the last Belgian soldier out of Ghent.

When I had first met him he was in the Hotel Royal writing his report of that day's action on the road beyond the Yser. This he permitted me to copy.

"From 3:04 P.M. to 3:16 P.M. fired 1280 cartridges; 120 German horsemen killed."

"You hear," he added, "killed. That doesn't count the horses or the wounded or those they may have carried off. When the others retreated, I counted the dead. I don't ask anything better. But if I weren't a lieutenant, I'd rather guard one side of the armored car with a rifle than handle *La Belle*" (his machine gun).

"Meanwhile risking being shot through the head," I commented.

"That is where all the fun lies. By the way, can you shoot?"

"A little. Why?"

"I thought perhaps, being a newspaper man, you'd like to take a ride with me tomorrow. I am not allowed to drive you out to the lines, but tomorrow morning just come over the bridge of boats across the Yser and ask for Burney. You'll find me in sight of the German trenches. Say you're my brother."

I tried not to show my reluctance. Being under fire was something to which I had become accustomed. But the prospect of standing beside Burney, guarding one flank of the "tin can" with a rifle, only thirty or forty yards from advancing Germans, while their comrades farther back took me as a target, was not alluring. Still, I accepted.

When, the next morning, I reached the bridge of boats, shells were bursting all around, the German machine guns were alarmingly close, and for the first time, my knees were shaking. Still, I had promised and I would perform.

Yet when a Belgian officer flatly refused to let me cross the bridge over the Yser I did not insist.

What was courage, anyway? I could understand a Belgian patriot welcoming the fight against a brutal invader. Tears had come into my eyes when, on the Grand' Place at Furnes, I had watched King Albert and General Joffre pass in review the Sixteenth French *Chasseurs-à-pied*, whom I considered the finest looking soldiers I had ever seen, and when, at another time, the King reviewed a heroic Belgian regiment of infantry, to the music of *La Brabanconne.*

Or one could be heroic for personal reasons. The ambulance driver who had taken me to Dunkerque on my way to London had exchanged places with an infantryman in the first line during a fierce German attack simply because a French girl with whom he had fallen in love asked him for a German helmet!

But the source of Burney's absolute fearlessness was a burning thirst for adventure.

How, I wondered, as the towheaded boy and I sat over a last drink and he wrote out his latest report, would such as he ever be satisfied in a world without war?

When he finished, we shook hands solemnly.

"Go to Ypres," he urged.

"Why not? Thanks for the tip, *Au revoir*, Burney. I hope we shall meet again." (We never did.)

Early the next morning, leaving everything in my front room at the Hotel Royal, I set out for three days in Ypres. Thanks to careful camouflage, a Belgian cap and my dirty raincoat, I reached that town toward evening, after an exciting twenty-mile hike. On the way I met a convoy of Paris motorbuses, endless guns and caissons, a regiment of Zouaves. Nine times I passed French sentinels without having to show my Belgian *laissez-passer,* which was valueless to them; eight of those times thanks to the old "pipe trick" of which I had read somewhere.

Approaching a sentry, one stops *before* being challenged, fumbles for matches, slowly lights a pipe, gives the challenger a reassuring smile and moves on. Such self-confidence is so reassuring that the sentry suspects nothing. The ninth time, I held out a Belgian cigar to the French sentry, muttered the single word "*Vlamsch*," and was waved on.

At Brielen, just north of Ypres, a group of French soldiers were hurriedly pulling down a captive balloon. A moment later the reason appeared—a German *Taube* looking for a target. Instead, three French biplanes rose and attacked it. The faster German crippled one of the French craft and might have downed the others as well, but for the miraculous appearance of a still faster French monoplane which so peppered the *Taube* that it escaped only by pretending to fall almost to the earth and then suddenly darting behind the nearby German lines. What a sight for a green war correspondent!

Ypres was larger than I expected; in the thirteenth century its 200,000 people had produced cloth on 400 looms. Most of its present 17,000 people had until the war been engaged in making Valenciennes lace. Not a large town, but of incredible beauty. The Grand' Place at Furnes with its two churches was elegant; the one at Ypres was magnificent. The glorious Cloth Hall, with the Gothic, former Cathedral of Saint Martin behind it, made me almost forget why I had come.

Still my first need was to find lodging. As I entered one of the two hotels on the Grand' Place, I heard the clerk tell a civilian just ahead of me: "Sorry, *monsieur,* but unless you have permission from the French or the British headquarters, I cannot give you a room."

Zounds! In a minute I was walking in the direction of the railroad station where I hoped to find an obscure inn. Ypres was in Belgium, not in France. Surely, the landlord would give me a room on the strength of my Belgian *laissez-passer*.

Turning in at a shabby place, I saw a buxom Belgian girl behind the bar. Here was my chance. I identified myself, told her of my sojourn with the Belgian army, persuaded her to have a couple of beers, and then asked if she could not put me up until the following day on the strength of my Belgian pass.

"Certainly, Monsieur." She smiled sweetly. "One instant and I shall prepare your room."

Five minutes later she was back with a Belgian gendarme who frowned and announced, "You are under arrest!" Served me right for trusting a waitress! I might better have gone straight to British headquarters and put a bold face on it. Instead I spent the night in a prison cell in the superb Cloth Hall.

Just before dawn a loud explosion almost jarred me out of bed. A German shell had dug a hole in the Place just outside my barred window. Claustrophobia seized me. Being shelled in the open was one thing; being crushed in a falling building with no chance of escape was something else.

Early the following morning my gendarme appeared: "Mr. American, do you wish to be brought before the French or the British?"

British censors were conspicuously more liberal than French and I had a lot to cable. "Before the British," I answered.

A nervous English major barely looked at me.

"Get that neutral journalist out of here and back to headquarters at once."

Off I went in an army truck under an armed guard, wondering at the anxiety the major had taken no pains to conceal.

It was November 2, 1914—the decisive day, I later learned, of what historians were to call the second German offensive of the First Battle of Ypres. Among the participants on the German side, a dispatch runner of the First Company, Sixteenth Bavarian Infantry, was an Austrian-born German named Adolf Hitler. . . .

At St. Omer, the Provost Marshal of the British Army, an immense man with bristling mustache, snarled at me and contemptuously tossed my Belgian pass aside. When I protested, he roared: "Don't you realize I can have you shot as a spy?"

"Certainly," I answered, "and if I had a large army behind me, I could have you shot." Whereupon, he laughed heartily and lightened the conditions of my arrest. But he insisted on keeping my passport and sending me to London without it—at my expense. When I pointed out the legal anomaly of expecting a prisoner to pay for going where he did not wish to go, the Provost Marshal bellowed: "That's right. You can go in chains in the hold for nothing, or first-class at your own expense." I chose to pay.

At Folkestone I hit another legal snag.

"Passport!" demanded the police.

"It was taken away by your Army at St. Omer."

"Sorry. You can't land here without a passport."

I appealed to the ship's captain. "Sorry. Saw you being put aboard. Know nothing at all about your passport."

Hours passed. Nine P.M., ten P.M. Since the French at Boulogne would probably be as obdurate as the British, I foresaw spending the rest of the war going back and forth on this channel boat, unable to disembark on either side. The situation called for drastic action.

Walking down the gangplank again, I approached the nearest policeman and shouted for the dock commander. Eventually a lieutenant appeared to whom I explained as patiently as possible the absurdity of punishing a traveler for not possessing a passport which his own Army had taken away. He saw the point. Exacting a promise from me to go to the War Office and reclaim my passport the first thing the following morning, he let me take the last train to London.

At the War Office bright and early, another officer, after giving me a lecture on the iniquity of being in a British war zone without British permission, poked a typed paper at me. "Sign this," he ordered. By doing so, I would recognize that if ever found again in the British zone of operations without proper credentials, I should be "held at the disposal of the Commander-in-Chief." Considering that I had, without serious harm, spent the last three days as a prisoner of the C.-in-C.,

I signed with alacrity, received my precious passport, and left the War Office.

By nine-thirty I was once more in the Chicago *Daily News* office on Trafalgar Square.

"My God," Bell exclaimed, "we were worried. Did you see this?" And he handed me a newspaper with a photograph of the Grand' Place at Furnes as it looked after a German shell had gone through the front of the Hotel Royal—it had been my room.

"Missed me," I commented. "Now I won't have to go back to pick up the things I left."

"The *News* will see to that," Bell reassured me. "But how did you get here?"

"Prisoner of the British Army. Don't ask me why."

"Tell me later. Now sit down at that machine and write everything you know. Precious little is appearing in America."

Again I described all that had happened—the final fighting on the Yser—the flooding of the estuary, the air battle over Brielen, what I had picked up about the Battle of Ypres, personal experiences. (British censors cut out my description of the still unfinished British and French defense of Ypres and of the scant courtesy I had received from the British Army, but left the rest.)

When after two or three days, I could write no more, Bell said, "Now, what do you plan to do next?"

"With your permission I shall rest here a day or two, for I haven't had much sleep since leaving Furnes. Then I'll go back to Paris. Obviously, I am through with Belgium."

"I doubt it," Bell said, with a puzzling twinkle.

6

Starving Belgium

*Therefore, thus sayeth the Lord God . . . I will
wipe Jerusalem as a man wipeth a dish, wiping
it and turning it upside down.*

II KINGS 21:12, 13

A FEW DAYS LATER I found myself back in Belgium, this time on the
German side, well behind the fighting front. Bell had sent me to verify
and describe the man-made hunger of the Belgian people. For, as he
explained, an American group, with the blessing of the Administration
in Washington, was in the process of creating a private organization,
the Commission for Relief in Belgium, to feed the Belgians. The local
German masters and the sea-ruling British had more or less given their
respective permissions. It remained for the American people to provide
the funds.

"Your job," Bell stated, "is to depict the situation in terms that
will loosen up American pockets." So there I was in Brussels, an attractive city which I had frequently visited before.

The reasons for Belgium's plight were plain. Normally, this highly
industrialized country imported about three-fourths of its food. The
German military government cut off outside food and brought the
economy to a standstill. Yet it continued to requisition Belgian food for
the German Army, pocketed Belgian taxes, and imposed fines on unsub-
missive communities.

On the other hand, the British fleet was blockading Germany, stopping and searching all foreign ships, and seizing any cargo suspected
of being destined, even indirectly, for the Fatherland. London said to
Berlin, "The populations of countries you occupy are, under the Hague
Convention, your responsibility, not ours." Berlin answered: "So long
as your blockade prevents outside food from reaching Germany, we shall
not let Germans go hungry in order to feed Belgian and French enemies."

As a result, in spite of heroic efforts by the Belgian authorities, a large number of the Belgian people were, by the middle of November, 1914, on the verge of starvation. At this point the American Minister at Brussels, Brand Whitlock, convinced the State Department that with proper guarantees, the United States should offer to feed the famished. Secretary of State Bryan concurred, but insisted that it be done by a private rather than by a governmental agency, with neutral diplomats as patrons and with the American and Spanish Ministers in Brussels as watchdogs rather than as executants. Under these conditions, the American Administration would do what it could to help.

With the approval of U.S. Ambassador Page in London, Baron Lambert and Emile Francqui of Belgium offered the job of heading the new organization to a successful American mining engineer with great experience abroad, one Herbert Clark Hoover. The latter, at considerable personal sacrifice, accepted, provided he could obtain iron-clad British and German guarantees of noninterference. Thereby he embarked upon a public career that was in time to lead him to the White House.

By the middle of November, Hoover felt he had sufficient assurances to go, with several assistants, to Belgium and set up his organization. This was the group which Bell had persuaded Ambassador Page to arrange for me to accompany. Somewhere between Tilbury and Flushing—the only route open—a young man whom the Chicago *Daily News,* in an editorial note, described as "one of its able staff of war correspondents," bearded Director Hoover in his cabin.

My first impression was of a typical American businessman, at the same time youthful and tired, serene yet worried, with scowling eyes under dark hair, and an impressive chin. Yet he told me of his plans with all the fervor of an evangelist: he had obviously accepted it primarily from a Quaker sense of duty. If any American can do this difficult job, he can, I told myself. At the end he said: "Don't wait for me. Go to Belgium and start writing at once. Whitlock says the situation is getting desperate."

Thus advised, I hurried to the Hague, where the U.S. Minister, Henry Van Dyke, persuaded the Germans to stamp my passport for Belgium. Remembering that Van Dyke was one of my mother's favorite authors, I tried to talk to him about his books. But the Minister refused, on the ground that he was totally immersed in world affairs, "of which, of course, you know nothing," he added. I suddenly understood why Minister Whitlock described Van Dyke as "the only living man I know who can strut sitting down!"

From Rotterdam, where I obtained further details from the Commisison's local representative, an American, Captain J. F. Lucey, I wired a first dispatch. After describing Hoover's request, I added a personal appeal: "This is an opportunity for 'inspired millionaires'; it is a far greater opportunity for showing the character of the American people without distinction of occupation or income. Come, you merchants—

Belgium also is a commercial nation though a small one; you lovers of peace, you idealists; here you may aid in conserving the very breath of their bodies to people who have become world renowned for their interest in peace and in spreading the feeling of human brotherhood. You trade unionists, socialists and workers, remember that Belgium is a stronghold of workers and a center of socialism that you could ill afford to lose. I challenge you to see who among you all will open his pockets the widest. . . . Belgium, though reduced in circumstances and dumb, looks its gratitude. It is turning its eyes toward us and they are filled with tears of hope."

The Dutch train went no further than Antwerp where I had just time to note with relief that the war damage was slight before climbing into an improvised horse-drawn bus whose driver promised to reach Brussels in a few hours.

But at lunch time, in a roadside *estaminet* at half-destroyed Malines, my tongue got me into trouble. Two German soldiers at the next table inquired where I lived, and when I told them, asked how the Parisians felt under German occupation.

They obviously needed enlightenment about the situation and I gave it to them—only to be arrested for my pains, and locked in a room at the German *Kommandantur*. There I stood on my American dignity and my German visa and refused to talk to anyone but an officer. Two hours later a German lieutenant appeared.

When he heard that I had come from Paris, he exploded into French: "*Mon Dieu, monsieur,* I am an artist. I have been living ten years in Montmartre. Ah, this absurd war! But now I must find some way of getting you to Brussels. Your conveyance left hours ago. There are no trains for civilians."

Back into another horse-drawn vehicle with a dozen other travelers.

At the American Legation, Minister Brand Whitlock and Secretary Gibson welcomed me cordially. With Whitlock, one-time Mayor of Toledo, a former newspaper reporter, and an author in his own right, I felt immediately at home. Though he was busy with the important people of the Commission, soon to be headed by Hoover himself, the Minister was available when needed, and several times lunched with me alone, when, forgetting Belgium, we talked of our common loves, books and writing. All during these exciting days, he worked at his poetry and novels and kept a journal. It was not surprising that he later clashed occasionally with the supremely practical Hoover.

Hugh Gibson persuaded the Germans to give me the necessary means of transportation for my investigations. He made appointments for me with important people—Baron Emile Francqui of the Belgian *Comité Central de Secours et d'Alimentation*; Millard K. Shaler, an American engineer, who had obtained a first shipment of outside food for the Belgians; and a certain rich businessman named Daniel Heineman. Heineman, American by birth, represented German business in Brussels, had studied and lived in Germany, spoke German, and, as

Brand Whitlock later put it, could "work marvels with the German military administration." Fifteen minutes' conversation with Heineman revealed the key to his power—the man was pro-German in the current conflict. However, having, since my misadventure at Malines, realized my dependence upon the Germans, I swallowed my urge to argue the question of war guilt and instead solicited from him valuable advice about where to go and whom to see.

Although the Commission's personnel was exclusively American, it enjoyed the protection not only of Whitlock, but of the Spanish Minister, the Marquis of Villalobar, to whom Whitlock sent me. The Marquis was reported to be a "synthetic man." Owing to faulty heredity, he had had to replace so much of his missing anatomy (two legs, one arm, one eye—all artificial) that, according to facetious Belgians, when he removed the orthopedic substitutes at night, there was "nothing left to go to bed." But he was marvelously courageous and made little attempt to conceal his dislike of the way the German military were treating the Belgians.

In due time, the Germans gave me permission to go by car anywhere in Belgium except to the battle front or to the "atrocity area" (a Belgian expression) of Louvain-Aerschot where they had destroyed the famous library and the entire town, respectively, as "warnings" to stubborn Belgians. They insisted that there was no hunger in either area although I filled a notebook with contrary accounts from refugees.

While waiting for permission to travel, I had found plenty to investigate in Brussels itself.

In appearance the city was about as usual—buxom women on the streets, but not after dark; shops and *estaminets*, open but empty: in one large beer hall I found myself the only customer.

Thirty-five percent of the inhabitants of the inner city were on relief. Of 3,500 formerly employed in the printing trades, exactly seventy were working, turning out the endless series of German proclamations telling the people what they might and might not do, and describing the penalties for disobedience. The great indoor panorama, where Mother and I had "witnessed" the Battle of Waterloo, was one vast soup kitchen.

What with the closed banks and the paralyzed economy, many formerly well-to-do people had no alternative to the breadlines. A family of musicians, a father and four sons, were literally tottering with hunger, as I saw when they insisted on playing for me to show their gratitude for part of my lunch. Yet all this time, the Germans were pumping Belgian food and money out in exchange for German currency, with which their soldiers seemed inexhaustibly supplied, and with which the people could buy almost nothing.

In the Marolles Quarter around the Palais de Justice nearly everyone was on relief.

The weather was so cold, fuel and clothing so scarce, that I felt ashamed to be warm. Yet tailors had had no work since June. The coal districts were bursting with coal—but with no means of transportation.

Belgium lay across the German lines of communication to the front, and the Army monopolized the railroads. Belgian peasants claimed they could tell how the war was going by noting the number of trains with fresh troops ("beet roots") going forward and those coming back with the wounded ("pulps").

The Mons-Charleroi district, which I investigated once I got permission, was one vast desolation. Accompanied by local Belgian officials eager to assist, I visited nearly every village. In each, picking a typical street, I went from house to house. To every family I put the same questions: What have you had for dinner? What provisions do you have in the house? How many children have you? Do they work? What is your trade? Do you lack work? How much do you earn? Is this your own house? And so on.

The answers were alike. In the Borinage no miners were working. The town and area of Bimche were shut down tight. The glassblowers around Charleroi had been unemployed since June. Before the town hall of Châtelet, near Charleroi, women and children stood for hours every day in order to devour anything which the Germans, bivouacked inside, were willing to throw to them.

At Charleroi itself, where I stayed in the house of an *échevin* (alderman), the German military had not only requisitioned all the food, but taken a census of the wine, forbidding the inhabitants to consume any more of it until German officers got around to "purchasing" it at seven cents a bottle. Since the Belgian bourgeois habitually stocked the best old Burgundies, their rage was limitless. Limitless too seemed the supply of forty-year-old Chambertin which, defying their captors, they offered to an American reporter, "lest the Germans get it, those uncouth louts."

Gradually the picture became precise. At first the Germans had terrorized and plundered the Belgians on the assumption that the war would quickly be over. Their failure to win on the Marne and in Flanders had left them with ten million hungry, embittered people on their hands. Most foreigners predicted that at some point the Belgians and northern French would stage a desperate revolt regardless of the consequences.

Every Belgian had an atrocity story to tell. True or false, they awakened a deep hatred of the Germans in all those Belgians who could not be terrorized.

These were the majority. To them, Belgium, in itself something of a synthetic state with a relatively short unified history, had suddenly become a primary reality and King Albert a national hero. Before the war, Whitlock explained, Albert, bourgeois king of two bourgeois peoples, went forth unheralded from his palace. No one cheered when he passed in the streets. Most of his subjects ignored him. Belgian capitalists deplored his lack of the "business ability" that his uncle, King Leopold, had displayed. In fact, before 1914, the average Belgian had remained primarily a city patriot, devoted to Antwerp, Brussels, or Liège. If a Fleming, he was interested in heating up the "language question"; if a Walloon, bent on deriding or ignoring it. Albert's heroic decision to defy mighty Germany and his magnificent leadership of the troops defending the last remaining corner of the country had suddenly transformed cities and ethnic groups into a nation to which the King and his courageous Queen, Elizabeth, were precious symbols. Though absent, they were the soul of the resistance.

This resistance, as I saw, took many forms. In Brussels, newsboys sold the "legitimate" *Nieuwe Rotterdamse Courant* newspaper, with a copy of the forbidden London *Times* hidden inside it. When the Germans trained guns on the unruly Marolles Quarter, the inhabitants from their windows poked stovepipes back at them. Along the Rue Haute, ragged children daily played at soldiers. At the sight of a German in uniform, the little captain gave the order: *"Achtung! Nach Paris!"* And the urchins goose-stepped *backwards* while passing citizens roared with laughter.

Belgian women complained of the Germans' disregard for Belgians' feelings—how, after the rape of the entire country, German traveling salesmen were astonished to be shown the door by Belgian shop keepers. German officers would not understand why the wives, sisters, and daughters of men whom they had imprisoned or shot indignantly refused their invitations to dance.

While the occupying authorities were generally courteous to me, they treated the most distinguished "natives" with contempt. At the Charleroi *Kommandantur,* a German officer, while greeting me warmly, before my eyes ordered my companion, a local alderman, literally thrown down the front stairs.

Nothing but the thought of my assignment kept me from going with him. By this time I had become convinced that the German Army had indeed done most, if not all, of the terrible things with which the Belgians and their Allies reproached them. This raised the question: to what extent were the German people involved in these mass murders, this wanton or deliberate destruction of whole towns and cultural treasures? Why were the "good Germans" so ineffective? For weeks this question perplexed me.

In any case, it was clear that the worse the Germans treated the Belgians, the more important it became to get American food to Belgium.

Just after my return from Charleroi, an American acquaintance excitedly told me of an unbelievable incident he had just witnessed.

At the Legation, in the presence of the American Minister, one of the newly arrived American members of the Commission (could it have been Jarvis Bell?) had angrily accused Danny Heineman of being a German agent. Heineman, acting for Baron von der Lancken, aide to the Civil Governor, had, this American insisted, originally proposed to Whitlock that America feed Belgium so as to lessen the effect in Germany of the British blockade. "We Americans, Mr. Minister," the accuser had affirmed, "are the victims of a German plot. If this is not true, let Mr. Heineman deny it."

"Lord God!" I exclaimed. "And what did Whitlock do?"

"He looked at his watch, remarked that it was his dinner time, and withdrew, leaving the dispute unsettled. The man who accused Heineman threatens to resign."

"And what do you think of the charge?"

"If it were not true, Whitlock would have made Heineman deny it."

True or false, what a headline: "American Food for Belgium a German Plot to Thwart Britain's Blockade!" It would rock the world. As the correspondent of a neutral country, I owed it to my public (and to my future career, perhaps) to tell all the facts. Yet by doing so I might condemn countless Belgians to famine. Toward the end of a sleepless night, emotion prevailed over ambition. I suppressed the story.

Actually, as I was to learn many years later, on about August 15, the German Minister in the Hague had asked the Dutch Foreign Minister to send food to the hungry Belgians via the River Meuse—and the latter had refused lest he compromise the Netherlands' neutrality. (The Dutch Government later changed its mind.)

On October 6, Minister Whitlock had wired the State Department that as early as September 12, Heineman had told him of discussing with the German authorities possible means of feeding Belgium. On October 14, Baron von der Lancken had told Whitlock that "the German authorities were ready to give assurances that none of the food brought in would be requisitioned or seized or in any manner utilized by the German authorities, but it would all go to the Belgian population." What more plausible fact but that Heineman *had* acted as the Germans' agent in persuading Brand Whitlock to take the initiative, along with his Spanish colleague Villalobar?

Certainly, that assumption would explain the failure by the American Minister or by Heineman to deny the indignant American's accusation.

The incident left a bad taste. Since leaving Rotterdam, I had not been able to send a line to the paper. I was the only American correspondent in occupied Belgium. But for how long? It was time to wind up my investigation, get out, and tell the world. One more trip, and goodbye to starving Belgium.

Accordingly, I once more rented a car and was driven to Namur, on the River Meuse. Even in that bleak wartime November, the town and its surroundings were exceptionally attractive.

To look at, not to investigate. In and around Namur, the German invaders, infuriated by the unexpected resistance they met, had done their worst. They had lined up the Mayor of nearby Dinant, a brother of the young man who showed me around, with his two little sons and about six hundred other people, old men and women, mothers with babies in their arms, and mowed them down with a machine gun. And always with the same excuse: *Man hat geschossen*—somebody shot at us. As if a free man did not have the right to resist an unprovoked invasion of his country!

Before I could look further, I was summoned to the German

Kommandantur in Namur where a stern-faced lieutenant informed me that my permission to travel by automobile had been canceled—why, or by whom, he refused to state.

What had happened? Had I expressed too freely my sympathy for the Belgians? In any case I would not give this pompous *Boche* the satisfaction of noting any dismay on my part. So I simply said: "I assume that I shall be allowed to drive back to Brussels."

"You may—and no farther."

Once in the capital, I confided the incident to Minister Whitlock, who promised to inquire. The next morning he broke the bad news.

"Edgar, I don't know what you have said or done, but the Civil Governor informs me that not only has he withdrawn your permission to circulate by car, but he wants you to leave the country as soon as possible, and by way of Maastricht. Antwerp is too close to the military operations. For your sake I suggest you go quickly."

I did not blame the Minister. After all, his overriding job was to keep on good enough terms with the occupying power to permit the feeding of the Belgians. Since I was leaving soon anyhow, what difference would a few days make?

"Very well, sir. I have already seen most of what I need except Liège. I can take a quick look at that and still go by way of Maastricht."

"Then I shall tell the Germans you are leaving soon. And Edgar, once you are out, do all you can for the poor Belgians."

What else had I come for?

Here I must go back a little. Shortly after my arrival in Brussels, Hugh Gibson had taken me to lunch at the Restaurant de la Monnaie, a rather sumptuous place behind the famous Théâtre de la Monnaie (a table d'hôte dinner without wine cost all of a dollar). Customers were few.

He introduced me to the proprietor, an American called Richards with a Belgian wife who, on the eve of the war, had inherited the restaurant from her father. Thereafter, whenever convenient, I had eaten at the Monnaie.

Usually Richards, by profession a musician, sat a few moments at my table and, as he warmed to my accounts of wartime experiences in Paris and on the Yser, made little contributions to my well-being, such as wines of a better bouquet than I would have cared to pay for. At the conclusion of our third conversation he said, "Would you mind having coffee with a friend of mine in the back room?"

There, seated at a table, was a thin man of perhaps fifty, with eyes as piercing as those of my father.

"Meet my French friend, *Monsieur* François."

"Delighted, sir, but with all the English here jailed by the Germans, Brussels must be a tough place for a Frenchman," I replied.

The stranger gave Richards a quick look, then apparently reassured, held out his hand.

"Colonel Jean François of the French Army. Sit down and tell me what you know about Paris, about the fighting you have seen on the Yser, about London, and about Mr. Hoover. Is he a competent and reliable man? Remember that we here in Brussels are terribly isolated— more on the giving" (with a glance at Richards) "than on the receiving end."

"*Sapristi,*" I thought to myself. "I come to Brussels with a German visa and within three days I am having coffee with a French colonel! This is something out of Conan Doyle."

Whether Colonel François (if his name was François) headed the French espionage network in Belgium, I never learned. But soon Richards was telling me how he and François were aiding young Belgians to slip out of the country and join the Belgian army. This they accomplished by pushing wooden barrels open at both ends between the electrified wires along the frontier. Fugitives simply waited near the frontier for a dark night and then crawled through to Holland.

Now, when I told Richards of my expulsion, he once more took me into the back room where I found the colonel. How did he explain it?

"Not surprised," he commented. "You have seen much too, and talked with too many people."

"Including you, colonel?"

"Shush! Not word about a colonel," Richards interrupted. "You never met a French colonel. Now look, Edgar! We desperately need somebody to take a few letters out of this country—mostly letters from Belgian families to their menfolk in the Army. You can turn them all over to a friend in Maastricht who will see that they reach their destinations. Please don't say no."

Bewilderment does not adequately describe my feeling. Suppose I got caught? The suspicious Germans might well be on the lookout. I could just see the newspaper headlines: "American Arrested as Courier for Belgian Spy Ring." Much as I wanted the allies to win, I found this an exaggerated request.

Yet here, as Father would say, was another test of my manhood. How live with myself if I failed to meet it?

"All right. Put the letters all in a plain sealed envelope with no address on the cover. Then if caught I can swear I know nothing of the contents."

The next morning I left Brussels with the sealed envelope in my suitcase. Why I went back to Namur, I cannot recall. Perhaps I had left something there on my previous visit. Yet, for whatever reason, on a late afternoon in early December, I found myself at the Namur station, without a car, inquiring in English of a German official when I could get a train for Liège.

His answer outran my German. But as I turned to another official, a gray-clad soldier offered his services—in French. He turned out to be a Lorrainer from Metz, delighted when he found he had assisted an American.

That night, at dinner with him and a group of other Frenchmen in German uniform, I came to understand the total bitterness of being compelled to bear arms against one's own country. At the end of the meal, my friend offered a toast "to victory." I did not need to ask whose.

At Liège, the next morning, the immediate departure of a large wagon for Maastricht left no time even for a quick glance at the city. In I climbed, along with several other passengers. Two immense, ankle-bewhiskered Percherons covered the twenty miles in less than four hours. I had had enough and wanted out.

"The frontier, ladies and gentlemen. Carry your baggage with you into the shed for examination."

I remembered those letters. What would be the penalty if I were caught? Obviously, it might depend upon the contents. If they were just personal messages of love and greeting, my offense would be venial. But if, as I suspected, they contained "hard" information about everything from German troop movements to plans for Belgian sabotage, I could expect the worst.

Too late for vain regret. Having read somewhere that nothing so arouses suspicion as attempted concealment, I had put the big envelope on top of the things in the suitcase. Now, remembering how well the pipe trick had worked on those French sentries near Ypres, as I faced the German baggage inspector, I slowly filled and lighted my pipe, smiling broadly at him the while. When he told me in German to open my suitcase, I pretended not to understand and instead proffered my American passport. Whereupon he shook his head, opened the suitcase himself, and asked in French what I had to declare.

"Nothing at all," I answered in that language, launching into a long description of my identity as newsman, of my assignment in occupied Belgium, and of my desire to help the German authorities persuade the Americans to feed the Belgians.

This had the desired effect. The police inspector laid one hand on the big white envelope and looked inquiringly at me. I shrugged my shoulders as though to say, "Go ahead if you don't believe me." For perhaps ten seconds he hesitated, then withdrew his hand, closed the suitcase, and handed it back.

"Would you like someone to carry it into Holland for you, *monsieur*?" No, thank you—*monsieur* was used to carrying it himself. Instead I offered him my hand, which he shook heartily.

"*Passez, Monsieur.*"

Why he did not hear my knocking knees I cannot say. But although by the time I had covered the twenty odd yards to the Netherlands and safety, my shirt was soaked with sweat, inside I was all triumph. Father, I knew, would have approved.

When the Dutch policeman at the frontier saw my passport, he asked in English, "What is life like in Belgium?"

"Hell," I answered.

An hour later, having delivered my envelope to a mild-looking

Dutchman in a small house, who asked no questions, I left Maastricht for England by train.

Back in the London office, I put everything I felt into three long descriptions of hungry Belgium, sparing no detail except my conviction that inducing Americans to feed that country had been a German scheme. This I withheld even from Bell lest he turn against the work of the Commission. The *News* in Chicago featured these dispatches and backed them with an editorial. So did a London editor to whom Bell gave them.

When, shortly before Christmas, I reached Paris, my brother remarked that I looked ten years older than when I had left two months before. How explain that I felt fifty years older? I had been face to face with the two faces of war, combat and misery.

Moreover, any lingering feeling of neutrality toward the world conflict had seeped away. Thereafter I consciously strove for the victory of the Entente.

7

Italy Acts On Its Own

*Barbed wire entanglements should be broken
by human breasts.*

GENERAL VANZO TO GENERAL CAPELLO

ABOUT THE MIDDLE of April, 1915, the Paris correspondent of the Rome
Giornale d'Italia let my brother in on a secret: Italy would soon de-
nounce the Triple Alliance and declare war on Austria-Hungry. When,
on April 27, the Italian whispered that the agreement with Britain and
France had been signed in London, Paul offered to send me as full
correspondent either to Rome or to Vienna, to cover the new phase of
the great struggle, at twice my present salary.

Had I chosen Vienna, how different my life would have been! But
during the Christmas holidays Lilian had again been in France and we
had agreed to marry as soon as we had the means. Here was the
chance. She adored Italy and, as an Englishwoman, was at war with
Austria. Rome for me . . . and when circumstances permitted, matri-
mony. Twenty-five dollars a week had been ample for a young correspondent of simple tastes—I had lived before the war on about half
that amount—but for two, it could have meant only that "life in a
garret" against which Lilian's father had warned her from the time I
appeared on the scene. Now I was on the road to affluence.

May 1 found me in Milan, where public demonstrations against
and for Italy's intervention were expected. The night before I had
boldly cabled that Italy was going to war. But was it?

At the Casa del Popolo, successive socialist orators hurled death
and defiance (so far as I could make out—my Italian was strictly that
of musical scores) at all imperialists and shrieked for peace. But afterwards one of them admitted to me (in French) that he thought war
inevitable.

74

Two hours later, in another smaller hall I heard a voluble, totally bald firebrand urge his listeners either to help Italy fulfill its "manifest destiny" by recovering Trento, Trieste, and Dalmatia, or to join with him in making a revolution.

When I introduced myself as an American journalist, Benito Mussolini, for it was he, told me, in French with a Swiss-Italian accent, how, in August, 1914, he had felt the call of country. He had therefore resigned as editor of the socialist *Avanti* and founded a new newspaper, the *Popolo d'Italia*, dedicated to Italy's greatness. Now, whether the Italians liked it or not, the country was going to war. On parting, he urged me not to miss the speech by Gabriele D'Annunzio at Quarto near Genoa, on May 5.

Only later I learned that the French government had made possible both Mussolini's interventionist journalism and D'Annunzio's triumphant return from exile to his own country by providing funds for the former's new newspaper and for the latter's unpaid creditors. Nonetheless, both men were sincere.

At Genoa the next day, sitting at the top of the Castellaccio watching the sunset glow over the beautiful harbor, I realized how little I knew about Italy. My studies had somehow skipped from late Roman to Elizabethan Europe, neglecting those Middle Ages and that Renaissance which were Italy's glory. Modern Italian composers and Benedetto Croce, the philosopher, were familiar figures. But of modern Italy's history and problems, aspirations, and culture, I knew virtually nothing.

My ignorance left me all unprepared to understand how a minority of Italians, led by the Cabinet, could decide to plunge into the biggest war of all time in the name of what they called "holy selfishness." Had they measured the full horror of what they were stepping into?

Though an internationalist, I was no pacifist. War in self-defense, war for freedom, war to "redeem" the Italians of Trento-Trieste (if there was no other way)—such I could understand. But war to justify a country's claim to be a "great power," war to conquer Slavic Dalmatia, war for what would now be called "kicks," as the Italian nationalists urged, was beyond my understanding. Only something great could be worth the loss of several hundred thousand young lives.

Moreover, Italy was poorer than I had realized.

Could it afford such a war? Not, of course, according to Norman Angell. But my favorite economist, Charles Gide, whom I had interviewed in Paris a month or two previously, had destroyed my trust in Angell. "France," he insisted, "is rich. England and Russia contain almost inexhaustible resources and could make war for over a century if necessary." Maybe Italy could afford the "little war" that its politicians had in mind.

But did it possess the needed psychological capital? In the old days, comparatively few participated in war. But this struggle was "total" and involved whole peoples. What would happen when the casualty lists started coming in?

D'Annunzio's speech at Quarto coincided with Italy's formal denunciation of the Triple Alliance, accepted in 1882 in resentment of
France's declaring a protectorate over Tunisia, which Italy coveted.
Physically, the poet was small, painfully histrionic, over- and under-
civilized, a decadent primitive. Yet his well-chosen rhetoric raised a
large crowd to delirious enthusiasm. Never had I seen people so responsive to highfalutin eloquence.

I could not but contrast D'Annunzio's verbal flights with the sober
words of King Albert to the victorious survivors of the Yser battle and
wonder what my friend Lieutenant Burney would have thought of the
Italian "bard," as D'Annunzio liked to call himself.

So wondering, I reached Rome. In those May days it seemed to
me a golden city, less formally handsome than Paris, but richer in the
harvest of twenty-five hundred years.

Thanks to Hendrik C. Andersen, the American sculptor whom I
had met in Paris the year before, and allegedly a relative of Hans
Christian Andersen, I soon found myself established in a pleasant
pensione kept by an aging, widowed *Marchesa*, close to Hendrik's own
sumptuous rooftop apartment on the Piazza del Popolo, Piranesi's
masterpiece.

The *pensione's* real manager, the spinster daughter, supplied the
rest of the family income by working as a qualified tourist guide to the
Eternal City. *Marchesina* Ilda Roero di Cortanze was about forty, spoke
English, French, and German as well as Italian, and was a passionate
nationalist. Though as a textbook for my Italian lessons she chose
Dante, personally she had little use for those glorious centuries of
Italian disunity, and steadily sought to direct my attention to the
surving glories of imperial Rome.

This, I gradually saw, was part of the same yearning for Italy's
former greatness that made her an interventionist. As we got better
acquainted, she poured out her rage and distress at having Italy and
Italians regularly patronized, or worse, by foreign visitors. Piedmont,
her own birthplace, had never bowed to foreigners, and Italians must,
she felt, demonstrate both to themselves and to the world that the
"Third Italy" was a Great Power. She swore by Mussolini and D'Annunzio, and read the *Idea Nazionale* newspaper, which I found intolerably
chauvinistic.

Here, I began to see, was an explanation of the government's
choice of war that went far deeper than an itch for Slavic Dalmatia.
Italy was out to show the world. . . .

With Ilda as a guide, I missed no detail of the interventionist
struggle in Rome. The decisive battle—to ratify or not to ratify the
Treaty of London—came, with the return to Rome from his native
Piedmont of Giovanni Giolitti, the former Prime Minister, national
political boss, and chief neutralist. Giolitti argued that without fighting
Italy could still obtain *"parecchio"* (considerable) from an Austria
which had finally become aware of the danger. Prime Minister Salandra
had already refused such an offer made by Germany in the name of

Austria-Hungry. Before Giolitti's arrival a solid majority of the Deputies had left their visiting cards at his Rome apartment as a sign of their support.

D'Annunzio led the interventionist drive. A hundred and fifty thousand Romans welcomed him on his arrival at Rome. Some of them had collected arms for a trial of strength. One street barricade was erected. In one of his speeches, D'Annunzio went so far as to call Big Boss Giolitti a traitor. When the Parliament assembled for the big debate, D'Annunzio's arrival in the visitor's gallery set off a tumult of applause. Instead of clearing the galleries, the cowed neutralist Deputies tamely confirmed the interventionist Salandra–Sonnino Government. Three days later, Italy declared war on Austria–Hungary.

Ilda was in the patriotic clouds. So were Editor Bergamini of the Rome *Giornale d'Italia*, a *Sonniniano*, to whom I had been introduced by his Paris correspondent, and Colonel Ricciotti Garibaldi, who had been fighting in the French Army and knew what modern war was like. On the other hand, Editor Malagodi of the *Tribuna*, a *Giolittiano*, darkly predicted national disaster.

Even Thomas Nelson Page, the American Ambassador, and like Brand Whitlock in Belgium, a professional writer, confessed his astonishment that Italy had taken the leap. "A month ago," he confided, "the people seemed unanimously opposed to war, and the affirmation of the Germans that war would be averted seemed well grounded. The government's Green Book may explain why it *wanted* war but not why war became the common will."

The Ambassador explained that Sonnino intended Italy to be only a limited belligerent, fighting exclusively against Austria–Hungary, but not to the extent of dismembering that empire, which would strengthen the Slavs who were contesting Italy's claim to rule the Adriatic. Nor did Sonnino wish to see the complete defeat of Germany, lest that leave Italy at the mercy of victorious France and Britain.

Moreover, as Sonnino saw it, Italy's war was to be cheaply conducted; the country had requested a loan from Britain of just fifty million pounds!

Salvatore Cortesi of the Associated Press agreed. More than twice my age, Cortesi was a "Roman of Rome," shrewd, cynical, kind-hearted, and always ready to impart something of what he knew to the American greenhorn.

Even to one as politically inexperienced as I, there was something unreal about all this, like undertaking, in the midst of a burning town, to put out the fire in just one street.

Some six weeks later I hazarded an explanation for the *News*. "Roughly speaking," I reported, "seven elements have been compounded in the Italian consciousness to bring about the entrance of Italy into the present war. These elements are: One grain of hatred (for Austria); one grain of laudable desire to unify and strengthen the country; four grains of fear (of Austria, of France, of the young Slavs backed by Russia, and of Germany); one grain of imperialism—ambition to satisfy commercial and military but not necessarily vital desires." Three years later I was to recognize an eighth element—sheer idealism.

But mine was not to reason why, mine was to get to the Italian front and describe that first "lightning advance" which was being announced. To show my good will, I sent to Chicago a short but flattering biography of Italy's commander-in-chief, Count Luigi Cadorna, a Spartan-like Piedmontese sixty-five years old.

My flattery had no effect: "neutrals" were not wanted at the front. Finally I took Commander Train's advice and simply left for Udine, a pokey little town in Friuli, seat of the Italian Headquarters.

No hotel would give me a room. At Headquarters the aide-de-camp of the general in charge—not Cadorna—answered my pleas to see something of the fighting by uttering seventeen "impossibles" in succession, followed by a warning to leave town or be arrested.

So after a brief visit to Milano, where I hired for the *News* the part-time services of a reporter on the *Secolo* newspaper, Tancredi Zanghieri by name, and had a second talk with Mussolini, whom I visited regularly thereafter, I returned to Rome to cover Italy's war from there as best I could.

Not but what I continued to travel. At Father's request, I met him for a brief visit in Lausanne and admired him more than ever. Moreover, in the Swiss hotel, I had the fun of first seeming to invite, then rejecting, the proposal of a young Viennese woman that I send her accounts of what was going on in Rome. Imagine me spying for the Central Empires!

Only in September, with English, French, and Italian correspondents, was I taken on a tour of the Italian front by the very *Ufficio Stampa* that had warned me to leave Udine two months earlier.

In the company of two civilian captains, Pio Pirelli of the famous tire company, and a German-Italian called Weill-Schott, we visited the lines from the Swiss border to the Adriatic at Grado, formerly an Austrian summer resort, from which one could look across the water to Trieste eight miles away—the nearest the Italians ever got.

The Italian fighting forces were at the same time full of *slancio* and lacking in enthusiasm. Between the General Staff, the professional field officers, the civilian officers, and the conscripted soldiers were vast distances. The first seemed competent in a Germanic sort of way. The field officers resented the staff officers' heavy hand, the civilian officers were amateurish, and the privates so deficient in curiosity that after two weeks in a village, many still did not know its name.

These things were evident enough. But the two captains resented mention of them by a young American who, with the exception of the famous correspondent, Luigi Barzini, was the only journalist present who had seen actual fighting. Moreover, I committed a dreadful breach of etiquette. Having just blistered my feet badly, I had, in anticipation of roughing it, shod myself with a pair of white tennis shoes. This, to our guides, showed a suspicious lack of *savoir-faire* on the part of a neutral; one officer complained that my white tennis shoes drew enemy fire. Only when it was too late to undo it did I recognize my mistake. I should have dressed not only conventionally, but elegantly like Captain Pirelli—and phrased my descriptions more tactfully.

Back in Rome, I plunged into modern Italian history, until names like Mazzini, Garibaldi, Cavour, and Crispi became almost as familiar as Jefferson and Washington. I also studied church history, for I was expected to send occasional, strictly noncritical stories about the Vatican. Through the American Seminary (*Collegio*) in Rome I got on good terms with two eminent churchmen, Monsignor Sincero and Monsignor Benigni. The former provided me with political information from the "other side" of the war until he was made cardinal. Then in what I had learned was typical "Vatican language" he said: "My son, in the past I knew nothing and told you everything, while from now on I shall know everything and tell you nothing." And so it turned out.

As the American Embassy had suspected, fighting a limited war proved difficult once the first Italian drive failed to reach Trieste and Trento. In December Italy signed a no-separate-peace pact with France and Britain and Russia and occupied Valona in Albania. Shortly thereafter, German troops drove the Serbs to the Adriatic and Italian ships transported the survivors to Macedonia to continue the struggle.

Among the few Albanians who fled to Italy was the notorious Essad Pasha Toptani, who many considered the symbol of all that was wrong in the Balkans. When I interviewed him, he cut me short by asking why he was having trouble in getting an American loan.

"Conceivably because of the American belief that you sold your country simultaneously to Austria, Serbia, and Italy," I suggested.

"Nonsense," said Essad. "It is true I took money from all of them, but there was no betrayal. I never did any of the things I promised."

Early in January, 1916, Lilian and I decided to wait no longer but to marry at once. In the previous three months I had taken on a second, purely technical, job for Cortesi, and by the end of the year had six hundred dollars in the bank. No garret for Lilian and me.

Once married in London, we returned to Rome and found a superbly oversized apartment in Palazzo Galitzin in the Via della Scrofa in the ochre-colored lower city. A plaque on the façade announced that from 1557 to 1590 the poet Torquato Tasso had lived there. Lilian shared my feeling that in Rome one should live as Romanly as possible. This we did for seven unforgettable years.

In May, 1916, a greatly reinforced Austro–Hungarian army launched in the Trentino the promised "punitive campaign" by what was probably to date the second largest artillery bombardment of any front. It was touch and go. Only when the Austrians reached the mountain rim from which they looked down into the Po Valley, did the Italians manage to stop them and recover a little of the lost ground. The first news of the failure of the Austrian offensive came to me, curiously enough, from no less a bigwig than General Brusati, aide-de-camp of King Victor Emanuel.

The shock to a people that had been lulled to complacency by Cadorna's uninformative war bulletins was tremendous. After a fist fight in the Chamber of Deputies, Salandra resigned and was succeeded by Paolo Boselli, a courageous if colorless octogenarian. Yet something had changed. The new Prime Minister begged me to assure America that Italy would fight to the end against all enemies. What had become of the "little war"?

Completely to my liking was a new Cabinet member, Leonida Bissolati, leader of the reformist socialists, who at the age of fifty-seven had fought for almost a year as a sergeant of Alpine troops. Now, as Minister, he frequently gave me exclusive information.

About this time an Italian engineer, Galletti di Cadillac, a distant relative of that Antoine de la Mothe Cadillac who founded Detroit, invited Lilian and me to inspect the "strongest radio transmitter in the world" which he had just completed at Popoli in the Abruzzi. There he also led us up a nearby mountain to visit the hermitage that had produced Celestine V, the only Pope who ever resigned—to Dante's disgust. The current hermit looked like a foetus, wore a derby hat, and whined for alms.

One day Hendrik introduced me to a retired judge, Gaetano Meale, who, under the pseudonym Umano, had since 1907, like Hendrik, been advocating a world authority to prevent further wars. Prince Gelasio Gaetani, a future ambassador to the United States, composer Ruggiero Leoncavallo, famous everywhere for his opera, *Pagliacci*, and Deputy Paul Milyukov, later foreign minister in the Russian revolutionary government of Prince Lvov, all gave me interviews.

Thus, though still unwelcome at the Italian front, I found plenty of interesting stories. Tancredi Zanghieri, now an officer participating in the successful Italian August offensive which finally took Gorizia, privately supplied the *News* with first-hand accounts of battles. And sure enough, as Boselli had implied, Italy declared war on Germany, though declining to send troops to assist the hard-pressed French at Verdun.

Nonetheless, any war correspondent denied access to a fighting front was a failure. My good friend Ambassador Page finally set himself to correct this. He intervened personally with Cadorna in my favor. I was permitted to visit Udine just in time for Italy's autumn offensive on the Isonzo. Once more the terrain the Italians gained was not worth the cost in human lives.

Meanwhile, however, thanks to Commander Train, I had established a working partnership with the admiral commanding the almost inaccessible Italian naval base at Venice, which the Austrians were bombing regularly. During a visit in August, I became close friends with the American consul, B. Harvey Carroll, a former newspaper editor from west Texas, a pudgy, literate, bouncy, indomitable man. Carroll refused to stay indoors during air raids (there were no cellars in Venice), and was always first on an afflicted spot to give aid. Thanks to my insistence, he finally consented to put on, during alerts, an Austrian helmet I brought him from the battlefields. He induced the admiral to extend to Lilian my permanent permit to enter Venice. In November, 1916, she and I stayed there several days in a *pensione* on the Zattere not far from the American Consulate.

Moreover, the friendly admiral recommended me to a big shot in the Navy Ministry at Rome. Soon thereafter I was permitted to make a scouting trip in the Adriatic on the cruiser *Quarto* (no Austrian subs to shoot at, but an awful case of seasickness). To compensate for the absence of action, the Navy offered me a ride in an open airplane. Although the pilot only circled half an hour at a few thousand feet over Brindisi harbor, that flight inspired a "rave" mailer to the *News,* of which this was the conclusion:

"Friendly pilot, you have made me understand the swallow and the frigate bird, and during this first flight I have stored faith. I believe in what is, and in the future. I believe that science may some day become art and art science, that matter may turn to spirit, that the ugliness of effort may some day engender beauty as the swamp the water lily. And I believe that the swamp itself must give place to the meadow, the hovel to the bungalow, greed and gluttony to apostolic charity. You have shown me how all men may be brought together in community of aspiration, as we were brought together, you the mechanic, I the humblest of writers."

Was D'Annunzio's style contagious?

Meanwhile, the world's interest had shifted to politics. In December, 1916, Wilson asked the several belligerents to set forth their peace terms. Germany and Austria did. The Allies refused. A month later, Wilson followed up with a "peace without victory" speech including an appeal for the creation of a League of Nations to prevent further wars.

To Hendrik and me, this seemed the promise of a new dawn. But to Italian nationalists, it was nonsense that threatened to deprive Italy of the fruits of its "holy selfishness." A few months previously, at an art exhibit of a "formidable and complex futuristic genius," Depero by name, someone passed out Marinetti's latest blast: "War . . . is a law of life . . . only war can rejuvenate, speed up, sharpen human intelligence, lighten . . . the nerves, free us from the daily burdens, give a thousand savors to life and give talent to imbeciles. War is the unique rudder of the aeroplanic life we are preparing. . . . War is the culminating and perfect synthesis of progress."

But after thirty months of tough fighting, the Russian soldiers of the east front had little use for Marinetti's kind of progress. They mutinied, and started a revolution that was to destroy the monarchy. The first news of it delighted me if only because Russian autocracy had been an obstacle to full American sympathy with the Entente. The Russians deserved something better than weak-kneed tsars and virile Rasputins. But now the Russian army was striking less against the monarchy than against further fighting, a step that might defeat us all.

In view of the lessened Russian pressure on Austria, one might have expected the Italian government to welcome America's declaration of war on Germany. But not Sonnino, who already suspected that President Wilson would seek to nullify the promises to Italy contained in the Treaty of London. Rome's only celebration of America's entry into the conflict was a luncheon for the American Ambassador given by the representatives of the Associated Press and the Chicago *Daily News*.

Indeed, presumably to forestall any such American pressure, Cadorna undertook new offensives between March and May, 1917, without any striking successes. In June, the Austrians counterattacked north of Trieste with even less result. Only, in August, by skillful maneuver, did the Italian Second Army take an all but impregnable position and cut the Chiapovano Railroad on which the Austrians depended for supplies.

A month later, the editor in Chicago ordered me to the Balkan front for a brief visit. It had taken the Allies a full year to reestablish themselves along a line from the mouth of the Voyussa River in Albania to the Aegean. The Italians held the Albanian sector and had sent a further division to Macedonia, where they distinguished themselves by their dash. On June 3, the Allies had (once more) proclaimed the "independence" of Albania in the hope of rallying as much of the population as possible to their side.

This was my first view of the Orient and I reacted in a typically American way: its filth, poverty, disease, and Moslem indifference outweighed its undoubted picturesque charm. Actually, the naked children, their bellies swollen by malaria, the veiled women in dismal black burkas, the white-fezzed loafers perpetually drinking coffee, gave a misleading impression of this essentially sturdy people. But as the guest of General Ferrero in the blue villa under the old Venetian castle of Kanina, I met no educated Albanians. The country was so fever-infested that at the Italian mess, huge quinine capsules, called "white coal," were a regular part of the menu.

After Valona I visited Argyrokastro and was almost consumed by bedbugs; then by car to Korcha, a center of Albanian emigration to the United States (nearly everybody knew a little English), and then across Macedonia to the Italian headquarters at Tepauci. From the ancient town of Monastir (where the officers set their watches by the Austrian bombardment which began each day at 5:00 P.M.), I climbed to the Italian trenches under the summit of "Quota 1050."

Of all my war assignments, this one was the most trying. First, two officers and I went several miles on horseback, along a way exposed to the Bulgarians' fire. Just when our group came into full view of the enemy, my horse persisted in neighing loudly in spite of all my efforts to quiet him by putting my fingers in his nostrils. Finally, for the last three hundred yards each of us walked separately toward the enemy trenches in order to be as inconspicuous as possible. I tried to overcome my nervousness by picking wild flowers and muttering reassuring phrases to myself. My relief at reaching shelter was monumental.

From Macedonia I returned to Italy by way of Corfu, a former resort of Kaiser Wilhelm, bringing with me an inkling of Balkan politics and a case of dysentery which it took three weeks of vacation with Lilian at Capri to overcome.

That beautiful island was almost empty of visitors. Among the few people whom we saw frequently, three stood out. The first was Marinetti, who occasionally visited our little villa and recited his latest examples of what he called "rumorismo" (noise-ism). The others were a pair of Italian writers, a very sensitive young man named Gilardi and his friend, a lady journalist, somewhat older, whom everybody called simply Capinera (linnet). Gilardi had expressed his reaction against the war in a little book called the *Real Gospel of Jesus,* in which he argued that Jesus had never claimed to be anything but a humanitarian. Between the belligerent Marinetti and the gentle Gilardi–Capinera pair, there could be no contact.

Daily swims in the incomparable Bay of Naples calmed our war-weary nerves. But not for long. Even while Cadorna was launching the greatest of all his offensives, Pope Benedict put out an appeal for peace—"defeatism," Marinetti called it. Whatever the Pope's intentions, the effect was to weaken the already drooping morale of the Italian army and people.

The causes of this slump have been much debated. Most critics have blamed General Cadorna. The general, it is said, repeatedly ordered his subordinates to undertake offensives without proper artillery preparation, and when they failed, replaced them. The turnover became so rapid that the soldiers immortalized it in an almost untranslatable song:

> 'Nu fesso è partito,
> 'Nu fesso è arrivato;
> Sarà silurato
> Senza pietà.

Cadorna and his staff officers further imposed a Prussian-like discipline upon a people whom centuries of tyranny had never made blindly obedient. Worst of all was his insistence upon frontal attacks— "uphill all the way, right to the very end"—which after thirty months had left the front still within gunshot of the old frontier. On their own inability to advance in spite of a hundred thousand casualties, the soldiers on the bloody Corso commented acidly in a song about the General. One of the best known verses went (in my rough translation): "General Cadorna said to the Queen, if you're looking for Trieste, it's on the map, to be seen."

Whatever the cause, the fight was oozing out of the Italian. Particularly, out of the typical infantryman. Of him I wrote: "He can bear suffering and privation but he cannot hate an anonymous foe. At first he fought and fought well though without political conviction. In time he became a hardened combatant, an expert and tried veteran. But the more he became aware of his progress in the sanguinary art, the more he wanted to get out of it. As his patience wore away, and the war continued without tangible result or hope of victory, his combativity dwindled."

In fact, to a foreigner the difference in morale among Italians was fantastic. Piedmontese were dependable. Wild Sardinians and Sicilians were magnificent in attack. Romagnoli rated high. At the bottom, Italian officers put Tuscans and Neapolitans, who allegedly (to revive an expression of Hemingway) "suffered from an overdeveloped sense of self-preservation."

Cadorna's answer to progressive demoralization was progressive punishment. When an entire brigade revolted, he had one hundred and eleven summarily shot.

Nevertheless soldiers who went on leave in good spirits continued to return full of incipient revolt. Not so much because of their families' privation (which was real) as because of spreading defeatism. Groups of unconverted neutralists, heartened by the Russian revolution and by the "peace without victory" appeals of President Wilson and of the Pope (who had called the war a "useless slaughter"), sought to force the Government to withdraw from the war. Rumors of Austrian peace offers also helped. Socialist Deputy Turati spread the slogan, "No third winter in the trenches." In Venice, after a particularly trying air raid, a large number of women gathered on one *campo* shouting, "We want peace!"

To most foreign correspondents, Cadorna and the Government seemed equally remiss. Neither had seriously tried to provide the combatants and the people the kind of ideal they would be willing to die for. "Holy selfishness," great power talk, the promise of Slavic Dalmatia, these moved very few. Even more than other peoples, the Italians responded to emotion.

In early September, thanks to my friend Comandante Costa, I installed Lilian in Venice within reach of Udine. Carroll found us an apartment on the Grand Canal, a gondola with a gondolier who also acted as houseman, a maid happy to find work in the all but hermetically sealed city. We would, I figured, remain there until Christmas. . . .

8

Caporetto

E tutto procede dalla debolezza dei capi.
MACHIAVELLI

IN CONTRAST TO, but also because of, the harsher reality of war, Venice in that autumn of 1917 was more beautiful than ever. The silence, the blackout, the absence of military activity except for the invisible movements of the warships, the growing emptiness—all contributed to the dream. And after three long years of strain and psychological jolts, I reveled in those long weekends in Venice with Lilian, and when I could, stretched them into full weeks justified (in Chicago's eyes, I hoped) by the stories I sent about the exploits of the Italian Navy, with one of whose finest officers, Lieutenant Commander Luigi Rizzo, I had become well acquainted.

Personally I should have been happy to live in Venice until the war's end (assuming that it would end, which many Italians were beginning to doubt). But around October 20, Carroll told me that he had heard talk of a possible Austrian offensive. The duty of a war correspondent was clear. I reached Udine around noon of Wednesday, October 24, 1917, to find myself in the midst of disaster.

At the Caffè Nuovo, the tall weedlike proprietor with the German mustache strolled over to my table to exercise his English.

"What's up?" I asked.

"The enemy is attacking us, very heavy, and he has Germans with him. Last night I went on the Castle and all the sky was fireworks and cannon in the ears. You came just in time."

The daily official communiqué was supposed to appear at noon. A typewritten copy, often signed by General Cadorna himself, was generally affixed to a board in the correspondents' room in the Press Office, the *Ufficio Stampa,* some time after lunch. On my way there, I met an English colleague, Percival Gibbon, a truculent Welshman of great literary talent. He confirmed the fact of an Austrian offensive on a vast scale—and with German aid. Correspondents, it seemed, were being asked not to visit the front. It seemed ominous, but such orders had been known before.

The bulletin was reassuring: "The enemy shock finds us solid and well prepared."

In times of temporary restriction, the events of each day were related to us in the evening by a staff colonel. On that Wednesday evening, the colonel spoke so fast that I had great difficulty in following. Yet the general feeling among the press officers and my Italian colleagues remained one of confidence. The army had given ground in many places, but no more than would strengthen defense.

That night we had a dinner party at the Caffè Nuovo. Will Irwin and Inez Haynes Irwin came in later and a dignified and well-meaning official from the British Foreign Office. The Irwins were leaving for Venice early the next morning. When the Caffè closed, we went in a group to Gibbon's room and were very gay and sang songs until midnight. Eight bells and all's well! But outside, a tall lean figure wrapped in a raincoat was pacing the streets under the low arcades, fearful of returning to his bedroom and sleeplessness. Luigi Barzini, war correspondent of the *Corriere della Sera,* knew already what we did not even dream: that the Italian Second Army was retreating faster than any army should retreat.

Next day a hush lay over the *Ufficio Stampa.* Our officers were uncommunicative. The Italian correspondents huddled over maps, watched in fascinated silence the finger of the least subdued among them, who traced and explained certain maneuvers. When we foreigners drew near, voices died away and the group dispersed. The day's bulletin failed to allude to incidents we had already learned from the staff colonel.

I heard a correspondent murmur over and over, "Our situation is serious, our situation is serious." Doubtless he found it difficult to convince himself of the fact. To me it was frankly incredible. The Austro-German forces were numerically quite inadequate to make any serious impression on the Italian lines. Otto von Below, though an estimable German general, was not a name to frighten anyone. The line of Monte Kolovrat, against which the assault must strike, fairly bristled with guns. The Fourth and Twenty-seventh Army Corps holding the critical point were among the best troops. I felt that any initial losses we might undergo, Plezzo, Caporetto, Monte Nero, could not seriously compromise the situation.

About nightfall, as I was leaving the *Ufficio Stampa,* Barzini's brown face bent above me.

"Do not tell the other correspondents," he whispered, "but to America you may say that the forces operating against us are directed by General Mackensen."

I started. Mackensen, the conqueror of Russia, Serbia, Rumania, was endeavoring to add the glory of another successful offensive to his chapleted name? It sounded bad. And yet should that make any difference? The staff colonel's lecture indicated losses, but did not explain the alarm now clearly written on the faces of our companions.

And so Thursday passed. On Friday, the third day of the enemy drive, we awakened to the sound of bombs falling in the streets of Udine. Still the sun shone. The Italian fights best in the sunshine. After breakfast a friendly Italian official touched me on the shoulder. There was such grief in his eyes that when we shook hands I held his palm a long time and tried to smile.

"I have just seen Cadorna." His voice went along in a queer stuffy singsong. "I have just seen Cadorna and he said, 'I am faced with overwhelming numbers: all of the conditions of victory are in my hands. But my men won't stand.' "

Something froze in me. The mystery began to clear.

By noon disaster was in the air. The effrontery of enemy airmen knew no bounds.

By evening our Italian colleagues had forgotten their reserve and broken into voluble imprecation. What were the generals doing? Where was the King? Why, in the name of God, had the army gone to pieces? No one could say, not even great-hearted Father Semeria, Cadorna's confessor, who paid a visit to the *Ufficio Stampa* in the evening.

When Gibbon came out of the censor's office he called me aside.

"The captain has allowed me to call the Italian retreat a 'débâcle.' "

The staff colonel did not use Gibbon's term, but he amply confirmed the latter's impression. Behind the second line, which had already been turned by the enemy at Monte Maggiore, a third line was being formed. When the colonel ceased, our press chief, General Barbarich, read an appeal of General Cadorna to the troops. It was full of fire and brought us to our feet with a cheer. The "old man" might save the situation after all.

Ten minutes later we learned that he had ordered a general retreat to the Tagliamento River twenty miles to the west of Udine. The foreign military missions had been asked to leave. The first of the trucks carrying the Staff archives were already rolling westward through Porta Venezia.

The enemy was in the hills above Cividale and the fall of Udine was only a matter of time.

Yet in the piazza, a crowd stood before a freshly printed proclamation signed by the Mayor, which assured the inhabitants there was no real danger.

Perhaps there was none—for those who would take the hint and go.

On Saturday, October 27, another day of sunshine, the General Staff left Udine. By noon the automobile parks were deserted. The big offices of the *Ufficio Stampa* were a picture of desolation. Packing cases, trunks, and valises were piled in the courtyard. The lofty ceilinged rooms were strewn with maps, newspapers, printed forms, useless stationery, old books. Chairs were overturned. The models of the Carso and the county of Gorizia were abandoned.

Officers, orderlies, and correspondents walked mournfully from place to place in chill silence. Gibbon voiced the feeling of all of us when he approached our guide and said: "Captain, in this moment, we are all Italians." Three Englishmen and myself were due to leave in the *Daily Mail* car.

But Gibbon and I had reached a decision: we would remain behind and see the Austrians enter Udine, then count on our intimate knowledge of the country to slip away and score a news beat. So we each put our suitcase in the headquarters car and casually told the other correspondents we were going for a drink. Once around a corner we ran to a caffè where we knew we would not be found, should anybody bother to look for us.

The *Daily Mail* car left without us.

From the roof of a tall building which had sheltered the offices of the Italian naval representative, Gibbon and I looked across nine or ten miles of green plain to Cividale, set against the foothills of the mountain girdle "where they had come through." Cividale was burning. A cloud of smoke rose half a mile in the still air and there were flames. The Italians had fired the magazine and storehouses. We watched the flashes of enemy shells breaking on the roofs.

In the streets of Udine, disaster walked with iron shoes. Everywhere, in home and office, people were making ready to go. That morning the first stores had closed. The hospitals were being rapidly emptied. But there was much to do, and the time was short. Men ran back and forth from this place to that, shouting orders. Women begged means of transport from the nearest passerby. The very wind whispered disaster—incomprehensible, unreasonable, utter disaster. Yet aside from a few officers and ourselves, no one knew why the army had had to retreat.

As the sun was setting, we sat on a wall just outside the Porta di Cividale and questioned the passing soldiers. There was a long, endless line of wagons, caissons, camions, and guns, with hundreds of men walking between them. They formed part of the Second Army from the Bainsizza plateau, south of the point where the break had come. Had they been beaten? Certainly not. Why were they retreating? Orders. Was the enemy behind them? Who could say? Cividale was being bombarded when they left it. Why had the Fourth Corps broken? They could not tell. But they were angry because four battalions of *Arditi* whom they met going forward to hold the roads above Cividale and gain time, had called them cowards.

When we reentered the town and reached the Via Manin, the *Ufficio Stampa* was deserted. And from that moment we felt very much alone.

There was no newspaper published in Udine on Saturday and no official bulletin. By nightfall no eating house, restaurant, or hotel dining room was open. We laid in a stock of bread, canned meat, fruit, and chocolate from a shopkeeper who was about to leave town. It would, we figured, carry us through the next day.

As Gibbon and I were leaving the Albergo d'Italia, a shot sounded, followed by the shuffle of feet and shouting. Then a man sped by in the half dusk, running at full speed. After him came a crowd of armed soldiers and fat citizens, the latter bursting with indignation. The fugitive was quickly run down and collared by a soldier on a bicycle. Two carbineers appeared and took charge of him. It all happened so quickly that when we reached the spot, crowd, carbineers, and prisoner had disappeared.

"What had he done?" we asked a soldier.

"Done?" was the contemptuous answer. "He tried to throw the town into panic. Fired a revolver in the open square and shouted, 'You Italians are all cowards.' "

Were we awake, or was this an example of enemy subversion?

That night we dined with a major of Alpine troops, several other officers, and some youths of the town, in an apartment on the upper floor of a main street. We were guests, but contributed all our stock of food to the table strewn with odds and ends. It was the strangest meal I had ever shared. The major who had commanded one of the battalions on Monte Nero—"cut off but still resisting, sending news by carrier pigeon," he explained vehemently—had been ordered out of a hospital in Udine, wounds and all, and told to take the first train to the rear or failing that, anything he could find. One of the lieutenants present had been wounded at Caporetto on Wednesday and gave us our first coherent story of the defeat. The other officers had been caught in Udine by the retreat. All were getting out that night by any means available. No one had any real notion where the Austrians were. Cividale had been occupied late in the afternoon. Had the enemy advanced further under cover of darkness? Had we a force capable of fighting a rearguard action between Cividale and Udine? Would the enemy enter town that night? No one knew.

"Why did the lines break?" someone asked.

The major drew an automatic revolver from his pocket, looked about the room significantly, and laid the weapon beside his plate.

"There was treason," he thundered.

The other officers nodded.

"And jealousy among our generals," the major continued, filling his wine glass with precision and emptying it at a gulp. "The infantry have always been weak. They tried to take Monte San Gabriele. We *Alpini* took it for them and then they could not even hold it. O God, God, God!" he suddenly groaned. "Why am I here? Why was I wounded? Why am I not with my men on Monte Nero, out of this rabble, where I could die like a man?"

We could not answer.

"When are you leaving?" I asked our host, a boy of about seventeen. He paled slightly and looked at another boy near him. "Tomorrow —no—how can I leave? All we have is our wineshop. I must stay and protect our property for my mother and sister."

"You mean for the Germans," commented a lieutenant with smiling bitterness.

The subject dropped. We dipped into can after can. Only wine was plentiful.

The major suddenly laid down his knife and glared at the door. And our gaze followed there, half expecting to see the helmet of an Uhlan appear.

"They may be here any moment," said the major. "But they will never have me as prisoner. There are seven of them here, the little darlings," he tapped the butt of his automatic, "six for them and one for me." Yet before the meeting broke up, the major had presented Gibbon with his revolver and seven little darlings.

"Take care of yourselves," he called out as we separated, "and remember that when an army retreats the men become ugly. Goodbye, goodbye." And he and the lieutenants were gone.

The sky was covered with clouds and the wind was rising. We climbed to the hilltop beside the castle and looked long toward Cividale. But we could see nothing.

At half past ten when I was sleeping in the Albergo Croce di Malta, a dull report shook the town. The night was too dark and rainy for an air raid. I slept again. Someone knocked on my door. It was another English colleague.

"Come, let's take a look before I leave."

Ten minutes later I was beside him in his car. At Cadorna's villa the sentries had disappeared, and though we knocked thunderously, no one appeared. In the piazza we passed a great rumbling something.

"Who are you?" I asked.

"We are the antiaircraft battery from the castle. Orders have just come by wireless for us to go."

"Are you the last to leave?"

"The last."

Then a second explosion shook the buildings to their very foundations.

The bottom had definitely fallen out of Udine.

The second explosion caused a stampede. Many Udinese had been unable to believe that the town was being left to its fate. Even the sight of the departing Staff had not shaken the middle-aged from their roots. Something would happen at the last moment. The Austrians would be driven back. Or else it was all a feint to draw them on. Besides, the Second Army had not yet passed through the town. Probably the retreat was only a tremendous farce of some kind. Even those who realized the extent of the disaster were reluctant to abandon all they possessed. But when explosions began to shake the houses, many of those who had intended to remain lost courage. Snatching up a few garments and their dearest possessions, they fled out into the night, spreading the canard that the enemy was shelling the city.

I could not sleep. About two in the morning the camions of the retreating Second Army began to pass through town at high speed. One of their roads led under my window. Horns sounded, whistles screamed, the old houses trembled from the heavy wheels. To me it seemed that the drivers were half crazy in a world gone mad! The clacking shutters, the shells, the rumbling and screeching automobiles continued for hours, years, centuries. . . . I turned on the light and tried to read. I could not follow a sentence. I could only feel the Austrians coming closer and closer. Finally I fell asleep and dreamed a strange dream.

It was broad day. The piazza in front of the giant statues of Caius and Hercules was empty, but at one side, in the open doorway of a tobacco store, stood a man. Tramp, tramp, tramp, the Austrians were entering town. Across the open park beyond the castle they swung, then under the tower and along the Via Manin. The first of them filed into the Piazza and as they did so, all their heads turned toward the man in the doorway and smiled in recognition. His eyes never left theirs. A dozen soldiers with rifles advanced and formed a line. They were going to shoot him, but he could not move. His eyes began to roll from side to side, but he never opened his lips. What was the matter with him? Could he not save himself? My God, it was myself!

In desperation I opened my eyes. It was still night. Boom! Why had I not left in the *Daily Mail's* motor car?

Toward dawn I dozed off and when I opened them day was at hand. Flinging open the shutters I leaned out, breathing the delicious air. It was still raining. A deserted wagon lay on its side in the street, spilling its load of household goods half across the pavement.

At half past six, washed, dressed, combed, calm, and smiling, I knocked on Gibbon's door. It was Sunday, October 28.

The last servant in the Albergo d'Italia brought us black coffee. After we had drunk it, we went into town. In front of the naval quarters stood a motorcycle big enough to carry two. It was tempting, but we put the thought from us. Someone might be counting on that motorcycle for a military purpose.

At the Porta di Cividale no one was visible, nor at the Porta di Gemona to the north, where we imagined the Germans would enter first.

But through the Porta di Aquileia, past the railroad station, around the center of town, and out again by the Porta di Venezia, what had been an army was passing. It had no form and no visible officers. Yet the men were keeping a certain kind of order. Standing at the railroad gate, we watched the moving column. Some of the soldiers looked at us with curiosity, others with a question on their lips, a few with unconcealed hostility. For Gibbon was wearing a correspondent's uniform, similar to that of a British officer. The men were from the Bainsizza, from Monte Santo, from Monte San Gabriele. A wounded sergeant limped along, almost alone. He had come on foot from the hospital at San Giovanni di Manzano, he said. The wounded who could walk had been turned out to shift for themselves, some of the others had been taken away in ambulances, some had been left behind.

The station at Udine was full of wounded, standing, sitting, lying on stretchers and on the bare floor, with no one looking after them. It was each for himself.

Around the outskirts of town the storehouses and munition depots in a dozen places were burning. Near the Porta di Aquileia, along the tracks, flames were shooting hundreds of feet in the air. Every now and then a great explosion shot flying fragments of fire two hundred yards, while the houses nearby rocked. These were the reports which had so shaken the town in the night. At three hundred yards, the heat was intolerable. Some trees near the fire were burning and it looked as though the entire town might go up in flames. At that moment no one would have cared. Even to us it did not seem to matter.

Most of the dwellings were bolted with closed shutters. From behind them, lonely dogs and cats wailed for the departed.

As we passed the gaping doorway of a large building on Via Aquileia, a dozen voices called to us. We stopped and looked within. More wounded men lay or sat on the cement floor. Again they took Gibbon for a British officer.

"*Signore*," they cried, "where shall we go?"

Gibbon and I exchanged a glance. "Tell them something in Italian," he said.

"Why aren't you in your beds?" I asked, for only a few were dressed.

"We didn't want to stay. They all went away."

"Who went away?"

"All of them, everybody, and all of us who could walk. But we cannot walk. Where shall we go? Someone must be coming back to take us away."

"Where are your doctors?"

"All gone away."

"Your nurses?"

"The same—all gone."

"But how did you get downstairs without help?"

"As we could; some of us slid, some crawled. We don't want to be left here. Please tell us where to go."

We knew no more than they. But Gibbon said: "There may be another train."

"Yes." And we both knew there would be no other.

"Go to the station," I said softly. "You will be better off there." I think some of them understood there was no hope.

"Where is the station?"

"Just down this street."

"Is it far?"

"Not far. Five minutes on foot."

"Oh," groaned a voice. "I can't walk so far. Don't leave us; we don't want to stay behind and be captured." The speaker stood up. One foot was a bloody bandaged stump, but he placed it firmly on the pavement without wincing. "We don't want to be captured," he said again. And then, I swear, he *walked* to where we stood just outside the door and fell at our feet.

"Don't leave me, don't leave me."

Had we been of finer stuff we would have stayed and looked after them and ourselves spent the rest of the war in prison. Instead, we left.

When we looked back, the man with one foot was fifty yards down the sidewalk, crawling on his hands and knees.

We did not blame the doctors and nurses who had gone. Their duty was to their country and it demanded that they be free. These wounded could not, I repeat, could not, have all been saved by any means the Italians possessed. Many were the examples of devotion among the hospital and ambulance corps. At Cervignano, south of Udine, a woman fifty years old, a volunteer nurse, remained at her post twenty-four hours after her son, who had commanded naval guns on the Carso, had retreated. She did not leave the hospital until the last wounded soldier had gone.

Soldiers abandoning a town to the enemy almost always try to carry away with them everything of value. They "commandeer" food and liquor, shoes, pass on to bicycles, and end by common robbery if they are not controlled. This is normal and in one sense logical. Why leave anything to the enemy?

The Italian *Arditi* sacked Udine as the French "captured" Verdun. While the majority followed the main way around the outskirts of the town, some who had apparently been ordered to defend the city, mingled with stragglers from other corps and set about systematic plundering. I remember seeing soldiers parading through the rain in silk hats and women's underwear, armed for the most part only with bottles. Yet I saw no civilians mistreated.

And where were the Austrians? Had they decided to surround Udine and come in from the west? Just before noon, we strolled out of the town in the direction of the enemy. Suddenly, just ahead we heard two shots. Rushing forward we saw a strange sight. In a stopped foreign car sat a dead Austrian general and his military chauffeur, both killed by Italian *carabinieri*.

It made us think. "Who," Gibbon asked, "ever saw a modern general out in front of his troops? Obviously the Austrian wings must be closing in on the town from behind. This is our last chance to get out."

I agreed. It was time to go—without our world scoop.

Before joining the retreating mob at the Porta di Venezia, we "commandeered" two bicycles standing before an empty house.

Nearly all day and then again in the evening, the rain fell in streams that a rough wind drove here and there in mighty gusts. The road was a lake of mud. Bicycles were almost as useless as pushcarts or perambulators, but we clung to them and twice succeeded in riding a few disconsolate miles.

There was no rioting, but no order. The center was occupied by a double row of automobiles, camions, carts, and donkeys moving about two miles per hour. Beside, between, behind, and around these conveyances walked a mixed congregation of men, women, children, and soldiers. A few of the latter carried loot. But the wineshops of Udine had proved too great a temptation for most of the pillagers. Officers were rare, and their men were taking orders from no one. Some few sang antiwar songs, others, popular tunes. Others talked in small groups of twos and threes, chiefly about peace.

"But are you certain we shall have peace?" a round-faced boy asked.

"Certain," replied his companion. "You can have no war without an army. An army cannot fight without arms. When we threw away our arms we ended the war."

This confidence in the midst of such appalling misery was astounding. "Where are you going now?" I asked.

Both stared. "Where? Home." It was their turn for astonishment.

"But if the Austrians come after you?"

"They won't come far. They too want peace."

"What did your officers say when you threw away your arms?"

"What could they say? It would not have been well for them if they had said anything. Some were ugly, but when they realized that we were serious they changed their tune. And if our officers do not understand now, we shall make another jump to the rear. We are tired, you understand, tired of all this business and we are going home. Why should we fight Austria?"

This message was droned into our ears. But among the talkers were many who trod along silently, and I saw tears rolling down the cheeks of one.

"All retreats are like this," muttered Gibbon. "I have seen three in this war. The Allied Governments ought to pay me to stay away. This is nothing compared to the Russian retreat from Poland in 1915."

This one was bad enough. If you can imagine an army with all its vehicles, supplies, men, weapons, shaken up in an immense bottle and then violently shot out of it along a muddy country road, then add many thousands of refugees, all under a torrential rain, and you begin to see what we saw.

Under my raincoat, heavy jacket, and sweater, in spite of the effort of pushing a bicycle through the slime, I was shivering. Yet beside me, peasant children trotted with bare feet, their bodies wrapped only in calico. Old men tottered under the weight of babies, women sank down exhausted beside ditches. Boys dragged unwilling livestock along. Families rode in wagons on top of household goods, or in donkey carts, or on donkeys. A few refugees found places in crowded military camions, but the drivers were impatient; children were separated from their parents, wives from their husbands.

A few moments after leaving Udine, we heard a great uproar behind us and a cry, "The Austrians, the Austrians!" A panic started. Chauffeurs left their cars, drivers their wagons, women and children fell and were trampled. A few minutes later, there came a sound of fusillade across the fields from the town. If there were any Austrians, their number must have been small. We saw none. There were enough Italian soldiers on that road to have repulsed a division had they kept their arms. But they thought only of flight.

We trudged on, going nearly twice as fast as the jam of automobiles, clinging tenaciously to our bicycles. Sooner or later we expected to emerge from the mess of traffic and mount them.

At Campo Formido, immortalized by history as Campo Formio, we turned aside to visit the aviation camp, hoping to find Italy's best aviator, Captain Baracca, whom we knew. Even as we approached, flames shot into the air, and by the time we drew near his pine shack, it was a roaring bonfire. Outside the largest hangar, two horses were tethered. Inside were the partly burned skeletons of at least twenty fighter planes, and a dozen motors intact. Then we noticed two cavalrymen busy in a corner.

"Who set these buildings on fire?"

"We did."

"What for?"

"Orders."

"Did you also have orders to plunder the aviators' baggage?"

"We weren't. We were only hunting for explosives to blow up the motors." A bundle of letters dropped from their hands.

We rode away with gall in our mouths.

The crowd on the road grew thicker. Twice we turned off on cross roads and gained a few moments on the bicycles, but each time came out on the main road again. On one of the side roads was a column of French artillery, proceeding with perfect discipline. Once we caught up with a column of British Red Cross ambulances. They too were doing well.

At Codroipo the station master said there were no more trains. If we desired to cross the Tagliamento River that night, we must walk. The shortest way was along the railroad track. We joined another dense column of soldiers quietly making their way along the tracks.

Our feet were weighted with mud, and the bicycles moved through the cinders like steamrollers. Gibbon's feet were hurting him. Then the soldiers ahead began to go more slowly and finally they stopped altogether. We had reached the entrance to the railroad bridge, a steel trestle with a narrow foot track and a hand rail on one side. Only two could march abreast. No bicycles were allowed. With a groan that was almost a paean we hurled the silly mechanical devices into the river.

Someone behind began to push. We went forward in little jerks, only to stop again. Some soldiers pulled knives. At this rate we would not be across the stream before morning. So heads high, working with elbows and shoulders, Gibbon and I wriggled our way forward through the gasping mob. Finally we cleared the crowd, jumped over the gates, and were on the bridge.

It was nearly a mile long. The Tagliamento River, ordinarily a meandering brook in the midst of a broad gravel bed, was swollen by rains to a broad torrent. It beat against the stone piers below and frothed terribly under the ties upon which we walked. By the time we reached the opposite bank we were reeling with fatigue.

Our immediate goal was Casarsa, a junction village a few miles farther. Once across the Tagliamento, most of the soldiers had halted. But we looked forward to a hot dinner and beds, or a train to Treviso. After further aeons of tramping we did reach Casarsa Station. Upon the tracks stood at least five trains, all headed west, all puffing, and all crammed with soldiers and refugees.

We left the station and went in search of food. One of the two restaurants was closed. There was light inside and the sound of singing, but the door was far too heavy to batter down. The other restaurant had been taken by storm. With exceptional wit, the proprietress had accepted the situation and picked a stout soldier as auctioneer, who sold everything at famine rates and passed the money to her. From this soldier we obtained a three-quart bottle of vermouth. He refused to sell less and insisted on tasting the contents before he relinquished the bottle to us. Perhaps he wished to make sure of the quality. I scooped up a couple of tumblers from a table and we sat down outside to our drink. But after a couple of glasses of the strong stuff our stomachs protested. They wanted food, not drink. At the critical moment somebody sold us eight eggs. Fried in greasy ashes and eaten with the palm of the hand, those eggs produced a sensation of immortality.

Refreshed in body and mind, we returned to the station. An hour later we found a few square feet of space on the coal of a tender, already occupied by twenty or thirty soldiers. It was bitterly cold and soon began to rain again. At midnight the train started, ran a few miles west —and stopped. After a few more hours on the coal, we struck out across a field toward a road. Fifty yards more and we splashed waist-deep into a ditch. When we finally reached the highway, we found it almost deserted. In vain we tried to induce an old woman at a door to give us shelter. At a nearby campfire we were again surrounded by soldiers in open revolt. To remain with them would have meant a fight. After an hour we gave up and headed westward again. It was half past four in the morning, October 29. We had been on our feet almost twenty-four hours.

Gibbon groaned. "The nails have come through my boots until my feet are like burning coals." I tried to persuade a soldier leading a pack horse to let Gibbon ride the animal to Pordenone while I walked, but he refused.

Gibbon groaned again. "Old man, I'm finished. Go on, leave me. I'd rather die than walk to Pordenone." He sat down on the wet step of a standing camion, his head dropped forward and he slept.

Finally, I persuaded an officer commanding a retreating auto column to take us to Pordenone.

For a solid hour we stood in line in a cafe in order to obtain the hot coffee substitute that was all the place offered. Finally the waiter placed two steaming cups on the counter.

Then the unbelievable happened. An impatient Italian captain pushed me—a mere civilian—aside with disdain, and reached for my cup. Five days of contained frustration exploded. From behind, I seized him by the collar, threw him over my foot to the floor with a schoolboy trip, and grabbed the cup with my free hand.

Lying on his back, he pointed his automatic revolver at me and hissed: *"Imboscato"* (shirker). Equally quickly, Gibbon drew the major's revolver and pressed it into my hand. I pointed it down at the captain. "Flower of the Second Italian Army!" I retorted.

How long we stood muzzle-to-muzzle I cannot say. But long enough for me to utter a prayer: "God, if he shoots, give me strength to pull my trigger before I die," still keeping my other hand on the cup of discord. A passing colonel interrupted the confrontation. "Put down those guns. What kind of behavior is this?"

The captain did so, struggled to his feet, and made off. I handed the weapon back to Gibbon.

Still no trains. Once more we hit the road westward toward Treviso. Gibbon's shoes were full of blood. But here military drivers were in less of a hurry and three successively succumbed to the lure of a fifty-lire bill held high and gave us short lifts. Just beyond Conigliano, we climbed into a curious looking vehicle. It had no seats. And then suddenly Gibbon cried: "What in God's name is the matter with us? It's an ambulance. We can lie down." We stretched ourselves on the bloodstained blankets.

Before nightfall we were in the fine old town of Treviso, the new seat of the Italian Supreme Command, had checked in with the *Ufficio Stampa,* found a hotel with a bathroom, and eaten our first real meal in thirty-six hours.

For us the Italian retreat was over.

The next day I hurried from Treviso to Venice, fearful lest the entire front collapse and my wife, who had been laid up with a sprained foot, be unable to leave, although I had urged her to do so by wire. Carroll reassured me. Lilian had found a place in the last train to Rome. And there I followed her, convinced that Italy must save itself in the capital before it could hope to do so on the field of battle.

9

Italy Saves the Entente

. . . Che l'antico valor
ne l'italici cor non è ancor morto.

PETRARCH

FROM NOVEMBER, 1917, until the collapse of the Ludendorff offensive in France, in August, 1918, the Italian front was a decisive battlefield. For after the defection of Bolshevik Russia, a total Italian collapse would have freed up to seventy-five Austro–Hungarian divisions for use on the Western front, a force that the United States would not have been able to offset until 1919—and perhaps not then. Of this fact, the Italian débâcle at Caporetto had made the Entente painfully aware.

Why had that happened? First-hand witnesses like me believed that it was more the result of a military strike than of a well-planned German-directed offensive against an Italian Second Army caught off balance by Cadorna's premature interruption of its previous advance. Unlike those French divisions on the Chemin des Dames, the two Italian corps at Caporetto had not so much mutinied as decided to "march for peace," in this case, to go home, on the assumption that equally peace-hungry Austro–Hungarian soldiers would follow their example.

Yet when the comrades and younger brothers of these "peace marchers" saw that instead of ending the war, unilateral pacifism had opened Italy to a barbarous invader, they underwent a spiritual change. Thereafter, freshly mobilized and undertrained peasants and workers who would not have given a plate of spaghetti for Dalmatia, fought magnificently for their homes and their families. And of the roughly seven hundred thousand Italians who deserted, the half who managed to escape capture suddenly realized their mistakes and, once reorganized and reequipped, returned to the front with a new belligerence.

In short, Caporetto did what no amount of rhetoric and song had been able to accomplish: it "awakened" Italy.

What had actually saved the country in those first awful days was the unforeseen size and speed of the Italian retreat. The German-Austrian commanders anticipated a success. But they certainly did not expect the Italians to surrender without fighting while singing the *Hymn of the Workers*, as four brigades did at Caporetto on the first day of the attack—still less to see the Second Army head for home.

Furthermore, they probably expected Cadorna to stand on the Tagliamento River. When instead the General retreated to the Piave River, some forty to eighty miles further west, he left a space which the battle-weary invaders could not quickly cover. By the time they brought up their matériel, the new Italian Commander-in-Chief, General Armando Diaz, had mustered enough die-hard troops to hold the shortened line.

Returning from Rome to the front in late November, 1917, after reassuring myself both as to the safety of my wife and to the resolution of the Italian Government, I shared with Gibbon an unheated apartment in Padua, the new headquarters town. Our two newspapers bought us an open car to which the Army contributed a soldier chauffeur, and we spent almost every day on the lines with the troops, returning each evening with frozen fingers, to type our dispatches, file them, enjoy a late dinner at the almost deserted Hotel Storione, and pile into icy beds to shiver ourselves to sleep.

In one particular, covering the war in Italy was entirely different from the job of our colleagues on the French front. The latter received necessary military information and the regular company of staff officers. The Italian *Ufficio Stampa* provided relatively little information, at least to foreigners, but gave each newsman a *Comando Supremo* pass that enabled him to go wherever he liked. Gibbon and I rapidly established a chain of acquaintanceships with commanders from the Adige to the Adriatic. In consequence, we knew *less* and saw *more* than correspondents on the Western front and had a greater sense of participation in the fighting. I remember the surprise of Wythe Williams of the *New York Times* when, upon his arrival at Padua from Paris, I took him straight to the front-line headquarters of a friendly major without bothering to inform the commanding general of the sector. If we on the Italian front missed anything big, it was strictly our own fault.

For about a month after Caporetto, the battle was touch and go. The invaders hurled their tired forces at the new Italian positions along a sixty-mile front in a frantic effort to eliminate Italy altogether. But by the middle of December, I was able to report with all the confidence of personal experience that what remained of the Italian armies was showing a new readiness to die rather than to yield further.

In Rome, too, after receiving a vote of confidence from the Italian Chamber, the new Prime Minister, Vittorio Emanuele Orlando, announced on December 26 that Italy had overcome the crisis.

No less salutary was the effect of Caporetto upon the other Allied and Associated Powers. Britain and France hastened to dispatch to Italy divisions whose requested presence a year earlier might have localized or prevented the Italian defeat. The United States rushed in a Red Cross mission of devoted and competent people whom my wife immediately joined, and somewhat later, the 302nd U.S. Infantry. In May, 1917, American volunteer aviators had begun training on Italian Caproni planes at Foggia. Now President Wilson's Committee on Public Information under George Creel sent a group of propagandists with the task of convincing the Italians that they were not alone but a valued member of an ultimately victorious alliance of democracies. At the head came a professor of political science from the University of Chicago, Charles E. Merriam.

At our first meeting I knew he was my sort of man, freedom-loving, internationally-minded, and tough. The enthusiasm that we both felt for the Fourteen Points, which Wilson had just hurled at a still skeptical world, immediately brought us together. When Merriam asked me to serve as his occasional interpreter and unpaid personal adviser on matters Italian, I gladly accepted.

For his offer lightened my growing depression. In part this was the effect of too much contact with the ceaseless slaughter, sorrow, and general demoralization of an apparently unending conflict. In part it was a feeling of personal guilt at not being an active military participant.

This feeling started with the United States' entrance into war. Before that, in spite of the desire to see the defeat of the Central Empires, I had considered that I could best serve as a war correspondent. Moreover, I had seen too much of what Alfred de Vigny had called military "servitude" as well as military "grandeur" to look forward to being bogged down somewhere in a trench, perhaps for years. What a contrast with the freedom of a newsman!

On the other hand, by what right could I, twenty-five and able-bodied, urge my countrymen to give everything if I excused myself, on whatever pretext, from sharing the dangers and discipline of the combatants?

Accordingly, in May, 1917, I wrote my brother, asking him to inquire from the American military mission in Paris whether I could enlist without going home for training. After some delay I got an answer: I would have to return to the United States and undergo several months' training—still longer, if I wanted to be an officer. In all probability, the source said, the war would be over before I could participate actively in it. As an experienced war correspondent with a knowledge of French and Italian, I could do more for my country by remaining on my present job. If I felt any qualms of conscience, I should put myself at the service of the American Embassy in Rome.

Somewhat unwillingly I accepted this advice, even though Ambassador Page had at the time no particular use for my services.

Had it not been for the Bolshevik Revolution and the Italian débâcle, that U.S. officer in Paris might well have been correct about the war's early end. But all during the retreat from Caporetto, while Gibbon and I were denouncing the Italians' behavior ("a mixture of stupidity and cowardice") I could not but ask myself: "And by what right do you, a newsman free to come and go as you please, judge soldiers some of whom have had thirty months' uninterrupted hell?" This doubt may well have nourished the violence of my reaction to the Italian captain who tried to appropriate my cup of hot chicory at Pordenone, calling me "shirker." Maybe I was a shirker. . . .

The reader may imagine, therefore, with what relief I accepted Merriam's offer to give the Committee on Public Information part of my time, while Lilian gave most of hers to the Red Cross.

Com Pub's job was to strengthen the Italians' morale. What better method than to aid the "fightingest" newspapers? Among these the *Popolo d'Italia* ranked high. Benito Mussolini, who, having volunteered for the *Bersaglieri,* had been invalided out because of an accidental injury, outdid himself as patriot during the post-Caporetto Italian crisis. Yet the *Popolo's* influence remained limited.

So when Merriam asked me if I could find out what sort of support would be necessary to increase its circulation, I assured him that I could.

"Find out how much money he needs to expand," Merriam said.

At the *Popolo d'Italia* office in Milano, Benito received me with his usual gusto and became attentive as soon as I informed him that Signore Merriam of Com Pub admired his efforts to keep up Italy's fighting spirit and would like to help him increase his influence. "Could that be done?"

"Naturally," he answered. "But I lack the necessary cash."

"And how much would it cost?" I inquired innocently.

"*Molti quattrini*" (a lot of money), replied Benito, sticking out his jaw.

I had not lived thirty months in Italy for nothing.

"In that case, I fear there is no use in talking further about it. Com Pub does not have a lot of money for this purpose. Still, if you wish to give your old friend Mowrer a figure, he will pass it on to Signore Merriam."

"Right," said Benito. "Shall we say"—he stopped to calculate how high he might safely go, then named what seemed to me an absurdly low figure.

Frowning to conceal my relief, I agreed that it was indeed *molti quattrini,* but that I would do what I could to persuade Com Pub that Mussolini's exceptional services merited exceptional support. Merriam was willing, but whether Benito actually obtained American funds I never knew.

Next, at Merriam's suggestion, I spent most of the month of February, 1918, producing a manuscript on Italy's share in the war, starting with D'Annunzio at Quarto and ending with the post-Caporetto miracle. Some of it consisted of carefully edited dispatches and mailers which had already appeared in the Chicago *Daily News*. But I added full connectives and explanations. And although I omitted nothing, the general tone was highly favorable. Certainly such a book would have added considerably to the little most Americans knew about Italy's changing intentions, improved performance, and general significance in the Great War.

I called the manuscript *Soldiers of the Third Italy* and dedicated it to the "Italian soldiers whose exploits it recounts" and to Ambassador Page, "without whose personal intervention it never could have been written."

On Merriam's advice, I sent it to the editor of the *Daily News* with the request that he assure immediate publication as a contribution to the general cause.

In vain. The editor reported no success with book publishers and no willingness on the part of the *News* to bring it out.

This was a painful disappointment. The publication of such a volume would have been a bridge between reporting and the book-writing to which I intended to return as soon as the war ended.

Next appeared three American socialists, picked by George Creel because he hoped that their enthusiasm for "Wilson's war" would convert, or at least silence, the antiwar Italian socialists. The three undertook a speech-making trip around the country under the guidance of Italian socialist, Edmondo Rossoni, who could outtalk most of a nation of talkers. Lilian and I went along to look after, and interpret for, the Americans.

Politically, in spite of Prime Minister Orlando's stubborn defense of the Italian claims incorporated in the Treaty of London, the nation's attitude was shifting. The Government could not overlook the fact that to many Italians Wilson appeared as a sort of savior.

Our dentist in Naples, Vincenzo Guerrini, one of those *originali* whom Southern Italy regularly produces, actually set up in his office an altar to Wilson, with the President's photograph upon it.

Moreover, to everyone's surprise, the Rome Government, which had originally opposed any dismemberment of Austria-Hungary, suddenly accepted it as a possibility. The result was the Pact of Rome of April, 1918, which committed the signatories to strive for the "total liberation" of the Habsburgs' "oppressed peoples." In this change my good friend Bissolati took the lead. As a result of the pact, Italy released and started retraining and reequipping those Slav prisoners ready to strike a blow for their respective nations' freedom.

The Pact of Rome did not necessarily imply the disruption of the Dual Empire. As late as October, 1918, President Wilson was at one with Emperor Charles in trying to preserve that country on a federative basis. The tenth of his famous Fourteen Points merely assured the member peoples of "the freest opportunity of autonomous development."

Why then did the Italians shift to a policy of dismemberment? One reason was the arguments of the Slovak leader, General Milan Stefanik, by profession an astronomer, who had served as a flyer in the French Army. Stefanik loved Italy and apparently convinced Sonnino that Italy's influence would be greater upon independent than upon federated Central European peoples. Through Stefanik, I visited a Czechoslovak training camp in Umbria and learned of the efforts of those other remarkable Czechoslovaks, Masaryk, Benes, and Osusky. Stefanik, after a brief but adventurous career with the seventy-thousand-strong Czechoslovak Legion in Siberia (which could have overthrown the Bolshevik regime if permitted by the Allies), died just before his country became formally independent.

My friend Monsignore Sincero repeatedly passed on to me reports from Austria-Hungary: economic shortages of all kinds; clashes between the discontented Slavs and the ruling Germans and Magyars; impending dissolution. Nothing but a great military victory (or just possibly President Wilson, whose emissary in Europe, Professor George Herron, was in constant contact with representatives of Emperor Charles as well as of the discontented Slavs) could save the Central Empires. Ever more American divisions in France would, in time, more than compensate for the Bolsheviks' defection. Accordingly, between March and August, 1918, the German commanders in the West tried repeatedly to smash the Allies.

In June it was the Austrians' turn to seek a knockout. They chose for their "hunger offensive" the low hills and coastal plain north and east of Venice, between the Montello and the Adriatic. The Veneto was a rich, smiling garden containing the loveliest villas in the world, where landscape itself was art. Nowhere was the desecration of war more conspicuous. Obviously it made the hungry Austrians' mouth water, for on launching their offensive the commanders instructed the soldiers to seize foodstuffs, textiles, leather, and soap—and post them home.

From headquarters at Padua, where, after Gibbon's return to England, I was living comfortably by myself in the apartment of a rich landlord who had fled (he considered daily baths as *abuse*, not *use*, of the bathtub and cut off the hot water while leaving behind his chambermaid, la Lena, to collect the rent and look after the tenants—it did not matter if the Austrians captured *her*), the faithful Carlo could drive me to almost any part of the battle line in less than ninety minutes.

The Austrians concentrated their offensives on two areas, one north of Treviso, and the other around San Donà di Piave, near the Adriatic. The latter was easily accessible by car from Mestre or by motorboat from Venice, where I often stayed overnight with the Carrolls. Along this line, for one terrible summer week, from June 15 to June 22, seventy-three Austrian divisions tried to smash their way through sixty entrenched Italian divisions, some of them undefeated veterans from the Carso, some composed of reequipped "military strikers" from Caporetto, and still others formed entirely of teenagers who had never fired a shot in anger. Both sides fought magnificently. Three times, if I remember correctly, picked Austro-Hungarians crossed the fateful Piave and established bridgeheads, only to be driven back by Italians who, finally, knew what they were fighting for. Although the assailants inflicted forty thousand casualties and took fifty thousand prisoners, they still could not win.

During those seven days I spent most of the daylight hours and two of the nights in the trenches. Once, at Carroll's urgent plea, I took him along to a battalion headquarters a hundred yards behind the Piave (at Pralungo). We arrived in the midst of an Italian counterattack and found shelter and lunch with my friend the major in the dugout headquarters. Carlo parked the car behind a ruined barn and covered it with green branches. After lunch we sat out behind a stone wall under a tree to talk a little before creeping forward to the front line. We never got there. The neighboring dugout housed a first-aid station. From it, the battalion doctor suddenly emerged and said to the major:

"An operation within the next couple of hours will save the life of that abdominal case. I lack what I need to do it here." Then he looked at us. And at this minute, a hundred yards away, enemy machine gun fire rose to a roar, while leaves cut from the branches by bullets rained down on our heads.

We had intended to stay all day, but I took the hint and looked at Carroll, who nodded. "We'll take him back immediately." I said, "Major, where's Carlo?"

"Right here, sir," said a voice and the chauffeur popped up from another hole where he had been lunching with the sergeants, for all the world like the servant in a Goldoni comedy.

"Get those branches off the car and back her up here."

"But, *signore*—"

"No buts, soldier."

The doctor and his assistants strapped the wounded soldier to a stretcher, and the stretcher to the seat tops front and rear. Carroll, a husky man, sat in the back seat and held the precious load while I mounted in front to steady Carlo.

"I'll give the chauffeur the signal when to go," said the major, going into the dugout to phone his advanced outposts.

A few minutes later he came back. "Don't dawdle on the road. Your chauffeur knows where the hospital is. Thank you for *his* sake . . .," pointing to the wounded man. "*Addio, Signor console, addio* Edgardo. Come again, soon."

The warning not to dawdle was unnecessary. Carlo, a sturdy Piedmontese with a sense of duty, covered the miles under enemy fire as though trying to win the Grand Prix. We heard the whine of bullets, but were untouched. Once we had delivered the wounded man at the hospital, we left Carlo at Mestre and returned to Venice. It was Carroll's baptism of fire and like a true Texan he had enjoyed every minute of it. Best of all, the wounded man eventually recovered.

Three days later, the Austrian offensive faded out, the Italians regained some of their lost ground, and the battle was over. Our side had won.

Not since that October with the Belgians on the Yser almost four years before had I been so close to the killing. I almost envied the American Red Cross lieutenant, Edward Mackay, a New York lawyer who had been killed by an Austrian shell in his army canteen near Pralongo the day before our visit. Mackay had asked to do the front-line job, explaining that since he was older than most of his associates —forty-two, to be exact—his death would be of less consequence than that of any of them. Now he was lying in Roncade cemetery while I was back in the front bedroom of the Hotel Danieli in Venice, after a good dinner with Carroll and his wife at the Vida, a charming *trattoria* in Campo San Giacomo dell' Orio.

From then on death never left me alone. In July, Mildred, my cousin and playfellow, died while pregnant with her first child.

During the Christmas holidays Lilian and I finished a magnificent walking trip between Viterbo and Rome, only to learn of the death of Olivia Andersen, Hendrick's widowed sister-in-law, who shared an apartment with him, his mother, and his adopted Italian sister, Lucia.

In March, 1918, at Padua, I received a telegram from Father announcing the sudden death of my mother. She had never been strong, and since that nervous breakdown when I was seven, never been well. Yet she had shown a remarkable ability to overcome her physical handicaps. Though the offspring of generations of pioneers, she was "no wife for a poor man," as her father had told mine. Only in those three Paris years, 1914 to 1917, had she lived as she had always wanted to. Then out of a sense of duty, she had gone home to Father, to whom Paris was an imposing but excessively foreign world into which he had no inclination to fit. Now she too was dead.

In July, it was the turn of her brother, Albert, whom I loved dearly.

All around me, young men were celebrating a sort of Triumph of Death like the chilling fresco on the walls of the cemetery at Pisa. The least a war correspondent could do was share the risk.

Opportunities for "special assignments" were waiting to be seized. Lieutenant Commander Luigi Rizzo, the only man in any Navy who successively torpedoed two battleships from a thirty-foot motorboat, had taken a fancy to me, perhaps because I publicized his exploits so thoroughly in America. That same July, I believe, he asked me if I would care to go "battleship hunting" with him. Would I not!

And what a night that was! I met Rizzo about sunset at the Venice Arsenal and our two *mas* (as the Italians called their armed motorboats) headed for Trieste, some eighty miles away. Shortly before we sighted the Istrian coast, we shifted from the gasoline to the electric motor and thereafter glided over a calm sea as silently as a swan. Rizzo and I stayed in the bow, while he peered through glasses into the starlit night. In vain. Not an Austrian ship of any kind to be seen.

"Pig misery!" said Rizzo to the engineer. "But we cannot take Mowrer back without letting him visit Trieste."

Half an hour later we drew along a dark wall-like something.

"What's this?" I whispered.

"The Trieste harbor pier. Let's go for a little walk on it and smoke a cigarette." So he and I walked along the pier toward the shore until we saw the faint glow of the Austrian guardroom against the dimmed lights of the city whose redemption was Italy's major war goal.

"If I could bring my torpedoes up here I'd let those sentries have them," growled Rizzo. "But if we start anything we'll only get killed or captured. Here," . . . and he stopped and handed me a large stone, "take this back as proof you stood with me on Austrian territory."

When at dawn we parted at the Venice Arsenal, he apologized for not having offered me a torpedo attack. "Perhaps another time."

With the indomitable Rizzo, there was no other time. But with Navy flyers I shared two other exciting escapades. On the first occasion my friend the admiral sent me in a hydroplane accompanying another charged with photographing Trieste harbor.

Flying well out to sea, our planes were over our goal in under an hour. While the photographer's "crate" dropped low to get pictures of the Austrian fleet and docks, mine circled lazily above the city more or less out of the range of guns.

Suddenly the pilot pointed down—our companion plane was landing on the harbor water! He put his hands to his mouth and bellowed into my ear: "Their motor has conked out. We must rescue the men." And down we started.

Something else started too. From dockside an Austrian torpedo boat darted out, and headed for the floating plane. It was a race. By the time we taxied alongside, the destroyer was only three hundred yards away, coming on at thirty knots, its bow gun blazing. Fortunately, it was too near and the shells whistled many feet over our heads.

"Get in," yelled my pilot to the others. "Quick or you are finished." At that very minute the other engine started and before we could move, rose out of the water and streaked away. With admirable coolness my pilot also bounced across the water, rose, and banked on one wing, barely missing the waves, in time to avoid the ship's shells. In a few moments both planes were out of range and headed for Venice.

My wife had been the only sufferer. I had promised to meet her for lunch. But when I arrived at the restaurant almost two hours late she had gone, convinced that something awful had happened. Ours was a happy reunion.

My most exciting "special assignment" was never reported. This was shooting up an Austrian trench along the far bank of River Piave from a roofless hydroplane. It started as a bombing expedition. My bomb struck a farmhouse which the pilot, Ensign Guazzetti (one of a group to whom we referred as "eighteen years old, know no fear and very little else"), insisted was full of Austrians. Next he set his plane down in the lagoon not too far from the river and suggested a "real thrill—

trench-raiding with you behind the machine gun." Major Baracca, greatest of Italy's "aces," had been killed while on a similar raid over the Montello.

I could not but accept. I practiced a few shots from the Fiat magazine gun, a type which I had never before fired, and then we flew straight out over the Adriatic to a point about five miles from the coast and a mile in the air. Here the pilot turned and took a downward course that would enable us to enfilade the Austrian front line.

Midway I had a disturbing thought: suppose we were taken prisoner? I saw the entire scene—capture after a forced landing on the Austrian side, trial before a military judge, my sentence as a civilian *franc-tireur*, death at dawn by a firing squad! But even as I flinched at the prospect, our plane roared down with open throttle and leveled off about six hundred feet above the Austrian trench. The pilot drove his elbow hard into my ribs, the signal to get busy.

Looking down, I could see the startled inmates first look up at us, then huddle against the parapet. I felt sorry for them, but I had a job to do. Aiming carefully, I raked the trench for perhaps half a mile. Just when the surprised Austrians started firing back, the machine gun stuck. Following the pilot's previous instruction, I tried to eject the faulty cartridge. Still no result. I cursed myself. "First, you are scared, then you botch the job."

But by this time we were back in safety over Italian territory and Ensign Guazzetti was digging me in the ribs. Finally, he shot the plane skyward to a safe height, took both hands from the controls, cupped them to my ear, and shouted: "The gun is empty."

Whereupon, to celebrate our "victory," he looped the loop while Italian troops on the ground cheered! When we landed at the Arsenal in Venice he said only: "I hope you enjoyed the hunt."

Certainly mine was a unique story.

Yet my dispatch, a thousand words long and full of the thrill of the new (to me) form of combat, never appeared. The Italian censors warned that revelation of my adventure as a trench-raiding civilian would embarrass the Italian *Comando Supremo*. Reluctantly, out of respect for the admiral who had made it possible, I tore up the most sensational personal report I had ever written.

10

Like To Die

Why should November come again, when all
Our days are now so like the dying year—
The same enclouded skies
And black, ill omened birds?
PAUL SCOTT MOWRER

DURING THE AUTUMN months of 1918, disease lent a hand to violence. Spanish fever, epidemic grippe, whatever the future may call the malady that ravaged the world, took a heavy toll from Italy. Its coming weighed horribly upon the nerves of all. And as an involuntary *embusqué,* who had lived beneath the war's great wing without too much exposure to its danger, I suspected that disease had come to reap those destined victims whom the machine gun had spared.

Curiously enough, despair was thicker the farther one went from the zone of actual fighting. Life in the faraway capitals was starkly depressing. Yet in stuffy Padua, noisy with soldiers, and in empty, beautiful Venice, it was cheerless enough. I tried in vain to reason with myself: so great a misfortune could only bring an equal benefit; no war could last forever; the disorder must eventually give way to a new and better order; all the glib phrases we had repeated for years. It was no good.

Such thoughts were not unnatural. When the death of an Austrian archduke opened the doors on chaos, I was twenty-two. Three or four years later the young men of my generation were emotionally old. Never were armies so sad and so heroic.

In mid-October, while Lilian was visiting me at Padua, Professor Merriam wrote from Rome, asking me to serve as his representative at Headquarters without ceasing my work as war correspondent. This double quality the *Ufficio Stampa* refused to recognize. I announced that I was leaving the front altogether.

Yet at the railroad station I found a conciliatory note from the

108

chief censor which brought me back to Headquarters after a brief visit to Rome and a talk with Merriam, during which I obtained a letter confirming my right to speak in his name.

In my absence my wife had a dream. She saw my prostrate body, fearfully mangled, and awoke, filled with a feeling of danger for me, so intense that she was only prevented from starting for Rome by the news of my speedy return to Padua. A subsequent dream, in which she was with me somewhere and the war was over, passed unheeded in the horror of the first impression.

That same Saturday morning, in Rome, I awoke with a bad cough. When in the afternoon I met a colleague, I felt the need to provide against misfortune.

"John, I must return to the front tomorrow night. If I should develop the flu, will you cover the situation for my newspaper?"

On Tuesday, my wife and I lay side by side in Padua, both victims of Spanish fever. Lilian managed to get off a wire to Chicago telling of our plight. Twenty-four hours later the answer came from the publisher: "Spare no expense. Call on us." This, at least, was a great relief. When the Italian doctor came the next morning, he listened attentively to my breathing and uttered a single word: "Pneumonia!"

Then began our purgatory. The doctor suggested a nurse, and there were no nurses to be had in all Italy. He prescribed a liquid diet, but of milk there was none, and meat for broth could not be found. Roused by the danger to me, my wife got up from her sick bed and saw to my needs. But it was no use. La Lena, terrified by the epidemic, all but refused to enter the bedroom. Only Carlo, the military chauffeur, who put his trust in brandy, continued to serve us faithfully.

I grew steadily worse. The caffein the doctor prescribed—there was no specific against pneumonia in those days—would not let me sleep, but despite the constant pain in my chest, I could hardly be said to be awake. A nurse came, I know, an American Red Cross worker, whom someone had spared for a few hours. She complained I was nervous and hard to care for, yet all through the night, in conformity with the doctor's orders, she continued to excite me with more caffein. And being new to the war, she could not understand my depression.

What did that woman know of the agonizing vacuum of European life in that year 1918? Could she not realize that not I alone was dying, one among many, dying in an old palace in a headquarters town, but that she herself, so healthy and strong, that all men, were slowly sinking into awful nothingness?

With each new shot of caffein my brain grew more wildly active. In the morning the nurse went away and I was left, half lucid, moodily resentful of the reproaches she had not uttered. And as soon as I was alone with my wife, herself too sick to see to everything, great resolutions began to form in me.

Was I afraid to die? Or only afraid of suffering, of the pain in my chest, of the fiery applications? My death was certain. But let it come all at once, not slowly, with padded lungs and a sleepless racing heart! At this point something occurred to decide me. Suddenly a great coughing shook me, causing unspeakable pain. Out of my lips shot a clot of greenish mucus. I stared at it there on the pillow. God, anything was better than slow corporeal deliquescence, anything . . . even death.

That was it: suicide was what I had been thinking of. It was so easy; you just pierced your throat beside the glottis and out on the red stream from the gaping jugular you hurried forth into oblivion. Or you blew out your brains with a revolver (but I no longer had a revolver: I had lent mine to one of Carroll's assistants). Or you drown —that was it! A mere washbasin would do, just enough water to cover nose and mouth, a little will-power.

Giddy but determined, I arose from the soiled pillow and tottered into the dressing-room. (How good the marble floor felt to fevered feet!)

You turned a faucet, and when the basin was full you plunged in your face and breathed the waters of release!

I tried hard. Twice I drew the liquid in through my nostrils; but then my nerve failed me; I raised my head and choking, crying with disappointment, I returned to my bed. I lacked the courage of suicide. And by my mad act, I had doubtless spoiled what little chance I might previously have had of recovering!

What humiliation! I had loaned my revolver, but there were my paper clipping scissors and I could reach my jugular. Just then Lilian came in and, like a maniac, I told her I had decided to take my life; whereupon I again got out of bed. She wrestled with me a minute and threw me back, telling me, I do not know in what words, of her two dreams and how God could not betray her . . . would save me.

Some time later men came in, big friendly Americans, who placed me on the floor of a camion and drove to U.S. Army Base Hospital 102 at Vicenza. My wife rode with me inside. And although the jolting tortured me, I did not utter a sound or complain, because I loved her. Once there, they put us to bed in separate wards.

There was a roaring in my ears that impressed me as strangely out of place in a hospital amid all those beds and the moving about of endless convalescents in bright colored cotton robes. Where did the noise come from and the crowd outside the hospital windows? Why, they were cheering me. I had been given three medals for bravery!

The first night at the hospital was an endless round of delirium and nausea. Yet in the morning, when my frantic cries for food had finally been answered, I managed by great effort not to vomit the precious nourishment. How recover if I did not eat?

Fever must have been lower that day. For hours I watched the patient in the next bed. After a long time the doctor came and spoke to him. I could hear nothing—I seemed stone deaf—but he smiled. Then a nurse brought a uniform. Before my eyes the man dressed and walked out of the hospital! It seemed some did get well. But probably the water in my lungs would finish me in spite of a hundred dreams. . . .

And it was night again. I could no longer remember how long I had been in the hospital. I had less pain and was conscious of a man, a doctor no doubt, a new doctor, who was listening to my breathing and tapping my chest. When he finished, he whispered to the nurse and went away. But before he left, his eyes rested a moment on mine in a look of tenderness. With the insight of the very weak, I knew, as certainly as though he had pronounced sentence, that he had given up hope of my recovery.

My fight had been useless. My wife would have done better to let me cut my throat, back there in Padua. The end would doubtless come that night or the following morning—the fatal fifth day. Seen close at hand death was no longer quite so terrible. If they would only give me more morphine so that I might sleep.

Now they were coming to prepare me for death. The lights shone in the ward in splendid brightness. First a purple robe—that was right. One might as well do this thing in style. But what did these nuns want and this priest in scarlet? No, I would not confess, I had nothing to confess! My belief had been good enough in life, it would do me in death. Ah, these Catholics, how persistent they were! Surely a man was entitled to die in peace!

"No, no, go away and let me die!" I begged my would-be confessor.

I heard the priest say that once dead I would be sorry; he held the keys of heaven! Well, we should see.

Then I was lying in the dark and the open air. Solemn in my mortuary purple, I lay on a cot amid thick undergrowth and waited for the end. Years passed and still it was dark. Then a lantern gleamed and a nun appeared. How persistent, these Catholics!

But she said nothing of confession, only gave me an injection of something, not the morphine I desired, and went away. More years; more injections; church bells; a return of pain. In utter weariness I looked forward to death. . . .

What happened then I cannot explain. Only I had a vision far more impressive than ordinary experience. Up in the sky, just where he appears in Renaissance paintings, I saw something I recognized as God. No words can tell what he looked like; imagination and memory fail me. But below him, like the Virgin in a Crucifixion, kneeling in profile against a background of dark pine trees, was my wife. For an age she had not entered my mind. Hers was now another world, one I had left and to which there could be no return. Yet there she was with God, pleading for me. I did not try to understand, only waited, knowing that the courts of heaven were deciding my fate. A long time passed; gradually it began to grow light. Then God spoke:

"Because of her love you shall not die!"

Dawn drove the vision from the sky, leaving only a blurred image of miracle. I seemed to be lying in a narrow boat, moored to the bank of a stream. About me the grey light brightened little by little. Surely I must be better: since they had put me out to die, they ought to bring me back indoors, now that I was going to get well. The doctor must realize that God himself had said that I should live. . . . And I was very thirsty.

But no. It was growing dark again; hospital and all had disappeared.

God had deceived me or I had dreamed it all. Death was upon me. My body shook with cold. My limbs were icy, my feet had lost consciousness. Death, if necessary, but not by freezing! What were the doctors and nurses thinking of to leave me so?

I protested.

A nurse appeared. This was my last chance. If I could convince her of the necessity of warming me, I might live. Otherwise the morning would find me stark. The effort was agony:

"Nurse, the most elementary science . . . any science . . . any mother knows."

There! Now she would understand and act.

"What do you want?" queried the nurse.

She had not understood. Yet it was so simple—and terrible. I must convince the woman.

"Any mother knows that . . . although in the early stages . . . the early stages . . . pneumonia . . . cold . . . early stages . . . cold may be beneficial . . . may help . . . at the point where I am now . . . like this—"

She laid a cool hand on my forehead. My heart was beating faster than it had ever beat before, faster than I could count.

"There, there," she said, "that'll be all right."

"No, no!" I protested in my loudest whisper. "Not all right. Any mother . . . mother . . . knows, instinctively for her child . . . for her children . . . he must have heat."

The nurse smiled pityingly and went away.

The chill of death grew sharper. My flesh no longer trembled, it ached, then slowly became less sensible. Finally night came, and I was lying at the entrance of a large building, tucked into a niche by the vestibule. All had become delightfully clear. Dr. Slaughter, as I called the physician, had married my nurse. The night before, hoping to make me a little more comfortable, he had brought me to his palace on the Grand Canal in Venice. I looked out on a vast hall of solid marble with windows on two sides.

It was a Sunday afternoon and the Slaughter family was holding a reception. Many people came in. The palace turned out to be neither very old nor very beautiful, but in compensation it contained a unique treasure, a rare glass organ of the *Sette Cento*, the work of an anonymous master. In the old days this instrument had been played by hydraulic pressure, but the mechanism had long been broken. Dr.

Slaughter had caused it to be pumped by electricity. A single performance cost fifteen hundred *lire*. A famous organist, descendant of a long line of musicians, sat at the keys this afternoon. Gravely, to the assembled guests, I expressed my satisfaction at being present at so rare an entertainment for once before I died. They did not seem to hear me.

Yet more and more people came in, chiefly by the gondola entrance. Many were Italians who chattered and looked at me closely. I spoke to them in their own tongue, but they did not reply. I judged them impolite, but understood that the living quite properly have no time for the dead. I belonged to the past.

The American consul came, a great friend. Gladly I took this opportunity of telling him farewell.

Then the voice of the glass organ rolled forth and I could think of nothing but the vast wave of sound. From this time on I noticed an added complication in a world of ever growing strangeness. My thoughts sounded as though spoken by another.

This double personality offered certain advantages. Although I was aware as from the outside of myself lying in bed, a dying man, that was only my body. The real *I* floated on melody, fuller, completer, than any ever heard before. The tune seemed familiar, but I had never heard anything so satisfying, so majestic! What a genius, the maker of such an instrument, what a master the organist, the last of his line! Toward the end, the excessive repetition began to pall, though each time I was swept away by the sheer power.

Again night was falling. In fitting silence the guests were leaving. Last of all, through the glass doors I watched my friend the consul stepping into his gondola, the last link with the life I was leaving.

Everything was going at terrific speed. In company with Mrs. Slaughter, I wandered through enormous empty rooms, looking for I could not remember what. At one moment from a lofty internal window, we looked down into a hall like a church, but bare and dilapidated. On a level with our eyes and near the ceiling of the empty room, a railroad ran, suspended on steel beams and cables. Trains followed one another in rapid succession, roaring and shrieking. At one moment we got aboard and whirled through total darkness. Then we were passing across England from coast to coast. Now the railroad ran through the study of an old friend in America. At one moment it ran out on a great dock where a British warship was lying. A group of officers were gathered on deck, drinking. They called to me joyfully to help celebrate the victory that marked the end of the war. (This was on October 25, 1918, almost three weeks before the Armistice of November 11.) But when I put foot to the ship's deck I found it to be shaking violently. Seasick and unhappy, I cried aloud for Mrs. Slaughter. She appeared and we climbed into her touring car and started across Italy. She drove, though a chauffeur in khaki appeared from time to time. Behind them

I rode alone. At times she turned and gave me advice intended, I thought, to aid in dying.

Dying I was, and by degrees, but what a strange process! It was like painless but progressive mutilation. I had already thrown most of my body through the car window. What was left seemed insignificantly small, while nurse and chauffeur loomed gigantic. It only remained for me to hurl the last bit over a convenient cliff and all would be over. I fully intended to carry out the plan (some last effort on my part seemed necessary), but before an opportunity presented itself the car abruptly reached Milan, turned quickly behind the railroad shed, and plunged down a coal chute. Everything was again confusion. When this cleared, we were returning to Venice across the Lombard plain. It was summer. All the little birds were singing. Hour after hour the engine whirred. Then the car stopped before a farmhouse. Mrs. Slaughter vanished. Soon I lay under a roof in an outhouse. After a long time another nurse appeared.

"When are we returning to Venice?"

"Very soon. Don't worry."

"Where have we stopped?"

"In Vicenza."

It was the same hospital.

Delirium gave way to a new kind of reality. One lung had ceased to function, the other rose and fell almost insensibly. I could not raise my hand for weakness. Perceptions of the outside world were hopelessly confused, my own speech was inaudible. But my mind experienced an unexpected yet voluptuous lucidity.

My entire past life paraded slowly before me and I scrutinized the threads. Many things displeased me in what I contemplated. A pity that I had never written the books I had planned. But it was too late for remorse. My wife, my father, my brother, these would grieve. But I could no longer grieve at the thought that I was about to leave them. It was all so simple, so natural, so right. For at this critical stage I no longer believed, I felt sure that life is unending, not only life in general but, in some strange sense, individual life. Why then be perplexed or worried. A soul was about to pass from a dying body.

It would be necessary to keep one's wits about one. In passing, one lost consciousness, said the theosophists, who claimed to know. I should try to keep mine. Once dead, I should try by all available means to communicate once with my wife, in order to reassure her. Perhaps my mother would be on the other side to meet me.

A nurse bent over me and I opened my lips in a last question:

"How long is the actual death agony?"

Perhaps she was inexperienced or perhaps taken aback by my directness, for she answered my question frankly, with sober compassion.

"Not long. Perhaps five minutes."

Well, I could stand so short a period of suffering.

Only it was not short. Lines from a poem by my brother, lines whose profundity I had not hitherto realized, came into my mind:

Let us become acquainted not too slowly,
Not in the gradual way of ebb and pain,
O hospitable death, but swift and fain,
Heart unto heart, and each accepting wholly!

For me the ebb was gradual, but there was no longer any pain. The final sensation was of being balanced somewhere between my body in the hospital bed and a point in the air a few feet above it. Breathing was difficult. Difficult or impossible. I began to smother. In spite of desperate efforts, I lost consciousness.

When I awoke, the living forces had won their fight with the microorganisms. For a few days I found it difficult to believe in my recovery. Yet each morning I gave thanks to God who had spared me. It was so good to be alive and with Lilian. Each night I seemed in sleep to come in contact with a source of health and peace. One morning I awoke with verses on my lips—incoherent, but how vividly felt. Outside the grimy hospital window a tree was still green.

Another source of thankfulness I shared with the world. The Italians, I learned from the nurse whom I had called Mrs. Slaughter and whose devotion probably saved me, had routed a retreating Austrian army at Vittorio Veneto. And shortly thereafter she announced the signing of the Armistice. The war was over.

PART THREE

Italia

Docet

Circumcize therefore the foreskin of your heart, and be no more stiff-necked.
DEUTERONOMY 10–16

11

Essence of Politics

The real is the only rational.

HEGEL

IT WAS MAY, 1919, before I resumed work in a world nominally at peace.

Shortly after I learned of the Armistice, my fever returned. The doctors diagnosed empyema, and operated. Only at the end of January could we return to Rome. Three more months, including one at Taormina, in full sight of snow-draped Mount Etna, restored my strength, in spite of a persistent fever, to cure which my local doctor insisted that I sleep on our terrace.

The decisive turn for the better came one morning in May. When I awoke, Monte Mario and the Janiculum still slept in a featherbed of mist. But day was lifting behind the Sabine mountains, and from beneath the ruddy tiles of the roofscape came the amorous purr of nesting swallows. The rising sun evaporated the last uncertainty concerning my health.

The world to which I returned was, however, a far cry from that of which we had dreamed during the war. Since the Armistice, a great many things had happened. President Wilson had come to Europe and been received like the Redeemer, and nowhere more than in Rome. But at Paris just about everything had gone wrong.

As described to me by Paul, who came to Rome on a brief visit, the Peace Conference was a catastrophe. He and I had felt sure that fifty-one months of human slaughter *must* lead to a *Novus Ordo Seclorum.* Instead, the victorious European powers were resuming the international rat race where they had left off in 1914. Had the slaughter of millions meant nothing? Where had the so-called statesmen been all

119

this time? Had they never read Barbusse's *Le Feu*, Duhamel's *Vie des Martyrs*, Arcos' deeply moving *Sang des Autres*, my brother's war poems, or John McCrae's warning:

> *If ye break faith with us who die*
> *We shall not sleep, though poppies bloom*
> *In Flanders Fields?*

Yet here was Britain already playing off enemy Germany against ally France, France seeking to annex the German Saar, and Italy demanding the Germans of South Tyrol, the Slavs of Istria and Dalmatia, and "Italian" Fiume (which had not been included in Italy's original war price). Months before, in the hospital at Vicenza, a tough Italian major whom I had met on the Piave, Rodolfo Graziani, had visited me to protest against any concessions to the Yugoslavs. (As General Graziani, he later became Mussolini's hatchet man in Ethiopia and Tripolitania.)

The only hope of a decent and durable peace, Paul believed, lay in an American–French–British alliance to keep the Germans quiet and a League of Nations to substitute collective security everywhere for national violence. But already the U.S. Senate was muttering against our participation in either.

Finding me well enough to resume working, my brother asked me bluntly which I preferred to do—revert to literature or continue with the *Daily News*?

As late as February, 1918, I had written Mother of my ambition to return to America to write. Yet to an admirer of Irving Babbitt and of Huneker, the prospect of dealing critically with many of the "new writers" was unattractive. I might, of course, wait until the novelty craze wore off, as I imagined it shortly would.

But would the *News* accept me as a *foreign* correspondent? I had no taste for reporting in Chicago.

Paul reminded me that, after almost five years of uninterrupted service abroad, I was in line for paid home-leave, and advised me to resume filing from Rome until I could talk it over with the editors.

Accordingly, I began describing Italy's hatred of the same President Wilson whom, six months before, it had deified. To show his feelings, my impetuous dentist, Vincenzo Guerrini, in my presence snatched the framed photograph of the President from its place on his political altar, and stamped it to pieces.

In July Lilian and I sailed for New York on an Italian liner, the *Pesaro*. From Naples to New York, by way of Genoa, Marseilles, where it took on over a thousand doughboys, and Gibraltar, where, after a week, these doughboys coaled the ship while striking Spanish dockers sat around in dirty worksuits on the passengers' steamer chairs and looked on, the *Pesaro* took twenty-three days! Aside from the impatience and boredom, the trip was not unpleasant. The weather was perfect. Assisted by an Italian poet businessman, Delfino Cinelli, we each day typed and posted up a "newspaper," *The Daily Wail,* full of nonsense and gripes that alarmed the unhappy ship's officers.

In Chicago, I underwent a second operation. Once more I nearly died. Yet three weeks later, I was playing one-handed golf, and finally, after several hearty talks with the *News* people, returned to Rome at the end of October as an accredited Bureau Chief.

This resolved my personal dilemma, but left me chastened in several ways. Two operations had left my chest wall permanently weakened. Certain sports I might successfully resume—walking, climbing, swimming, tennis. For golf, canoeing, rowing, wrestling, boxing, gymnastics, I was forever handicapped.

Since from birth I had suffered from what my wife calls a "morbid craving for perfection," deploring, like the poet Yeats, "all things uncomely and broken," I faced the future with some misgiving.

There was, however, a job to be done. In postwar America. Senator Lodge and his fellow isolationists seemed to be trying to resign from the human race at the moment their active membership was most needed. Since obviously the world needed to be changed, a good place to start was Europe, and journalism an appropriate profession.

Yet neither my studies—small history, no solid economics, no political science—nor my war-time experience had given me sufficient understanding either of international, or of Italy's domestic, politics.

Fortunately one of the most remarkable political thinkers of our time, the Italian judge, Gaetano Meale, who, since his retirement from the Milan bench, had chosen to go by the name of Umano, jumped into the breach.

Umano was devoting his life to urging mankind cure its two "political sores," *despotism* and *international anarchy.* Ten years earlier, he had submitted to the (second) Hague Conference on the Pacific Settlement of International Disputes a pamphlet, *Attempt at an International Constitution (Essai de Constitution Internationale).* In this he demonstrated that war is the inevitable outcome of a multi-sovereign state system.

The argument, which perhaps owed something to both Machiavelli and Hobbes, and has since become commonplace, made no impression upon the learned jurists in the Netherlands. They were more interested in regulating the laying of automatic submarine contact mines. And in consequence, Europe in 1914 had slipped into a war that Umano had predicted.

Also, about 1907, my friend Hendrik Andersen, after studying sculpture at the Ecole des Beaux Arts in Paris, had set his heart on inducing the nations of the world to create a world center of communication, to be adorned by his own monumental statues.

Aided by Olivia, née Cushing, the widow of his dead painter brother Andreas, Hendrik enlisted the services of two highly competent French architects, the Hébrard brothers, and in 1914, shortly before the outbreak of hostilities, submitted a beautifully illustrated volume, *A World Center of Communications*, to a number of European politicians, who applauded and did nothing.

Undaunted by this, Hendrik in 1918 published and circulated a second volume, *Creation of a World Centre of Communication*, of which Umano furnished the political part, Jeremiah Jenks, of New York University, an economic argument, and the Hébrards the architectural plans. The immediate targets were the delegates at the Paris Peace Conference.

In those early months of 1919, Pope Benedict, whose bust Hendrik was modeling, had become enthusiastic about such a World Center (where but in immortal Rome?). But as America cooled to Wilson's League, so did His Holiness.

When, after resuming work for the *News*, I politely asked the Papal Secretary of State for permission to quote some remarks on world government which Benedict had made to Hendrik, Cardinal Gaspari refused, informing me that *not only had the Pope said no such things, but he was unacquainted with any Signore Andersen!* Since Hendrik was seeing His Holiness several times a week, it was puzzling that the Papal Secretary of State should be unaware of the fact.

I saw more and more of Umano. As I absorbed his basic theses, I began to understand not only why the war-time victors were behaving so ineptly, but *why they could hardly do differently*. Umano believed that the basis of any stable order is dominion under law exercised for good or ill by the strongest group. Since, in the absence of effective international law, a people depends for survival upon its own physical, mental, and economic resources, it cannot avoid war. Sometimes, exasperated by my reluctance to accept the primacy of power, my mentor would complain, "But Edgar, at the bottom you are still just a literary man."

Yet when, in 1922, he published his *Positiva Scienza di Governo*, his work was ignored. Umano, unhappily, was not only a political analyst of unequaled perception, but an intellectual eccentric who had original theories about almost everything, some of them farfetched. Instead of limiting his masterpiece strictly to his main theses, he had written a 1,200 page *omnium gatherum*.

It included his views on biological evolution, on the survival of the fittest, on man's sex life, and on religion. He summarized the history of mankind in ten bulky "meanders" (in order to demonstrate a recurring pattern), added a long and vituperative *Speech to Their Last Majesties*, and concluded this bulging volume with a series of illustrations that looked like microscopic slides of microbes. His, he proclaimed, was the *only positive science of government*, all previous theories being "quackeries and assininities."

Wiser political scientists would have dug the gold and left the dross. After all, Machiavelli, whose *Prince* I had just read, became a political authority in spite of his offensive insistence on transforming his accurate descriptions of amoral political practices into an illogical amoral imperative. But not even my admired friend, Charles E. Merriam, had the patience to extract the wisdom from Umano's irrelevancies.

That I did just this was due to my good fortune in hearing Umano's doctrine directly from him and thereafter confirming it by direct observation of events. In the process I became convinced that Umano and Hendrik Christian Andersen would be recognized as ancestors of whatever genuine international authority humanity eventually accepts.

Meanwhile, the Paris Peace Conference had adopted a pale substitute for such an authority, the League of Nations, an "American infant," left, according to Giuseppe Borgese, "unused on the threshold of a foundling hospital in Geneva." Still, it offered a frail hope to a world which, wherever else one looked, presented little but disorder, bickering, and violence.

As early as June, 1919, the Italian historian, Guglielmo Ferrero, warned that division among the war victors was playing into the hands of Germany and Russia. What had happened to the Fourteen Points?

France, supported by Britain, prevented Czechoslovakia from divesting itself of that German Sudenten rim which later served Hitler as a pretext for dismembering Czechoslovakia.

France and Britain, after slicing up Turkey's Arab empire for their own benefit, pushed the only too willing Greeks into annexing Turkey's coast.

Yet London and Paris were dead set against giving Italy a colonial mandate like those they planned to take for themselves. Moreover, since Britain showed no sign of relinquishing Cyprus, what valid argument was there for asking Italy to abandon the Dodecanese Islands? And if Yugoslavia and Greece were to be allowed, against all decency, to partition Albania, why not let Italy keep Valona?

President Wilson, with inexplicable inconsistency, accepted Italy's claim to the Germany of South Tyrol and the Slavs of Istria, while opposing its itch for the indubitably Italian enclave of Fiume.

Major Rejna of the Italian Grenadiers reacted by occupying Fiume and turning that normally humdrum seaport over to Lieutenant-Colonel Gabriele D'Annunzio.

D'Annunzio's daily fare of rhetoric and sex ("the name of all the Fiume women is Passion," he proclaimed) attracted nationalists, adventurers, and pleasure-seekers. During the sixteen months of his *Italian Regency of the Carnaro*, he wrote numerous diplomatic notes to other "sovereign states," flirted with the Hungarian communists, received Lenin's baptism as a "genuine revolutionary," introduced arson and castor oil as political weapons, and provided Mussolini with a first draft for what was to become the corporative state.

During the war at Venice I had become acquainted with the self-styled bard whose nocturnal visit to Trieste pier, similar to my own with Rizzo, had first gained him fame as a hero, and found his arrogance insufferable. Personal courage and skill with words he certainly possessed. But to me his patriotism was just an aspect of the worship of that ego which he identified with the Superman. From my first visit to Fiume I brought back only a faint chuckle and a lingering distaste mixed with alarm. For, just as D'Annunzio had led a reluctant Italy into war, so by his words and conduct at Fiume, he was focusing the collective fanaticism that was to bloom as *fascismo*. Serious thinkers like Leonida Bissolati the Deputy and Gaetano Salvemini the historian shared my view of the bard (and said so). Yet *Marchesina* Ilda almost swooned with expectancy each time D'Annunzio threatened to "march on Rome." Others, like dentist Guerrini, made me, as an American, personally responsible for the Fiume farce.

Britain, meanwhile, was up to its old trick of restoring the European balance and normal trade, regardless of the effect on German reparations payments. The argument against reparations was persuasively presented by a young British economist who had attended the peace conference, John Maynard Keynes. His book, *The Economic Consequences of the Peace*, convinced many that no capitalist country could make a heavy unilateral transfer of wealth.

Far from disappearing, the disagreements among the victors seemed to grow worse at each successive conference. The early meetings, held outside Italy, concerned me only indirectly. But in early 1920, the Supreme Allied Council (from which the United States had withdrawn) met in San Remo on the Italian Riviera, a town of sunshine, sea, and flowers.

Where was a more delightful place in which to launch a career as international reporter? I found the assembled leaders more interesting than the issues. Lloyd George, handsome, vain, sensitive, and superficial, dominated the conference. What he lacked in substance he made up in manipulative skill. Never again did I meet a politician so gifted in handling delegates and press alike. His colleague, Lord Curzon, could, like Henry Van Dyke, "strut sitting down."

Walrus-mustached Alexandre Millerand, a former socialist, was unprepossessing in appearance. But after observing the French Premier for a week, I diagnosed unusual will-power under that dull exterior and was not surprised when this "mediocre" statesman subsequently saved Europe by sending General Weygand and a French military mission to help the Poles defeat the Bolsheviks at Warsaw.

Substantially, the conference was disappointing. Once the delegates had brushed off an absurd request by Germany to double its military forces and formulated an unrealistic peace treaty with Turkey, they settled down to "dividing the war swag," meaning Rumanian and Mesopotamian oil and colonies disguised as "mandates."

The United States both was, and was not, represented at the conference by the new Ambassador to Rome, Robert Underwood Johnson, a poet whom the stricken Wilson had appointed to succeed the ailing Thomas Nelson Page.

Johnson turned up unexpectedly at San Remo and immediately had long talks with the chief delegates. Yet in a first interview in the hotel garden, he nervously informed me that he was on the Riviera by accident and did not know what, if anything, he was supposed to do.

Most of the delegates considered this a diplomatic fiction. Americans were not without interest in foreign oil. . . . But after watching the ambassador's subsequent career in Rome, I found his original story convincing. He *never* seemed to know what he was supposed to do.

Much as I enjoyed San Remo in the springtime, I was happy to return to Rome. When I complained to Umano that the San Remo conference was clearly not what millions of young men had died to bring about, he grinned sardonically: "What else did you expect from those buffoons?"

Certainly I had expected something else.

In Rome, Prime Minister Francesco Saverio Nitti, despite his sharp wit, had been unable to deal with either the internal or external Italian crisis. His successor was none other than the old political boss, Giovanni Giolitti, who in 1915 had been hooted out of power for opposing the Italian war. Unscrupulous as Giolitti was, he had political savvy and courage. For his foreign minister he chose a professional diplomat, Count Carlo Sforza.

At our first meeting, Sforza and I became friends and political allies.

Having been accredited for two war-time years to the Serbian Government-in-Exile, he believed that close Italo-Yugoslav relations were both possible and desirable. Within a few months after taking office he had negotiated with Belgrade the Treaty of Rapallo establishing a not unreasonable frontier between the two countries.

But for Fiume to become a free state as planned, D'Annunzio had to be ejected.

The bard boasted that Giolitti would take the city only over his "bleeding body." Three six-inch shells on his windowsill from the Italian dreadnought, *Andrea Doria,* changed his mind. Announcing that the Italians were "a nation of cowards for whom it was not worthwhile dying," the hero fled. Subsequently he retired to an estate at Gardone on Lake Garda. There he regularly extolled his guests and himself by firing a cannon, dreamed of dying at the North Pole as the "axis of the world," and ended his life as Prince of Monte Nevoso, writing apologies for fascism.

Foreign Minister Sforza's next achievement was granting independence to Albania. To be sure, to achieve this, the Albanians had been compelled, the previous June, to drive the Italian Army out of Valona while Italian nationalists howled.

Since 1917, Albania had been part of my news territory. Now in November, 1920, Mehmet Konitza, Albania's acting Foreign Minister, asked me, as an American, free of those European entanglements from which the little country had so long suffered, to become its King!

Though flattered, I politely refused. The Albanians plumped for a republic, which lasted until President Achmet Zogu Bey Mati proclaimed himself King Zog I in 1928.

In April, 1921, anticipating a good time and a fine story, I set off for Tirana, specifically, as I wrote, to "witness the rebirth of a nation free of foreign domination for the first time since the Roman conquest of Illyria in 229 B.C."

During the Great War I had been able to visit only the more modernized Tosk section of the country. Now I was fascinated by the tall Gheg mountaineers of the north, who had for centuries preserved their arms, their dress, and their customs against all comers. And what customs—Scotland at the time of Macbeth, with its clans continually "in blood" with each other! The Ghegs faithfully observed what they called the Law of Lek, allegedly given them by a former (mythical) hero called Lek Dukadjyn.

Half way to Scutari, by sheer accident I met and had a picnic lunch with that fellow Albanophile, Rose Wilder Lane, one of the few Americans who at that time really understood the country. I greatly admired her courage and enterprise.

Riding from Tirana toward the eastern mountains to investigate one of the incessant revolts, an English official and I were stopped by the chief of police, who asked if we were properly armed for the excursion.

My friend explained that we saw no profit in being armed in a country where everyone else carried a weapon, and was accustomed to shoot first.

"Nonsense," replied the chief, pressing his own huge Mauser automatic into my friend's hand. "Take this, and if anyone offends you, shoot him."

"And then be killed by his avenging relatives?"

"Maybe, but always remember that in this country, no matter whom you kill, you are sure to have done someone a favor."

Helping such people maintain their independence appealed to me. And shortly after my return to Italy I was able to render them a service. Though the Italians had withdrawn their troops, they still insisted that the Albanian Republic, as a "successor government," honor the concessions which Italy, like other countries, had squeezed from decadent prewar Turkey. In Italy's case these would have deprived infant Albania of a considerable portion of its scant revenues.

Summoned to Rome to discuss the claims, the inexperienced members of the Albanian delegation asked me for help. In consequence I spent a whole day at the American Embassy reading in a big digest of international law everything I could find on foreign concessions.

Not unexpectedly I learned that each country had consistently taken the side of the argument that fitted its particular interests. So I carefully copied out some twenty significant cases when either Washington or London had refused to be bound by the economic decisions of a previous government, translated them into Italian, and turned them over to my Albanian friends.

Imagine the confusion of the slick Italian lawyers when these barely literate primitives overwhelmed them with arguments from the most respected authorities! A few days later Italy dropped its claims. "Now you understand the absurdity of what 'they' call international law," Umano guffawed, when I told him the story.

In consequence, when, in March, 1922, I returned to Albania, this time with Lilian, the Albs entertained us in princely fashion, and arranged for us to travel by car and horseback wherever we wished, accompanied by an armed gendarme, for, as usual, parts of the country were in revolt.

Yet my most vivid memory is not of the heavily armed, white-fezzed, white-trousered, handsome tribesmen of Shoshi or Shala, but of an evening in the smallest of Tirana's three mosques. There for hours I watched a Ramadan dance by about a hundred Howling Dervishes (Rifais) led by a sheik wearing a hodja's green turban. I had been taken through the crowd of faithful who blocked the entrance by a young American woman, a member of the Red Cross mission that, since World War I, had aided Albania in so many ways. To get in, she simply said, in proper Albanian, to the soldier guarding the door: "Tell your pals that important personages from Cross the Red American have come to honor the dance by their presence." So in the company of another "unbeliever," *a woman* at that, I watched the whirls and heard the howls of people who, seeking personal contact with God by what we would call hypnotic means, wounded and burnt themselves with no apparent pain. A few skewered their cheeks without bleeding. One ardent Dervish ran head-on against the brick wall of the mosque, and arose, apparently unharmed. At one moment I almost succumbed to the temptation to jump down, spin, howl, and repeat the sacred word, *Ullah.* By the time we left I knew, if I had ever doubted, that Western science had not and perhaps never would plumb the human possibilities. There would always be miracles.

Back in Europe, I followed Albanian affairs by correspondence with the U.S. diplomatic representative in Tirana, Grant Smith. This trained diplomat talked like a finicky old maid, but made it his business to know exhaustively each country to which he was assigned.

Yet I had little time for the Albs. By 1922 the Germans were brazenly ignoring parts of the peace treaty.

The big powers, in the absence of the United States, still sulking behind its oceans like Achilles in his tent, summoned the Genoa Conference to decide what to do about the Fatherland. Almost forty states attended including a gleeful U.S.S.R. My task was to backstop my brother, the C.D.N.'s chief correspondent. So Paul left the planning to me. Before leaving for Albania, I visited Genoa, a rich and bustling seaport with a superb history, full of magnificent buildings, whose inhabitants spoke among themselves a language which might have been Swahili for all it meant to me, and to many Italians. I secured comfortable quarters for my brother, my wife, and myself, a necessary precaution since hundreds of newsmen were due to attend, including a famous Dutch correspondent called Marc Van Blankenstein and a youthful American named Ernest Hemingway.

At the first session in famous San Giorgio's Palace, the former seat of Europe's first bank, the conference nearly broke up when Russia's Chicherin proposed general disarmament, which would have meant the end of the *cordon sanitaire*. The Soviets no longer needed large forces for they had finished recapturing their former subject countries, the Ukraine, Armenia, Azerbaijan, and Georgia, which had sought to use the Russian revolution to escape from the Bear's clutch. Colonialism was "criminal" only when capitalistic.

France's fiery Barthou replied that if the Soviets deviated by a hair from the original agenda, France would call off the conference. Lloyd George temporarily patched up the quarrel.

It was good theater, and from my seat on the floor between the delegations of Denmark and Estonia (each of which assumed I belonged to the other) I enjoyed it thoroughly. But it boded ill for success of the conference.

Russia was feeling its oats. Leonid Krassin, Soviet delegate, a bourgeois by birth and a former engineer, invited me to lunch and explained that the Soviet Union was prepared to make to capitalism those concessions which would make socialism work—the coming NEP.

On the seventh day, the news that the Russians and Germans had signed the Rapallo Treaty canceling all further financial claims on each other and including certain secret arms agreements whose details became known only later, practically blew up the meeting.

The French went around saying "we told you so." And although for almost five weeks more the British made determined efforts to get the thing off the ground, we newsmen knew it was a dead duck.

Baron Riddell of Walton Heath, owner of the sensational crime-sex weekly, *News of the World*, explained to me Lloyd George's difficulties in dealing with the elusive Russians:

"Several times in the evening we thought we had an agreement with Litvinov, for he is a Jew of the Jews and smells money. But instead of going to bed like a Christian, Litvinov each time reported to Chicherin, who is, if I may say so, anything but normal. And by six o'clock in the morning, the deal was off."

I returned to Rome with more confidence in my ability to report international politics. And with a deepened conviction that Umano was right—peace between sovereign states could never be more than a truce.

It was in this frame of mind that, in September, 1922, I reached Geneva, Switzerland, to cover the Third Assembly of the League of Nations.

The League was an organization of jealously sovereign states, anything but the international authority that could, at·least in theory, compel the members to observe law and eschew violence.

At this Assembly, the main interest lay in disarmament. Yet even as eloquently expounded by Britain's Lord Robert Cecil while he sat on the back of his neck and scratched his long thin legs, I found this impractical. American pioneers had disarmed only after, not before, the appearance of a U.S. marshal or a sheriff able to protect them against bad men, horse thieves, and marauding Indians.

Nonetheless, I succumbed emotionally to the so-called Spirit of Geneva, along with other visitors. Several U.S. Senators who had voted against American membership came to scoff and remained to approve the League.

Secretary of State Hughes, who had at first simply ignored communications from Geneva, was now acknowledging them and acting "like a non-resident associate," as I duly reported. League officials like Secretary General Sir Eric Drummond, Jean Monnet, Arthur Salter, Henry Bonnet, Ludwik Rajchman, were passionately dedicated to their great undertaking, and determined to make the organization work, if necessary without American participation. So too were Pierre Comert, Adrien Pelt, and Arthur Sweetser (at this time the only American employee), three members of the efficient Information Section.

On the concluding day, I ventured a verdict:

"In the view of Americans here, an international body which administers the Saar Valley and Danzig successfully, which has compelled the arbitration of the Aaland Islands and Syrian disputes, which has solved the Upper Silesian question and which is now asked to assume the guardianship of the freedom of the Dardanelles and the Bosporus and of the Christian minorities in Turkey and perhaps even the government of Thrace is no longer a body which the American Government, even from a political point of view, can afford to ignore."

Whereupon, at Chicago's behest, I boarded the famous Orient Express train for Athens. My assignment was to report on the Turkish deportation from Anatolia of its Greek inhabitants. The Turkish Government had signed the Treaty of Sèvres, transferring Thrace and the zone around Smyrna to Greece. But some Turks refused to comply. The governments of Italy and France, enraged by the victory of the pro-German king at the Greek election, withdrew their troops from Turkey.

Yet King Constantine rashly attempted to seize even more of Anatolia.

Before I reached Athens, Kemal Pasha routed the advancing Greek armies. Turkish soldiers advanced to the coast, plundering and murdering Greeks, eliminating some three thousand years of Greek culture from Asia Minor. Close to a million Greek refugees had somehow to be evacuated and resettled.

The beaten Greek commander, Nikolaos Plastiras, set up a Revolutionary Committee, sent King Constantine into a second period of exile, and executed several members of the Cabinet. Unable to cope alone with its refugee problem, poor Greece sent out a cry for help, directed chiefly to America.

Though I interviewed a member of the revolutionary committee, a Navy Captain called Alex Hadjikyriakos, I never understood why the officers who had welcomed Venizelos' first offensive against Turkey, should have condemned King Constantine's subsequent offensive. I was convinced that the Turks under Kemal would have opposed a "little Greece" around Smyrna as fiercely and as successfully as they did the enlarged zone sought by the King.

My basic assignment was awakening sympathy for the innocent Greek refugees. I found it inhuman that the Greek government refused to house homeless people in the innumerable churches, where thousands might have found shelter. "At Piraeus," I cabled, "they sit around quietly and passively on the docks or in churchyards, or lie on the cheap, gaily colored Oriental rugs which nearly all have brought with them. Few have money or jewelry; the Turks saw to that. Few complain. The East is habitually silent."

The Revolutionary Committee liked my dispatches so much that an official offered to allow me to charge them against my newspaper and pocket the price. I answered that I never accepted *small* bribes. . . . Several other Americans were helping the refugees and I felt proud of them. Wealthy Greeks were helping too, but some went about it in a curious way. At the hotel in Athens, the wife of a rich shipowner asked me as a "practical American" just what she and her lady friends could do. "Write out the biggest check you think you can afford and turn it over to the relief organization," I promptly answered. Her discomfiture was comical. "But we wanted to knit," she protested.

On the first free evening I walked by moonlight to the Parthenon and found it open. Since then I have seen the art treasures of many lands, but never again became so drunk on architectural beauty as in those three hours alone in the moonlit ruins.

Modern Greece was part Western, part Levantine. Its inhabitants suffered from an overdeveloped individualism and itching palms. Yet many followed Western culture with avid understanding.

Salonika, where I had my interview with Hadjikyriakos, and talked theology for hours with the chief Rabbi (who was delighted to hear that American professors taught Sephardic Hebrew like his, rather than the East European variety), illustrated why continental Europeans called any helter-skelter salad of fruits or vegetables a *Macedoine*. Here people of rival nationalities were inextricably mixed and forever squabbling. The Slav majority, who claimed to be the "real" Macedonians, were undoubtedly closer to the Bulgars than to the other neighboring peoples. Yet it was obvious that the victorious allies had no intention of allowing them to opt for a country that had fought on the side of the Central Empires.

In Belgrade I interviewed Foreign Minister Nintchitch, who was a picture of worry—worry about the Turks' return to Europe, about the Bulgars' alleged flirtation with Moscow, and, above all, about the unreadiness of the Croats and Slovenes to accept domination by their Serbian Redeemers.

Belgrade struck me as an unfinished amalgam of Germany and the American frontier, with a touch of old Turkey. The Americans there blamed Washington for Turkish militancy. One of them confided that "we could have prevented the insane Greek adventure into Asia Minor or ended that war by a mere word. Failing this, we could have thwarted the Franco-Italian plan for the Turks' return to Constantinople and prevented the expulsion of nine hundred thousand Greeks." Thanks to isolationism, we had done nothing of the sort.

From Belgrade I took the Orient Express to Sofia. The difference between Serbs and Bulgars astonished me. Sofia struck me as almost Methodist in feeling, although most of the inhabitants attended the Greek Orthodox church.

At the Genoa Conference, I had become acquainted with Prime Minister Stamboliski's secretary, a beautiful young professional diplomat called Nadezhda Stancioff. Thanks to her, my requests for interviews were promptly granted. Although of a leading family, Miss Stancioff had rallied to Stamboliski's Agrarians, who, having deposed the German King Ferdinand who had led the people to defeat, undertook sweeping economic reforms, dreamed of creating a so-called "Green Internationale" of farmers, and accepted Communist aid for the purpose. Nintchitch had insisted that Stamboliski was a communist. The proof, Nintchitch argued, lay in the fact that he had just ordered the White Russian refugees to leave Bulgaria.

Nadezhda violently denied this charge. "You will hear for yourself," she insisted. Sure enough, Stamboliski insisted not only that Bulgaria was not communist, but that it had had nothing to do with the Soviets since the Genoa Conference. He was seeking to save "Bulgarian Thrace" from Greece or Turkey by having it put under the League of Nations.

King Boris refused to discuss Balkan politics with me. Yet in the course of a long interview devoted to almost everything else, His Majesty made some memorable statements. At one point, perhaps thinking of his unhappy father, he said:

"Autocracy may be successful for a short time but sooner or later it creates forces that destroy it." Profound—yet less than twenty years later Boris made the same mistake his father had made before him, entered a world war on the side of autocracy, and paid an even higher price for his folly.

The *News* in Chicago in a special editorial compared the style of this interview to that of Walter Pater.

Returning from the royal palace, I found in my hotel a message from Paris ordering me to return at once to Rome, and, by sheer luck,

I managed to catch the Orient Express that same night. I missed the connection at Venice and continued to Milan. An Italian newspaper made clear the reason for my brusque recall—Italy was on the verge of civil war! At the office of the Milan *Secolo* my friends were in a dither, but managed to get me a berth on the night train to Rome.

The railroad station was surrounded by nervous *carabinieri,* and only persons with tickets were allowed on the platform. No wonder: it was crowded with armed *fascisti* in uniform. In the midst of them I saw Mussolini.

"Signor Mussolini, tell me what's up?"

"Don't you know? I am going to Rome to install *fascismo.*"

"Congratulations," I stammered, and boarded the train with the triumphant Benito.

12

The Triumph of Rhetoric

Thou shalt not follow a multitude to do evil.
EXODUS 23:2

REMEMBERING ITALY as I knew it between March, 1919, and November, 1923, I find it difficult to believe that such a place existed. Anarchy was rampant. Yet most citizens acted as though neither the strikes, violence, local insurrections, and killings by the Communists and Socialists nor the Fascist "counter action," "punitive expeditions," arson, beatings and murders, concerned them. On the other hand, thanks to Mario Borsa, editor of the Milan *Secolo*, to Maffio Maffii of the Rome *Tribuna*, and, a little later, to Guglielmo Emanuel, Rome correspondent of the outstanding *Corriere della Sera* of Milan, I kept abreast of the political chaos.

Italy's near-revolution and counterrevolution had little in common with the bloody French upheaval of 1789, or, for that matter, with Admiral Horthy's ruthless anticommunist repression in Hungary.

Nonetheless, to a young American, the behavior of the Italian people was as unbelievable as it was disturbing. They left all responsibility for law and order in the hands of the government, and when it failed to act, shrugged their shoulders and went about their separate businesses. Four successive Premiers proved unequal to the task of suppressing relatively small groups of fanatics "polarized" against each other.

The Socialists began it.

Along with many Catholics and old-time politicians like Giolitti, they had opposed the war. So presumably had a majority of the conscripted soldiers. In 1917 the Russians showed how a determined minority could exploit war and defeat to overturn an established regime, and create a "Workers' and Peasants' State" based on a minority dictatorship.

Italians were, I had assumed, too civilized and cynical to be easily stampeded. Now the returning soldiers, schooled in violence, reacted to years of stern discipline and casualties.

Officers and noncoms who had risen from the ranks resented returning to their former inferior incomes. Families at home could not forgive the loss of fathers, husbands, brothers, and sons in a war which, the Nationalists were now insisting, had been useless, since victorious Italy had been "robbed" of its victory by ungrateful allies. Demobilized soldiers, unable to obtain immediate jobs, were ready for anything.

Here was inflammable material to stoke an insurrection. The Labor bosses' first step was to direct the people's wrath against the authors of the war. Socialist Deputy Treves set the tone by inviting a mob to "sweep the streets of Milan clear of interventionist filth." The Socialist Congress of the autumn of 1919 called for the expropriation of capitalists, if necessary by violence.

Twice, in Rome, I witnessed gang attacks upon isolated officers, one a much-decorated major. In the North, screaming workmen set upon anyone in uniform; privates tore epaulettes from officers' shoulders, and decorations from their breasts.

At Ancona a mob burned a colonel's house to the ground. Trainmen held up trains until generals got off. Revolutionaries tore down the national flag on Armistice Day and raised the red banner in its place.

Nor were the police spared. At Milan, hoodlums killed a plainclothesman discovered at a labor rally. At Trieste, female furies danced around the body of a Royal Guard whom someone had killed.

During the previous June election, patriotic orators were compelled to be silent or cry "long live Socialism." In industrial centers like Turin, Milano, Genoa, Florence, any bourgeois, particularly if elegantly dressed, or wearing a monocle, or in a motorcar, was liable to attack. Groups of workmen sang: *"Per i signori ch'han voluto la guerra, C'è la galera, C'è la galera"* (roughly: prison for the warmakers).

Life in the country, particularly in Tuscany and the Po Valley, became an orgy of labor violence. Red Leagues, representing half a million landless farm workers, cowed landlords, burned the houses of well-to-do, terrorized scabs and dissenters, and generally did what they pleased. In Sicily priests carrying crucifixes led Catholic peasants to "expropriate" big estates.

Life in the cities was disagreeably enlivened by never-ceasing strikes of one sort or another. In Rome, in 1919, striking garbage collectors twice allowed the streets to be filled for a week with refuse which might well have started an epidemic. In December, a general strike paralyzed the entire country. Next buses and streetcars vanished. In January, 1920, I found the central post office at San Silvestro closed by striking postal, telephone, and telegraph workers. A few days later it was the turn of the railroad men. At first the unions merely demanded higher wages (already well above the prewar level) since inflation was steadily boosting living costs.

But in March, their leaders demanded the right to organize workers' committees in every plant and business house. Deputy Bombacci, a communist, boasted to me that these committees would develop into Soviets. The unions themselves would become super-Soviets to which the small plant Soviets would send delegates. During the San Remo conference, a strike at Turin paralyzed the main line between Italy and France; union bosses in a Fiat plant struck because the management insisted on their working on solar time—it reminded the workers too much of wartime conditions! June saw another wave of strikes, and in August "anarchists" at Ancona prevented the departure of a shipload of Italian soldiers to Albania.

Meanwhile, the unions had launched a second type of offensive. At the Mazzoni cotton mills near Turin, the management refused to accept a factory committee. Since some other companies had consented, the union took the case to an arbitration board, which, with the management absent, decided in favor of the workers. Still the Mazzoni brothers refused to submit. Premier Nitti then enjoined them (illegally, some insisted) to accept the board's decision. When the Mazzonis did not budge, the workers took violent possession of the mills, set up the disputed factory committee, and started to carry on business. The company surrendered. The unions were jubilant. The revolution was at hand.

But by this time nearly every employer in Italy felt compelled to do or die. When in May, the always turbulent metal workers union demanded higher wages, the owners refused. Thereupon the union boss, Bruno Buozzi by name, proclaimed a slowdown. The companies countered by a lockout.

As a result, the Milanese awoke to find that workmen in every foundry, forge, and metal workshop in town had locked themselves in the night before, and armed themselves with machine guns.

A wave of terror ran through the Italian *bourgeoisie*. Some individuals started exporting their capital; a few got ready to leave the country on short order.

Francesco Saverio Nitti, the former Premier, a financial expert from Naples, who laughed with his whole fat body, might well have done nothing. He had explained to me how, by yielding to labor demands, he was "letting the steam out of the revolution." I heard him tell a group of American correspondents, "We Italians do not make revolutions, we make speeches."

But Giovanni Giolitti was now Premier, and from him I expected action. Not for nothing were Piedmontese called the "Prussians of Italy."

Ever since 1902, Giolitti, except for the war years, had governed the country, cynically, arbitrarily, but not illiberally. Though he organized gangs with clubs to determine the outcome of elections, he slowly molded provincial Piedmontese, Tuscans, Sicilians, etc., into a nation. At seventy-eight he seemed the one politician who, by a proper mixture of force and persuasion, might save Italian democracy. His age was in his favor. Italians, I had learned, shared with Chinese a reverence for advanced years. A political leader was considered ripe at about sixty, worthy of authority (*autorevole*) around seventy. At the height of the Caporetto crisis the Parliament had replaced the discredited Salandra with the aging Boselli. A few months earlier, France had called on the seventy-six-year-old Clemenceau to save it from defeat by taking stern measures against all who opposed the war effort. The Italians expected something similar from Giolitti.

Giolitti was, unhappily, no Clemenceau. He did not lack courage. Instinctively he relied on balancing one illegal extreme against the other rather than on suppressing both. Hence he chose to let the rebellious workmen in the factories stalemate themselves.

When after three days the government had done nothing to end the illegal occupation, I went to Milan. My friends at the *Secolo* newspaper were pessimistic. Visit an occupied factory? Impossible. Dangerous. Nevertheless I took a cab to the Stiegler elevator works in the south part of town. A red flag was flying over it!

Leaving the cab some fifty yards from the closed main door, I found myself looking down the barrel of a machine gun, while a stern voice cried: "Halt! Who are you?"

It was too late to run. "Let me come a little closer and I'll tell you." And raising my arms above my head, I slowly approached.

"Stop or I fire."

"Easy, comrade. I am just an American newsman come to report what you are doing."

"A socialist newspaper?" asked the voice, somewhat mollified.

"Certainly not—a *bourgeois* newspaper. Socialists know your side of the argument already. Don't you want the American people to read your story?"

"All *bourgeois* are liars. How do we know you will tell the truth about what you see?"

"If I wanted to lie, I could have stayed in Rome. I'll show you my dispatch before I send it, if you like. Now, open the door and let me talk to somebody."

"It's against the rules but I'll ask. Mind you stay just where you are." And he disappeared.

Never taking my eyes from the muzzle of his machine gun, I inched closer to the door. After about three minutes it opened a crack. "Come in," another voice ordered. "I am in charge here and I'll give you ten minutes if you promise to write exactly what you see."

"It's a bargain," I answered, and slipped inside before he could change his mind. There I found myself in the presence of an intelligent looking foreman, who led me to what had been the director's office. "Sit down," he commanded. "Now what do you want to know?"

I stayed an hour. After twenty minutes of tranquil discussion, my host graciously showed me around the plant. "Note how everything is working just as if the managers were here. We can run the factory without them. Be sure you write that."

"I surely will."

"Then write that you think we shall succeed."

"Everything but that. I am almost sure you will fail. For although you can make electric elevators, to whom will you sell them? Do you see the owners of buildings taking them from a socialized factory? No, to succeed you must nationalize the whole economy. Are you able to do that?"

"You mean we shall have to let the managers come back and run things as though nothing had happened?" demanded the foreman in so crestfallen a voice that I almost felt sorry for him.

"Just that."

"You are wrong, but you are honest. Before you leave, have a drink." Solemnly he poured two *Americanos.* "To the revolution!"

"To Italy," I responded. He took me to the big door, we shook hands, and with a last glance over my shoulder at the machine gun, I returned to my hotel and wrote a first-hand description of what could be the beginning of the Italian revolution.

But in my heart, I felt it was not. Whatever they might do or say, people like the foreman at the Stiegler factory were not Lenins or Trotskys.

As foreseen, the steam gradually leaked out of the movement. Soon workmen slipped home to sleep and managers began moving back to their offices.

But the near-panic which labor violence provoked was not without results. In October, 1920, I heard rumors of a move to oust the "do-nothing" King and replace him by his cousin, the Duke of Aosta, an army general and outspoken nationalist.

In November, perhaps in order to strengthen his reputation abroad, Victor Emmanuel gave me a nonpolitical audience, the first he had granted to a newsman since the war. He did not conceal his nervousness about the future.

Although the Socialists issued a new appeal for the abolition of private property, it soon became evident that the Italians preferred their growing economic security to the risk of violent upheaval. During the previous summer, Lenin had made the mistake of inviting certain foreign union leaders to Moscow. Deputy Serrati, editor of the Party newspaper, *Avanti,* returned to announce publicly that Russia was a "land of hunger, pestilence, and the gallows."

In the autumn municipal elections, the Socialist Party lost conspicuously, and at the subsequent Socialist Congress, it split into three factions. A dedicated few remained faithful to Moscow. A middle group, led by the intrepid Serrati, advocated cautious advance. Conservative Socialist leaders like Turati urged extreme caution lest the Party provoke a disastrous reaction. Better wait to realize Socialism the fifty or hun-

dred years predicted by Giolitti than undergo a dictatorship of the
Right! When Lenin's official observer at the Congress, the Bulgarian
Kabakchev, solemnly excommunicated the Party in the name of the
Red Pope in Moscow, the majority replied derisively, *"Habemus Ponti-
ficem."* The powerful Confederation of Labor sided with the moderates.

Giolitti was jubilant. His jiujitsu tactics were working. In an interview he had outlined to me his plans for legalizing those workers' committees which the Communists considered embryonic Soviets.

Here the wily old man went astray. His policy of "social neutrality"
created so much parliamentary opposition that he had to call for new
elections. At this point, following his traditional tactics, he shifted sides
and allied himself with the very Nationalists and Conservatives who
were reproaching him for his weakness.

This, too, turned out to be a mistake. To be sure, Socialists and
Communists lost badly. But almost before the voting was over, Giolitti's
Nationalist and Fascist allies in the Chamber of Deputies turned upon
the Premier and forced him out. For the first time, they felt free to
embark upon the decisive anti-Socialist counteroffensive they had been
afraid to launch while the Socalists were riding high. In mid-summer,
1921, their emerging leader, Benito Mussolini, publicly admitted that
"to claim that a Communist danger still exists is to take one's fear for
reality."

By holding a balance between the retreating Socialists and the
emerging Fascist squads with their "punitive expeditions," the new
Premier, Ivanoe Bonomi, still hoped to keep both sides within the
democratic limits.

But public opinion was now largely on the side of the Fascists, and
they moved to conquer the country. In this undertaking, armed forces
and police increasingly sided with them. Officers who had not forgotten
the Socialists' antipatriotism and cowardly attacks, sometimes participated in the "punitive expeditions" without even bothering to remove
their uniforms.

For the most part, these met little or no resistance. In fact, to
Americans in Italy, the amazing thing was the failure of the two
"private armies" ever to meet in real battle. When the Socialists were
riding high, few if any Nationalists or Fascists had stood up to them.
Now, as Bonomi wrote later:

"The revolutionary leaders paid for their sin of having, during the
war, scorned the moral values of courage and sacrifice; nor were they
able to demonstrate, not indeed heroism, but firmness; nor could the
masses without leaders limit the damage."

This was true. But the Fascists showed no more courage. At
Sarzana, target of a "punitive expedition," three soldiers and eight
policemen under a resolute officer routed five hundred armed Blackshirts. Mussolini's *squadristi* were no more ready for martyrdom than
Socialists.

A determined Italian Premier would have had little difficulty in
restoring order. And the Italian upper and middle classes, having had

their revenge, would, I felt sure, have insisted on a return to legality. Was it to achieve anarchy or dictatorship that Cavour and his successors had united Italy? At the front with the Italian armies, I had met few extremists. Given time, the Fascist reaction, like the Socialist insurrection that provoked it, would peter out.

So great was my confidence that I settled down to writing a book on modern Italy.

This was my fourth start. Part of a manuscript on contemporary French poetry lay mouldering in my desk. A study of idealistic currents in contemporary European thought had never got beyond an introduction and a table of contents. *Soldiers of the Third Italy* had found no publisher.

Now I deliberately planned a book to appeal to the nonspecialized American with a real interest in world affairs. The title, *Immortal Italy,* was at the same time sentimental and indicative of my thesis: Italy must be considered as a unique depository of almost three thousand years of unbroken history. This explained its peculiarities.

In conclusion, I stated that Italy had "settled down into a condition of normal anarchy." The government was acting "like a fat old lady amid . . . unruly sons. Since she cannot make them behave, she is forced to set one against the others." Admittedly the Italians' "fatal preference for rhetoric, futile passion, and violence" could still cause trouble, say, a temporary military dictatorship. Yet although "bad government has partially discredited democracy, there is no room for social or political reaction in Italy." (No weak reservations here!)

Appleton accepted the manuscript with alacrity. Gaetano Salvemini welcomed the volume. Twenty-five years and another world war later, he told me that *Immortal Italy* was still "the best book on the subject, written by a foreigner."

Yet even as *Immortal Italy* appeared, parliamentary cabals overthrew Premier Bonomi and the premiership remained unfilled for weeks, since none of the leading politicians was willing to undertake the job of restoring order. Finally it went to Luigi Facta, a well-intentioned nobody.

During the interval, Fascist squads shifted from burning Chambers of Labor, and harassing union leaders to "capturing" whole towns, Ferrara, Rovigo, Reggio Emilia, Modena. When in June, 1922, sixty thousand armed Blackshirts seized the town of Bologna and tossed out the Red administration, I hurried to that city and interviewed the leader, or *raz* (a title Italians had adopted in jest from the Ethiopians), one Dino Grandi. Affable, but a braggart. A single company of *bersaglieri* under a resolute captain would have routed the Fascist occupiers, Facta's only reaction was to repeat his assurance that all would be well. The incurably irresponsible Deputies overthrew Facta, were unable to fill his job, and finally put him back!

More and more influential citizens were applauding the armed liquidation of the Red Terror, among them the editor of the influential *Corriere della Sera.*

But how explain that my friend Giuseppe Prezzolini, editor of *La*

Voce magazine, showed signs of rallying to the *Duce*? Obviously, I underestimated the influence of those "realistic" philosophers, Vilfredo Pareto and Gaetano Mosca, and the depth of the nationalism that bubbled in Prezzolini and his close associate, Giovanni Papini. Yet how could anyone swallow the line: "In fascism is the salvation of our freedom"?

In midsummer, 1922, at the railroad station of Civitavecchia, I witnessed an exceptional scene. Several hundred Fascists from Grosseto, armed with rifles, had attacked the "Socialist" town and been repulsed. When the citizens launched a counterattack, the colonel commanding the local garrison first huddled the demoralized assailants into the station and then bundled them on to my train. Once it was moving, these heroes started shooting at the windows of the houses! The townsmen returned the fire, broke several car windows, and, incidentally, put a bullet through my hat half an inch above my head.

Behavior like this colonel's convinced "important people" Rome had decided that, having done their duty, Mussolini and his Fascists should go. From what I knew of Benito's past, and from personal contacts, I considered him to be without the necessary qualifications.

As a young man he had fled to Switzerland to escape military service (he served later, to be sure) and opposed Giolitti's nationalist adventure in Tripolitania. Yet in 1913 he proclaimed, along with Marinetti, that Italy "needed a blood bath." In 1914, encouraged by French friends he turned against his neutralist comrades.

After the war, he secretly sabotaged the Fiume adventure, because it was led by someone else. His intellectual baggage was a hodgepodge: Nietzschean arrogance, a belief in "élites" borrowed from Pareto, and in direct action inspired by Sorel. Though Mussolini still called himself a Socialist, everyone knew he was extracting funds from capitalists by a promise to smash the Reds!

Here at most was a potential Cola di Rienzo, not a Bonaparte. Such a man might, I conceded, talk his way to power in San Marino but in Italy, home of Dante, Petrarch, and Machiavelli, the country of Mazzini and Umano—impossible!

In September, 1922, before Chicago sent me to Geneva and the Balkans, a friend in the Italian Ministry of War had remarked that both General Badoglio, the country's top commander, and General Pugliese of the Rome garrison, were ready to crush *Fascismo* once and for all, at a word from the Premier. With luck I might be back in Rome in time to report that happy event. . . .

Instead, on October 29, there I was, making the threatened March on Rome from Milan with Benito, whom the King had designated as Premier.

Once the train was under way, I settled back to self-examination: where had I gone wrong?

First of all, I had ignored Machiavelli's warning that "men change government easily, thinking to get something better."

Again, I had failed to appreciate the appeal of nationalism and of *Romanità* to a king and a people who felt that their prolonged disunity had made them vulnerable to foreign "trampling and scorn."

Also, I had overlooked the Italians' acceptance of the *compulsion of polarization*. Millions of Italians, once convinced that they had to choose between incipient communism and fascism (presumably temporary), had opted for fascism as the lesser evil.

Finally, I had underestimated the Italians' susceptibility to rhetoric. Just as D'Annunzio had elocuted Italy into the Great War, so Mussolini, though in a less flowery key, had verbally hypnotized his countrymen into accepting a new tyranny, and him as tyrant.

Well, at least the first interview with the new Premier should be mine. Boring my way through the Blackshirts blocking the corridor with the remark, "I am a friend of the *Duce*," I reached the compartment where Benito sat making plans for his arrival in Rome. And, as I expected, he consented to answer a few questions.

Yet all I heard was big talk about Italy's becoming a strong military power through the revival of *Romanità* and totalitarian discipline enforced by a single political party as in Soviet Russia. For the rest, the Duce would play it by ear.

Nothing is less welcome to a newsman than to have to report without bias the doings of a government he dislikes. Mussolini remained friendly and even went out of his way to see that I attended his press conferences. With Alberto de Stefani, the new Finance Minister and a tepid Fascist, I was on excellent terms. But a party in power whose unruly Blackshirts continued to take "revenge" upon its former opponents, administered castor oil and beatings to those who complained, raised the ugly banner of anti-Semitism (there were only 50,000 Jews in all Italy) and refused to accept Free Masons as members, outlawed all other parties, and, above all, allowed itself to be ruled by one man who claimed to represent the "general will"—this I found odious.

Mussolini took several ministries into his hands, used the new "Fascist militia for national safety" as his personal instrument, and compelled the fear-stricken Parliament to let him govern by decree. By the spring of 1923, newspapers were referring to him grandiosely as the *Signore* of Italy, the title used by petty Renaissance tyrants. In April I wired that the last opposition had vanished, in May that in this "second phase" of the Fascist revolution the Duce's authority was absolute, and in late July, at *his* request, that he would tolerate Parliament only so long as it accepted his will as law.

Nonetheless, most Italians welcomed total tyranny if only because it slowly put an end to three long years of disorder and civil strife. They applauded when he demanded naval parity with France, strengthened the Army, and shortly thereafter offered to conclude an agreement with the U.S.S.R. to allow Italians to cultivate parts of famished Russia. By March, 1923, his troops had reconquered half of that portion of Tripolitania lost during the World War. Looking ahead, I could see a real danger that this unabashed demagogue would talk his country into a new major conflict.

How then explain the enthusiasm for Fascism expressed by foreigners? Not mainly because Mussolini had smashed the unions, driven beggars and prostitutes from the Roman streets, increased the Italians' self-esteem to the point of arrogance, and made the trains run on time.

There was a deeper reason. Fascist parties sprang up in other countries, notably in Germany and Hungary. At a meeting of the Italian–American Society in Rome, Ambassador Child, presumably with President Harding's approval, publicly praised the Duce for having saved Italy from "impractical humanitarianism and whining weakness . . . worse than war."

Mussolini was almost delirious with joy. "Never before," he gloated to me, "has an ambassador openly approved of a political party in a country to which he was accredited." Child later became a member of the Italian Fascist party.

Fascism, I began to see, was a mixture of nationalism and socialism, combining the worst features of both. Early humanitarian reformers, even including the somewhat less than humanitarian Marx, had sought to eliminate injustice and inequality by advocating the public ownership of the means of production. That this could substitute state oppression for capitalist exploitation was obvious. Marx tried to soften the threat by promising that at some future date the state would "wither away." Some British Socialists sidestepped it by proposing pluralistic (guild) ownership. Lenin, however, extended the (temporary) dictatorship to everything, thus creating, or borrowing from Robespierre, the *totalitarian state*, the most efficient form of despotism ever devised.

Mussolini saw that the one-party state could dominate the national economy without formally collectivizing it, ostensibly in the name of the nation, actually for the benefit of the party hierarchs. And, as in Russia, the identification of the people with the state and the ruling party required making the Big Lie "the art of government and the rule of life."

Here lay the attraction of Fascism for foreign Nationalists, adventurers, reactionaries, and purblind capitalists (who imagined they could buy control of the ruling party by supporting it). Obviously, there were everywhere incipient Fascists waiting for the chance to acquire a *Duce* of their own.

By the summer of 1923 I had had enough of Italy—and the Fascists had had enough of me.

So when my brother suggested I take Berlin, a major foreign post, I accepted.

13

Encounter With History

We understand by substance whatever is constant in change.

SANTAYANA

EIGHT AND A HALF YEARS are a long time in a young man's life. No others so influenced my outlook as those spent in Italy. Both because I was young enough to learn and because that country had so much to teach.

Italy had no single recognized center like London, Paris, or even New York. From each of these, a foreign newsman could pretty well cover the respective country, but not from Rome.

Rome was the political capital and the seat (or *see*) of the Roman Catholic church, with an unbroken history of almost three thousand years. But in those days both Milan and Naples were larger. Genoa, the country's chief seaport, proudly trailed its long maritime glory like seafoam on the moonlit Mediterranean. Florence, though incredibly stuffy, never forgot it had been a second Athens, and continued to produce outstanding citizens. "Prussian" Turin, in addition to its industrial prowess, always remembered that from there, the House of Savoy and Count Camille Cavour had given the country unity after centuries of frustrated efforts by others. Venice, even in decline, remained, in the minds of its inhabitants, the *serenissima* among cities. It emphasized its uniqueness.

Italians from Dante to Mazzini had bitterly envied united peoples like the French, British, Spaniards, and Poles, and sought to make an end of foreign invasions and humiliations by bringing all Italians together. Under ancient Rome, Italy had been master of the Western world.

To sensitive foreigners, however, Italy's unequaled appeal lay, in

143

large part, in the cultural pluralism resulting from its former divisions. Where else could one find so many different "subcultures," all Italian to be sure, but enormously varied? Where else could one change cultural climate with so little effort?

Italy, moreover, was not only culturally more varied, it was richer in natural beauty and in man-made things sifted by time. Here the hills literally bloomed into houses as in Anticoli Corrado behind Tivoli, beloved of artists! The cause may well have been the prevalence of malaria at lower levels. But the resulting harmony was no accident.

Modern Italians resented foreigners' neglect of present achievements in favor of their past. But pretechnical Italy was Europe's finest example of organic harmony between man and nature, the thirst for which can never truly vanish, as the efforts of Frank Lloyd Wright attested.

In 1917, I had written Mother:

"I have begun a course of study that would make Methuselah sigh. Beginning with a book on the excavations in ancient Crete, which show the existence of a society contemporary with that of ancient Egypt, I shall pass from the study of Egypt to that of Greece, from Greece to what is known about Etruria, from Etruria in a straight line to ancient Rome. Afterwards one must take up theology, history, architecture, and general conception of the church with special reference to Byzance, then coming to Medieval Italy and the Great Renaissance, and so on down to today. Some of this is already done but the rest must be accomplished during the three years more I expect to remain in Italy."

Lilian and I plunged into Italian cultures, from the mysterious Etruscans to Benedetto Croce. During our Italian years, we saw most of what Italy offered. From the northern lakes and smiling Venetian villas to the plain, bright colored cottages of Calabria, from bustling Milan to Pythagoras' Syracuse and Barbarossa's Palermo, we knew and loved it all.

By the time we left, we had vacationed at half a dozen seaside resorts, and swum at many more, from primitive Porto Santo Stefano to Capri, Pesaro, and Venice.

We had walked through Tuscany and Umbria, across the Sorrentine Peninsula and on the lower slopes of Vesuvius, and climbed the Abruzzi. We read Browning at Pippa's Asolo and Lilian had translated Petrarch at Arquà Petrarca in the Euganean Hills where the poet died.

Moreover, on various news assignments, I had tramped the Alps and Dolomites and swum at other odd places such as Acquileia and Brindisi.

One such assignment remains particularly vivid. Early in the summer of 1923, Mount Vesuvius started smoking more heavily than usual, but this was so common that nobody noticed it until suddenly Mount Aetna erupted, burying a number of villages on the slopes. Ambassador Child invited me to go to Catania with him on the U.S. cruiser *Pittsburgh,* which happened to be in Naples.

It was dark as the *Pittsburgh* finally came in sight of the great volcano. And what a spectacle! Against the sky, flames were rising thousands of feet over the snow-covered peak, suggesting nothing so much as a medieval vision of hell, magnificent and terrifying. The following morning the crest was covered by dark smoke with only occasional flashes of fire. A motorcar took us up to the bottom of the flow. A huge grey ribbon of lava, a hundred yards wide and twenty feet high, was slowly rolling down over a village at the rate of two or three feet a minute.

When the three-mile column of molten rock touched a building, the latter crumpled like a wilting flower and disappeared under stones. Nothing I had ever seen in nature, not even midwest cyclones, could match its awesome power. "Aetna," I wired the *News*, "is a white mystery of super-natural power and super-natural convulsions which suggests something titanic." Returning to Naples on the *Pittsburgh* that night, after a last long look at the gorgeous flaming monster, I remembered Professor Craig's favorite psalm, "When I consider thy heavens, the work of thy fingers, the moon and the stars which thou hast ordained, what is man that thou are mindful of him and the son of man that thou visitest him?" In the arms of an aroused nature, mankind, I mused, is about as much master of its fate as a mosquito in a tornado.

Among Italy's so varied provinces, I developed strong preferences. Much as I relished Tuscany, say, at Delfino Cinelli's villa outside Florence, I loved the Veneto more.

Among cities, I preferred Rome—not the bloated, traffic-bound capital of the 1960's, cheapened by Mussolini's ventures in neo-*Romanità* and ugly new living quarters—no, the pre-Fascist Rome lying for the most part comfortably within the old Aurelian Wall, still overwhelmingly the city of the Popes and of the ancient Romans. For nowhere else were so many historical landmarks in so small a compass.

From our apartment on the top floor of historic Palazzo Galitzin in the Via della Scrofa ("our" half of it attributed to the great Bramante) it was an easy walk to any part of town, including, when we chose, which was not often, the Via Veneto. And walk it we did, day in and day out, becoming familiar with every museum, monument, church, ruin, piazza, street corner, view, and, of course, good, inexpensive restaurant.

Among places to eat we preferred, in summer, the *Castello dei Cesari* on the Aventine Hill from whose terrace one looked across the once great Circus Maximus to the ruins and cypresses on the Palatine. Convenient at any season were the *Concordia*, not far away at the back of a courtyard; a sidewalk cafe on the Piazza del Popolo; and, closest of all, a small trattoria, *Alfredo*, which produced the best home-made *fettucini* in Rome until Sinclair Lewis, whom I introduced to Alfredo, made the place internationally popular.

Of the Roman museums we could never get enough. Each one— the Vatican, the Capitoline, the Villa Giulia with its incomparable Etruscan Apollo of Veio—held something out of the ordinary. Since I preferred sculpture to painting, and Greek sculpture to any other, my favorite was the *Museo delle Terme,* largely on account of the Apollo of the Tiber, the incomparable Venus of Cyrenaica, and that other "Venus rising from the sea" on the side of the marble sarcophagus.

Yet our tastes were catholic. Although I had been taught to look down my nose at baroque art and to sneer at rococo, I came to enjoy Bernini and to soar with the "fly-away" ceilings of Tiepolo. I even admired Pius the Ninth's monument to the Virgin Mary on Piazza di Spagna directly opposite the new and sumptuous office which, at Chicago's bidding, I installed on the "noble floor" of a building on adjacent Piazza Mignanell.

Among fine piazzas the world over, I put Saint Peter's first, equal or superior to St. Mark's in Venice, Paris's Concorde and Place des Vosges, and Brussels' Grand Place. But I never tired of the monumental Piazza Navona with its obelisk and fountains (also a former Roman circus), of Piazza di Spagna, or of Michelangelo's incomparable Campidoglio. And everywhere rose those old Roman palaces, medieval, renaissance, or barocco, with their heavy, forbidding but grandly proportioned façades and inviting courtyards, notably those of Palazzo Borghese and of Palazzo Farnese, the latter, with the Cancelleria, the finest building in Rome.

Where but in Rome could an incurable walker discover new beauty after eight years—a corner in an otherwise nondescript church (Rome had that kind too), a charming little ex-voto on an outdoor wall, or a previously unnoticed vista?

What other town had such a setting as the Campagna, as melancholy as the Veneto was smiling and rich, but just as fascinating? And within easy reach, for Rome then had no suburbs and in most directions the city stopped abruptly at the gates.

In summer when it was too hot to walk, we swam daily in the Tiber at Ponte Milvio, then well outside the city, or, if we had a free half-day, took the train to Maccarese and walked through the deserted woods to the empty beach near Fregene.

Swimming at lonely Fregene could be something of an adventure. Even a calm sea was subject to a mysterious undertow. Once, having swum out a quarter of a mile, we spent almost an hour getting back to shore—exhausted.

On another occasion, two giant white bulls, with immense dewlaps and six-foot horns like those on a Roman frieze, demonstrated their masculinity to admiring cows by chasing us into deep water.

In cooler seasons, we tramped over Monte Mario or along Via Appia Antica, with its confused pagan and Christian memories. On weekends we sometimes took the trolley car to the Castelli Romani (or, less often, to Tivoli and Hadrian's Villa). Occasionally we trudged the fifteen odd miles back to Rome, as Ruskin had done, stopping to dine on fettucini, raw ham, and melon, washed down with plenty of good Frascati wine, at one of several rural trattorias.

The secret charm of the Campagna Romana, aside from the usually transparent atmosphere that brought out each trace of color, was its emptiness. In ancient time this area was almost as populated as it is today. But after the year 537 A.D. when the Gothic King Witigis cut the aqueducts and flooded the farms and villas in an effort to reduce the city, the campagna became the abode of that most ruthless of enemies, the anopheles mosquito, and so it remained until the advent of DDT. Human beings who defied him succumbed to malaria or fled and gradually it became an almost vacant prairie out of which rose the ruins of long deserted dwellings and great gates leading nowhere. Yet to me no other landscape in Italy was as appealing as this, especially under the glow of the setting sun.

In short, when one could forget politics, both national and international, life in Italy in the years immediately after the First World War was an unending satisfaction.

Pleasant too were my nonpolitical assignments and the friends they brought. One of these was covering the Vatican. During the war, my instructions had been to keep Church dispatches to a minimum. But thereafter the *News* expected coverage of all the "high spots" provided it contained nothing "controversial" or "offensive to Catholic readers."

In the somewhat narrow Protestant atmosphere of my father's house, the Catholic Church itself was "controversial," a perverter of the "true doctrine" that had been happily restored by reformers like Luther, Calvin, Knox, and Wesley. Considerable study of comparative religion had erased this family prejudice from my mind. Yet the American priests whom I met in Rome seemed to me unnecessarily doctrinaire.

Not so the Italian prelates. The Italian Church dignitaries with whom I became familiar had supple minds. Monsignore Sincero, of the *Rota*, had dropped me when he became a cardinal. But Monsignore Benigni came frequently to the apartment to dine and talk. Benigni had been an assistant to Cardinal Secretary of State Merry del Val and was both broadly international and elastically conservative.

Shortly after we became acquainted he set out to convert me. For several months I simply parried his hints. Then one evening he let go: "My son, what is there in the teaching of the Church which you find difficulty in accepting?"

"Well, monsignore, may I mention, among other things, the Pope's claim to temporal power?"

Benigni's face grew stern and his voice rose. "Young man, on the day of judgment, when the skies are falling and fire is devouring the earth, the last voice to be heard on this doomed planet should be that of the Holy Father, crying, 'I want my temporal power!'"

I could not but admire an institution that had, for almost two thousand years, in the face of all sorts of heresy, and of growing historical and social "relativism," stood fast on its claim to possess absolute truth.

My admiration for the Church was somewhat marred when Pope Pius, who had, as Cardinal Ratti, given an interview to me and to an Italian colleague, later denied having received us! I had described the Cardinal as the "most cultured, experienced, versatile and superior man to become Pope in many generations." A deliberate untruth from such a man resulting in harm to my innocent Italian colleague would have been shocking.

When Pius acknowledged his mistake, I came to believe that he had misstated the facts inadvertently.

To my surprise, the American Cardinals turned up late at the Papal Conclave. This, the Cardinal Primate of Ireland explained to me, was a not unusual precaution on the part of those Princes of the Church who preferred not to commit themselves in the choice of a new Pope. "What did you expect?" my friend and early mentor, Salvatore Cortesi, asked. "To go very far, a churchman must be a good politician. In Rome any politician learns to be *fermitur in re, soavitur in modo*." Unfortunately for Italy, as I was learning, most lay politicians were *fermitur in verbis, soavitur in actis*.

The more unpleasant the current trend in Italian politics, the more eagerly I welcomed personal friendships with interesting Italians. Cosmopolitan society in Rome resembled that in all European capitals, and we knew any number of diplomats and Italian high officials.

A good many of the richer Roman aristocrats, among them some married to foreigners, were addicted to the kind of *dolce vita* later pictured in the film of that name and in the novel *S.P.Q.R.* My Italian secretary, Count Cesare Brenda, while too poor to participate in the life of easy pleasure and personal exhibitionism to which he was born, daily reported the more extravagant doings.

A notable exception in that society was Don Gelasio Caetani, a son of one of Rome's oldest historical families. Don Gelasio had studied at the Colorado School of Mines and became famous during the war by blowing up the Austrians on Monte Sabotino. We had first met at the front. Although he later became Mussolini's ambassador in Washington, he was no Fascist and was recalled from the United States because he opposed the organization of Fascist groups by Italo-Americans. Back in Rome, he became famous a second time through devising the plan for draining the famous Pontine Marshes, which had belonged to his family. Just when he was about to become Governor of Rome, he suddenly died. I can not but think how different Rome would have been if more aristocrats had possessed the character and broad interests of Don Gelasio.

Most Italian writers were more bourgeois than bohemian. For one D'Annunzio, Italy had ten authors of the Manzoni or Verga type, devoted to describing normal humanity. In the office of *La Voce* magazine, high above Piazza de Spagna, Giuseppe Prezzolini had introduced me to several outstanding writers including his former close collaborator, Giovanni Papini, a mocking Tuscan who had published that ironical autobiography, *Un Uomo Finito* (*Played Out*) at the ripe age of thirty-two, and then switched to religion. And we were always welcome at the country villa of Adolfo de Bosis, the poet businessman, who translated into Italian verse the complete works of Shelley mostly while riding the streetcar to and from his office.

Little by little, more and more "foreign" writers dropped in on the Mowrers, Sinclair Lewis, Ezra Pound, Edna St. Vincent Millay, among others. Edna recited her poems in the most beautiful speaking voice I have ever heard. Pound was even then cultivating an impressive arrogance.

Through de Bosis, we became acquainted with an instructor of philosophy from Harvard, B. A. G. Fuller, who had just completed a *History of Greek Philosophy—Thales to Democritus* and was eager to talk about it. Fuller not only knew his subject thoroughly, but in the tradition of Santayana, wrote it beautifully in nontechnical language. His brilliant, learned expositions and the discussions which followed reawakened all my latent love of metaphysics. As a result, Lilian, de Bosis, and I helped him with the proofs of the book, and otherwise did all we could to make it a success.

During the war René Arcos and the charming Renée he was soon to marry had been our guests (after the Italians released him from the fortress at Messina where in spite of his French passport, they had held him as a presumed Turkish spy!). In 1922 René filled me in on the postwar intellectual climate of Paris. Julien Benda had shattered a lot of complacency by his book called *La Trahison des Clercs*, meaning those French intellectuals who had written and spoken unintelligent anti-German demogogy during the war. For the rest, French artists and men of letters still reflected the shock of the war. The former were taking refuge in formalism and mad experimentation, the latter in a subjectivism that expressed a dream rather than reflected the world. Arcos found the experiments interesting. But noting my deepening preference for the classical, he felt sure I would not much like them. Later, of course, things would settle down. . . .

Also from Paris came Arcos' friends, the novelist Luc Durtain and his wife, whom I had met in 1913. Durtain traveled everywhere and described what he had seen as only a French raconteur can.

Since Lilian was an accomplished pianist, several musicians frequented her little salon. Giuditta Sartori, herself a concert performer, brought along some of the young Italian composers, Casella, Malipiero, Pizzetti, and Respighi, whose endless discussion of the new tendencies in music also reminded us of prewar Paris. Albert Spalding looked us up when he came to Rome. And from the American Academy on the Janiculum, where he was a pupil, came a gifted fellow-Chicagoan, Leo Sowerby, who once brought another young composer, Howard Hansen. Sometimes the British-Russian conductor, Albert Coates, dropped in for a change of shirt and a hearty snack after a concert. Fascinating, too, was a Sardinian guitarist whose peasant wife was endowed with what fellow Sardinians considered the supreme gift—she could sing quarter tones loudly enough to be heard a mile!

Harry Stickroth, a pupil at the American Academy, who had an uncommon gift for drawing, made a Signorelli-inspired portrait of Lilian which he liked so much he kept it and gave her an inferior copy. Before he could fully develop what seemed a major talent, he died.

Six months before I left Italy, to our intense delight, we had a daughter, Diana Jane, so named that she might later use either sobriquet (she chose the first); she was an irresistible baby and Lilian had never been so handsome. Years before Dr. Hoffman in Chicago had remarked that "motherhood makes holy virgins of women" and so it was with my wife.

In September, 1923, I took ship for the United States. Editor Dennis in Chicago briefed me on what would be expected in Berlin, and sent me back to Europe by way of Washington, D.C., my first visit.

Another capital! What Washington lacked in variety of human activities—business, art, intellect—it made up in charm, informality, and "normalcy." But where was the "association of nations" President Harding had promised the American voters in 1921?

President Coolidge never asked me about Italy (as I had foolishly expected he would), and I left him wondering what sort of joke God had played upon the American people. Secretary of State Hughes, though vastly impressive, praised the naval disarmament treaty as a more effective path to peace than the League of Nations, which America had fathered and repudiated.

While in Washington I read a recent popular novel, *Soldiers Three,* by an American ex-Doughboy called John Dos Passos. One of his heroes deserts from the American Expeditionary Force in France when he can no longer stand the "injustices" and downright meanness of his superiors in a war in which he sees no meaning. Yet in so doing he imagines himself as a sort of John Brown struggling to make men free! At the end he is turned over to the American military police by a French girl whom he has begun to love.

I sympathized with the French girl. To be sure I had, as a student, fancied myself as an anarchist. But in the intervening years I had lived through an impressive sample of history. Germany's conduct, though odious, was similar to that of previous would-be conquerors whose aggressions make up the bulk of history. Perhaps the war might have been prevented, but once started, it had to be won.

Certainly, throwing down one's arms and refusing to fight further (deserting, in short) did not settle anything. The Italians had tried it at Caporetto with baneful results. If the Russians had succeeded by some such method, they owed it exclusively to the Entente. Had the Entente permitted the Czechoslovak prisoners in Russia to overthrow the Bolshevik regime, they could almost surely have done so. Or had the Entente not defeated Imperial Germany, the latter would have gobbled up choice parts of Russia and thrown the communists out of the rest. The Bolsheviks owed their continued existence to, among other things, those Americans who fell in France. Wise men, from Socrates to Alfred de Vigny, had always known that the price of freedom was the readiness to defend it, whatever sacrifice that entailed.

Yet a good many American veterans shared Dos Passos' apparent feeling that American participation had been a mistake. They had fought to make the world safe for democracy—and just look at it! But to eliminate or even temper man's aggressivity would be no easy job. And to succeed at all, one had to begin with an understanding of the overwhelming role of power in human affairs.

This understanding seemed absent from the isolationist America of the early twenties. Provided they could overcome the last trace of the brief postwar economic depression and be let alone, all too many citizens thought it safe to let the rest of the world drift by itself.

So many years' residence spent in Europe had taught me that a people is nothing but the summation of its history. In fact, until modern times, every people seems to have looked back, and not forward, to a Golden Age or a lost Eden. As one might read in Deuteronomy, "Giants dwelt therein in old time; and the Ammonites call them Zamzummins." Older countries revered their Zamzummins. I loved my country, particularly its absence of fixed classes, generosity, and vast open spaces. The richer a people's conscious heritage, the fuller its existence, its history.

For this reason I failed to share the current optimism of young American intellectuals concerning the Russian revolution. Louis Fischer, in particular, called my scepticism "un-American." To him, then, the Soviet Union embodied mankind's latest hope.

In 1917, I too had welcomed Kerensky's revolution and even, for a while, Lenin's. Since then doubts had arisen. Two close friends in Rome, Nicolas and Katya Volkov, while not attempting to hide the cruelty of the tsarism in which they had participated, he as a general's son, she as as princess, gave us a harrowing picture of subsequent life in the Russian Utopia.

Moreover, I had shortly before provided my old Paris friend, Vladimir Michailov, with enough money to permit, first him and then his wife, to escape from Leningrad—a "hell on earth," as he described it—by buying passports from corrupt Red officials. Yet far from being a reactionary, Vladimir had been imprisoned by the tsarist government for participation in the uprising of 1905. Obviously the U.S.S.R. *de facto* was the denial of everything the American Founding Fathers had stood for.

Any such statement, to many reformers, constituted a denial of the future in favor of the past. In my view it was an essential recognition of human continuity. Even beauty, in a painfully transitory world, frequently increases with age. Much magnificent poetry is sheer nostalgia. Italian buildings owed some of their charm to the fact that they were built to last. Adolfo de Bosis' son, Lauro, had had an apartment in a (renovated) segment of Rome's Aurelian Wall. American builders practiced built-in obsolescence—and I resented it. The more a people (or an individual) is familiar with its past, the more "objective" its judgments are likely to be.

This conclusion indicated to me why, among modern countries, only Italy produced a philosopher like Benedetto Croce. For Croce identified experience itself with history and argued that, as a mere part of history, philosophy could be nothing but the application to life of historical insight. Was this not what Pascal had in mind when he urged considering the entire succession of men through so many centuries as a single man, existing always and learning continually? All peoples are equally "old."

Something like this, I concluded, was what, in 1923, my countrymen needed to remember before we could make our maximum contribution to mankind.

I returned to Rome in time for Christmas with my wife and fascinating baby daughter and to say farewell to the city which not even Mussolini could permanently spoil.

The Fascist Government was delighted to get rid of me. But one friendly newspaper editor risked a dose of castor oil by publicly and extravagantly commending the "exact picture" which Edgardo Mowrer had given, not only of Italy's war effort, but of the "difficult years of reconstruction." He even added a good word about *Immortal Italy*.

PART FOUR

"Civilization, that Frail Reed...."

The psychic task which a person can and must set for himself is not to feel secure but to be able to tolerate insecurity.

ERIC FROMM

14

The German Neurosis

Du bist verrueckt, mein Kind,
Du musst nach Berlin . . .

—POPULAR SONG

EARLY JANUARY, 1924, found me living in the Hotel Bristol, Unter den Linden, Berlin, a hostel less famous than the nearby Adlon but practically next door to the *News'* office. Although I had by then spent some twelve years in Europe, this was my first meeting with the Fatherland.

And I knew very little about Germans. In Belgium, in 1914, I had seen the German Army at its worst. But now that the people had replaced the Kaiser, I thought they merited better treatment than they were getting from the French and Belgians. In this, I inclined to agree with Keynes' *Economic Consequences of the Peace*, which I later recognized as one of the most harmful books ever written. In fact, because Keynes' arguments persuaded Washington as well as London that the beaten Germans were not dangerous, and encouraged the Germans to think they could defy the victors with impunity, any list of the ten non-Germans most responsible for the Second World War would include John Maynard Keynes. Yet I blamed my own government for having stupidly signed a special peace treaty instead of ratifying that of Versailles and then getting its terms eased. In short, I was inclined to see the postwar Germans rather through the eyes of my friend Count Sforza than through those of my brother Paul or of Frank Symonds of the *New York Times*.

In any case I was unprepared for what I found. Yet I had been warned. Shortly before leaving for Germany I had asked advice from Marc Van Blankenstein, one of Europe's ablest newsmen, who had spent a decade in Germany, including the war years.

155

"One thing only, Edgar—never imagine you understand the Germans."

"But surely you understand them, Marc."

"Certainly not. After years of contact, like an entomologist who has studied ants, I can predict pretty accurately what the Germans in a given situation will do. But *why* they do it I am unable to say. Nor will you, no matter how long you remain in Germany."

I never did. After almost ten years in the Fatherland, I was still finding German reactions, both individual and collective, *sui generis*.

Which was exactly what many Germans felt themselves to be, especially after their still unimaginable defeat in 1918. To them the years of disappointment, trial, and never-ending crisis seemed like a lunatic's dream.

In 1918, the military leaders who had, to the last, fed the Germans a diet of victory talk, suddenly ordered them to overthrow the august House of Hohenzollern and create a republic which few of them wanted.

Most expected a "negotiated settlement" and instead found themselves at Versailles facing a *Diktat* on a take-it-or-leave-it basis, long after any possibility of their reopening hostilities had disappeared. That this *Diktat* was less severe than the Treaty of Brest-Litovsk, which they themselves had imposed on Russia the previous year, meant little. For Russia had been defeated and physically invaded while Germany had sued for peace while its soldiers were still everywhere on foreign soil. Unlike Wilson, Kaiser Wilhelm had never talked of a peace without victors or vanquished. . . . How compare the two treaties?

As if military defeat, with the loss of over six million in killed and wounded, was not bad enough, a people with a mania for "quiet and order" found themselves subject to years of bloody insurrections, unceasing disturbance, and pressure from France and Belgium.

As a result, unrepentant nationalists successfully launched the legend that unbeaten Germany was betrayed by a revolutionary "dagger thrust" at home. This encouraged Right radicals and the "new" Army to organize armed bands which fought not only against Poles, Communists, and left Socialists but against the new Republic as well. In fact, Oswald Spengler, that strange hybrid of historical seer and German jingo, had already announced that the Weimar Constitution was doomed.

The Republic refused to hand over the hundreds of "war criminals" demanded by the Allies. Berlin developed a device for circumventing the agreed limitations on the size and nature of their new armed forces at home, and, finally, under the Rapallo agreement, began more or less secretly to develop forbidden air and tank forces on Russian soil. If the other countries did not disarm, why should Germany?

Republican leaders, many of whom had applauded the Kaiser's war and approved annexations while things were going well, contested the government's "technical" admission of Germany's war guilt. For they rightly saw in it the basis of the Allied policy of making them pay for a large share of the war damages done to France and Belgium by the imperial armies.

In this, they counted on the support of Washington, which had washed its hands of the Versailles treaty and of every trace of its wartime "association" (except for its insistence on the repayment of the inter-Allied debts). Even more, they counted on the support of Britain, whose leaders, of whatever party, not only disapproved of France and Belgium's insistence on substantial reparations (Britain had not been invaded), but were engaged in one of those balance-of-power acts upon which British statesmen had long prided themselves.

Imperial Germany had financed its losing war almost exclusively by internal loans and currency inflation. The industrial and landed barons realized that the burden of meeting both the heavy internal obligations (which they had expected the beaten enemy to pay) and the promised reparations would rest on them. Under their influence the "democratic" Republic repudiated its agreed payment schedule—and almost ruined the German people in the process.

For when Germans ceased paying, the French and Belgians sent an army of sixty thousand soldiers into the Ruhr, the heart of the German economy. Britain said tut-tut, and I later met a British official whose business it had been to urge the Germans to print and sell new marks abroad each time the pressure for reparation payments became irresistible. Coolidge in Washington showed his disapproval by withdrawing the remaining American occupying forces from Germany. Thus encouraged, Berlin organized passive resistance against the invaders.

Passive resistance temporarily prevented the French and Belgians from exploiting the Ruhr but at the price of utterly debasing the already weak German currency and ruining millions of small savers. On January 9, 1923, the Allied Reparation Commission solemnly accused Germany of violating the peace treaty.

In the Ruhr the French stood firm, sent recalcitrant industrialists, agitators, and workmen to jail, took over the industries and railroads, shot saboteurs, and despite British resistance, organized a Rhineland separatist movement that, given more time, might have persuaded the inhabitants of the left bank of the Rhine to secede from Germany.

Although the Reichsbank raised its discount rate to 30 percent, exports fell to almost nothing. The people were in despair. In Bavaria, monarchists and fascists combined under General Ludendorff to overthrow the Republic. In Saxony and Thuringia, communist-leaning local governments acted in defiance of the Republic.

At this point Chancellor Gustav Stresemann called off passive resistance, which, in a few months, had cost the Republic several billion dollars in real income, and offered to negotiate with President Poincaré.

General von Seeckt forcibly dissolved the "Black *Reichswehr*" and the Labor Commandos. He also sent a Prussian Army to the Bavarian border and cut short any further agitation for separation from the Reich. Expert financiers like Helferich and Schacht set about stabilizing the currency (six trillion marks to the dollar on November 22, 1923), thereby saving a situation which Stresemann had characterized as hopeless. The "catastrophe policy" was over. Sullenly, German leaders settled down to a policy of fulfilling the peace treaty.

Premier Poincaré finally agreed to discuss reparations with the Germans (the French franc had sunk during the Ruhr "war" from 12 to 26 to the dollar) and President Coolidge consented to allow Americans to participate privately in two expert commissions to study the German situation.

All this I had to learn upon reaching Germany in order to understand why that winter of 1923–24 was the grimmest the Germans had known since the Thirty Years War three centuries earlier. Inevitably they tended to blame the victorious foreigners for their misery.

Yet nowhere have I met more friendliness, particularly from my own employees. Frau Magda Kluge, my secretary, an admirer of Otto H. Kahn, understood the political situation, frequented artists like Max Reinhardt and intellectuals like Kurt Tucholsky, editor of the weekly *Weltbuehne* (who wrote under five different pseudonyms), and seemed delighted to introduce me to Berlin's Bohemia and to the "German soul." To advise me she brought to the office two knowledgeable writers, Dr. Erich Podach and Leo Lania, the latter an Austrian who described German events in fluent Italian.

Richard Kant, the office man-of-all-work, had spent the war in the navy and, on the rebound, become a communist. He had a way of correcting my not infrequent linguistic mistakes (he spoke some English), beginning "Pardon me, sir, but," which I found irresistible.

When later the *News* in Chicago authorized me to hire a German assistant, I was lucky enough to have in succession two highly intelligent young men, Richard Winners and Otto Brok, both passionate republicans, the first a Ph.D., the second a doctor of political science and a respected member of the (Catholic) Center Party.

Thanks primarily to my office associates and to Herbert von Hindenburg, a nephew of the Field Marshal, I had not been two weeks in Berlin before I was meeting all sorts and kinds of Germans, within, out of, for, and against the government. And although I had early taken as my goal "few news sources but the best," in no other country have I acquired as broad an acquaintance as in the Weimar Republic.

In contrast to the Italians and to the French, most Germans were genuinely hospitable, and, I thought, mildly "daft."

Take the Bohemians at the Romanisches Cafe to which Frau Kluge and Lania soon introduced me. There, at the near end of Kurfuerstendamm opposite the Gedaechtniskirche, artists, actors, writers, *Akademiker,* and newsmen sat for hours with their wives or with their "steadies" over a single coffee or beer and talked, argued, and quarreled about everything in the world. At a side table the former world's champion, Emanuel Lasker, took on all comers at chess, for two marks a game. It reminded me of prewar gatherings in the *Closerie des Lilas* in Paris. In both places, the same passion for ideas, the same delight in epigrams and intellectual fireworks, the same absence of "moral prejudice." But with a difference. Most of these Germans recognized no morality beyond a vague humanitarianism, unmindful of Théophile Gautier's remark that despite unceasing efforts mankind had never been able to invent an eighth deadly sin. Prostitutes on the Tauentzien Strasse were incredibly, even comically, brazen.

The homosexual and lesbian *Dielen* publicly emphasized the nature of their custom. The artistic and not-so-artistic balls to which my wife and I occasionally went in subsequent years were remarkable not only for their size, but for the exhibitionism of the participants.

Not by chance, I came to believe, had the philosopher Hegel, ruminating on world history in Berlin, been led to see the former as an oscillation between subsequently synthesized opposites.

Slow-moving in mind, Germans were addicted to "depth" of thought, matter-of-fact yet passionately sentimental. Despite defeat, the soldier remained "the finest man in the whole state."

Strangers stopped my wife on the street to inform her that walking on the grass was *streng verboten*, or to warn that my daughter's shoelace needed tying.

The *bourgeoisie* adored titles as much as the nobility and the army. I collected several "Dr. Dr.'s" and saw on a front door in Luebeck: "Dr. Dr. Dr. Schmidt."

Yet at the same time, no people held more individual notions about everything. In spite of the pressure for conformity, the Weimar Republic probably boasted more "originals" per thousand than Southern California.

Among the many incredible characters who came to my office was the Hungarian-born Ignatius Trebitsch. Few persons have played so many roles, all of them dubious. After adding the name Lincoln, this smooth-talking individual passed himself off in the United States, Canada, and England as a minister of the gospel, became secretary to a British millionaire, and, with the help of Winston Churchill and David Lloyd George, got himself elected to the British Parliament. During the war he spied successfully and simultaneously for Britain, France, Russia, and Germany. Denounced in England, he drifted inevitably to postwar Berlin. When the combined action of the victim wartime governments finally drove him from Europe, he moved to China on borrowed money, some of it from me, and after professionally advising a Chinese warlord, and becoming a Buddhist monk, he took service with Japan and the puppet emperor of Manchukuo.

I did not believe the fantastic tales of his past which he related as the basis for soliciting small loans, but I was sorry when he left.

Another bizarre creature was the "hunger artist," Siegfried Herz, who, under the name of Jolly, lived for forty-four days on mineral water alone in a glass cage visible to the public, collecting about twenty-five thousand dollars and a gold crown for his pains.

Where but in Germany could one find 150,000 organized nudists?

Religious sects of all sorts and kinds throve in a way to make Los Angeles envious. At Frohnau, a suburb of Berlin, stood a Pali Canon Buddhist monastery, whose German head, Dr. Paul Dahlke, had written a book on Hinayana Buddhism which I read with intense interest. On one of our visits to the place, he first invited us to discuss religion with him and then told me to go home and pursue the path of Enlightenment.

Berlin, and presumably other German cities as well, swarmed with self-styled prophets, clairvoyants, mediums, magnetisers, hypnotists, medical quacks, and minor freaks. Among our friends was a successful iron pipe salesman whose profitable inventions were, he explained, suggested to him, in exchange for chocolate, by his friends, the gnomes living in the forests of Brandenburg (Heinzelmaeden).

Only Germany filled the forest and mountain trails with young *Wandervoegel* protesting against industrial civilization, the forerunners of the American youth of the sixties.

Berlin boasted an M.D., Olga von Ungern-Sternberg, a friend of ours, who spiced general medicine with psychoanalysis, and relied, in difficult cases, on astrology for final diagnosis. At home her husband contentedly looked after the household and helped with the horoscopes. His uncle, a Baltic general in the Tsarist army, Roman Nicolaus von Ungern Sternberg, had been the Buddhist "mad baron" who, in 1920, carved out for himself a personal empire in Mongolia and for a year successfully maintained it against the hated Bolsheviks.

At the School of Wisdom in Darmstadt, Count Hermann Keyserling, another Baltic nobleman, who had married Bismarck's granddaughter, alternately flayed the Germans for not speaking the "cultural language of the rest of Europe," and boasted that Germany would eventually lead the world back to authoritarianism. "Germany has nothing in common with the West and nothing in common with the East," was a remark one frequently heard.

In politics this *Eigentuemlichkeit* became sensationally clear at the Beer Hall Putsch trial in Munich, whither Lania accompanied me as interpreter, three months after my arrival in Germany. Although Ludendorff had been the nominal leader (and was acquitted), the real culprit, a queer looking "state-less" ex-corporal named Adolf Hitler, virtually took charge of the proceedings, the judges consenting. In a four-hour harangue, he calmly boasted of seeking to overthrow the Republic and predicted he would make himself dictator. Yet, one learned, the *Reichswehr* had been employing Hitler as its agent in combatting not only communism and pacifism, but socialism and democracy.

Partly because of its loony atmosphere, Germany turned out to be anything but an unpleasant spot to work in.

I travelled considerably, and soon realized that late political unification had left Germans as diversified as Italians. There were broad differences between Catholics and non-Catholics and between regions.

Among German cities, I immediately liked Berlin best. Berliners had a personality of their own, scornful of the "provincials" who flocked to their theaters, concerts, university, industries, and corporations: they were friendly and courageous and witty, at top levels proudly cosmopolitan, responsive to European fashions, and delighted to be called the Americans of Germany. Physically Berlin reminded one of a better kept, better governed, better looking Chicago. It was greener and far more full of flowers, but its climate was roughly similar. Like Chicago, it lay in an area of barometric high pressure, the kind that has always made me feel my best.

True, in those first years after the currency stabilization, living was hard. Taxis were few and shabby. It took me three months to find an apartment to which to bring from Rome my wife and baby daughter, half way between the Center where I worked and the West, where one played. But it was nightmarish with paintings by the artist-owner, who had a preference for naked females portrayed in expressionist style.

After six months with the fat nudes, we fled to the rather handsome apartment of a widowed Prussian, a self-pitying baroness who used her own, and her country's misfortunes, to extract the last possible penny from her foreign tenants. Not until thirty months after my arrival could I obtain the coveted "white certificate" which enabled us to rent an empty apartment and fill it with our own furniture from Italy. This was a duplex giving on the Tiergarten, which we divided with Dorothy Thompson, my erstwhile newspaper colleague. We remained at Haendelstrasse 8 until the end.

To us, Berlin grew more attractive from year to year. Under the zany influence of the Weimar Republic, it was becoming more and more the cultural center of Germany. Munich might scoff, and ancient universities like Goettinger, Tuebingen, Marburg, Heidelberg, Freiburg, and Bonn emphasize lack of tradition. But artists and writers seemed irresistibly drawn there, not only Germans, miscellaneous Central Europeans, and Russian exiles, but, as time went on, Westerners as well. Indeed, by 1930 Berlin was well on the way to outstripping London and Paris as the intellectual and artistic mecca of Europe. Certainly it had the finest theaters, something that mattered enormously to Lilian, who had become a full-fledged dramatic critic.

The Germans had always been a highly schooled people with a passion for learning. This meant that wherever a foreigner went, he could, once he had enough of the language, find interesting discussion. Almost every German knew a good deal about something and was ready, even eager, to talk about it. He favored abstractions and had theories about almost anything. Unlike the Frenchman and the Italian, he took a genuine interest in other countries.

High officials, businessmen, shopkeepers, politicians, occasional waiters, and ex-sailors like my office man, Richard Kant, all had interests outside their immediate callings. They were almost uniformally accessible. President Hindenburg was, I think, the only German who ever refused my request for a talk.

A surprising number spoke some foreign language so that it was very rare, even at the beginning of my Berlin career, that I found myself unable to get the information I needed.

Nonetheless, reporting in France, Italy, and Belgium had convinced me of one thing: nobody, newsman or other, could hope to know a foreign people until he was conversant in their language, whether Basque, Chinese, or Mandingo. Therefore learning German became my first, and for a time, my principal task.

Fortunately, I remembered from university days a few of the language's syntactical convolutions. In Rome I had chosen to cut my linguistic teeth on Dante's *Inferno*. In Berlin I started with Count Keyserling's *Travel Diary of a Philosopher*, and found it fascinating.

At first it took me two hours to read half a page. And it was eighteen months after my arrival in Berlin before I felt linguistically qualified for my job. I still share the feeling of a newspaper colleague at the Adlon Bar who, being told that an Indian politician called Das was dead, remarked: "I wish to God that *Der* and *Die* had died with him."

Always, too, I remembered the warning of my friend Marc. War, defeat, inflation, and robbery might for a time leave a legacy of queerness in any people. But in Germany idiosyncracy went deeper. To explain it, I fell back on a remark of a great German physician, mentioned to me by a young doctor friend, "God bless the neurotics: but for them we would still be living in the caves," a thought which had occurred to Marcel Proust.

Many Germans were, I felt, doing their best to stay out of the caverns.

15

The New Sachlichkeit

For the first time since the Reformation,
Germany seems to be ready for a great
human future.
　　　　—COUNT HERMANN KEYSERLING, 1923

ONE OF THE words heard most often in Germany was *Sachlichkeit*. The dictionary defines this as "realism." To the half ruined Germans of January, 1924, the new *Sachlichkeit* meant, among other things, recognizing the failure of their ruinous, (not so) passive resistance to the Versailles Treaty and the need of seeking "equality of status" by fulfilling their obligations.

It is possible to view the years of treaty observance as a scheme to secure the evacuation of foreign forces from German soil—and then to defy the victors. And to German nationalists it was precisely that. But to me the Weimar Republic was much more than a contrived "incident between two wars." Millions of war-weary, peace-minded citizens wanted nothing better than the democratic republic, provided that it did not delay too long the restoration of that equality of status for which most of them never ceased to clamor.

There seemed therefore a reasonable chance that these reasonable citizens would, if only by sheer weight of numbers, prevail over the unreconciled few and ease the Fatherland back into the mainstream of European life.

In spite of its manifest handicaps, lack of legitimacy, a peace treaty that fell between the two stools of punishment and reconciliation, contained an admission of exclusive war guilt by Germany and what amounted to its unilateral disarmament, the Weimar Republic, I am still convinced, would have survived but for the world-wide depression of 1929 which hit Germany harder than any other European country and fostered the proliferation of communists.

Certainly, in those early fulfillment years, most Americans in Germany nourished a legitimate hope that Germany's defeat, humiliation, inflation and internal disorders had brought home to most citizens the folly of again seeking European hegemony.

Not but what the opposing forces were strong. I had an early warning. In the train that brought me from Rome to Berlin, German industrialist informed me that Germany would rid itself of the Versailles Treaty or perish. "And if we perish, Europe will perish with us," he shouted.

It was clear that the German revolution, having been made on order, was no true revolution at all, and the Scheidemann's proclamation of the republic was more or less an accident. The spectacle of Adolf Hitler defying his judges at Munich, and the eulogies of war which I heard from young "racist" ex-soldiers around Count Ernst zu Reventlow —these two were not without effect. In fact, after some months in Berlin I informed my brother that while over half of the Germans unquestionably supported the republic, its opponents were on the whole more energetic and influential.

For while the Weimar constitution was in some ways a model of democracy, it offended the inhabitants of the smaller federal states by its centralization and gave the President the right to rule by decree law for three months without parliamentary confirmation whenever he chose to declare a national emergency. Even worse, it prescribed the election of the Reichstag members by proportional representation. A similar system had proved to be the ruin of postwar Italy, as I had witnessed. How provide a firm and lasting parliamentary majority with twenty-five or thirty competing parties in the field, some of them intent on overthrowing the state?

The election to the presidency of the elderly Field Marshall Paul von Hindenburg, the very leader whose defeat was responsible for Germany's misery, was another eye-opener. Hindenburg got a plurality of a million votes. Two million other Germans, whose votes could have elected the Catholic democrat, Wilhelm Marx, and thereby changed the course of history, wasted them on the communist candidate, Ernst Thaelmann. Clearly, to survive, the Weimar Republic must last long enough to build up an unshakable consensus among the new generation. As Santayana had written, "Existence itself is not a good but only an opportunity."

In January, 1924, what mattered most to the German people was economic relief. Production was almost stagnant, the cost of living the highest in the world. Impoverished Germany was again paying reparations, but under new conditions to be devised by the recently appointed International Committee of Experts, headed by the Chicago banker and erstwhile general, Charles G. Dawes of Chicago. So the Germans bent all their efforts to this end.

During my first six months in Germany, I sent thirty or more dispatches on the subject of reparations, currency, trade, bankruptcies, living costs, and the like. In the process I interviewed many authorities: Finance Minister Hans Luther, a technician rather than a politician; Foreign Minister Gustav Stresemann; Reichswehr Minister Otto Gessler, the Bavarian Democrat whom many held responsible for keeping the army free of civilian control; Geheimrat Hermann Buecher, head of the powerful National Association of Germany Industry, and his gifted assistant, Erwin Respondek; the nationalist editor, Cuno Westarp, at that time the chief opponent of any reparations plan; and a little later, the "great" industrialist Karl Fredrich von Siemens. For the *News* I wangled an article from a former Vice President of the Reichsbank, and became friends with two gifted economists, M. J. Bonn and Melchior Palyi, as well as with Edmund Stinnes, the "dissident son" of the Ruhr magnate.

Finally I extracted an interview from Germany's "savior," Reichsbank President Hjalmar Horace Greeley Schacht, the chief author of the currency stabilization. Schacht characteristically bade me "warn" the French: no evacuation of the Ruhr, no more reparations! Schacht, I saw, was a neurotic whose outstanding ability was accompanied by an unusual appreciating of his own greatness. Tall, thin, with narrow shoulders and a long neck encased in a two-inch stiff collar, he looked at the world through or over his glasses with the expression of an indignant pouter pigeon. Yet a little flattery immediately melted his *hauteur*. Noting this, I solemnly assured him that no other living German could so forcefully yet lucidly have expounded his country's viewpoint—and received an invitation to visit him again whenever I had other questions.

My most useful economic contact was, however, a partner in the *Berliner Handelsgesellschaft*, Siegfried Bieber, who knew the United States. Bieber made me a member of his weekly lunch club, or *Stammtisch*, at the excellent Peltzer Grill in the Neue Wilhelmstrasse. From him and his friends I regularly learned what was going on in business and financial circles. In consequence, my cabled explanations of the various ramifications of the reparations problem astonished not only my brother but the Chicago editors as well. Where had Edgar learned so much about finance? For thanks to the *Stammtisch*, I was able to bone up on a given subject before putting questions to the experts. Another friend in time of doubt was Gustav Stolper, editor of the weekly *Deutsche Volkswirt*, similar to the London *Economist*. When other sources failed, a telephone call or a visit to Stolper usually filled the lack.

I also struck up a lasting friendship with Owen D. Young, of the Dawes Committee, and through him with the subsequent young Agent General for Reparations, S. Parker Gilbert. From the Agent General's able assistant, Shepard Morgan, a former newsman, I obtained several scoops. Nowhere is the proverb, "To him who hath shall be given," more appropriate than in news reporting. Soon a leading German newspaper was asking the former "man of letters" for an article on the attitude of American business toward Germany.

But I anticipate. After a new parliamentary election in December, 1924, produced a majority in favor of the Experts' Plan, Germany obtained a series of loans whereby foreigners provided the reparation funds which organized domestic industry and labor *would* not, and the German masses *could* not, supply. (At Christmas, 1924, some fifty Berliners committed suicide because of economic misery.)

Among American, and some British, financiers the lending epidemic raged much as the St. Vitus dance mania had in certain medieval towns. Impervious to objective political facts, deaf to warnings by newsmen like me who pointed out the abnormality of the Germans' thirst for *unprofitable* loans, foreign bankers rushed to Germany and handed out the billions they and their depositors had made as profits during the war.

Their fixation on Germany was the more remarkable because both France and Belgium were not only in greater need of reconstruction, but showed no signs of the political instability always present beneath the surface of the Weimar Republic. Yet these otherwise rational bankers had almost unanimously decided that defeated Germany was the most dependable country in Europe.

The result was the maddest financial bat since the tulipomania of Holland in 1637 when people paid as much as twenty-six hundred guilders for a single bulb. But the Dutch buyers obtained a flower, whereas most of the American and other lenders to Germany got, after a few years of exaggerated interest, nothing at all.

The Chicago *Daily News* maintained in Berlin, as in other capitals, a visitors' bureau where tourists could write, read the newspapers, and, with special permission, dictate to the secretary. About 1927, on instructions from Chicago, I moved the bureau to the finest site in all Berlin, the "Kranzler Corner," where Friedrichstrasse intersects Unter den Linden. It was directly above the most famous café in the city, in a building which, according to a police document, was "one of those which have been built by His Majesty the King" (Frederick the Great) "whose permission is necessary for any changes in it." The Weimar Republic made no objections to my turning the second floor into a very attractive headquarters for American visitors. And a great many dropped in, including bankers who sometimes discussed their plans with their host.

Thus I renewed an old friendship with David Friday, formerly on the economics faculty of the University of Michigan, and made the further acquaintance of Henry Goldman, Harry Stuart, the great Otto Kahn, and that boldest of business buccaneers, Samuel Insull.

With Friday and Goldman I argued long and heatedly over the advisability of extending so much credit to the Germans. The former was convinced, as I might have been had I been living somewhere else, that since the Germans had disowned the Kaiser, they were irrevocably democratic, "much like us."

Goldman went further. He considered that innocent Germany had been pushed into the war by Russia (the untenable thesis of American historians, Henry Elmer Barnes and Sidney Fay) and had then been subjected to the "criminal" Treaty of Versailles. Postwar Germans wanted nothing except to cooperate on an equal footing in the maintenance of world peace. The Kapp Putsch, illicit rearmament, ritual (*Vehme*) murders of republicans by fanatical nationalists—all these were in his eyes normal by-products of French mistreatment. Nothing pleased him more, he insisted, than to leave vindictive and decadent France for peaceful *gemuetlich* Germany.

Otto Kahn, another pro-German, insisted that it was the mission of the United States to save the world.

Certainly, the Germans were taking all they could get. The Reich used part of its borrowings to pay reparations and part to improve roads and railroads. Federal states and cities put theirs into new public buildings, schools, gymnasia, playgrounds, swimming pools, planetaria, which the victorious countries managed to do without, and often reserved half of the principal to pay the interest.

In March, 1928, Owen D. Young, in an interview with me, expressed his own alarm at German borrowing to finance extravagant home consumption. In May, the Agent General warned against further unproductive loans and at the same time urged the creditors to fix a date for the end of reparations, which the original Experts Committee had been unable to do. Borrowing continued merrily. And although I reported my belief that the "ruling elements" in Germany intended to meet their obligations as they fell due, I felt bound to add: "All that one might ask is whether the Germans are not artifically doing all in their power to diminish their capacities of payment."

This suspicion had been publicly expressed by, of all persons, Ernst Thaelmann, as early as 1925, when he flatly stated that the Americans would never recover the money lent to, or invested in, Germany. But who would listen to a communist?

My *Stammtisch* acquaintances insisted that the affluence was artificial. Certainly, as planned by the wily Dr. Schacht, the state remained poor. When, in 1928, the loan stream slackened, unemployment rose sharply.

Meanwhile, I had become aware of a plan to compel the Allies to concede ever more *Gleichberechtigung*.

To the success of this plan, the election to the Presidency of the old Field Marshal, von Hindenburg, was probably essential. It enabled German negotiators at crucial moments to point out to the Allies what might happen should the current fulfillment policy fail to benefit the Fatherland. Various signs of popular devotion to the former empire were also effective: revival of the old flag and wartime uniforms, handsome compensation to the former sovereigns, consistent pardons to "nationalistic" rioters and assassins on those rare occasions when the courts condemned them, and, above all, the maintenance of the Reichswehr "above politics," meaning uncontrolled by the civilian government.

The chief actor in the plan was Gustav Stresemann.

Externally Stresemann had none of the marks of a successful diplomat except for an attractive wife. He looked like a Prussian barkeeper, overweight, bald, with undistinguished features, a harsh voice.

And nonetheless, as Foreign Minister from 1924 to his death in October, 1929, this "reformed" imperialist went a long way toward obtaining "equality of status" for Germany. This he achieved by what he called *Schaukelpolitik*, a seesaw policy between the Western powers and the Soviet Union, without full commitment to either.

On the one hand, by accepting the Dawes Plan, signing the Locarno Pact, and entering the League of Nations (strictly on his own terms); by discussing the settlement of other disputes with Briand at Thoiry, and verbally approving the latter's dream of a United Europe; by accepting the second, or Young, plan on reparations and signing the utopian Kellogg-Briand pact "outlawing" war, Stresemann got the Allied Military Commission and the last occupying troops out of Germany three years ahead of schedule.

On the other hand, he refused to sign an "Eastern Locarno" or to accept the new frontier with Poland! For eighteen months he secretly negotiated a "treaty of friendship" with the U.S.S.R., holding off his signature until he had lulled French suspicions by the Locarno agreement. Yet four days before he signed that agreement, he granted the Soviet Union a huge credit. This, Herbert von Dirksen, a leading German diplomat, gleefully called a "little Locarno" and "a revivifying injection . . . into the organism of Russo-German friendship." Stresemann further developed the secret military cooperation between Berlin and Moscow whereby the latter obtained ever more German-built arms factories, while the former used Soviet facilities for training German officers in flying, tank strategy, submarine warfare, and the like, all forbidden at home by the Versailles Treaty.

In seeking drastic treaty revisions, as in previously encouraging inflation, Stresemann had the support and advice of the British. At the Peace Conference in Paris, as I wrote in *Harper's*, "the realistic British took their swag in cash—ships, colonies and German investments and thereafter they were quite willing to make peace and get down to business." Germans called the British Ambassador in Berlin, Lord D'Abernon, the "Lord Protector" of Germany's secret rearmament. They credited him with first suggesting to Stresemann the Locarno Pact and the Thoiry discussions with Briand. On one occasion in Antonina Vallentin's salon in Berlin, D'Abernon personally explained to some of us that Britain's interest lay in reducing France's military preponderance as rapidly as possible.

In my opinion, *Schaukelpolitik* was something that Stresemann and D'Abernon worked out together. And successful it was. Even disarmed, Germany was, by 1927, again a Great Power.

Schaukelpolitik was made easier by the fact that the German Foreign Office contained both "east" and "west" oriented diplomats whom the Minister played against each other. Leading among "Easterners" were Baron von Maltzan, the real author of the Rapallo Treaty, with whom I had become acquainted at Genoa, and Count Brockdoff-Rantzau, the German ambassador in Moscow. Maltzan was a shifty-eyed man with a cynical humor who went in 1925 as Ambassador to Washington in order to wangle American support for Stresemann's policies—and died in an airplane accident two years later.

Brockdorff-Rantzau was an outspoken nationalist who considered an exclusive "east orientation" as the quickest road to a revival of Germany's lost power. A German-Russian partnership would be unbeatable. No *Schaukelpolitik* for him.

Whatever else it did, German-Russian "friendship" made Soviet diplomats and German communists more socially acceptable than in other Western capitals.

Literally "everybody," except diplomats of countries that (like the United States) did not recognize the U.S.S.R., attended the Russian November receptions in the sumptuous former tsarist embassy Unter den Linden. During this period the guests "evolved" from tieless workingmen to dignitaries in white tie and tails, a remarkable de-proletarization. There was little political conversation but much overcrowding. To most guests, the climax of the evening came when the dining room doors opened and they could rush upon a mountain of the finest Molossol caviar brought specially from Russia. Those who had waited too far from the dining room door often got none.

Yet Ambassador Krestinsky was a courteous, if informal, host. Furthermore, he was not afraid to discuss matters with a "bourgeois" newsman or introduce a visiting Soviet Ambassador, Madame Kollontai. He also encouraged me to talk with the Soviet Minister of Public Instruction, Anatoly Lunacharsky, the most civilized Russian communist I had met since I lunched with Leonid Krassin at Rapallo in 1922.

Ivy Litvinov, English-born wife of the Soviet Foreign Minister, scandalized German communists by writing a newspaper article in which she commented favorably on the elegance in the Berlin shop windows. I had an almost human relationship with Mironov, then press attaché in Berlin, and with his successor, Sergei Vinogradov, a handsome masculine type who never hesitated to express an opinion. Certainly the Russian officials one met in Berlin in the twenties and early thirties had little in common with the browbeaten double-talkers of later years. Perhaps this explained why nearly all were eventually murdered by Stalin.

Berlin in the nineteen twenties was a kind of stopping off place not only for Russians heading west, but for Americans entering or leaving

the Soviet Union, including those who lived there and needed occasionally to come up for air. Among these were newsmen like H. R.
Knickerbocker, Frederick Kuh, Walter Duranty, Eugene Lyons, William
Henry Chamberlin, and the author, Maurice Hindus. In addition,
Samuel Harper, the Russian specialist of the University of Chicago,
never went in or out of the Soviet Fatherland without pausing in Berlin
to report and enjoy a few good arguments.

These men had varying views of communism. Chamberlin, Kuh,
Hindus, Lyons, and Harper were for some years hopeful about the
revolution. Duranty always got along well with the Kremlin. He argued
that the Russians deserved nothing better.

Knickerbocker, on the other hand, recognized from the first that
the U.S.S.R. was at war with the world and prophesied that no good
would come of it. I trusted Knick's judgment.

Junius Wood of the Chicago *Daily News* looked on the Soviet
Union with such disdain that the Bolsheviks, unable to believe that
anyone would dare treat them as he did, let him get away with it.
Arriving in Russia for the first time, he immediately wrote a highly
critical piece. Promptly the censor called him in and said: "Mr. Wood,
you are new here, but I must warn you that if you write any more
dispatches like the last, which I have stopped, you will wake up some
morning to find yourself in Riga."

To which, Junius said: "Is that a threat or a promise?"

"I don't understand you, Mr. Wood."

"Do you believe I came to your God-forsaken country because I
wanted to? The greatest favor you can do me is to expel me and get
me sent somewhere else."

At another time, when foreign correspondents were called to the
Foreign Office in the middle of night only to be handed an "important
news announcement" at the door, Junius went home and wrote:

"According to the doorman at the Soviet Foreign Office," etc. etc.
Again the censor intervened, but Junius remained in Russia as long as
the paper wanted to keep him there.

And gradually, one by one, several of the original enthusiasts,
Chamberlin, Lyons, and, in 1939, even Sam Harper, turned thumbs
down on the "great experiment."

Thanks to the comings and goings of these and other Soviet experts, Berlin was probably better informed about events in Russia than
other Western capitals.

Furthermore, it was to Berlin that the Russians first brought their
highest accomplishments in stagecraft, movies, ballet, and music. Soviet
theatrical producers made me realize how influential Marinetti's futurism
had been in stimulating revolutionary art in faraway Russia, the last
place one might have expected to find it.

German communists and fellow travelers we saw less often, although there were plenty of them. Occasionally, we met the playright,
Ernst Toller, and the more gifted Bertold Brecht, the former fairly

oozing sentimentality, the latter more anarchist than communist, with an almost sadistic view of life. Boris and Lili Keith we met frequently. Boris, an apolitical Russian painter, was at most a nominal Bolshevik. His German wife, Lili, was the Berlin correspondent of Soviet newspapers, and passionately procommunist. Ernst Toller, the Munich revolutionist of 1919, may have influenced the Soviet theater with his dramas, *Massemenseh, die Maschinenstuermer,* and *Hinkemann.* But personally he seemed unbelievably unrevolutionary, a pathetic figure.

Otto Katz, a Czech, some thought an agent of the Kremlin. Good looking, sharp of mind, he turned up regularly in Bohemian society.

His wife, a shapely little creature, regularly astonished social gatherings by standing on the nape of her neck with her legs straight in the air—like a "candle." I have a notion that she was some kind of gymnastic teacher. During subsequent years I ran into Otto, now calling himself André Simone, in the strangest places, Paris, Mexico City, and the like, only to read in December, 1952, that he had been done to death by the very communist killers whom he had done so much to put in power in Prague.

Another remarkable revolutionary, introduced to us by Dorothy Thompson, was "Red" Count Michael Karolyi, who had been successively Prime Minister and President of "Red" Hungary. Karolyi resigned after a few months and escaped when the Rumanians overthrew the "People's Republic" and established the regency under Admiral Horthy. He found refuge in Czechoslovakia and came frequently to Berlin. Although after the Second World War he became communist Hungary's diplomatic representative in Paris, I still believe, in the absence of conclusive evidence to the contrary, that Karolyi was a sensitive idealist whose hatred for the sternly enforced privileges of his and other highborn families drew him to the side of those "underdogs" for whom he imagined communism to be speaking.

A unique and exotic friend was the Liberian Consul General in Hamburg, who lunched with us regularly when he visited Berlin. Momelu Massaquoi had unsuccessfully run for President against President King and managed to get out of the country in time to escape Mr. King's retaliation. Whereupon the latter generously made him the country's highest diplomatic officer in Germany.

About 1930, I should say, he invited me to visit Liberia. When I expressed my inability to persuade Chicago to send me there, Momelu insisted that the *News* would be shortsighted if it overlooked his offer.

"Edgar, if you go to Liberia, I guarantee that you will see things no white man has even seen before."

My journalist's ears twitched. "What, for instance?"

"I shall have you initiated into my tribe, the *Vai,* one of the largest in West Africa. Look"—and he stripped off his shirt. From shoulder to shoulder and from neck to waist, his back was divided, apparently by a knife, into squares the size of a finger nail. "This is the sign of our tribe," he explained.

As one who shrinks from a simple injection, I shuddered at the prospect of undergoing similar "vaccinations." Still—"What else?" I asked hopefully.

"I'll see that you go out with the Leopard Men."

"I've heard of them, but who exactly are they?"

"They are the people who descend from leopards. You think all men come from monkeys. We believe they spring from various animals."

"Anatomically, that theory poses a problem, but I have known tiger men and rabbit men. What do Leopard Men do nowadays?"

"Once a year, to commemorate their ancestry, they strip and put on a leopard skin, attach iron claws to their hands, crawl into the cabins of sleepers, slit their throats, and drink their blood."

In a flash I saw myself crawling half-naked through the jungle in the dark, fearful of snakes.

"Indeed, an unforgetable experience," I commented. "But between us, Momelu, just why do they wish to pretend to be leopards?"

He looked at me firmly. "Because they *are* leopards." And suddenly between us I felt the presence of three thousand years. . . .

Among "West-oriented" German diplomats, Otto Kiep stood out pleasantly. He had been born in Scotland, spent most of his young life in the British Isles, and served the Fatherland with distinction during the First World War. As a subsequent diplomat in Berlin and Washington, he never wavered in his hope of seeing Germany a full-fledged member of a West European community. Logically, therefore, he took part in the July, 1944, conspiracy against Hitler, and was executed by the Nazis. In the early twenties we saw a good deal of him and his beautiful young wife, Hanna.

Two other invaluable "Westerners" were Karl Ritter, head of the economic and reparations division of the Foreign Office, and Hans Schaeffer, State Secretary (highest permanent official) first of the Economics and then of the Finance Ministry.

Ritter, a bachelor, kept himself in fine condition by engaging in track. The Weimar Republic encouraged middle-aged people to run, jump, ski, and the like. My wife distinguished herself among her age group in running. Ritter became an inexhaustible source of information. In fact, in 1931 he tipped off Frederick Kuh and me to Germany's coming attempt to form a customs union with Austria as a prelude to political union, thus giving the United Press and the Chicago *Daily News* a world beat. The reports set off a European crisis that brought about the failure of the Viennese Credit-anstalt.

Schaeffer, a lawyer by training, with a broad understanding of economics, was hospitable and intelligent. At his *kleinbuergeliche* beer evenings (the favored form of entertainment in Berlin), the food and drink were plain, but the discussions magnificent. Although Schaeffer was a Social democrat, he regularly revealed how far the demand for "equality of status" had penetrated the German Left as well as the Right. This required, in his eyes, not only the departure of foreign soldiers, but the rapid return to the Fatherland of Germans unjustly separated by the Versailles Treaty. Usually the claim did not include the inhabitants of Alsace-Lorraine, who for half a century had demonstrated their preference for France. But it covered the Saarlanders and the people of Eupen-Malmedy, a territory which had been allotted to Belgium subject to subsequent plebiscite. And above all, it emphasized the recovery of the Polish Corridor and the "lost portion" of Upper Silesia. In some respects Schaeffer was contemptuous of Poles.

Friends of Gustav Stresemann have subsequently claimed that he felt that the age of nationalism was dying and that power was passing (in the West, at least) from national governments to economic combines. Certainly in 1926–27, he favored the creation of what I called, after long talks with its creator, Emil Mayrisch of Luxembourg, "probably the greatest economic organization in the world," namely, the Continental Steel combine. Even while the French and German governments were feuding about nearly everything, the industrial magnates of the two countries found no difficulty in cooperating.

In any case, Stresemann was in this respect an optimist. Far from "withering away," nationalism in Germany became more virulent with each French concession.

Did not Stresemann forsee this? Or did he really expect his use of the Russian threat abroad and the nationalist threat at home to make the French value his "European" outlook? Shortly before his death in October, 1929, he expressed his disappointment:

"I have worked with all my heart for peace and reconciliation, and have subordinated everything to reaching an understanding among Great Britain, France, and Germany. . . . It is now five years since Locarno. If the Allies had made one single concession, I could have kept the support of my countrymen. But the Allies have given nothing in return. Their few small concessions always came too late. Now the youth of Germany, which we had hoped to win for peace and a new Europe, is lost to both of us."

Certainly, to me it seemed that Germany was ridding itself of the burdens of defeat slowly but surely. Yet on one point I agreed with Stresemann: to expect Germany under the new Young Plan to transfer 121 billion more marks over the next fifty-nine years was incompatible with a policy of reconciliation. And for this the United States had to bear some of the blame. How America could legitimately expect France and Belgium to let off a beaten enemy, while maintaining its own demand for repayment of inter-Allied wartime debts baffled me. Yet that is what Coolidge and Hoover did—until the worldwide depression made myths of further reparations *and* debts.

To us it seemed no coincidence that Stresemann should have died on the very day of the break on the New York Stock Exchange which ended the era of beautiful nonsense in the United States and in a great many other countries as well. Two years earlier, a crash on the Berlin exchange had suggested that something was lacking in the picture.

After the New York stock débâcle and Stresemann's death, Germany's *Sachlichkeit* gave way gradually to a new irrationality. Thenceforth those too young to have fought in the great war listened to the pied pipers of nationalism leading them on to a new one. Rising unemployment, the startling growth of communism, and the deliberate sabotage of the Weimar Republic by infatuated conservatives and frenzied racists—these and not Allied intransigence were driving toward catastrophe.

One who bore a heavy responsibility for this was Dr. Schacht. The Reichsbank President originally went along with the Young Plan, then at the last moment refused to sign. Once the Reichstag had accepted the Plan, Schacht resigned from the Reichsbank with as much reverberation as possible. At the news, prices on the Berlin stock exchange sank fifteen points. Though he refused publicly to state his reasons for resigning, a phone call to his office brought him to the phone.

"How about letting me tell the American people just why you are quitting?" I asked.

"I have nothing to say."

"Dr. Schacht, *you* cannot do this. *You* are an international figure of the first magnitude. In fact, to people all over the world *you* and *you alone* really represent Germany. *You* owe these people an explanation," I rhapsodized.

A pause.

"How soon can you get here?"

Twenty minutes later I was hearing his explanation: he would not agree to Allied sanctions in case of nonpayment. Again the interview ended with an invitation:

"I hope you will come and see my pigs for I am going back to the farm. Before that, I shall take a trip around the world."

Thereafter Schacht used his leisure to induce German financiers and industrialists to throw their political and financial support to Adolf Hitler.

Looking back, it is clear that the German democrats missed whatever chance they had. As late as 1927, the former imperial regime was still in disrepute. The republicans had created a strong paramilitary organization, the *Reichsbanner*, which theoretically could checkmate any rebellion by the "patriotic" associations and the Black *Reichswehr*. They had the most read German newspapers.

Since the French could at that time choke off a German political movement by reoccupying the Ruhr, I saw no immediate danger. Nonetheless I predicted that any future overthrow of the republic would most likely start with a proclamation of an "exceptional condition" (emergency) by President Hindenburg.

In June, 1930, the departure of the last French troops (which I went to witness) was the signal for which the nationalists were waiting. Into the German celebrations of that event appeared a new note of defiance. Meanwhile, Social democrats in the Reichstag brought down the cabinet of Socialist Hermann Mueller. Foreign Minister Curtius, who had succeeded Stresemann, suddenly lost interest in any understanding with France that did not compel the Poles to restore the Corridor. Out of the blue, Hindenburg dissolved the Reichstag. Heinrich Bruening, who had succeeded Mueller as Chancellor, was given the power to rule the country by decree under Article 48 of the constitution, exactly as I had foreseen. As though in preparation for the new regime, the commanding general of the Reichswehr, Wilhelm Heye, was dismissed for wanting to proceed against officers involved in antirepublican plots, in favor of the "grey eminence," Kurt von Schleicher, a general with a taste for intrigue and an impenetrable ego, who confidently assumed that he could keep control of the "healthy" nationalism he was doing his best to foster.

With reaction literally "before the gates," the republican politicians entered into the election campaign with unusual zest and habitual blindness. Twenty-four separate parties competed for Reichstag seats. These included a "humanity party," a "house owner party," a "retail merchants' party," a "cultural party of the intellectual callings," and, for the first time in Germany, a "prohibition party." Political fever rose. So too did public cries for a dictator who would put an end to the "shameless intrigues and bickering of the politicians."

I missed the election itself. The Berlin Mowrers were due for home leave that very September, 1930. Since my brother generously volunteered to come to Berlin and cover the big event for me, Lilian, seven-year-old Diana Jane, and I embarked on the *Europa* at Bremerhaven, just two days before the voting. Only after the handsome liner cleared Cherbourg for New York did we hear the news from Germany: one hundred and seven of Hitler's Nazis had won seats in the Reichstag, thus becoming the second largest party. The communists had gained twenty-three seats. The lid was off, and with it the "great human future" foreseen by Count Keyserling.

16

Europe Between Wars

Europe, civilization of man in movement.
—EDMOND POGNAN

THE CHICAGO *Daily News* not only encouraged, it insisted on first-hand reporting. Editors Dennis, Smith, and Binder took it for granted that "the man on the spot is always right." No argument by cable; no tampering with his copy. Above all, no sitting tight in one spot and rewriting from local newspapers. Let him go look at a story and describe what he sees.

To a dedicated traveler like me, this demand was music. And Berlin a wonderful place from which to start. Strictly speaking, my territory consisted only of Germany, Poland, and, later, Denmark. But it could be occasionally stretched to include fringes like the "contested" Saar Territory and the districts of Eupen and Malmédy, Luxembourg, and even the Netherlands. Part of the time, too, the *Daily News* had no fixed correspondents in Vienna, which meant exceptional assignments to Austria, Czechoslovakia, Hungary, and, once, to Rumania.

Moreover I was frequently called to Paris, sent two or three times to Geneva and once to London, substituting for the regular correspondent.

Counting vacations, perhaps a tenth of my "Berlin period" was spent outside Germany.

Though the smallest of the continents, Europe offers a greater variety of scenery, peoples, political regimes and problems, art, ideas, and scientific achievements than any other.

A first task was investigating those areas that had been taken from the defeated Fatherland in 1919.

Saarbruecken was a smaller, duller Pittsburg in the midst of a landscape that must have been inviting before industrialization turned it into a drab mine and factory complex. It contained a few old churches and a baroque castle where I once lodged with the League of Nations High Commissioner, the Canadian, George Washington Stevens. French occupying troops were present but inconspicuous. Hatred of France was, however, as omnipresent as the mountains of coal that disfigured the landscape. In the mouth of the leading German industrialist, Hermann Roechling, whom I visited in his castle at Dillingen, anti-French feeling positively sizzled. In vain did I quietly remind him that just before asking for an armistice in 1918, the German army had deliberately flooded coal mines in France. In his inflamed mind, nothing his country did during a war could justify countermeasures in time of peace. A first visit to the Saar revealed that, given a chance, the Saarlanders would vote to return to Germany.

The Grand Duchy of Luxembourg also gave me a salutary political jolt. The countryside was similar to the Saarland, only prettier. The people looked Germanic. Among themselves they spoke an almost incomprehensible Teutonic patois. Yet their official language was French, and in sentiment they were more pro-French than the Belgian Walloons I had met during the war.

The village of Malmédy which Belgium had, for strategic reasons, annexed in 1919, presented a similar paradox. The German-speaking inhabitants of German-appearing Eupen naturally wanted to return to Germany. But so did most of the Francophonic citizens of Malmédy, who had names like Dupont. For France they had only a vague respect, and for Belgium a real dislike.

Luxembourg and Malmédy posed a moral and political problem. As a grandson of a Union soldier, I had always believed that the Southern States had no legal right to secede. But suppose that a common language and origin are not the primary elements in nationality? Suppose it is essentially a matter of choice? If a whole people is to be granted the right of "self-determination," why not part of it?

The same problem was even more starkly apparent in the East: the citizens of Danzig were a tight German island in a Polish sea.

Moreover, the majority of the three hundred thousand Polish-speaking *Masovians* around Allenstein in East Prussia (*Masurians* to the Germans) were satisfied to be German—in spite of Polish propaganda, as I verified on the spot.

Yet most citizens of the neighboring corridor were passionately Polish. The prewar German minority had largely packed up and left. Since Poland obviously could not depend upon hostile Germans for access to the sea, the Danzigers paid the price. Nor, in view of the previous mistreatment of Poland by Prussia and Russia combined, could I find this unjust.

Logically, of course, there was no good reason why the ancient

Hanseatic port of Danzig, as a Free State protected by the League of Nations, should not have gladly served as outlet for Poland's sea-borne trade. It had been a free port under Napoleon. But by 1924 the Poles were busy building the rival port of Gdynia allegedly because Danzig was unable to handle so much traffic. Another, perhaps more basic, reason became clear to me during a first visit there.

To nearly all Germans, *Polnische Wirtschaft* was a synonym for inefficiency and improvidence. To this condescension the Danzigers added a hatred that made cooperation a problem. A few hours in Danzig instilled the conviction (confirmed by the League's High Commissioner) that most Danzigers would rather vegetate *as Germans* than thrive as Free Staters!

Yet, politics aside, what a charming old place Danzig was! During the better part of its history, it had been the leader of the Hanseatic towns on the Baltic. It was certainly the most beautiful, with its brick Gothic and Barocco churches, its Dutch-type houses in the Frauengasse with their un-German stoops giving directly on the street. If only its atmosphere had been as scintillating as its *Goldwasser*.

Were the Poles being needlessly provocative? I had to find out. The signing in April, 1926, of the German-Russian Friendship Treaty directed against Poland was an invitation to visit Warsaw.

I immediately liked the city and the people. True, it was less tidy than Berlin. Parts of it, including the fascinating old ghetto near the River Vistula, were sadly dilapidated. Yet the *Old Square* was one of the world's finest and the Fukiera Tavern in the basement of a fine old house served an ancient Tokay wine superior to any I ever found in Hungary.

As a whole, the Poles were incredibly courageous and, understandably, nationalistic. They had no liking for Germans and even less for Russians. Materially, most of Poland was underdeveloped. But the officials whom I met were trying hard to catch up with the West. The intellectuals were gifted, entertaining, and very individualistic.

Unfortunately, their type of individualism was proving as great an obstacle to effective government now as it had been in the eighteenth century, when it brought Poland to ruin. Then any member of the Sejm could block a piece of proposed legislation by his single veto. Now with twenty-one parties represented, the parliament was behaving so irresponsibly that both the economy and the state finances were shaky. As I wired the *News,* the words most heard in parliamentary debate were *zloty, katastrofy,* and *skandall.*

Eight days after I (unfortunately) returned to Berlin, Marshall Pilsudski, the socialist hero of the battle of Warsaw, marched on Warsaw with his troops, overturned the government, and imposed a new constitution, with himself as boss. Thereafter, Polish political life went from bad to worse.

I visited Poland repeatedly; not only Warsaw, but the countryside. The counselor of the Polish Embassy in Berlin, Count Tadeusz Jackowski, welcomed the three Mowrers to his estate in Wronczyn, a few miles north of Poznan.

Society at Wronczyn was half feudal, half bohemian. Peasants knelt in the road to kiss the hand of the Count's guests, a procedure I found embarrassing. But how they could dance!

On the other hand, at Wronczyn we always met writers, actors, professors, and journalists. Conversation was witty and cosmopolitan. Countess Jackowska, née Anna Schiller and a vague relative of the great German poet dramatist, had been a well-known actress. Her brother, Leon ("Lulek"), managed a repertory theatre in Warsaw and was an acknowledged communist.

The farming on the estate of the German von Wegeners at Ostaczewo near Torun, the birthplace of Copernicus, in full Polish Corridor, was no more efficient than at Wronczyn.

In the thirties, when after Pilsudski's death, Poland fell into the hands of the "colonels," the amosphere became almost fascist. But where then in Central Europe was it otherwise?

In 1926, during a summer vacation at Abbazia, near Fiume, on the Gulf of Quarnero, then Italian, now part of Yugoslavia, I found the ever-present fascism so disagreeable that thereafter I avoided my beloved Italy as much as possible. The Italian ambassador in Berlin, Count Luigi Bosdari, became a sort of secret confederate. When once I hinted that Mussolini risked being assassinated, the Duce's ambassador said quietly: "That might be the solution."

Mutilated, disconsolate Austria was something else. One morning the newspapers carried an almost incredible story: easy-going Vienna was in the hands of striking socialists and communists who had burned the Palace of Justice in resentment against alleged judicial discrimination in favor of fascist "front fighters."

In Austria, as all newsmen knew, no situation, however "desperate," was "serious." Yet the following morning a cablegram from Chicago said laconically: "Go Vienna immediately."

Lilian brought a valise to Tempelhof Airport and I was off in the first plane. The frightened pilot would go no nearer Vienna than Bratislava, on the Austrian border.

Yet I reached the capital comfortably by taxi, found a room at the luxurious Hotel Bristol, and the next day, after the traditionally superb lunch at Sacher's, cabled Chicago that tourist buses were moving normally through the paralyzed streets and that the general strike would end at midnight. The mayor had conceded to the Social democrats ("responsible labor") the right to create a Republican militia. "War" between the Christian Socialist national government and Socialist Vienna was to go on, but in the *gemuetlich* Austrian manner, as I learned both from the commander of the republican guard, Dr. Julius Deutsch, and from the Catholic Minister of Trade, Josef Schurf. For a "scientific" explanation of the riot I turned to the eldest disciple of Sigmund Freud, Paul Federn. It ran like this:

The old Austrian empire had been the father. Once he had discredited himself and his children by losing a war, Viennese socialists tried to substitute a brother image. When continuing economic misery destroyed the people's faith in brotherhood and a new father started to appear, the disillusioned and furious children sought to destroy the physical basis of paternal authority, namely, the records and legal documents in the Palace of Justice. And by firing on the children, the police revived the latters' ancient fear of castration by the father. "The Vienna riots," Federn concluded, "were in the deepest sense a family row." So that was it.

By coincidence, just as I was about to return to Berlin, the death of King Ferdinand of Rumania brought a new cablegram: "Go Bucharest cover funeral." Thanks to my newspaper colleague, Marcel Fodor, whose knowledge of Central European and Balkan politics was encyclopedic, I wired from Vienna a full description of the political situation in Rumania left by Ferdinand's death and set off in the Orient Express.

In the same sleeper were Prince Babu Stirbey, an important Rumanian politician, the Rumanian Minister from Paris, and a former Rumanian chargé d'affaires in Washington, Radu Djuvara, who immediately took charge of me and greatly eased my task in Bucharest.

In much of Europe, Rumanians were an object of sarcasm—allegedly unstable, slightly effeminate, morally unprincipled, gifted at writing, "not a nationality but a profession." Stories of strange behavior in high places at Bucharest were standard lunch fare at Geneva.

Yet prepared as I was, I was startled when, shortly after reaching my room in what was reputed to be the best hotel, a bellboy brought me an album of photographs—naked call girls, any of them available.

My next impression was one of streets colorful with people; boyars and their pretty wives in European clothes, sturdy peasants in long white shirts, tight white trousers, and black sleeveless vests, their womenfolk in short white skirts and one, or sometimes two, colored aprons, all right out of the stories of Panait Istrati, a writer whom I greatly enjoyed. In the Calea Victoria bishops in black rubbed elbows with red-sashed workmen. I eagerly tasted the shashlik and caviar.

Djuvara and U.S. Minister Culbertson, a friend of the deceased king, got me the credentials that allowed me to pass beside the royal corpse on the catafalque in the Cotroceni Palace; all unperceived to watch six-year-old King Michael playing in a garden; and to attend the open air funeral at Curtea de Arges, in the foothills of the Transylvanian Alps.

Both the lying-in-state and the funeral were moving spectacles.

Yet in Rumania even the most solemn event can have a ludicrous touch. At Tempelhof, Lilian had provided me with the clothes she felt were appropriate for riots, nothing more. But protocol at the royal funeral required a black suit. Even as I was seeking to rent one, two young Rumanian acquaintances offered to lend me a tuxedo. But when, the hot sunny morning of the funeral, they brought to my hotel the coat of one, the trousers of the other, I found that the latter were six inches too voluminous around the waist! Too late to find others. I strapped my belt and buttoned the coat to hide the captive bulge.

Then off to Curtea de Arges. I happened to share a compartment in the train with the Rumanian representative of a Paris newspaper. When we reached the funeral chapel, he took me not to the press gallery fifty yards from the catafalque, but to the covered platform before the chapel entrance where lay the King's body.

"Stay here and pretend not to understand if anybody objects. I cannot be with you, I am too well known," he said in French. And back he walked to the press seats.

I found myself standing conspicuously at one side of the bier behind four black-robed Primates, while three queens and two princesses in black took up a position six feet away on the other side. I was able to describe everything, even the stones in the queens' abundant jewelry.

Yet each time I took my right hand from my belt to scribble in the notebook in the other hand, my trousers started falling! The deep voices of the priests were already chanting the litany: it was too late to withdraw. I spent the next half hour shifting my fingers rapidly from pencil to belt, barely avoiding a catastrophe.

When at the end I sought to follow the King's body and the royal ladies into the chapel, I found the stairs blocked by the Primate of Bessarabia on whose shoulder I had almost been leaning.

Again I heard the voice of the Rumanian newsman: "Go into the church." In reply I pointed to the obstructing Primate. "Push him, push him," he yelled, still in French. "Such people do not count in this country."

Dutifully, I elbowed my way past the Primate, entered the church, with the royal family inspected the still open crypt into which the body had just been lowered, made a few notes, and started on foot back to the funeral train. Everyone else had returned to the railroad station. Had I lingered too long? Anxiously I reached for my watch.

Gone! Hastily I went back over my itinerary, searching every foot of ground, stairs, and chapel. No watch. Someone must have taken it. Since last noting the time, I had been in contact with nobody but the Primates! The local chief of police grinned cynically when I explained my misfortune, accepted two dollars, and promised to forward the watch to Berlin—"if it turns up, but don't count on it."

From Berlin, I filed a political description of the country which the censors would not have passed in Bucharest. In spite of rumors, I wired, Rumania under the two Bratianu brothers, Jon and Ventila, was stable and at peace—"peace like that of Mexico under Porfirio Diaz, of Italy under Mussolini, of the Kingdom of Mother Goose under old King Cole."

I might have added, like the peace of Hungary under Admiral Nicholas Horthy, "regent" for the nonexistent "king," most of whose subjects passed their time muttering "no, no, never" to signify that they would not accept the mutilation of their former territory sanctified by the Treaty of Trianon.

Politically, Hungary made little sense. But what compensations! The people, particularly the young women, were the best looking I had seen. The cafés were filled with argumentative, brilliant intellectuals and chess fiends. Music and dancing were omnipresent even in the countrysides, and wild with the Gypsy strain. Budapest between the two wars provided little copy for an international newsman. But for a vacation it was unequalled, as many an American was finding to his surprise.

Prague was something else. A handsome old governing center on a hill, the Hrad, overlooking the lovely Moldau River, in the midst of a modern, almost Germanic-looking city. The people as industrious as Germans, as musical as Hungarians and Poles. Hiding a sort of magic medievalism under modern realism, democratic, highly literate, lacking in that desperate Polish will to resist alien violence at any cost, yet capable of an unyielding if slightly comical passive resistance of the type embodied in Jaroslav Hasek's *Brave Soldier Schwejk*.

Most Czechoslovaks in Prague refused to admit a knowledge of the German language. The correct approach for an American ignorant of their tongue was to start off in English, switch to French, then to Italian, and, still obtaining no response, finally to smile apologetically and say, "I fear we must speak German." At least in my case, it always worked. And everywhere I went, I found Czechoslovak friends.

Next stop, Copenhagen. In Europe, Denmark could be considered the antithesis of Rumania, the former orderly, totally literate, individually responsible, the latter, well, different. Yet in one respect the two peoples were alike: in their love of pleasure. Whereas Swedes and Norwegians, when sober, struck foreigners as somehow dour, Danes had, or seemed to have, a happier temperament. Nowhere but in Copenhagen did an amusement park play such a large role in the life of the citizens.

I liked the Danish mind. As a child I had been fascinated by Andersen's fairy tales. In my student days, Maude Edwards introduced me to the essays of the Danish critic, Georg Brandes, whose principles of criticism I greatly admired. In Austria, Lilian and I met the Danish novelist, Karin Michaelis, and several delightful young Danes. The newsmen at *Politiken* in Copenhagen were highly competent, well-informed, and generous to an American colleague.

But Denmark revived the suspicion I had acquired in Switzerland —that abstracting one's country from the main currents of history produces an unrealistic outlook. What could one think of a people who, having just retaken North Schleswig from defeated Germany, then imagined they could safely abolish their armed forces?

Not that I ever really knew Danish. During my several professional stays in the capital, I managed to decipher enough of the written language to follow simple events in the newspapers. But I never understood the speech. Danish pronunciation departs as greatly from written phonetics as English, which is saying a great deal.

Fortunately most educated Danes were polyglot.

Stockholm I got to only once. It was early in March when the ice was breaking up and the first whiff of spring in this raw latitude was even more intoxicating than elsewhere. My job was to find a replacement for a stringer whom the *News* had felt obliged to dismiss. Arriving at the Grand Hotel late one Saturday night, I weakly put off the distasteful task until Monday. Instead, on Sunday I presented an introduction to a Swedish family—and was invited to a formal dinner that same evening.

Originally stiff in manner, after four hours during which I was toasted six or eight times in aquavit, had champagne for dinner, and topped it off with whiskey after a game of bridge, my Swedish companions notably relaxed. When, to sober up a little, I expressed the intention of returning to my hotel on foot, one of the by now brotherly fellow guests accompanied me through the still snowy streets. At one point he stopped dead.

"I live here. You may not know it, but I am the greatest skater in Sweden. Come in and see my cups."

"Humm," I thought, "you are in them." Nonetheless, I entered to find myself in a great library-like room whose shelves were heavy with the silver trophies he had won on the ice. When I repeatedly declined a whiskey, he insisted on accompanying me to the Grand Hotel and having it there. Fortunately for me, if not for him, the bar closed before we arrived.

The next day, I visited the beautiful town hall with my hostess of the evening before, hired the stringer for the *News,* and left for comparatively sober Berlin.

However unfortunate for Europe, 1929 was a fascinating year for me.

In Munich, I interviewed the Bavarian Minister President, Heinrich Held, who had been publicly exchanging epithets with the Prussian Minister President. "Bavaria," I wrote, "is frothing like the foam on March beer in the vast chambers of the Hofbraeu House." Hence my visit was opportune. Herr Held emptied his Bavarian heart to me. What his countrymen wanted, he thundered, were "rights similar to those of a sovereign American state," thereby recovering enough "lost independence to remain Bavarians."

These were such fighting words that I secured his permission to submit my story for approval to the Bavarian Minister in Berlin. Having secured this gentleman's *placet,* I cabled the piece and departed for

Paris. The interview caused such an uproar in the German press that three weeks later I learned that Herr Held had declared my text to be "inexact." Since I still possessed the original with the Minister's signature, I wrote an open letter to the editors of newspapers in Munich, Frankfurt, and Berlin, giving full details. Whereupon the dispute shifted to the Reichstag with Herr Held still frantically protesting he had been misunderstood.

On the way to Geneva for a League of Nations Council meeting I spent a fantastic day in the train with the unaccountable theatrical genius, Gordon Craig, an old acquaintance. When he found me reading *Hamlet,* he immediately asked what I thought the play was all about. I replied that to me *Hamlet* was the greatest of all plays because, unlike *Macbeth* or *Lear,* and quite regardless of the crimes of Hamlet's mother, the real subject was the inescapable tragedy of *all human life.* Whereupon Craig fell upon my neck and announced that he and I were the only people who understood the play.

France remained the country I had known and loved. Yet in spite of Briand's persistent attempts to create a united Europe without war, there was a new emptiness in French public life. Some attributed this to desperately heavy wartime losses in a society where male children were scarce, to the nearness of revolution and defeat in 1917, and to the postwar "abandonment" of France by the "Anglo-Saxons."

Intellectually the atmosphere was different too. Many of my old friends were still there and active. Romains and Duhamel had both embarked on their respective series of novels, *Men of Good Will* and *Les Thibault.* Arcos and Bazalgette were editing a broadly international magazine, *Europe.* The former was also publishing magnificent books in richly illustrated *Editions du Sablier,* including several by Romain Rolland, and impressively masculine woodcuts by the Flemish engraver, Franz Masereel.

The Latin Quarter was thick with foreigners, many of them American. I talked regularly with the gifted young Chicagoan, Ernest Hemingway, whom I had first met in Genoa in 1922. Since then, he had written several books in a new, very American style which was to affect all Western writing. Joyce had published *Ulysses.* Gertrude Stein was deforming the language to the plaudits of all experimenters. Why, I wondered heretically, did Joyce and she insist on a new medium when they had nothing particularly valuable to say in the old one?

From Paris Chicago sent me to London to fill in for an absent correspondent. After the worried continent, there was a delightful stability about that great city and one felt the late war far less. Bloomsbury was a-blooming. Dominant in literature seemed to be D. H. Lawrence (all of whose books I had read with interest but without excessive admiration) and the young American poet, T. S. Eliot.

I took over the correspondent's desk in the *News'* office on Trafalgar

Square just in time to announce the opening of the first London-Bombay airline; to watch the eighty-first Oxford-Cambridge boat race from an airplane ("too much study at Oxford," old Oxonians complained when Cambridge won again); to chronicle the perennial Anglo-American business disputes; to register the "unseasonable" heat wave (almost seventy degrees!); to see the triumphal entry into Parliament of the "flapper M.P.," Jennie Lee (whom I got to know); and, best of all, to become well acquainted with my wife's family. With her brother Leslie, an ex-flight officer, I took long and fascinating walks through the immense city. Father Leo seemed to me to represent unconquerable England at its best. Thanks to the assistance of Lord Thomson (born Christopher Birdwood), a former general who had joined the Labour Party, my political dispatches were considered highly informative.

Somewhat earlier, the plainsman Mowrer and his London-born wife had become mountainers for at least three weeks each year. Just who persuaded us to take up skiing at Tre Croci in the Dolomites I cannot remember. Lots of Germans were "running ski" (pronounced shee, Norwegian fashion). But we both loved walking. Lilian had the physique of a born climber, and little Diana Jane was soon practicing vehemently.

For several years we "went to school" to the Austrian ski teacher and novelist, Hubert Mumelter, a rugged out-of-doors man who loved mountains more than anything in the world. He was also an amateur caricaturist and his cartoons of the various guests, his pupils, took some of the smart out of the many bruises that are, I assume, the fate of every ski-learner. In fact, we became so attached to Mumelter (called Bill for short) that when he shifted to another winter hotel at Monte Pana nearer Innsbruck, we dutifully followed him.

Skiing was a sport in which my missing ribs were no handicap. And Bill was such a good teacher that in the course of ten or twelve years, after further instruction at the famous ski school at Zuers, we were able to "do" most of the famous runs in Europe, whether in Austria, Germany, Switzerland, France, or Italy.

Winter vacations at high altitudes seemed even more restorative than Mediterranean swimming. Above all, I found those otherwise inaccessible snowcaps beautiful beyond description. Never have I felt a sweeter thrill than when swishing down a two-mile slope in new snow under a blue sky with the sun glinting on great peaks above glistening trees.

The Giant Mountains on the German-Czech border were more accessible. On winter weekends we took the train from Berlin to Hirschberg and then climbed up over the frontier to a Sudeten German *Baude* on the Czech side.

On one occasion, with Raymond Swing and his family, we spent a few days skiing in the Harz Mountains, including a climb to the top of the Brocken.

At Arosa I made long overland trips with a Swiss army lieutenant.

Undoubtedly the most grandiose of my ski excursions was a climb from the Britannia Hut above Saas-Fee to the top of the fourteen-thousand-foot Impfischhorn. The view was superb. Coming down, my career almost ended when, on an icy ridge near the top, the guide slipped and for a moment, five roped climbers tottered above a two-thousand-foot drop. Never have I known anyone so penitent as that Swiss guide.

In the course of these years, I came to feel that I knew Europe as well as I did my own country.

17

This American World

Others appeal to history; the American appeals to prophecy.

A LONDON PERIODICAL, 1821

IN 1917 Chancellor von Bethmann-Hollweg had wisecracked that since Americans could "neither fly nor swim," no significant number of them would ever reach Europe. Eighteen months later, weary German armies faced two million fresh American doughboys.

By the early twenties signs of Americanization were appearing all over Europe, and nowhere so conspicuously as in Germany. This puzzled me for a while: why should the demonstration of American military power produce mimesis in nonmilitary fields? Previously it had existed only in dentistry. Thinking hard, I came to see that such mimesis had regularly occurred. As I described it shortly thereafter:

"Military activity stirs such deep places in the human heart that the conquering soldier knows no rival in popular prestige, if only his success be dazzling enough. Brilliance is essential; it was not homely Republican Rome which dazzled the world—it was the visibly triumphant Empire of plundered province and plutocracy. Not the fear but the glamor of Islam's triumphant scimitar converted men wholesale to Allah. . . .

"Spanish pikemen and colonial conquistadores spread Spanish culture and customs throughout Europe. A century later, it was the turn of France. For a whole century there was hardly a reigning princeling but sought to reflect some of the radiance of the Roi-Soleil. When, after a series of smaller successes, Britain finally downed Napoleon, she acquired not only territory but French prestige. Her pre-eminence lasted until 1870 when Germany gave France a drubbing and blossomed out as a pattern for the world. . . . No amount of Rhodes scholars or exchange professors from France could shake the belief of Americans in German academic superiority—until the Great War. Then it was no time before they discovered a fact hitherto negligible: that German life and education were organized to the ideals of a social and political order almost completely alien to our own. . . . But had Germany and her allies won the war within the first six months? . . .

"It is as the military power that successfully raised millions of armed men from the ground at Myrmidon speed, brought them to Europe through infested seas and gave the *coup-de-grâce* to mighty Germany that America today impresses most of the world." And drastically hastened the Americanization of Europe.

Obviously, this was not the whole story. In part, Americanism moved into a vacuum created by a European civil war. But it was also deliberately imported by admiring Europeans.

As early as 1922, German intellectuals like Hermann Keyserling resurrected de Tocqueville's prediction that the United States and Russia would dominate the future. And like Keyserling, most of them were of two minds about it, at one moment welcoming the development, at another warning darkly against the American people's shocking lack of *Geist*.

Both attitudes struck sympathetic, if opposing, chords in me.

I was proud of my settler ancestors, of their self-reliance, their readiness to cooperate, their attachment to what Santayana properly called "English liberty," and above all, of their classless democracy. Europe offered less of all these.

But the latest developments in the United States rubbed me the wrong way. Even while accepting the benefits it conferred, I disliked mechanized industry with its brutal devastation of natural beauty, its pollution of once pristine rivers, its excessive emphasis on ever greater consumption. Although I remained devoted to my businessman father, I disliked government of, by, and for business. America the free had become primarily America the prosperous, the land of unlimited (economic) opportunity.

France first revealed to me that some societies not only esteemed modest-living artists and intellectuals, scientists, and educators more than successful politicians and businessmen, but on the Left Bank in Paris, in Soho in London, in Berlin, in Munich, and in Warsaw, took pride in them as nonconforming individuals. This became to me a test of civilization.

Moreover, our American democracy, however genuine, did not preclude a pharisaical assumption that we were, thank God, not like other men, particularly not like "class-ridden Europeans" with "their eternal wars." In his book, *Our Foreign Policy*, my brother Paul had severely criticized the self-satisfaction that was preventing (or serving as a pretext for preventing) our wholehearted participation in the postwar world. I was convinced that the Administrations' attempt to substitute endless talk of peace and international law without teeth for membership in both an Anglo–French–American alliance and in the League of Nations proposed by Wilson, was irresponsible folly.

Something of this feeling was, I think, common to those many American expatriates who remained in, or flocked to, Europe after 1919. Even when I did not share their artistic tastes, I knew only too well why they were there.

Shortly after my return from Chicago in 1923, René Arcos asked me to write my impressions of my country for his magazine, *Europe*. The result, published in May, 1925, was critical to the point of injustice. The war had left "Europe's organic society moribund." So the future, obviously, belonged either to Russia or to the United States. But "if there be any civilized morrow for a society rooted in intellectual democracy and plutocratic industrialism, the United States should see it first." To reach that morrow might, I suggested, take fifty to a hundred years.

The article provoked a certain reaction, favorable from Europeans, unfavorable from all but expatriate Americans. I had expected the criticism. But the Europeans' praise made me realize how incomplete my description was. Even while I wrote, the conditions I deprecated were spreading from the United States to Europe, to be decried or welcomed as Americanization. Obviously, in my article I had said too much or too little. What had made, what still made, us Americans different from our European cousins? I spent the next years trying to find out. The result was my second book, *This American World*.

The basic theme was that after a long period of spiritual separation, the United States and Europe were drawing together again. But this time, because of Europe's cultural decline and recent disastrous war, the tide was running from the New Country back to the Old Country. To demonstrate this, I had not merely to cite the spread of chewing gum, but also to ask what *were* those elements in America which first distinguished it from Europe and were being imitated abroad? How far would Americanization go in Europe? And finally, what would come of it, anyway?

All in all, quite a task for a newsman. But very appropriate for an American writer culturally conditioned to both continents. Particularly, if he lived in Berlin. Of all the European peoples, the Germans were offering less conscious resistance to what European traditionalists were beginning to call the "American blight."

In my newspaper reports, I identified 1925 as "the first great American year in Europe" and noted how "that complex of factors, personal democracy, technique and the standardization of produce," along with Taylorism and advertising methods, "had bitten deep into the German soul." Shortly thereafter my economist friend, Dave Friday, announced, during a visit to Berlin, that the introduction of mass production was making Germany "the United States of Europe."

The year 1926 saw the introduction of installment buying there. Someone at the National Health Week Conference solemnly warned that "prohibition had demoralized American public life." In 1928 I reported that while the men were faithful to beer, German women were happily devouring ice cream sodas. A Chicago-type gang war (some Germans had previously organized a chapter of the Ku Klux Klan!), an American-type women's suffrage convention, U.S. movies, a mink coat scandal involving Berlin Mayor Boess—all signs of the current running ever more strongly from America to Europe. The famous Austrian novelist, Jacob Wassermann, let out a warning blast: America was indeed a hope for Europe but also a danger because ruled by women! None of which prevented German diplomats from competing for Washington posts. . . .

Berlin had become the mecca of American visitors to Europe. In Berlin a repentant Isidora Duncan, after her unhappy adventure as the wife of Serge Essenin in Russia and her stupid plaudits of communism, begged me to announce that "a dancer, homeless . . . nameless and moneyless, would like to marry an American in order to regain her American citizenship." American actors, musicians, writers from Anita Loos to Sinclair Lewis, singers, dancers, Sonja Henie, ocean flyers, politicians like Jimmy Walker, all flocked to Germany to be feted. Oscar Hammerstein sought to purchase a Berlin theater. German actor Werner Kraus and producer Leopold Jessner admitted that acting in the United States was generally superior to that in Europe. Alfred Palitzsch wrote a play about Henry Ford.

All these items were grist to the writer of *This American World,* which J. H. Sears and Company published early in 1928. Curtis Brown had found me an English publisher, Faber and Faber, and managed to secure a preface from no less a celebrity than T. S. Eliot. In it, with an enthusiasm as genuine as it was unexpected, Eliot summarized the purpose and content of the book:

"Mr. Mowrer's book is a study in the philosophy of history, in the same sense as the work of Spengler, but written with a lighter hand and with no hard and fast theory into which to fit his facts. It is a study of the future of Americanism both within and outside of America.

"The majority of American criticisms of America, however intelligent, suffer from a pre-occupation with the local aspects of the problems. . . . The majority of foreigners think either of Americanization as something to be welcomed and exploited, or as a plague to be quarantined; and either point of view is apt to be superficial. Mr. Mowrer goes farther. He inquires into the origin, as well as the nature, of Americanism; traces it back to Europe; and finds that what are supposed to be the specifically American qualities and vices, are merely the European qualities and vices given a new growth in different soil. Europe, therefore, in accepting contributions the danger of which Mr. Mowrer certainly does not palliate, has contracted a malady the germs of which are bred in her own system. Americanization, in short, would probably have happened anyway: America itself has merely accelerated the process.

"This is an idea which must have occurred to many thoughtful minds, but which has never been so fully and cogently developed as here.

"Mr. Mowrer's observation is given greater force and more particular interest by the brief account of his own origins and beginnings:

" 'Not to have the frontier in one's blood makes emotional understanding of the United States impossible. On this account Americans divided into two groups, the older stocks and the new-comers. The latter are strong in the cities. They almost monopolize certain branches of our life, they dress, conduct themselves, talk and think like descendants of old settlers—but they do not feel as they. That is why so much that is admirable in American arts and letters, the work of the later arrivals, does not touch the older stocks, why to the sixth generation American, New York often seems as alien as Vienna or Amsterdam.' "

Eliot's words filled me with pride. Perhaps I could manage to be both a good newsman and a significant writer.

In retrospect, my conception of Europe as a unit and my prediction of a single Atlantic bloc (unless communism seized Europe first) seem more timely than my very qualified acceptance of Oswald Spengler's theory of history. Meanwhile, I insisted, "although the period be 'American,' the epoch is still 'European' and Americanism is merely the form in which Euro-American civilization will conquer the earth." Even my anticipation of America (not Russia!) as the "new Rome," although previously made by others, seemed new to many.

The English edition attracted attention in Europe, if only because of Eliot's preface. Arnold Bennett gave it a favorable review. My brother-in-law, Charles Maltby, an insurance man with a voracious appetite for reading, who had never quite understood how his wife's sister could marry an American and a "scribbler" at that, was moved to send me a cordial, reasoned dissent from my assumption of Europe's essential unity. He wrote:

"I am afraid my insularity prevents me from assenting to many of your premises, at least so far as this country is concerned. They may of course be perfectly correct for the rest of Europe; but it requires quite a serious effort for an Englishman to remember that—geographically at least—he is really part of Europe and this feeling has been intensified rather than lessened by the war. After all, we are hardly four generations removed from the days of the Georgian squire."

Here then was an explanation for Britain's dismaying postwar shift from defending France to supporting Germany, and for its dogged (and successful) efforts to thwart Stresemann's and Briand's efforts to bring their countries together. Ever since losing its last bit of French territory, Calais, in 1558, Britain had prospered by keeping the Continent divided. To do so, it had had to consider itself as somehow not part of Europe.

Even after two shattering wars many Englishmen still felt the same!

The Germans had ignored the American edition of *This American World* but upon seeing the English edition, Ernst Rowohlt, the publisher, asked permission to bring out a German translation. When I assented, he assigned Annemarie Horschitz, the translator of Hemingway, to do the work.

Amerika: Vorbild und Warnung must have hit the German public at the right moment, for thereafter I received a number of requests to write about the subject. Among the first, and particularly welcome to me, was a bid from the *Europaeisches Revue,* a rather intellectual magazine published in Berlin by Prince Karl-Anton Rohan of the Austrian branch of that very distinguished family, and by former Ambassador Wilhelm Solf, an Islamic specialist who had translated the Rubaiyat into German. The *Revue* was broadly cosmopolitan.

My piece, entitled *Americans and Germans,* predicted the permanence of the current German-American cooperation, but *only* if both countries continued to nourish the same ideals, economic and political....

A little later, the *Technische Hochschule* in Stuttgart invited me to lecture on America and Americanism and develop my theories about what people twenty years later were to call the "Atlantic Community."

These were our banner years in Berlin. For by the time of our next visit home in 1930 everything had changed. The gloom in Germany was as nothing compared to that in the United States. In spite of exceptional measures, unemployment was rising and bankruptcies too.

Prosperity, as President Hoover said, might be just around the corner, but it seemed to have gone to sleep there. Exploiting our association of 1914, I visited the President in his office in the White House. He was not overly depressed. But I could not share his trust in either the Briand-Kellogg Pact or the London Naval Disarmament Treaty to keep the peace. Moreover, the new Hoover-MacDonald cooperation in favor of Germany and against France seemed to me to have come at a moment when Germany was ceasing to deserve either support or confidence.

Needless to say, my reservations concerning the latest developments in Germany made no visible impression upon the President.

Meanwhile Walter Strong had moved the *News* into a fine new plant and was, I understood, having some difficulty in meeting the payments on it. But I was sure if anyone could hold on until economic recovery, he could. After all, there had been depressions before and none had lasted more than a very few years. . . .

Then at the end of autumn, 1930, back to a Germany in which the election of all those Nazis to the Reichstag obviously foretold a crisis. Only Dr. Schacht, a fellow passenger on the transatlanic liner, was undisturbed. Things were moving along to his taste.

Moreover, much of the Germans' former cordiality toward the

United States seemed to have disappeared with the advent of the American depression and the emergence of the Nazis. Whereas in previous years most European writers had described America with benevolence if not with enthusiasm, they now attacked it. Egon Erwin Kisch brought out *Paradise America*, one long sneer at the alleged heartlessness and lack of culture of Americans. An opera, *Foreign Soil,* described the delight of some Europeans who managed to escape the "degrading" living conditions of both North and South America, and return to civilized Europe.

In France, where André Siegfried had written a description of the United States so perceptive that Americans could learn from it, the novelist-physician Georges Duhamel, my friend of prewar Paris days, published a travel book, *Scenes from the Coming Life,* which I found comical in its lack of objectivity and understanding.

Small wonder that Sinclair Lewis, returning from Scandinavia with the Nobel Prize, reacted so violently to Berlin's rising anti-Americanism that just before New Year's Day, 1931, he included in a newspaper interview the flat statement: "I am absolutely for my country, right or wrong."

18

Berlin's Golden Twenties

Eucharistisch und thomistisch,
Doch daneben auch marxistisch,
Theosophisch, communistisch,
Gotisch, kleinstadt-dombau mystisch,
Aktivistisch, erzbuddhistisch,
Ueberoestlich, taoistisch,
Rettung aus der Zeit-Schlamastik
Suchend in der Negerplastik,
Wort und Barrikaden waelzend,
Gott und Foxtrott fesch verschmelzend.
      —FRANZ WERFEL, *Spiegelmensch,* 1920

TO THIS DAY, elderly Berliners sometimes greet each other with the friendly query: "Were you too a Twenty-er?"

Those who were, often look back upon those particular years in the German capital as pure gold. And with much reason—all through that decade Berlin was the center of social and cultural effervescence such as has rarely ever been equaled, certainly not in our time.

Bluntly put, Berlin was a cultural riot, the wilder for the lack of such deep traditions as still held sway in Paris and London. Even before 1914, there was a sarcastic saying that the Berliner not only "knows everything but knows it better." In the twenties, Germans from elsewhere sometimes remarked acidly that the Berliner not only did everything but did it more.

In fact, that shrewd social philosopher, William Schlamm, looking back, found the spirit of the time best expressed in one film and two novels: *The Cabinet of Dr. Caligari,* Thomas Mann's *Magic Mountain* (why not his *Death in Venice?*) and Robert Musil's *Mann ohne Eigenschaften.* In the film, the characters are insane; in the *Magic Mountain* they are dying of tuberculosis; and in Musil's book, already existentialist. To these three I would add that other weird novel, *The Golem,* by the German Czech, Max Brod. This retells the ancient legend of how Rabbi Jehuda Loewe, of Prague, invented a robot like the one that destroyed Frankenstein which, thanks to his negligence, became a monster and ran amuck.

Schlamm rightly considered the society that produced these works moribund. And yet at the time one could say to the twenties, as Francis

Thompson to the setting sun, "Thou dost thy dying so triumphantly."

In Berlin, these years offered everything from Dada to Bertold Brecht; from the dire prophecies of Spengler to the greatest scientific discoveries of all time; from bearded nudists to the ultra-mondaines of Kurfuerstendamm with their monocles and cropped hair. Setting aside tradition, good taste, and not infrequently moral scruples, artists, writers, intellectuals, and plain viveurs, in their effort to "stay alive," pursued extremes—"the more evil, the better; the more perverted, the more natural; the more provocative, the more attractive," as Schlamm remembered them. Precisely for this reason, Englishmen, Frenchmen, and Americans flocked to the place where they could "experience their own time at its most excessive." For, in Berlin, as Werfel indicated in the verses at the start of this chapter, they found more of everything, except binding rules by which to live.

To be sure, within the overripe fruits of the twenties, the worm of despair never ceased gnawing. Despair at what? At one's inability to find a faith that could overcome the fear of living in a world where existence had become an "absurdity." And not all the Coué-like attempts at self-mastery through auto-suggestion could expel the worm.

The lack of any ethical compass was particularly hard on the younger war veterans who were frantically seeking a justification for their sacrifices, and on the immediate postwar generation who found themselves growing up among fireworks full of sound and fury, signifying—what? Why, according to Oswald Spengler, signifying the downfall of the West!

My first assistant, Dr. Richard Winners, by nature a moralist, considered the Berlin cultural riot obscene and sought consolation in the German classical writers and the novels of Dostoievsky. Otto Brok, who succeeded Winners in the *News* office, was sustained by his Catholic faith. Yet he was intrigued by the existentialist philosophers, Heidegger and Jaspers, with whom he had studied; by the dead Czech, Franz Kafka, who had put the existentialist predicament in its most drastic form; and by the forerunner of all these, the Dane, Soren Kierkegaard.

Since Brok found me hospitable to metaphysical discussion, he repeatedly urged me to read Kafka and Kierkegaard. But I had never seen any reason why Nietzsche's arrogant proclamation that "God is dead," or the unproven theories of Marx and Freud, should affect my own belief that Hindus, Platonists, Christian mystics, and even a few moderns like Emerson, Bergson, and William James, had something more solid to offer. Rightly or wrongly, I attributed the emergence of existentialism to three main factors: to the rationalists' substitution of historical and cultural relativism for fixed doctrine; to the contemporary decay of ethical and artistic standards; and to the overwhelming shock of a lost war. The Germans' traditional tendency to self-pity had been heightened by an unthinkable military defeat that caused the more introspective to sit, preferably facing a *schnaps,* wondering "Where is my ego?"

At the depth of my own adolescence, aged eighteen or so, I had wallowed in the sorrows of Thomson's *City of Dreadful Night*, and later, in Italy, admired Leopardi. But there was a difference. Thomson's gloom was the result of concrete and objective causes, his personal misfortunes, that suffering and callousness all about him. Leopardi *sought* suffering—"*e il naufragar m'è dolce in questo mare.*" But Kafka's woes were beyond remedy, for they lay in existence itself.

His self-pity struck me as pathological. If life was as meaningless as he said, how had previous generations overlooked the fact?

Just when, I asked myself, had human life been anything but paradoxical—sorrow in joy, pain in pleasure? When had it been free of horror? When Tamerlane piled up the skulls of the entire population of Samarkand? When, during the Thirty Years War, bigoted Catholics and Protestants killed off half the population of Thuringia? For "civilized" man, as Santayana had noted, war, not peace, had been the normal condition, and would continue to be so until he found a substitute.

When men were not killing each other wholesale, God had done his share. In the fourteenth century the Black Death had wiped out a quarter of Europe's population. If our ancestors' morale had withstood shocks like these, why should we cringe? Not life, but existentialism, was "absurd." Certainly, back in the twenties I never dreamed that, thanks to Brok's professors and to the literary skill of Jean-Paul Sartre, it would one day become the hallmark of intellectual sophistication or that books by these gloomy nihilists would sell like popular novels.

Meanwhile, the unstilled thirst for meaning was driving millions of young Germans into living for kicks: wild artistic, moral, and political experimentation. Chaotic as it was, social and cultural life in Berlin was magnetic. Many a foreigner who came to carp remained to participate.

Perhaps nothing else was so characteristic of Berlin's Golden Age as the annual Press Ball. This was held in the immense Zoo Restaurant. Though in theory a private affair, almost everyone of any consequence got an invitation and few refused. For it was unlike any ball anywhere else in that it brought together the leaders of totally different worlds. The Reichs Chancellor and his Cabinet, officials, foreign ambassadors, high society, politicians, professors, artists and writers, newsmen of any standing, all met once a year at the Zoo. It was as though Paris had merged the Elysée, the Opéra, and the *Beaux Arts* Ball into one vast get-together that opened with the dignity of a state reception and ended in a bacchanal. Every guest found at the Press Ball just what he or she sought. For a foreign newsman it was a unique opportunity to talk with the people who made the news.

There Lilian and I first met the great theatrical producers, Jessner and Reinhardt, the orchestra conductor Furtwängler, and, once, Richard Strauss himself, who had come from Vienna to conduct one of his operas. Outstanding playwrights like Zuckmayer and Brecht never missed a year and on one occasion we saw the venerated Gerhardt Hauptmann, one of the few modern writers who combined a social consciousness with fanciful poetry.

Among artists, we knew best George Grosz and Rafaello Busoni, the half-Swedish son of the great Italian musician, Ferruccio Busoni. Grosz was the most gifted pictorial satirist of his day and had not forgiven the Germans for getting him into the war.

Through the people we met at the Press Ball and elsewhere we gradually became familiar with the many facets of Berlin's vaunted *Kulturleben* and could study its triumphs and "excesses" from close up.

As in France, I found most "new" art and literature neither beautiful nor significant. Take architecture. To a devotee of the majesty of French Gothic and the classical and Renaissance mastery of proportions, Gropius' Bauhaus stuff and the "machines for living" of Le Corbusier were merely interesting. I often wondered what Vitruvius would have said about them.

In the theatre I preferred Reinhardt's frank romanticism to the "modernity" of Jessner and the experimentalism of Piscator, whom we knew well. Why make *Hamlet* a study of unemployment or play it in modern clothes?

In music I liked Wagner, Brahms, and Debussy, could take Mahler and Stravinsky, and drew the line at Schoenberg. My preference was music which could be felt rather than analyzed. Therefore, I enjoyed most the uncompromising melodic line of Toscanini, whom German critics found "superficial." But then Germans had a habit of finding superficial anything which they could understand, unlike the French to whom "that which is not clear is not French." The *Maestro* answered that he played Mozart and Beethoven according to the original scores and challenged the Germans to improve upon them.

For the same reason, I liked Rilke's poetry, and could not stand Mallarmé's German disciple, Stefan George, and his pretentious "circle." The claim of George's biographer (a member of the "circle"), that from the master's poetry "has come the new soul; from his hands, the new man; from his vision the new behavior," I found ludicrous. In fact, whether disguised as "stream of consciousness" or "higher meaning," deliberate obscurity bored me. Life itself was obscure enough.

Imagine my joy when in Goethe's *Faust* I found confirmation of something I had long suspected: to be great, a poem need be neither unintelligible nor complicated. In fact it could be written in something close to doggerel—so long as the author was a genius.

Among novelists, Lyon Feuchtwanger had just written his successful *Jud Suess* and was enjoying the social eminence it brought him. And of course, the two Manns stood out above all others. Thomas may have been the better writer, but his novels fitted well into Spengler's *Untergang*. Decadent Heinrich certainly was not. During the war he had resisted the pan-German frenzy to which Thomas had succumbed. His sharp satire was exactly what the Germans needed.

The sad fact was that many modern artists and writers had become so alienated from society that they could not bear to delineate nature without distortion. Some preferred to substitute for nature's language their own subjective protests. These people dared not face the fact noted by Heraclitus: "The waking have one and the same world, the sleeping turn aside each into a world of his own." In short, reality is the dream we share.

Therefore, even for a scientific half-illiterate like me, it was a relief to turn from the creeping disorder that infested German arts to positive achievements in communications, transportation, medicine, and, above all, pure science.

Then, for the first time, Zeppelins crossed the ocean, to be shortly replaced by commercial airplanes. I took part in the test flight of a new airship at Friedrichshaven piloted by Dr. Eckener. To describe the floods of the Oder River Valley I hired a small Junkers plane at Tempelhof, and was back in my office within four hours, a new sort of reporting.

The German radio transmitted twenty-five thousand points a second across the Atlantic, thus laying the ground for commercial television. It transmitted facsimiles of checks from country to country. Somebody broadcast a concert from the bottom of the Baltic Sea—I forget why. Dresden put a loudspeaker into the railroad station. A citizen of Leipzig piped music into his barbershop. Leipzig University set up a chair of cinematography, the first, I believe, in Europe, if not in the world.

The world's first rocket-propelled automobile successfully ran along the Avusbahn near Berlin.

A German invented a way to fertilize the soil by electricity. An ingenious chemist made "real silk" from lobster and insect shells. I. G. Farben began the commercial production of gasoline from coal, thus enabling a country that lacked petroleum deposits to wage modern war.

In the field of health, German physicians announced new methods of treating leprosy, gallstones, and yellow fever, and of diagnosing and curing cancer—this last a false hope! While one M.D. treated diabetics by hypnosis, another claimed to relieve nervous disorders, sleeplessness, and melancholia by air travel!

A Heidelberg professor of hygiene swore that palmistry was science and claimed to tell the character of defunct individuals by examining their corpses' hands.

Contrariwise, anticipating modern worries, Professor Martin Hahn of Berlin complained that gas-driven automobiles were poisoning millions of city dwellers and should be replaced by electric cars. Going further, a Dr. Arnold Sach of Heidelberg found the health of contemporary Germany to be worse than that of ancient Egypt.

And nonetheless Professor Eugen Steinach proclaimed a "biological law of adolescence," based on his discovery of a rejuvenation germ which he modestly called the "world hormone." His disciple, my friend, Dr. Peter Schmidt, popularized this therapy in a best-selling book, *Conquest of Old Age*.

Last, but not least, Sigmund Freud of Vienna, the father of psycho-analysis, brought out *Das Unbehagen in der Kultur,* which I reviewed for the *News.* Subsequent talks with his disciples failed to allay my impatience with the master's dogmatism. Yet I could not but admire the keenness of many of his perceptions. Civilization had indeed imposed disturbing inhibitions, unfortunately, with too little success.

Not the least of the paradoxes of the twenties, and not only in Germany, was the fact that just when the Western peoples were succumbing to decadence or some political *Ersatz,* communism or nazism, scientists were undermining the philosophical materialism which was the cause of so much "alienation." While philosophers and writers, artists and intellectuals bemoaned (with Spengler) the collapse of the Faustian spirit and faith in progress, British astronomers like Eddington testified to a profound faith in God ("the Supreme Mathematician"). And in the Physics Institute at Berlin University were four Nobel Prize winners—Einstein, Planck, Schroedinger, and Heisenberg, who, between them, had discovered something called relativity and an *indeterminacy principle* which together legitimized the ancient belief in human free will.

Einstein I visited first in 1924 when he publicly supported one of the humanitarian causes to which he was dedicated. After he told me his story, I ventured to ask him for an explanation of a phase of relativity which I found illogical. Einstein smiled and said:

"Quit bothering your mind about it: mine is a mathematical, not a logical theory. Here—" and he snatched up his violin and began to play Bach. In all but physics, Einstein remained a traditionalist.

When, some years later, the newspapers announced that he had found the long-sought *universal equation* applicable to all natural forces, I applied to my Scottish friend, Lancelot L. Whyte, also a member of the Physics Institute, for a simple explanation. Instead, he invited me to lunch near Potsdam with Einstein's "house mathematician," a young Hungarian named Cornel Lanczos. When over coffee I asked for a simplification which I could cable, Lanczos answered:

"Forget it: there is a basic flaw in the Master's equation." Then seeing my amazement, he added: "Why not? After all, Einstein was never very good at figures."

Somewhat earlier Einstein had been involved by a disciple, one Leo Szillard, in another false alarm. Having announced a joint discovery of a new type of ice-box, they failed to produce it. Years later, Szillard explained that Einstein would not permit the manufacturers to use his name for publicity. Yet the new principle was later incorporated, according to Szillard, in the atom bomb!

Meanwhile Lance had made the *indeterminacy principle* as clear to me as my lack of higher mathematics would permit. Like me, he was convinced that the universal disorder around us was largely the result of the absence of anything in which thoughtful people believed. Learning that I had "sat at the feet of" Bergson, whose theory of time fascinated him, Lance revealed his own goal: a synthesis of physics, chemistry, biology, and psychology, an understanding of being as a single process from disorder to order. This was pretty thin air for an unscientist like me. I simply could not believe that an understanding of natural forces could ever substitute satisfactorily for the medieval cult of the Virgin Mary, Henry Adams notwithstanding.

To remain a creative civilization, the West needed a belief in something beyond itself.

When the Berlin magazine, *Neue Rundschau,* asked me for a contribution, I chose as subject "A New European Culture?" After insisting that the problem was common to both sides of the Atlantic, I outlined what I considered the basic questions:

"First, how can democracy be made as inspiring to the mind as it is beneficial to the body?

"Second, how can we get the best out of the limitless capacities of machinery?

"And third, how can we produce, in a machine age, where mere utility holds sway, an ideal of such spiritual potency that it can unite us and the machines in a vast cultural creation, a new *Lebenstil?* . . .

"Therefore either reason, or reason's child, science, must press forward into a realm of spiritual values both have so far consistently denied, and reveal a divine hierarchy of idea, or this hierarchy must be established by religious faith—I am skeptical of science's power to establish it. Therefore I see no hope save in religion—a new wave of Christian fervor, a renascence of the *Tao,* an incarnation of the Lord Buddha, or the strengthening of some other belief (call it prejudice) to a religious fervor."

I failed to make a convincing case, for the publisher of the *Rundschau* returned my manuscript with a polite letter expressing his inability to believe in a religious revival.

Just about the same time, Karl Anton Rohan, for whose magazine I had previously written, invited me to become a member of the German *Kulturbund,* an organization German in name but European in spirit, which endeavored to combine the best in tradition with something (not too much) of the new spirit.

Membership in such an august organization almost miraculously increased my "cultural acceptability." Until then, in any gathering of German intellectuals, somebody was sure to turn on me at one moment and put the ritual question: "And where have *you* studied, *Herr* Mowrer?"

The first time I was thus challenged, I hardly knew what to answer, the question seemed so irrelevant. But I came to realize that to the self-conscious German *intelligentsia,* "higher education" or a recognized talent was essential to acceptance. So instead of answering, "What has that to do with the argument?" I learned to reply nonchalantly: "At the universities of Chicago, Michigan and—ah—Paris." (The last was a clincher: even the most *Kultur*-proud German respected the Sorbonne.)

"*Ach so?* Then you are not a genuine American. Your name suggests a German origin."

"About one-sixteenth, perhaps. The original Maurer came from the Rhineland a couple of centuries ago. All other known ancestors were English, Scotch-Irish, or Dutch. Not much German influence, I fear."

"Remarkable. You think almost like a German."

Thinking like a German, of course, meant dedication to a "problem," the more insoluble—"deeper"—the more attractive.

The German, Dr. Max Clauss, head of the joint committee for French-German understanding, insisted that only a corps of incorruptible civil servants could maintain the needed balance between society and the individual.

I liked Clauss, but his faith in those very *Beamte* who had docilely followed the Kaiser and his generals into the Great War amazed me. Foreigners from Madame de Staël to Santayana had insisted that the Germans did not understand Western freedom. Was this why *Kultur* did not exactly mean culture?

Santayana said so flatly. *Kultur,* he wrote (*Essays in England*) "is not to be extended to other nations" who would only "pollute it." Foreigners who show the proper kind of genius, Shakespeare, Dante, and Christ are "virtual and unconscious Germans." In 1914 Thomas Mann had insisted that the whole prewar world including Germany had been "infested with the vermin of intellect and stank with the poison of civilization."

On the other hand, *Kultur* was, though national, not that which probing anthropologists discovered in every society. Some peoples had *Kultur,* others had none! And among peoples, Germans were more cultured than others, as Thomas Mann so clearly indicated (*The Magic Mountain*) in the dialogues between the "profound" German, Castrop, and the "superficial" Italian, Settembrini.

It was this assumption of superiority, I reflected, even more than its physical aggressions, that had made the Germany of Bismarck and the Kaiser unpopular elsewhere.

Fortunately, most members of the *Kulturbund* were anything but chauvinist, and I learned much from their discussions, particularly of politics.

In 1929, thanks, I believe, to Lance Whyte, the London publishing house, Kegan Paul, Trench, Trubner and Company, asked me to do a volume for its *Today and Tomorrow* series. Lance had contributed *Archimedes, or the Future of Physics*. Other volumes treated the futures of everything from laughter, leisure, monogamy, swearing, Ireland, and women, to mankind's emancipation and the war against the moon. Since most previous authors had chosen an appropriate classical figure as title, I chose to symbolize politics in *Sinon*, the Greek who persuaded superstitious Trojans to carry a wooden horse full of soldiers into Troy. Every successful politician is, I argued, something of a Sinon.

This doctrine was pure Umano, to whom I gave credit in a footnote. Yet it proved unacceptable to both tender-minded and tough-minded readers. The former gagged at admitting that the heart of politics is force and that justice, rightly defined, is the rigid application of sovereign law, ethical or unethical. On the other hand, my master's rigorous demonstration that sovereignty made war between nations inevitable, hence, that to eliminate war states must eliminate or "pool" their separate sovereignties—this outraged nationalists everywhere, and nowhere more than in isolationist America. They could not admit that their choice lay between internationalism and further catastrophic conflicts.

I had set down my views with what I now consider unnecessary cocksureness, perhaps in a desire to shock my countrymen out of their current complacency. In any event, *Sinon or the Future of Politics* was unfavorably reviewed.

The *Kulturbund* was devoted to preventing the next war by uniting Europe. Since Washington persisted in seeking peace by sentimental talk, a pact "outlawing" war, more efforts at partial disarmament, small economic adjustments, and threats of "moral sanctions" (means I considered futile), I gladly participated in my friends' European campaign. For I had become attentive to what I was later to call my three-fold heritage: American by birth, Western by heritage and culture, and human by race. A united Europe would not necessarily prevent another war. But it would be a start. Understanding required the harmonizing of conflicting national myths. So long as the school histories of Germany and France gave such variant versions of a common experience, say, of the War of 1870, how could the two peoples be anything but enemies?

Thereupon I persuaded some Berlin officials to allow me to tell a similar group in France (where Aristide Briand was urging Europe to unite) that Germany would welcome setting up a two-nation group to prepare a single history manual for schools in both countries. What is more, the French in Paris received the proposal with apparent sympathy, and, given more time, something might have come of it.

Nonetheless, I already foresaw difficulties. As early as 1928 I reported that the drive for European unity was going badly in Germany not only because too many groups were working at cross purposes, but for a more profound reason: a rising wave of truculent nationalism. Instead of rushing to accept Briand's offers of a merger, or, at least an alliance with France, the Germans wanted to be paid for it at the expense of Poland and of the French and Belgian taxpayers. Over in England the British Labour Government of Ramsay MacDonald was following the traditional policy of keeping the Continent divided.

Subjected simultaneously to the grievous economic crisis and the flood of rising nationalism, the glamor that was Berlin was slowly fading. Perhaps it had been too hectic to last.

19

Germany Puts the Clock Back

*There is something deep and irrational in the
German soul, which makes it appear alarming,
alien, even repulsive and savage, to other,
shallower nations.*

THOMAS MANN

THE STORY OF THE GERMAN PEOPLE'S SURRENDER to the one-time Bohemian corporal needs no repeating. Yet even when all is said, there
remains something inexplicable about it. How many times did I find
myself remembering my wise friend Marc's advice: "Never imagine
that you understand the Germans."

The depression had hit them less hard than it had the Americans.
And nevertheless, by the end of 1930, millions were muttering that
"something has to happen," "better an end with terror than terror
without end," or even echoing Bert Brecht's prayer (*Die Massnahme*):

Submerge us in filth,
And embrace the executioner,
But transform the world.

In some ways, the Germany of 1931 resembled that of 1924:
economic stagnation, another frantic attempt to cast off the reparations
burden, and new efforts at blackmailing the victors of Versailles into
granting Germany union with Austria and restoring the Polish Corridor.

Unemployment remained between four and five million. The price
of bread stayed high. Yet, in March, Chancellor Bruening, under pressure of a budget deficit, reduced the dole!

In May prices fell sharply on the stock exchange. In June foreigners
staged a run on the German banks and Bruening raised the bank rate.
In July the huge Darmstaedter Bank failed and all other banks temporarily closed their doors. President Luther of the Reichsbank frantically sought help from Washington, London, and Paris. Hoover proposed

a moratorium on war debts and reparations. But because Bruening still insisted on the customs union with Austria, he got a cool reception from the French.

In revealing the "inside story" of the German financial breakdown, I argued that the government was deliberately using the crisis to force the abrogation of the Versailles Treaty and had determined to "go for broke" and see which side could hold out longer.

Britain's abandonment of the gold standard and fear of inflation brought about a second flight from the mark. German cities, which had squandered their foreign loans on vast public improvements, were no longer making ends meet. By October foreigners were withdrawing their credits at the rate of some ten million gold marks weekly. Government printing presses were replacing the loss. In December, 1931, a desperate Bruening raised import duties.

Yet all this time, he was stubbornly going ahead with a new super-modern armored cruiser at great expense. The courts imprisoned the pacifist, Carl von Ossietzky, for revealing details of the country's illegal rearmament.

Melchior Palyi warned that politics would be Germany's ruin. Another economist, M. J. Bonn, told me for publication that foreigners should expect no more reparations but a return of the people to a pre-1914 mentality. Both democracy and capitalism in Germany were on their deathbed.

My news file for this year was grim indeed. A temporary ray of light was the visit to Berlin of Premier Laval and Foreign Minister Briand of France to discuss a possible customs union of France, Germany, and, I believe, Austria as well. Thanks to a French newsman, Fernand de Brinon, who accompanied the French delegation, I talked with both ministers.

Neither was personally attractive. Laval was shrewd but basically ignorant of world affairs, a bad combination. Briand looked as shabby as ever and ill, in addition. His policy of gradual Franco-German reconciliation had become acceptable to the French exactly when it could no longer satisfy the Germans. Nothing but a new French occupation of the Ruhr could have cut Germany's demands down to size. Yet such an occupation was virtually forbidden by the Treaty of Locarno! Unable to choose between the policies of Briand and Poincaré, France was soon to pay a terrible price for its indecision.

Among Frenchmen in Berlin not even the warmest champions of the Franco-German customs union, Oswald Hesnard of the French Embassy, who had a remarkable knowledge of German affairs, and René Lauret, correspondent of the *Matin*, had much hope.

After the Laval-Briand visit, many Americans in Berlin felt apprehensions which they sought to impart to visitors from home.

This was not always easy. Some of these, including Mayor Cermak of Chicago and those "kings of the rum runners," Bill and Ben McCoy, showed more interest in German nudism than in German politics. I

enjoyed the McCoy brothers' hair-raising stories of the close escapes of
their ship, the *Arethusa*, as it brought to the United States rum from the
West Indies and Christmas champagne from the French islands of St.
Pierre and Miquelon. But they considered Hitler's threats so much
bombast.

On the other hand, two brilliant members of Charley Merriam's
political science staff at the University of Chicago, Harold Lasswell and
Frederick Schuman, understood at once, and thereafter did what they
could to alert Americans at home. So did the New York economist,
Alexander Sachs, the same one who later brought Einstein to F. D. R.
After listening to me for a long time, Sachs urged me to write a piece
on the "real" financial situation of Germany for *Barron's Weekly*, and
later collaborated with me.

Faraway U.S. citizens had some excuse for their blindness to
National Socialism. Europeans, I felt, had none. One of the least alert
was the Swiss "analytical" psychoanalyst, Carl Jung. Since I preferred
Jung's theories to those of Freud (perhaps prejudiced against the latter
by an earlier contact with his daughter Anna), this was a shock. I had
gone to Zurich hoping to get a neutral analysis of Nazism for the paper.
Instead Jung amazed me by warmly defending the Nazis. Perhaps he
felt Hitler represented the Germans' "collective unconscious."

The French in France were blind to the rising German threat.

Among the worst was Romain Rolland. In May, 1931, while at
Geneva covering the fruitless Franco-German debates over the suggested
customs union, I slipped off to Villeneuve for a talk with the great
French pacifist writer, whose refusal to take sides during the First
World War had made him the target of French nationalists.

As an incorruptible human being Rolland drew my admiration.
But in his hatred of the "corrupt" Third French Republic, he had
painted for himself an idyllic picture of the Soviet Union. Nor would
he believe that the nation of Beethoven and Bach (and of the hero of
his own great novel, *Jean-Christophe*) could be carried away by an
Adolf Hitler. And anyhow, it was all the fault of the Treaty of Versailles.
. . . I left the great man in his Swiss garden, smiling defiantly in the
direction of Paris, totally proof against argument.

In Germany, Europeans like Emil Ludwig were becoming seriously
alarmed. So was Helmut von Moltke, with whom we had become close
friends. Helmut later heroically gave his life in the struggle against the
Fuehrer.

Rohan, Coudenhove-Kalergi, and Stern-Rubarth also feared the
worst. The latter had for many years participated in all international
negotiations as head of the "officieux" *Diplomatische-politische Korre-
spondenz*, which expressed the views of the German government. Although "independent" newsmen frequently referred derisively to Stern-
Rubarth as "his master's voice," he was a wealth of useful information
and had, I believe, striven for Franco-German reconciliation since 1924.

Another Cassandra who never ceased to warn was our friend,

George Grosz. With his artist's antennae, Grosz early detected the revival of all that he detested in his countrymen. His drawings for Piscator's staging of *Schwejk* were positively ferocious. At each new Nazi outrage, Grosz shook his head and muttered that the world "had seen nothing yet." Too few in Germany saw what he saw.

I like to think that it was because of his experience as a worker in a Ford factory in Detroit that Prince Louis Ferdinand of Hohenzollern, son of the ex-Crown Prince, proved impervious to Nazi infection. Although his uncle, Prince August Wilhelm, joined the Nazi Party, and his father for a time supported Hitler in the hope of a monarchical restoration, "Doctor" Ferdinand, as the prince called himself, remained untouched in his honor and his intellectual integrity. Had monarchy still been in fashion, what a Kaiser Louis Ferdinand might have made!

Conspicuous among clear-sighted politicians was the Catholic mayor of Cologne, Konrad Adenauer, reputed as a friend of the West. In fact, according to Brok, himself a *Zentrums* man, some in the party suspected Adenauer of having looked wistfully, if not favorably, upon the Rhineland separatist movement of the early twenties and refused him a decisive influence in shaping party policies. Nonetheless, although I had met him only a few times, when asked, in 1930, by Richard Moennig to write, for foreign circulation, a description of the leading German politicians, I predicted a great future for the mayor.

An agreeable but disturbing adversary of Adenauer was Hans Zehrer, who resigned his job as foreign editor of a democratic daily to found and edit the monthly magazine, *Die Tat*. A brilliant if verbose writer with a smattering of knowledge from many fields, Zehrer and two friends, Ferdinand Fried and Giselher Wirsing, waged in these years an insidious campaign to induce the politicians to create a "new" Germany, national, socialist, and outside the world economy; to renounce the "decadent" liberal West; and to ally itself with the "younger peoples of the East," including the U.S.S.R.

Like many doctrinaires, Zehrer did not mind inconsistency. In January, 1932, he announced that the Nazis would certainly become the majority; in May, that they would never take power; in October, that there would be no revolution; and a week before Hitler became Chancellor, that there was "no fascism in Germany."

While personally too civilized to welcome Nazi barbarism, Zehrer and his friends, by their reassuring articles in *Die Tat*, unquestionably helped make Nazism palatable to worried Germans who might otherwise have combined to defeat it.

Zehrer had a Jewish wife, a "Kurfuerstendamm type," monocled, good-looking, socially ambitious. We saw them frequently though I was never able to reconcile Zehrer's humanity and intelligence with his "East orientation."

Toward the end of 1931, Adolf Hitler felt sure enough of himself to make a first massive appeal for the support of the foreign press. Actually, I had already had one conversation with the self-styled leader in the Party Headquarters, the Brown House in Munich, and confirmed my 1924 impression of a slightly comical but dangerous man, brutal, guileful, and willful.

Now I had two other talks with Hitler at the Kaiserhof Hotel in Berlin, which had become the headquarters of Nazi bigwigs in the capital.

During the longer interview, the *Fuehrer*, at a question from me, rose from his chair, stared over my head into space, and launched into a five minute speech on his favorite text, Germany's "fourteen years of infamy." At first I thought this sheer theater, then gradually realized that this voluble man believed what he was saying, that, in fact, he was capable of believing whatever he wanted to believe, and intended by sheer will to make it come true. Thanks to this realization, I predicted that he would endeavor to carry out literally the program he had outlined in *Mein Kampf* (which I had recently read).

Ernest ("Putzi") Hanfstaengl, the Nazi press chief, remained an enigma. Big, dark, blessed with a cultured New England mother, subjected to American society at an early age, he should have been Nazi-proof. According to Robert Murphy, Hanfstaengl's attention had been first directed to Hitler in 1922 by an American Army officer, Captain Truman Smith, who already surmised that Hitler might become a German Mussolini. After the failure of the Beer Hall Putsch of 1923, the Hanfstaengl family hid him from justice and, unfortunately, persuaded him not to commit suicide, as he intended. In consequence, though "Putzi" set small store by Nazi ideology, he did a good job in playing down the repulsive aspects of Nazism for visiting correspondents. Drinking with him in the Kaiserhof occasionally, I met others of the band who were always ready to imbibe a whiskey at the expense of an American newspaperman. Thanks to their thirst, I obtained advance information concerning the Party's plans.

An unexpected source of information was a small cripple, Dr. Paul Joseph Goebbels. Goebbels had nothing in common with Hanfstaengl except a dark complexion and a craze for women. Unlike the other Nazi leaders, he was not a paranoiac, a pervert, a crackpot, or a brute. Except when deliberately lying, he always communicated something. This made him the only Nazi orator who could convince rather than hypnotize his auditors.

He came to my attention of his own volition. Some time before 1930, I received a request for a job from an unknown writer. I might have known that, though a Rhinelander, Goebbels was already a leader of the Berlin Nazis, but I did not. Therefore, while refusing his offer, I suggested that he drop in and see me. Some time later the little man with the sharp face limped in, and for half an hour we discussed the world. Goebbels soon revealed that he had become a follower of Hitler in order to remove the "Jewish blight" from Germany.

"Less than 1 percent of the total population," I objected.

"Numerically yes, but dominant. Just imagine, no Jewish theater producer would put on my last play. Too German. No, we shall get rid of them all."

So that was it: his Nazism was pure resentment. He was far too intelligent to believe *Mein Kampf*. For some time after Goebbels became editor of the Berlin Nazi newspaper, the *Angriff*, we remained on speaking terms. Occasionally he phoned personally to offer news or to invite me to a Hitler rally in the huge Berlin *Sportpalast* at which thousands went wild and girls in the front row became delirious.

Goebbels was, I believe, the master manipulator of our time. When, on one occasion, I was too busy to attend the oratorical orgy at which Hitler was slated to announce the Party's economic program, I asked Goebbels for an advance text.

"No need. Here is our program in one sentence: under National Socialism everything will be different."

It took me a few moments to appreciate the magic of those seven words. In the prevailing German atmosphere they were worth millions of votes. What a public relations man was lost when the lame doctor turned to politics!

At the Kaiserhof Bar, Hanfstaengl presented me to Rudolf Hess and Hermann Goering, both of whom became outstanding among Nazi leaders. Hess was a dramatic looking nobody, a faithful Achates who showed nothing of his mental unbalance.

Goering was full of human traits, most of them distasteful. Praiseworthy were the primitive courage that had made him a famous war ace, and, one might argue, his doglike fidelity to the *Fuehrer*. Repellent were his insensitivity, general laziness, addiction to drugs, kleptomania, personal vanity and love of show, and, toward everybody but Hitler, mania for personal domination. Even while he was threatening the "hostile" foreign press (as he did at one conference), I had the impression that he was coquetting for our favor.

If 1931 was a year of warning, 1932 was one of betrayal.

Most professional officers had never ceased to regret the monarchy and the first to abandon the republic it had sworn to uphold was the *Reichswehr*.

Early in 1932, in the person of General Kurt von Schleicher, it set itself up as kingmaker. This ambitious officer was the head of the unacknowledged "political department" of the armed forces.

The pretext was the "failure" of Chancellor Bruening. By March, half of the young males between the ages of sixteen and thirty were unemployed. Bands of Nazi rowdies paraded the streets shouting, "Let the Jews croak." "Germany is getting ready to defy the victors of 1918," I reported.

When the spring presidential election revealed that only the combined efforts of the remaining republicans had reelected Hindenburg over Hitler, Schleicher, who previously had called Bruening the "greatest Chancellor since Bismarck," persuaded Hindenburg to replace him with another Catholic, Franz von Papen, a former career officer, an outspoken nationalist, and the owner of the Berlin Catholic daily, *Germania*.

Papen was a figure whom (to quote the French ambassador in Berlin, André François-Poncet) "not even his friends took seriously." His cabinet consisted of four counts, five barons, four simple "vons," and two commoners!

Schleicher was hardly more prepossessing. Yet in his "political" work, he was assisted by a group of capable officers known as the "three musketeers." Two of these, Major Erich Marcks, the son of a historian, and Captain Erwin Planck, son of the "quantum theory," were among my best news sources.

Schleicher's vanity was anything but reassuring. Once, around midnight at the Koenigin Bar, we found the general seated with a group of people, including the Plancks. Invited to join them, we sat down just in time to hear the general say: "The Herr Reichspraesident needs a strong man. And he knows just where to find him—here." And he slapped his breast in self approval.

At the congress of the nationalist Steel Helmet (veterans' organization) in Magdeburg, I reported their demands for the revival of monarchy and militarism with a certain sympathy. Reactionary these people might be. They were neither lunatics nor sadists. Moreover, like Bruening before him, Papen really sought understanding with France. Unhappily, when it looked as though France might concede enough to satisfy the Germans (at least for a while), Britain intervened to prevent agreement.

The May election to the Prussian Landtag brought another communist gain. This set the stage for a second betrayal, that of the Catholics.

Brok, a bachelor, occasionally turned up showing traces of the night before. One morning he rushed into my office shouting: "It is all over, it is all over." And burst into tears.

"Otto," I said, "go down to the café and have some coffee and you'll feel better."

"*Nein*, I don't have a hangover."

"Then what's the matter?"

"Last night at a meeting of the leaders of the Center Party, which I attended, our Party leader, Monsignor Kaas, read a letter from the Secretary of State at Rome, Cardinal Pacelli, whom you knew in Munich as Nuncio."

"Yes?"

"The Cardinal wrote that the Pope was worried about the rise of communism in Germany and advised our Party to help make Hitler chancellor. The *Zentrums* leaders agreed." He sobbed.

"Yes, go on," I said.

"But, Edgar, that means Hitler in power! Hitler wants a new war and he will get it." Once more he broke into tears.

"Otto, may I report the Cardinal's message and the Party's decision to cooperate with the Nazis?"

"*Nein*. It was a secret meeting. But you will see."

And see we did. From that day the Center regularly supported

Hitler. In November, the Party urged Hindenburg to take Hitler as chancellor. Even when in February, 1933, the Catholics realized it was too late to hold him to the Constitution, they voted an Enabling Act doing away with personal freedom, democracy, and law in Germany. This they called "clarifying the situation."

Years later when some were denying that, as Pope, Pacelli had favored National Socialism, I remembered Brok's story.

Next to run out on the Republic were the Socialdemocrats. They dominated, if they did not entirely comprise, the *Reichsbanner*, an organization three million strong. Yet when challenged by the Hindenburg-Papen cabal, the *Reichsbanner* faded without resistance.

The climax came in July when the Chancellor invoked his "exceptional powers" to suppress the socialist government of Prussia. Clearly, to survive, German democracy must thwart this. Nor was such defiance utopian. The Prussian Minister of the Interior, Carl Severing, had at his orders sixty-seven thousand well-trained, devoted military police, some of whom had served in the *Reichswehr*. He could threaten the President with the prospect of civil war.

So on the morning Papen intended to eliminate the Prussian government by military force, Knickerbocker and I sat down in the Ministry of the Interior to see the show. After a couple of hours Severing's personal secretary received us.

Wringing his hands and almost weeping, he said, "It is terrible. But what can we do?"

We snorted. "If I disposed of almost seventy thousand devoted Schupos as well as the *Reichsbanner*, I can imagine what I might do," I answered.

"Just what?"

"It is now half past twelve. The Chancellor is at lunch. Suppose the Minister sends police to the Chancelry, arrests Papen, locks him up at police headquarters, proclaims military law through Prussia, and informs President von Hindenburg that he is holding the Chancellor on a charge of treason—and will submit to no interference by the *Reichswehr*. What could the President do?"

The secretary looked at me in shocked amazement. "But Mr. Mowrer, you are bloodthirsty!"

Seeing that his surrender was total, Knick and I made our way along Unter den Linden. What a story—but how convey its full significance to American readers?

Then Knick had an idea. We turned down Friedrichstrasse and stopped the first two streetwalkers we met. After they had each had a couple of brandies, Knick said:

"We are American newsmen and wish to know what you girls think of the ousting of the Prussian government?"

When they finally realized that we were serious, one said:

"We are for the new gentlemen."

"You mean for Papen?"

"Naturally."

"But why? Do you happen to be the daughters of Junkers?"

"No. But these damn socialists with their free love have made it almost impossible for an honest whore to earn a decent living. The gentlemen will change all that and give us a chance!"

Knick and I cabled the conversation literally. Unfortunately, the Chicago *Daily News* decided it was too hot to publish.

Like their Italian comrades in 1920, the German communists had driven the frightened bourgeois into the arms of the verbally most anticommunist group, namely, the Nazis. True, while in the middle of 1932, communism drew over five million votes, the Nazis were piling up nearly three times that many! Many citizens still believed that they had to choose between Hitler and Stalin.

It was a ridiculous assumption. Never at any time during my stay in Germany did the communists have a real possibility of taking over the country, either by an election or by a *Putsch*. The *Reichswehr* and the republicans combined would have made short work of them, if they had tried the latter.

Now, however, the communists did not *oppose*, they *welcomed* the approaching advent of Nazism. Stalin, I was informed, had decided that, according to the immutable laws of history, fascism was the last stage of capitalism. The sooner the Germans adopted fascism, the sooner communism could replace it.

I first met this argument in 1929 when Harold Nicolson of the British Embassy in Berlin joined me in trying to convince the communist party head, Heinz Neumann, that, in assisting Hitler, communists were handing him the rope with which he would hang them!

Neumann was an intelligent adventurer who, as A. Neuberg, had carried out communist subversion in China. He had been selected by Moscow to teach the theory and practice of Soviet Communism to the Chinese Reds who had followed his manual, *The Armed Uprising*, in staging their early revolts. Nicolson's arguments had seemed to make some impression on him. But Moscow commanded and Berlin obeyed. Until Hitler as Chancellor abolished the communist party, confiscated its property, and imprisoned or murdered its leaders, the latter tacitly cooperated with him against the republic and the Socialdemocrats, occasionally siding with the Nazis in street fights and riots.

A number of rich Jewish industrialists and bankers still could not believe that Hitler intended to carry out his promise of liquidating them.

I could see reasons why Hitler and the paranoiacs, fanatics, cynics, ne'er-do-wells, hoodlums, and plain primitives who followed him concentrated their propaganda against the Jews. As rabble rousers, they needed personal targets identifiable as broadly as possible by their names, appearance, and way of life. As deliberate barbarians, they and their camp-followers (the "I'm–not–really–a–Nazi–but" people) could not but resent the general Jewish commitment to the liberal, Occidental civilization which it was their aim to destroy.

Yet Jews in Germany were proportionally far fewer than in the United States. Both Heinrich Heine and Karl Marx had been baptized Christians. Most of our many Jewish friends *felt* German, *spoke* German, and *acted* German. They shared the Germans' condescension toward the "East Jews" who flocked in after 1919. Why then the sudden hatred?

Conceivably the Jews' emergence as a successful and conspicuous element in the Republic sparked it. Under the monarchy, they had played a smaller role. Occasionally German nobles and officers, in need of cash, married Jewish heiresses. "Aryan" working girls sometimes preferred Jewish husbands. In banking, trade, medicine, the theater, and the newspapers, Jews were prominent. But before 1919 they had had small political influence.

The Weimar Republic gave them their chance and they made the most of it. Any number sought integration into German society. By 1933 this process had gone so far that when the Nazis started identifying Jews, they found less than 600,000 full-blooded, but well over a million "grandmother Jews"—persons, including a few Nazi leaders, with at least one quarter "Jewish blood"!

A Jewish industrialist, Walther Rathenau, became a Cabinet Minister (and was assassinated for his effrontery). In Berlin's artistic and cultural flowering, Jews played a leading part. As well they might, for in the cultural revolution of the twentieth century, three Jews, Marx, Freud, and Einstein, each in his separate field, were acknowledged leaders.

As a result few successful Jews believed in the Nazi threat to their existence until it was too late. When at the weekly *Stammtisch* I repeated the anti-Semitic threats made by Nazis at the Kaiserhof Bar, my friends laughed at me as a gullible American.

Toward the end of 1932 we visited a banker named Arnholt. After dinner, while the men, all Jews but me, sat over coffee, several boasted of giving money to the Nazi party at the request of Aryans like Schacht and Thyssen! My face must have betrayed my amazement. The host politely asked what I was thinking.

"Merely wondering how the People of Israel have managed to survive so many thousands of years when they obviously have a strong suicidal urge."

Arnholt raised his eyebrows. "But you don't take this fellow seriously."

"Unfortunately I do—and so should you."

"Just talk," insisted the banker while his friends nodded. They too thought me incapable of understanding the German soul. . . .

My growing belief that, given a chance, Hitler would realize the promises of *Mein Kampf* was based not only upon my experience with fascism and contacts with leading Nazis at the Kaiserhof. From June on, I worked on a book to be called *Germany Puts the Clock Back*. My overconfidence in the basic sanity of the Italians had devaluated *Im-*

mortal Italy. This time I would forego prophecy and stick to facts. Therefore I opened with Papen's rape of Prussia, described in detail the decline of the Republic, traced the historical reasons for that decline, and ended as follows: "The fact was that at this juncture (early November, 1932) the vast majority of even highly cultivated Germans did not themselves know what they wanted. . . .

"A great, a religious people was seeking a faith. A geographically and psychologically shapeless people was seeking an outline. In the task it shrank from no extreme, seemed to eschew no prevarication or folly. The result was a new 'particularity' of a type that could obviously prove dangerous. . . ."

Germany Puts the Clock Back appeared in New York on December 31, just five weeks after the publisher received the manuscript.

After a November election in which the Nazis suffered their first real defeat, Schleicher informed the senile President that the army could not guarantee order unless he, Schleicher, became Chancellor! So Chancellor he became.

Under the General, the advent of the Third Reich looked somewhat less inevitable. Marcks and Planck, both anti-Nazi, assured me that Schleicher now realized that cooperation with Hitler was impractical and had made the latter's elimination a major task. Even more important, in December at Geneva, Britain, France, and Italy agreed to sign a Convention giving Germany "equal rights in a system providing security for all nations." What more could the Germans expect? The Christmas trade had shown an economic improvement.

Yet shortly before Christmas I ran into Dr. Schacht and inquired as to his holiday plans.

Sardonically he looked at me over his two-inch collar. "I am going to Munich to talk with Adolf Hitler."

Indignation overcame politeness. "You too, my fine Democrat!"

Schacht snorted. "*Ach*, you understand nothing. You are a stupid American."

"Granted. But tell me what you expect from Hitler in words of one syllable and I'll try to understand."

"Germany will have no peace until we bring Hitler to power."

"Good. Pleasant journey."

Three weeks later, I met him again.

"How did your conversation with Hitler go, Dr. Schacht?"

"Brilliantly. I've got that man right in my pocket."

From that moment I expected the worst.

It was not long in coming. In the last days of January, the tragedy of the Weimar Republic rose to its shrill climax. This time the betrayers were Franz von Papen and Paul von Hindenburg.

20

Witness to Murder

The Third Reich is the Germanic Ideal,
an eternal tomorrow.
　　　—OSWALD SPENGLER
　　　The Decline of the West, 1922

THE FIRST EIGHT months of 1933 were a nightmare, relieved, for me, only by the brief periods I spent outside Germany.

The bad dream began in January, when Franz von Papen ousted *Reichs-Chancellor* Kurt von Schleicher in favor of Adolf Hitler, with himself as Vice Chancellor!

The trick lay in persuading the dotard President to refuse Schleicher permission to dissolve the moribund *Reichstag* on the ground that Schleicher's proposed legislation would adversely affect landowning Prussian Junkers, including Hindenburg and his son.

Papen's intrigue ripened so quickly that as late as January 15, Schleicher told Austria's visiting Chancellor Kurt von Schluschnigg that Hitler was no longer a problem! Two weeks later, this mustachioed "nonproblem" dissolved the *Reichstag*, called for new elections, and began eliminating the remnants of the Weimar Republic. He took control of the Prussian police away from Papen and gave it to Hermann Goering, confiscating the passports of real or supposed enemies.

On February 27, after his bully boys blamed the burning of the *Reichstag* on communists, Hitler declared martial law and launched a series of arbitrary arrests while his followers embarked unhindered upon wholesale blackmail, robbery, violence, and murder. Two days later he put the entire country under a state of siege.

On March 5, the people gave him 44 percent of their votes, but by excluding communist and some socialist deputies from the *Reichstag*, he obtained, with the support of the *Zentrum*, a majority vote, brushed aside the Constitution, and made himself dictator.

214

The Third Reich was born. The *Fuehrer* set about making the Republicans "atone" for the previous fourteen years.

On April 1, declaring the Jews to be a "guest people," the government declared a boycott of them and decreed an amnesty for Nazis convicted of torturing these "guests." The boycott meant the economic strangulation of Jewish business and professional men. To provide enough lawyers to fill the vacancies, the regime ordered that examinations be made easier for Aryans! Not even proven "nationalists" escaped the anti-Jewish rake.

Distinguished Jews like Albert Einstein and Karl Tucholsky had left the country earlier. Others now followed. Among these were close friends of ours like Wilhelm Haas, a highly original professor at the *Hochschule fuer Politik* in Berlin who became an adviser to the ruling Shah-in-Shah in Teheran, and publicists like Leopold Schwarzschild of *Das Tagebuch*. Edgar Stern-Rubarth, convinced that Hitler would not last long, lingered on though deprived of his job.

In New York, another Jew, the German Consul, Dr. Paul Schwarz, though immediately fired by the Nazis, remained in America and became a formidable foe of Nazism.

So did our "Aryan" friend, Otto Kiep, the Consul General, who resigned, courageously returned to Germany in order to oppose Hitler, and became a martyr to the anti-Nazi cause.

On the other hand, Dr. Schacht eagerly accepted from Hitler his old job as head of the Reichsbank. Certain office officials, of whom we expected better, such as Friedrich Gauss, Hans Dieckhoff, and Hans Thomsen, apparently found no reason not to serve the new regime.

At the end of April, Hitler set up a Soviet-type secret police known as the *Gestapo*, under a lawyer bureaucrat called Rudolf Diels, which immediately made mass arrests. Adversaries like Konrad Adenauer found themselves accused of "corruption." Monsignor Kaas, coauthor of Hitler's triumph, found it convenient to move to Rome.

Hitler's birthday became a national holiday. On May 1, 1933, he addressed a million people on Tempelhof Airfield, the largest and best orchestrated meeting I have ever seen. Somewhat earlier the regime had abolished independent labor organizations. Shortly thereafter, following the examples of such fanatical iconoclasts as Chinese Emperor Chian Sian-Wong, the Caliph Omar, and Savonarola, students of the nation that had produced Meister Eckhart, Bach, Leibniz, and Goethe, solemnly burned "impure" books in sixty-four bonfires. Among American authors thus honored were Hemingway, Dos Passos, and Upton Sinclair.

Knickerbocker had once described to me his horror when, as a boy in Texas, he watched a white mob burn a Negro. Bookburning was not inhuman, but it was a formal repudiation of civilization.

In June, the government "nationalized" the Lutheran Church, including a special ghetto-ized branch for Christianized Jews.

Before the month was out, Hitler annexed the nationalist Party of Hugenberg and Duesterberg, without whose assistance he could not have become Chancellor. Goebbels boasted that Germany had a world-wide mission to overthrow democracy. Crude totalitarianism, which Lenin imitated from the Incas and which was first publicly proclaimed by Mussolini, now reigned in the country of "poets and thinkers."

The Fuehrer's *sbirri* rounded up unemployed youths and sent them to work in the harvest fields. Nazified universities started expelling students at the first sign of opposition to the regime.

All this Hitler called maintaining Germany's acknowledged eminence in art and culture!

From the beginning there was something unreal about it. As I stood in the Wilhelmstrasse that night late in January watching thousands and thousands of uniformed ruffians parading before Adolf Hitler at the Chancery window in frock coat and Chaplinesque mustachios, I felt that it could not be so.

"No, no, no, no," I kept saying to Lilian, standing beside me, and as incredulous as I was.

Any doubt I may have had was dispelled the next day by my friend, Erwin Planck. The captain informed me that both he and Major Marcks were immediately seeking refuge, Planck in China, the major at the head of a *Reichswehr* battalion, safe in barracks.

"Just what will the Nazis do?"

"Play Indian—but for keeps!"

Hitler's dissolution of the *Reichstag* gave me a brief respite in which to forget Germany while skiing at Monte Pana in the Dolomites. John Gunther came from Vienna to fill in.

Eight days later I received an order to return immediately to Berlin! Whereupon I went out for a last run with Mumelter, crashed through the snow crust, and broke my leg.

Hardly was I back with my leg in a "walking cast" when Gottfried Bermann of the *Fischer Verlag* telephoned: he hoped I would understand that the publishers could not afford to put out the planned translation of *Germany Puts the Clock Back*.

I understood. Not for anything would I have brought harm to Bermann or his wife, "Tuti," daughter of the owner, with whom we had often gone swimming in the Havel River. Gottfried and "Tuti" were Jews.

Watching the *Reichstag* burn, John Elliott of the New York *Herald Tribune* expressed our common thought: only Hitler's death or the armed intervention of a foreign power could prevent the worst. Intervening was, however, the last thing the French had in mind. Poincaré or Barthou perhaps, but not Tardieu, Laval, or Flandin. When, eight months later, Poland proposed invading Germany, Paris and London refused to listen. The London *Times* all but disowned its indomitable correspondent, Norman Ebbutt, for his critical attitude. President Roosevelt had his hands full with the crisis at home and the coming economic conference in London.

The new owner of the Chicago *Daily News*, Frank Knox, had not had time to acquire the faith in his foreign service of his regretted predecessor, Walter Strong. When in March I reported that Germany had become an "insane asylum," even my brother began to wonder if I were not breaking under the strain.

Allen Dulles of the State Department, whom Paul requested to look me up during a visit in Berlin, assured me I was taking the German situation too seriously.

Shortly after Hitler obtained his Enabling Act, a government spokesman summoned me to announce that the *Fuehrer* had read *Germany Puts the Clock Back* and disliked it. (An edition had appeared in London while I was in the mountains.)

"That's all right," I countered. "I feel the same way about *Mein Kampf*. He writes for Germans, I write for Americans."

Whereupon the official informed me that until I resigned the chairmanship of the Foreign Press Association (to which I had been elected in January), the German government would have no further contact with that body.

An appeal to Dr. Goebbels merely drew a biting condemnation of my mendacious reporting. From that day detectives waited on the railing opposite our apartment and followed me wherever I went.

I had reported one such revolution in Italy. Why undergo a second and worse? Why not ask Knox for another assignment? On the other hand, how could I run away when everything I stood for was being challenged? I decided to fight it out.

Obviously I could not commit the Press Association. Calling a meeting, I reported Goebbels' threat and submitted my resignation. Somewhat to my surprise, my colleagues asked me to remain chairman by an overwhelming majority, including a courageous Italian fascist, Paolo Monelli, the author of an amusing book about the Germans, *Io e i Tedeschi*.

My "duel" with Goebbels was widely reported. In London, Wickham Steed declared *Germany Puts the Clock Back* to be the "clearest and fairest account of the German situation that I have read for many a day."

The London *Times* praised my colleagues for upholding our right to report things as we saw them.

Fortifield in spirit by such support, I went abroad for a few days' relief. In Paris I convinced my brother that far from having exaggerated, I had actually underplayed the German terror. In Holland it was tulip time. For two wonderful days, Marc Van Blankenstein drove me through the rainbow splendor of miles of flowers, a sight which could not have been more restorative.

In Berlin, the Nazi near-pogrom of Jews was in full swing. On this point Lilian and I decided to make no concessions. She repeatedly brushed past glowering storm troopers to trade in Jewish stores. On April 1, I had gone to a Jewish surgeon to have my "walking cast" removed. Challenged by Brown Shirts downstairs, I announced my nationality in English and went upstairs. It took four knocks to induce the frightened physician to let me in. He had, he said, expected no more patients.

In May at the house of a friend, the hostess took us quietly into the back room and showed us a released Jew, his back beaten to pulp.

Berlin newspapers carried no accounts of Jews murdered or tortured, or of synagogues burned. The Nazis persecuted those who passed such information to foreign newsmen. Accepting the challenge, Brok and I spared no effort in ascertaining the facts. We combed medical journals and provincial newspapers for possible clues or inadvertent revelations.

One unexpected informant on what rank-and-file Nazis were doing and saying was a young American newsman, Charles Hewitt. Charley came into our office one spring day and asked what he could do for the *Daily News*. Blue-eyed, blond, and "ultra Nordic" in appearance, he had been welcomed by the Nazis as a "true American." What he had seen had turned his stomach to the point where he wished to join the battle against them. Therefore he drifted naturally to Brok and me. We advised him to continue cultivating the Nazi Party, keep his mouth shut—and report regularly what he saw and heard. This he did for several months, with great profit to the Chicago *Daily News* and, I think, to his father's journal, the *Tonawanda News*, to which he also sent reports.

Yet another source of news, which the Nazis never detected, was a physician, the son of the Grand Rabbi of Berlin. About once every two weeks I phoned and complained of "pain in my throat." At his office I waited my turn among the other patients. Once he had me in the chair, he sent his assistant out of the room, and in her absence, thrust a tightly rolled typed sheet into my breast pocket. Back in the *News* office, I copied on my own typewriter the outrages he described and burned the original document.

One night, after dismissing the assistant, the doctor said: "You are a marked man and were followed here. I can't afford to see you any more. Unless you have some other suggestion."

Lose such a mine of information? Indeed, I had a suggestion and he accepted it. Thereafter, each Wednesday at precisely 11:45 A.M., he and I stood at neighboring urinals in the public comfort station under Potsdamer Platz, the most crowded spot in Berlin. Since we never spoke and left by separated entrances, my waiting snoops outside never suspected the messages that he dropped on the floor, which I pocketed unobserved.

Those Berlin Jews who had failed to leave Germany when they might have done so now found themselves without passports. Several came to me for advice.

"Get out, and fast," was my invariable answer. "Can you and your wife walk a few miles?" If the answer was yes, I furnished each a map of the German-Czechish border, marking a little used international ski trail which led to safety in Czechoslovakia.

At least one family did get out, since I received a postcard from Prague. Of those who complained that escape was impossible and that their only remaining course was to commit suicide, I always asked:

"If so, why not do it in the way that will do the world the most good?"

"Which is?"

"Something you must figure out for yourself," I answered as I rung for Richard to show them out. Any one of them might have been a Nazi agent sent to trap me into saying something that would justify my arrest.

To discredit my reports of anti-Semitic outrages, "Putzi" Hanfstaengl started the story that Mowrer was a "secret" Jew. How otherwise account for his biased outlook? This Knickerbocker scotched with a single remark. To a group of Nazi leaders who repeated the charge, Knick answered: "Edgar a Jew? Of course! As Jewish as Ludendorff!"

Extirpating Hebrews was, of course, only one detail of the Nazi plan for "nordicizing" the Germans.

This fantasy was deepest in two top leaders, Alfred Rosenberg, who had drunk deeply of previous racialism, and Walter Darré, Minister of Agriculture and self-appointed "eugenicist" of Germany.

Solemn as only a fanatic can be, Darré explained to the foreign press that the key to nordicization lay in the German women. Henceforth these were to be divided into four classes under government supervision.

Class One women, tall, long-legged, blonde, blue-eyed, and high-breasted, would mate exclusively with leading Nazis. (Never mind that many of these were dark!)

"Ordinary" German specimens, Class Two, would marry anyone they chose—and produce privates for the future army.

Class Three women, physically defective or conspicuously "un-Germanic," would be sterilized before marriage.

Class Four women, consisting of Jews, Slavs, and "other sub-humans," would be permitted neither to reproduce nor to marry.

In a few generations the Germans would be overwhelmingly Nordic.

This was too much even for newsmen inured to Nazi nonsense. Knickerbocker put the first question.

"Herr Minister, would you tell us why you wish to give all the advantages to Class Four women?"

Among roars of laughter the indignant Darré broke off the meeting.

Hitler never applied the Darré plan. But some months later, a magazine called *Das Wissen der Nation* prescribed proper eugenical behavior. Blond German males, the author specified, should avoid dark, Mediterranean-type girls, particularly those "with short legs, black hair, hooked nose, full lips, and inclination to plumpness."

The day after the book burning, I had an appointment with the economist, Werner Sombart, author of internationally famous studies of modern capitalism and himself an advocate (somewhat like Zehrer) of a "German socialism."

Assuming him to be normal, I opened by describing my distress while watching the bonfire before the university. What, I queried, was the matter with such students? Nothing at all, he replied. They were patriots engaged in extirpating un-German elements from the national life. Shocked, I asked:

"Are you aware just where this sort of patriotism will end?"

"Where, then?"

"In a new 'fresh and jolly' war!"

"And so what?" answered the unperturbed professor.

"Do you favor such a war?" I stammered.

"Not precisely. But I must admit that I see in war between great nations the highest manifestation of the Divine Will."

To us foreigners, almost more obnoxious than avowed Nazis were those nationalists who had secretly helped bury the Weimar Republic and now boasted of their work. One pleasant spring day, Camille Lemercier and I were having an *aperitif* on a café terrace at the corner of the Tiergarten, then at its most delightful. Camille had been my brother's assistant in Paris, and now represented *Havas* in Berlin. A sensitive man of great integrity, he found Germany's regression horrible in itself, and dangerous for France.

A German colleague approached. Wolfgang Schwarz had been foreign editor of the socialist *Vorwaerts*. He was an agreeable fellow, and I frequently pooled information with him at international conferences. But with the advent of Hitler, he boasted that he had for years been a *Reichswehr* agent charged with reporting on socialists. We greeted him coolly.

"Have you something against me?" he asked.

"Wolfgang," I replied, "can it be true that you think this new regime is good for Germany?"

"According to my conviction, yes," he said in French.

Camille turned white and, using the second person singular to express his contempt, said, in French, in a low intense voice:

"Thou! Thou hast no convictions. Thou art venal, thou art vile, I spit on thee."

Schwarz raised his fist, dropped it, shrugged his shoulders, and walked away.

"Camille," I asked gently, "do you see a chance of avoiding a war with these barbarians?"

"How can one be sure? All I know is that we can always count on their stupidity."

In June each year the Foreign Press Association gave a dinner for the German foreign minister at which the latter outlined the latest developments in his policy—as far as he wished it to be understood abroad. Since the government was boycotting the Association, we decided instead to give a luncheon for the diplomatic corps, with no government officials present. We did, however, send invitations to Schacht and to "long" Sahm, Mayor of Berlin, both of whom surprised us by attending. Every ambassador in Berlin accepted, including those of fascist countries. Then suddenly the dean of the diplomatic corps, the Papal Nuncio, sent regrets. Remembering Brok's story of Cardinal Pacelli's intervention in favor of the Nazis, I understood the Nuncio's change of heart. A month later he signed a concordat with Hitler.

To circumvent diplomatic protocol at the luncheon we seated the guests at small tables, each including one or more newsmen. No ambassador sat "above" any other. I made the only set speech, welcoming the guests. To express the Association's feelings without precisely attacking anything, I feigned difficulty with German grammar: "In this country where we are—I mean *have* been—so happy . . . that some of us have sought relief—I mean recreation—abroad . . ." etc., etc. By the fifth such "correction" the diplomats were roaring. The French ambassador almost rolled off his chair.

Their hilarity so angered Schacht that he asked permission to reply, and launched an attack on the foreign press for substituting opinion for facts. When I solemnly thanked him for the compliment to the American press, famous for its factual reporting, the diplomats again guffawed and Schacht sat down, his face scarlet.

This meeting was a blow to Goebbels. Even more distasteful to him was the subsequent news from America that I had been given the Pulitzer Prize for foreign reporting in 1932. Yet flexible as always, he switched completely and began offering me "favors." Among these was inclusion in a group of correspondents taken to a concentration camp in order to see for themselves how "humanely" political prisoners were treated.

Among the prisoners, the best known was Carl von Ossietzky, former editor of the *Volksbuehne*, a pacifist weekly that had specialized in revealing details of Germany's secret rearmament.

On the way, Knick and I devised a scheme to ascertain from Ossietzky, even in the presence of his guards, what sort of treatment he was receiving. Sure enough, after taking us for a tour of the obviously prettied-up camp, at our request they brought out Ossietzky, heavily guarded, but with no visible marks of physical mistreatment.

After greetings on both sides, Knick asked:

"Are you allowed to receive books, Herr Ossietzky?"

"Certainly" . . . without changing expression.

"What sort of books would you prefer?"

"Whatever you have . . . history perhaps."

A good beginning. I took over.

"History then . . . but what period? Ancient, medieval, modern—which do you prefer?"

After a long silence, Ossietzky replied in a monotone: "Send me a description of the Middle Ages in Europe," and, for an instant, looked squarely into my eyes.

We needed no further information. Instead we shook hands and watched silently while the guards led Carl von Ossietzky back into Europe's New Dark Age.

Yet even in the Third Reich life was not without comic interludes. As I said, Lilian and I had for years maintained formal social relations with, among others, Soviet diplomats. One morning the Russian embassy counselor invited me to lunch, explaining that he was returning almost immediately to Moscow. Since he had barely noticed me before, I judged that something unusual was up. It was. After an overabundant meal ordered in advance, with too much good Moselle wine, Brodovsky began:

"We Russians greatly admire your reports on the Nazi regime, Herr Mowrer."

"Delighted."

"In fact your line is so like ours that I want to ask you something —why aren't you a communist?"

Remembering the Communist Party's previous support of Hitler, I grinned. "Presumably because I do not believe in communism," I answered.

"Have you read Marx?"

"Yes. That may be the reason."

"Don't you realize that only communists can understand current events? Bourgeois are blinded to the meaning even of their own actions by their ignorance of the dialectic."

"That probably explains my failure to understand. My father is a businessman."

"Not at all. Intellectuals can transcend class blindness. Lenin came from the petty nobility."

"Seriously," I queried, changing the subject, "what good would I be to you if I gave up my job and went to Moscow?"

"Who said anything about giving up your job and going to Moscow?"

"My boss is a tolerant man. But I doubt if he would keep a communist on his payroll."

"Why tell him?"

"I see. I should stay here as an unidentified communist and you would help me write my dispatches. Well, . . ." enjoying the situation, "supposing I did, what would I get out of it?"

"No other regime so rewards intellectuals."

"Provided they follow the Party line," I corrected.

"Naturally. But they have no difficulty because they know it is right."

"May be. Concretely put, how much would you pay?"

"I don't know how much you earn now."

"I am a well-paid foreign correspondent."

My questions seemed to raise Brodovsky's hope. He raised his wineglass. "Shall we say twice as much?"

I drank, then laughed heartily. "So that's how you do it! Sorry I can't be of any help to you. But glad you like my dispatches."

We parted, he to Moscow to be "purged" by Stalin, I to continue an exhausting struggle which I could not win, but which self-respect would not allow me to abandon.

Before leaving Berlin, the press chief of the Czechoslovak Legation in Berlin, a great friend, had promised me an interview with his country's eighty-three-year-old President, Thomas Garrigue Masaryk.

Late in the afternoon of July 4, I entered the great castle on the hill where so many Holy Roman Emperors had reigned, ascended the monumental staircase, and, with no ceremony at all, was shown into the President's book-lined study. I noted his erect figure, his deep-set, twinkling brown eyes and the strong thin hands which, in his youth, had swung a blacksmith's hammer . . . even as had my Grandfather Mowrer.

"You have had much experience both as a thinker and as a patriot. Many people consider you the greatest living democrat," I began. "I wish to know your opinion concerning the most striking symptom of our times. I refer to the revolt against civilization."

President Masaryk: "What do you call civilization?"

E. A. M.: "Put it this way: from time to time down the ages, a sprinkling of human beings have, against the society around them, striven for the recognition of better things. Among these were beauty and intelligence; also reason, tolerance, mercy, social justice, and personal liberty. . . . In the West, suddenly, today, we are faced with an almost worldwide movement which denies their value. What ought those who still hold to the old-fashioned idea of civilization do to combat the new trends?"

President Masaryk: "There is no formula. . . . The situation is never twice the same."

E. A. M.: "Then you feel perhaps the apparent danger to the democratic ideal is not serious?"

President Masaryk: "If democracy is in danger, that only proves that its leaders were tried in the balance and found wanting. . . . Perhaps this temporary period is necessary to call the people back to the beauty of freedom, to abandon violence in favor of collaboration. . . . Democracy needs leaders, like everything else. . . . Society needs a common faith and the intellectuals had none. People wanted truth. The intellectuals said one thing today and another tomorrow. How can one expect to be followed by common men if one has ceased to understand their needs, material and spiritual?"

E. A. M.: "But these new leaders' success showed that it was as easy to sell a third-rate political philosophy as a third-rate toothpaste. Is there not a deadly danger for democracy in this demonstration?"

President Masaryk: "Not in the long run. . . . If the new rulers can satisfy the fundamental human needs they will remain in power. If not, they will be driven out."

E. A. M.: "In the meantime, years and perhaps decades may pass."

President Masaryk: "Quite so. . . . But if I am right, democracy will come because in the end it must come. . . . If, on the other hand, people continue to prefer tyranny, oppression, and intolerance, then I am wrong. How short the periods of liberty, how limited the geographical area covered! But in the end it will be different. There will be democracy."

E. A. M.: "How can we most speedily bring it about?"

President Masaryk: "Follow your convictions. Live your politics. Tell the truth and do not steal. And, above all, do not be afraid to die."

Thus, we parted. Walking down the great staircase of the castle, I rejoiced at the old President's call to courage, but found it difficult to accept his fatalism. Would whole generations be willing to die for an ideal which only their great grandchildren could hope to see?

In Berlin I welcomed our publisher, come to see for himself what the Third Reich was like. Frank Knox was an experienced newsman, limited in outlook but objective in judgment. After thoroughly questioning me and other American correspondents, he listened to the Foreign Minister Baron Konstantin von Neurath, a "renegade" professional diplomat who had curried favor with Hitler, and to certain American diplomats. Then he returned to Chicago convinced that the Germans were living under a terror and that his Berlin correspondent was reporting it accurately.

Before leaving, Knox informed me that he wanted to shift me to Tokyo. If I remained in Germany the Nazis would do me physical harm.

Lilian was surprised but not unwilling. Japan and Italy had been her childhood favorites. She admired Japanese poetry and plays. I was less enthusiastic. The big show was in Europe, now more than ever.

Still, the Germans would sooner or later throw me out. Here was a chance to know that Orient whose philosophy had meant much to me. I gratefully accepted Knox's offer, and without saying much about our coming transfer, Lilian and I began buying books and laying in the kind of wardrobe Tokyo's climate and etiquette required.

Washington's replacement in July of Ambassador Sackett by William Dodd was a blow to freedom. Sackett was a coal mine owner who, knowing nothing of foreign affairs, had relied upon a staff which for a time included two of our best diplomats, John C. Wiley and DeWitt Poole. Dodd considered himself an "expert" on Germany—he had studied in Leipzig in 1904! Since he brought a letter of introduction to me from Charley Merriam, I tried, over a long dinner on my balcony overlooking the Tiergarten, to explain what was happening. To no purpose: he knew better. Obviously nothing but time would correct this purblind professor's misapprehensions. In fact, his obnubilation was such that even after thirty Americans had been mistreated by

Nazi hoodlums, Dodd announced he had no wish to mix in Germany's affairs. In case of difficulty with the regime, we American correspondents had only Consul General Messersmith, Commercial Attaché Miller, and Consul Raymond Geist, to rely upon. What was worse, the Nazis knew it.

Truly exasperating was my inability to convince two American editors whom I admired, Oswald Garrison Villard of the *Nation*, and George Shuster of *The Commonweal*. Neither man was ready to accept the hard facts of the Third Reich. I remember wasting two hours in a vain attempt to persuade Villard that Hitler meant war. During a similar conversation, Shuster at one point became too indignant to continue. If such intelligent Americans refused to face the facts, how be confident that the West would react in time to prevent the worst?

Early in August, the German wife of Dr. Paul Goldmann, Berlin correspondent of the Vienna *Neue Freie Presse*, telephoned in anguish to announce that the Nazis had arrested her elderly and ailing husband in reprisal for the Austrians' arrest and deportation of the Nazi press officer in Vienna. Whereupon Knickerbocker and I hatched a plot: Knick would tell Goebbels that, in exchange for Goldmann's immediate release, I would resign the chairmanship of the Foreign Press Association.

And so it happened. When several American colleagues heard of my offer they went to *Gestapo* chief Diels and offered successively each to sit in jail for a day (with appropriate publicity) for the overaged and innocent Goldmann, until the Germans had had sufficient "reprisal satisfaction." This was something that Diels could not accept and did not want publicized. Although I did not know of my colleagues' offer at the time, it helped persuade Goebbels to accept my offer. Knick sent to the *News* an unsigned dispatch describing the "solemn treaty" between its correspondent and the German Government. And the latter's press bureau put out a communiqué stating that according to the agreement Goldmann had been released and Mowrer had resigned!

The matter did not stop there. The British and American press not only printed the account of the "deal with Goebbels," but added, with visible glee, that since Mowrer was soon to be transferred to Tokyo anyway, he had got the better of the bargain.

Whereupon the Berlin *Zwoelf-Uhr Blatt*, Hitler's *Voelkischer Beobachter*, and the *Boersenzeitung* informed German readers that their government had eliminated from the chairmanship of the Foreign Press Association a "sworn and proven enemy."

The Nazis stationed storm troopers outside my office and our apartment, shadowed my friends, and threatened my office associates. (Messermith never went out in the evening without giving me the telephone number where I could reach him—in case of need!) In Washington, Ambassador Hans Dieckhoff, a career diplomat and former friend who was now supinely serving Hitler's aims, informed the State Department and Colonel Knox in Chicago that because of the "people's righteous indignation" (*die kochende Volkseele*) against that liar, Mowrer, the German government *could no longer guarantee his physical safety.* A thoroughly alarmed Knox wired me to leave Germany at once.

I had assumed we would leave for Chicago and Tokyo in October. Now Goebbels was trying to force me out in mid-August.

My inclination was to hold to the original schedule. Masaryk's last words echoed in my head: "Tell the truth and don't be afraid to die!" In particular, I wanted to attend the Nazi Party Celebration in Nuremberg on September 2, thus showing my contempt for Goebbels' threat. But Dodd, Messersmith, and Knickerbocker were all against it. They insisted that the Nazis were quite capable of having me "shot while trying to escape," their favorite formula in such cases.

Lilian was magnificent. She could see my point: yielding to a Nazi threat was repugnant. On the other hand, why risk one's life in an inevitably losing duel? Better stay alive and carry on the good fight elsewhere. Finally, I consented to leave Berlin on September 1, the day *before* the opening of the Party Congress. Lilian would stay behind, get rid of the apartment, and ship the furniture to Tokyo; then, with Diana Jane, join me in Paris and together sail for America.

Once it became known I was leaving, expressions of sympathy poured in, not only from foreign and German friends, but from people I did not know. In spite of my protestations that I had done only what any of them would do, a group of British and American colleagues and friends gave us a party and presented a silver bowl to a "gallant fighter for the liberty of the press."

On the final day, several Germans, headed by Helmut von Moltke, ignoring the dirty looks of the ever-present snoops, were at Bahnhof Zoo to see me off. George Messersmith had canceled his office appointments to appear. In a loud voice he promised to see to it that Lilian and Diana Jane would soon follow me and with no interference from the Nazis.

In spite of everything I felt a deep sadness. I had enjoyed Berlin and learned much from the Germans. Yet just as the train was pulling into the station, the young German official sent to make sure I actually left, asked in a sweet-sour voice: "And when are you coming back to Germany, Herr Mowrer?"

I sought a reply that would put this scoundrel in his place.

"Why, when I can come back with about two million of my countrymen," I answered loudly enough for all those present to hear.

It took the official a full minute to take it in. Then he almost shouted:

"*Aber nein.* Impossible."

"Not for the *Fuehrer*. The *Fuehrer* can bring anything about . . . even that."

PART FIVE

The

Great

Refusal

Easy the way
Down to Avernus; night and day the gates
Of Dis stand open. But to retrace thy steps
And reach the upper air—here lies the task.
VERGIL

21

Some Uses of Adversity

What's so good about prosperity?
—RUSSELL LYNES

AT THE *News* in Chicago, Colonel Knox, Editor Dennis, Hal O'Flaherty, Laird Bell, Carroll Binder, Harry Smith, and others welcomed us as the happy survivors of a battle—as indeed we were, our heads "bloody but unbowed." Also, I realized, among newsmen a Pulitzer Prize meant more than its accompanying five hundred dollars conveyed.

Business leaders friendly to the paper, like Lawrence Houghteling, Benjamin Becker, Kellogg Fairbank, and Lessing Rosenthal entertained us royally and introduced us to other Chicagoans, some of whom were eager to hear first-hand about the German madness.

Yet in spite of their kindness to us, we could not but realize that to most Americans, the United States was a country which God had abandoned. In 1930 they had been still too stunned to realize what had happened. Now their self-confidence had gone. The land of unlimited opportunity saw itself as the home of millions and millions of unemployed, their number swollen by adolescents who would have been in school if their fathers had found work. Into this atmosphere, to be sure, with the New Deal and President Roosevelt's reassuring talks, there had come a note of hope.

But not for businessmen. At our first talk, Colonel Knox informed me that to meet his payments on the Chicago *Daily News*, he was obliged to dismiss one-tenth of his employees.

"Don't do that," I remonstrated. "Just reduce by one-tenth all salaries, beginning with mine and yours, and fire nobody."

The Colonel smiled sarcastically. "You sure are out of touch with

229

this country. The unions would rather I fired nine out of ten than reduce wages. Your suggestion is quite impractical."

Such it may have been. But when an entire society is involved in a crisis, the least it can do is to demand equality of sacrifice. Yet how convince union leaders nurtured on the conviction that what goes up must never come down? Their stubbornness was just another example of the national fixation on something for nothing that had brought about the stock exchange crash in 1929.

On the other hand, business leaders in Chicago were not speculators but manufacturers and traders and railroad executives who, by no stretch of the imagination, could feel themselves responsible for the nation's disaster. Their opposition to the New Deal was free both of hypocrisy and of secret guilt.

Nonetheless, as I came to believe later, the New Deal put a permanent crimp in Chicago's future. Until the Depression, the city on the lake was not merely the second largest in the country, but felt itself the coming leader. The *Daily News* foreign service appeared in New York and in Philadelphia as well as in a large number of lesser places. The Chicago school of writers rivalled the ex-patriate group in Paris. Many Chicagoans had felt that it was only a matter of time before the "central city" would outstrip "foreign" New York.

The New Deal destroyed completely any chance of this happening. For by hobbling Big Business and concentrating outstanding individuals in Washington, it drained Chicago of the necessary energy and self-confidence.

But there was worse: the apparent inability of both Hoover and Roosevelt to deal effectively with unemployment convinced many Americans that communism was indeed the wave of the future. In their eyes capitalism had revealed its basic inability to supply the needs of modern society. They began to think of themselves as revolutionaries. Among them were a large number of writers.

Since some of them were my friends, their apostasy disturbed me. They had no excuse for failing to investigate the facts of communist life before jumping. These facts were in most respects appalling. After sixteen years the Communist Paradise was a terror-haunted slum. In some respects, Soviet Russia was worse than Tsarist Russia. Economically the Bolsheviks had set the country back by at least twenty years. This was not my personal opinion. I had never been in the U.S.S.R. It was the verdict of scores of foreign observers who had returned from Moscow through Berlin and unburdened themselves of their disgust. The facts were available in any number of books.

Life in the United States in 1933 was still more abundant than in anywhere else. The American living standard during the worst of the Depression was as high as that of Britain at its most prosperous. Why then were Americans so sorry for themselves?

Obviously I had yet to learn, with Schopenhauer, that happiness is a matter of the relation of reality to expectation: you can increase it by improving the reality or by lowering the expectation. Since Americans were unable to do the former and unwilling to do the latter, they embraced a sophism: since capitalism was a failure, its avowed enemy, communism, must be a success.

Paradoxically, indirect support for these rebels was furnished by the business community. Despite Washington's steadfast refusal to grant diplomatic recognition to Moscow, Stalin, after 1927, had let out huge contracts to American companies to build plants, dams, and other essentials in his country. Skilled Russian propagandists feted and brainwashed the builders and managed in addition to convince American business that American recognition of the U.S.S.R. would bring a flood of Soviet orders. A prominent Democrat like William E. Bullitt, the Philadelphia patrician who had tried to "mediate" at Prinkipo in 1919 and later married John Reed's widow, had urged diplomatic recognition. Convinced that he could thereby relieve the Depression, foil Hitler's threats, and hasten the transformation of the Soviet regime, President Roosevelt, in exchange for certain promises from Soviet Foreign Minister Maxim Litvinov (whom I had met at Genoa in 1922), did so, sending that same Bullitt and a selected group of American diplomats to Moscow to represent the United States.

Although Stalin kept none of Litvinov's promises, diplomatic recognition by the United States Administration unquestionably fortified the belief, or at least, the hope, of rebellious or self-pitying Americans that the U.S.S.R. was indeed the "future." This one could understand.

Incomprehensible, on the other hand, was the Chicagoans' apparent indifference to the gangsterism that fattened on the fruits of the Eighteenth Amendment (shortly thereafter superceded by the Twenty-First Amendment). In Chicago, the profits of bootlegging had made gang warfare endemic. So long as Americans persisted in consuming illicit alcohol, the leaders could do little to control the resulting lawlessness. Yet they could have tried harder.

In fact, three years earlier I had put to Samuel Insull, the self-assured head of giant Midwest Utilities, the blunt question: "Why do you prefer to have crooks in the City Hall?"

Since at each of our luncheon meetings, he regularly plied me with questions about the international situation, he could hardly refuse an answer to mine.

And out came the truth. "Because, Edgar, in your country" (Insull had remained British) "one has only the political choice between a crook and a Methodist minister with no understanding of business. By coming to terms with a crook I can protect my franchises." So there it was, the moral indifferences of the old frontier.

The story of my "duel" with Dr. Goebbels, culminating in his threat to my "physical safety," had been widely publicized throughout the United States. One consequence was an invitation from the Foreign Policy Association to tour the country talking on the New Germany. These lectures were to be in the form of debates with an official from the German Embassy in Washington, who would argue that the Nazis were seeking nothing but "equal status" with France and Britain.

This offer bothered me. Though loquacious by nature, I had lectured relatively little and never engaged in public debates.

Moreover, Lilian and I were extremely tired. Only after reaching America did we feel the full effect of those seven months of fighting Hitler. We had a craving to forget Berlin and the *Daily News* for a while before embarking on any new ventures. Still it was the crying duty of those who knew the facts to warn America concerning the nature and intentions of Nazism. So I accepted the Association's offer of a debating tour to start after a canoe trip with Albert and Marie Green on the Flambeau River in Northern Wisconsin. Never since our marriage had we overlooked an opportunity to paddle an Indian-type canoe on anything from a mill pond to a spring torrent.

In 1933 the Flambeau Valley was still wild country, the woods thicker and more primitive than those I had known as a boy in Michigan, totally different from the stately, manicured European forests with which we had become familiar.

Now for about a week we paddled down the Flambeau, shooting occasional rapids, camping on the shore where night found us. Adventure we had in plenty—an encounter with an inquisitive bear that poked its nose into our tent early one morning, an overturn in going over a small waterfall, one night in a lonely cabin whose lock we forced open—and finally returned to Chicago, relaxed and ready for anything.

There Knox abruptly informed me that he had changed his plans. My brother Paul would become editor in place of the retiring Dennis and I could take Paul's place as correspondent in Paris. How about it?

The prospect of life in Japan had been exciting and our furniture was already somewhere between Berlin and Tokyo. Still, Paris was unique. Once Knox assured me that the paper would meet the expense of getting our belongings back from the Orient, I accepted his offer with enthusiasm.

A few days later, I set out on my debating tour with a slippery-tongued member of the German Embassy in Washington. For me it was a very qualified success. My opponent concentrated on making me appear "anti-German" and ignorant of German affairs despite my many years in Berlin. Even though I knew that he had to lie to keep his job, I resented his charges and at the beginning overreacted to them. In consequence, he won the first three or four of our debates. Not until we reached Minneapolis had I learned to deal with his innuendoes and half truths and hold up to ridicule this diplomat "sent abroad to lie for his country"—and such a country as Nazi Germany. And also to prepare my own arguments more carefully.

They needed every bite I could put into them. Most Americans were still unprepared to believe the shocking truth about the Nazis. They "knew," from contacts in America, that Germans were "not like that." Other listeners were still victims of the legend that in the Great War we had fought on the wrong side. A number had swallowed the myth propounded by, among others, my news colleague, Walter Millis, that the United States had been maneuvered into that war, not by German submarines, but by those "merchants of death," the domestic armament makers.

An overwhelming number of citizens were determined that, come what might, the United States must never again be drawn into one of "Europe's eternal wars." Hence they resented my making them uncomfortable by pointing out that in the course of its independent existence our country had fought at least as many wars as any European country and that if, this time, the British and French did not stop Hitler, the United States might have to do so. Even when they accepted as accurate my analysis of Hitler's intentions, many still argued that this was no business of ours. Some were already asking Congress to pass "neutrality legislation" that would prevent a rash or purblind future President from "helping England again."

I found this a strange way of "keeping faith" with those Americans who had died in the Argonne. But so things were.

Some German-Americans were creating anti-Semitic *Bunds* in imitation of their former Fatherland. Pro-Germans like George Sylvester Viereck, in a supreme effort to discredit *Germany Puts The Clock Back*, were accusing its author of being "pro-socialist if not pro-communist." The fact that no American newsman had been more closely associated with conservative, European-minded Germans like Prince Rohan, they soft-pedalled.

Once the lecture tour was over, we hastened to St. Petersburg, Florida, to visit Father, now seventy-five years old. Since the death of my Aunt Sarah, he had lived alone. Each day he went to one of three golf clubs, played eighteen holes, had his lunch, and returned to town to read his son's dispatches. His welcome betrayed a new respect for he felt that in the conflict with Dr. Goebbels I had done as he would have done.

Yet all too soon we were back in Chicago. Father took comfort from Paul's coming presence in Chicago, well within reach, and had hoped that we too would remain in America. Still, stoic as always, he followed his life-time principle of "taking it as it comes," and uttered no word of regret or protest when we left.

Thanks to my travels throughout the country I perceived that the Depression had brought to prominence individuals who accepted hardship cheerfully and set about overcoming it by their own efforts. Among their satisfactions was the fact that the customer was again king.

Yet the chief beneficiaries of the Depression, it seemed to me, were American intellectuals—professors, writers, artists—all those whose interest lay outside the prevailing pattern of getting and spending. For perhaps the first time since the Founding Years, these people were receiving almost as much consideration as their counterparts in Europe.

Not only their opinions, but their works commanded respect. After Sunday dinner at his home in Evanston, Editor Dennis read us poems by Carl Sandburg—not new, but newly popular. I found them interesting in the way Whitman was interesting. For the first time since Eugene Field, Chicago seemed proud of a poet.

Moreover, I was impressed by the New Deal's help to indigent artists which seemed bound to attenuate the ugliness of American cities.

To make sure that his new Paris correspondent "understood the United States better," Colonel Knox had decided that I should carry out some Chicago assignments before returning to Europe.

"Go out to our so-called universities and find out what the professors are doing or thinking that is of interest to us ordinary folks," he told me.

Ever since I all but became a philosophy teacher, I had felt the pull of the academic world. For the next two weeks I divided my time between the Midway and the Evanston campuses, interviewing outstanding educators. Introduced by the *News* as "illuminating articles giving the impressions of a correspondent trained to analyze the ideas and personalities of university men," my eleven stories struck many readers as something new in Chicago journalism.

For the sake of the headline, I led off with Chicago University's "boy-wonder," Robert Maynard Hutchins. In a speech to the December graduating class, President Hutchins had announced that "fact-finding science" was bankrupt! In its stead, he advocated the acceptance of a set of rational principles based on "fixed and immutable ideas."

Scientists should prepare the way for a new era of "collective synthesis." The "proper subject matter of a science" was its abstractions. A university must be "intelligible as well as intelligent. The modern American university seems to approximate a kindergarten at one end and a clutter of specialists at the other." This conception led, I believe, to what became the controversial Great Books program.

At both universities, certain faculty members were deep in politics, city or national, led on the Midway, by my friends, Charles E. Merriam and T. V. Smith, a pragmatist philosopher. Along with Louis Brownlow and Augustus B. Hatton of Northwestern, these professors hoped to reform the American government, its administration, its tax system, its criminology. This was something new.

Local political scientists agreed with me that the world had recently passed from a *post*-war to a *pre*-war period, and that hostilities would follow unless the free countries stopped Hitler and the rambunctious Japanese. Unlike most other citizens, they felt sure that the United States would be drawn into whatever major war developed. Particularly insistent on this were Bernadotte Schmitt of Chicago and Kenneth Colegrove of Northwestern, two remarkable intellects. Schmitt was still involved in a running feud with rival historian, Harry Elmer Barnes, who had tried to exonerate Imperial Germany from primary responsibility for starting the world war. Since my experience had led me to the conclusion that Germany was chiefly responsible, I supported Schmitt. Colegrove, a Far Eastern specialist, predicted that the Japanese military would "do it first."

Among themselves, of course, my interviewees disagreed fundamentally on what type of knowledge was most important. Arthur Compton, the great physicist, plumped for science, not only for its practical benefits, but for its inculcation of "that veracity of thought which springs alone from the search for truth."

Sociologist William P. Ogburn, on the other hand, insisted that material inventions accounted for most changes in human life. Since inventions were occurring with increasing speed, Ogburn prophesied "no rest ahead for conservatives."

Harold Lasswell, so melancholy when we had known him in Berlin, had returned in high spirits from a Freudian immersion in Vienna. Thanks to his analysts, he now accepted "infantile and childhood experience" as the keys to the understanding of people. The key to better politics was psychotherapy. Abraham Lincoln owed his historic role as liberator to a mother fixation. . . .

Arthur Isaac Kendall, a bacteriologist at Northwestern University, argued without exactly saying so that knowledge of mankind's relation to microorganisms held the key to the future of both. Human illnesses might come from ailing bacilli. "Instead of treating ourselves, we should treat our microbes, learning to keep them in their harmless, domesticated state of partnership with us rather than allowing them to revert to some primitive savagery." A brilliant mind.

Thirty odd years later, I look back with joy to those days among the Chicago professors. I found them better educated and wiser than those with whom I had studied, eager—perhaps a little too eager—to help society; empirical rather than dogmatic, radical in belief (some with ill-concealed sympathy for the Soviet system). Paradoxically, the humanists tended toward atheism, the scientists toward a religious attitude which was scorned by the psychologists, whose loose theories in turn awakened the laughter of the logicians.

Beneath it all, however, I thought to discern a trend away from agnosticism and doubt and a hunger for the kind of fixed principles Hutchins advocated.

"Mankind," I wrote optimistically at the end of my last story, "is like a Greek chorus singing a Negro hymn. In one age, the strophe leads the choir and loudly it carols, 'Ah'm on my way to Heaven I know.' This makes for an age of faith. But after a time the antistrophe comes in with the next line: 'Keep on a-goin',' you've a long ways to go'—which makes for an age of skepticism. Now for several decades, mankind has been listening to the second line and become a trifle weary. Analysis has taken the charm from too many pleasures. Unless I am much mistaken, we shall soon again be hearing about the path to Heaven."

The result of the current ferment, I further predicted, would be a merger and classification of knowledge. If unsuccessful, science itself might be temporarily eclipsed in the popular unrest that lack of doctrine was almost sure to bring. If too successful, it could introduce a new kind of intolerance. But if even 50 percent successful, if it satisfied men's consciences without doing violence to their intellects, the new synthesis might be the finest fruit of the new age. "To have felt the coming of this synthesis is to this reporter the most interesting result of the investigation of the academic mind at Chicago."

Never again could the United States be quite so sure of its superior and special destiny. Sooner or later the professors' vision of a technologically integrated world would prevail. The vital question was, when.

The day after I turned in the last of my university articles we were on our way to Paris.

22

Encore La France

*Paris . . . the symbolic city of human experi-
ence.*

—RICHARD LE GALLIENNE

ALMOST BEFORE WE KNEW IT, we were temporarily established in a
hotel on the Rue de Rivoli facing the statue of Joan of Arc, surely a
symbolic location: Joan had stood for what the contemporary democracies needed most: freedom, courage, faith. . . .

Yet it did not take long to realize that while the city was the same,
the French people had changed. Something was missing.

It took a little time to identify that something. It was not a result
of economic depression. France was feeling this, though less than
Germany or the United States. Public finances, except for one brief
period, had been unstable since 1914. Since the government refused to
deflate the franc again, the people now found themselves once more
with too high prices, diminishing exports, a capital hemorrhage, and
excessive corruption; all in all, a fertile seed-bed for communist propaganda.

What we missed was not the people's faith in the franc. It was
their faith in themselves. Instead of the confidence that had led Joan
(and almost five centuries later, Georges Clemenceau) to victory, a deep
uncertainty; instead of the *Pucelle's* total courage, timidity; instead of
the traditional realism, wishful thinking.

The situation called for a Poincaré. But that dour old man was
desperately ill. And his alleged truculence toward the Germans (*"Poincaré la guerre!"*) had made him anathema to the entire French Left
and to much of the financial Right.

The people seemed hopelessly divided. Uncompromising ideologues
like the French have always taken sides. Civil strife, like that between

the Armagnacs and the Burgundians, with the Paris carpenters on one side, the butchers on the other, had been endemic. Ever since 1789, republicans had been at loggerheads with an irresponsible monarchist minority. Nonetheless, the victorious Jacobins had not only firmly established republican rule, but had planted those irresistible seedlings, liberty, equality, and fraternity, all over Europe. Yet in 1934 Europe's antidemocratic epidemic was spreading to France and the chief carrier was the "hereditary enemy."

How, I wondered, was it possible for so democratic and intelligent a people to make light of this danger?

Two old friends provided an answer. Most of the "men of letters" I had formerly frequented were dead or had become national figures, equally remote from the world of newsmen. Verhaeren had died in a stupid accident during the war. Rolland was still living in Switzerland, unreconciled to his own country. Duhamel and Romains were famous novelists. Vildrac and Arcos, now respectively a leading poet and a successful publisher, were, however as accessible as before.

But as our paths had been different, so were our current views. Though we shared a passion to prevent a new war, we differed totally as to method. Arcos and his associates placed their hope in disarmament. The last war, in their eyes, had demonstrated the futility as well as the horror of any armed struggle; it left the victors no better off than the vanquished! In a wartime poem, Arcos had stated this in an incomparable line: *"Les morts sont tous d'un seul côté."* One of his earliest books had been called *Poets Against War.*

Furthermore, he, his wife, Renée, and the Vildracs were convinced that all peoples, including Germans and Italians, shared their aversion. In their eyes, Mussolini's rodomontades were for internal consumption only. Hitler might rave and promise the Germans rule over Europe. But if either dared start a new war, his long-suffering people would turn against him and toss him out.

Meanwhile, over in Russia, Stalin had eliminated the capitalist "merchants of death" and created a peaceful-loving state, moving, however slowly, toward social justice.

So my friends asserted.

Experience had taught me otherwise. In 1920 I had been deeply shocked by Santayana's prediction of more wars to come. Since then, the world's passive acceptance of communist, fascist, and Nazi barbarism had made me suspect Santayana was right. Several centuries earlier Machiavelli had warned: "Men remain so simple and governed so absolutely by their present needs that he who wishes to deceive them will never fail to find willing dupes." Now Mussolini and Hitler were finding further dupes in France.

Fascism could not be checked by appeals to reason, humanity, or faith in moral progress, but only by superior force and the readiness to use it. Fortunately, the free West still had both. . . .

I liked my friends as much as ever, but since my arguments had no effect upon them or theirs on me, political discussion languished.

Most of my time, anyway, had to be spent with politicians, officials, and diplomats. I had little time left for intellectuals, even those few with whom I found myself in agreement.

Quite accidentally, the shift in companions was symbolized by the location of our new apartment. Lilian had in vain sought a place to live near the Luxembourg Garden. Finally we took an apartment near the Esplanade des Invalides, on the western edge of the Faubourg Saint-Germain, only a hundred yards from the Seine. It was less than half an hour's walk from the *News* office on the Place de l'Opéra, and the way led along the river and then either across the Champs Elysées or over the smiling Place de la Concorde (once the bloodiest spot in Paris!) and through the Garden of the Tuileries, where I sometimes dawdled, watching the *Parisiennes* scattering crumbs for the birds. What relaxation! Once I became mildly lyrical:

In summer in the Tuileries
The sparrows eat their filleries;
Kind people throw them crumberies
That swell their tiny tummeries.

Attracted by their squealeries,
Fat pigeons join the mealeries.
At length, with bloated drummeries,
They sit and preen their flummeries.

Since our new apartment was part of a former *hotel particular,* its rooms and fireplaces were magnificent.

"*Bel apartment mais très bourgeois,*" Arcos commented.

Before returning to America, my brother had offered us the use of his country house at Crécy-en-Brie, an ancient walled village thirty odd miles from the capital, on the "Big" Morin River—sixty feet wide at most. After we acquired a motorcar (our first), we spent all available weekends there. Since the countryside was hilly and wooded, Crécy was just what the family required. The garden sloped down to the river, which offered tolerable swimming and ideal canoeing. Diana Jane soon became an excellent paddler, and together we took up cycling, French fashion, and soon were familiar with the entire Brie area.

Crécy had made Paul an honorary citizen and the villagers talked readily with his brother. They confirmed our fear that during the war something more than young men had died in France. The village electrician argued that if, as I said, the Germans were again a threat to the world, the fault lay with Washington and London. Why had these governments not stuck to the Versailles Treaty and the Three-Power pact accepted by Clemenceau, Wilson, and Lloyd George? Moreover, the "dirty parliamentarians" in Paris were selling out France. And anyhow, who could expect the war-weary French people to admit, even to themselves, the need for a vast new effort? The country could not stand another wholesale hemorrhage like that at Verdun and/or the Chemin des Dames! If the worst did happen, while the Germans were smashing their heads against the impregnable Maginot Line in the east, French and Belgium troops on the Belgian-German border would invade the demilitarized Rhineland. So reasoned the electrician.

A neat military conception and, at the time, perhaps a sound one. But it hampered Frenchmen's ability to recognize, still less to counter, Hitler's plans.

Industrialists, like Guy de Wendel, were cheerfully cooperating with their German counterparts. Hitler was playing his propaganda cards with skill, alternately tearing up a part of the Versailles Treaty and insisting on his love of peace.

Britain, backed by the United States, refused to see that Nazi Germany had become a danger. President Hoover still insisted on the sanctity of war debts. The Poles, once France turned down their 1933 offer of a concerted invasion of Germany, had signed a nonaggression pact with Hitler.

At times, I wondered if the Mowrers would not have been happier in Tokyo. But the Japanese had seized Chinese Manchuria and had set up a puppet regime.

And what had the outside world done about it? When the Lytton Commission formally confirmed the facts for the League of Nations, the Japanese walked out of a stunned international organization. Sanctions against the aggressors were the last thing the other member states contemplated. As for the United States, why Secretary of State Stimson had announced a "doctrine" of nonrecognition of territories acquired by force. That would show those generals and admirals in Tokyo. . . . In an early weekender from Paris I coldly predicted that unless stopped by American power, Japan would soon embark upon a real war against China.

We were still living in the Rue de Rivoli when the Stavisky scandal served the semifascist *Croix-de-Feu* as a pretext for bloody riots before the Chamber of Deputies. A few days later, counterrioting communists and hoodlums sacked shops a hundred yards from our hotel. Unable either to prevent the riots or to allay the charge of corruption that had served as their pretext, Premier Daladier resigned. Parliament replaced him by former President Gaston Doumergue, whom the Left charged, unfairly, I believed, with sympathy for fascism. A socialist deputy, Gaston Bergéry, proclaimed the need of a Popular Front (meaning a union of Left republicans with communists) to cope with the fascist peril.

Only French individualism kept the various rightist groups from merging into something really formidable. Nevertheless, for at least two years after the *Croix-de-Feu* riots, the danger of a fascist revolution seemed always present.

Shortly after our arrival, the potential international front against aggression was further weakened by the death of King Albert of Belgium, an indomitable character and a firm ally of France.

Few public spectacles have moved me more deeply than the funeral ceremony in the beautiful church of Sainte Gudule. Here a people worthily expressed their grief. And to me, the death of this sovereign whom I had not seen for twenty years was almost a personal loss. Young King Leopold struck me as a man of lesser kidney.

Moreover, Brussels was full of disquieting stories about rising tensions between Flemish and Walloon citizens which could only lessen the people's preoccupation with the German danger.

Yet in spite of such interludes, the Paris assignment remained overwhelmingly political. Intimately as I had known a certain France, the French political world was strange—and complicated beyond belief.

In such a situation I turned for help to French members of the newspaper fraternity.

Some of them, nobody was sure how many, were in the pay of a foreign government. Mussolini boasted of his influence on the famous *Temps,* one of Europe's leading journals and a frequent mouthpiece of the *Quai d'Orsay.* The German Embassy in Paris had the "support" of at least three French newsmen and one whole newspaper, *Le Matin* (which sharp-tongued Parisians called the "Paris edition of the *Angriff*"). Fernand de Brinon, Laval's close friend, was consciously serving Hitler, among other ways, by successfully preventing the publication of a French translation of *Germany Puts the Clock Back.*

Even Moscow managed to find suitable mouthpieces in the French press. French colleagues who regularly "touched" the secret funds of their own government were understandably loath to reveal to a foreigner, however friendly, those matters which their paymaster wished to keep quiet.

Nonetheless, several distinguished French writers, Pertinax, Marcel Ray, Genevieve Tabouis, a niece of the famous Cambon brothers, gave me timely assistance.

So much of the news was "managed" that an American correspondent in Paris needed to read not only the French press, but the German, the Italian, and the British as well. The last was nominally free. But two or three of the best known British writers were hopelessly pro-Nazi and regularly assured readers that the *Fuehrer* or the *Duce* wanted nothing so much as peace. Reading them reminded one of the professional quip:

> *You cannot buy or bribe or twist*
> *That saint, the British journalist;*
> *But, seeing what the man will do*
> *Unbribed, there's no occasion to.*

Fortunately for me, French politicians were more accessible than those of other countries and, at a certain degree of intimacy, became invaluable informants.

Of them all, I came to know best Edouard Herriot and Léon Blum. Herriot, whom I met occasionally at Geneviève Tabouis' apartment, was a former professor and literary critic of great intellect, delightful wit, and reputed awesome virility. (Producing a book or two and cultivating a knowledge of gastronomy seemed to be the prerequisites of success in French politics.) Two years later he bestowed on me the Legion of Honor.

Léon Blum, a student of philosophy and of law, occasionally invited me to dinner at his tasteful apartment on the Ile Saint-Louis behind Notre Dame, perhaps the most attractive site in Paris. Once or twice he included another socialist, one Vincent Auriol. ("I hope you don't mind, my little Edgar, if I invite dear Vincent. He is not very intelligent, but he is so nice." I did *not* mind.)

Blum regularly filled me in on the political situation. Yet our conversations ranged mostly over general topics, literature, and philosophy. Only concerning the German danger did I find him unresponsive: he could not take Hitler seriously.

Edouard Daladier was affable, well intentioned, and indecisive. Pierre Flandin's towering stature and unconcealed antifascism could not hide a basic lack of political courage. Yvon Delbos, personally attractive, somehow lacked iron. So long as Britain and the United States were so confident of inducing Germany to accept disarmament and peace through agreement, why should the French people be alarmed?

Among available politicians, either Georges Mandel or Louis Barthou might have checkmated Hitler. But Mandel, a former protégé of Clemenceau and a man of similar courage, was politically out of favor. Barthou became my choice. Hitler's murder of the diminutive Austrian Chancellor, Engelbert Dollfuss, had convinced the little Frenchman with the bristling beard, still tough at seventy, that the Germans, like the Japanese, were definitely on the prowl.

Though no friend of the Soviets (as I had noted at the Genoa Conference in 1922), he succeeded by skillful diplomacy in inducing a frightened U.S.S.R. to seek to enter the League of Nations and thus prepared the way for the subsequent Franco-Russian alliance. He also tried to firm up France's alliances with the Little Entente and with Poland.

As time went on, I depended less on newsmen and more on various French officials willing to showing me the ropes and letting me know who was pulling each.

Boss of the *Quai d'Orsay* under successive Ministers was Alexis Léger, a subtle diplomat and an even subtler poet, who never failed to tell me how he regretted the departure from Paris of that "fellow poet," my brother.

My old friend, Pierre Comert, who had resigned from the League to become press chief in the Foreign Office, went out of his way to save me from mistakes. We sometimes dined with him and his American wife, and he regularly took me to lunch at a little restaurant in Grenelle which he was proud to have discovered.

Welcome, too, were the friendship and valuable advice of Henri and Hellé Bonnet. Henri had been a member of the League of Nations Secretariat, unquestionably the finest bureaucracy I have ever known, and become head of the Institute of Intellectual Cooperation, with headquarters in Paris. What he did not know he was ready to find out and communicate.

Each time that Ambassador André François Poncet returned to Paris from Berlin, he gave me the latest news of Germany.

To most Americans the Japanese invasion of China was more disturbing than anything in Europe. Since I occasionally wrote about Far Eastern matters of which I had no first-hand knowledge, I sought the advice of specialists. Among these was Paul M. Linebarger, a former American judge, who had been the intimate of Sun Yat-sen and was currently advising Chiang Kai-shek. Each time Linebarger passed through Paris, he described Far Eastern developments in exchange for my analysis of the European situation.

International politics in the thirties centered around the League of Nations at Geneva, to cover which was part of my assignment. As time went on, meeting succeeded meeting there with such rapidity that my daughter once remarked that all I had to do was to say "Geneva" to our Ford in Paris and the car would need no steering.

The year 1934 chiefly saw disarmament talks. Of these I was always skeptical. No disciple of Umano could believe that great powers would disarm and entrust their safety to an undependable, international vigilance committee—or indeed, to anything else, short of an effective international authority.

These doubts brought me into friendly dispute with the American representatives at the disarmament meeting, Minister Hugh Wilson from Bern and Norman Davis from Washington. The latter was an outspoken champion of the current American policy of substituting words—the Kellogg Pact, the Stimson Doctrine (and later the Neutrality Laws)—for a concrete political policy. Davis agreed with some Britishers that it would be a mistake to get rid of Hitler, since the latter could be succeeded only by a communist, which would be worse. To me this notion was little short of insane. But what could a correspondent do— except report and report and report?

To the Fifteenth League Assembly in 1934 Maxim Litvinov, the Soviet Foreign Minister, made a long impassioned and, to his hearers, largely unintelligible speech. After listening in perplexity for five minutes, Geneviève Tabouis turned to me: "Edgar, what language is he speaking?"

I explained that the Bolshevik was speaking "Whitechapelese," an exotic tongue which he had acquired while an exile in London, along with an English wife whom we newsmen considered too good for him, the former Ivy Low.

Most member states were reconciled to, if they did not actually favor, the acceptance of the Soviet Union as a member. Yet that majority split over a typical League question: should the Soviets receive from the organization a formal invitation to join and a welcoming banquet, or should they be compelled to request membership? Would Moscow be willing to come in "without roses"? delegates asked. This was finally settled by allowing a large number of members "individually" to invite

Stalin to join while officially the League remained silent. And as usual, the Soviets showed a realistic indifference to the presence or absence of "flowers." What they wanted was defense against Nazi Germany, which they hoped to obtain from the League.

For that period Lilian and I had taken an apartment on the *Route de Lausanne*, not too far from the Assembly Building known to correspondents because of its glass walls as the "Reptile House." It was her first long visit to the League, and she wanted to see everything and meet everybody. Few towns can be more delightful than Geneva in the autumn.

Gourmet newsmen spent considerable time trying to discover enticing restaurants. Nearby France was full of such places. One, the Père Bise, on Lake Annecy, was incomparable. Another, at Thoiry, was famous not only for the 1925 meeting between Briand and Stresemann, but also for the nine-course luncheon upon which these two statesmen had gorged themselves before seeking a political agreement.

On the Swiss side of the frontier, the lake-side taverns were less attractive for their food than for their sites, with outdoor tables overlooking that most hospitable of inland seas.

The city of Geneva had little to offer. To be sure, the Bavaria *Bierstube*, which became the correspondents' unofficial headquarters and was later famous for having acquired the original caricatures of those two heretical Hungarians, Dersö and Kelen, served excellent German beer. But in the course of some twenty visits, I found but two Geneva restaurants that impressed my spoiled Parisian palate. High on the hill in the old city, the Plat d'Argent offered a few good specialties. My favorite was Chez Longchamp, a tiny place on the very edge of the city, convenient only to the cemetery and the cantonal rifle range ("no mere coincidence," we newsmen commented sarcastically). There in two or three rooms a French family served to perhaps two dozen people a superb lunch or dinner.

One day at the Assembly Building, I ran into the Soviet chargé d'affaires from Paris, Marcel Rosenberg, a dark little man with a permanent stoop caused by tuberculosis of the spine. He was reputed to have been a "soft-hearted" terrorist who could not bear to hear the shots that killed his victims. On this occasion, to my surprise, he suggested that we lunch together. Yet he declined my offer to pick him up at his hotel.

"No. I shall leave the Assembly precisely at one P.M. and walk along by the lake. You come by in your car and I'll get in." And so it was.

When we reached the suburban restaurant beside the water, he sought a table out of hearing of the other guests and still refused to talk. Only after the meal, as we sat in a hired rowboat several hundred yards from the shore, did he feel safe. Then he discussed not only American but Soviet affairs with a freedom I had never found in other Russian communists. Once ashore, he again went mum. A block from his hotel he left the car: none should know with whom he had been lunching.

When thereafter I met him in Paris, he acted as though we were strangers. Truly, as Chip Bohlen once wise-cracked, the two most dangerous opinions a "bourgeois" diplomat can harbor are: first, "Alcohol does not affect me," and second, "I know how to deal with Russians."

Yet my most astonishing experience was with a German. In the "Reptile House" Wolfgang Schwarz, now an acknowledged Nazi, had greeted me warmly, but I had had enough of Wolfgang in Germany and refused to respond. After two or three attempts, he wrote me a letter: we had been such good friends . . . should we let politics estrange us? I left it unanswered. But on the day of my departure for Paris, he approached me:

"Edgar, I have a message for you from the German *Fuehrer.*"

"Do tell!" I answered. "And whom would Hitler ask to deliver it but you! Be serious, Wolfgang."

He reddened. "Actually Hitler entrusted the message to his personal representative at the disarmament conference, Colonel von Haselmeyer. Haselmeyer asked my help. Am I to tell the Colonel that you refuse to listen?"

"I'd listen to the devil if he had anything to say. Go ahead, Wolfgang."

"*Gut. Der Fuehrer laesst sagen*: You, *Herr* Mowrer, completely misunderstood the nature of National Socialism. Therefore he had to ask you to leave Germany. But he also admires you. And if you now admit your mistake, he will not only welcome you back to Germany, but make you his favorite foreign correspondent. How about it, Edgar?"

I was staggered. The reference to the colonel precluded the possibility of a hoax. And I resented the implication.

"Whom does your *Fuehrer* take me for? He expelled me, not because I do *not* understand National Socialism, but because I understand it only *too* well. He is even less of a man than I thought he was. Tell him I shall return to Germany when he is no longer there."

It was Wolfgang's turn to be staggered. "All right. I'll give your answer to the Colonel. But Edgar, one personal question: what would you do if your country came under National Socialism?"

"I would become Swiss. Goodbye, Wolfgang."

That same evening, as I afterwards learned, Wolfgang related the whole story to my friend, Malcolm Davis, the local representative of the Carnegie Foundation.

"Just imagine Edgar saying that to escape National Socialism he would become Swiss. Isn't that depressing."

"Very," Malcolm replied darkly, "for if National Socialism ever came to the United States, I would be dead. And I had always counted Edgar among those who would die with me. And now you say the so-and-so would run out and become Swiss."

Wolfgang stared at him. Try as he would, he could not understand these Americans. . . .

Nor sometimes, when I considered our foreign policy, could I.

23

None So Blind. . . .

The startled flocks in the European poultry yard fluttered around, lead by capons.
— WINSTON CHURCHILL

WHATEVER HOPE the U.S.S.R.'s admission to the League raised, soon faded. Hardly had the delegates gone home from the Fifteenth League Assembly when Croatian fanatics (*Ustachis*), trained in terrorism at Janka Puszta in Hungary and incited by Italy, assassinated their Serbian "enemy," King Alexander of Yugoslavia, at Marseilles. With him, by tragic coincidence, they killed France's foreign minister, Louis Barthou, on whose courage and energy I had based my hope of peace.

The outraged Yugoslavs, who had been complaining for years of Hungary's illegal activities, demanded a meeting of the League Council.

The meeting turned into a theoretical debate concerning the right of states to "agitate" for revision of imposed treaties which they did not like. Finally, the Council adopted a resolution "admitting" that Hungary had wrongly failed to suppress acts of political terrorism, set up a committee to draft a "convention" embodying this obligation, and closed the book on the assassination of Alexander and Barthou. We newsmen, who had hurried to Geneva hoping to hear the League condemn Hungary as an aggressor under the Charter, wasted our time.

In January, 1935, the city of Saarbruecken was even uglier than I remembered it. The same "coal town" look—dingy buildings and drab looking people. Lilian and I had driven there from Paris to meet Wallace Duell, the brilliant young *Daily News* correspondent from Berlin, and together report on the League-supervised plebiscite whereby the Saarlanders, after fifteen years under League control, were to decide whether to remain under the League, to join France, or to "go home to the Reich."

246

Before the advent of Nazism, a decision to "go home" had been a foregone conclusion. But in 1935, not all Saarlanders were ready to exchange personal freedom under the League administration for tyranny under the Brown Shirts. A month before, in Paris, the "separatist" leader, Max Braun, had assured me that if the French wanted they could secure a majority for the *status quo*.

Braun did not know that Barthou's successor as Foreign Minister, Pierre Laval, wanted to get rid of the Saar. Three days after taking office, he had decided it should go back to Germany. He had even promised Hitler's Foreign Minister, the former champagne drummer, Joachim von Ribbentrop, to allow "neutral" troops to supervise the voting. The *Fuehrer* had stated publicly that the Saar was the "only remaining obstacle" to Franco-German peace and amity. Laval was taking him at his word. Britain and Italy provided the bulk of the supervising troops. And responsibility for the plebiscite was given, not to the current Chairman of the League's Governing Commission, Geoffrey Knox, a courageous Englishman who opposed Nazism regardless of his government's view, but to a special commission head by a Swede named Rhode, who like most Scandinavians at the time, had no intention of getting himself labeled anti-German. Roman Catholic bishops in Germany had appealed publicly to the Catholic three-fourths of the Saarlanders to vote for reunification, another example of the Vatican's unwavering support of the Nazi regime, as I sadly noted.

Our hotel was full of Germans from the Reich who had come to "observe" the proceedings. Through the streets wandered little groups with typical Nazi faces who, I felt sure, were storm troopers in civilian dress.

The League's technical adviser on plebiscites, the American, Sarah Wambaugh, complained of the unusual number of "errors" in the voting lists. These she had some difficulty in correcting since self-proclaimed Saarlanders living in Germany were allowed to return "home" and vote.

Over a luncheon in the *Schloss*, Geoffrey Knox informed us that the neutral troops were being kept off the streets, that their commander, a Major Hennessey, was suspected of belonging to the British Fascist Party, and that the German government had sent agents, both voters and intimidators, into the territory. He blamed the British government, the Plebiscite Commission, and the French for letting it happen.

Max Braun confirmed all of these things. True, a hundred thousand Saarlanders had attended a recent public meeting in favor of the *status quo*. But without the certainty of French support few would dare take the risk of Hitler's vengeance if Germany won. Braun and his trembling little wife were making preparations to get out immediately after the announcement of the voting results, while the way was still open.

On voting day, Lilian, Wally, and I patiently toured the hilly countryside, stopping at a dozen different polling places and inquiring of the "neutral" supervisors how things were going. None of them had any complaint. Personally we saw no violence. But everywhere young

Teutonic stalwarts hovered in the background, while courageous voters complained to us of threats and other forms of intimidation. Duell aptly described the atmosphere as one of "political paralysis suddenly broken by spasms of fear."

The final count gave 90 percent to the Reich, a bare trickle to France, and only 8 percent to the League. Some suspected that the ballots were tampered with, while stored in the Wartburg before counting. Within an hour of the announcement, toughs wearing swastikas were stopping cars with French licenses (including ours) and indulging in a public celebration which only Knox's Saar police kept within limits. The "neutral" troops apparently considered it no business of theirs. Germany, which had evaluated the "loss" of the Saar at 1,028 million gold marks, paid to France 140 million.

On the next day, as we drove back to Paris through the Vosges the fog was so thick Lilian walked ahead of the car to help me keep it on the road—a fitting symbol of Europe's plight!

Worse, while Laval and most of the League members were happy to be rid of the Saar, a "red rag to the Hitler bull," the bull himself was so encouraged by his victory that a fortnight later he boasted publicly that Germany already had an (illegal) airfleet second to none, and denounced the Versailles Treaty.

Italian Stresa in April, 1935, was outwardly as cheerful as Saarbruecken in January had been depressing.

Viewed as a spectacle, the Three-Power Conference there was a success—"flowered pomp and theatrical splendor," as I wired the *News*. Mussolini utilized it to exhibit Italy's new military might. The streets and the air above them were never free of Italians in uniform.

But as a method of curbing defiant Germany or of protecting Austria, its avowed purposes, the meeting was a farce. Through Rudolf Kircher of the *Frankfurter Zeitung*, a one-time democrat who had become a Nazi mouthpiece, the absent Hitler also made his position clear. He would accept an air agreement or a disarmament pact only on the basis of complete equality, as offered by the Three Powers in December, 1932. But under no circumstances would the Third Reich take action against an aggressor or make any promises which could thwart its "need" for expansion to the east.

To make Germany accept less, the Stresa powers would have to stand together and mean business. Mussolini proposed war, if necessary, to prevent Hitler's threatened seizure of Austria, provided Italy was given a free hand in Ethiopia. Britain and France would have no part in such an undertaking. In fact, on the second day of the Stresa meeting, one Neville Chamberlain, a Tory provincial who had somehow become Britain's Chancellor of the Exchequer, had announced that Britain would make no commitments on the continent without Germany. All the delegates could agree upon was a new meeting. . . .

Driving to Milan for a brief visit, Marc van Blankenstein, Lilian, and I passed thousands of semi-uniformed school children lined up along the new *autostrada* waiting for Mussolini and saluting every passing car with shouts of *"Duce, Duce, Duce."* To this, I mused, had *fascismo* reduced the children of Dante, Machiavelli, Galileo, Giordano Bruno, Mazzini, yes, and of those intrepid Italians with whom I had stood on the River Piave in June, 1918.

After Stresa, Britain slightly accelerated its lagging rearmament. France and the Soviet Union signed the military alliance that had been the goal of the murdered Barthou. The British, French, and Italian governments induced the League to "rebuke" Germany as a treaty breaker.

Yet almost at the same time Britain undercut its effect by signing a Naval Agreement authorizing Germany to construct a fleet equal to 35 percent of Britain's.

When the Japanese seized another chunk of China, the United States did nothing but grumble. Philippe Bertholet, the former Secretary General of the French Foreign Office, described the United States as "without will . . . a congeries of little groups in which the noisiest prevails." But what was France willing to fight for?

Mussolini's designs on Ethiopia had clearly appeared during the Wal Wal incident at the end of 1934. In the following June he publicly boasted that nothing would prevent his Italy from acquiring its promised *impero*. We newsmen did not know that Laval had, in January, promised Mussolini a "free hand" in Ethiopia in exchange for the latter's pledge to let France send a full division of troops over the Brenner Pass to Czechoslovakia in case of a German threat to that country.

By midsummer, the democracies were, I reported, "seeking some good way of sacrificing the Abyssinians without driving the Italians from the League or openly violating the Covenant." But until the Assembly in September, the Powers stalled.

As the Italians saw it, Italy was doing only what the British, French, Portuguese, Dutch, and Arabs had previously done—in fact, what the early colonists had done in America: subjugate a backward people.

Many British and French Conservatives agreed. And anyhow Italy's support against Germany was worth more than rigid observance of the League Covenant.

On the other hand, most Britishers saw in the international organization the surest guarantee against another European war. Provided of course that League members undertook the sanctions against aggression prescribed by the Covenant. Mussolini had gone so far as to threaten Britain with war and the League with his withdrawal if either tried to hinder his imperialistic design. Any effective sanction such as closing the Suez Canal to Italian shipping or supplies would infuriate French Conservatives and American oil companies. On the second day of the September Assembly, I cabled that Laval was ready to hand the Ethiopians to Mussolini not only bound hand and foot, but "with their tongues cut out as well to keep them from protesting."

Nonetheless, the League voted to ask the members to take economic sanctions against Italy. The British fleet stood ready to close both Suez and Gibraltar to Italian shipping. True to the spirit of the Neutrality Acts, Roosevelt imposed an American arms embargo on *both* belligerents.

Yet for the next nine months the League members sought to find a compromise that would prevent Italy from leaving the League. Delegates from verbally bold but inwardly wavering countries spoke in hushed tones of "preventing a war." The notion that Mussolini would embark upon a war against Britain was a joke!

Early in October the Italians launched the invasion. As Robert Vansittart later wrote, "This was the moment when the world might have been saved by united resistance to aggression—if it had any arms; but it hadn't, and scarcely blushed, though it was angry at being found out." Instead, Prime Minister Baldwin, in a speech to the British Peace Society, said, "I give you my word there will be no great armament." The League's report, drafted primarily by the clear-thinking French member of the Secretariat, Henry Vigier, formally charged the Italian government of "resorting to war in disregard of its covenants under Article 12 of the Covenant of the League of Nations."

Yet only the Soviet Union and little Haiti openly condemned Mussolini. By October 16, it was clear that no member state was willing to carry out its full commitment under Article 16 of the Covenant. In fact, Laval, with the support of French Conservatives and fascists, turned down the British offer of a new *Entente Cordiale* rather than join that country in imposing serious sanctions. Even partial application of the oil boycott could have brought disaster to Italy.

In mid-November, Mussolini staged the bluff of moving a couple of divisions to the French frontier.

It worked. Out of the blue, on December 11, 1935, came the incredible news: the Foreign Ministers of France and Britain, meeting secretly in Paris, had agreed on a "fair exchange" of territory between Italy and Ethiopia. The former was offering Ethiopia an outlet to the sea with some three thousand square miles of territory, and receiving in exchange sixty thousand square miles and the right of economic expansion and settlement in the entire southern half of Ethiopia—a fair exchange, indeed!

This my colleagues Pertinax and Geneviève Tabouis simultaneously published in Paris even before the plan had reached the British Cabinet in London. Someone in the French Foreign Ministry had deliberately leaked it.

Would public opinion force the repudiation of the Plan? Americans were particularly indignant. Back in Geneva once more, we heard Hoare's successor, Anthony Eden, pledge Britain's support of the League. A month later Laval resigned. Perhaps the League could still save Ethiopia.

Instead, the Powers stalled again. And by the time Britain and

France may have been ready to apply an oil embargo, the Italians, using poison gas, had conquered the Ethiopians. Noting this, Hitler on March 7, 1936, denounced the Locarno Treaty and marched his troops into the demilitarized German Rhineland. In three years he had created an army of thirty divisions, larger than that of France! Thereafter, for Britain as well as France, Italy's support against Germany seemed more important than upholding anything so "purely juridical" as the League Covenant.

Two days after Mussolini, from the balcony of Palazzo Venezia, announced the founding of the new Roman Empire, the League Council turned the matter over to the special June Assembly. There the scene was unforgettable. When Haile Selassie went to the rostrum of that once august forum, Italian newsmen whistled and stamped until the Rumanian delegate, Titulesco, scornfully asked the chairman to "silence this *canaille*," and the Italians were hustled out. Only then did the tiny black-bearded emperor begin speaking.

"I am Haile Selassie, first emperor of Ethiopia. I am here to demand the justice which is due my people." And so on, to the dramatic conclusion: "God and history will remember."

Moving words but vain.

I accepted an offer from an American network to put the exiled Conquering Lion of Judah to go on the air, and almost failed. For although he immediately accepted, in calculating the time needed to get him from the hotel to the radio station high on the Geneva Hill, I underestimated the deliberation of His Majesty's "royal gait."

We reached the broadcasting building just in time for me to dash up four flights of stairs and start introducing the distinguished speaker. When I finished my three-minute piece, he was still not there. So for three more endless minutes I improvised on Haile's past, present, and probable future, sweating like a soul in pain, until His Majesty arrived and, speaking mostly in Amharic with an English translation following, made a moving appeal to the American people. Little good it did.

Hitler's military reoccupation of the Rhineland, which reduced Italy's seizure of Ethiopia to insignificance, came as no surprise to me. Two months earlier I had received an official invitation to come to Holland to report on German military preparations on the Dutch-German frontier. Would I, as a neutral American, inspect the situation on the spot?

I would. In the company of a Dutch Staff Officer and of Marc van Blankenstein I drove along the border from Maastricht in the south to the North Sea, seeking through glasses whatever could be discerned on the German side. This was plenty: formidable German military establishments, new soldiers' quarters, fifteen new airfields, new roads mysteriously ending just short of the frontier.

Each evening a local Dutch officer interpreted what we had witnessed during the day—nothing less than part of a German "Van Epp plan" to overrun half of the Netherlands in a first attack. To do this,

German forces had, however, to reestablish themselves in the demilitarized Rhineland Zone to the south, with whatever risk of war with France this might entail.

My articles jolted the Dutch people, temperamentally disposed to be complacent about Hitler's intentions, and, when published in the London *Times* and the *Echo de Paris*, British and French readers as well.

Though without political effect, they made me better known in Paris, and in London led eventually to a "working partnership" with leaders (some of whom had read *Germany Puts the Clock Back*) such as Sir Robert Vansittart of the Foreign Office, Robert Boothby, M.P., a few courageous Labor Party M.P.'s, Allen Lane of Penguin Books, and somewhat later, Winston Churchill.

When Hitler did exactly what the Dutch officers had urged me to predict he would, France had another opportunity of scotching the German menace. Under the Locarno Treaty, France and Belgium were entitled to consider Germany's violation of the demilitarized zone a direct attack on their territories, to take what military action they chose against it, and to call on Britain and Italy for assistance.

But instead of instantly mobilizing and ordering the Germans to withdraw within twenty-four hours in which case, as we learned much later, the German generals intended to depose Hitler, the French let the British induce them to put the case before the Council League in London, of all places. King Edward VIII took credit for having averted a war!

Pierre Laval's chickens had come home to roost. Had he not, in the previous September, turned down the British offer of a full *entente,* Britain would have been obliged to join France in compelling the German troops to withdraw.

In London I found quarters in an "exclusive" little place on the edge of St. James' Park convenient to St. James Palace where the conference was held.

John Gunther, whom the *News* had transferred from Vienna to London in 1934, shared the assignment, he covering the "natives" of the British and Commonwealth delegations, and I the "foreigners." Never was there a more depressing job.

To Britishers, the Locarno Treaty meant little. The Rhineland was German, wasn't it? I heard them applaud a newsreel showing Hitler's army being welcomed by "liberated" Germans.

At the opening session, an irresolute Pierre Flandin told a wary Council that while France had a legal right to act alone, because of its belief in collective security, it was asking the League to prevent a violation of a sacred treaty. Paul Van Zeeland of Belgium asked only for a declaration that the Locarno Treaty had been broken. Whereupon the Council invited nonmember Germany to send a delegate to London.

During the forty-eight hours Hitler let them wait, Anthony Eden pled for a rebuilding of confidence and Dino Grandi reaffirmed Italy's devotion to peace in Europe—no mention of the Rhineland or Ethiopia.

Munch of Denmark, speaking for the neutrals, "viewed with alarm" the widening gap between the two parts of Europe. Colonel Beck of Poland denounced the Franco-Soviet Treaty!

Only Litvinov for the Soviet Union denounced Hitler's entire policy and asked the League to stop it by all necessary means. Nobody but the press paid any attention to the representative of a revolutionary country whose own intentions were suspect. . . .

When Joachim von Ribbentrop finally condescended to appear, he read aloud Hitler's original explanation of his act, then sat with closed eyes through the rest of the seance.

So after solemnly deciding that Germany had violated the Locarno Treaty, which Hitler had already admitted, and then humbly waiting a few days in vain for Mussolini in Rome to send instructions to his representative, the Council adjourned.

Hitler had won again. Britain's Prime Minister Stanley Baldwin had, I wired, "been jelly-fishing as usual." Even that champion of democracy and world order, Edouard Herriot, had warned the French delegation in London against any "imprudence."

Gunther and I feared the worst. Though the League Council might sit until the delegates' pants became shiny, as long as Hitler could deceive the League members by his tactics ("just one more little drink and I'm off the stuff forever"), he had nothing to fear.

The French General Staff had planned to defend France on the east and invade Germany through Belgium to the north. But by permitting the German divisions to reoccupy the Rhineland, and eventually erect their own Maginot Line there, Paris condemned its armed forces to static defense or worse.

Certainly, this was the conclusion which the Belgians drew. A few months later, under pressure from two Socialist deputies, De Man and Spaak, King Leopold's government denounced the military alliance with France and reverted to the same sort of neutrality that had failed to protect the country in 1914.

On the wall of Saint James' Palace, the invisible handwriting had been clear. John and I, in a joint dispatch, translated it for our readers:

"The present push is not likely to cause war. But unless something is done to change the situation, the next one, or the one after next, surely will."

24

Rehearsal in Spain

Most men are not guided primarily by rational or economic considerations, by aspirations of economic betterment, or by enlightened self interest, but by collective passions and emotions which silence rational considerations.

—HANS KOHN

JULY, 1936, was the rainiest summer Paris had known since 1873. Nevertheless, the fourteenth of July was literally a red-letter day for I found myself walking as an observer with a huge parade from the Place de la République to the Place de la Bastille: French Radicals, Socialists, and Communists were celebrating together the formation of a Popular Front government which promised to end the Laval policy of appeasing the fascist countries. They might, I felt, just do the trick.

"Not so," insisted my fellow parader, S. Pinkney Tuck of the American Embassy. How, he asked, could we be sure that the Reds would not treat a Popular Front as Lenin treated Kerensky? Would not communism be worse than fascism? After all, some fascists were gentlemen. . . .

Fascism and communism were both abhorrent. But first things first. Once we overcame the more urgent danger, we could concentrate on containing bolshevism. So I argued. Kippy remained unconvinced.

Three days later, the Spanish Army mutinied and shortly thereafter I found myself at the railroad station of Cerbère on the Franco-Spanish frontier, trying to reach Madrid and the Spanish civil war.

The driver of the lone taxi refused even to try to drive me to Port Bou in Spain. "Useless, Monsieur. No one is allowed to cross the frontier. Save your money."

Since I intended reaching Madrid one way or another, I sat down to think the situation over.

For years the Spanish situation has been seething, as I knew in detail from my colleague in Madrid, Jay Allen. The Liberals and Socialists had come to power in February. But the new "unlimited" freedom was a heady brew for a brave, passionate, and politically inexperienced people prone to excesses. Certainly, it was a drink which Conservatives refused to swallow. It came as no surprise when, after a series of "Hatfield and McCoy" murders on both sides, the army blew its top and, supported by the Catholic hierarchy, the feudal lords, the money barons, and the fascists of the *Falange,* launched a revolt against the democratic republic.

The Spanish ambassador in Paris, Ferdinand de los Rios, had given me a letter to all Republican authorities. But how contact them across a closed frontier? Should I return to Marseilles and inquire about planes for Spain?

Then suddenly I leaped to my feet with a grin: in front of me the railroad tracks disappeared into a mountain.

"Tell me," I asked a passing porter, "what is at the other end of that tunnel?"

"But Spain, Monsieur"—sarcastically, as if any fool should know that.

"Is it far?"

"No, Monsieur, a few kilometers."

I drew a good-sized bill from my wallet.

"How about taking my valise and walking through to Spain with me?"

Two minutes later the porter and I were stepping from tie to tie between rails that served as guidelines through the blackness of the tunnel. But not for long. First a glimmer, then a gleam, finally dazzling sunshine.

"You are in Spain, Monsieur, at Port-Bou," said my guide. Gleefully I handed over the bill, picked up my suitcase and typewriter, and started toward the nearest building.

"Halt!" a voice cried.

A Spanish frontier guard in shabby khaki, with a cocked hat of black oilcloth, shoved a rifle muzzle against my belly.

"How did you get here and who are you?" he demanded in heavily accented French.

I pointed to the porter just disappearing into the dark hole on his way back to France and produced my passport and the Spanish ambassador's letter.

He looked at them uncomprehendingly, then growled: "Come along. You're under arrest."

But when a police captain read Los Rios' recommendation, everything changed! I spent the night in a simple but comfortable hotel and the next morning went on to Barcelona with several other passengers in a bus driven by two workmen. Written on its side were the letters POUM, which one of my companions explained stood for *Partido Obrero de Unificación Marxista.*

"We are Trotsky-ite communists," he said proudly. "The *fascistas* fear us most."

By midmorning we reached Barcelona. The recommended hotel looked deserted. Finally a frightened proprietor appeared. Most of his employees and all guests had left, he explained. Still he could give a room with bath to an American newsman.

When he had personally carried up my bags, I asked him what had happened in Barcelona.

"The military tried to seize the town last week, but the Republicans defeated them. Now the workers have seized it and we are in complete revolution."

This I had not read in Paris.

"How do I get to Madrid?"

He shrugged his shoulders. "No trains are running and the main road around Zaragoza is in the hands of the Nationalists."

"Good. Then please get me a taxi to go to the American Consulate."

"But, *Señor,* the revolutionaries have confiscated all cars. You'll have to walk. I'll show you the way."

The American Consul General explained the situation. All Catalonia, practically severed from the Republican government at Madrid, was being governed, "if you can call it governed," by a *Generalidad* under an Anti-Fascist Committee of fifteen members, ten of them Leftists, which had suppressed the military revolt and killed its leader, General Goded. The Committee had seized much property and he and his colleagues were having a hard time protecting that of U.S. citizens.

For the rest, the picture was not pretty. The wholesale looting and the summary executions of alleged "fascistas" (nuns were still being shot every night on Mount Tibidabo above Barcelona) seemed unworthy of a "democratic republic" that claimed to be defending itself against "reaction" and was calling on other democracies to help it.

What a story—and still largely unpublished. It could never pass the censors. "How," I asked a Spaniard employed as bookkeeper in the consulate, "can I tell the world what is going on in Barcelona?"

He looked suspicious. "Will you report the facts as they are?"

"That, *Señor,* is like my asking you if you cheat on your books. But no use in writing what I cannot get out."

"Some Americans are leaving tomorrow for Marseilles. I'll ask one of them to file your story if you give it to me."

Promising to do so, I walked to the *Generalidad* and asked to see the nominal boss, Luis Companys. The guards would not let me enter the building.

The following day, having written two dispatches, I took one (innocuous) to the telegraph office, the other (blood-curdling) to the consulate for transmission via Marseilles. I also complained that nobody at the *Generalidad* would talk to me. A Catalan employee who had been in the United States laughed.

"Why," he asked in broken English, "do you bother with Companys who is just a figurehead? Why don't you see Buenaventura Durruti at the Anti-Fascist Committee?"

"And who is Durruti?"

He looked at me with astonishment. "The head of the FAI, the *Federación Anarquista Ibérica.*"

A few minutes later I brushed past armed guards before another building—and ran straight into a Catalan newsman I had known in Berlin. When he heard what I wanted, he pointed to a door.

"Durruti is in there."

It was no time for tact. I knocked and immediately entered. The *Caudillo* of Catalonia, a man with fierce eyes, was sitting alone.

"Who are you?" he roared.

My passport and Los Rios' letter reassured him.

"The only way to Madrid is through Valencia. But I have no means of sending you there. You might report the fighting around Zaragoza."

"Thanks. If I cannot get to Madrid, I shall accept your offer. Meanwhile, are you planning to establish an anarchist society here?"

"Yes, once we have put down the rebellion everywhere. What do you know about anarchism?"

"I have studied Max Stirner and Kropotkin."

"Really? Then you are an anarchist?"

"By no means. Too impractical. But thanks for your offer."

Later that day, Lawrence Farnsworth, an American newsman based in Spain, told me that a British destroyer was in port and might be going to Valencia. Perhaps. . . .

Once more I trudged to the waterfront. Sure enough, there lay a warship bravely flying the Union Jack. I talked my way past a suspicious sailor into the presence of the commanding officer, showed my credentials, and explained my desire to go to Valencia en route to Madrid. Would he take me?

After damning all Spanish Republicans as anarchist terrorists, he said: "It's very irregular, but these are irregular times. Be here tomorrow evening by eleven p.m."

The rest of the day I spent writing up my notes and walking miles, including an evening stroll on the *Ramblas,* full of guards, armed workers and their wives.

Superficially, as I had already noted, Barcelona seemed peaceful, even orderly in spite of a profusion of red signs in windows, damaged churches and convents. The rare bourgeois I met turned out to be foreigners. Except for the cars flying a foreign flag, a few ambulances, and the conveyances of physicians, all autos were in the hands of workmen in overalls and each bore a label: POUM, CNT, or FAI.

About midnight, early for Spain, I went to bed. An hour or so later the gasping proprietor knocked at my door: "Señor Durruti is downstairs and wants to see you immediately."

In the bar I found the fiery *caudillo* and four armed workmen. Durruti wrung my hand heartily.

"Proprietor, bring us some bottles of your best wine."

Then to me: "I've thought of what you said. Sit down and tell me why you are not an anarchist."

For the next three or four hours—I lost count after the second bottle of wine—I argued with this self-taught anarchist who was eager to pit his own philosophy against that of an informed unbeliever. We discussed radical thinkers from Helvetius to Nietzsche. He spent some time explaining his feud with the communists.

"But here in Catalonia *we* are on top. Moreover, you, with your interest in freedom, should be on our side. For in Spain today we are the only alternative to communism's suppression of the individual. Our use of compulsion is only temporary."

Remembering what I had been told of the prevailing terror, I could not but smile inwardly. Yet when, a year or so later, I learned that a Spanish communist had killed Durruti, the latter's warning came back to me. Perhaps, without the intervention of the Soviet Union, anarchist influence might have balanced communist influence within the Republican government. If so, the outcome of the civil war could have been different.

Before leaving me at dawn, Durruti shook hands warmly and promised that he would soon be sending me to the Zaragoza front.

The next day I sent a second uncensored dispatch "via courier to Marseilles." In the evening the hotel proprietor managed for a consideration to persuade an armed anarchist with a car to take me and my baggage to the British destroyer.

The officers, most of whom had been forbidden to go ashore in Barcelona, kept me up until three in the morning asking questions about the reign of terror. They were pleased to learn that foreign property had generally been spared and that foreigners were free to move about. But they were incredulous when I reported that Americans believed that most of Barcelona, if not of all Catalonia, opposed the officers' rebellion. They looked forward happily to a prompt victory by General Franco, who, they said, had been in command, since the deaths of Generals Mola and Sanjurjo in plane accidents, and was bringing Moorish troops from Africa in German airplanes.

Forty winks and a British breakfast later, I went ashore at Valencia, firmly in Republican hands after an unsuccessful uprising by the military, and caught a crowded train to Madrid.

There, too, armed workmen were in possession of most motorcars and had occupied the apartments of *fascistas*, a word applied to conspicuous opponents and to the rich.

My first visit was to the American Embassy. This handsome, not very large, building had become a boarding house and sanctuary for about a hundred frightened Americans who slept everywhere, even in the courtyard. The host was the U.S. Military Attaché, Colonel Stephen Fuqua. The chief housekeeper appeared to be the Third Secretary, Eric C. Wendelin. The rebellion had found Ambassador Claude Bowers and most of the Embassy staff in summer quarters in the old fortress town of Fuentarrabia in the north. They had not returned to Madrid. Since I knew he favored the Republic, I could not understand our Ambassador's absence from the center of the conflict. Spanish Republicans bitterly resented it.

The "boarders" in the Embassy, who were getting out of Madrid as fast as they could find facilities, spoke of wholesale murder and looting by the Republicans and called the regime communist. They could not understand how I dared live at the Palace Hotel, half of which was now a military hospital. Didn't I realize that I might be robbed or murdered?

Actually, the only time I felt threatened in Madrid was late one evening when, returning to my hotel room, I saw two armed ruffians trying to open the door. Hearing me approach, one of them readied his rifle. But when, in English, I shouted, "What are you doing there?" they disappeared without answering. The hotel clerk said they must have made a mistake.

My former colleague, Foreign Minister Julio Alvarez del Vayo received me with characteristic enthusiasm, gave me a pass to go where I liked, put a car at my disposal, and described the situation. He denied that there had been any "reign of terror." During the fighting, the military rebels had killed workmen and workmen had killed a few soldiers and some of their active sympathizers. It had been necessary to commandeer all motorcars for military and supply purposes and to keep enemies from escaping. Now Madrid was quiet, as I could see for myself.

The military situation was still chaotic. The Franquistas were holding the Alcázar at Toledo and approaching the Sierra de Guadarrama from the north. They occupied the southwest, the northwest, and part of the north of the country and were moving to unite their areas in Estremadura. Then they would attack Madrid. But in spite of General Franco's Moors from Africa (so it was true, then), they would never take Madrid without massive German and Italian help, which they would probably receive. In that case, he wanted to know, would Britain or France help their Spanish fellow democrats?

Remembering the attitudes of the British naval officers and the Americans in Barcelona and Madrid, I had to reply that I found it unlikely. Did the much travelled Vayo expect respectable *bourgeois* to support a regime which was apparently giving free rein to communists, Trotsky-ites, and anarcho-syndicalists?

"And who would have defended the Republic without them?" Vayo demanded. "And there is not a communist or an anarchist in the government."

At the time this was true. The only communist whom I met in Madrid was Claud Cockburn of the London *Daily Worker*. How this educated, well-born Englishman could be a follower of Stalin baffled me. Vayo hoped for volunteers from abroad, but if any had already arrived, I did not see them.

He showed me my chauffeur and armed gunman and told them specifically that the car, an Italian *Lancia,* was mine to go wherever I chose, for so long as I needed it.

He also introduced me to his colleagues in the Cabinet. President Azana and Premier Giral Prieto were impressive, but in energy they seemed inferior to Largo Caballero, a blunt, popular type. Two months before the generals rebelled, this Socialist had wanted to arm the workers, but the Cabinet had declared that unnecessary: it guaranteed the loyalty of the armed forces!

Caballero invited me to go with him to a mountain headquarters. What I saw was disturbing. There was at this time, literally, *no* Republican army, just a few officers, a scattering of trained soldiers, and a mass of armed volunteers. Most of the officers were unimpressive. In the front line on the Sierra de Guadarrama, a major commanding a sector that was expecting a rebel attack, explained that lack of military experience was no handicap. He and his men would defend the Republic to the last man.

"Why no trenches?" I asked.

He looked at me scornfully. "Trenches are for cowards. We Spaniards do not take cover from our enemies." Argument was useless. Obviously this boaster had never imagined, still less experienced, modern machine-gun fire or an artillery barrage.

Some of the volunteers were what Americans in Madrid called "rifle wenches." One such, on sentry duty, waved her rifle and demanded to see our papers. She was not over five feet high. But what a beauty—flashing blue eyes, classical features, and shapely figure colorful in blue jeans, with a red scarf around her black hair! Her name was Jesusa Lopez.

Another day, Vayo asked me to take my colleague, Karl von Wiegand, on a quick visit to Toledo where nationalist troops were successfully defending the forbidding old Alcázar above the river against what seemed to me amateurish assaults by Republicans. Sniping was continuous on both sides. After talking with a voluble Republican commander, previously a labor leader, Karl and I wandered through the ancient town, admiring the old gates and regretting that the Republicans had covered or removed the fine pictures normally visible in the cathedral.

As we left Toledo, someone in the Alcázar spotted our car on the Alcantara bridge and fired several shots which pierced the back seat. But for their nimbleness in slipping to the floor, two American correspondents might have ended their careers there and then.

During my second trip to Guadarrama, enemy shells started exploding on the road just ahead. The chauffeur refused to proceed farther.

Vayo had said the car was mine to command. Though I understood a little of what I heard, I could not speak the language. Instead I relied upon Italian uttered one syllable at a time, which most Spaniards could follow. To the unlettered, I explained it was a Spanish dialect.

On this occasion, my protests failed to move the obdurate chauffeur, who replied calmly that if he and the gunman were seeking danger, "we would be in the infantry." At which point, the latter touched his rifle significantly.

Yielding would have been disastrous. "And I did not come four thousand miles from America to write about your war just to be prevented by a couple of cowards. If you don't put that gun down and drive on to headquarters, I shall ask Ministro del Vayo to send you to the infantry."

Since they had seen me with the Foreign Minister, the bluff worked. They drove on. The nearest shell landed half a mile away. Just before reaching our destination, the chauffeur stopped again.

"Please do not tell the general at headquarters," he pleaded.

Magnanimously, I agreed, "provided it never happens again." Back in Madrid, I treated both my companions to manzanilla and thereafter had no trouble. Yet Madrid, in spite of my fruitful talks with superb Republicans like Luis Araquistain and Luis Quintinilla, was becoming oppressive. I was relieved to learn from Chicago that I might return to Paris.

At a last lunch, Vayo reviewed the situation with me. He had received disturbing news: the British Cabinet was almost openly pro-Franco and France would not help the Republic alone. Yet both knew that Italy and Germany had begun recruiting airmen for the Nationalists even before the latter launched the rebellion. It looked bad for the Republic.

At the end of the meal, Vayo, with that frankness which charmed even his opponents, looked at me appealingly.

"Now that you have seen everything, Edgar, tell me that you are sure we shall win."

I was grateful for the many facilities which had made possible my coverage of the civil war, but determined to speak out.

"Julio, I like you too much to tell you a lie: I am not sure you will win."

"But why not, Edgar? The people are with us."

"Because you Republicans are waging too much revolution and too little war. But I certainly *hope* you will win." Solemnly, we said *adiós*.

At the airport bar, after more manzanilla, my gunmen began talking to each other too quickly for me to follow.

Finally, the chauffeur turned to me. "We are real friends, aren't we?"

"Of course," I answered.

"Like brothers?"

"Absolutely."

"We should like to do the *Señor* a favor," the chauffeur continued.

"Thanks, but my plane leaves in a few minutes."

"We can still do it. Has the *Señor* no enemies in Madrid?"

"Everyone has enemies, but I haven't been in Madrid long enough to identify them." Then laughingly, "But suppose I named an enemy?"

The two looked at each other and giggled. Slowly the gunman drew his finger across his throat. And I went cold, realizing that as a "favor," these reluctant warriors would "eliminate" any "enemy" whom I might designate, naturally, in the name of the revolution.

In the plane I typed a dispatch describing the Spanish situation. "Underlying everything," I wrote, "is the abyss of personal hatred between the two camps. The rebels butcher women and intellectuals, the Republicans kill priests, fascists, and monarchists. . . . The war will be fought to a bloody and bitter end, with no quarter given by either side."

I reached Paris to learn that the French government had issued a declaration of nonintervention in Spain's war. Nonintervention by France meant not only a probable victory for Franco, but for Hitler and Mussolini as well. What was the matter with Léon Blum? I got an appointment with him for the following day.

Blum received me in the sunny garden behind the Palais Matignon.

I wasted no words. *"Monsieur le Président,* this nonintervention business . . . what have you done?"

"I hope, my little Edgar, that you are not going to talk to me about the Germans. Tell me about Spain."

"I *am* going to talk to you about the Germans—*in* Spain. There they and the Italians are waging the next European war by proxy. If they win, there will be no holding them.

For half an hour we argued. Then suddenly he raised his voice: "I am going to tell you something: my political position is not strong enough at home to allow me both to realize my domestic reforms and to intervene in favor of the Spanish Republicans. I have chosen to carry out my reforms. And that's that."

It was, indeed.

25

Two Revolutions

The rich and poor shout, clash and heave and
*   strain.*
The 'have nots,' ultimately, always reign.
But then among them, fat 'haves' rise anew,
Until again the many hate the few.
                              —PAUL SCOTT MOWRER
                              School For Diplomats

THE ATLANTIC CROSSING on the *Normandie* was the first I ever enjoyed.
What beauty of proportions and of furnishings; what savory food; what
smoothness, now that my friend André Labarthe had eliminated the
original vibration by changing the type of propellers; all under a glorious late August sun. Three weeks of fishing with the Greens at Knife
Lake, Minnesota, a remote wooded spot on the Canadian border, and
a similar period with Father in Florida's sunshine left me eager to
understand my own country.

Father, a former Theodore Roosevelt Republican, now seventy-
eight years old, considered the 1936 presidential election crucial to our
future development. To the *Daily News* it was more than that, since
our publisher was the Republican candidate for the vice presidency.
Neither Knox nor Landon could be called reactionary, but both saw
little good in F.D.R.'s "reforms."

For the first time I understood the full impact of the New Deal and
the clash of emotions which it was causing. Immersed as I was in
foreign, chiefly European, affairs, I had not realized that Franklin
Delano Roosevelt and fanatical henchmen like Harry Hopkins were
intent not merely upon economic relief and recovery, but upon drastic
social change as well, in short, upon a legal revolution.

The President had transferred control of the country from Big
Business to Big Government. This he had done by putting together a
unique election coalition, Southern Democrats, national minorities, a
sprinkling of Northern "Wasps," liberals, intellectuals, and a few well-
to-do business people, called by Republicans "traitors to their class."

I considered it high time that all Americans enjoyed their full rights as citizens. Yet I had serious doubts about the viability of a permanently pluralistic society.

If it turned out that way, the "Wasps" could only blame themselves. Instead of restricting immigration to an assimilable size, Anglo-Saxon business leaders, seeking cheap labor had, since about 1890, induced millions of poor Europeans to migrate to the "land of unlimited opportunity." Now the latter had harkened to the call of reformers, who proclaimed the bankruptcy of capitalism, meaning, generally, of classical capitalism, and voted for Roosevelt. This my brother called an "alliance of the plebs and the king against the barons."

Roosevelt had not made a serious dent in mass unemployment or accomplished much in economic recovery. Nevertheless, by sparking law after law, each conferring some benefit on a special group, and by showing unremitting interest in underdogs and attacking "economic royalists" (all duly expressed in his Fireside Chats), he had literally created a new and different United States.

This was what the Republicans, with the backing of most newspapers, and particularly of the Chicago *Daily News*, promised to undo.

The New Deal left me with mixed feelings. The Republicans could not disavow responsibility for the Depression. On the other hand, in my table of values the rights of the individual came first.

Hence, I found myself unable to support either party.

Washington, that once tranquil capital, was literally buzzing with activities, both sane and insane. How any legislator with a grade school education could have approved, still less voted, the Neutrality Acts, I found incomprehensible. In obedience to them, President Roosevelt was, like the British, refusing to sell to the Spanish Republic the essential arms and ammunition which the rebels were getting in quantity from the fascist countries. This pleased pro-Franco American Catholics and those others who were counting on Nazi Germany to crush bolshevism.

"And then?" I always asked, and got no adequate replies. Most heads were buried in the sand of wishful thinking. There were exceptions, like the bibliophile lawyer, Lessing Rosenthal, and Rabbi Stephen Wise in New York. But one did not meet many. Yet—American paradox —some citizens who were unwilling to see their own country oppose aggression by Italy, Germany, or Japan, severely condemned European appeasers. Happily, even under Knox, the *News* had remained unshakably internationalist.

Just before I left Chicago for Europe, in answer to Carroll Binder's complaint about ever stricter Soviet censorship, I suggested replacing our permanent representative in Moscow by a series of visitors. Carroll asked me to be the first of these.

For years I had felt the need of first-hand experience of the Communist Paradise. I could reach the U.S.S.R. in time to cover the coming ratification of the new Soviet Constitution.

After an uneventful trip to England on the *S.S. Queen Mary* and a brief visit to Lilian's Father in London, Lilian and I reached Paris before Thanksgiving, and thence set off for Moscow, by way of Austria and Poland: Nazi Germany was forbidden territory to me.

In Warsaw, between trains, after a long talk with former Foreign Minister Zaleski, we strolled through the beautiful *Stari Miast* and along the Vistula.

Finally, Moscow! My excitement was acute. Ever since I had met Maroussia, Sonya, and Vladimir in 1911, I had wanted to visit their country. Yet physically, aside from Red Square with the imposing crenelated wall of the Kremlin and Saint Basil's onion dome, the street where rich merchants had lived and collected art works, and the river, Moscow was disappointing. Most of it was run down and what was new was already rickety. The Victorian furniture in the once luxurious Metropole Hotel was shabby and when we opened the faucet in the bathtub, sewer water welled up through the outlet.

Happily for us, Soviet officials were going out of their way to please known opponents of Hitler. Foreign Minister Litvinov offered us an official meal with quantities of caviar even better than the Hotel Metropole served for breakfast. At the censor's office, my old Berlin acquaintance, Mironov, did what he could to ease the sending of the rare dispatches I submitted.

Yet of the ten or twelve other Russians to whom I wrote immediately, only one accepted an invitation to visit us. The others either did not answer or pleaded overwork. The single exception was another Berlin acquaintance, Sergei Vinogradov, a tall good-looking man with kindly eyes.

Much of what I learned of the political situation came from the American Catholic chaplain in Moscow, Father Leopold S. Braun, a laughing young priest whose courage, religious devotion, and charity shone from his face.

The reason for the apparent xenophobia of most of our former Russian acquaintances, he explained, was fear. *Russia was in the grip of the most gruesome terror the world had ever seen.*

The Russian revolution had taken nearly twenty years to reach the stage at which the French Revolution arrived in four—namely, that of devouring its own children. Stalin, the Georgian, was revealing himself as a combination of Nero, Genghis Khan, Tamerlane, and Abdul Hamid of Turkey. The murder of his favorite Kirov in Leningrad two years before—which he had probably ordered—was serving as a pretext for the killing of the "Old Bolsheviks," without whom Lenin could not have toppled the Kerensky regime.

In fact, Stalin was carrying out a "second revolution" directed against any individuals whom his Interior Commissars told him might become obstacles to his total power. In August, Zinoviev, Kamenev, and a group of secondary leaders had been shot after confessing complicity in the murder of Kirov. Boguslavsky, Sokolnikov, and the brilliant Radek, perhaps the most successful Bolshevik propagandist, were currently undergoing a well-staged trial as Trotsky-ite deviationists, meaning that Stalin was afraid of them. Many more were to follow.

"Is it possible these former comrades are guilty?" I asked Father Braun.

"Don't make me laugh."

"Then why do they confess to imaginary crimes?"

"Under the Soviet system a political prisoner must prove himself innocent. They arrest you and tell you you are a camel. It is very difficult to prove you are not a camel. In prison you are tortured and brainwashed until you begin to think you may be a camel. Those not ready to say so publicly never come to trial.

"Moreover, some communists are so committed to their ideology, that they accept anything the Party, in this case, Joe Stalin, decides is good for the revolution, even their own deaths."

So this was what the workers and peasants' government had come to! No wonder that the Russians whom we did meet refused to discuss politics. Father Braun's description was confirmed by non-Russian communists who had sought refuge in the Soviet Union from fascist governments at home. Lili Keith, a refugee communist from Berlin, was almost tearful about Stalin's false charges against Radek and the threat hanging over "that great theorist, Bucharin," not to speak of his "neglect" of German "comrades." A number of Austrian communists had even sought refuge in the Austrian Legation (one saw their noses pressed against the basement windows) and had asked to be sent home at the risk of being imprisoned rather than be murdered in the Soviet paradise, like so many other foreign refugee communists.

In fact, among the foreigners we met in the U.S.S.R., only Walter Duranty still saw any virtue in the regime. Duranty relished the favored status which his "understanding attitude" had gained him with the Soviet officials. When, in January, 1937, two old Bolshevik stalwarts, Radek and Sokolnikov, were in the dock facing charges so ridiculous that all Moscow was laughing at them, Duranty solemnly wired the *Times*: "This trial does stand up and the evidence rings true." Other Americans explained that his Russian wife and child were "hostages" for his good behavior.

U.S. Embassy officials had no illusions about what was occurring. William C. Bullitt, who had persuaded President Roosevelt to recognize the Soviet regime and became our first ambassador in Moscow, had quickly soured on the regime. Counselor John C. Wiley had been strongly anticommunist even before seeing Russia.

By the time of our visit in December, 1936, both men had been shifted to other posts. First Secretary Loy Henderson, confirmed all that Father Braun had told me.

So did the British Ambassador, Lord Chilston, and his phenomenally informed Consul, Major McCrea, who had been born in Odessa. After a genuinely British lunch at the Embassy, the Major spent an hour explaining what was happening. Rule by the Communist Party "in the name of the workers and peasants" was a fraud masking the rule of a single man—and he a human monster!

Nor was this surprising, according to the major. Years before, the

Russian socialist Plekhanov had prophesied that an attempt to build socialism by force "would lead to a political deformity after the image of the Chinese and Peruvian empires, a renewed tsarist tyranny with a communist lining."

Yet no amount of argument by enlightened foreigners in Moscow had been able to dissuade those two Fabian idealists, Sydney and Beatrice Webb, from publishing a two-volume travesty of reality, sententiously entitled *Soviet Communism,* based on literal acceptance of what Russian communists told them. Most foreign correspondents in Moscow insisted that the Webbs' description bore to Soviet reality the same relation as the *Little Flowers* of Saint Francis to Pope Borgia.

In the second Soviet Constitution, whose ratification by the Extraordinary Eighth Congress of Soviets had been the immediate pretext for my visit to Russia, the regime skillfully camouflaged its inherent fraud. While it verbally conferred almost normal civil rights upon all Soviet citizens and even specified the right of any federal state to secede from the U.S.S.R., it specifically preserved the "leading position of the Communist Party of the U.S.S.R." Microscopic examination also revealed another catch: two articles prescribed a severe penalty for any lack of total loyalty to the communist state. This meant in practice that so-called political crimes would continue to be exempt from due process. The secret police had only to label any real or suspected dissent as political to remain free to dispose of the criminal as it saw fit. Hence, instead of hindering, the new Constitution in a way authorized Stalin's massacre of fellow Bolsheviks.

The right to secede was bound to remain a dead letter so long as the Communist Party remained in control of every federal republic.

Nonetheless, formal ratification became the occasion for a public holiday and the government permitted foreign correspondents to attend the ceremony in the Great Hall in the Kremlin. Penetrating that somber fortress was exciting. Guards at the gate in the great red wall examined our identity papers. Inside at the foot of the stairway more guards frisked all entrants. Even high-ranking Soviet officers in uniform were compelled to check their arms.

Upstairs, delegates, many of them Asians in exotic costumes and furs, packed the huge hall. Opposite the press gallery, in the midst of Commissars, two of whom, Molotov and Litvinov, I recognized, sat Great Stalin, a figure with hips too broad for the shoulders and drooping mustache—insignificant looking but for the hard shifty eyes and steel features.

We did not need to follow the delegates' speeches to note that every speaker paid humble tribute to the Georgian. Here was a "personalism" which reduced all other Russians to trained seals, expected to leap through any hoop at the trainer's bidding, as Plekhanov had predicted.

To avoid the annoyance of constant NKVD surveillance, I had asked *Intourist* for a Party member as interpreter and guide. The morning after our arrival, a pleasant looking young woman about thirty appeared at the hotel, introduced herself as Mrs. Angarskaya, Siberian by birth and wife of a communist professor. Knowledgeable about the Soviet Union, indefatigable in her efforts to show us Moscow at its best, with enough status to make any other spy unnecessary, she was the perfect *cicerone* except in one respect—she never expressed an opinion of her own.

To factual questions, she gave factual answers. But a question as to what *she* thought of even the most innocuous aspect of Soviet life elicited a noncommittal answer: "Lenin told us . . ." or "Stalin says. . . ." In view of the current atmosphere of terror, I assumed this was an example of what George Orwell later immortalized as "double-think."

Yet toward other Russians, Angarskaya's attitude was anything but noncommittal. On one occasion she arrived at my hotel room in time to see me tipping the waiter in order to get the breakfast dishes removed before we started reading the newspapers. She excused herself and dashed after the waiter, shouting at him as she went. Curious, I followed her far enough to hear her reading the riot act to the hotel manager. Then I returned to my room and waited.

When she arrived, I looked at her, saying nothing. After perhaps a minute she became nervous. "Shall we read *Komsomolskaya Pravda?*"

"No. Let's talk. Just when will you learn to mind your own business?"

"I don't understand you, Meester."

"You understand perfectly."

"That waiter should not have touched your dirty money. Tipping in Russia is strictly forbidden."

"No one in Moscow has refused my tips yet. Perhaps if you paid the waiter properly, he would not take tips. Just what did you say to the manager downstairs?"

"I told him that if I saw that waiter taking your money again he might find himself in a labor camp in Siberia."

"I see. A generous nature you have, Mrs. Angarskaya. However, now please translate the leading article in *Pravda*."

We had no further trouble.

In Moscow at the end of 1936, no male foreigner could cross Red Square after dark without being invited (usually in German) by one or more buxom ladies to *"komm mit."* It reminded me of the Friedrichstrasse in Berlin in the brave days before Hitler.

Not astonishing, of course. But a day or two later, in the Press Bureau, Mironov boasted: "At least we in Russia have abolished those two capitalist stains, mendicancy and prostitution.

"Really, Mironov? Come and have dinner with me at the Metropole and afterwards we'll go out on Red Square and you'll see not one but several willing dames."

"I know all about them. They aren't prostitutes."

"No? Just the victims of my irresistible masculinity, perhaps?"

"I'll explain. Prostitution is a capitalist phenomenon resulting from hunger due to joblessness. But those Russian women on Red Square have jobs."

"Then what do they want from strangers?"

"Extras, mostly fur coats."

And at this point I gave up.

Yet of all my Moscow encounters, the most unforgettable came from an encounter in the newsmens' section of the Hall in the Kremlin. This was with an old Berlin acquaintance, a writer for the *Deutsche Allgemeine Zeitung,* an organ of the "big business" *Volkspartei,* which had, so far as I knew, never sold out completely to the Nazis. Still. . . .

My former colleague expressed his sincere admiration for my stand against Hitler three years before. *"Das war wirklich schoen.* Come to lunch at my apartment and bring your wife. I want so much to discuss the world situation with you."

What foreign correspondent could resist? In the designated apartment, the D.A.Z. man introduced the fourth person at table as *Kapitaen-zur-See* von Baumbach, Naval Attaché at the German Embassy. Over a relentlessly German meal, we chatted amiably of old times and listened to funny stories about Russia. But when the (German) servant had brought the coffee and disappeared, my friend said: "By way of introduction, I should inform you that the Captain is also the head of the German Intelligence Service in Russia. He will tell you something."

My bewilderment grew greater.

"Mr. Mowrer," the officer began, "we of the German officer corps understand why you refused to yield to Hitler. As Americans we would have done the same. You were brought up to cherish individual freedom. But you must realize that the era of freedom is disappearing. The new epoch will be one of nationalism and to play its appropriate role in it, Germany simply must have more territory.

"We military have no great respect for the Bohemian corporal. But he is conditioning the German people to support our coming expansion into Eastern Europe where our future lies. And nobody can stop us.

"In so doing we shall have to fight Soviet Russia. We hope France and Britain will not interfere. If they do, so much the worse for them. France is decadent and will succumb in three months. Without France, England can do nothing. Once we have defeated Russia—not too difficult an undertaking—and created Greater Germany by annexing part of the Ukraine, we of the *Wehrmacht* will get rid of Hitler and seek the friendship of the Western countries."

"But," I interjected, remembering Ludendorff's similar ambitions during the first world war.

"No buts, Mr. Mowrer. I am telling you this so that you will realize that Nazism is just a necessary interlude in our history. Basically we respect Western values. But today's Germany is too small for the number and energy of its people."

He stopped and waited for my comment.

"Shades of Bismarck . . . or Bonaparte!" I thought, determined to show no feeling.

Then, aloud: "Very interesting. But aren't you omitting one factor of some importance from your calculation? What makes you think we Americans will sit quietly while you defeat Britain?"

"Are you not aware of the American neutrality legislation and the determination of your people to keep out of the next war? Besides, you are not a military people."

"In 1917, you Germans belittled the impact of America's declaration of war. A year later there were two million Americans in France and it was all up with you. I would advise you not to take the neutrality legislation too seriously, *Herr Kapitaen.*"

"Then you really believe that your country would fight Germany to save Britain?"

"I do indeed, even if we had to do it alone."

He laughed incredulously.

"There you are wrong, Mr. Mowrer. We have no quarrel with the American people. But the creation of Greater Germany is for us a matter of life or death."

"Even by war?"

"By war if necessary."

It was time to go. We thanked our two hosts for an unforgettable lunch, pulled on our *galoshi,* and left. My mind was seething and I needed fresh air and exercise in order to think. Why had this professional soldier revealed a (presumably) secret German politico-military plan to an American newsman—even off the record? Was it to strengthen the American people's reluctance to involvement in another European war or, by giving the scheme premature publicity, to prevent it? To this day I cannot say.

Both Angarskaya and Mironov were surprised that after describing the ratification scene in the Kremlin, I had not sent more frequent dispatches to Chicago. According to the agreement with Binder, I was saving my fire until I returned to Paris, when there would be no censor to protect sensitive targets.

However, a friend in the U.S. Embassy drove us out of Moscow to see the convicts, most of them political, working under police guard on the new and impressive Volga-Moscow Canal. How many such convicts were there in the U.S.S.R.? No foreigner knew exactly, but diplomats and newsmen agreed that there were certainly many millions.

This use of political prisoners impressed me greatly. So when Mironov asked if there remained anyone I should like to interview, I named Yezhov, Stalin's recently appointed head of the GPU.

I had already talked at length with Litvinov and been really impressed by that great developer of the Soviet Arctic, Otto Schmidt, about whom I was able to write enthusiastically. This Mironov knew. Therefore he replied that, though unusual, it might just be possible for me to see Yezhov.

Yezhov, however, insisted on knowing what I wanted to question him about. "That's easy," I told Angarskaya. "Russia obviously leads the world in the quality of its convict labor and I want to ask Yagoda's successor just what is the secret of its efficiency."

Yezhov's reaction to this proposal was vehemently negative.

Thereafter, I sought no more interviews. Just before Christmas, I left for Paris alone, Lilian having previously returned through Germany from Leningrad. With me I took a piece of political contraband whose discovery by the Soviet frontier authorities would surely lead to its confiscation and perhaps to serious trouble for me, since I had solemnly promised not to reveal the source (a foreign newspaper correspondent) "under any circumstances!" This compromising object was nothing less than a complete list of *all* the members of the Soviet Politburo since its formation, with the present "condition" of each. Thanks to Stalin, it read like an aide-memoire of the fates of Henry VIII's wives which I had learned in school—"divorced, beheaded, died; divorced, beheaded, survived," with two additional categories: "somewhere in prison" and "whereabouts unknown."

At the Soviet frontier, I had the choice between hiding it on my person or putting it in my briefcase between pages of an English translation of one of Stalin's speeches. I chose the latter.

The venture turned out well. When the guard opened my briefcase and saw Stalin's name on the top document, he looked no further. But what a relief half an hour later, to know that the earth beneath the train's whirling wheels was no longer Stalin's!

Less than a month's exposure to what the Webbs called a "new civilization" had affected my vision. Strolling through the streets between trains, I saw Warsaw with new eyes. How magnificent the city! How fine the buildings and rich the shops! Even the former ghetto seemed less dreary than it had a month before.

Chicago agreed that I had earned a vacation. We spent the Christmas holidays at Kleine Scheidegg under the shadow of the towering Eiger, Moench, and Jungfrau peaks. It was mid-January before I posted my final Russian mail story. This gave, in dramatized form, the hitherto unrevealed fate of all the Politburo's members since its formation. After describing the servile adulation given Stalin by all his present followers, I suggested that sometimes, at twilight, even the *Vozhd* might think back to what he had done to his old comrades. And after listing in detail the diverse fates of about a hundred and fifty of these, I concluded: "All, all are gone, the old familiar faces."

This story made a considerable stir. And not only in America. When, some months later, Carroll Binder applied to the Russians for a new entrance visa for Mowrer, Moscow refused bluntly.

I did not mind. Samuel Johnson had rashly written: "I would not give a half-guinea to live under one form of government rather than another. It is of no moment to the happiness of the individual."

Contrariwise, I knew now that I would give all the guineas I might ever possess rather than live under the Soviet form of government. If necessary, I would give my life.

26

Toward Catastrophe

We ought never allow a disorder to take place
in order to avoid war, for war is not thereby
avoided but only deferred to one's disadvan-
tage.

—MACHIAVELLI

BY THE BEGINNING OF 1937 it was clear that only a complete change in British political thinking could spare the democracies an ultimate choice between war and surrender to the Axis. From this time on, French policy was largely made in London. This was the result of pacifism induced by tragic memories and by current weakness. The French (elementary) Teachers Federation was openly advocating surrender. One of their leaders argued that "servitude is preferable to war." In Paris the group of liberal Catholics around *Esprit* magazine shrank from the grim facts, as I learned when I spoke to them on Hitler's policies.

At the end of my talk, amid a conspicuous absence of applause, the Chairman, Emanuel Mounier, said:

"I think I should tell you that most of us disagree with your thesis."

"With precisely *what* do you disagree?" I countered.

"*Eh bien,* first of all, Hitler is a man like everybody else—"

"Stop right there," I interrupted. "First, according to the *Fuehrer's* friend, Leni Riefenstahl, the German movie actress whom many of you must have seen, Hitler is something less than a man. And second, if he is like everybody else, then God help the rest of us, including you and me."

This drew a laugh, but made no converts.

In Britain ever more citizens seemed to agree with those students of the Oxford Union who had passed a resolution declaring that "this house refuses to fight for King and Country." Prime Minister Neville Chamberlain (whom Churchill once characterized as "a turnip mesmerized by a rabbit") saw no reason for opposing Nazi Germany. A

272

number of Tories, beginning with American-born Lady Astor and the "Cliveden set," and an Anglo-German Fellowship, sometimes called by their all too rare opponents the "Heil Hitler gang," accepted as good wine the anticommunist propaganda offered by Ambassador von Ribbentrop. The Fellowship included Lord Mount Temple; Lord Redesdale, father of that Unity Mitford who was to fall in love with the *Fuehrer*; Lord Lothian, a coming ambassador in Washington; Sir Rennell Rodd, former ambassador in Rome; and Sir Horace Wilson, soon to supplant Vansittart as the government's chief adviser on foreign affairs.

As a result, Europe's drift toward catastrophe lacked the dignity of an authentic tragedy. For tragedy, as the old Greeks conceived it, contained an element of inevitability, while there was nothing necessary about the misdirected appeasement of Nazi Germany and fascist Italy, about the Western democracies' inability to recognize the real stake of the Spanish Civil War, or about their indifference to Japan's invasion of China.

In January, 1937, the French government considered putting a ban on the passage of foreign volunteers going to help the Spanish Republic. Some of these were admittedly Soviet agents. Others were, however, friends of democracy and freedom who recognized the Spanish Nationalists as the tools, if not the conscious allies, of world Fascism.

Against such a background, the much-touted Conference Against Piracy (held at Nyon in Switzerland since the Germans and Italians refused to come to Geneva) could only be a farce.

The new Spanish Premier, Juan Negrin, a highly intelligent, energetic, and sincerely democratic physician, implored the League to declare Italy and Germany guilty of aggression and to proclaim the right of the Republic to import fuel oil without outside attacks. All to no purpose.

Thanks to Jay Allen, to Richard Mowrer in Madrid, and to correspondents John Whitaker and Frances Davis on the Nationalists' side, I missed few details of the developing Spanish tragedy. And I continued writing in favor of the Spanish Republic, trusting that humanitarians like Negrin would be able to prevent a communist takeover in case of a Republican victory.

In France, in spite of, perhaps because of, such reforms as the forty-hour week, the trade unions failed to complete on time the widely advertised Paris Exhibition of 1937. Only the German, Italian, and Soviet pavilions were ready on the opening day. Paris waiters and hotel employees discouraged tourists by lackadaisical service. Endemic strikes were giving a new sort of French fascists, the *Cagoulards* (or Hooded Men), a pretext for further illegality. Meanwhile the politicians elbowed for high office as though nothing were happening. When in March, 1938, Hitler seized Austria, there was no French government.

In physics positive attracts negative. But in human relations, like attracts like. Most of the Mowrers' friends were outspoken anti-Hitlerians. Among these Jean Monnet, the Pan-European, combined political ideals, intellect, and an unrivaled ability to convince people. Two of France's outstanding economists, the Conservative Charles Rist and the "Leftist" Francis Delaisi, were at one in their opposition to Nazism. At Yvonne Michel's we met Minister Pierre Cot, already strongly pro-Russian, and newsman Georges Boris; Henri and Louise de Vilmorin; Jean Prouvost; a gifted professor called Louis Joxe; René Pleven; Pierre de Lanux and his American wife; Jacques Kayser, a friend of Daladier; Socialist Pierre Brosselette (who later died heroically for freedom); and a charming young woman, Eve Curie, all unforgettable. They too shared our political uneasiness.

So, in most respects, did the American Ambassador, William Christian Bullitt, and his brash but competent secretary, Carmel Offie. Bullitt was unique, the only American diplomat who knew his country of residence as well as any American correspondent. To do so, he introduced news techniques. To each French social or political group he assigned a member of his staff. Bob Murphy, a conservative, was assigned to "cover" what remained of the aristocrats of the Faubourg Saint-Germain. Larry Higgins, a New Englander, was to cultivate the Communist Party! Since Larry had never met a French Communist, I introduced him to the daughter of the party leader, Marcel Cachin, who brought him into touch with her father. Cachin himself was so personally attractive that one could believe his claim to have become a communist only "in order to be a better man."

Bullitt, thanks to his system, to his knowledge of France and of the French language, and to his political perception, kept President Roosevelt, to whom he telephoned almost daily, fully informed concerning Europe from Moscow to Madrid. Until 1940, he had a decisive influence on American foreign policy toward Europe and the Soviet Union.

On only one point our views differed. Realizing the essential aggressivity of the Kremlin, Bullitt condoned the readiness of Poland and Rumania to seek a German counterweight to potential Soviet pressure. To me, constantly noting how at Geneva the U.S.S.R. steadfastly urged collective action against fascist aggression, Polish and Rumanian fears seemed grossly exaggerated. Subsequent events proved Bullitt's judgment to have been the better.

In June, 1937, Frank Knox and his wife came to Europe. Their planned itinerary included a visit to Rome and a ten-day steamer trip from Venice down the east shore of the Adriatic, thence through the Western Greek Islands to Athens. Knox extended a boss's "invitation" to Lilian and me to go along, as friends, political counselors, and interpreters.

This prospect we found attractive in spite of our repugnance to fascism. Umano was long dead. But Hendrik Andersen was still pushing his plans for a world city, aided by his adopted sister, Lucia. We hoped once more to meet old friends like Maffio Maffii, the Emanuels, Giuditta Sartori the pianist, Alfredo Casella, and Francesco Malipiero.

The *Duce*, however, informed Knox that never again did he wish to set eyes on that "enemy of Italy," *Signore* Mowrer.

Verbot number three! Hitler, Stalin, and Mussolini simultaneously found me *persona non grata*. What a distinction!

Colonel Knox arrived in Europe an isolationist ("we must keep out of that dogfight") and returned to America a resolute antifascist.

Mrs. Knox, on the other hand, had remained a small-town egotist, basically uninterested in what her husband was doing—or in Mediterranean civilization. She complained constantly.

Still, familiar cities like Venice, Trieste, Fiume, Tirana, Durazzo, Valona, Corfù, and Athens, and new (to me) ones like Zara (home of maraschino, baptized by D'Annunzio "blood of the Morlachs") and marvelous Split within the ruins of the nine-and-a-half-acre palace of Roman Emperor Diocletian—these helped me forget Annie's monotonous demands for boiled carrots and tea in little bags.

Promising to rejoin the ship at Valona two days later, the four of us went from Durazzo to Tirana where I felt sure I could induce King Zog (whom I had known as Achmed Zogu Bey Mati) to receive us. Our request, when transmitted by the American Legation, he immediately granted, only specifying it was for men only, properly dressed in frock coats, striped pants, and high collared shirts. These Knox and I borrowed from members of the Legation. Zog received his sweating visitors in sports togs and greeted me as an old acquaintance. Though he said nothing of any moment, he impressed the Colonel.

Thence to Valona by car and by ship to Corfù, past Ulysses' rocky Ithaca, and through the Corinth Canal to Athens.

Lilian and the Knoxes were seeing Athens for the first time and even Annie felt the charm of this unique though noisy city. The Greeks had just fallen victim to the harsh dictatorship of General Metaxas. To us, the odious atmosphere of tyranny was all too familiar, but it made the Colonel think. The day before our departure, leaning on an ancient ruin, he remained silent for a moment, then announced: "It isn't property that counts; it's liberty."

When we left Athens Lilian returned directly to Paris to complete the manuscript of her first book, *Journalist's Wife*. The Knoxes and I stopped in Belgrade (where I learned of Stalin's liquidation of three former communist acquaintances, Ambassador Krestinsky, Marcel Rosenberg, and the German communist leader, Heinz Neumann). In Vienna the Colonel interviewed the wobbling Schuschnigg—already secretly condemned to death by the *Fuehrer*. Then while he and Annie went to Prague and Berlin, I returned to Paris.

When the Colonel, indignant at what he had seen in Germany, also returned to Paris, I surprised him with an invitation to a stag dinner with Léon Blum, who had just resigned as Premier. Knox was flabbergasted to meet not a wild-eyed socialist, but a soft-spoken intellectual who disliked Fascism and Communism equally.

Yet Blum still minimized the Nazi threat.

In London, Sir Robert Vansittart had read *Germany Puts the Clock Back,* recognized a natural ally, and invited me to visit him at Downing Street as often as I could. He regularly gave me the latest diplomatic information from Berlin, often letting me read the dispatches, and together we plotted what might still be done.

Only on Italy did we differ. To the end, Van (as everybody called him) remained convinced that Mussolini could be kept, or weaned, from Hitler, and that without the Italian's support, the German would not dare wage war. I felt that the common goal of empire linked the two indissolubly. Seeking to mollify the *Duce* was effort wasted.

Unhappily, Neville Chamberlain soon replaced Van with Sir Horace Wilson, who, with Editor Geoffery Dawson of the London *Times,* hastened the course to catastrophe.

In London, Lance Whyte was now working as scientific adviser to the bank house of O. T. Falk. To the manager, Sir Maurice Bonham Carter and his wife, Lady Violet, Lance described my antifascist stand. She read *Germany Puts the Clock Back* and spoke of it to Gerald Barry, then editor of the London *News-Chronicle,* who in turn advised Allen Lane, the astute and enterprising head of Penguin Books. Lane published *Germany Puts the Clock Back* as one of the first four "Penguin Specials."

In hard cover, this had sold considerably less in England than in America. As a Penguin product, it was thrice reprinted as originally written and then again in 1938 with additions bringing it up to date—in all, some three hundred thousand copies. These, according to Allen, "may reasonably be said to have been the beginning of a real awakening in the British public to the inherent dangers of the trend of affairs." In 1942, it appeared in braille.

Truly, as Brother Paul was to write years later:

Be right too late and every one is bored;
Be right too soon, your word will be ignored.

The year 1933 had been too soon. Was 1937 too late?

Not too late to attract further kindred spirits in Britain's three political parties. Lance Whyte's employer, the banker, O. T. Falk, organized in the London City an anti-Hitler rally at which Harold Nicolson, Bob Boothby, M.P., and I spoke. Conservatives like Lord Robert Cecil, Lord Cranborne, John Wheeler-Bennett, and Labourites like Hugh Dalton, Philip Noel Baker, Nye Bevin, Jenny Lee, and Herbert Morrison, whom I made a point of seeing during each visit to England, were recommending my book. Leftists like Harold Laski and the Hungarian economist Thomas Balogh sought my acquaintance. Sad to say, Opposition Leader Lansbury of the Labour Party was a Christian pacifist, who opposed Nazism and at the same time the massive British rearmament that might have given Hitler pause. Lansbury's successor, Clement Attlee, talked bravely but refused to disown the party's stand. The international situation deteriorated from week to week.

In the spring of 1938 I received an invitation to visit China. During the previous three years I had become well acquainted with China's ambassadors in London and Paris, Quo Tai-chi and Wellington Koo, respectively. Although the invitation allegedly came from a French group, I suspected that the Chinese government had a hand in it. Yet once I received the assurance that I could go where I liked and write what I liked, the temptation became irresistible. I prepared to fly to Hong Kong in a French plane.

Before I left, Dr. Ludwik Rajchman, head of the Health Section of the League of Nations, filled me in thoroughly on the Chinese situation. "Lulu," as even his family called him, was a Polish physician and one-time close associate of Jozef Pilsudski in securing Poland's independence from Bolshevik Russia. Before becoming a senior League official, he had organized Institutes of Epidemiology and of Hygiene in Poland.

For the League his master work had been the organization, in cooperation with T. V. Soong, the banker brother-in-law of Chiang Kai-shek, of technical assistance for New China, the first ever undertaken by the League. Thereafter the doctor spent much time in China. Some felt that it was the success of the Rajchman-Soong project that had caused Japan so precipitately to leave the League and seize Chinese Manchuria.

I had been for two years waiting for a Western reaction. But until the "second phase," when the Japanese seized Shanghai, Lulu explained, no Great Power did anything serious to save China. True, a German military mission was turning Chinese peasants into soldiers, the German Lufthansa linked a few Chinese cities together, and the Soviet Union was sending some supplies to Chiang Kai-shek. But the Stimson Doctrine grandiloquently proclaimed by Washington and the half-hearted Report of the League's Lytton Commission proved to be as ineffective as the Kellogg-Briand Pact Outlawing War.

At long last President Roosevelt had replied with his "Quarantine Aggressors" speech at Chicago. Eight of the nine Powers that had signed the Nine-Power Treaty of 1922 promising to respect China's sovereignty, independence, and territorial integrity, had met at Brussels to decide what to do about Japan. We Americans in Europe raised our chins and squared our shoulders.

Another deception! "Peace-loving" editors at home raised such objections to the President's proposal that at Brussels, even before the conference began, its failure was obvious. The Belgians, though boasting of their "services to peace," wanted chiefly to know who was going to pay for the meeting. After two distressing weeks and several long talks with the U.S. chief delegate, Norman Davis, I had returned to Paris convinced that the conferees would do nothing but talk.

Shortly after the Brussels meeting, Japanese flyers revealed their estimate of the United States by deliberately sinking the U.S. Gunboat *Panay* on the Yangtse River near Nanking. Subsequently, the one-hundredth meeting of the League Council fizzled into more words.

Now, in April, 1938, I dutifully presented myself at the Pasteur Institute in Paris and asked for whatever preventive injections were needed for China.

"Central China?" The attending physician peered into a book containing the latest medical reports from all over the world. "You will want protection against the plague, cholera, typhoid, and para-typhoids A and B. Three shots, each a week apart."

When I expressed my intention of leaving within ten days, he looked at me quizzically. "If you insist, I can do it in one shot . . . un petit cocktail . . . if you can stand the kick."

I stood it, and left for China precisely as planned.

The flight to Hong Kong took eight days and I would not have had it shorter. East of Athens, all was new to me: Beirut, interesting if venal; cedarless Mount Lebanon; Damascus and the covered Street Called Straight; Baghdad; Karachi and a British Army polo match; Calcutta; Rangoon, with the golden Pagoda of Shwe Dagon and Bangkok, from the Emerald Buddha to the water-life on the klongs! On the way to Hanoi, flying over a dense jungle, the pilot sighted a herd of elephants, spiraled down close, and stampeded them—a scene from the Wizard of Oz! Finally we reached bustling Hong Kong.

The colony's governor, Sir Geoffrey Northcote, was courtesy itself, but when I expressed my belief that the United States would do nothing serious to help China, not even stop the sale to Japan of those warplanes which were making a hell of Chinese cities, I could not tell whether he was worried or relieved.

To many of those foreign "masters" in Hong Kong, Kuomintang China was just a burst of Canton firecrackers, all noise and smoke destined shortly to disappear without trace. Yet with the exception of the Italians among them, they were not pro-Japanese.

For my geographical and human itinerary, I depended on Rajchman's friend, T. V. Soong, leading male member of the incredible Soong family, head of the Bank of China and allegedly China's richest man. Burly T. V., as I was soon calling him, received me in the inner office of a Hong Kong bank, in his shirt sleeves with a revolver in a holster on his left hip. Apparently, he was subject to frequent attempts at assassination and told none but his relations and close associates of his future movements.

Thanks to T. V., I met his sister, Ching-ling, better known as the widow of the great Sun Yat-sen whose memory all Chinese revered. Her fragile beauty was singularly attractive, but with her devotion to her dead husband went an irrational affection for the Soviet Union where he and she had spent several years. When at her request, I described how Stalin was murdering his old companions, she refused to listen. "Stalin," she answered, "is the greatest man alive since the death of my husband, Dr. Sun. He is the hope of mankind." As a "true believer," she preserved the purity of her faith by denying discordant facts.

This shocked me until I recalled that Moscow had supported the new Chinese Republic in its early years and that Chiang Kai-shek, for whom Ching-ling seemed to have little use, was now accepting communist aid against Japan.

In the train for Canton, I had no sooner sunk into a seat than T. V. unexpectedly sat down beside me. He too was going to Hankow.

Though I spent only two months in China, rarely has so short a period been so vivid. And the longer I stayed the greater my delight. Most remarkable about China was its "Chineseness." Though a dedicated traveler, I found for the first time a country sufficiently "foreign." When, following T. V.'s advice, I had calling cards printed in both languages, Edgar Ansel Mowrer became, in Chinese, *Mao La*. Even commercial flights turned into adventures.

During that first one, from Canton to Hankow, while I was standing in the aisle talking with T. V. Soong, the plane suddenly hit a down current and plunged, banging the top of my head on the ceiling, inflicting a deep cut on T. V.'s leg, and injuring most other passengers. "This," I thought, "is *finis* . . . before I see China." Only a few hundred feet above the ground could the experienced German pilot pull out of the drop.

A second flight was even more fantastic. At Chungking airfield, while I waited for a Chinese "crate" (vintage of about 1920) to take me to Chengtu, a modern plane piloted by two Americans in white ducks dropped out of the sky. Chinese soldiers with fixed bayonets rushed to surround it. And from out of a shed came a long line of coolies, each staggering under the weight of a single smallish package which he loaded into the baggage compartment or placed on the floor between the seats. The Bank of China was prudently transferring its gold reserve to Lanchow, out of reach of the advancing Japanese! I persuaded the Americans to take me as far as Chengtu. During the flight an elderly Chinese official in a gray robe and I sat alone in the midst of two and a half million dollars.

Where else were cities more unlike? In Canton where the China clippers from New England used to wait for cargoes of tea, a hundred thousand people lived permanently in houseboats anchored twenty deep along both banks of the Pearl River. What a contrast between the masses who trembled at the wanton but murderous Japanese air raids, and the alert modernity of Provincial Governor Wu Te Chen, Mayor Tseng Yangfu, a Pittsburgh-trained mining engineer, and Dr. K. T. Chu, of Indiana University, the physician in charge of first aid to bomb victims! For Governor Wu I drafted a statement in English describing the wanton slaughter of civilians by the Japanese flyers, which, when signed by him and issued to the mayors of the world by the International Peace Campaign in Paris, helped turn public opinion against Japan.

Wuhan on the Yangtse, whither the government had moved from Nanking, now contained thousands of refugees who had come from the east generally on foot, sometimes bringing whole factories.

In Hankow I lived at the *Hotel des Wagons-Lits et Terminus* under the protection of French troops, a last remaining example of the kind of "master" rule of which China had had more than enough. Yet I met no French people. Instead I enjoyed total Chinese hospitality, conversational and gastronomic.

At my first dinner, given for some thirty guests by Hollington Tong, American-educated Vice Minister of Information, the menu, "because of war-time restrictions," was limited to a mere forty dishes.

In fact, my most meager Chinese meal, offered by a poor professor, consisted of five dishes, any two of which would have satisfied most Americans.

Thanks to T. V., to the American Ambassador, the erudite Chinese-speaking Nelson T. Johnson, and to the U.S. Naval Attaché, Major James McHugh, I saw everyone I needed to see, beginning with the Generalissimo and Madame Chiang.

From the Gimo, polite and inscrutable, I remember only the memorable remark: "We are buying time with space," a formula which had been first used by the early Bolsheviks in accepting the harsh Treaty of Brest-Litovsk.

His wife, Mei-ling, youngest of the Soong sisters, slim, attractive, and vivacious, discoursed eloquently on the nature and purposes of the war. She seemed to hold me personally responsible for America's continuing sale of those planes and bombs wherewith the Japanese were crushing Chinese cities.

The third Soong sister, Ai-ling, and her husband, H. H. Kung, famous as a modern financial wizard and a seventy-fifth lineal descendant of Confucius, gave me tea and cakes. But whereas I found H. H. friendly and hard to envisage as China's chief pawnbroker, Ai-ling lectured me so sternly on America's political failings toward China that after an hour I was not sorry to leave the only woman I had met who inspired something like a sense of fear.

Others to whom I listened at great length were the War Minister, Ho Yin-chin; the energetic Kwangsi general, Pai Cheng-hsi; Chen Li-fu, former "Tammany boss" in Shanghai and organizer of the pious New Life Movement dear to Madame Chiang; and handsome Wang Ching-wei. Wang expressed doubts about a Chinese victory in the absence of massive foreign help. Shortly thereafter he tried to avenge himself on those who ousted him from political power by becoming a Japanese puppet.

W. H. Donald, the Australian former newspaperman who had become the indispensable adviser of the Generalissimo and Madame, remained as unhampered in criticizing China's weaknesses as in refusing to eat Chinese food or to learn the Chinese language. His very frankness and common sense made him a power in the regime.

As I was to witness. The day before I had visited the nearby cholera camp housing several thousand sick. Never had I seen such dehydrated bodies. There the League of Nations epidemiologist, a young Englishman, revealed that, for some unfathomable reason, his Chinese medical colleagues no longer cooperated with him. So he was returning to Geneva. I persuaded him to wait until I had informed Donald of the difficulty. Two days later the Englishman appeared in my room at midnight to tell me that Donald had pacified the other doctors. To show his gratitude he gave me there and then an anti-cholera shot three times as powerful as the one I had received at the Pasteur Institute where, he commented, "they know about cholera only from hearsay." For whatever reason I remained immune in a time of serious epidemic.

Chungking combined trade and war, old and new China. My bedroom on the top floor of the Mei Feng Bank, a concrete and steel construction with an electric elevator, offered a choice of five spittoons and the silken sheets concealed any number of unelegant and voracious bed bugs.

Chengtu, however, the capital of present Szechwan and of the former Kingdom of Shoo, would have offered few surprises to Marco Polo. In spite of the presence of foreign-trained Chinese, including my Geneva friend, Victor Hu; in spite of several universities, some of them transplanted from the coast; in spite of a Y.M.C.A. and Missionaries, Boy Scouts, and Girl Guides; of a modern brewery, ten daily newspapers, and a feminist weekly edited by twenty-two-year-old, incredibly pretty, Japan-trained Chu Zho-hwa; and even of a few youthful communists acting out a play in the public square, Chengtu was still Cathay.

Imagine a primly square town of several hundred thousand inhabitants, encompassed by miles of wall forty feet high, with gates that closed each night at 10:00 P.M. to keep robbers out and soldiers in! A city of shops selling superb silks and legendary embroideries made in shop fronts by weak-eyed little boys of ten; of coppersmiths and curio dealers selling old jade carvings and coral and malachite rings straight from the pigtails of Tibetan women; a city that fermented its wine from oranges.

There I conversed at length with two old scholars who disliked everything modern, and visited an opium-smoking French consul, immensely cultured, whose large house outside the walls was protected day and night by fifteen savage police dogs. At his dinner table a fabulous French authoress, Madame Alexandra David-Neel, told of her repeated trips on foot through mysterious Tibet, and of monks several hundred years old.

From a neighboring table in the town's chief restaurant, "Marshal" Yang Chi-yi, Civil Governor of the Province of Szechwan, challenged Mao La to a drinking contest. The American chose beer instead of orange wine and thanks perhaps to some earlier training at student Kneipen in Germany, managed to achieve a draw.

Kunming, capital of Yunnan Province and soon to be the terminal of the legendary Burma Road, was, in 1938, still idyllic, and amazingly

French. Situated 6,500 feet above sea level, with temples, lovely West Mountain, and a nearby lake, it was enough to make Californians envious. Many of its inhabitants and most of the country people around it were not Chinese, but Shans, Miaos, Lolos, and Wahs. Though conquered by Genghis Khan, and physically incorporated into China in the eighteenth century, Yunnan had remained spiritually closer to French Indo-China than to the Middle Kingdom.

In Kunming, the French government maintained a French school and a French hospital. Most of the foreign businessmen were French and French was the predominant foreign language.

The Governor, General Long-yun, lived in French style. Guests at the dinner to which he invited me sat at an oblong table, were served one dish at a time by servants and drank French wine or water.

Nonetheless, the Governor had sent three divisions of soldiers to fight the Japanese, and with French help was training two hundred thousand more.

War fever was running high. The public squares were full of fiery speakers and enthusiastic listeners. China could not lose.

I had become doubtful of a Chinese victory while spending several days on the Yellow River with a retreating Chinese army.

Shortly after reaching Hankow I applied to Hollington Tong for permission to see some fighting. Tong suggested visiting the quiet "East Front" beyond Kuling. When I argued that I had not come from Paris to have dinner with Chinese generals but to see military action, he relented. So in due time, equipped with bedding and food for an emergency, three of us, Belgian correspondent Jacques Marcuse, a Chinese interpreter, and Mao La set out by train for the "North Front" along the Yellow River.

We hoped to reach the town of Lanfeng on the Lunghai railroad where the Chinese claimed to have penned against the Yellow River an entire Japanese division under famous General Doihara.

At Chengchow, where we waited a few hours between trains, a dust storm brought us a taste of the Gobi Desert and turned the sky black as night for several hours. And at Kaifeng, the passenger train stopped for good. While we were seeking some means of moving onward, Japanese planes raided the town. Canton possessed a few shelters. Here it was naked murder. When the last bomb had crushed the last cluster of houses and the planes had zoomed away, I saw in the streets about a hundred corpses, including several headless babies.

General Cheng Sheng, the Yellow River Defense Commander, was away from headquarters and his subordinate refused to help us proceed further. A minor officer at the headquarters three miles out in the country proved equally unhelpful. China was again retreating and the generals were reluctant to allow foreigners to witness the process.

However, we stood on our passes from the Generalissimo in Hankow.

Noting that our intended goal, Lanfeng, was forty kilometers distant, he finally let us depart. A truck driver gave us a lift for a few miles, then returned to Kaifeng without us, but carrying our interpreter, who feared falling into Japanese hands.

Thus "alone in China," Jacques and I sat down under a tree in the rain to decide what to do next. Out of nowhere appeared a Chinese war correspondent, C. C. Chen, who offered to accompany us to Lanfeng on foot. Accepted. Yet difficulties persisted. While Chen, another young Chinese who scattered propaganda leaflets, their two coolies, and Jacques and I groped our way through the darkness, we ran into a prowling armored car whose Japanese driver had heard our voices and was trying with his searchlight to locate us where we lay on our bellies in long grass. He failed, but since his car remained between us and the local headquarters, we slept in an abandoned farmhouse, for all the world like the one described in Pearl Buck's *Good Earth*.

Still no luck. A few miles farther on, an unseen Japanese machine gunner suddenly opened up and all but got us. Lanfeng and the penned-in Japanese division were inaccessible! Reluctantly we turned back expecting to board a train at Kaifeng.

Too late! The American Mission where we had stayed was empty, the last west-bound train had departed, and it was raining heavily. Nothing to do but tramp the fifty odd miles back to Chengchow where we might still find a train bound for Hankow.

We became part of an endless procession of fleeing soldiers and civilian refugees. Aside from the presence of an occasional mandarin and several Chinese ladies in silks mincing along on deformed feet, it resembled the Italian retreat from Udine almost twenty-one years earlier.

The going was even tougher. Chen, Jacques, and I had already walked some seven hours. Worse, having been assured at Hankow that army transportation was everywhere available, I had neglected to choose walking shoes. By this time, each heel bore a blister the size of a silver dollar.

Once more the resourceful Chen came to the rescue. After we had plodded some ten miles, he first borrowed bicycles for Jacques and me, and then talked an Army truck driver into letting us four pile into his vehicle, already loaded with retreating Chinese soldiers.

At Chungmow, where the truck stopped, Chen found us shelter from the pouring rain in a bathhouse, where Jacques and I dried our soaked clothes, shared the roll and peanut supper of a Chinese postal clerk, cadged a brandy from the bathhouse keeper, absorbed countless cups of boiling tea, and slept like stones on bare benches.

In the morning, we set off alone on the last twenty odd miles. By the middle of the afternoon, the pain in my feet was bringing tears to my eyes. No alternative but to press on.

Suddenly out of nowhere a Chinese medical general halted us and finding out who we were, brought us in an ambulance to the American Baptist Hospital in Chengchow. He did this to repay America, he said, for hospitality shown to his student son in America.

Compassionate American doctors dressed and bandaged my feet, gave us a plentiful dinner, and, toward midnight, managed to find us space on to the floor of the baggage car of a crowded local train. Early the next morning we shifted to a sleeping compartment in the Hankow Express, with which our train had miraculously caught up, I never knew how. Thirty-six hours later, having survived on hard boiled duck eggs bought from women at the various stations, we reached the shimmering Yangtse.

It had been a rough week. But once the Navy doctor on an anchored U.S. destroyer certified that my heels were free of gangrene, I realized how worthwhile the adventure had been. Few foreigners had then witnessed what Jacques and I had seen. After dutifully reporting to Ambassador Johnson and Major McHugh, I left, as described above, for Chungking, Chentu, and Kunming.

Only in the train from Kunming to Hanoi and again in the airplane for Paris did I settle down to weigh, for Chicago readers, China's chances of successfully defending itself.

The negative side was impressive: in modern terms, China had no army. Soldiers from southern China went barefoot. Almost none had long coats. Steel helmets were few, umbrellas frequently substituted for bayonets. I saw one antiaircraft gun, something that looked like a trench mortar, a dozen machine guns, perhaps half a dozen batteries of field guns. Not a single Chinese airplane while Japanese flyers were everywhere. Iron kettles on bamboo poles served as kitchens and each soldier seemed to scrummage for food where he could find it. There was a lively trade in, and pilfering of, chickens and ducks. So much for the passive side.

On the other hand, these same ragged soldiers were indefatigable marchers who neither lost nor, like other fleeing armies, threw away what arms they possessed. Retreat meant nothing: apparently, one place was as good or as bad as another. Most privates smiled broadly at the spectacle of two foreign "masters" hoofing it out of reach of the Japanese. The rare officers joked with us in English. Not once did I see signs of anger or despondency. Some offered us portions of their scant food and water and often shared both with refugees. Morally they were unbeaten.

Over dinner T. V. Soong had smiled a little sadly when I asked him on what the Chinese based their hope. He replied:

"Our strategy is to hold on and wait for a break."

27

Over the Dam

Amid a roaring and bellowing and thundering
of ocean and tempest, the ship is quivering—
Oh God—and going down.

        EDGAR ALLAN POE
        Manuscript Found In A Bottle

IN PARIS, I heard the glad news: Lilian's book, *Journalist's Wife,* was a great success. Its author had been invited to go to America in the autumn for a two months' lecture tour. She was already making her preparations.

Her publisher, Thayer Hobson of William Morrow and Company, who had previously brought out my *Germany Puts the Clock Back,* wanted me to do a "quick" volume on China—"a mixture of description, personal experience, and politics." So, when he heard about it, did Allen Lane of Penguin Books.

By working every weekend in Crecy, I soon finished a manuscript.

Yet when I reached what I had thought was the end, I became worried. I had insisted that "a renascent nation of four hundred million could do almost anything, provided it had the guts to suffer, the patriotism to hold on, the leadership to trust." But did this apply to the rumpled disorderly China I had seen?

Would a victory by China promote the cause of democracy and individual freedom, both of which that country lacked?

These were questions which I owed it to myself, as well as to my readers, to answer. So as a postscript I added a "Dialogue With My Conscience Which May Be Omitted by the Uninterested," of which this was the essence:

"In thwarting Japanese aggression, the Chinese will have hamstrung one of the contemporary world's three Public Enemies. By fighting and immobilizing one of them it has seriously reduced the chance of successful aggression elsewhere by the other two. . . . Already the Chinese are conceivably saving the finest Occidental youth from premature death and the Continent of Europe from devastation. And even supposing that . . . China should . . . emerge some ten or twenty years hence as a new and more powerful aggressor, I would answer that the danger to democracy is *now*, not in a decade or two when the wave of resurgent barbarism will either have triumphed or passed. Since more democracy is absolutely essential if civilization is to progress . . . the Chinese are truly defending the future of civilized man.' "

The book appeared simultaneously in America as *The Dragon Awakes*, and in England as *Mowrer in China*.

By this time, Germany was well on the way to annexing Czechoslovakia. My chagrin was personal as well as political. At least a year earlier, Ambassador Bullitt had asked if I would like to be the U.S. Minister in Prague. The actual representative, J. Butler Wright, was leaving. He, Bullitt, would recommend me to President Roosevelt as Wright's successor. I was, the Ambassador thought, the kind of man the United States needed in Prague. Hitler was plotting mischief. While F.D.R. could not promise any direct American involvement in Europe, his choice of a Minister known internationally for his opposition to Nazi Germany would encourage the Czechoslovaks and emphasize Washington's condemnation of further aggression. If I said the word, Bullitt thought he could get me appointed. So how about it?

My immediate reaction was bewilderment. Long before, I had decided that if I left newspaper work, it could be only for literature. Yet how could I pass up a unique opportunity to confront Adolf? Seeing my predicament, Bullitt accorded me time to think over his offer, with the advice to decide quickly since the State Department might have another candidate in mind.

The problem was, whether after a couple of years in the diplomatic service I could get back into newspaper work. While cruising the Adriatic with the Knoxes, I had cautiously sounded out the Colonel. He found my question silly. How could an established foreign correspondent, a Pulitzer Prize winner, consider such an offer? Diplomats, as everybody knew, were striped-pants cookie-pushers, not to be taken seriously. As for Czechoslovakia, its protection was not, thank goodness, the responsibility of the United States. Rather than lose me, he would consider raising my salary. (He never did.) But if I left, his taking me back into the *News* Foreign Service would depend upon circumstances.

As a result, I had wrestled with the problem so long that when, finally, I said yes the job had gone to a State Department official, Wilbut J. Carr.

Less than a year later what Bullitt had expected occurred. Hitler issued a peremptory demand for the cession to Germany of the Sudeten Germans of Czechoslovakia. His unopposed annexation of Austria had convinced him that he could take them without a major war. Yet should France and Britain oppose his design with arms, he was ready.

The presence of three million German-speaking individuals near the German frontier was political dynamite that could, if skillfully used, become a step toward the realization of Haushofer's "geo-political" Germany.

Germans and Czechs had for centuries lived together yet in separate societies. Even after independence voluntary segregation continued.

We had noticed this with astonishment during skiing vacations on the Czech side of the Riesengebirge. In the particular German mountain hotel where we stayed, one saw no Slavs. At the Czechish *Baude* a few miles away, where we occasionally stopped for a drink, there were no Germans and the employees became civil only when satisfied that we were indeed Americans.

The Sudeten rim of Czechoslovakia was not only industrially rich but, since totally fortified, a powerful barrier to a possible German attack.

Shortly before I left for China, Hitler had stirred up a revolt which Benes, backed by France and Britain, quickly snuffed out by mobilizing four hundred thousand soldiers. Britain, for the first time since the armistice of 1918, sent its sovereigns on a formal visit to France. The *Fuehrer* backed down, at least in appearance, only hastening the construction of a Siegfried Line opposite France's Maginot Line.

Hardly had Their Majesties returned to London than Neville Chamberlain sent his friend Walter Runciman, not to Berlin to tell Hitler he must be quiet or else, but to Prague to "help" the Czechoslovaks decide to what extent they would "satisfy" the Germans!

Hitler confided to his generals with what glee he awaited the "hour of his destiny." The latters' reaction was, however, anything but gleeful. Although General von Blomberg had completed a military plan for crushing Prague's military resistance by a *blitz*, Germany still had only a handful of divisions on its western border.

What followed was a surrender which, as minutely described by William L. Shirer in his *Rise and Fall of the Third Reich*, stands out as perhaps the most ignominious in a period of democratic ignominy. Even while the German chargé d'affaires in Washington, Hans Dieckhoff, was warning Berlin that in case of overt war, the United States would support Britain, and while the British were officially assuring the French that Britain would not allow France to be defeated, in London, the Prime Minister and the Foreign Secretary were working to avoid trouble at Czechoslovakia's expense.

As the drama developed, ever more details leaked out. By August we knew that various Germans had told Churchill and Vansittart in London that if Hitler made war on Czechoslovakia, Germany's military leaders, headed by Generals Beck and von Brauschitz, planned to get rid of Nazism by force. On the other hand, the London *Times'* hints of a coming British "peace" sellout gave heart to the *Fuehrer*.

Hitler maneuvered skillfully. First he pushed the Sudeten Germans' claim to join Germany. Benes replied by offering to yield small portions of the territory, a first costly mistake. Next, Germany demanded territory containing part of the Czech fortifications. Under nocturnal pressure from the French and British representatives in Prague, Benes again consented.

Only when the German once more raised the ante, did Benes say no and mobilize the rest of his armed forces. Fighting behind what may have been the strongest fortifications in Europe, his forty divisions might well have strained the valor of the Germans. Hitler, meanwhile, was insisting on his intention of obtaining what he wanted by arms. To this not even Chamberlain could consent. For about a week, our hopes of a showdown rose.

In vain. Chamberlain, aided by Mussolini, persuaded Hitler to accept peaceful transfer of the territories. This removed the last obstacle to convoking what became known as the Munich Conference.

Czechoslovakia was represented by observers only. The Soviet Union was not invited. Yet for hours Chamberlain's hatchet man, Sir Horace Wilson, worked on the Czechs, insisting that if their country fought, it would fight alone. When informed of this, Benes surrendered to Hitler's demand. Thanks to this, Chamberlain and Daladier masked their spinelessness as "deference" to the will of an ally. Hitler seized the fortified mountain rim, thereby making any future defense of the country impossible. No German general would dream of overthrowing a leader who had peacefully "redeemed" the Sudetenland.

Most people in both Britain and France welcomed Munich as what Chamberlain said it was, namely, "peace with honor," "peace in our time." The London *Times* burbled that "no conqueror returning from a victory on the battlefield has come adorned with nobler laurels." Presumably its editor, Geoffrey Dawson, knew, as we did not, that Britain's Minister had also signed a secret "nonaggression" pact with Hitler.

In Britain, two powerful Conservative voices rose against Chamberlain's catastrophic mistake. Alfred Duff Cooper, the First Lord of the Admiralty, resigned from the Cabinet and warned a hostile but spellbound House of Commons of the danger. Winston S. Churchill, M.P., told the House that Britain had sustained "a total, unmitigated defeat"—and was shouted down.

Liberal and Labor opposition to Chamberlain did not count since neither party offered an alternative policy. From America, President Roosevelt wired Chamberlain: "Good man."

Meanwhile Polish colonels and Hungarian nationalists, scenting a kill, were moving in to seize parts of the Czechoslovak corpse.

At the League Assembly, among major delegations only the Russians professed readiness to help the Czechoslovaks. In an interview with the *Daily News*, Maxim Litvinov insisted that Britain had "sold the Czechs down the river from the moment Runciman appeared." As matters stood, only complete resistance to Franco-British pressure by Benes could, he felt, save the situation. Hearing of this interview, Britain's chief delegate (in the absence of the Foreign Minister), Herbrand Edward Dundonald Brassy Sackville, Earl de la Warr, asked me to introduce him to Litvinov so that he might report the Russian's views to London. Nothing came of their meeting.

But though my coverage of the crisis was secondary, my emotional involvement was total. I had long known a number of leading Czechs, including two of the three chief "founders," Masaryk and Stefanik. During a ski vacation at Mégève, I had become friendly with the Minister in Paris, Stefan Osusky, like Stefanik, a Slovak. Moreover, I was corresponding with the editor of a leading Czech newspaper, Hubert Ripka.

What a fool I had been! Why had I not accepted Bullitt's offer to try to make me American Minister in Prague. In view of Roosevelt's failure to condemn Germany's grab I could not have changed the outcome. But the thought that a prompt answer to Bullitt might have offered me an opportunity to try to avert the Czech tragedy embittered me for weeks.

The Munich Agreement delighted friends of Germany, foes of Russia, and doctrinaire pacifists. It also brought antifascists even closer together. Knickerbocker's apartment on the Ile Saint Louis and ours in the Rue de l'Université became centers of anti-nazism.

Not all Americans in Europe felt as Knick and I did. Shortly after Munich, on the doorstep of the American Embassy in Paris I met one who did not. When I expressed my disgust at the sellout, he contradicted me so sharply that we almost came to blows. At the last minute, reason prevailed. Embassy Counselor Robert Murphy went on his way and I on mine.

Another eminent American champion of appeasement was Ambassador Joseph Kennedy. From Bullitt I had heard of the unusual interests and attitudes of our London Ambassador, and could not understand President Roosevelt's choice of him for a critical position at such a time.

During the Christmas holidays in 1938, while skiing in the Engadine, we were joined on a descent from the famous Diavolezza, a breathtaking run, by a young man who introduced himself as Joe Kennedy, Jr. Though a tyro on skis "Old Joe's" eldest son repeatedly tried to slip into the lead. After he crashed for the third time we slowed down lest he injure himself seriously.

In the late spring of 1939, Ambassador Kennedy told me that the United States had no vital interest in the outcome of a war, even if there were one, which he doubted. Several years later, he expressed a similar indifference to the spread of Soviet power.

Shortly after Munich, Bob Boothby invited me to explain to a large group of Conservatives in a room of the House of Commons why Munich meant not peace but war—and sooner rather than later.

At the end, one M.P. objected hotly.

"I find the Munich settlement quite right. Ever since Versailles, we have treated Germany badly. I think we owed something to the Germans and I am glad we have paid it."

"Any answer, Edgar?" Boothby, as presiding officer, asked.

"Only this—if I felt as our friend does, I would have considered it more ethical to give Germany something that belonged to me rather than the territory of another."

"And what would you give them?" the M.P. challenged.

"Give them the county of Kent," I answered.

Boothby took advantage of the ensuing uproar to end the meeting. A few days later Winston Churchill invited me to have Sunday lunch with him at Chartwell Manor outside London.

There were no other guests. Mrs. "Clemmy" Churchill explained the delay in serving: Winston was laying bricks in the garden, his favorite way of forgetting a worry. His constituents at Epping were, she explained, angry at his failure to support the Munich settlement.

After a while Churchill came in, mortar on his overalls, hands, eyebrows, and thinning hair, greeted me, sat down, and poured us large glasses of port (he was temporarily off brandy). This was my first conversation with the greatest public figure of our time. In the early thirties, in his dislike of the "foul baboonery of Bolshevism," he had briefly defended Hitler. He still favored Franco. But among politicians he possessed an almost unique quality, the ability to stick to what he believed at the cost of losing his following.

At table he talked for an hour about the European situation, eloquently, brilliantly, objectively, first of "poor France, corrupt, divided, floundering, without compass (though bound one day to recover)," then of Britain, "prostrate with sleeping sickness," which had "almost given Europe to Hitler." When he fell silent, I put the crucial question: "Do I understand that you would welcome an alliance with the Soviets?"

His voice became hard: "To save England I'd pact with the devil."

This was what I had come to Chartwell to hear—and never forgot.

Less than three years later he did so pact. But unlike F.D.R., he never expected he could persuade the devil to join the heavenly host.

Events developed as Churchill expected. Although both Chamberlain and Georges Bonnet publicly promised that they would sacrifice no more allied territories in their quest for peace, few believed them.

The Spanish Republic collapsed. Whereupon certain French Senators, perhaps mistaking the Rockies for the Pyrenees, blamed the United States for refusing to sell arms to the Spanish Republicans! Bullitt, I knew, felt that the United States dare not let Britain or France go down. In the middle of March, 1939, Germany seized the rest of Czechoslovakia, including the magnificent Skoda arms works, and a few days later, occupied Memel.

Being in London at the time, I smiled bitterly at the consternation of those Englishmen who had believed that they had really purchased peace in their time at the modest price of Czechoslovakia's independence. Chamberlain was in a tizzy. In his first speech to Parliament, he announced that he would not let the rape of Czechoslovakia deflect him from his peace policy. Yet two days later in Birmingham he reproached the *Fuehrer* with a complete breach of faith, and promised to offer a security guarantee to both Poland and Rumania!

The only existing instrument of collective security was the League of Nations. Once the stronger members failed to apply the enforcement provisions of the Charter, some of the weaker sought protection by withdrawing from the organization. Others argued that since the world would not fit itself to the League, the latter should fit itself to the world by watering down Article 16.

Those who feared communism more than they did fascism suggested that by forcing out the U.S.S.R., the League might induce Japan, Germany, and Italy to return to the fold.

Secretary General Joseph Avenol, a former French inspector of finances of impeccable conservatism whose real interest was in paintings, could, by abolishing the Disarmament Section and merging other Sections, pension off the thirty or forty officials most devoted to democracy and the original League idea, thus making the Secretariat less objectionable to the dictators.

Among those he considered throwing to the Nazi-Fascist wolves were Marcel Hoden, his own Chief of Cabinet, a favorite of the newsmen, whose "attitude" had made him *persona non grata* to the pro-Fascist members; Henri Vigier of the Political Section, a sharp thinker and a fine draftsman of documents; and Ludwik Rajchman, hated by the totalitarians for his vehement championship of China, Ethiopia, and Republican Spain.

Hoden and Vigier proved flexible enough to keep their jobs. Rajchman preferred to resign and with his pension bought a fruit farm at Chenu not far from Tours. With him went some of the League's remaining integrity. The original outstanding League Secretariat was badly depleted. Salvador de Madariaga had resigned to start a brilliant diplomatic and literary career. Two American officials, Arthur Sweetser, an original member of the League Secretariat, who had become head of the Information Section, and Ben Gerig, found themselves politically orphaned.

Late in May, 1939, I covered my last League Council meeting. Germany and Italy were celebrating their political marriage, the so-called Steel Pact. To the *News* I wired that the new Palace of Nations had "become a mausoleum haunted by the ghosts of braver men."

Britain and France were making little progress toward forging a convincing deterrent. Although Britain signed a military alliance with Turkey, we felt sure that both Chamberlain and Bonnet would rather satisfy "Germany's just claims against Poland," meaning Danzig and the Corridor, than oppose them by war. In France men like Henri de Kérillis, André Tardieu, and even my former friend, Georges Duhamel, were asking: "Why die for Danzig?"

Poles and Rumanians were willing enough to be protected. So were the little Baltic peoples. But none of them wanted an alliance that permitted Soviet troops to enter their territories as defenders. As Churchill put it later, they "did not know whether it was German aggression or Russian rescuers that they dreaded more." Ambassador Lukasiewicz even intimated to me in Paris that Poland, rather than accept an alliance with Russia, would take on Germany single-handed.

The loss of Czechoslovakia had, in a sense, left the Soviet Union the arbiter of Europe's future.

Although Hitler talked bigger than ever, early in March, 1939, I learned that, immediately after Munich, Germany had made a first faint friendly overture to Moscow. Stalin publicly warned the democracies that the Soviet Union would be no country's catspaw. On April 16, Litvinov solemnly offered a full-fledged pact of mutual assistance to Britain and France, and if possible to Poland, on a take-it-or-leave-it basis. Yet the following day the Soviet Ambassador in Berlin told the Germans he saw no reason why Russia should not live on a normal footing with Germany.

The French wanted to accept Russia's offer immediately. Chamberlain was in no hurry. He did not move quickly even when, on May 2, Stalin ostentatiously replaced Maxim Litvinov as Foreign Minister by the surly Molotov.

Knick and I were puzzled. Stalin's feeling toward Germany was obviously a love-hate complex. This had ideological roots in the belief that fascism was a step toward communism. An alliance with Hitler could secure Russia during the period in which National Socialism "evolved" toward a Soviet pattern. Moreover Stalin admired the "fearless" Germans as much as he despised the "spineless" Western democrats.

Ever since 1922, the Soviet Union and Germany had collaborated happily in increasing the military potential of both countries.

Yet in early 1936, Marshal Tukhachevsky, on his way back to Moscow from the funeral of King George V in London, had urged France's General Gamelin to lose no more time in repressing German expansion by all means, including force. During the First World War, Tukhachevsky had been captured and imprisoned by the Germans at Ingolstadt, where he might have made the acquaintance of a French captain called Charles de Gaulle.

Talk of a military conspiracy to assassinate Stalin was current in Prague in early 1937. Tukhachevsky was brought to trial on June 11 of that year, charged with *serving the Germans*, and executed along with thousands of the better Soviet officers. Stalin considered their existence an obstacle to his plan of possibly changing camps. From that time on, he was for sale to the highest bidder.

As late as May 25, 1939, despite Bullitt's warning, I tried to believe that an Anglo-French-Russian agreement was imminent.

We outsiders never suspected to what extent Britain and France were lagging behind Germany in rearmament. Since 1933, Hitler had put the achievement of military superiority regardless of the cost at the top of his list. During the year 1938–39, Germany spent five times as much on weapons as Britain. Conservatives in Paris continually sniped at Air Minister Pierre Cot for failing to build enough modern fighters and bombers.

Yet Cot told me that France's airplane program was in good shape. France's military leaders did not believe that airpower could contribute very much to a French victory. . . . The truth was that bitter memories of the million and a half young Frenchmen killed in the previous war had created a defensive mentality that nothing could shake. No more bloody offensives. Let the Germans grind their youth to death against the impregnable Maginot Line.

All through June international relations were unnaturally calm.

At the request of an acquaintance in the Quai d'Orsay, Etienne de Crouy, I had taken into my office as an unpaid volunteer a young former Egyptian diplomat, Paul Ghali, who, in exchange for learning the trade, provided me with whatever information he could acquire. As the son of a Coptic Egyptian judge and a French marquise, Ghali had excellent news contacts. He was seeing de Crouy every day—to the profit of the Chicago *Daily News*. To protect the latter, I described his revelations as the "guesses of a retired diplomat." Among these was the fact that what Ghali called the "French military outlook" included war in August!

How could I take my scheduled home leave on the presumed eve of the war I had expected ever since Hitler came to power? We agreed that Lilian and Diana Jane would go to Wyoming as planned, and I should follow them if, and when, the situation permitted.

Instead it worsened from day to day, bringing to Paris two interesting visitors. One was John Gunther, who since resigning from the Chicago *Daily News* service, had written two admirable books, *Inside Europe* and *Inside Asia*, which popularized world affairs in terms of personalities. Late one summer afternoon, we sat on the sidewalk at Fouquet's on the Champs Elysées. What, John asked, did I think would happen?

"The Soviet Union is about to sign a pact with Hitler and most people think there will be war before September."

"Dreadful," John gasped.

"The pact will be dreadful. But war is necessary unless Hitler and Stalin are to be the masters of Europe and Hirohito the master of Asia."

"But think of the millions of dead."

"I do—and God knows how sadly. I also think of the millions doomed to be tortured or killed, of whole new countries subjected to one or the other forms of modern tyranny, if there is no war."

"But is there no alternative?"

"I see no alternative to war but submission to fascism."

John left me shaking his head sadly.

The second visitor, the representative of a big movie producer, had heard in America that Mowrer had expected war.

"Come to Hollywood and write scripts about it," he said, naming what seemed to me a princely figure.

I almost yielded. But how could a correspondent abandon his ringside seat just when the bell was about to ring? When I declined, he suggested that I try my hand at a single script on the Munich crisis, which I agreed to do.

The drama moved ever faster. In July the French arrested certain Nazi spies, expelled the German "journalist," Otto Abetz, and arrested a couple of Frenchmen as traitors. Because the trail led "too far" into French political life, this charge was soon dropped. Abetz was a friend of Laval's henchman, Fernand de Brinon, the same one who had skillfully prevented *Germany Puts the Clock Back* from appearing in French. In the middle of August, Eugenio Pacelli, now Pius XII, publicly urged the Poles to save the peace by yielding Danzig. Warsaw refused.

Shocking as it was to so many Western liberals, the fateful Nazi-Soviet Pact merely confirmed the suspicion of those throughout the world who considered Stalin capable of any felony. Yet in Berlin, U.S. Congressman Hamilton Fish, stated that Germany's claims were fully justified. In Paris, Theodore Dreiser defended the Russians.

In the French capital five thousand U.S. tourists stormed the American Embassy in the search for facilities to get home. On August 29, I watched long lines of French women and children at the railroad stations, seeking to leave the city. Mrs. Dora Delano Forbes, President Roosevelt's aunt, refused to abandon Paris. At her age, she explained, she knew no better way to die than in Paris in a war. France already had five million men under arms.

Early on September 1, before his phone was cut off, Richard Mowrer managed to tell me from Poland: "The lunatic of Berchtesgaden has struck." British planes started dropping propaganda pamphlets to the German people. Yet only after four days did French divisions cross the border into Germany.

"The coming of war in 1939, not for the first time in Stimson's life, was a relief." So wrote Stimson and Bundy after it was over.

Certainly it was preferable to further surrender.

PART SIX

Three-Cornered Combat

And were I alive today, mankind would tremble.
> Inscription on Tamerlane's
> tomb at Gar Emir

28

The Phony War

The god of war hates those who hesitate.
— EURIPIDES

WHILE GERMAN TANKS, preceded by dive bombers, crashed through courageous, ill-armed, and ill-disposed Polish armies and destroyed Polish cities Hitler had promised to respect, we in Paris waited from hour to hour for France to attack Germany. How many times had I heard German officers attribute their defeat in the First World War to the Kaiser's "insanity" in fighting simultaneously on two fronts! Now Hitler was similarly engaged. The French, with more divisions mobilized than the Germans could put behind the Siegfried Line, might even win a quick victory. At the least, while most of Hitler's airplanes were busy in the east, French and British bombers could destroy Germany's war industry. This the hard-pressed Poles were begging the French to do.

Instead, after quickly occupying most of the ground between the two fortified lines, the French stopped. Six weeks later they retreated to the Maginot Line. Between the two armies, farmers continued to plow their fields. Paris also insisted there must be no shooting across the Rhine! Premier Daladier almost plaintively begged the British air force not to attack German targets lest the Germans in reprisal destroy "indispensable French war industries."

How could this happen? People then and afterward attributed this Franco-British passivity to the "Maginot Line complex." Or to lack of adequate military means. Or to Commander-in-Chief Gamelin, whom some of his military associates called a "noodle."

But the truth went deeper. The Allies were trying, not to win the war, but to persuade Hitler to call it off. Some French nationalists had become conscientious objectors! Democratic patriots like Premier

Daladier were unable to face the prospect of a second wholesale slaughter.

Britain's reluctance had been rationalized by Captain Liddell Hart. The Captain had had moments of brilliance. Before Charles de Gaulle, he had urged that a new war be fought not by masses but by skill and initiative—including massed tanks. But by 1939 he had concluded that (at least for Britain!) "our chief risk of losing a war lies in trying to win the war." A serious land effort on the continent would "diminish" Britain's sea and air defense. And anyhow, the "chief hope for our civilization lies in nobody winning the next war."

These jewels we had read in a book, *The Defense of Britain*, published three months before Hitler attacked Poland. What more could the *Fuehrer* and his generals want? That a Chamberlain should accept such tragic nonsense was only natural. But by the time two British army corps finally reached France, even Churchill, perhaps influenced by the Hart theories, felt that it was too late to attack Germany. As a result London and Paris sought to "contain" the Axis, relying on the Maginot Line and a naval blockade. Yet while Chamberlain and Daladier stubbornly refused to wage war, they also declined Hitler's repeated peace offers. How be surprised that newsmen from America who visited the *Daily News* office regularly asked, "What's going on here?"

Assuming that the aim was victory, thousands and thousands of French, chiefly women and little children, left Paris. Those who remained carried gas masks against attacks that never came, and scurried to shelters at the first warning siren. The authorities imposed a blackout on buildings and motorcars and reduced city lights to a minimum. Otherwise, nothing happened. It was eerie.

Meanwhile, though the Poles were holding out in Warsaw and attacking German tanks with cavalry, elsewhere defeated Polish soldiers and civilians were streaming southeastward toward Rumania, as Richard Mowrer vividly reported.

On September 18, a Polish diplomat telephoned. "Edgar, the dirty Russians have invaded Poland and are killing, disarming, and imprisoning our troops. They call this 'helping us.' It's all over."

So it was. And not content with having done literally nothing to aid a faithful ally, Paris and London did not even charge the Kremlin with violating its own declaration of neutrality. Polish political refugees set up a government in exile as the Czechoslovaks had done. Military refugees served with the French or the British.

So far as newsmen were concerned, the major event of September was the establishment of a Ministry of Information in the Hotel Continental on the Rue de Rivoli, under the direction of the sophisticated writer, Jean Giraudoux. Cynics sarcastically attributed the Premier's choice to Giraudoux's authorship of the play, *The Trojan War Will Not Take Place*—"obviously hoping to duplicate the experience now."

The Ministry of Information obstinately refused to let newsmen visit the front. Finally, on September 21, four American correspondents, weary of waiting for military *laissez-passer* that never came, set out by car well before dawn "to find the war." Since I spoke French and knew the country, I drove.

The main roads were virtually empty. When police challenged us, we showed our United States passports and grinned. Turned back twice, we shifted to less frequented highways and returned to the main road beyond the check points. After some four hours I pulled up just short of the Saar River—the frontier. The four of us walked across the bridge into Germany, unchallenged. At least we had the dateline we came for. But no story. It was uncanny. Were there no French troops between us and the German lines? We decided to present ourselves to the nearest French military post and ask for further directions.

A bewildered French captain finally accepted us for what we were, gave us a bite to eat—and sent us back to army headquarters under guard. At dinner that night, the commanding general produced an answer to the question that was baffling the world: how could one win a war by doing nothing? He explained: Britain and France were counting on the blockade and naval warfare while they built up superior forces. Hitler must either attack the impregnable Maginot Line, try to break out elsewhere, or come to terms. In the evening we drove back to Paris through a countryside that had suddenly come alive. The lightless roads were jammed with soldiers, supply trucks, and tanks. Some of the last moved as nimbly as terriers; others, big as small houses, clanked along with the gait of mechanical elephants, fearsome in the darkness. Once I heard the faint deep baying of distant guns. So far as I know, ours were the first reports from the "fighting front."

Only later did some of us visit the Maginot Line in the Warndt Forest, this time in uniform upon invitation from Minister Giraudoux. Never in the history of man were there such fortifications, invisible, almost entirely submerged, incredibly protected and equipped with weapons of the latest types. They so impressed me that, back in Paris, I wired that Hitler would have to attack France through the Low Countries where there was no Maginot Line. . . .

After a third visit to the front by me, and one by Ghali, the *News* was represented with the French Army by Robert Casey, a crack feature reporter, famous around Chicago for his verbal embroidery. In the First World War Casey had served in the American artillery and afterward described his experience in a book, *Cannoneers Have Hairy Ears.* He was a splendid addition to what we modestly considered the best foreign service in the world. William Stoneman was doing a superb job in covering British forces in France.

For Casey I had bought a motor car, indispensable under existing conditions. I had also, without asking Colonel Knox's permission, promoted Ghali from volunteer apprentice to paid assistant, with the right to sign cables in my absence.

With Knick, I even shared a world "beat." The British intelligence service secretly provided us with full details on the amount of private loot, millions and millions of dollars, which Goering, Goebbels, Ribbentrop, Himmler, Hess, and Ley, the labor boss, had stashed away in stocks, bonds, and insurance policies in neutral countries. We revealed everything, down to the amounts and places of "investment."

Goebbels personally broadcast denials. He would, he said, gladly give a division of troops to lay hands upon those lying American so-and-so's, Knickerbocker and Mowrer.

Never had I received a greater compliment.

In spite of continual rumors of German preparations on the Dutch and Belgian frontiers, the autumn months slipped away without the expected German offensive. Perhaps the loss of an authentic copy of the German war plan compelled the German Staff to formulate another, which took time. It need not have. Dutch and Belgian politicos felt the plan was a "plant," and took no notice of it. Why should Hitler attack neutral countries? Paul-Henri Spaak opposed a Dutch-Belgian military alliance lest it be judged provocative. Instead, King Leopold and Queen Wilhelmina offered their combined good offices to end the war.

At the end of November, 1939, the Soviet Union attacked neutral Finland in order to strengthen its Baltic defenses. Conservatives with no visible urge to fight Hitler or Mussolini thrilled at the chance of fighting Stalin and called upon their governments to rush British and French expeditionary forces to help the heroic Finns. But since any serious aid had to cross Sweden and the prudent Swedes said no, the Finns defended their country alone, and for many weeks repulsed Great Stalin's armies. Finally, on December 4, a League of Nations that had lacked the courage to take sanctions against Japan, Germany, or Italy solemnly expelled the U.S.S.R. President Roosevelt refused to consider Russia a belligerent under the Neutrality Act or to support the League. On the other hand, Congress amended the Neutrality Acts in a way to permit our sending war material to Britain and France on a cash-and-carry basis.

The French people were becoming restive. Where were all those promised British divisions? Nobody told them that at General Gamelin's request, the British were training their own troops in England. By the middle of December, Germany had no less than a hundred divisions on its Western frontier—almost as many as France, Belgium, and Holland combined.

A bright spot in a dark winter was a letter from Knox permitting me to return to Chicago and spend Christmas with the family. To save time I booked a passage on one of Pan American's recently inaugurated transatlantic air flights.

Misplaced optimism. The weather was unfavorable. After waiting four tedious days in Lisbon, the hydroplane got as far as Horta in the Azores—and stopped. Soon it was joined by another of the four planes that comprised the service. Thirty-five thoroughly disgruntled passengers spent disconsolate Christmas holidays. I took walks and stared longingly across several miles of rolling water at seven-thousand-foot

Mount Pico. The rest of the time I talked politics with Avra Warren of the State Department, economics with Graham Towers, the Canadian banker, and wines with *Vizconde* Domecq of the great sherry firm, Pedro Domecq.

An oil expert from Bahrein, Max Thornburg, later to write a superb book, *People and Policy in the Middle East,* produced on the local newspaper press several issues of a gossip sheet, *The Horta Swell,* and illustrated it with his own woodcuts.

Finally, the local officials, weary of complaints and abuse from passengers who had missed Christmas holidays in America, hired the Italian steamship *Rex* to stop at Horta and take most of them to New York. Three, however, were allowed to encumber a single "service flight" to Baltimore. By exerting newspaper pressure on the company, Colonel Knox got me included.

It was a rough trip. For almost twice the scheduled flying time, the hydroplane, bumping along a few hundred feet above monstrous waves, bucked a westerly gale. Knowing that the pilot had only so much gas, I prepared myself for an Atlantic landing, presumably my last. We finally made Bermuda with enough fuel for another half hour's flying. So much for transatlantic air travel in those pioneering days.

Thirty-six hours later I reached Chicago, much to the relief of my anxious family.

Everyone, including Father, who had, at the age of eighty-one, just broken ninety on the golf course, asked the same question: where is the war? I tried to answer in a speech before the Chicago Council on Foreign Relations. When I explained that the Allies were planning either to starve the Germans out, or to force them to commit suicide against the Maginot Line, listeners snorted their unbelief. What, in the name of Bonaparte and Lord Nelson, was the matter with the French and British? I explained that both peoples had been so unprepared for war that I had given my cherished Colt revolver to my friend, Etienne de Crouy of the Quai d'Orsay, when he was called to arms. His government had none left for reserve officers.

Yet even while they criticized the Allies, most Americans seemed determined under no circumstances to give them active military support, and approved President Roosevelt's peace initiatives, which if successful would have left Germany and Russia in permanent possession of Poland.

The men around Roosevelt, as I learned during a week in Washington, were sharply divided. Bullitt, who happened to be in town, and my old Berlin protector, George Messersmith, now Assistant Secretary of State, believed that the United States should under no circumstances permit a victory by Hitler, Mussolini, and Stalin.

On the other hand, Under Secretary of State Sumner Welles (Bullitt's *bête noire*), Assistant Secretary Adolf Berle, Ambassador Hugh Wilson, and, naturally, Ambassador Joe Kennedy from London, while wasting no affection on the aggressors, considered their victory preferable to American participation in a second European war. Welles had, in Bullitt's absence, persuaded the President to let him undertake a peace mission to the principal European capitals. Nobody seemed interested in what Secretary of State Cordell Hull advocated.

F.D.R., as I gathered from a conversation with him, stood squarely in the middle. He certainly wanted the defeat of the Axis. He had also decided to keep America out of the struggle. This first interview with our President was disillusioning. That he had no interest in anything I might tell him about France I could understand—he had Bullitt for that. But behind his insistence on telling me all about the Azores (whence I had just come) there loomed an overgrown vanity that enabled sycophants like Harry Hopkins to lead and mislead him by the flattery upon which he fed. I had met Harry in Paris. At the dinner table Bullitt had asked me to answer Hopkins' questions about France. Instead, this newly "arrived" social worker (soon to become Secretary of Commerce) solemnly told two old "French hands" what was going on in France!

Our policy toward Japan was no less incoherent than that toward the Axis. In a long confidential report to Paul in Chicago, I suggested that the *Daily News* advocate preventing the victory of Germany in Europe, of Russia nearly everywhere, and of Japan in China, by *limited* assistance. Such a policy would, I felt sure, receive the support of three-quarters of all Americans.

Seven weeks of absence from Paris had sharpened my perceptions of wartime conditions in France. If, indeed, the country *was* at war. Sometimes, I felt about the phony war much as an old acquaintance, the historian Oscar Browning, had felt about the Bolshevik revolution of 1917. "I have," he insisted, "been writing about revolutions all my life and they simply do not happen like that."

Yet phony or not, the struggle had separated five million men from their families. It crippled business, closing many small shops and the upper floors of department stores, reducing transportation and shipping facilities, making some luxuries and a few necessities scarce. About a fourth of all motor vehicles had been commandeered. Gasoline was rationed. So was use of the telephone and telegraph. It took me six months to get my phone at Crécy reconnected. Auto lights were still dimmed, but, unlike London, Paris was incompletely blacked out. Shelter signs were everywhere, and there were occasional alarms. But almost no enemy bombing. Most of the women and children who had left Paris in early September were back. Formal entertaining and dress were out. Yet there were, if possible, even more cozy little dinners and lunches where the chief topic was the war and when would it be over?

I described a typical meal:

"Yesterday was Friday and a day of food restrictions so I really did not expect very much.

"At the restaurant there was, in French parlance, almost nothing to eat: a choice among seven kinds of oysters; sea urchins; French clams called *praires*; six or seven sorts of fish including bouillebaisse;

no 'butcher's meat,' meaning, of course, no veal, beef or mutton, but only rabbit, chicken and curry.

"There were not even sausages or other delicatessen products; we had to be satisfied with vegetable hors d'oeuvres, caviar, anchovies and sardines; no cakes, French pastries; no chocolate dishes or candy; just a choice among fruit salad, pineapple with kirsch and a soufflé à la liqueur. Thanks to a couple of fairly decent wines, we managed to get this sort of thing down. We might, I thought, be excused for remembering between gulps that by our abstemiousness we were helping to win the war."

Nonetheless civilian morale was worsening. At dinner one night, when I had suggested that we should use the war to prepare a better world, François Michel exploded: "*Sans blague!* We French are fighting simply to save our skins."

In mid-March, the vastly outnumbered Finns collapsed and the "heroic" Soviet Union occupied the coveted frontier lands. Sumner Welles' untimely and self-promoting peace mission to Europe was the failure Bullitt had expected.

I spent two pleasant weekends skiing in the French Alps, one of them on the Italian frontier with the Alpine *Chasseurs*. Neither their skiing nor their morale was impressive.

In America, Lilian was becoming restless. She had been too long near the center of world events to feel comfortable in neutral Chicago. Diana Jane, on the other hand, had found herself for the first time among children in a child-centered society—and took to it like an astronaut to outer space. When the Greens offered to take our daughter into their house, Lilian accepted and returned to Paris. Whatever lay ahead we would face together.

With her, she brought my movie manuscript which Warner Brothers, after a long delay, had rejected. Entitled "If Fight We Must," it described the conversion of a young American Quaker journalist from pacifism to the use of force against aggression through a series of adventurous experiences, the Munich crisis, his arrest and detention in a Nazi concentration camp, his final escape. I had tried to make the point that in deference to our deepest convictions, the United States should fight where necessary to defend freedom—and at the same time try to make this the last war by subsequently participating in a world authority. The letter of rejection explained that while the material was very interesting, Warner Brothers did not "want to do anything with this subject at this time." I did not bother to submit the script to another company.

Nonetheless, the shock of a second world war was having some effect in the United States. In Chicago, Mrs. Anita Blaine, the sister of Colonel Robert McCormick (called by the *Daily News* "Colonel McCosmick"), had organized a federalist movement called *World Citizens* and commissioned me to send her a series of reports on the developing war and peace aims in Europe.

Upon my return to Paris, I got in touch with interested persons and organizations and read everything I could find on the subject. Virtually all planners agreed that the Allies' aim must be "an intelligently organized world," with something more effective than the League of Nations to keep the peace. There unity ended.

Premier Daladier was ready to discuss "federal links" with Great Britain and "the various states of Europe." Others favored a federation of democracies as advocated by Clarence Streit. The largest group sought an "organized Europe" including a Germany whose "fangs had been permanently drawn."

After a vast amount of investigation I concluded that rather than press schemes upon Europeans, Americans had better concentrate on persuading their own Administration and countrymen that only world unity and cooperation could prevent a future disaster on a more gigantic scale, and so reported to Anita.

At the same time, I was doing all I could to help Colonel Paul Rockwell persuade the French to let him organize a second Lafayette Escadrille, composed like the first, of American volunteers.

Finally, the amiable but hesitant Daladier yielded the premiership to Paul Reynaud, an outspoken opponent of Munich, who had in September advocated a French offensive to help Poland. Reynaud had read a book published a few years previously by that prison comrade of Tukhachevsky, Captain Charles de Gaulle. This was entitled *Toward a Professional Army* and in it the author had demonstrated the futility of defensive warfare against offensive drives by massed tanks. Solemnly, the new Premier warned of coming total war.

Lilian's return from America had coincided with Germany's blitz of Denmark and Norway. The Danes did not try to resist, the Norwegians held out only long enough for the royal family to escape to Britain, for the French to send some Alpine *Chasseurs,* and for the British Navy to sink several German warships in two battles off Narvik.

While allied forces were still occupied in Norway, the Germans launched in the Belgian Ardennes, to the consternation of the French General Staff, the great offensive they had postponed from the previous autumn. In five days they occupied the Netherlands, exactly as the Dutch officers five years before had told me they might. The Dutch Queen and government followed the Norwegians to London. Marc Van Blankenstein, whose outspoken anti-Hitler stance had cost him his position with the *Nieuwe Rotterdamse Courant,* managed to leave Holland one jump ahead of the Germans only thanks to a friendly British intelligence agent.

The Belgians, though reinforced along the German border by French and British divisions, surrendered on the eighteenth day.

Worse, the main German thrust through the "impenetrable" Ardennes split General Corap's bewildered French Army, reached the Channel on the eleventh day, and cut the Belgian, French, and British forces in the north off from the rest of the army. On May 24, the British headed for England. Only the superb courage of forty thousand French defenders of Dunkirk enabled most of the British to escape. The French lacked the men, the tanks, and the planes to resist the superbly executed German offensive. Far too many soldiers were stationed in the useless Maginot Line. French tanks were scattered instead of being concentrated, and France had failed to make or buy enough planes. Winston Churchill, now Britain's Prime Minister, refused to send more of his growing air force to France. Yet Germany's strategic blitz was the brainchild of a French officer and twice before, in Spain and Poland, with all the world looking on, the Germans had tried it out.

Another French officer, Colonel Menu, at the Ecole de Guerre had in 1932 predicted the coming of the atom bomb. The French Staff had in the meantime slept.

By mid-May near panic reigned in Paris. On one Sunday morning thousands of Parisians knelt and prayed before Notre Dame Cathedral. The government again urged parents to send away small children.

Even more revealing was the sudden laxity of the censors. While they still clamped down on factual news, they let me wire that this was the "battle of the century" (what an exaggeration!) and that the Germans might win it. So when I learned that Hitler's tanks were at St. Quentin, ninety miles from Paris, I cabled Chicago that the French government's intention was "very similar to what it had been in September, 1914." Paul caught on, and the *News* was the first to announce that the French government might retreat to Bordeaux.

Reynaud named General Weygand commander-in-chief in place of the indecisive Gamelin and appointed Marshal Pétain, the savior of Verdun, Vice Premier. Weygand, an ultraconservative, had been chief of staff under the great Marshal Foch. Surely, Ghali and I thought, two such patriots would insist on fighting to the death.

Hundreds of thousands of Belgian and French refugees, already cluttering the northern roads, indicated clearly what the exits from Paris would be like as the Germans approached the capital. Since I had no intention of becoming Goebbels' prisoner, Lilian and I needed a sure route for a last-minute escape.

After studying various roads from Paris to Chenu, I chose one and carefully reconnoitered the first ten miles so as to be sure of finding the way in total darkness. In case of separation, I gave Lilian a second carefully marked *Sorties de Paris* map.

The Germans, perhaps mindful of their defeat in 1914, advanced cautiously. While one powerful force turned eastward to close in on the Maginot Line from behind, another, as in 1914, swept westward, crossed the Seine near Rouen, and advanced on Paris.

At the French headquarters near Soissons, I learned that the army had orders to hold just long enough to permit the government to abandon Paris without panic haste for Tours.

During my absence Lilian had taken Ghali's advice and left for the Rajchmans' house in Touraine. At least she was safe. Gone too were Alexis Léger and other officials of the French Foreign Office. The courtyards of the Quai d'Orsay were heaped with those archives which had not already been destroyed. Reynaud had previously advised friendly embassies to do the same. Yet Ghali informed me that the Premier had publicly announced that Paris would be defended.

Seeing a chance for easy loot, Mussolini's Italy had that day declared war on France.

At the office I hastily packed a suitcase with private correspondence and my clipping books and took it to the apartment.

At two o'clock that night Colonel Horace Fuller phoned me. "Edgar, the Germans are at Saint Germain. Please get out of Paris at once."

Fifteen miles from Paris! "Thanks for the tip. I'll leave tomorrow morning."

"They may be in Paris tomorrow morning. Let me tell the Ambassador you are leaving tonight."

"All right, I'll leave now. See you in Tours."

According to a previous agreement I telephoned Ghali to come to my apartment and share the car with me, packed two more suitcases, wrote a good-bye note to Zénobie, the faithful cook; took a last glance at the beautiful furniture and pictures I was abandoning; grabbed my portable typewriter; awoke the concierge and told her that I was following the government to Tours. When Ghali finally arrived, we set out without lights through the dark streets to the Châtillon Gate and the road I had previously reconnoitered. Aside from some small infantry units we met nobody. Nobody bothered to demand our papers. Only when, in the faint light of dawn, we crossed the main Paris-Tours road south of Chartres, did we see what we had missed: thousands of motorcars, buses, and trucks, tens of thousands of refugees, some of them in uniform, jammed together in a solemn column moving southward at about three miles an hour. From time to time, an unopposed German warplane swooped low over them to spread further disorder.

Still following side roads, we reached Chenu in the early morning. Lilian had not arrived.

Any one of twenty things, most of them bad, could have happened to a woman alone in a tiny car among half-crazed refugees. Immediately after breakfast I set out for the prefecture at Tours where my friend Mandel, now Minister of the Interior, had taken up quarters, and asked his aid in locating my wife. Within half an hour he had asked every police prefecture between Tours and Paris to look out for a French-speaking *Américaine* in a beige Simca motorcar. Should she not soon appear, I intended to drive toward Paris and seek her myself.

From Mandel I learned that Churchill, now Prime Minister of Britain, was about to pay a third visit in an effort to induce the French government to continue the war from Brittany. He had promised immediately to send to France his three best divisions with twenty-five more to come in October. Churchill's greatest opponent was not General Weygand or the pro-Germans, fascists, and defeatists, but Reynaud's "official" mistress, Hélène de Portes, who wanted to end the fighting.

On the second morning, there, by God's grace, was Lilian. Her car had broken down and she had been two nights on the road.

Her return was the only sunlight in a lowering sky. Reynaud was frantically appealing to Roosevelt for a declaration of war. To do what I could, I sent Knox a personal cablegram: "New presidential declaration in name of all American states promising enough war material to ensure victory one year hence can keep torch of resistance burning fiercely. President already has necessary figures of all requirements but declaration must come quickly." Knox never bothered to reply.

That evening Ghali telephoned from Tours that the French were on the point of destroying the Loire bridges: unless we crossed that evening we might be stranded on the German side. Around ten o'clock the Rajchmans, several refugee friends of theirs, and the Mowrers drove bulging cars into Tours, slept in the house of a friend of Yvonne Michel, and the next morning, along with Knickerbocker and Ghali, set off, not for Brittany, but for southwest France. Before leaving I wired the *News* from "somewhere in France" that without American intervention "the war will soon be over."

On June 15, we reached Bordeaux. Several thousand people, including the French government, had preceded us and more were to come.

Tours had been disorderly. Bordeaux was bedlam.

Hotels, restaurants, cafés were bursting. People stood in line for hours to have a drink or eat an oversized meal. Many seemed indifferent to their country's fate. Cabinet members lived in hotels with office room where they could find it. Newsmen found neither lodging nor work space. Lilian slept at first in the house of the American consul general, later in the improvised offices of the company for which she had for some weeks been broadcasting to America, finally, with acquaintances in the suburbs. Ghali and I passed four nights on the seats of the Ford, carefully locked and parked on the esplanade before the Hotel Splendide.

Since we had no fixed abode, Ghali, Lilian, and I chose a certain café table as an improvised headquarters. When we found it occupied, we loitered nearby or occupied another. When the table was free, we used it as a desk. At other times I typed dispatches on two park chairs. Once I used the hood of the car.

Nearly all our copy dealt with the one question that mattered: would the French government continue the war from somewhere outside France or would it capitulate? Thanks to Georges Mandel and to U.S. Deputy Ambassador Tony Biddle, Ghali and I followed the crucial Cabinet debate in detail. For Mandel's use, I recruited the names of several foreign correspondents who, like me, were ready to follow a fugitive French government anywhere, even to Madagascar, to give it "legitimacy."

Within the Cabinet, the situation "oscillated" from one hour to the next. Reynaud had told President Roosevelt: "We will fight before

Paris. We will fight behind Paris. We will lock ourselves up in one of the provinces. We will go to North Africa and, if need be, to our American possessions." He had invited General de Gaulle to meet him in Algiers. President Lebrun actually set out for that city. But Pétain and Weygand opposed this as adamantly as they had the suggested transfer to Quimper in Brittany. Weygand wanted a military armistice to "save the honor" of the French army through avoiding the military surrender that would have followed the departure of the government. What happened to France was secondary. Over in the City Hall, Pierre Laval, Hitler's not-so-secret weapon against France and Britain, was whipping up sentiment in favor of capitulation. Camille Chautemps suggested that the Cabinet first "see" whether Germany's armistice terms were "acceptable," and then make up its mind what to do. Premier Reynaud agreed, on condition that the British would accept this derogation from the "no separate peace" agreement.

Britain first ruefully accepted the Chautemps plan and then dramatically substituted an offer of "indissoluble union" between the United Kingdom and the Government of France which had been concocted by three Frenchmen in London and Bob Vansittart. General de Gaulle read it over the telephone to the Premier.

Newspapers in Paris and London had repeatedly proposed formalizing what they considered a common destiny. Now the chance had come. Yet before we newsmen heard of Churchill's offer, the French Cabinet had rejected it, and Reynaud had resigned as Premier in favor of Philippe Pétain.

Pétain's Cabinet was a salad of ultranationalists and defeatists. Here were pro-Hitlerites, at least one admirer of Mussolini (Baudouin), several who could not forgive the British for their policy toward France since 1919—including the absence of a really large army and air force on the continent nine months after the outbreak of this war! All of them expected a German victory over Britain within weeks. The new Cabinet's first act was to ask Franco's ambassador, Lequerica, to invite Hitler to reveal his armistice terms.

That evening, Ghali and I called upon Mandel at his hotel and from him received the full story of Reynaud's surrender. Why, we asked, could not France fight on when militarily insignificant states like Norway, Holland, and Belgium already had governments in exile? France could assemble in North Africa some of the half million mobilized young men waiting in the depots, and all its forces from Syria and from Norway. It still had planes in North Africa, with more on the way. The combined British and French fleets could thwart a German attempt to cross the Mediterranean.

Could the majority of the Cabinet be pro-German? I asked bitterly.

I can still hear Mandel's harsh reply: *"Mais non, mon ami, mais non.* Don't look for complications where none exist. These men are cowards and they behave like cowards. What could be more natural?"

Pétain personally was no coward. The eighty-four-year-old one-time war hero was merely "periodically" senile! He attributed France's unprecedented defeat to the substitution of electric military communications for carrier pigeons. He accepted this defeat as deserved—and as the necessary prelude to a "national revolution" and the creation of a fascist state like the one in Spain. Better Hitler than Léon Blum! Ever since the beginning of the war, enemies of the Third Republic like Senator Lémery had tried to persuade the Marshal to become Premier.

At first Pétain wobbled. On June 20, the government seemed on the point of moving to Perpignan, whence it could depart unhindered for Algiers.

One morning a crowd of uniformed men, officers, and soldiers, gathered on a public square, I think before the stock exchange, and startled the Cabinet by shouting, "We are betrayed. Lead us to battle."

Betrayed they surely had been. Still, Hitler might demand more than even Pétain could concede, so until the armistice was signed, Ghali and I hoped that France would produce a second government somewhere abroad.

On the first day of the Pétain era nearly all Britishers departed from Bordeaux, a bad sign. The city was suddenly full of motorcars for sale. To increase the confusion, German planes dropped a few bombs on this "open" city.

By offering not to occupy two-fifths of France "in order not to favor the establishment of a French Government in England or elsewhere," Hitler made sure of the acceptance of his other conditions.

On June 22, the French emissaries at Compiègne duly affixed France's signature to an armistice agreement at least two of whose provisions Ghali and I found shameful. One left uncertain the status of the French fleet. Another specified that all French nationals caught fighting with another country against Germany were to be immediately shot as *francs-tireurs*. An embittered but defiant Mandel and three other stalwart republicans set out for Morocco on the steamship *Massilia*. Lilian promptly departed for Lisbon, in my Ford, leaving me the Simca.

Though Bordeaux lay well within the zone marked for occupation by the Germans, many French *bourgeois* were undisturbed. Restaurants and cafés were more crowded than ever.

Ghali and I planned to report the enemy's triumphal entry before leaving. Then we found that someone had stolen the Simca. While we were discussing what to do, a diplomatic car appeared at the café and the driver gave me a message: "Please see Ambassador Biddle at once."

Tony, fresh and handsome as ever, came directly to the point. The Germans were, he said, already at the Dordogne bridge, a few miles from Bordeaux. By tomorrow they would surround the city, thus cutting off exit. Would I please leave for Spain at once?

I would not . . . and for three reasons: first, I counted on seeing the Germans enter the city; second, I had invited our friend, Jeanne Lemercier, the widow of my old newspaper colleague, to dinner this evening; and last, I no longer had a car in which to flee.

Tony was unconvinced. "You've got to get the hell out. I feel responsible for your safety and I won't have you sleeping under my bed. I would have to leave you sometimes to go to the toilette. If I find a car you can buy cheaply, will you leave today? If you lack the money, Uncle Sam will lend it to the Chicago *Daily News.*"

We compromised. I bought a Hillman Minx left behind by a British official, and promised to leave Bordeaux *after* dinner that same night.

Should I go to Lisbon or to Vichy? To find out, I called upon the new Minister of Information, Jean Prouvost, a newspaper publisher, who was already censoring all information "that might shake the French people's confidence in Marshal Pétain," as he admitted to a British diplomat. He received me with barely veiled hostility. Disregarding this, I asked what he would think of my leaving immediately for Vichy. Here was his chance.

"For a man of your particular convictions," he answered icily, "Vichy will hardly prove to be a hospitable place."

That settled it.

That same day, Knickerbocker met Laval in a hotel lobby and put the key question: "*Monsieur le Président,* have you considered what the Germans will do to France?"

Laval, an eager co-author of the armistice, smiled broadly over the dirty white necktie that he always affected. "No, no, Mr. Knickerbocker, you are mistaken. France has only one enemy—the Soviet Union."

During the afternoon, while I practiced driving the Hillman, Ghali and I agreed that he would go to Vichy for the *Daily News* while I went from Lisbon to wherever an alternative French government might establish itself.

In the evening we had a farewell dinner at the Chapon Fin restaurant, one of the best in France. Nothing could still Jeanne Lemercier's tears or lessen our common grief. Toward ten o'clock Ambassador Biddle walked over from a neighboring table, with a reproachful look. "Edgar, when are you clearing out?"

"Shortly."

"Good. If you run on any Germans in the dark, step on the gas. And remember, if they should catch you, make them get me on the phone immediately."

A few minutes later, I left my friends and walked to the Hillman. Sitting inside were a soldier and a girl.

"What the hell—excuse me, Arthur, just what are *you* doing in my car?"

Arthur Koestler, in the uniform of a private of the French Foreign Legion, gave me an appealing look. He presented the girl, English and pretty. "As you drove up two hours ago, we heard you say you would shortly be leaving for Biarritz. Unless a known antifascist like me can get out of here, you know what he can expect from the Germans. So we waited in the hope that you would take us with you. This is my last chance."

How refuse? "On one condition, Arthur, this is *my* car and it goes *where* I wish *when* I wish. If you agree, let's go."

"Agreed."

Without lights, the Hillman rolled southward toward Spain. Nothing stood between us and safety but the possibility that the Germans had already blocked the road ahead. If so, well, I would have to decide whether to crash through a road barrier or to turn around and try to reach Spain by some other road.

The drive was uneventful. At Biarritz in the early dawn Arthur got out.

"I dare not enter Franco's Spain, so I shall find a boat here for England. Please take the young lady with you to the border. Thanks for saving my life." And he was gone. After a couple of hours' sleep, we drove on.

At Hendaye on the French side of the Bidassoa River, the English girl left me. Whereupon I drove across to the Spanish side, stopped at the barrier, and presented my passport. The guard turned directly to the Spanish visa which Lilian had "purchased" from the Spanish consul in Bordeaux, looked at it a second, and handed it back.

Then in pidgin French: "Visa from Bordeaux no good. No enter Spain."

"And what do I do now?"

He shrugged his shoulders.

"How should I know? Go back to France."

I decided it must be a mistake. I would wait until they changed the guards and try again.

Making myself comfortable in the car I typed a dispatch describing those features of France's surrender which I had been unable to wire from Bordeaux. "The France of Cambronne, of Denfert-Rochereau, and of Ferdinand Foch," I concluded, "has ceased to exist."

Even as I typed, scores of cars and hundreds of walking refugees streamed by, all headed for Spain and safety. Among them were acquaintances who stopped to say a word.

By late afternoon the half dozen other cars parked behind me, headed back to France and the Hillman remained alone. A change in the Spanish guards brought no hope. I still could not enter Spain.

Nor, since my name was not on his list, would a young U.S. diplomat from Madrid let me join a group of Americans the Embassy there was vouching for.

So there I was, in the middle of a bridge over an international river, with Goebbels' Germans only a few miles away.

What a situation!

About 10:00 P.M., I carefully measured various articles of clothing along which, tied together as a rope, I might slide down into the Bidassoa. Once in the water, under cover of darkness, it would be simple to swim ashore somewhere on the Spanish side. My presumed arrestation would not matter.

Unhappily, my improvised rope reached only half way to the rock-filled stream. If I then dropped the rest of the distance I could expect a broken leg.

Early the following morning a passing Polish colleague recognized me and asked what I was doing with the Germans only four miles away. What indeed! Sadly, I took from my wallet a suitable bribe for the French frontier guards who would, I hoped, let me reenter France and make a dash for the unoccupied area.

Just as I was turning the car around, an idea hit me like a dive bomber! Six months before I had passed through Spain with a visa from Paris. I studied it intently. Originally it had said nothing of the number of times I might enter the country in transit. Some Spaniard had, with a pen, limited this to one trip. If I could erase that ink stroke, a guard unfamiliar with my previous attempt to enter might let me pass. I set to work.

No professional counterfeiter ever took greater pains with a false thousand dollar bill than I did in removing that pen scrawl. First an eraser applied so delicately as to leave no scratch. Then I licked the paper for five minutes, and carefully scrutinized the result. The ink was gone! Next I rubbed dust over the entire page until it was uniformly dirty and showed no trace of tampering. Saved, provided the new guard showed up before the Germans and was unaware of my previous rebuffs.

Luck was with me. At noon the new Spaniard appeared. Smiling broadly, I walked into the guard room and presented my passport open at my invisible masterpiece. Without looking further the guard stamped it, the barrier went up, and I drove into Spain, mentally thumbing my nose at Dr. Paul Joseph Goebbels, wherever he might be; and ironically humming *Giovinezza*.

But not for long. A few miles ahead more *carabineros* blocked the road.

"Step this way!"

One of them led me into the office of a hard-faced officer.

"Excuse me, I just wish to make sure your name is not on our list of undesirables," said he in French.

I almost collapsed. Here was the famous "blacklist" of Franco's enemies. Yet even as he fingered the cards I started to smile. According to Spanish custom he was looking for my name, not under the letter "M" but under "A" for Ansel. Naturally he found nothing.

"Bon voyage, monsieur."

I headed for Lisbon singing not *Giovinezza*, but the *Battle Hymn of the Republic*.

29

Uncle Sam Girds Up His Loins

Until, in God's good time, the New World,
with all its power and might, steps forth to the
rescue and liberation of the Old.
                        —WINSTON CHURCHILL

NEUTRAL LISBON WAS as crowded as Bordeaux. Here were the same myriads of international refugees seeking accommodation in hotels, restaurants, and cafés—and often not finding it. Competing with them were any number of tourists who had come to the capital to see the exhibition commemorating Portugal's eight centuries as a colonial power. All steamship and air passages were sold out for a month ahead. Nonetheless, after the misery of Bordeaux, Lisbon seemed a blessed city.

Among the refugees were old friends, including U.S. military and naval attachés from countries the Germans had overrun, and local U.S. diplomats who filled me in on what the Lisbon newspapers and radio left unsaid. Moreover, we met a few Portuguese, including the Russian-looking poet owner of a bookstore with whom I had accidentally become acquainted during my stay in Lisbon the previous December. Now I again sought him out once or twice in order to talk books. Other acquaintances offered the welcome news that the presence of so many refugees had finally opened Portuguese minds to the danger of a Hitler-dominated Europe.

In fact, a Portuguese diplomat sent a message that if I would "solicit an audience," Dictator Salazar would be happy to grant it. I refused. I had nothing to demand of any friend of a friend of Hitler! A foolish attitude and, I now think, an ungracious one.

Soon, thanks to the aid of a colleague stationed in Lisbon, the Mowrers moved from a noisy hotel room on the crowded plaza to a luxurious suite in the British-owned Palacio de Monserrate, near the town of Cintra, high in the hills seventeen miles from Lisbon. In the absence of other guests, we had the eighteenth-century landscaped park, which some considered the finest in the entire world, to ourselves, with servants to look after our comfort.

Upon reaching Lisbon I had filed the dispatch written on the Bidassoa bridge and received from Chicago instructions to remain in Portugal long enough to complete a full account of France's shocking defeat. In the beautifully proportioned library of the palace I poured out several thousand words, sparing nobody, while emphasizing the influence of both communist and anti-Soviet fifth columnists.

France had been "out-prepared, out-organized, out-generaled and out-fought." Only by listening to Charles de Gaulle might the commanders perhaps have avoided defeat.

After work, we read in the library, walked in the landscaped park, dined in Lisbon, or drove to such beauty spots as Cap da Roca, where Europe stretches its finger furthest into the Atlantic. Once we swam at Estoril (chilly), that luxurious refuge of discarded royalty.

The news remained bad. At Casablanca, a calculating General Noguès had kept Mandel and his intrepid companions under arrest and prevented Churchill's emissaries from seeing them. Thereby, he killed the last chance of a French government in exile.

On July 4, the British fleet sank a number of French warships at Oran after the latter's commander, Admiral Gensoul, refused either to side with Britain, or to sink his own ships, or to take them to a port in the Caribbean. I understood Churchill's motive—possession of the French ships might be what the Germans needed successfully to invade Britain.

Yet I shuddered at the inevitable effect in France. Here was Laval's opportunity. Speaking to what remained of the French Parliament at Vichy two days later, he insisted that France had no more implacable enemy than England and accused that country of using France for its own protection rather than for mutual victory. Certainly, without the Oran attack, far fewer French legislators would have favored the suicide of the democratic Republic.

Since 1919, the French, British, and American peoples had followed unrealistic foreign policies. France was paying an appalling price for having done so. Only, at long last, were the British being led by the man who, given a chance, would have nipped aggression in the bud. Was it too late? Now I should see for myself. Knox had ordered me to fly to London and put myself at the disposal of his friend, Colonel William J. Donovan, famous in the previous war as head of the "Fighting Sixty-ninth." Airplane seats were at a premium in Lisbon, but by a combination of intrigue, influence, and bluster we finally flew to England and found rooms at the Dorchester Hotel in London.

From the first I liked "Wild Bill": plenty of will behind a smiling but realistic shrewdness. What could I do for him? He explained: at Knox's request he and I were to collect and publish information on the

"Fifth Column" activities which had so helped the Germans in Norway, Holland, Belgium, France. What were the British and Americans doing about the problem? Beyond this, however, lay his real assignment— finding out for President Roosevelt the thing he needed most to know: would and could the British hold out against the Germans?

Ambassador Joe Kennedy had reported to Washington that the democracies had lost the war and that the British should seek immediate peace with Hitler. But the President had lost confidence in his London Ambassador's judgment and accepted Knox's suggestion that Donovan, with Mowrer's help, take a fresh look at Britain. Knox knew of my intimacy with members of the Churchill government. As a newsman I could legitimately poke my nose into everything and ask indiscreet questions. Was I ready to start at once?

During the next three weeks I visited several defense centers and shuddered at the lack of military preparation. Lilian and I saw everybody we could and questioned all who would answer—foreign and English. Among the foreigners were Russian princes, Polish refugee gentry, Hungarian socialists, members of the Czechoslovak Government-in-Exile, and American businessmen.

Particularly, I listened to the Chicago *Daily News*' perceptive London representatives, William Stoneman and Helen Kirkpatrick, and to our old friend, John Wheeler-Bennett, who knew the Germans well.

At the House of Commons I talked with Cabinet Members and M.P.'s of all three parties and met others at informal dinners and receptions: Anthony Eden, Alfred Duff Cooper, now Minister of Information, Sir Charles Peake, Lord Halifax, looking more than ever like an Anglican Rector, with whom we had dinner and Robert Vansittart. To top it all off, we had lunch with the Prime Minister and Mrs. Churchill at Number Ten Downing Street.

Winston talked incessantly and gaily of Britain's prospects and his own intentions, quizzed me about both Hitler and President Roosevelt's next moves, noted his predecessor's inability to detect a "bad smell," and seemed to relish the impending crisis, remarking, as he said in a subsequent speech, that he found England's isolation "rather exhilarating." If the worst came to the worst, he, after defending Britain to the last, would send the fleet and the air force to Canada and fight from there. In 1918, Clemenceau had promised the French that "we will fight in Paris, we will fight on the Loire, we will fight on the Garonne, we will fight on the Pyrenees. And if we are off the Pyrenees, we will fight at sea. But never count on me for peace."

During that month in England I wrote just one news dispatch. In this I took issue with Ambassador Bullitt's claim that the Pétain Government, being neither subservient to Germany nor fascist, should receive American support. In my judgment, any government led by puppets like Laval and Baudouin would eventually do whatever Hitler wanted. Far from preventing this, American aid would delay that clean break which would require the Germans to police all of another country, thus having fewer resources to use elsewhere. America should help those Frenchmen who were fighting, or ready to fight, against Nazi Germany.

Chief among these was Charles de Gaulle. Shortly after our arrival in London, Duff Cooper asked me if I knew the General. Yes, I had met the latter once, admired his prescience about the nature of the present war, and, in Bordeaux, heard his appeal to the French government to unite with Britain or go into exile rather than accept a degrading armistice.

"The P.M.," Duff continued, "is hesitating whether or not to give some sort of recognition to de Gaulle and his Free French. What do you think, Edgar?"

"A curious question. How many allies has Britain now?"

"None" (sarcastically), "not even the United States."

"Not yet. How then can you hesitate about recognizing de Gaulle? If he turns out well, you have a minor ally. If badly, what does Britain lose?"

"That's exactly what I told the Prime Minister, and I shall tell him what you said. He respects your knowledge of France. Just when would you give de Gaulle official recognition?"

"But surely on July 14."

Duff agreed. On that day, 1940, Frenchmen in arms paraded behind the Cross of Lorraine to the Cenotaph and there paid homage to the British dead of the First World War.

Twice thereafter, a French officer brought me a message that *le général* had heard of my advice to Duff Cooper and hoped I would visit him and receive his thanks. The second time I accepted, though explaining that I had only fifteen free minutes before an important luncheon.

In small offices in Saint Stephen's House on the Thames Embankment, a towering French brigadier with an oversized nose and a truculent expression thanked me warmly for what I had done for France.

"Unnecessary, *mon général;* we are on the same side in this war." He beamed, then suddenly asked: "And now, what would you like to know from me?"

I gasped. I knew about de Gaulle's efforts to enlist the fighting services of the more than thirty thousand French soldiers and sailors in England. About Britain's situation I probably had more knowledge than he. Still, he was the man who had said: "The flame of French resistance must not and will not go out."

So I spoke out boldly: "*Mon général*, I saw the French army go to war in 1914 and its spirit was superb. I saw the army in 1939 and its morale was inadequate. How do you account for the difference?"

I expected him to be offended. Instead he smiled and answered: "That is a very good question. Sit down and I shall explain it to you."

For a long hour, having canceled my luncheon date by telephone,

I listened to de Gaulle's analysis of why France had fallen. In subsequent years I heard many explanations but never a more profound, objective, even pitiless description of that national débâcle. At the end, the general expressed his confidence that Germany would eventually be beaten either by the United States or by Russia.

What a remarkable man, Churchillean in dimension, with the same unconquerable spirit and gift of words—in short, another great seventeenth-century liberal!

Before Lilian and I left London, Donovan and I agreed on what he would report to Roosevelt: *Britain under Churchill would not surrender either to ruthless air raids or to an invasion.*

After a last weekend with Viscount Cranborne, then Secretary of State for Dominion Affairs, a resolute anti-appeaser, we flew to America via Lisbon. Many times, both before and since 1940, I have been critical of Britain's obsolete policy of keeping Western Europe divided. But no experience has ever been more "exhilarating" (to quote Churchill again) than that of England in July, 1940.

In Chicago my daughter, hale and happy at the Greens', was ready for the university. Equally satisfying was the fact that wiser Chicagoans, including the *Daily News* staff, favored "saving America by aiding the allies." In New York, a Mrs. Natalie Wales Payne had successfully organized "Bundles for Britain."

On the other hand, the America Firsters and other isolationists were successfully pushing the slogan, "T'aint our war." Moreover, a group of leading, politically illiterate citizens inspired by people like Ambassador Joe Kennedy and the Lindbergs, considered Nazism the "wave of the future" and predicted an early British collapse. According to Paul Mowrer and Carroll Binder, it was touch and go whether the American people would wake up in time.

Lilian and I restored our energies by a few days at Glen Lake, Michigan, swimming and tramping over the great dunes of Sleeping Bear Point. Then back to work. While Lilian successfully sought the most appropriate college and a scholarship for Diana, and prepared a series of lectures, I prepared to go to Washington as a "diplomatic" correspondent.

Before leaving Chicago I wrote several pieces predicting that to invade Britain successfully, Hitler would have to make up his mind quickly for "already the days are growing short, the nights foggy and the North Sea rough."

On August 19, the *News* started publishing Donovan's and my series on Fifth Column activities in Europe. Quisling in Norway, Mussert in the Netherlands, Degrelle in Belgium, and the combination of the pro-Nazis and defeatists in France, skillfully nourished by "pro-French" Germans Otto Abetz and Friedrich Sieburg, all were part of Hitler's diabolically effective plan of softening up his adversaries. As the *Fuehrer* had put it: "The results at which I aim are only to be obtained by systematic corruption of the possessing and governing classes.

Business advantages, erotic satisfactions, and emotion are the three main elements of our propaganda organ."

In France those classes were assisted by women who could never forget the slaughter of the first war and by a defeatist officer group. Even in Britain, pro-German organizations like the British Union of Fascists, the Link, the Anglo-German Fellowship, and the Christian Fellowship had had a devastating influence on public opinion.

In the United States the *Bund* was still openly pro-Hitler. A German official, Captain Wiedemann, publicly boasted that he had prevented revision of the American Neutrality Acts. I warned: "It is conceivable that the United States possesses the finest Nazi-schooled Fifth Column in the world, one which, in case of war with Germany, could be our undoing."

Knox offered the Donovan-Mowrer articles free to all editors "as part of a national defense program," and they made a considerable stir.

On Labor Day, I set out happily in a new Mercury motorcar for Washington, D.C., one of the two American cities which I preferred. (The other was San Francisco.)

What did I find so attractive in the capital, aside from the presence of those national policy makers on which my work depended? Washington was unique for its spaciousness. What other world capital had such broad avenues and comparatively rapid transportation? Where else was there such profusion of majestic trees and flowering shrubs? Never shall I forget the lift of spirit as I drove over the last hill and saw across the Potomac, the Cathedral, the Washington Monument, and the Capitol Dome against a pale blue sky.

Paul Leach, the experienced *News* correspondent, not only showed no resentment at sharing his field of activity with me, but gave me the necessary information: who was who in the capital, and why.

In the Navy Building, Colonel Knox thanked me for my services to Donovan and to our country and completed the political picture: the President encouraged by Donovan's report, was determined quietly to save Britain in spite of the neutrality legislation. His most active supporters in the Cabinet were Stimson, Morgenthau, and Knox himself. They were quietly encouraging William Allen White's *Committee to Save America by Aiding the Allies*. Shortly after I reached Washington, Steve Early, the White House Press Chief, offered me the job of preparing statements for the Secretaries of State, War, and Navy to issue, an opportunity which I politely and perhaps foolishly declined.

The United States' greatest weakness was lack of military preparation. Hypnotized by its early belief in peace through words, the Roosevelt Administration had for years failed to react to Hitler's rearmament or Japan's denunciation of the naval limitation treaty. Those most conscious of this failure, the generals and admirals, were even more cautious than the leading civilians. Although Secretary of State Cordell Hull had expressed the view that "there is no such thing as appeasing Hitler any more than a squirrel can appease a boa constrictor," he, too, was slow to move.

Roosevelt, as Knox made clear to me, was, moreover, committed to keeping out of the war; there would be no American expeditionary force in Europe this time, just supplies and money. F.D.R.'s immediate task was to get the people's support for his revolutionary "destroyer-for-bases deal" with the British, which, he told Congress, was "the most important action in the reinforcement of our national defense since the Louisiana Purchase." As a small step in this direction, Knox asked me to lunch in New York with the publisher of the *New York Times*, Arthur Hayes Sulzberger, who wanted my view of the situations in Britain and France.

The meeting in the *Times* Building was pleasant enough, with Sulzberger repeatedly interrupting my somewhat lurid descriptions with the exclamation: "But this is dreadful—much worse than our correspondents have reported." To which I had no reply. Having followed the *Times* regularly since my return from Europe, I had been disappointed by its failure to take a clear stand on the President's policy.

Justice Brandeis thanked me for "standing up to Hitler," and urged me to support the Zionist movement, which Germany's persecution of Jews had made "mandatory." With Justice Frankfurter I exchanged Central European persiflage.

My news beats were the White House Conferences (shared with Paul Leach), the State Department, and foreign embassies. At his meetings with the press, generally attended by no more than twenty newsmen, Secretary Hull was not greatly communicative. Even during an hour's personal interview, I learned little. Perhaps the President had not bothered to keep him informed. With Sumner Welles, with Assistant Secretary of State Adolf Berle, with Mike McDermott, Loy Henderson, Ray Atherton, and John Wiley discussion was rich and varied.

It took a little time to overcome my distrust of Knox's Under Secretary, Jim Forrestal, who had been a partner in Dillon, Read and Company, an American bank which had, in my eyes, demeaned itself by transactions with Nazi Germany. Eventually I came to recognize him as an unusually courageous champion of freedom. In the perceptive Navy press chief, Commander Berry, I found a political ally.

Another contact was Oscar Cox of the Treasury (a shrewd, articulate lawyer as passionately devoted to the defeat of the Axis as Secretary Morgenthau). On rare occasions I received tips from Harry Dexter White, whose openly pro-Russian attitude never led me to suspect any closer tie with Moscow.

The Assistant Secretary of War, Jack McCloy, and General Marshall pooh-poohed my suggestion that, to survive, the United States would have to build as many as fifty thousand planes a year. Three White House cronies, the handsome poet, Archibald MacLeish, now Librarian of Congress, witty Thomas Corcoran, and earnest Ben Cohen saw to my domestic education. At MacLeish's hospitable house we met Attorney General Francis Biddle and his poetess wife. Thanks to so many insiders, I managed to keep abreast of the slow development of American policy during those darkest months of the war, which were, in my opinion, not only Britain's but Franklin Roosevelt's "finest hour." For he personally contributed, perhaps decisively, to saving Britain in spite of the Neutrality Acts, the isolationism of so many honest citizens, and his own feeling that to be reelected he had to promise the voters never to "send your sons into a foreign war" (an obscure phrase, since all save civil wars are necessarily foreign). F.D.R.'s destroyers-for-bases deal, Lend-Lease, and the use of American warships to convoy supplies to Britain rate as supreme statesmanship.

Unfortunately, it seemed to me, our President was going astray in his scorn of the Free French and his support of Pétain.

The Vichy crowd were irrevocably—or almost—on the side of the Rome-Berlin-Tokyo Axis. Hence I steered clear of the Vichy French Embassy where the stodgy former Mayor of Versailles, Gaston Henry-Haye, had supplanted my friend, de Saint Quentin. Of the treacherous Italians I took no notice and avoided contacts with our one-time German acquaintances, Ambassador Dieckoff and Minister Hans Thomsen, both of whom were working with American isolationists. Nor did I seek to extract information from the arrogant Japanese.

On the other hand, the new Polish Ambassador, Jan Ciechanowski, gave me invaluable scraps of information about occupied Europe. Of the Yugoslav Ambassador, Constantin Fotitch, and his attractive wife, Tatiana, we saw much. Strangely enough, in view of Stalin's refusal to let me reenter Russia, the Soviet Ambassador, Constantine Oumansky, occasionally had me to lunch with him alone. During these meals he affected an anti-Hitler pose. This did not prevent him, as I found out later, from passing on to the Germans everything he learned from me.

In view of my inexperience of the Far East, I was delighted to find in Washington Chiang's special emissary, T. V. Soong, who was employing as his adviser Ludwik Rajchman, all of whose family were by now in America. T. V. eventually persuaded Roosevelt to allow Brigadier General Claire Chennault, an impressive soldier, to recruit American volunteer flyers, the Flying Tigers, and endow China with something like an air force able to stand up to that of Japan. "Why," T. V. asked me early in 1941, "do American officials who have always opposed communists in their own country show such tender solicitude for communists who happen to be Chinese?" I could not answer. In my opinion, the U.S.S.R. had triggered Hitler's war by its 1939 agreement with him. At a *Fortune Magazine* Round Table on Peace Aims in Princeton, which included, among others, Raymond Leslie Buell, John Chamberlain, Herbert Agar, Quincey Wright, Pertinax, George Shuster, Gustav Stolper, Max Ascoli, and George Fielding Eliot, I took the lead in inducing the meeting to adopt a resolution calling for immediate steps "for reconstruction of the postwar world and holding out hope for the creation of a New Order of Free Peoples." From such peoples the U.S.S.R. was conspicuously absent.

Lord Halifax (who succeeded the "reformed" Cliveden-ite, Lord Lothian, as Ambassador) and the former London *Times* correspondent, Wilmot Lewis, provided a valuable background. Sir Walter Layton, whom we had known in Berlin, introduced me to Britain's chief purchaser, Arthur Purvis, a remarkable man who met a premature death. And the British Information Service high up in Rockefellew Center in New York, occasionally slipped me "exclusives."

At Eugene Meyer's house, on one occasion, I heard John Maynard Keynes somewhat patronizingly insist that we Americans should ask from Britain nothing in return for our aid, since Britain was really saving us from Hitler and the Japanese.

From month to month F.D.R.'s public utterances became more belligerent. He urged the United States to become the "arsenal of democracy." He described Lend-Lease as an offer to a neighbor of the garden hose to put out a fire.

By this time, Germany was invading the Balkans and threatening all of North Africa, particularly Egypt and the Suez Canal. Admiral Darlan turned over to Rommel for use in Africa hundreds of invaluable trucks. Nothing but the exorbitance of Franco's political price had prevented Hitler from joining Spain in seizing Morocco. His submarines were playing increasing havoc with British shipping. Under the influence of a gang of bankers (the "synarchists"), Vichy France was moving ever closer to Germany.

On the other hand, the Free French were spreading their control over Central Africa and some isolated islands, much to F.D.R.'s and Bob Murphy's disgust. In spite of a message smuggled out of France by a group of French writers, thinkers, and scientists, warning that the French people did not support Pétain, Washington was sending supplies to Pétainists in North Africa.

When Congress failed, by just one vote, to repeal the American Draft Act which had created the new U.S. Army, I was so depressed that Paul Leach gently jibed at me for "carrying the weight of the world on those thin shoulders." World affairs were not Paul's forte.

In late March, Adolf Berle communicated the latest shocker. From T. V. Soong, the Department had learned that Hitler would shortly attack the Soviet Union! Yet Britain was stronger than ever, and Hitler's troops were bogged down in North Africa. The United States was openly helping his enemy. To take on the Soviet Union at such a time would be insane. Nonetheless, Berle insisted, such was Hitler's intention.

Like Joe Stalin, I could not believe that Hitler's generals would take such a gamble. So I missed a world beat by ignoring Berle's tip.

At the end of May, 1941, President Roosevelt, in a fireside chat, hinted at impending events of great importance and declared a state of national emergency at home.

In June, Nazi Germany turned on its Soviet associate, just as Berle had said, and started carving the enlarged Third Reich out of Russian territory. Roosevelt replied by sending U.S. forces to Iceland, tightening up commercial sanctions against Japan, and ordering Harry Hopkins to London and Moscow as his personal representative. The great war had entered a brand new phase.

F.D.R. responded to the Republicans' charge that he was a "traitor to his class" by bestowing even greater confidence and responsibility on those socially or financially outstanding figures who supported him. Among these were Bullitt, Averell Harriman, Francis Biddle, Ed Stettinius, and Dean Acheson.

Yet Harry Hopkins, now the unquestioned presidential favorite, had already ousted Bullitt as F.D.R.'s chief adviser on world affairs. This not only weakened the President's anything but firm grasp of such matters, but introduced into American policy a social reformer's indulgence of the Soviet Union. Some in Washington whispered that Walter Duranty, the *Times* correspondent in Moscow, had during an American visit communicated to the President his and Ambassador Joe Davies' touching trust in the Bolsheviks.

The Fields, Henry and Patsy, kept open house to visiting foreigners. Henry had worked in Russia as an anthropologist and, almost alone in Washington, predicted that the Russians would defeat the German invaders.

At the Washington homes of Jean Monnet, Pertinax, and Pierre Cot, we saw other French friends: Raoul Roussy de Sales, ailing but indomitable; Jules Romains; Geneviève Tabouis; Eve Curie; and Alexis Léger.

I found for Henri Bonnet a job in Chicago with Mrs. Anita Blaine, head of *World Citizens*. Although she was Robert McCormick's sister, her dislike of his political policies was allegedly keeping her alive. When she awoke in the morning tired of living, a mere glance at the Chicago *Tribune* caused such a rush of adrenalin that she determined to see the day through—and did. Bonnet's handsome Greek-born wife, Helle, had opened a hat shop in New York.

In May, 1941, René Pleven, a former assistant of Jean Monnet's, came to Washington on behalf of General de Gaulle in order, as he put it, "to secure from the American Administration as much consideration for the Frenchmen who are fighting democracy's battle as you give to the traitors who sold out to Germany." The President refused to receive him. Only months later, after failing to include the Free French, now the Fighting French, among the signers of the Atlantic Charter, F.D.R. consented to give them the benefits of Lend-Lease.

Everything depended on Germany's campaign in Russia. It had begun late, thanks to Hitler's insistence on previously conquering Yugoslavia and Greece. Yet the Nazis were going ahead rapidly, taking literally millions of prisoners, and, in the Ukraine, being welcomed as "liberators." Would the "aid without strings" which Roosevelt, imitating Churchill, had begun giving Stalin be enough to save Russia?

Knox was not worried. U.S. armament was increasing. There was a growing belief in Washington—or so I wrote—that the Soviet Union would somehow manage to hold out. The signing of the historic Atlantic Charter by Roosevelt and Churchill, identifying their peace aims with what amounted to a new heaven and a new earth, revived the spirit of peoples everywhere.

Late in August, Knox asked me once more to see Colonel Donovan, the recently appointed Coordinator of Information—a cover name for a new, superintelligence and information service—who lived in Georgetown only a few hundred yards from us.

As was his custom, Donovan received me over a hearty breakfast. "I want you to go to Southeast Asia. You will size up the situations in the various countries; judge what would be the best information setup and the possibilities of disseminating American information; and finally bring back to me whatever you may learn concerning Japan's intentions in the near future. Knox will provide a letter identifying you as his personal representative, but you will pass as a newspaper correspondent just as you did in England. When you come back, I want you to enter the information service as my personal adviser. How soon can you leave?"

Here was the opportunity to become familiar with Far Eastern problems for which I had been waiting. After a week of research and reading I was ready.

Since Donovan did not lack for information concerning the Philippines, after talks with General Douglas MacArthur and Admiral Hart (who saw no reason for the creation of a new intelligence service under Donovan), from Manila I hastened to less-chartered places—Singapore (twice), Java, Thailand, Burma, Kunming, Chungking, and Hong Kong. In each of these countries I talked with scores of individuals. In Indonesia I visited the Buddhist temple of Borobudor, which made me temporarily regret having deserted literature for journalism. In Bangkok, city of *wats*, tricycle rickshaws, and *klongs*, I interviewed Prime Minister Bipul (whose current worry was how to get the Thai women into hats, gloves, and stockings); in Rangoon I listened to nearly everybody including a newsman, U Nu; and at Toungoo, to Colonel Chennault of the Flying Tigers and to Joe Alsop, now with the latter.

At Kunming I breakfasted in the town hall with my old acquaintance Y. T. Miao, the rich mining engineer; and in Chungking, chief target of Japanese air raids, with Chinese, American, and British experts, from the Gimo and Madame down to my American friends, Jim McHugh, General John Magruder, and Leland Stowe, my colleague on the *Daily News*. Ambassador Clarence Gauss was hostile to Chiang and anti-British as well.

British Ambassador Sir Archibald Clarke Kerr predicted, without apparent alarm, the ultimate success of the Chinese communists. In fact, what he said was strikingly similar to what Jimmy Sheehan (with whom by chance I had traveled from Singapore) and I heard from Chou En-lai, the bland, double-talking representative of the Communist Fourth Army. Clarke Kerr and Owen Lattimore, official American advisers to Chiang, argued that Chinese communists were not "agrarian reformers." Bishop Yu-pin prophetically insisted that Chiang was being too lenient with his "Reds."

On the plane to Hong Kong I reviewed my conclusions. Singapore, I thought, could resist against attack once the powerful British battleships announced by Duff Cooper, arrived from England. Yet the command of the area was dispersed among no less than seven generals and admirals, some of the lesser of whom referred to the top commander, Air Vice Marshall Sir Robert Brooke Popham, as "Brooke Pop-off" or "Brooke Popcorn."

Java's fate also depended upon the British and Dutch navies. Thailand and Burma were ready to succumb at the first Japanese attack unless the West sent troops to help them.

China, on the other hand, was, according to most specialists, militarily better off than in 1938. Chiang could hold out, once the Flying Tigers went into action, so long as supplies arrived regularly along the Burma Road. On the other hand, some leading Chinese believed that they had done enough and that it was now up to the United States to come in and expel the Japanese.

But all this left unanswered the vital question: what would Tokyo do next? I had heard the guesses of several of the greatest Western experts on Japan.

In Singapore Sir George Samson, quiet and competent, had stated that the ruling Japanese war lords had not yet made up their minds concerning their next move, but were likely to plump for an attack on Vladivostok.

Mynheer Lovink in Batavia had dwelt on the limitless ambition of the Tokyo authorities ("these people can never turn back") and expected a lunge into Southeast Asia, including the Dutch East Indies. He thought that "we" (meaning chiefly the United States) "should precipitate matters" since "the fight is inevitable."

Wong Pun-son, a fat, unmilitary person in a blue uniform, chief Japanese specialist of the Chinese Intelligence Service, hid his activities so well from foreigners that even Colonel Jim McHugh had not heard of him. (His obscure office in a kind of shanty high up over the Chialing River bore the noncommittal label, "Head of the International Relations, Chungking.") He had spent half his life in Japan, and Japan, he believed, must expand or burst. For the present, the Japanese would do whatever their German ally indicated and the Germans did not want them to attack the United States but to invade Siberia when the moment came to "make contact" with the Germans advancing from the west. Therefore Tokyo was maintaining thirty divisions on the Siberian border. Only after Russia's defeat would the Japanese turn south and finish off the British. Actually a good-looking German newspaperman in Tokyo,

Richard Sorge, actually a spy for the Soviet Union, had informed Moscow in that same October that Japan was not going to move against Siberia, thus enabling Stalin to transfer to Moscow the divisions that saved that city.

While the Hong Kong plane tossed about in three successive thunderstorms I went over these conflicting views, recognizing that of Japan's next move I still knew little more than when I left the United States. In Tokyo I might be able to learn something more definite.

But one of those things happened which preserve the mystery of life against the encroachments of reason. Emerging on the terrace of the house on the Peak at Hong Kong where I was a guest, I sniffed the northeast breeze, looked down fourteen hundred feet at the ships in the harbor, and said automatically to myself: "I am not going to get caught in Japan." That day I exchanged my flight to Tokyo for one to the Philippines.

In Manila I reported what I had heard to MacArthur, who listened intently. He was, he said, convinced that thanks to sheer extension of territory, Russia, like China, would wear out the invaders. Of Japanese intentions elsewhere he was less sure. The Philippines, he said, were not yet fully prepared to resist attack. Yet he did not believe the Japanese would dare confront the United States.

Thanks to Carlos P. Romulo, the Philippine newsman, I interviewed President Manual Quezon, a frail man who indicated that, once independent, the Philippines would wish to become a member of the "American Commonwealth" which the United States was sure to create one day.

The following night after dinner I prepared to sleep for a few hours before rising to take an early plane for the United States. But in the hotel lobby, Ernest B. Johnson of the U.S. Maritime Commission, who had just arrived from Tokyo, beckoned me to his table.

"Have a drink," he urged. "You can sleep on the plane. I need somebody to talk to." This last in so unusual a tone that reluctantly I sat down with him.

"Mr. Mowrer, when in San Francisco, do me a favor. Call up my daughter Barbara and give her her father's love and greetings."

"Of course. But don't you write to her?"

"Frequently. But now I need something more intimate than a letter." He drained his glass and ordered more. "I don't ever expect to see my daughter again."

Too much whiskey, I thought. "Does your daughter refuse to see her father?"

"Of course not. But the Japs will take Manila before I can get out. Something tells me I shall never see America again."

"Take Manila? That would mean a war with us."

"Of course . . . and soon. Didn't you know the Jap fleet has moved eastward, presumably to attack our fleet at Pearl Harbor?"

"No. What makes you think so?"

"The Japanese military crowd are desperate and for them it's all or nothing. They'll move against the Philippines at the same time. MacArthur's forces are too weak to hold these islands. And I shall never get out of here. So please call my daughter, say you've seen the old man and he sends his love."

Suspecting that Johnson knew something the source of which he was withholding, I gave up any idea of a nap and until midnight sought unsuccessfully to obtain more details. Then with his daughter's address and telephone number in my notebook, I said goodbye, assembled my belongings, and drove to the airport, my head buzzing.

Returning across the Pacific, I had the ritual swims at Guam (unattractive), Wake (alive with sooty terns and the ubiquitous brown rats), Midway, and Hawaii. At Midway I found myself in the midst of those most amazing and attractive of all birds, the goose-sized goonies (Layson's albatross, to the learned) then in their mating season. Even hardened seabees deferred to the traffic rights and wishes of these incredible feathered democrats who scorned human beings, enjoyed their love dances, and persisted in taking off for flight downwind rather than against it.

At Pearl Harbor, Admiral Kimmel warned me of coming war with Japan, but like Admiral Hart, urged Washington to delay it as long as possible.

In San Francisco, after lunch with Paul Smith of the *Chronicle*, I invited Barbara Johnson to the Saint Francis Hotel and over a drink gave her reassuring news of her father, even as he had asked.

In Chicago, the recently founded *Chicago Sun* offered me the position of foreign editor.

This compelled me to decide promptly what I was going to do during the coming year. I now had no less than five such offers. Knox, before I left, had suggested that I help him build up Naval Intelligence. Donovan had asked me to become his personal adviser. A former U.S. Military Attaché in Berlin had urged me to sign up for Military Intelligence with the initial rank of major. In Chungking I had received a wired offer from MacLeish to join the Office of Facts and Figures which the President had asked him to create. And now an editorship in Chicago. However, one talk with the editor, Rex Smith, convinced me that his views and mine were incompatible. So I politely refused.

In my absence from Washington things had changed. During the First World War, Wilson had delegated full control of American propaganda, as well as of information, to just one man, George Creel, whose organization was tiny (by modern bureaucratic standards) but effective. This was the last thing Roosevelt wanted. He preferred entrusting similar or overlapping jobs to several individuals or setups.

To Nelson Rockefeller, Coordinator of Inter-American Affairs since 1940, he turned over propaganda to Latin America. Domestic propaganda he was giving to MacLeish. From Donovan he had stripped Latin American "intelligence" in favor of the F.B.I. Thus, in November, 1941,

Donovan no longer wanted me as his personal assistant, but suggested that I take over propaganda to the Far East under Sherwood.

To him and his civilian and military experts, I reported: "The Japanese war lords are again on the prowl. They will soon strike again somewhere, against the Russians in Siberia, against Southeast Asia and Indonesia, or even, according to one well-informed American observer, against the United States at Guam and Hawaii. Just where the blow will fall I do not feel able to say. Meanwhile, Admirals Hart and Kimmel desperately beg the Administration for more time in which to prepare."

The experts looked at each other sharply when I suggested a possible attack on the United States. But after a few questions Donovan dismissed me, urging me to spell out certain points immediately in separate memoranda and thereafter to turn in a written report for the official record.

Knox informed me that the United States was close to a showdown with Tokyo. Once the new Japanese Premier, General Hideka Tojo, announced that there was no longer any place in the Orient for Britain and the United States, the President had little choice. Even while Secretary Hull was offering a "compromise" that included Japan's withdrawal from China, he had little hope of an agreement.

On December 7, as we were driving to a one o'clock luncheon, the news came over the radio: Japanese warplanes had attacked the American fleet at Pearl Harbor and put five of our fifteen capital ships out of commission! That evening Colonel Knox, in the Georgetown house of our friend Adlai Stevenson, who was now working for him in the Navy Department, corrected the original story: not *five* battleships sunk or disabled—*eight!* His consternation demonstrated that he at least had not foreseen the Japanese attack, still less sought to provoke it.

I could not sleep. Ernest Johnson had been right! And if a member of the Maritime Commission knew the destination of the Japanese fleet, why had the President, why had Knox and Stimson and Hull who were expecting war, not known it and taken the necessary precautions? And so on, through endless hours. Only in the early morning came the saving thought:

Nothing but *a direct attack could have brought the United States into the War!* Here was the "break" for which both Churchill and T. V. Soong had been waiting. Our side still had the power to win and win we would. By their imprudent action the Japanese warlords had saved the free world.

30

Misfit Bureaucrat

*And I returned, and saw under the sun, that
the race is not to the swift, nor the battle to
the strong, neither yet bread to the wise, nor
yet riches to men of understanding, nor yet
favor to men of skill; but time and chance
happeneth to them all.*

—ECCLESIASTES

THE YEAR 1942 started badly for the United Nations, as the President called our camp.

In the Pacific, the Japanese took full advantage of their destruction of half the American fleet and of MacArthur's airplanes. In the Philippines only Corregidor held out, temporarily. Once Japanese airplanes had sunk two British capital ships off the coast of Malaya, seventy-five thousand British surrendered at Singapore.

In North Africa, Rommel's Germans and Italians were threatening Egypt. German submarines in the Atlantic had rendered precarious the essential traffic between the United States and Britain.

At home, as Oscar Cox informed me, our war production was still hopelessly inadequate; the United States, Cox thought, badly needed a Ministry of Supply.

And for me too, this was a year of personal sorrow and professional frustration.

Shortly before Christmas we heard that Father was dying in St. Petersburg. This was no less a blow for being expected. In November, after Father had had his ailing mouth examined by a specialist, Paul had told me the sad news: cancer. So we had arranged that as he approached the end, Paul, Lilian, and I would visit him successively so that one of us would always be with him.

After Christmas Lilian sent word to me to come quickly or I would be too late. From his hospital bed, Father gave me a smile of recognition and pointed to his swollen mouth and throat. He could no longer speak. For hours I sat beside him, occasionally holding his hand, whispering loving words into his ear, shuddering at his accesses of pain. Toward the end of the third day I realized that he was no longer aware of my presence. The event I had dreaded all my life was at hand.

How I loved this man! Since the age of seventeen I had, God knows, seen little enough of him. He was a self-made Midwesterner, practical in his approach to life, the epitome of common sense. He combined courage, integrity, human understanding, cheerfulness, sense of humor, and total lack of self-pity. Intellectually he had little in common with his writer sons. Yet he was proud of us and we of him.

From childhood I had had a recurring dream in which he was dying. Now watching him go in the bleak Florida hospital, I had an experience which I felt compelled to jot down even as it occurred.

Nothing was moving on the bed except a pair of old hands. They wandered over his face, from cheek to throat and back to nose, hesitantly feeling out the murderous intruder's advance. Occasionally, the distorted mouth beneath the straight nose and high fine brow twitched with something closer to horror than to pain.

He showed no sign of yielding, but my Father's agony was almost more than I could bear. Anything but this creeping decomposition!

Suddenly I had to look around. There was no one else in the bare sanitary room. Yet in a corner I half-saw a tall impressive figure seated writing at a half-seen desk. I did not need to be introduced.

"Have you come for him?"

"You know I have. Why do you ask." Said firmly but not unkindly.

"Take him—take him now!"

"All in good time."

"No, now! How can you let horror like this go on?"

"I have my reasons—which are his."

"Reasons? How much longer must he strain to break away?"

"Only so long as he himself decides."

"He?"

"Who else?"

"Yet he is trying to live. See the vitality in that old face, how the steely eyes flash when he makes the effort to—to emerge from his pain. Why let this go on?"

"I do not let it go on . . . the decision is not with me. I told you, he decides."

"You mean he wants this? Well, it does not look like a free decision—that thing entering his mouth, seizing him, growing, swelling, strangling him," I choked.

The figure waited a moment before answering. "You," it said slowly, "see only the Outside Man, the one that will be left behind. These things are decided by the Inside Man. Strange as it appears, this Inside Man would not forego a single instant of this in spite of the agony."

"Impossible. No man could choose to die like this. There are a thousand ways—and this is one of the worst. Down here where he has been living, life is easy. The sun shines and the earth is green and gold. That is why he loved it here. How could he have turned from this and 'chosen,' as you say, to succumb to the intruder. His body was still hale. Left alone, he could well have lived ten years more and on a sunny afternoon, have slept himself away. He was at bottom a gentle, kindly man. Not a child or a dog but loved him. Why could he not die peacefully . . . if his was the choice?"

"You ask what I cannot answer," the figure answered softly. "Perhaps because he loved too much—you, your brother, his grandchildren, his old cronies, smiling faces, and sunshine and nature. Love is a chain. See how great must be the strain of detachment—how he pits his sinkink vitality against—me! You see him in this final misery—he can barely speak, eat, or breathe. Yet still his hands return with horror to those lumps whose hated growth is his release. Already, even you, for whom he has waited these last weeks, are just a dim loving presence to him, nothing more. When he finally gives up and accepts, that will be the end—or the beginning."

"Yet he has been trying to die, calling you with all his strength. . . ."

"That is why I am here. Now the Inner Man is seeking to go. Only what is nature in him still fights to live."

"Nonetheless," I protested, "ten years from now he would have accepted you not as half enemy but as whole friend. Then the parting would have been easy. Why must you take him now?"

"I do not know," Death answered. "Only he knows—and you."

"I? But I do not know."

"Why then all your life long have you so feared—this? Why did the little boy of four linger so anxiously at the end of the brick walk, quietly sobbing for fear Daddy might not come home? Why, after not thinking of him for weeks, have you repeatedly dreamed of his death and wakened sobbing? Must one not say, you felt his death and were rehearsing yourself to bear it—hard as it was?"

I was silent. Death returned to his shadowy writing.

Finally I spoke again. "Will it be long now? Tell me."

"I think not. He is calling me more loudly. Can't you hear him?"

Nothing. The old man's hand was slowly wandering over his ruined face.

"I must leave this place soon. Shall I see him again?" I whispered.

"If you like."

"When?"

"You know that too. And when the time comes, I shall be there to help."

Then, for the first time, my Father groaned.

We buried him three days later.

Returning from St. Petersburg, I became a Deputy Director under

Archibald MacLeish at the United States Office of Facts and Figures (OFF).

Archie was a handsome man, a good poet, and an inspiring librarian. I particularly relished his *Hamlet Of A. MacLeish*. As a propagandist, he found his task complicated from the beginning. For as a war measure, F.D.R. turned over to military leaders political and informational decisions to an extent that must have amazed Hitler, Mussolini, and Stalin.

As a result none except the military on the inevitable Committee for War Information Policy ever seemed to know precisely what our organization was supposed to do.

Least of all, Director MacLeish, his Deputy Directors, and the assorted cluster of miscellaneous mavericks who met with Archie each day to discuss current problems.

Archie was brilliant. So were most of his subordinates—too brilliant, regular bureaucrats in other Departments complained. Each of us had opinions of his own and was disposed to defend them heatedly. Here was the Speaker of the Massachusetts State Legislature (Chris Herter); two brilliant law professors from Yale; a number of newsmen and ex-newsmen; successful writers, both male and female; at least two reputed magazine editors; one pollster and two professional bureaucrats from, of all places, the Department of Agriculture.

Among us we discussed almost anything. Yet except for the few to whom Archie assigned specific tasks, our main jobs were fighting hangover isolationism, preserving the national morale, and selling war bonds.

I found it hard to promote the sale of war bonds because I believed that, so far as possible, Americans should pay for the struggle out of current income. Or at least, that since so many millions of Americans were serving in uniform to the detriment of their previous incomes, the President should rigidly stabilize not only prices (so far as possible) but wages and profits as well. Nor was it proper to argue—as we did—that, in purchasing a war bond, a citizen was not only helping to save his country and human freedom, but *making a sound financial investment*. Wartime investments should profit nobody. A people at war should accept equality of sacrifice. This view clashed with the President's scheme of bribing both labor and business to do what he should, if necessary, have compelled them to do.

My field was foreign politics. At Archie's request I occasionally delivered a lecture. On foreign policy my associates were, for the most part, of little help. All but Chris Herter and myself were in various degrees New Dealers. Until Hitler broke loose, their interest had been chiefly domestic. Two or three were admirers of the Soviet Union, now our noble ally.

For information I gravitated to certain State Department officials and to foreigners. The British were particularly qualified: David Bowes

Lyon, brother to the Queen; Harold Butler; Bill Ormerod; Isaiah Berlin; John Foster; Admiral Parsons; and some others. With Minister Casey of Australia, with Adrien Tixier, de Gaulle's testy but dauntless Washington representative, and with Robert Valeur, head of the General's information office, I often exchanged views.

My first explicit job was that of liaison officer to the State Department. This included a daily talk with Hull or, more frequently, with Sumner Welles.

Generally such visits were routine, but one morning the tall, usually imperturbable Under Secretary of State frowned and handed me a sheet of paper. "Read this, Edgar."

When I did, I gasped. Here, taken from a secret protocol to a proposed Anglo-Russian treaty of alliance, were Soviet territorial demands going beyond what the U.S.S.R. as Germany's jackal had seized in 1939: Poland as far west as the Curzon line of 1919; the three little Baltic states, half of East Prussia. It was dismaying that the British government could consider countenancing such insolence.

Handing the paper back, I said ironically: "Magnificent! Just let it become officially known that the United States, or Britain, for that matter, has consented to any such Soviet grab and the majority of Americans will agree with those America-Firsters who insist we are fighting on the wrong side."

Sumner nodded. "Stalin has signed the Atlantic Charter promising each people the form of government it wants as well as an agreement with Poland recognizing that territorial changes in Poland made in accordance with the Stalin-Hitler Act of 1939 were no longer valid. Yet here he is demanding almost as much by going back to the Curzon Line of 1919. The President must not accept any such grab."

To me Soviet territorial claims were ridiculous. In 1938 I had tried in vain to persuade the Bolsheviks whom I knew to support Czechoslovakia physically. A year later Stalin had triggered World War II by his agreement with Hitler. When the Germans turned upon him in 1941, the Georgian got only what he deserved. As an American who considered Nazi Germany a greater menace than the U.S.S.R. I was all for giving aid to the latter—to the extent to which Stalin played ball with us.

Nor did I fear that the monster in the Kremlin could wangle a separate peace from the Nazis. He had changed sides twice since 1938. But I knew Hitler well enough to feel sure that so long as he had the remotest chance of appropriating the Soviet Ukraine by force, he would never offer an acceptable separate peace to Joe Stalin. Those Americans who felt that we had to handle the Kremlin with kid gloves were misinformed.

Roosevelt characteristically got out of the difficulty by inducing the British and the Russians to omit any mention of territorial settlements in their treaty. And we in OFF breathed easier. We did not know that the President had already told Ambassador Litvinov that while it was too dangerous to put anything on paper, the United States would, after the war, support Russia's efforts to achieve "legitimate security."

Once or twice, MacLeish sent me to confer with the Coordinator of Latin American Affairs. Nelson Rockefeller had surrounded himself with a corps of skilled advisers and assistants, thanks to whose support he went on, like MacLeish, to become an Assistant Secretary of State.

Two other contemporary conversations remain vivid in my memory. At the Polish Embassy, early in the spring, Jack McCloy blithely announced the Administration's decision to remove from their West Coast homes and intern U.S. citizens of Japanese origin, whether born or naturalized. For who could be sure they would be loyal to America?

Some of those present concurred. In time of war. . . .

I dissented sharply. *Nisei* were as full-fledged citizens as any other group. We had not shanghaied the German-Americans in the previous war nor were we about to do so now, in spite of the anti-American activities of the *Bund*. Discrimination against *Nisei* was contrary to the American spirit. The Supreme Court would strike it down.

"After the war is over," Jack answered complacently.

"Take care, Mr. Secretary," I warned ironically. "If you do that to Japanese-Americans today, somebody else may do the same thing to Irish-Americans next time."

Our host intervened, and we both laughed. Yet in my judgment, this act, and the Supreme Court's supine affirmation of its constitutionality in 1943, constitute a blot on the American record. Years later I was gratified to learn how the Nisei 442nd Regimental Combat Team had avenged their relatives' persecution by becoming the most decorated fighting unit in American history.

On another occasion, the Secretary of the Navy, in answer to T. V. Soong's sad conjecture that without more American help, China would succumb to Japan, cheerfully answered: "Don't worry, Mr. Soong; we'll beat those *yellow* bastards yet!"

"How long," I wondered, "will it take us Americans to overcome our unconscious condescension to foreigners?"

In 1941 Marthe Rajchman, had published in cooperation with *Asia Magazine* a *New War Atlas of China*. Now she proposed that we collaborate in producing *Global War: An Atlas of World Strategy*. Once I found that Thayer Hobson of Morrow would gladly publish such a book, I accepted. I had studied maps from the age of seven, traveled over a great deal of the earth, and seen something of four wars. Marthe, a Geneva-and-Paris-trained geographer and cartographer, did some fifty maps and charts while I wrote the text. Our aim was to illustrate in geostrategical terms some of the more obvious possibilities of the world conflict. The Secretary of the Navy, who contributed a preface, called it "an ambitious undertaking." But we dedicated the book to "the uncounted other amateur strategists of the United Nations."

Some of the descriptions were prophetic. For instance, I defined

Russia as "part of the great central European plain whose inhabitants have never been willing to stay at home."

The Indian Ocean, Sindbad the Sailor's playground, was strategically interesting as a "center from which to go places," for instance, into Burma and Southwest China.

Italy, I assured readers, as the world was soon to learn again, was "almost as badly placed for defense as for expansion."

Having cleared the Mediterranean of enemy forces, the United Nations could, I indicated, "invade Axis-dominated Europe on its *soft* southern side," an adjective which Winston Churchill was to echo. Yet I slipped, in predicting that the likeliest place for the Allied invasion of France was the southern part of Brittany.

Marthe's simple but highly illuminating maps enabled a reader to follow my whimsical but precise texts without much effort. On Knox's instructions, I sent a copy to every member of the American Cabinet. One or two military training schools used *Global War* as a text in military geography and a few readers wrote to express interest. Almost all the many reviews were laudatory and for several weeks it was among "best sellers." I had expected that, if only because of the preface by the Secretary of the Navy, the Office of Facts and Figures would distribute it officially. Vain hope.

In June, Roosevelt finally merged four information offices, including our OFF, into a single something called the Office of War Information (OWI) under a new director, the writer and broadcaster, Elmer Davis. MacLeish and Sherwood remained, each in charge of his respective territory.

About a month later Sherwood asked Archie to transfer me to the Overseas Branch. I welcomed the shift. Yet before leaving OFF, at MacLeish's request, I submitted a critique of our work to date: fair as to encouraging domestic morale; handicapped by the cacophony of government voices; utterly inadequate on war information owing to interference by the armed services.

At dinner in our Georgetown house, Sherwood, a giant man with a perpetually funereal expression, explained what he wanted from me: to act as critic of programs for foreign countries.

To me Bob remained an enigma. He spoke of the President in the tone of a pious Roman prelate referring to the Holy Father. Next to F.D.R., he admired Harry Hopkins the most. Though a successful playwright and favorite presidential speech writer, he always seemed to be wondering just how he happened to be dealing with those foreign peoples of whom he knew so little. I myself never ceased wondering.

Elmer Davis was a man of my own sort. In addition to brains and literary ability he had real knowledge of Western Europe. Yet he too was bedevilled by the need to correlate OWI's line with that of the Pentagon. Administration he left to Milton Eisenhower, brother of the general whom the President had chosen to command the coming campaign in North Africa.

Sherwood's deputy director was none other than James F. Warburg, the same one whom I had first met at the Arnholts' in Berlin, and seen occasionally during the past six months when he had served as liaison with the British, whose advice the Overseas Branch followed in most matters. A Britisher sat in on our top-level meetings in New York.

Joseph Barnes, a deputy director like me, had worked in the Far East and Russia for the Institute of Pacific Relations and the New York *Herald Tribune* and then, at the age of thirty-three, had become that newspaper's foreign news editor. Joe had energy, charm, and a pronounced gift of self-salesmanship.

Yet in our New York office the executive with the broadest knowledge and experience of the world was the former Associated Press correspondent and editor, Edward "Tuck" Stanley, now in charge of OWI publications. After the first meeting we were not only friends, but allies.

Sherwood entrusted me first with reviewing the broadcasts by our East Coast senders to Europe, the Middle East, and Africa. What I read did not please me. To begin with, we aimed the same broadcasts at friends, neutrals, and enemies alike. This was being done over the objection of several of our foreign or foreign-born speakers, who recognized the necessity of appealing to each target people in its own terms. A young Arab complained, for instance, that among his anti-Semitic countrymen, each account of Nazi atrocity against Jews increased Hitler's popularity!

We agreed that whenever timely, subsequent broadcasts to Arab countries would emphasize some weakness of the Nazi leaders: Hitler's sexual deficiency, Goering's addiction to drugs, the infidelity of Goebbels' wife, and so on. Whether or not OWI followed this plan I never knew. For that depended upon Warburg and Barnes, neither of whom liked criticism.

Next Sherwood sent me to the West Coast as interim director of overseas operations for the Pacific area. I found our broadcasts naïve. The broadcasters knew their business—domestically. Therefore they sought to attract Asian listeners by "entertainment." This might be effective with neutrals or with Japanese enemies. But I could not imagine Filipinos or Dutchmen under Japanese occupation risking their freedom or even their lives to listen to American jazz, or expect our hard-pressed Chinese friends, impatiently waiting for news of more U.S. assistance, to waste time on American "shows."

I ordered more straight news, chosen for each target people separately. Yet a few weeks later, I learned in Washington that after my departure the now acting director had put things back as they were. My effort had been wasted.

A third disappointment came shortly thereafter. Wendell Willkie, F.D.R.'s defeated Republican rival, with the President's blessing, was going on a worldwide, goodwill tour and wanted a member of our staff to accompany him.

After considering me, Sherwood picked instead Joe Barnes and

Gardner Cowles, the Iowa editor, to look after the famous man. Sherwood's failure to include me in our plans for the invasion of North Africa (about which Donovan had asked my political opinion months before) was also mortifying. And yet I guessed the reason.

Since September, 1940, I had made no attempt to hide my disapproval of Roosevelt's Vichy gamble. My first job for MacLeish had been asking Secretary Hull what he intended to do about the French Gaullists' seizure of tiny Saint Pierre and Miquelon Islands off the coast of Newfoundland. In a public denunciation, the Secretary had referred to this act by "three so-called Free French ships" as "aggression comparable to Hitler!" A dissenting editorial writer in a New York newspaper had replied by referring to "our so-called State Department," a jibe which infuriated Hull.

To me, the Secretary first invoked the legal arguments against the upstart French brigadier. Roosevelt had steadily assured Pétain that the United States wished only to maintain the *status quo* in North Africa and the West Indies. A year before, the American countries had agreed for the second time to prevent any change in sovereignty in the Western Hemisphere. But how, I wondered, could anyone call a transfer of French territory from German-dominated Pétain to independent de Gaulle a change in sovereignty?

"So what shall I tell MacLeish the Department intends to do, sir?"

"Tell him if that French so-and-so does not voluntarily withdraw from these islands, I shall ask our Navy to throw him out."

Absurd! Forgetting my inconspicuous position in the government, I blurted out, "But you can't mean that, Mr. Secretary; the Gaullists are fighting on our side."

Hull gave me an angry look and dismissed me.

Unfortunately, his was the viewpoint of the President, even though the latter did nothing to oust the Gaullists. F.D.R. believed that "Pétain had a unique position in the hearts of the French people."

I did not question Roosevelt's or Bullitt's low opinion of those prewar Republican "gravediggers of France." But I had, I felt, nothing to learn from either man concerning the French people, among whom I had spent nearly a year as student, another year as "man of letters," and seven and a half years as foreign correspondent. Even though millions of French had, *faute de mieux,* turned to the eighty-four-year-old victor of Verdun for respite from defeat, a majority, I felt sure, would have preferred the creation of a French government in exile like those of the Norwegians, Danes, Dutch, and Belgians. Sooner or later, every decent man or woman in France would rally to de Gaulle and his *Fighting French,* if only because they impersonated the spirit of France at its most unconquerable. If Hitler won, then France, Pétain or not, would become a German *Gau.* As far back as December, Pétain had admitted to Ambassador Leahy, "I am a prisoner." Leahy had thereupon recommended a change in our policy toward Vichy.

But F.D.R. had decided to write France off until, after liberation by us, he could graciously restore independence to the French people. Meanwhile, as William Langer later explained, "Since we were at war, expediency was paramount." If our aims of an unopposed landing and of saving the French fleet in North Africa required dealing with Murphy's friend, General Weygand, or even with a fascist like Admiral Darlan, what was the harm? Although British intelligence reported that common people in North Africa favored de Gaulle, Murphy knew better. Anti-Gaullists in Washington strengthened the President's view that "war had put a moratorium on politics."

When, in April, 1942, Sumner Welles, at my request, received the Gaullist emissary, Emmanuel D'Astier de la Vigerie, the Under Secretary brushed him off with the statement that the Free French were "rapidly falling to pieces." Completely ignoring that at Bir Hacheim, Gaullists under General Koenig had turned the tide of battle.

Washington had omitted France from the newly formed United Nations, yet invited Vichy's ambassador to the 1942 Memorial Day Celebration, ignoring de Gaulle's permanent representative. Even after the United States started giving lend-lease aid to the Free French directly, it refused to follow Britain, the Soviet Union, and no less than six governments in exile in recognizing de Gaulle's French National Committee.

Our successful landing in North Africa, in spite of unnecessary casualties, further hardened the President's opposition to de Gaulle. For few leaders were ever more unlike. F.D.R. personalized the most abstract issues. De Gaulle, though equally emotional and devious, intellectualized his every feeling. Each misjudged the other.

Eight months earlier, a significant scrawl had appeared on Paris walls:

"*Pétain au dodo, Darlan au poteau, de Gaulle au boulot.*" (Pétain to sleep, Darlan to the stake, de Gaulle to the job.)

Happy as all Americans were over our success in North Africa, millions demurred when they learned that Bob Murphy had persuaded the President not only to exclude the Free French from participation in the liberation but to rely upon a disreputable collection of French fascists, opponents of Britain, and *synarchistes* interested only in saving their own wealth, all under the command of a decent but colorless French general called Giraud. It was no accident that Admiral Darlan, informed of the coming American landing by Murphy's friend, Pierre Pucheu, had hurried to Algiers and sparked the French resistance that cost many American lives before reversing himself and persuading his friends to lay down their arms while he ran things for the Americans. One could forgive Pétain, a "great man who died in 1925," as de Gaulle called him. But Darlan had been, with Laval, the most ardent of collaborators with the Germans.

The Administration's acceptance of him aroused the deep indignation of the British and of millions of Americans as well. To quiet them, F.D.R. hastened to explain that the deal with the treacherous French admiral was only a "temporary expedient."

Fate, however, played a trick on the President. On Christmas Day, lunching at the Fields', we heard of Darlan's assassination. The old French spirit was not dead! In an instant Lilian sprang to the piano and started playing the *Marseillaise*. We stood up and sang lustily.

About a month before, Ed Stanley had asked me to draw up a plan for the "confidential" distribution of our written material to some fifteen foreign countries, both friends and enemies. I was to plan and supervise these very diverse programs with a small suborganization of my own. This was something that Britain and the Soviet Union were already doing. Accordingly I wrote a memorandum for Davis and Sherwood arguing that such "confidential operations" would be the most effective means of heartening our friends and dismaying our enemies. Davis, who shared my misgivings about our Vichy policy, approved promptly but deferred to Sherwood.

While the latter hesitated, Warburg countered by offering to make me permanent director of the Oversas Branch in San Francisco. This would have got me out of New York and Washington and removed me from contact with Western Europe, which he and Barnes considered their private preserve. Naturally, I refused (the job went to Owen Lattimore, Joe's former colleague in the Institute of Pacific Relations).

Just after New Year's Day, 1943, Elmer Davis received a letter from Ed Stettinius, Foreign Economic Administrator, asking the former to let him send me for a few weeks to North Africa and report back on the need for civilian supplies under lend-lease. Davis urged me to accept.

This was a dish to my taste. Early in January, 1943, I completed the arrangements, started taking the prescribed injections, and bought appropriate clothes and medicines. Elmer requested the State Department to furnish me with the necessary papers.

Here was Secretary Hull's chance. The State and War Departments were sending to Algeria as governor the notorious Marcel Peyrouton, hated former head of the Vichy police. Eisenhower was faithfully following the Murphy policy. In Morocco, General Patton was fraternizing with General Noguès, the same man who had arrested Georges Mandel and fired on the American landing forces.

I was the last person Hull wanted to visit North Africa and report on the economic result of our policy.

Jack McCloy, perhaps remembering my jibe at his internment of the Nisei, convinced Stimson that I was "too emotional." Somebody circulated a story that in speaking to Hungarian Americans some time back in Chicago, I had recommended a postwar revival of the "pinkish" Karolyi government in Hungary. (This was a myth, but why, if true, it should have disturbed an American Administration prepared to back Stalin's claims to East Europe escaped me.)

The incident was more disturbing to Davis than to me. It was a concrete instance of a State-Army policy of withholding vital information from OWI representatives both at home and overseas; of allowing them to travel only with the consent of the two Departments; of permitting local military commanders to exclude OWI representatives from "their" territory without explanation, and of accepting or refusing to distribute our propaganda leaflets; and finally, of keeping "psychological warfare" strictly under military control.

To prevent my going, since their "jurisdiction" over Davis was merely assumed, Hull and Stimson adopted characteristic bureaucratic tactics. First State "lost" my application for a passport. Then I heard that the Department was "making difficulties." Next both suggested to Davis that my visit be "temporarily" held in abeyance. Hull put the responsibility on Stimson, Stimson on Hull. Then somebody persuaded Stettinius "not to press the matter." Finally McCloy insisted that everybody await the President's return from Casablanca and let him decide the question of basic jurisdiction.

Elmer reacted superbly. He stood on his right to send his employee wherever necessary to gain information. He assured both Secretaries that I was not going to North Africa to "agitate against a policy." As a U.S. official, Mowrer would, Elmer wrote, conform or resign. To imply otherwise "is a slur on his honesty and patriotism and upon the honesty of the direction of this office." (To me, Elmer hinted that he too might resign.) Hull and Stimson quickly repudiated any slur upon anyone's honor, but still thought that my visit should wait until the conclusion of the current policy conference at Casablanca.

Elmer urged me to be patient. But I had had enough. After two more inconclusive talks with McCloy, I asked Elmer to tell Stettinius that I would no longer accept the mission for him, and sent my boss a courteous but real ultimatum: either put me in charge of an organization for "secret operations overseas" or let me get out. When Elmer replied that he could not take an immediate decision I sent him an official resignation, effective two weeks later. Still Elmer demurred. Warburg was preempting "confidential operations" for himself. But Elmer added: "I would add some remarks about appreciation of what you have done for us except that I know you feel you haven't had a chance to do anything. Nevertheless, your contribution looks fairly sizable to me and I am grateful."

And he played his trump card: would I not take charge of propaganda to the Soviet Union—with no outside interference?

It was a tempting offer. Unfortunately, recent remarks by Harry Hopkins seemed to indicate that the President intended to ignore Stalin's monstrous territorial demands, and continue to treat him as a trustworthy ally. How could I in good conscience defend such a policy? Reluctantly I shook my head.

During the next few days I wrote for Elmer an appraisal of our agency's work to date, dictated a chronicle of the circumstances of my departure which Elmer initialed, and with the help of my secretary, Florence Sugar, packed up my personal papers.

Yet the comedy continued. Drew Pearson published the incident, contrasting Secretary Hull's treatment of me, "a fervid interventionist," with that of Marcel Peyrouton, who had arrested Gaullists and jailed Jews. The following day at his press conference, Hull ducked the question why he objected to my going to North Africa, but added that he had known Mr. Mowrer well for years and admired him very much! Before the date of my departure from OWI, permission to go to North Africa arrived.

What did they take me for? The sooner I left government service, the better for everybody, especially for Elmer Davis.

As bureaucrat I had failed, and through my own fault. Why had I not held my tongue in the presence of my betters? War was no time for indulging personal feelings. Ptah Hotep, Lord Chesterfield and Castiglione, whose books I had read, should have taught me how to flatter people like the Secretary of State. If unwilling to do so, then why, of the five jobs offered me after Pearl Harbor, had I accepted the one for which I was least ready?

On the other hand, what a relief to be out of the bureaucratic jungle! Driving home to Georgetown with my personal papers, I thought of my wife's remark that during the previous year I had been too taciturn to live with. Well, no more gloom. Surely, I could find some way to help in the great struggle that would leave me free to speak my mind.

31

The Flawed Victory

We can do business with Stalin.
                    —HARRY HOPKINS

*Alice laughed. 'There's no use trying,' she said.
'One can't believe impossible things.'
'I dare say you haven't had much practice,'
said the Queen.*
                    —LEWIS CARROLL

APRIL 1, 1943, was a banner day: I became a syndicated columnist on world affairs. As such I was again free to speak my mind. When later, my friend Charles Hewitt of the Tonawanda *Times* complained that whereas in Europe I had "written like an American," in America I was "writing like a European," I considered it a compliment. Nonetheless, in the ensuing years, I twice got high marks in "readability" from self-styled analysts in the United States.

Before April, I had had six weeks of joblessness. When I resigned from OWI, I had assumed that Frank Knox would welcome me back to the *News'* staff, either in Washington or overseas. But the Colonel had deferred to his Cabinet colleagues, Hull and Stimson, and flatly refused me a position on the staff of the newspaper which I had, in my small way, helped to make famous.

Helen Reid of the New York *Herald Tribune*, with whom I often exchanged political expressions, thought I would "cost too much." The Chicago *Sun* no longer needed a foreign editor. *Time* suggested I head its London office, but I did not welcome the anonymity of the Luce publications. A.B.C. had no vacancies.

Rescue had come unexpectedly. Upon hearing of my resignation, Louis Bromfield wired me an urgent invitation to lecture before the Franco American Club in New York. Here was an opportunity to emphasize the inadequacy of Roosevelt's French policy. To a dinner crowd that included most of my French friends, I argued that an American policy of non-recognition of Vichy would have opened North Africa to a bloodless Anglo-American landing. There would have been no

341

"execution" of French warships by the British, no fratricidal killing of French by French at Dakar, no French warships rotting away in stale neutrality in Egypt and in Martinique, no harbor of Toulon littered with the hulks of sunken French vessels. "We cannot," I concluded, "honorably contrive at keeping in power any authoritarian regime that has opposed us. . . . For that will not hinder but promote the spread of bolshevism."

The moment was propitious. Publications, from *Time* to the *Daily Worker,* carried long reports. *PM* published nearly two full pages of text.

Commendatory telegrams and letters poured in from unknowns as well as from old friends, like Gaetano Salvemini. On the strength of what I said, Democratic U.S. Representative John M. Coffee demanded that the State Department furnish him a list of other patriotic Americans to whom, as to Edgar Ansel Mowrer, it was denying the right to travel. Republican Congressman George Bender urged Secretary Hull to recall Ambassadors Murphy, Hayes, and Standley, respectively, from North Africa, Spain, and the Soviet Union.

And Ted Thackrey of the New York *Post* offered me a job as commentator on world affairs.

News comment can contribute little to winning a war, but it may, with luck, help win a peace.

Roosevelt had brushed aside the advice of those diplomats who most understood what the war was about—Bullitt, Joe Grew, Loy Henderson—in favor of palace favorites, generals, admirals, and those few diplomats who agreed with him and with Harry Hopkins.

Churchill's judgment was sounder. Concerning the U.S.S.R. he had always been right. The predominant problem of peace-keeping was, how thwart a Great Power bent on expansion, as the Soviets seemed to be?

Convincing the American people of this truism was the task to which I set myself. My first column in the *Post* argued that unless the Big Four (including China) managed to reach agreement on essential points, we might still lose the war and the peace. Yet "never were four partners less prepared to dance a common quadrille."

Response from readers was immediate and heartening.

Bernard Baruch sent warm congratulations. My admired Italian friend, Count Carlo Sforza, now a leader of the exiled Italian Action Party, gleefully sent me a clipping from the Italian Communist Party newspaper in Paris accusing me of having "more hair than brains." Shortly thereafter the German newspaper, *Pariser Zeitung,* attacked Elmer Davis and OWI for appointing as his "deputy" (sic) a "notorious Communist leader, Ansel Mowrer." Wendell Willkie, with whom I had become intimate, promised to back my views during some "straight out talking" to the State Department. In October, 1943, *Publishers' Weekly* gave a couple of pages to a description of the three writing Mowrers— Paul, Edgar, and Richard.

Lecture offers poured in from various groups, and in fulfilling them, the exile of twenty-six years became familiar with most parts of his own country and friends with Natalie Wales Payne, later Lady Hamilton, whose Common Cause and Bundles for Britain had roused latent sympathy for that country.

Thayer Hobson of the William Morrow Company was begging me to write a book on foreign policy in answer to *Foreign Policy: Shield of the Republic.* "I just don't like the idea," he wrote, "of the American public exposed to Walter Lippmann for very long without some good strong cathartic to ease the cramps. . . . What would tempt you? Gold? A brass band to play to you in your leisure moments? Fair women to amuse you when Lilian is bored with you? Some nice Rhode Island Red pullets that will begin to lay in September?"

As a beginning columnist I simply lacked the time.

To Lilian's and my deep satisfaction, my temporary conspicuousness enabled me to help still other European refugees. For some I got jobs, for others, American visas or visa extensions. I did what I could for Poles like Ordynski, Lechon, and Karski (the last, a man of incredible courage who had traveled regularly between London and occupied Poland). I was able to aid Count Sforza, my Moscow friend Basseches, Marcel Ray, Kurt Loewenthal, Ernst Erich Noth, Eric and Elli Marcus, Philippe Soupault, Henry Bernstein, and through Senator Elbert Thomas of Utah, Luis Araquistain, the Spanish Republican. In 1942 I had tried in vain to get Herriot released from a Vichy prison.

Thanks to a careful hoarding of strictly rationed gasoline, Lilian and I were able to drive to the Food Conference at Hot Springs, Virginia, in her diminutive Crosley. As news, that conference offered little. Chiefly I remember the Administration's unsuccessful effort to keep the delegates physically segregated from the press. But the mountain surroundings were restorative and we drove back to Washington almost as lighthearted as from a vacation.

The Quadrant top-level Conference in Quebec in August, 1943, was full of news—when one could get it. Entrance to the counsel chambers of the Great within the Château Frontenac Hotel was all but impossible for newsmen. Luckily for me, Churchill's secretary, Brendon Bracken, regularly described to me some of the goings-on, while we walked up and down the superb promenade overlooking the mighty St. Lawrence.

Not that I much liked what I heard. The conferees agreed on a four-power declaration to set up an international organization based on the "sovereign equality of all peace-loving states." But the Big Two also made hair-raising decisions: dropping loyal Mihajlovic in favor of communist Tito in Yugoslavia and accepting in principle Stalin's territorial demands in Europe. At Quebec, though I did not know it, Roosevelt had said to Cardinal Spellman:

"The world will be divided into spheres of influence: China gets the Far East; the U.S., the Pacific; Britain and Russia, Europe and Africa. But as Britain has predominantly colonial interests, it might be presumed that Russia will predominate in Europe. . . ." Roosevelt "hoped that, 'although it might be wishful thinking,' Russian intervention in Europe would not be too harsh." (See the Cardinal's statement in the New York *Herald Tribune,* March 16, 1962.)

The Atlantic City Conference which saw the foundation of the United Nations Relief and Rehabilitation Administration (UNRRA), provided a few restful days.

Most of my energy went into columns where I hammered above all at a peace that would stand—unlike the last.

Americans differed sharply on how this could be brought about.

I could only gasp when, in April, 1943, Forrest Davis expressed Roosevelt's opinion: this was "a war of countries, classes, and color." Well, every modern war was one of countries. Germans seeking to create the Third Reich of four hundred millions, in accordance with the "geopolitical" theories of Haushofer, were our enemies, whether or not they approved of the "Bohemian corporal," of his gutter ideology, or of his crimes. But classes played absolutely no part in this one nor, except in Japanese propaganda, did color. World War II was a clash of individual freedom with totalitarian fascism, originally supported by totalitarian communism. Unless our victory eliminated or crippled fascism, it would not bring peace.

The Germans were a great people gone wrong. Much as I admired those individuals, both civil and military, who had always repudiated Hitler, I had no faith in those who turned against him only as it became clear that he could not win.

Roosevelt continued to subordinate "French domestic politics" (whether France should be fascist, communist, or free!) to military considerations. To be sure, Admiral "Betty" Stark in London began helping de Gaulle to create a secret army in France. But the President discussed replacement of French officials and changes in French law in Africa as if these were matters for Americans to decide and was planning to encourage extensive reductions in the French Empire, including the amputation of Dakar! In the same spirit, the President contemplated separating Walloons from Flemings in Belgium and Croats from Serbs in Yugoslavia, and was urging Churchill to give up Hong Kong "as a gesture of good will." Secretary Knox urged me to condemn those French sailors who, in American ports, "jumped" from Vichy ships to Gaullist vessels.

Once de Gaulle became top man in Algiers, it was clear that F.D.R. had lost that battle. The French general played his still unimpressive cards with superb skill. An irritated State Department began referring to us who criticized its policy toward him as "typewriter statesmen."

Nor did the Administration show more political principle in Italy. Mussolini, by his attack on France in 1940, had forfeited any claim to indulgence. Yet the man ultimately responsible for Mussolini's usurpation was King Victor Emanuel. Had His Majesty, in October, 1922, given the order, Italian *Bersaglieri* would have suppressed the march on Rome.

Instead, the little king chose Mussolini as Premier. This, decent Italians would never forgive, as I knew from Count Sforza.

Winston, however, supported by American politicians with an eye to votes at home, wanted Italy to change sides with as little disturbance as possible, to remain a monarchy, and to remain under the Allied Control Commission as long as possible.

Even today I accept Count Sforza's dictum that "Churchill's 'blind and stubborn' adherence to the notion of supporting the king and his weak Badoglio Government were playing into Russian hands."

In March, 1944, the *S.S. Queen Mary* put out from Brooklyn for "somewhere in Europe" with fifteen thousand American soldiers and: "Item—War Correspondents 2," of which I was one.

The giant liner, though stripped of all nonessentials, was so overloaded that when the G.I.'s lounging on the various decks rushed to port to see the Statue of Liberty, it listed ten degrees. Soldiers slept literally everywhere, even on the lounge steps. "War correspondents 2" were lucky enough to get cots in a converted (windowless) bathroom and, being "assimilated" to the rank of captain, to eat in the Junior Officers' Mess.

The ship's course remained secret. But the North Star and a map indicated that it was proceeding toward the Azores. Thence it steamed almost due north to a point near Iceland, and finally eastward to Scotland. Twice we had submarine alerts which lasted until protecting planes (we had no visible naval escort) appeared from nowhere, when everybody relaxed.

At dingy Glasgow, soldiers and correspondents herded into a crowded train and, after an endless night, found themselves dumped in a remote suburb.

The manager at the Hyde Park Hotel in Knightsbridge insisted no rooms were vacant. Finally, however, he gave to an "old client" a front bedroom on the *empty* top floor: London was undergoing the "little Blitz." (The German V-1's came a little later.)

What a satisfaction for an old war correspondent to be back in a war area! To news colleagues like Bill Stoneman, Helen Kirkpatrick, and Ed Murrow and to my British, Dutch, Belgian, Spanish, French, Yugoslav, Czechoslovak, Polish, and anti-Nazi German friends, only one thing counted: the coming invasion of France. Nothing would have thrilled me more than to be among the first Americans to land on French soil. But my purpose was to estimate the chances of a sound political peace, about which I was increasingly doubtful because of Russia.

Sir Archibald Clarke Kerr, whom I had known as British Ambassador in Chungking, was, as I wired (everything went by cable or radio), still "piping for Stalin." Ambassador Wynant's Russophilia alarmed me. From George Kennan I learned that the United States was offering about two-fifths of Germany to Soviet occupation, in full confidence that the Russians would reach the Rhine before American and British invaders could do so. This would leave the U.S.S.R. the master of Europe!

President-in-exile Eduard Benes went even further. Embittered by the Munich sellout of his country, he had in Washington encouraged

F.D.R.'s confidence in Stalin, thence gone to Moscow, and, inspired by the renegade Fierlinger, thrown his country irrevocably upon Stalin's mercy. After the war, as he now explained to me during a two-hour talk in the Czechoslovak Embassy in Belgravia, Czechoslovakia would seek protection against Germany chiefly from the Soviet Union. My polite reminder that Stalin had in 1939 betrayed civilization to Hitler, he brushed aside almost angrily. Had not France and Britain betrayed Czechoslovakia at Munich in 1938?

Canny Bob Vansittart (at whose Denham house near London I had dinner) shrewdly predicted that Stalin's future behavior would depend entirely "upon the amount of naked military power revealed by the American and British armies in the coming invasion of Europe—and how far eastward they go." De Gaulle's representative in Britain, Pierre Viénot, and Poland's Foreign Minister, Raczynski, deplored America's failure to use Stalin's need for our assistance to secure a peace without annexations. At dinner one night, Pierre revealed that some months previously, four leading German generals, von Rundstedt, von Mannstein, von Bock, and von Brauschits, had sent an emissary to the British at Lisbon, to offer a separate peace.

Toward midnight, as he was walking with me to Sloan Square, we heard an air-raid alert. While he hurried home, I ducked into the tube station. Emerging at Knightsbridge I heard the fearful din of the antiaircraft guns stationed behind the hotel in Hyde Park, interrupted occasionally by exploding bombs. Hastening to my top floor room, I opened the shutters. Flames were rising luridly against the skyline in no less than five places.

Four days later (mostly spent waiting at New Quai, in Cornwall), I found myself in a U.S. C-54 plane carrying the U.S. air squadron which Stalin had finally permitted to proceed to Russia by way of North Africa. Bucket seats were something Dante had spared his sinners. Nonetheless, I finally dozed off. Suddenly a violent shaking awakened me to hear the sergeant in charge demand anxiously:

"Pardon me, sir, are you dead?"

"Not yet," I gasped.

"Well, sir, the plane is at eighteen thousand feet and going higher and I should have put you on oxygen long ago. Here—" and he popped a tube into my mouth. I had frequently suffered from mountain sickness at an altitude of barely twelve thousand feet. So perhaps I was lucky since my only ailment was a sharp headache that oxygen soon cured.

The next moₐning, April 10, saw me in the white city of Algiers, full of uniforms, Arab robes, bare-legged French girls, with Italian prisoners in American uniforms serving as chambermaids in the hotel. It was my first visit to the home of the Barbary pirates. The high spot was dinner with General and Madame de Gaulle at *Villa Les Glycines*. There was only one other guest, and the general welcomed us with no trace of haughtiness. During an excellent meal whereof he partook freely, he discoursed on politics.

De Gaulle no longer had any doubts concerning his country's future. In fact, he was already planning to unite Europe—"that is to say, humanistic, Christian, and democratic Europe," as he explained. He predicted that the Soviet Union would play a major role in the Middle East and might defeat the United States in a coming war! Only in one respect did he surprise me: his distrust of Churchill was even greater than his dislike of Roosevelt, whose Great Design he considered a system of "permanent American intervention."

Obviously there were two de Gaulles, the one an intellectual Frenchman conscious of man's frailty, the other who spoke of himself in the third person and identified himself with France—or was it the other way round?

The Liberation Committee in Algeria consisted of representatives of all French political parties except Vichyites, including my friends Bonnet and Monnet. So reserving the General's European plan for a future commentary, I ventured in a column to advise Eisenhower how to get along with the French in France. They were, admittedly, a sick people, rendered neurasthenic by defeat and German occupation. All the more reason for treating them as equal co-belligerents. "Clinch the friendship between the American and French peoples for the years ahead," I urged. "The United States will surely need such friendship."

To a former student of Biblical literature, Egypt and Palestine meant far too much to be omitted from this trip. In Cairo, I spent much time in the museum and wandering around the Sphinx and the Great Pyramid, wondering at all that had been. Still I took time to interview that once great adversary of the Italians in Lybia, Idris Mohammed Ali el-Senussi, the unquestioned leader of his people, a small, finely featured long-fingered, indomitable man who was claiming independence "under British and American protection."

Sailors of the Greek war fleet in Alexandria, who had mutinied shortly before, were still unruly, allegedly because of Britain's insistence on restoring the King who had invited the semifascist dictatorship of General Metaxas. Yet behind their revolt were communists planning to transform liberated Greece into a little Soviet Union.

In Jerusalem, the Holy City, I talked with Britishers, Arabs, and Jews, visited a *Kibbutz* at Ain Geb on the romantic Lake of Galilee, marveled at the Mosque of Omar on the site of the former Temple of King David, and took a chilly swim at Tel Aviv. "The Jews," I wrote, "after two thousand years, are again pitching their tents on the same spot, stubborn as ever."

Flying back to Cairo through a pitch-black dust storm, I sat uncomfortably on a box with a projecting knob. Only when we landed in Cairo did I examine my seat. On it was the inscription: "To explode the bomb, push the lever down." Once or twice during the dark part of the flight I had attempted unsuccessfully to do just that! The two British airmen considered it a huge joke. Life was cheap in 1944.

From Cairo a U.S. Army plane brought me to Italy. En route, the only other passenger, a middle-aged man wearing a uniform with no insignia, introduced himself as "the Coca-Cola man, just off to our bottling plant in Italy to see that the boys get their Cokes." Wnat a contrast with Washington's hungry, tattered soldiers at Valley Forge!

In Naples, my brother-in-law, Colonel Dick Adams, a member of the American Military Government, commandeered a comfortable room for me near his, at Posillipo, and I occasionally ate with him and his fellow "AMGOTS," as the Neapolitans called them. "Allied Italy," Dick explained, "is a co-belligerent enemy. As enemies, the Italians are permitted to die for the Allies. Get it?"

During a long day with Benedetto Croce at Sorrento ("Torna a Surriento, famme campà," Lilian used to sing), he informed me that the Italians were shrugging off *fascismo* as nonchalantly as they had previous tyrannies, and no amount of oppression or disorder could shake their will to live. Croce had, in 1932, brought out a volume dedicated to liberty and was a strong partisan of my friend Sforza.

Italy was politically a "British responsibility," so at Caserta I dutifully reported to General Sir Noel Mason MacFarlane, head of the Allied Control Commission, a whimsical Scot who wore shorts all year round, and who gave me permission to visit the "American front" beyond the River Garigliano under Cassino.

Only a few days before, battle-hardened Germans had scored a second "Kasserine Pass" victory over green Americans. An American major at headquarters explained that the boys of the Thirty-fourth and Thirty-sixth Divisions, from Iowa and Texas, respectively, had attacked, been routed, and "were still running." Obviously, there was no substitute for combat experience. The best soldiers on the Cassino front, the major continued, were the Poles and the French who "knew what they were fighting for. . . . Pint-size French girls drive their ambulances right to to the front lines during battle, and several have lost their lives in the process."

For the first time since 1918, I spent a day with U.S. soldiers on a battlefront. Defeat had aroused their combativity. Yet their innocence of the why's and wherefore's of the war was amazing. Many read only comics, and some read nothing at all. A public relations captain at headquarters protested: "They are not illiterate. Put up a sign, 'Free drinks here tonight,' and every man jack will turn up."

I had hoped to enter Rome with our conquering troops. But at headquarters they considered this a long way off. Reluctantly, I flew back to the United States on a Navy plane. It was early May, 1944.

A month later Allied forces landed in Normandy.

President Roosevelt had at first refused to allow French troops to participate in this landing in their own country, then made a last and futile attempt to keep Charles de Gaulle out of France. It was October before the United States reluctantly signed the "landing agreements" initialed in August, which were tantamount to a recognition of de Gaulle.

Eisenhower had wisely permitted Leclerc's French troops to be among the first to enter liberated Paris which the German commander, by God's grace, had disobeyed Hitler's order to destroy.

Among the first correspondents in Paris was Helen Kirkpatrick. Lodgings were hard to find, and with sure feminine instinct she went directly to our apartment in the Rue de l'Université, obtained from the concierge the address of our former cook who had the key, and not only persuaded Zéno to let her move in but to get breakfast for her. Paul Ghali, who had gone to Switzerland for the *News* when the Germans occupied Vichy, returned to Paris shortly thereafter. French refugees streamed home from America as quickly as they could obtain transportation. And soon letters were keeping us abreast of what was happening in France.

F.D.R., finally impressed by the French people's dedication to Charles de Gaulle, invited him to Washington, lodged him in Blair House, and treated him almost as a chief of state. The general twice expressed to me his gratification at America's "recognition of France." But F.D.R. excluded France from the Bretton Woods and Dumbarton Oaks Conferences. At the second Quebec Conference in September Admiral Leahy urged the allies to rely in France upon Pétain! In Paris, American and British officers were still refusing to accept the French as brothers-in-arms. De Gaulle reacted by journeying to Moscow and signing a Franco-Russian treaty of alliance which gave him some "freedom of maneuver" between the super-power.

In the United States, American opinion was turning ever more strongly in his favor, in part because of a pamphlet, *Concerning France*, which Lilian brought out shortly after de Gaulle's visit. On the basis of personal experience and several months of research, she painted a vivid description of France's fall, the reasons thereof, and the cynical maneuvers of the Vichy-ites. It remains one of the best brief analyses of a heart-breaking period.

Dictator Francisco Franco of Spain had become our *de facto* enemy by sending a Spanish "Blue Legion" to fight against our Russian ally.

Only after our invasion of North Africa and the Russians' victory at Stalingrad did the cunning *Caudillo* change his tune. "Quick, *amigos*, a life raft, a parachute, a change of heart, a change of life, a new regime, powerful new protectors and a camouflaged umbrella: '*arriba España!*'" was how I described his flip-flop. After the war, I believed, the Spanish people would get rid of him.

Mexico, at the time of the Inter-American Conference at Mexico City (Chapultepec) in March, 1945, swarmed with Anti-Yanquis. Most powerful were certain Roman Catholics who called themselves *sinarquistas*, maintained contact with Franco, preached "Spanishness," successfully opposed Mexico's participation in the war against the Axis, and cooperated with the German Nazis active in their country. From the Czech communist, Otto Katz, then living in Mexico City, I obtained the names and addresses of some three hundred Nazis and when I returned to Washington, handed it to General Donovan for appropriate counteraction.

Palestine was also beginning to loom as a problem. Before my visit, though I knew and admired Chaim Weizmann, I had not taken Zionism seriously. Now I was a convert to the idea of a home for the Jews, the same which Bonaparte had promised them if he won in Egypt. The perfidy of those Palestinian Arabs who had happily sold land to Zionists at twice the normal price, then plotted to expel or massacre their customers, and the role of the Grand Mufti of Jerusalem, Haj Amin el-Husseini, who had not only opposed the allies but encouraged and abetted Hitler's wholesale massacres of Jews, with the support of many Arabs—together these convinced me that we owed the Arabs nothing. Thereafter I regularly spoke and wrote in favor of Zionism.

More and more, the chief political problem confronting the United States, and Britain was, however, how defeat the Axis without simultaneously subjecting half of Europe to Moscow? General Sikorski's plan for an East European Federation powerful enough to hold its own against either a resurgent Germany or an itchy-fingered Soviet Union was obviously sound. Unfortunately, at Moscow and Teheran, respectively, first Hull and then the President had, at Stalin's insistence, repudiated any such Federation.

This was due in part, his intimates explained, to his postwar plan of ensuring peace by dividing the world into major spheres of influence. Britain's sphere would lie in West Europe, the Mediterranean, and the Middle East, ours in Latin America and the Far East. Why therefore should not Russia establish a "Monroe Doctrine" over East Europe even if this led to the communization of the victim peoples? Most important to the President was inducing Stalin to enter the coming world organization.

F.D.R. had, according to Forest Davis, convinced himself that "the right of conquest is a valid element in international affairs" (though not for Germany, Italy, or Japan). Thanks to this he could justify his planned seizure of Dakar from France and of various Pacific islands from Japan. At bottom, in spite of his talk of democracy and liberation, our President was a *Machtmensch* in whose eyes power conferred privileges. Since the Soviet Union would emerge from the war as the second most powerful country in the world, the United States should defer to its desires. Though I did not know it, he had told Bob Murphy that "he wanted to make the Russians feel that Americans trusted them implicitly and valued Soviet-American cooperation in war and peace above any other prospective alliance."

This was not too difficult since, partly owing to Soviet victories, partly to endless eulogies of our "glorious ally" in the American press and radio, and partly to pro-Russian propaganda such as the motion picture of Ambassador Joe Davies, *Mission to Moscow*, the American people had discarded most of their previous distrust of the Soviet Union.

The first victim of this infatuation was Poland. Here Roosevelt, in Bullitt's words, "left the dirty work to Churchill." The British Foreign Office offered to compensate Poland for territories ceded to Moscow at the expense of Germany—provided that Stalin keep his hands off remaining Poland. This the Georgian accepted, tongue in cheek. His treatment of Poland had been ruthless. Particularly Hitler-like were the slaughter of thousands of captured Polish officers at Katyn Forest; the immobility of Russian armies outside Warsaw while German forces suppressed the revolting anticommunist Poles within the city; and, subsequently, the murder of two leading Polish Social Democrats whom he had himself invited to Moscow.

Nonetheless, passionate pro-Russians, like Ambassador Wynant in London, severely chided less naïve diplomats like Jimmy Riddleberger, who had no faith in Soviet intentions.

Late in 1944, Soviet officials set about communizing the "liberated" Balkan states. Churchill sought to divide the area, leaving Greece in the British sphere, Yugoslavia "divided," and the rest under Stalin. Tito, however, ignored his English dupe, and once he "escaped" to his country, successfully turned for help to the advancing Russians.

Toward the end of 1944, after Roosevelt's election to a third term, I put the question squarely to readers: "Do we want Soviet cooperation at Stalin's price?"

Apparently we did. The Yalta Conference, with neither France nor China present, was the West's last opportunity to stop Stalin in Europe or Asia. Roosevelt returned with the belief that Stalin had committed himself to creating democratic regimes in East Europe. And although F.D.R. mendaciously informed Congress that he had not discussed Pacific problems, actually his efforts to obtain Stalin's participation in the war against Japan had laid the way for the future communist take-over of China.

With the President I shared one conviction: durable peace had to be enforced either by a preponderant single nation, by an alliance, or by an international authority. The last was obviously preferable.

The peace debate was in full swing. The President had entrusted no fewer than twenty-eight governmental bodies with the task of "studying" the postwar world. The Chicago *Tribune* ironically suggested that Britain could become a state in the American Union. Dorothy Thompson believed we should "share our interest" with Russia, which will "want to strengthen Europe, including Germany and China." Howard O. Eaton put his faith in the enforcement of existing international law. Walter Lippmann urged us to build peace on a great power alliance that had disarmed all lesser powers. Sumner Welles defended the need for force in keeping the peace within the framework of the Atlantic Charter. Henry Wallace counted on economic reforms to make the world one neighborhood. David Lawrence and the *NAM News* urged a return to the original League of Nations. Hamilton Fish Armstrong and Roscoe Drummond argued that voluntary cooperation among sovereign powers had proved inadequate.

Early in 1945, Emery Reves, a Hungarian whom I had known in Paris, brought out a book, *The Anatomy of Peace*, which argued the case for world government.

American participation in a new and better League of Nations was the necessary first step. To this cause, from April, 1943, on, I had given as much time as I could spare from writing, broadcasting, and lecturing. While Lilian became the Washington head of the Women's Action Committee in favor of the United Nations, Waymack's and Mowrer's *Non-Partisan Council to Win the Peace* called for "an international organization with authority to deal with disputes between nations and with delegated power sufficient to enable it automatically and immediately to employ force in whatever degree may be necessary to prevent aggression and maintain peace."

In 1944 William Agar, Mark Ethridge, Lisa Sergio, and I launched a *Committee for a Democratic Foreign Policy* which we hoped would bolster the supranational idea.

But both American political parties advocated buying peace on the cheap. The Republicans wanted nothing beyond "cooperative organization among sovereign nations." The Democrats slid around the issue by demanding "adequate armed forces to meet the needs of preventing war and of making impossible the preparation of war." The House passed the noncommittal Fulbright Resolution. But a Senate subcommittee was holding up the so-called B2H2 resolution introduced by Senators Ball, Burton, Hatch, and Hill, which provided for a United Nations with limited but sufficient authority to suppress military aggression by force. Finally, the Senate passed the Connally Resolution favoring U.S. participation in *an* international organization.

This was as much as F.D.R. and Joe Stalin wanted. Their idea was a world actually run by a Holy Alliance of the largest powers, drawing legitimacy from a universal organization wherein the lesser states would be free to talk and devote themselves to nonpolitical activities.

In consequence, the blueprint which Dumbarton Oaks offered to a war-weary world incorporated the very weakness that killed the League; no possibility of legal action against an aggressive Great Power. Nor could such a Power be expelled for wanton aggression as the League members had expelled the Soviet Union in 1939 for attacking Finland.

Still, any organization would be better than none. And no world peace organization, as F.D.R. properly insisted, could be wholly effective unless it included the U.S.S.R. Our job was therefore to restrain Soviet expansion with all necessary firmness while at the same time persuading Moscow that it could obtain future security only through the United Nations.

By the time the San Francisco Conference opened, Roosevelt was dead and the war in the West was over. Bullitt later wrote:

"God was kind to President Roosevelt. . . . He died before the actions of the Soviet Government in Poland, Hungary, Austria, Rumania, Bulgaria, that portion of Germany occupied by the Red Army, Iran, Manchuria, and Korea had forced him to admit that he had lost his gamble 'for stakes as enormous as any states had ever played for.' "

The war in the West was over.

Before leaving for San Francisco I wrote, at the request of the *Iowa Law Review*, an article on the lesson of the League of Nations. That organization had failed, I argued, because it had remained an *international vigilance committee*. Like previous vigilance committees, it had regularly failed to tackle tough horse thieves and cattle rustlers. Bad men had continually got away with murder. The new League, to be half way effective, had to be a true sheriff or a town marshal charged with keeping order and enforcing the law. Here was the task confronting the delegates at the conference.

The editor of the *Review* called it a "delightful and brilliant article, somewhat of a bombshell in our staid and technical legal journals."

Thus encouraged, in my first column from the U.N. Conference at San Francisco, I sought to jar readers out of their complacency. "This," I wrote, "is the most important human gathering since the Last Supper. . . . The choice (here) will not be between war and peace but . . . between *sure-fire* war and *possible* peace. If this conference fails, then God help mankind."

This "exaggeration" drew the mirth of my colleagues.

Yet further world wars would make life on earth intolerable. There might still be time *to create a true superauthority*.

I spent two hours trying to persuade Senator Vandenberg, a U.S. delegate, not to extend the Great Power veto to proposed amendments in the Charter, thus closing the door to improvements. The old League could have taken action against a major aggressor—Japan, Italy, or Germany—and did not. The new United Nations would not be able to. Moreover, even in the Assembly, a minimum number of inhabitants should be required as a prerequisite to a vote. States with fewer people could combine. "Van" explained that neither of my demands would be acceptable to Congress. For the U.S.A, as for the U.S.S.R., with its three votes in the Assembly, any relinquishment of sovereignty was taboo.

Nevertheless, I enjoyed the conference. Newsmen and delegates had traveled from the East Coast in a special train, and had a good time on the way. Most entertaining was the British Ambassador, Lord Halifax. At each stop, the Noble Lord got out, introduced himself to everyone in the station, and solemnly shook each by the hand, as though he were running for office in the United States.

At San Francisco, France's foreign minister, Georges Bidault, regaled me with a French-size luncheon and a magnificently revealing story. When General de Gaulle entered Paris in August, 1944, Bidault as head of the French underground had welcomed him at the Hotel de Ville, accompanied him on his tour of the city through millions of delirious citizens, and finally gone with the weary General to the latter's quarters in the Ministry of War. There, over a drink, Bidault raised his glass: "What triumph, *mon général.*"

"Yes," de Gaulle grudgingly admitted, "but what disorder!"

Yet no personal enjoyment could offset my disillusion with the conference itself. The delegates, in my judgment, missed the boat. They concentrated on high-sounding phrases, theoretical ideals, and social goals (which I called "global hypocrisy"), and on short-term political aims, while skimping the job that mattered most—preventing war.

Conference Secretary-General Alger Hiss reproached me for criticizing Russia's ambition to dominate Poland. Vera Micheles Dean of the Foreign Policy Association earnestly tried to induce me to take a more "understanding line" toward the U.S.S.R.

On June 23, Moscow set up a predominantly communist "national government" in Poland. In a column, I quoted a "candid Bolshevik official" (I cannot remember who it was) who told me: "Certainly, the Soviet Union is expanding, but only into empty seats. We would not have moved in if you had been there. We shall not be moved out now that we are comfortably seated." None of which prevented Harry Hopkins in Moscow from signing a new agreement with Russia and reporting to Truman that we "can do business with Stalin."

The very Latin American states which had, in 1920, rushed into a Europe-dominated League of Nations through fear of "American imperialism" were now begging Washington to protect them against a "coming Europe dominated by the Soviets."

Thanks to Stalin, ours was a worse world than when the League's First Assembly convened beside the blue Swiss lake in 1920. Now, almost twenty-five years later, many delegates at San Francisco laughed bitterly at the promise that this would be the last war.

Yet Truman had no misgivings. Why should he? The new President went to Potsdam prepared to pay Stalin's price for entering the Pacific struggle.

Yet he had been warned. T. V. Soong visited Washington in the hope of persuading Truman to support a Chinese refusal of the Sino-Soviet agreement drafted at Moscow. When he failed, he invited me to lunch and poured out his misgivings. Rather than open China to Soviet penetration, he would resign as Prime Minister.

On August 6, an American A-bomb on Hiroshima opened a new epoch in human history.

My first reaction was one of horror: humanity, as it had revealed itself to me, was totally unfit to be trusted with any such ghastly weapon. Almost a year before, my friend André LaBarthe, former head of the Institute of Technical and Scientific Research at Paris, had predicted in the refugee magazine, *Tricolor*, that the world was entering the "rocket age." He explained that "as soon as a chemist finds the fusing combination adopted to a super-atmospheric motor, there will no longer be any obstacle in the way of bombing America from Europe and vice versa." And LaBarthe concluded: "The last war ended at the place where the mass use of airplanes and tanks was impending. The democracies forgot this. . . . (Now) "no city in the world is beyond the reach of sudden attack. There are no ocean barriers, no isolated continents, no man who can afford to be unconcerned with the aggression that menaces his neighbors." This I had quoted for my readers. Obviously, these coming rockets would carry not old fashioned limited charges of TNT, but an atom monster. Unless speedily abolished or controlled, the A-bomb could force free men to choose between serfdom and utter catastrophe.

At the moment, our monopoly of such a weapon could enable us to "nudge" the Soviets out of Eastern Europe without an armed conflict, as Churchill advocated. But Churchill was no longer Prime Minister. Would Truman follow his advice?

After a second A-bomb destroyed Nagasaki, Japan formally collapsed. The war that had taken fifty million human lives was over. Yet there was no real peace.

Why, why, why? I asked myself. Yet the answer was simple. Unlike the first world struggle, the second had been essentially a *three-cornered combat:* first Nazism and communism against freedom; then freedom and communism against Nazism. But communism was still determined to destroy freedom. Roosevelt as leader of the free had refused to see or, seeing, to admit this sinister fact. Another struggle, I knew, lay ahead.

"... condemned to repeat it"

Now that the victory was won, the democracies were free to return to the follies of their past.

— WINSTON CHURCHILL

32

The Aftermath

We looked for peace but no good came;
and for a time of health, and behold trouble!
—JEREMIAH 8:15

SHORTLY AFTER HIS return from Potsdam, Harry S. Truman received me in the White House. Here was the politician who had remained unsoiled in the swamp of Kansas City politics, the Senator who had struggled tooth and nail to eliminate profiteering on wartime government orders, and the quietly courageous captain of Battery D in the First World War.

But when I asked for his impressions of the Conference, he startled me. "They told me I would have trouble with Stalin. I had no trouble with Stalin. I got everything I wanted from Stalin."

Lord God of Hosts! In March, 1945, Ambassador Averell Harriman in Moscow had, I knew, warned Roosevelt that Stalin's postwar cooperation was no longer certain. A month later, the French communist leader, Jacques Duclos, had, upon instructions from Moscow, written a letter to American communists denouncing any further cooperation with "capitalists."

Forgotten, at least by the President's closest advisers, were the Georgian's toast to Hitler in 1939, his public assertion that France and Britain had attacked Germany, and his telegram to the German *Fuehrer* extolling the friendship "sealed in blood" of the Soviet and German peoples! Nobody remembered Molotov's toast to Hitler for his victory over Poland.

Why, in May, 1945, had Truman not harkened to Churchill and occupied Berlin and Prague until Stalin withdrew his forces from Central Europe? Only some years later, he told me why. He had barely become President ("and nobody was ever less prepared for that job")

359

when Eisenhower informed him that American forces had crossed the Elbe: should he, the General asked, order them to occupy Berlin before the Russians? "So, Mr. Mowrer, I did exactly what anyone else in my position would have done, I asked my military advisers about it, and they told me to let the Russians take Berlin. I did. As simple as that." Truman had missed the message.

Only after Stalin told Harriman, in November, 1945, that he had decided to go his "own way" did the President begin to understand his mistake. In January, 1946, he referred to Russia's occupation of Poland and of that part of Germany allotted temporarily to Poland as "high-handed outrage," and ordered Secretary Byrnes to make no more concessions to Moscow.

Nonetheless, he continued demobilizing our armed forces with the result that by the spring of 1946, the "strongest country in the world" could have put no more than six army divisions in the field. His chief aims were ending "economic slavery" at home and colonialism abroad.

Most Americans agreed. Had we not always been for the underdog? How delicious were peace, normalcy, and the return to private concerns! And nowhere more so than in Washington, D.C.

A few officials were disturbed when in February, 1946, the Georgian denounced "monopoly capitalists"—who happened to have saved Russia in 1941. Winston Churchill caused a minor stir when, in a speech at Fulton, Missouri, he deplored the "iron curtain" dividing Europe (an expression that had been used in 1914 by Belgium's heroic German-born Queen Elizabeth), stated that the Russians sought the indefinite extension of their rule and proposed the merger of the United States and the British Commonwealth.

Not much came of that warning.

Most Americans were more concerned over the Atom Bomb. In the pamphlet he wrote for the War Department, Henry De Wolf Smyth of Princeton gave the world a frank description of the nature and potentiality of the new weapon. In October, 1945, Smyth warned some of us that any industrialized country could, given time and the requisite effort, produce a bomb.

"You said you had no part in manufacturing ours. Could you make a bomb?" I asked him.

"Certainly, given the requisite material, a building as large as a commercial garage, and about two years. There is no way to prevent the spread of these things save by immediate action."

"Such as putting to death all persons with more than a high school knowledge of physics?" I suggested cheerfully.

"No, Edgar. Unless you also destroy every textbook of physics, some monkey will get hold of one and think out the answer."

A pleasing prospect, indeed! Our swords had, indeed, in Shakespeare's phrase, "become too massive for our strengths." Shortly thereafter, the witty Hungarian physicist, Leo Szillard, made the round of Washington columnists to urge the abolition of the new weapon. In the twenties, when he had been working with Einstein in Germany, Szillard had been considered a smart aleck. At Los Alamos, while working on the bomb, he had repeatedly been fired for insubordination by General Groves (and promptly reinstated at the insistence of Harold Urey). Now he was gravely worried over the existence of the device which he had helped to shape.

I had begun breakfasting occasionally with Senator Brian McMahon at his house around the corner from ours. The Senator was already deep in the problem of atomic control.

U.S. Admiral William Sterling Parsons, a tall handsome Mid-westerner, related his experiences at Los Alamos and described his mixed emotions when, as Senior Military Technical Observer, he dropped on Hiroshima the atomic bomb that opened a new era in human warfare.

Coached by experts such as these, I never underestimated the problem of superweapons. Yet the basic problem facing mankind was less that of controlling A-bombs than of controlling the Powers that either had or would inevitably acquire them. The first depended on the second.

Meanwhile, the world remained in turmoil.

The immediate danger, in my eyes, was the slow débâcle in China. The end of the war found Chiang Kai-shek's government struggling ineffectually with war-weariness, inflation, a communist revolt, and a hostile campaign in the United States. Many Americans had swallowed the legend (at which I had myself nibbled, but *only* nibbled, in 1938) that the Chinese communists were "agrarian reformers" who sought primarily to clean up and modernize China.

Truman had inherited F.D.R.'s deep distrust of the Chinese Generalissimo. Once Japan surrendered, our President, taking a tip from Secretary of State Byrnes, decided that Chiang should settle his "internal problems," meaning that he should form a coalition government with the Chinese communists who, after receiving vast quantities of captured Japanese arms from Russia, were spreading through China, executing landlords, and half terrorizing, half cajoling ordinary Chinese people into accepting their rule.

Since he lacked confidence in Ambassador Hurley's judgment, Truman decided, in December, 1945, to send to China General George Marshall, the "greatest living American," to pressure Chiang into accepting Mao and his friends as governmental colleagues.

The new Director of the Office of Far Eastern Affairs in the State Department was an idealistic official with considerable Chinese experience, John Carter Vincent by name. He admitted to me that Marshall's mission was a veiled ultimatum: take the communists into your government or forfeit essential military and economic aid from the United States! Marshall had convinced Truman that even with American weapons Chiang and his "corrupt" associates would be no match for the "agrarian reformers." Vincent had, in August, drafted an American note to Chiang: cooperate or face a "redefinition" of America's China policy, meaning no more help from the United States.

American insistence on cooperation between the communists and Chiang was tantamount to compelling the Kuomintang to commit suicide. This possibility did not greatly disturb Vincent. Many liberals still saw no evil in communism. At a Christmas, 1946, meeting of the Institute of Pacific Relations in Cleveland, which I attended, Edward Carter and Owen Lattimore actually asked the audience to "help Chinese communist patriots." Their formula for handling Russian and Chinese Reds could be expressed in a paraphrase of a Mother Goose rhyme:

Leave them alone
And they will come home,
Wagging their Dialectics behind them.

In a similar frame of mind, Ludwik Rajchman, socialist, Polish patriot, and internationalist, became a member of the communist-dominated Polish government's delegation to the United Nations. As such he fathered the U.N. Children's Fund, which he persuaded his American friends Fiorello La Guardia and Maurice Pate to take the lead in realizing. They were so successful that the United Nations established UNICEF in December, 1946, with Rajchman as its first chairman.

Inevitably, the Doctor's enemies denounced him as a communist. This I do not believe. When in 1945 he told me of his decision to work with the new Polish government, he explained that he wanted to accomplish one more thing for Poland and for humanity before he died. He cooperated with the Polish communists in the same spirit as Hendrick Andersen had sought the support of Mussolini in readying his dream of a World Center. When I questioned the wisdom of his decision he wrote me: "You will live to see ONE FREE WORLD—even though at the expense of the evolution of your views."

Actually I found myself agreeing with three "reformed" pro-Bolsheviks, Bill Bullitt, Eugene Lyons, and Louis Fischer. Bullitt, in *The Great Globe Itself*, urged resistance by every means, including, if necessary, the atomic bomb. "To execute a murderer is not an immoral act," he argued. And he added, "When we know that the Soviet has a bomb, we shall have to create a Federal Government of democratic states."

In *The Great Challenge*, Fischer warned: "If the democracies win, there will be no war with Russia. If the Russians win, there will be no democracy."

By the end of 1945 reports of conditions in Europe had become terrifying. I decided to see for myself.

Armed with military credentials, new visas, and my old correspondent's uniform to wear in occupied Germany, I flew to Britain.

London was almost as desolate as Gander in Newfoundland. Truman's abrupt stoppage of Lend-Lease had been an unexpected blow. One in thirty-one Londoners had been killed by German bombs or missiles. Few war ruins had been repaired. Necessities were still rationed and

Socialists like Aneurin Bevan, a Cabinet Minister, and his wife, Jennie Lee, M.P., seemed to feel that continued austerity was not only necessary but good for people. Yet at their own residence they served me an abundant meal based, as Jennie explained, on gifts from farmer constituents. Lunches and dinners at the Hyde Park Hotel were outrageously expensive. Liquor prices were almost prohibitive.

Nearly everyone seemed dissatisfied with the political situation.

Chiefly, the British people were suffering from the failure of their magnificent heroism to produce the better life to which they felt victory entitled them. They reminded me sadly of the French and the Italians after the First World War. Vanquished find it easier than victors to accept harsh postwar reality. . . .

Nye and Jennie saw nothing alarming in Russia's securing "friendly neighbors" along its western border. But Conservatives like Viscount Cranborne asked impatiently when the United States intended to help Britain put a brake on Soviet expansion. Had Englishmen and Americans given their lives in order that the East European nations should exchange Hitler's blight for that of Stalin? Bob Vansittart darkly predicted that by not restraining Russia during the war, our two governments had created a situation where some future Germany could again take up the "see-saw policy" between East and West—at the expense of both. Frederick Voigt, my former Berlin colleague, now editor of the *Nineteenth Century*, argued that by allowing Poles and Czechs to seize territories formerly inhabited by Germans, Churchill and Roosevelt had laid the ground for the next world war.

Most of the M.P.'s whom I met at the House of Commons, as well as certain high officials, complained that victorious Britain had become the "tail of a two-headed dog and was being wagged vigorously by both sides."

Churchill had been right about Greece: most Greeks were now begging the British forces to remain and defend them from their own communists, operating from inviolate bases in Albania and Yugoslavia.

At the first United Nations Assembly in the cobalt blue and gold Methodist Central Hall, near Westminster Abbey, the West and Russia wasted no time before disagreeing. The former wanted the United Nations to be the precursor of a world commonwealth. Gromyko for Moscow insisted that it must remain a meeting place where Great Powers could thrash out their differences and impose common decisions on the smaller countries. Reluctantly the Russians agreed to withdraw their troops from Iran. This seemed to me the only real accomplishment of this crucial meeting—and it turned out to be fraudulent.

Holland still offered a dismal picture of the destruction and desolation of war and foreign military occupation. Rotterdam was a shambles. So was the section of The Hague destroyed by Allied bombers in an effort to annihilate the German V-1's established in the nearby park and dunes. As the day of liberation approached, the Dutch had paid dearly for their stubborn refusal to bow their neck to the invading barbarians. The Gestapo had run riot, picking up resisters without mercy. Before retreating, the Germans stripped the country to the bone, even driving Dutch cattle into Germany.

In reaction the Dutch had given their Canadian liberators so warm a welcome that when their government called them home, some Canadian soldiers told their Dutch friends: "In the next war, do not expect us to come back: but we are leaving you our sons instead."

The Dutch government was maintaining a less stringent austerity than the British, hoping to make up the capital lost in Indonesia. (This policy paid off.) Some officials hoped to create a Dutch-Indonesian commonwealth. Marc Van Blankenstein thought otherwise. His hope was in a Dutch-Belgian customs union.

Belgium had come out of the war relatively unhurt. The returning refugee government immediately raised wages, thereby sparking a boom. This, in Brussels at least, was fanned by the expenditures of thousands of American soldiers on leave from occupation duty in Germany. Prices were high. Several old friends, including members of the government, whom I had known abroad during the war, thought that Britain and the Netherlands were "clamping things down too hard." Certainly, the relatively festive atmosphere in the Belgian capital reminded me of kermesses in old Flanders. So much so that I was not sorry to board the unbelievably crowded train for France.

With what emotion I found myself once more in Paris! I remembered not only the tragic days of 1940, but my first confrontation with the city in 1911. Since it was late and I could not remember the old telephone number in my apartment, I called my old friend Paul Winkler and asked him to fetch me in his car. He and his wife Betty put me up for the night and the next morning he drove me to our apartment in Rue de l'Université.

There my brother and his wife welcomed me "home." So did our former cook, Zénobie, now working for them. Zéno had, with incredible devotion, looked after and protected our belongings from the Germans ever since we fled the city. She cried when I kissed her.

In 1914, Zéno's home in French Flanders had been occupied by the *Boches*. But that period, she explained, had been paradise compared with four long years in Paris under the "dirty" Nazis. Now the latter were gone, but the *chagrins* of their presence still remained.

The picture of postwar France Paul and Hadley gave me was disturbing—political division, profiteering, apathy, a refusal to choose between the United States and the Soviet Union.

General de Gaulle, who had recently resigned as Prime Minister and retired in a huff to nearby Marly, was bitter that the people had dropped him as coolly as they had Clemenceau in 1919—or as the British dropped Churchill in 1945. Léon Blum, de Gaulle's socialist successor, was, I knew, a cultured humanist. But how trust a sentimentalist who had expected the last war to "free humanity from the last convulsions of barbarism and despotism"? Where, Paul wanted to know, had humanity produced a more barbarous despot than Joseph Stalin? The same French communists who had supported Hitler when he was Stalin's friend were now claiming ever more power because of their substantial part in the resistance movement!

In an effort to bring some quick relief to the long-suffering French, René Pleven had accepted a "controlled" inflation that favored the few at the expense of the many: farmers, grocers, butchers, some types of organized labor were profiteering happily while many old people and children went hungry. Waiters earned more than university professors. Although our friends, René and Renée Arcos, got enough to eat from their little property in Seine-et-Oise, other intellectuals and writers like Pierre Cot and Emmanuel d'Astier de la Vigérie were turning to communism. Paul believed that the strain of war and defeat had all but broken France's morale.

On the other hand, Chip Bohlen, in Paris on a U.S. government errand, endeavored to persuade me that Americans should welcome the withdrawal of "dangerous" de Gaulle. All of Europe, he predicted, would soon be socialistic, whether we liked it or not.

It was with regret that I left for Frankfurt.

A dozen years before, without conviction, I had assured the Nazi official engaged in registering my enforced departure from Berlin that I would return to Germany "only when I can come with about two million of my compatriots." Now the two million had come—in uniform —and although most of them had gone, my return was somehow a fulfillment. And I was curious to see what war and defeat had done to the German people.

Americans at the I. G. Farben Building in Frankfurt reported a strange combination of sullenness and servility on the part of the population. U.S. soldiers had orders to "hoot up" German males in the presence of an Allied officer, meaning, to make them take off their hats (*"Hut ab"*). American officers had little good to say of the vanquished. Nor had German anti-Nazis. Our old friend, Hans Deichmann, brother-in-law of the martyred Helmut von Moltke, was thinking of moving to Italy. Most Germans had stood by the *Fuehrer* to the end.

The German generals' revolt in 1944, however well intentioned, had come much too late. Now there was an abundance of self-pity.

A sorry, not unexpected, picture! In Berlin (reached in an American military train), an Army jeep brought me to a commandeered room in the once smug suburb of Dahlem. As soon as I had fulfilled the military formalities, another jeep with a German civilian driver bore me on a tour of inspection through the vast, still familiar city.

What desolation! Three-quarters of all the buildings were uninhabitable. The population had sunk from over four to two million.

Most of the bridges were gone. The inner city, with the once impressive Unter den Linden, was a shambles. The Kranzler Building had simply vanished, along with my old office. Ruined were the aristocratic and diplomatic Tiergarten Quarter and the section between the Luetzow Platz and the Gedaechtniskirche, including the church itself.

In the Hansa Viertel where we had lived for so many years, the mosaic-ed façade of our apartment still stood, but through the yawning windows as far as the River Spree one saw only rubble.

"This is the rejoicing city that dwelt carelessly, that said in her heart, I am, and there is none beside me: now is she become a desolation, a place for beasts to lie down in!" (Zephania.) Only there were no beasts: the remaining population had eaten them.

As if destruction were not enough, the Russian troops had literally commandeered the younger women and confiscated everything they could remove, particularly watches. What they had not stolen they had bought with U.S. occupation marks, the plates for printing which had generously been handed them by Harry White of the U.S. Treasury. The Germans had asked for this, I told myself. But how awful!

At the American *Kommendatura* our local commander, General Frank Howley, described the Germans as "suspiciously docile" and disapproved the easy fraternization with them of the newly arrived young Americans, who had not been in the war. Too many were courting German girls and believing what the latter told them. Our main hassle was, however, with the Russians who were acting as if they had won the war alone. Howley predicted that something would "have to give soon."

Out of curiosity not untouched by *Schadenfreude,* I visited a well-known bookstore and roughly asked the salesman for "Jewish literature" (forbidden to be sold under Hitler).

He forced a smile and brought from under the counter a volume of Heine's last poems. While he was wrapping it, I saw on a shelf another book—the original pamphlets of Thomas Paine bound together in London in 1795! For both, I gave him twenty American cigarettes (he asked for fifteen).

Even in traditionally anti-Nazi Berlin, too few Germans as yet saw anything amiss in their late government.

Driving home from a visit to Spandau, my civilian driver, a former banker, suddenly pointed to a ruined factory and said: "See, *Herr,* what you did to us."

I looked him in the eye. "We did none of this."

"You mean the English did it?"

"Certainly not. Every German corpse, every mutilated person, every ruined factory or dwelling, you owe to Adolf Hitler."

A pause. "But those were your bombers. I don't understand."

"Who first bombed cities?"

"Not we, not Germany."

"No? Did you ever hear of Warsaw, Rotterdam, and Coventry?"

A longer pause. "Yes," he conceded. "But those were not German."

Further argument was obviously futile.

At Nuremberg, on the prisoners' bench, twenty-two evil men sat facing the American newsman they had expelled. Himmler looked the picture of reproachful innocence (he loved animals). Goering, thinner than I remembered him, maintained a dignified defiance. Franz von Papen looked shifty as ever. Only Hjalmar Horace Greeley Schacht betrayed his anxiety. "What a pity," I thought, "that Hitler and Goebbels are missing." And yet . . . was it a pity?

Their crimes shrieked for retribution. But about this particular tribunal, I had serious doubts. Telford Taylor, one of the prosecutors, tried to convince me of its legitimacy.

Someone, he insisted, had to make sure that the Nazi example would never be followed. I agreed. Punishment, to be sure, but for what precisely and by whom? Waging international war, in spite of Grotius, had never been a crime and the Kellogg-Briand Pact had not made it so. Atrocities against one's own nationals should be judged by them. Only atrocities against foreigners, those millions of "Jews, Slavs, and other subhumans," were properly an international concern. The Nuremberg trials could serve humanity only if they set a legal precedent or served as a deterrent to some future Hitler. But would they?

I spent five days in Vienna, after Berlin and Nuremberg, a blessed relief. The city was intact, Russian pillage had been limited. The Viennese maintained something of their traditional insouciance, and U.S. High Commissioner, General Mark Clark, was nowhere yielding to Soviet presumption or intrigue. Viennese officials with whom I spoke seemed relatively serene.

Our friend, Maria Schanda, now a well known actress, who had spent most of the war in Berlin, described walking miles through the subway during Allied air raids, and the martyr's death of Helmut von Moltke, murdered by the Nazis. Unlike the military rebels of 1944, Helmut believed that only complete defeat could regenerate the German people. His resistance to the regime had been passive—but absolute. He practiced nonresistance in the spirit of the early Christians, and died like one.

I returned to Washington convinced that our policy in Europe was defective. We had not yet returned to the Netherlands the cattle the Germans had stolen from them; UNRRA, with our consent, was aiding double-crossing Tito; and the United States was feeding Germans while Frenchmen went hungry.

The Russians were welcoming little (and not so little) Nazis into the Communist Party. To prevent this it might be necessary to divide Germany along zonal lines.

Reports from Poland and the Balkans confirmed the steady communization of those countries, in defiance of the Yalta agreements.

In Washington, I learned of worsening situations in Iran, China, Turkey, and Greece. Stalin was reaping the hay of victory, sure that the precipitate demobilization of our armed forces left Truman with only limited means of enforcing our will.

Press Secretary Charley Ross informed me, however, that our President had finally decided to resist further encroachment by Stalin—and had so informed Secretary of State Byrnes. By dispatching U.S. warships to the Mediterranean and the Persian Gulf, Truman saved Turkey. When the American Ambassador at Teheran, George Allen, informed a hesitating Iranian Prime Minister that he could expect "no assistance without resistance," the latter mustered up his courage and reoccupied rebellious Azerbaijan, which the Russians had failed to evacuate.

Moreover, at Stuttgart in September, Secretary Byrnes warned the Kremlin that the United States would be forced to unite the economy of the three western zones of Germany, unless Stalin changed his line.

A few days later, Henry Wallace, a member of Truman's Cabinet, publicly demanded that the President "cease interfering with Russia." The United States, he had previously opined, had no more in common with imperialist England than with the U.S.S.R. Once Truman accepted his resignation, Wallace threw himself wholeheartedly into the arms of a communist, left Liberal group that saw nothing wrong in the forcible expansion of Soviet power and ideology. I was not surprised. I had known Henry since 1940. Whatever his familiarity with hybrid corn, about world affairs he knew less than Harry Hopkins.

In the summer, Lilian and I flew once more to Paris for the "Peace Conference," which Pertinax told me "could not possibly make peace," a shrewd prediction. Brother Paul agreed with Pertinax.

Again my memories are chiefly of two lunches. One was with Paul-Henri Spaak of Belgium at the Ritz. Spaak asked me how the coming peace treaties looked to newsmen. I replied that to me they seemed likely to be inferior to the much criticized Treaty of Versailles. Spaak admitted that until 1939 he had been one of that treaty's severest critics.

The other luncheon was at my once favorite restaurant, La Perouse, as guests of the Czechoslovak delegation to the Conference. To our amazement, we were greeted not only by Jan Masaryk, but by communist Otto Katz, whom I had last seen in Mexico City, and by other Red brothers. Jan assured me that Benes' decision to rely chiefly upon the Soviet Union was working out splendidly. . . .

When Tito of Yugoslavia shot down two American military passenger planes guilty of flying over a tiny corner of his country, I hurried to Italy to cover the inevitable crisis.

The view from my hotel window at the top of the Spanish steps in Rome was as superb as always. But the city was crawling with fascists, now opposing communists in the name of "democracy," and with communists working to give ever more of their country to Tito. The draft peace treaty with Italy had conceded most of Istria. Tito had, in July, judicially executed his wartime Serbian rival, General Draja Mihajlovic, in typically communist manner. Now Tito had deliberately killed Americans. Only by an ultimatum did Truman compel the insolent Croat to return the bodies of our murdered airmen, pay a large indemnity to their families, and order his representative at their public funeral in Trieste humbly to express his master's regret and a promise of better behavior.

Further east, the picture was equally grim. Though the monarchists in Greece had won a plebiscite and restored King George and Queen Frederika, the communists, thanks to their sanctuaries in Albania, Yugoslavia, and Bulgaria, were causing so much trouble that the British Labor government announced that it was withdrawing its forces from that country.

By the end of 1946, the euphoria that followed V-J Day had given place to an indefinable frustration. The twin threats of Soviet imperialism and the A-bomb were driving millions into wishful thinking, cynicism, greed, or isolationism. Too many Democrats wanted Truman to limit our commitments to the Western Hemisphere and Europe. At the United Nations, our representative, Warren Austin, was pushing for full and rapid disarmament of a kind that would leave the world open to further communist encroachment. Even that "converted" Republican, Arthur Vandenberg, could not see why the United Nations, unless radically strengthened, might suffer the same fate as the League of Nations.

To help prevent this seemed to me a solemn responsibility.

How to save peace by strengthening the United Nations was the subject of a five-day discussion at Dublin, New Hampshire, by a group of United World Federalists. Among the participants were lawyers, educators, editors, a publisher, businessmen, several young war veterans including Marshall Field, Jr., writers like Emery Reves and Michael Straight, my Jesuit friend, Father Edward Conway, physicist Henry De Wolf Smyth, and a syndicated columnist on world affairs. Among the silent observers were several young officers in uniform. Leading the discussions were former Supreme Court Justice Owen Roberts, Grenville Clark, former Governor of New Hampshire, Robert F. Bass, and Thomas K. Finletter. We agreed that permanent peace required some contraction of national sovereignty. On other points we differed sharply. At the end a comfortable majority, including me, signed resolutions calling for a Federal World Government with limited powers. Five participants, led by Justice Roberts and Clarence Streit, believed that "nuclear union" of democracies should come first. Thirteen, including U.S. Senator Styles Bridges, refused to sign, putting their faith in the evolution of the United Nations.

Most American newspapers were satisfied with the United Nations as it was and considered World Government either undesirable or utopian. Our three-way split at Dublin reflected the division among the American people and sparked public debate over the next few years, in which Lilian and I participated as fully as possible.

World Federalists, who had entered the field last, rapidly gained ground. Truman publicly predicted that one day "the peoples of the earth will live under one government just as the American Federal States do now." (Toward the end of 1947 a Gallup Poll indicated that a majority of Americans desired a "world government to control the forces of all nations, including the United States." In May of 1948, Chicago and Minneapolis staged a "world government week." By April, 1949, the State Legislatures of California, New Jersey, and North Carolina supported an amendment to the Federal Constitution permitting the United States to enter a world federation.)

In 1946, in the house of Eleanor de Bekessy, I had suggested to Senator J. William Fulbright that Congress might properly authorize the use of so-called counterpart funds in foreign countries to finance an exchange of scholars, thus cementing international relations. The result was the Fulbright Act.

In January, 1947, having learned that the State Department had informed Truman that "Soviet pressure against the free institutions of the Western world is something that can be contained by the adroit and vigilant application of counterforce," I accepted Elmer Davis' invitation to become a founding member of *Americans for Democratic Action*, in the belief that that organization would put the defense of freedom above any other preoccupation.

The replacement of Secretary of State Byrnes (who, Truman complained, "was beginning to think of himself as an assistant President in full charge of foreign policy") by George Marshall was no comfort. How trust the judgment of a general who had, in 1945, told Eisenhower, "I would be loath to hazard American lives for purely political purposes." What did he think wars were—Olympic Games?

Then the needed miracle happened: when Britain withdrew its armed forces from threatened Greece and the State Department further recommended that the United States take Britain's place as the protector of Greece (and, thanks to diplomat Loy Henderson, of Turkey as well), the President solemnly addressed a joint session of the Congress.

"I believe," he said, "it must be the policy of the United States to support free peoples who are resisting subjugation by armed minorities or by outside pressures." The Truman Doctrine was born.

This speech rocked the world. Aside from Russia-Firsters, Wallaceites, and unrepentant isolationists, the whole American people, including Congress and the ADA, applauded. For too long the United States had put up with injury and insult from a country which only massive American help had preserved from conquest and destruction. F.D.R.'s policy of appeasing Stalin had succumbed to its own inherent folly.

33

Truman Chases Ambulances

The Soviet Union selling democracy, prosperity and peace is about as convincing as a bald barber trying to induce his clients to buy expensive hair tonic.

—RAUL VARENGO, former headwaiter at the Algonquin Hotel, New York

LATE IN NOVEMBER, 1947, for the third time since V-E Day, I flew to Europe, this time to attend the Four-Power conference on the future of Germany. For me this would be the test: was the Truman Doctrine a call to action or just another of the slogans American Presidents so frequently substitute for a positive foreign policy?

Over the preceding years the United States had made several costly mistakes: trusting in Stalin's good intentions; demobilizing; failing to acquire a substantial stock of A-bombs while trying to reach an international agreement for their internationalization; and finally, forcing de-colonization upon friendly states.

Were our generals and businessmen relaxing military controls too quickly in our occupied zone in Germany? Did the Russians intend to keep Europe, including Germany, divided?

Moscow, having plucked bare its own part of Germany, was coolly demanding ten billion dollars of reparations from the rest of the country. To emphasize its demand, the Kremlin had, a month previously, instigated a communist-led general strike in France, which Premier Ramadier broke. Shortly thereafter his successor ousted the communist members from the Cabinet where the Party had been represented since 1944. Maybe the West did mean business.

Even before the failure of the Four-Power meeting, Georges Bidault confided to me in London that he and Britain's Foreign Minister Bevan had agreed upon what was to become the *European Union.*

It was high time. The British people had had more than enough austerity. Two years before, I remembered, only Conservatives had grumbled about it. Now individuals of all parties were in revolt.

A former colleague, American-born Virginia Cowles, the wife of the Labour M.P. Alden Crawley, explained the change. The Labour government was still rationing necessities as well as luxuries. Imports, though a "must" for trading Britain, were at a minimum. Corruption, Virginia asserted, was corroding John Bull's honest face. Among the "lower classes," taxi drivers, butchers, milkmen, and liquor-shop owners were profiteering. As a result, many other Britishers, like Americans under Prohibition, were black-marketeering.

Not since Oliver Cromwell had the English been so divided. The camps were much the same now as then—Cavaliers against ruling Roundheads. "How," an indignant Tory hostess asked me, "can the Americans expect us to worry about world government, united Europe, or Soviet expansion when we spend all of our time thinking about food, half of our time standing in line waiting for food, and a quarter of our time scheming how, by hook or crook, we can obtain more food!" Never, she felt, had any British government enforced such crass class legislation.

Yet Sir Stafford Cripps, over an excellent dinner, insisted that the English were finally enjoying social justice. Nobody was suffering from lack of nourishment. Clothes, though old and shabby (like his own), were adequate. Though Truman had cut off Lend-Lease too soon, the new American Loan and the Marshall Plan would soon lift England out of the postwar slump with its head held high. Cripps, if I remember rightly, ate no meat, neither smoked nor drank, and brooked no compromise with Evil. Nonetheless, I returned to America uncertain how much longer he and his friends could make austerity acceptable.

As Bidault had confided, Bevan in January, 1948, revealed his plan for a Five-Power Western Union. In March, the Kremlin struck back. Czechoslovak communists, with the support of Soviet divisions, snuffed out the last democracy in Central Europe, to the complete surprise of anticommunist Czechs. Four months before, at a dinner given by John Gunther in New York, Czechoslovakia's foreign minister, Jan Masaryk, had mocked Dorothy Thompson and me for suggesting that the Kremlin had designs on his country. In fact, Jan said, President Benes had in 1946 been worried lest the communists receive too *few* votes. Now an insignificant communist minority took over the country unopposed. Benes did not even suggest that the American troops stationed just across the frontier should come to his assistance. Once their paw was firmly fixed upon Czechoslovakia, Soviet representatives walked out of the Allied Control Council in Berlin.

In May, further emboldened by the West's passivity, Moscow set off a second communist revolt in Greece and communists in China stepped up military action against the Kuomintang.

Almost simultaneously, Stalin, annoyed by Marshal Tito's presumption in seeking to create a Balkan federation without Russia's permission, withdrew his military and civilian advisers from Yugoslavia. "Vile degenerates, a gang of hired spies and murderers headed by the Belgrade *Fuehrer,* Judas Tito, assumed the role of executors of a bloody plan of imperialist reaction," was the official explanation. And the *Vozhd* ordered the *Cominform* to expel Yugoslavia. In the United States, the Communist Party campaigned for Henry Wallace as President.

Happily, the Administration in Washington had not been idle. Truman made "containment" official and offered to Europe the economic assistance known as the Marshall Plan. The Occupying Powers and Benelux agreed upon a constitution for Trizonia, henceforth West Germany. When they introduced the new *Deutsche Mark,* thus depriving the Russians of further profit from those American-made currency plates which Harry Dexter White had given them, Stalin reacted by a total blockade of the city whose inhabitants he had failed either to win over or intimidate.

The United States, Britain, and France met the Russian challenge by launching a full-scale airlift to Berlin. The Cold War was on in earnest and by chance I played a minor part in shaping its political strategy.

In April, Charles Burton Marshall, an expert employed by the House Foreign Affairs Committee, told me that his brother, Colonel S. L. A. Marshall, soldier and journalist, had been recalled to the Army to write—or rewrite—policy for the Army Chief of Staff, General Omar Bradley, and wanted my advice about Europe. When we met, "Slam" and I agreed that the urgent need was for an Atlantic Alliance.

But was Europe ready for it? To find out, I asked Paul-Henri Spaak, now Belgium's Premier and Foreign Minister, which, if any, European countries would welcome an alliance with the United States. Spaak named several. These Marshall listed in a detailed paper for the Army Chief of Information and unobtrusively suggested that we ally ourselves with them. His memorandum found concurrences right up to the Secretary of Defense, James Forrestal, who put the Pentagon squarely behind what became the North Atlantic Treaty Organization.

Not long thereafter he and I collaborated successfully on a second project. The General Staff feared that pro-Stalinists in Yugoslavia would either murder Tito to please Stalin or manage in some other way to bring that country back into the Red fold. Only if Tito's breach with Big Brother in Moscow was truly unbridgeable ought he to receive economic aid from America.

When "Slam" told me of this situation, I invited to lunch with both of us Yugoslavia's former Washington Ambassador, Constantine Fotitch, and three other refugee Yugoslav diplomats. All four insisted that Tito's quarrel with Stalin was irreparable. This too Marshall told the Pentagon. Thus reassured, Forrestal helped convince Truman to give economic aid to tottering Tito.

As a result, Tito ceased assisting the Greek guerrillas, thus making it difficult for them to continue using Yugoslavia as a privileged sanctuary. Further American military aid to Greece soon became unnecessary. Though I felt that Truman should have obtained a bigger *quid* for his *quo,* the neutralization of Yugoslavia deprived the communist regime in Albania of effective outside protection. Here I saw our chance. A small number of Albanian refugees, armed, transported, and otherwise supplied by the United States, could spark a successful armed rebellion against communist Tirana by the Ghegs of the northern mountains. This would close the former Italian naval base on Sasenj Island to Soviet submarines.

During three lunches, I tried to convince Frank Wisner of the Central Intelligence Agency that this was desirable, feasible, and not too risky. Frank seemed unresponsive. Only fifteen years later, I learned that the Truman Administration, with the British had tried to foment and support an anticommunist coup in Albania, which failed because Russia's British spy, Kim Philby, revealed the plan to Moscow.

Shortly before, during a charming Guatemalan vacation with Lilian, I had suggested to President Juan José Arevalo that he offer federation to neighboring Honduras and Salvador. Never had I seen such "timeless" faces as those of the Indians around Lake Atitlan. To bring such as they into the twentieth century, Latin American countries needed to pool their educational efforts and their markets. Arevalo was not interested.

In September, 1948, Lilian and I went to Interlaken, Switzerland, where the European Parliamentarians were discussing European federation. The hero of the occasion was Richard Coudenhove-Kalergi, who had, in the twenties, converted Briand to his dream of Pan-Europa. The most eloquent partisans of the plan were two English M. P.'s, Bob Boothby and R. W. G. Mackay. Churchill had, in 1946, at Zurich relaunched his proposal of June, 1940.

Another gathering of world federalists from several countries brought us to Luxembourg. Though America was well represented, most of our delegates spoke no foreign language while many Europeans knew no English. The results were disappointing.

Yet Garry Davis, a young American federalist in Paris, ostentatiously turned in his American passport in order to emphasize his world citizenship. André Gide and Albert Camus organized *Les Compagnons de Garry Davis* with the same purpose. Federalism remained in the air.

The high point of our eight weeks in Europe, literally as well as emotionally, was a flight from Frankfurt to Berlin in a U.S. Army DC-3, as part of the airlift. The plane and its very young pilots had left Guam only three weeks before.

From my seat in the pilot's cabin I followed every detail of the flight, including a buzzing by two Soviet pursuits. Our plane was unarmed.

The Berliners' enthusiasm was obvious in the speed with which they emptied and refueled arriving planes, thus dispelling my previous doubts about the success of "Operation Vittles." Generals Clay and Howley and diplomat Bob Murphy were doing an incomparable job.

Yet in the Ruhr, British authorities were permitting communist-inspired coal miners to strike. This the British Deputy Lieutenant Governor, General Sir Richard McCreary, defended to me as part of "educating the Germans to democracy."

Ambassador de Saint Hardouin, at a lunch in Baden-Baden, stated that France stood for no such nonsense. "Alcatraz is not the right place to learn democracy," he insisted. Yet of the Western military occupants, the French were the most popular, perhaps because of their severity.

In Paris, in his office in the *Rue de Solférino*, General de Gaulle, whom I had not seen since Algiers, explained that France needed above all to postpone any possible showdown with the Soviet Union. The French people were still sick and he wanted to demonstrate his ability as a physician. From the General's associate, Christian Fouché, I learned of the high hopes de Gaulle placed in his newly organized *Rassemblement du Peuple Français*, the political party that refused to call itself a party.

We got home a few days before the presidential election in the States.

I had found it difficult to choose among the presidential candidates. At the time Truman announced his Doctrine, I would without hesitancy have supported him for a second term. Now I hesitated because he was hesitating. The Doctrine did not discriminate among "free peoples threatened by communist aggression and subversion." Yet instead of opposing communist expansion everywhere, Truman was, in the words of Congressman Walter Judd, "chasing ambulances" in a very selective way: Greece and Turkey received our help, China did not.

My support of Chiang Kai-shek was more than Ted Thackrey of the New York *Post* could take. During the war, Ted had seen no harm in sending an acknowledged communist to represent the *Post* in Moscow. For years my criticisms of the Soviet Union had galled him. Now his patience was exhausted. He informed me that I was so far out of touch with the *Post's* readers that he could no longer use my services.

I liked Ted and had striven to improve both his chess and his politics. But I had no intention of abandoning my convictions to please a Wallace-ite, and would carry on without the *Post,* and, if necessary, eke out a living by lecturing, writing books, and providing articles for such heterogeneous publications as *Better Homes and Gardens,* the *Zionist Quarterly,* the *Saturday Review, Coronet, See, Collier's,* and *Reader's Digest.* This proved unnecessary. George Little of General Features took over the column.

In November, 1948, my *Nightmare of American Foreign Policy* appeared. In it I noted that F.D.R.'s substitution of phrases and slogans for a positive foreign policy had encouraged Germany and Japan to unleash the Second World War and that his war-time Great Gamble had cost us the peace.

Truman's (for America) revolutionary decisions to defend Greece, Turkey, the Dardanelles, and Iran had, I continued, changed the world atmosphere. Yet even the Truman Doctrine and the Marshall Plan could save freedom and peace only if they led to the unity of the noncommunist world, and, ultimately, to a world federation. Until then we Americans would be plagued by dark uncertainties.

The concluding paragraphs read:

"Yet . . . in such a crisis it seemed to many observers that the drowsy leaders of the world's greatest democracy were aiming at nothing more than the preservation of an outworn system of sovereign states. . . . They were continuing their country's dreary diplomatic pattern of weakening potential allies and strengthening potential enemies.

"This was the nightmare of American foreign policy in 1948."

The reviewers' reaction was enthusiastic. The New York *Times* called the *Nightmare* "incomparably the best study of American foreign policy for this period that has yet been written." The Cleveland *News* gave it an eight-column head on the book page. Another newspaper called it a "devastating exposé" and a fourth praised the style ("epigrammatic and terse").

In England the volume had what the French call a *succès d'estime,* with the London *Times* and the *New English Weekly* on my side and liberal mandarins, led by Max Beloff, brushing off my criticism of F.D.R. as "querulous staccato."

To implement his Doctrine, Truman made Acheson Secretary of State, an obvious improvement over the "nonpolitical" George Marshall. Yet even as Acheson was launching the North Atlantic Treaty Organization and strengthening it by military bases in Spain, he was abandoning the Chinese Nationalists.

To me, this bordered on lunacy. In the late war, the United States had defeated Japan while simultaneously making a mighty contribution to the defeat of Germany. Lenin had predicted that the way from Moscow to Paris led through Peking and New Delhi. The communists had Peking. Madame Chiang, during a visit to Washington, had warned that Russia had equipped no less than five Chinese communist divisions with Japanese arms. Her husband could not hold out much longer. What was the United States waiting for?

On November 7, 1948, Stalin had told the Kremlin's inner circle that once communist comrades stood on the Indo-Chinese border, the positions of the French in Indochina would become helpless. "But we shall not stop with Indo-China," he had continued. "From there we shall spread southward into Indonesia and Malaya and westward into Siam and Burma. India itself will be threatened. As for Korea, the Yankee half will fall into our hands like a ripe plum. Even in Japan our friends will not be idle . . . . But we are counting most upon our gains in Latin America to paralyze the United States. . . . The revolution is well on the way."

There was no indication that these remarks disturbed the self-styled

China experts of the Institute of Pacific Relations. They already were calling those of us who urged assistance to Chiang, the "China Lobby." This, Congressman Walter Judd remarked later, was the invention of Americans who knew themselves "responsible for the loss of China to the communists."

In March, 1949, Jim Forrestal, who had just resigned as our first Secretary of Defense, invited me to Sunday dinner and poured out his troubles. Since 1941 he had repeatedly warned, first F.D.R. and then Truman, of the need to take the counteroffensive against communism. Now Truman and Marshall were washing their hands of China. His efforts to "federate" the three armed services had drawn the hostility of all of them. His family life had become impossible. He had been foully slandered, he charged, by a notoriously pacifist newsman who had accused him of physical cowardice. He had reached the end of his rope.

Jim listened patiently to my rejoinder that man achieves greatness not by casting off burdens but by taking them on. His troubles were the measure of his stature. But my argument made no impression. After dinner, I accompanied him to the Defense Department where he was posing for a portrait. At the door, with unusual solemnity, he said goodbye. Two months later he leaped to his death through an open hospital window.

In April, 1949, I became a consultant to DeWitt Poole, director of the new, nominally private but government-supported National Committee for a Free Europe, which was soon to inaugurate Radio Free Europe. Thereafter, until illness compelled Poole to resign, I spent four days a month in the office in New York, planning political warfare. During a trip to Europe I persuaded the French Ministry of Education in Paris and the University of Strasbourg to let the Committee establish in the latter city a *Free Europe University in Exile* (with its companion *College de l'Europe Libre*), of which Malcolm Davis became the first head. These provided instruction, particularly about their own countries, to young refugees from communist East Europe. They lasted until 1958 when Adolf A. Berle decided there were no longer enough young refugees to justify further assistance of this sort.

In July, 1949, following a suggestion I made to Carlos P. Romulo, then Philippine Ambassador to the United Nations, President Quirino and President Rhee of South Korea made a public appeal for a Pacific anticommunist pact. In August, Yuri Zhukov, a Russian Goebbels, violently attacked me for urging the immediate formation of a single freedom bloc.

Shortly thereafter, the Soviets exploded their first nuclear "device" several years before most American experts expected it. Truman's enthusiasm for any extension of containment to Asia dropped sharply. While Secretary Acheson waited for "the dust to settle" over the Far East, Chiang Kai-shek conceded his own total defeat by retreating to Formosa.

Truman still refused to promise him American protection. Assistant Secretary of State, Dean Rusk, publicly compared the communists' rebellion in China to the American Revolution! Acheson, in a speech that had worldwide resonance, conspicuously omitted Formosa, Korea, and Southeast Asia from America's defense perimeter. George Kennan, in our house, solemnly assured Congressman Walter Judd, who knew better, that it would be fifty years before Red China could "jeopardize America's security." Only after Mao concluded a military alliance with Red Ho of Indochina did the United States start giving financial support to the French in that country.

I was gloomy about Indochina. "If Washington and Paris," I wrote, "do not cease playing 'button, button, who's got the button' in Indochina, they are going to wake up some morning to find that particular button sewed to Great Stalin's coat." When *Americans for Democratic Action* publicly attacked Chiang Kai-shek, I resigned from that organization.

Truman was concentrating his efforts on Europe. Once the Soviets capitulated to the Berlin airlift, the United States, Britain, and France gradually restored sovereignty to West Germany. The European Economic Administration, headed by Paul Hoffman, was accomplishing wonders, as I knew from my daughter, Diana Jane, who was working with that organization in Paris.

Stalin's hostility was angering more and more Americans. In April, 1950, George Creel, who had headed President Wilson's Committee on Public Information, warned me that a Republican Senator, one Joe McCarthy, an "unscrupulous black Irishman," according to Creel, was impugning the loyalty of whole categories of citizens without adequate evidence.

This was the more regrettable because, as most newsmen in Washington were aware, the Administration was employing a number of pro-Russians, some of them merely "pink," others members of the Communist Party, who should have been dropped years before. In 1939, Premier Daladier in Paris had warned Ambassador Bullitt of the presence in the State Department of a Communist agent called "Eece."

"Eece is not a name, it is the sound a snake makes," objected Bullitt.

When he identified "Eece" as Alger Hiss, he passed the word on to Washington, with no result.

Truman demanded "conclusive proof" of any charge before firing anyone and did not always act when he had it.

As a meticulous defender of personal and civil liberty, I sided emotionally with Truman. The danger to America came primarily not from Party members but from the far greater number of honest pro-Russians, doctrinaires, and dupes who could not bring themselves to accept Moscow's and Peking's enmity as a fact of life. Unquestionably the Senator's attacks eliminated some undesirables. Yet by doing injustice to others, they sparked the popular revulsion against "McCarthyism" that cleared the way for the procommunist revival of the sixties.

North Korea's invasion of the South, in June, 1950, caught the entire West off base. U.N. Secretary General Trygve Lie sputtered: "By Gott, dot is aggression." To me it seemed a God-given opportunity for the United States to reunite Korea under Syngman Rhee.

The former U.S. Battery D captain skillfully mobilized the United Nations and in their name ordered General MacArthur to save South Korea. Lilian and I flew to Europe—again!—to ascertain the effect of this decision upon our allies.

Conservative Britain, as represented by Anthony Eden, by Bob Boothby, and by the Marquis of Salisbury, now dwelling in his ancestors' spacious Hatfield House, approved Truman's reaction. So, I gathered, did Winston Churchill, whom I heard speak in the Albert Hall ("he is dying to be Prime Minister again," Lady Bonham Carter confided). Yet though he talked with something of the old fire, he was no longer the peerless leader of 1940.

Officially the Labor government supported the United Nations' action in Korea, but the hostility of the "Keep Left" boys became apparent when, over a luncheon on the terrace of the House of Commons, Nye Bevan assured me that, were he Chinese, he would be a communist. Nye had been one of the few Laborites to urge British action against Nazi Germany in the late thirties. Communism was "different." Nye had imbibed too heavily of those articles in *The New Statesman* which conservatives called "Kingsley Martin's bottled belly-ache." Never thereafter did I seek his company, or he mine.

The Netherlands were bringing a hundred thousand men home from lost Indonesia. Having been constrained by America to abandon their colony, why should Dutchmen worry about Korea?

Belgium was looking inward for a different reason. Most Walloons and some Flemings had never forgiven King Leopold for surrendering too quickly to the Germans, for remaining in Belgium and visiting Germany during the war, and for remarrying a Flemish commoner. Unless Leopold abdicated, they threatened to split the country.

Brussels was paralyzed. I had to appeal to Bob Murphy, now U.S. Ambassador there, to get my baggage from the station to a hotel where for two days I was the only guest. The others had fled the city through fear of civil war.

Leaders of all three major political parties, bankers, shopkeepers, policemen, embassy servants, were insisting that Leopold must go. Crowds tramped the main streets shouting insults and obscenities at the King and "his Liliane." On the third day, when Bob Murphy confided that Leopold had agreed to abdicate in favor of his son, Baudouin, I hurried to the *Maison du Peuple,* the Trade Union Center, talked my way in past the guards, and waited for Spaak, who had led to the Royal Palace at Laecken the crowd that obtained the King's abdication.

When Spaak arrived, he grinned broadly and shouted, "Yes, my

friend, it's all over, and now let's go into the pastry shop." We celebrated the event in true Belgian fashion by washing down chocolate
eclairs with glasses of beer.

Ten days in Frankfurt, Berlin, and Bonn demonstrated how much
the German people owed to Konrad Adenauer—and to Joseph Stalin.
Without both, they would still have been atoning for Hitler's war. Over
an excellent lunch, Jack McCloy argued that in view of Russia's transparent ambition to communize all Germany, we had no alternative but
to accept West Germany under a trustworthy man like Adenauer, as a
member of the anticommunist front. Jack conceded that the phrase,
"*ohne uns*," was on too many German lips and that Left Socialists,
along with the communists and some Lutherans like Pastor Niemoeller,
were defiantly nationalistic. Still, he insisted, we had no sensible alternative to treating the West Germans as, well, *step*-brothers.

I could not but agree. The Germans were a powerful people whom
we should keep on our side.

The Allied forces, McCloy said, were still too few to defend the
Rhine, still less, the zonal demarcation line, against a determined
Russian ground attack. (An American correspondent wisecracked that
by putting into uniform our civilian committees in Germany we could
provide five divisions more.)

Berlin was, as always, unconquerable in spirit. I was not surprised
when the "Assistant" Mayor, Dr. Ferdinand Friedensburg, a remarkable
man who had, I believe, spent many years in the United States, assured
me that *his* Berliners could be counted on to defend themselves against
any aggression with everything they had. . . .

In Strasbourg, the Consultative Assembly of Europe was struggling
to promote European unity. Winston Churchill was urging the formation of a single European army. In this he was supported by Robert
Schuman of France and by Count Sforza of Italy. Unhappily, my
esteemed friend, Hugh Dalton, opposed any such internationalism.
When, I wondered, would the Labor Party understand that to remain
creative and influential, Britain must join the continent?

France's Premier, René Pleven, was ready not only to provide
troops for an Army of Europe, but to admit a German contingent.

Charles de Gaulle was not. The general, in the course of a long
talk in his villa, *La Boisserie*, at Colombey-des-Deux-Eglises, answered
my question, "off the record, of course." His views had not changed.
Only France could provide leadership for a united, humanistic, Christian, and democratic Europe. Postwar France was neither a true state
nor a true society—"governed by phantoms and puppets, undermined
by communists, socialists, and selfish industrialists." To rebecome a
nation France must "straighten up" (his favorite expression). Only

Charles de Gaulle could reawaken that sleeping soul without which France would go from bad to worse. When conditions in France and the world became bad enough his people would call on him to lead them out of "the mess in Paris."

Meanwhile he was penning his own memoirs. From time to time he raised his eyes from a page, and looked west across the rolling hills of the former Duchy of Bar toward the city from which the summons would surely come.

After a few days of almost supernal rest in the none too accessible Grand Hotel at Chandolin in Switzerland, Lilian and I motored to Marina di Massa in Italy to have lunch with Sforza. While we were looking for his villa, Sforza, who had been successively Europe's most experienced diplomat, Italy's youngest foreign minister, Mussolini's most formidable enemy, and Winston Churchill's *bête noire*, hailed us from over a stone wall. Imagine a tall old gentleman with a noble head, the face of a Renaissance patrician, white hair, white mustache, and small, white, pointed beard, dressed in an apple-green silk robe that hung to midleg over white silk sox and dark blue canvas shoes with rope soles. It was hard to say whether he more resembled a Roman senator or a Chinese mandarin.

Sforza painted a vivid picture of contemporary Europe: a continent still suffering from an inferiority complex; fearful of being involved in an extra-European war by the United States, yet unable to forego America's protection.

"Americans," Sforza added, "are popular in Italy. Your soldiers were sometimes rough and not too honest, but they loved and fed our children. That won all Italian hearts. Italy is the paradise of children, just as France is of women, and England of horses."

In Venice, no longer the incomparable ghost-like city of 1918, U.S. Ambassador "Jimmy" Dunn exuded optimism. "Never forget," he said, "there are two kinds of strength, the ability to inflict suffering and the ability to endure it. Italians are unique in their ability to take punishment. Expecting nothing, they are satisfied with little."

Italy captivated us as easily as it had thirty-four years earlier. Imagine the Piazza del Duomo in Reggio Emilia at ten o'clock at night with two trapeze artists performing on a wire sixty feet above the pavement while half the town's population looked on!

In Greece I interviewed, among others, former Prime Minister Plastiras. Should not his country, and Turkey as well, enter into European defense? I asked. He replied that America should put more pressure to do so on both countries. The Greeks were a passionately democratic people living under the threat of communist or reactionary dictatorship, burdened with selfish economic monopolies, partly because of their own inability to practice responsible democracy. As a result, the area from Greece to Pakistan was still incapable of self-defense. (In mid-October Greece and Turkey joined NATO and the prospect for Europe improved.) From Athens we flew home to Washington.

By this time General MacArthur had saved South Korea and begun the liberation of the North. Averell Harriman complained that MacArthur "has a strange idea that we should back anyone who will fight communism."

Forty-two nations were fighting communism in Korea. Yet many Leftists, like Nehru and Prime Minister Attlee of Britain, were doing what they could to prevent MacArthur from advancing to the North Korean-Manchurian border or from bombing China beyond the Yalu.

A few days later, Red Chinese troops entered North Korea as "volunteers."

How did they dare? Without landing a man, the United States could blockade and half starve China and destroy a large part of its industrial plants. Had the Indian Government assured them that these things would not happen? According to General MacArthur (*Reminiscences*), the Chinese commander, General Lin Piao, later confessed, "I would not have risked my men and military reputation if I had not been assured that Washington would restrain General MacArthur from taking adequate retaliatory measures against my lines of supply and communication."

To me the Red Chinese intervention was an opportunity to assist Chiang's forces in liberating the mainland.

But instead of punishing the new aggressor, the United Nations allowed them to send as their representative to Lake Success a certain Wu, whose speeches reached a new high in insolence. By this time MacArthur's troops were in retreat. At the United Nations, defeatism was now rampant. To make matters worse, Truman's vague reference to the possible use of the A-bomb brought Prime Minister Attlee flying to Washington to argue against any escalation. Truman agreed. "The United States was not," he believed, "in a position to assume the burden of a major war." But if not, whose was the fault? When MacArthur again drove the invaders back to the Thirty-eighth Parallel, Truman ordered him to stop there.

Once the American people realized that Truman was not seeking victory, they wrote off the undertaking as "Truman's War."

Two months later, McGraw-Hill brought out my new opus, *Challenge and Decision* ("Edgar is hard on publishers," one of my friends commented on my shift from Alfred Knopf). The book not only offended the pacifists and pro-Russians, but shocked many friends. For in it, I described twenty *irreconcilable* differences between the communists' regimes and ours. The existing "balance of terror" made a nuclear war unlikely. But no "balance" had in the past ever preserved peace for long. Communist governments seeking to expand their ideology and rule by all means short of major war could not accept a system of law that would put an end to any such hope. Nor could the free countries accept the type of world sought by communists. Disunited, the former must expect a never-ending series of Korean-type little wars. United, they could use their preponderant power to take a political offensive that included subversion and revolts in the satellite countries, and in Russia's internal colonies—in short, follow a *policy of liberation.*

This was the thesis of *Challenge and Decision.*

More favorable reviews. Newspapers in Manila and in Bloomington, Illinois (my birthplace) serialized the book. Doctrinaire pro-Russians, pacifists, and champions of the United Nations attacked or ignored it.

Their criticism did not disturb me too much. I was demanding of the free peoples, beginning with my own, an effort as devoid of sentimentality as of cynicism, which they still seemed incapable of making.

In December, 1950, I declined to renew my membership in the Foreign Policy Association, too pro-Russian for my taste, and three months later resigned from United World Federalists, with whose officers I had been in increasing disagreement over the need for successfully scotching the communist threat in Asia.

34

Containment Leaks

What I am asking you in the name of your principles, I am refusing you in the name of my own.

—LOUIS VEUILLOT

TRUMAN'S ACCEPTANCE of a stalemate in Korea upset so many Americans that, in my judgment, it cost his party the next presidential election. Some of the dissatisfied were Democrats. Senator Paul Douglas, always a fighter, urged Truman to create an American army of six million men. The brilliant Polish general, Wladyslav Anders, suggested that the President recruit a European Freedom Corps to aid in liberating East Europe. My own suggestion of an immediate peace treaty with, and rearmament of, Japan had a considerable echo.

Together, Congressman Abraham Ribicoff of Connecticut, Charles Burton Marshall, and I sought to arouse the American people to the choice confronting the Administration: of winning in Korea or fighting elsewhere. Once or twice Ribicoff took Marshall and me with him on lecture engagements on the assumption that three voices were more convincing than one.

On one such occasion, talking to students at Hollins College on the difficulties of the undeveloped countries, I suggested that college graduates could help the cause of freedom if, as government employees, they would each go for a year or two to a backward country, live with the natives, help in whatever way they could, and receive most of their pay in a lump sum after they returned. President Everett was skeptical, but when I put the question to a group of seniors majoring in political science, half said they would like nothing better than to join a Freedom Corps. This may have been one of the seeds from which the subsequent Peace Corps sprouted.

384

Late in March, 1951, I purchased from Pan American Airways two round-the-world tickets. Four months earlier, speaking at the Dutch Treat Club in New York, I had called for an American foreign policy going beyond selective containment. "We do not," I argued, "have to sit like hypnotized rabbits while the Soviet Union devours ever more unwilling peoples. We have all it would take to make each new act of aggression too costly for the Kremlin. The Cold War need not be a one-way street."

When I finished speaking, those present stood up and cheered. DeWitt Wallace, whom I barely knew, invited me to Pleasantville and bluntly asked what sort of job I wanted with *Reader's Digest*. I explained that I preferred to remain unattached, but would gladly write for his magazine.

Now I found myself with Lilian encircling the planet for the *Digest,* an experience that excited even incurable travelers like us.

During the next nine weeks we visited the "new Asia" from Karachi to Korea, an experience that caused me to modify a number of opinions. To begin with, talks in Karachi and New Delhi revealed that whereas the Pakistani rulers (soldiers and farmers), never claimed to be pacifists, the Indian government was schizophrenic. To foreign governments it preached "nonviolence." But it brazenly used force to seize anything that it wanted, with no nonsense about "self-determination."

Hindu philosophy, as filtered through Dr. Hoffman in Chicago, Vladimir Michailov, and the theosophists, had made a lasting impression upon me, deeper even than the Moslem Persian poets. Most of my Indian friends were Hindus, including Eric Da Costa, objective editor of the *Eastern Economist.* In Washington we were on friendly terms with India's Ambassador, Madame Vijaya Lakshmi Pandit, an attractive woman full of common sense, through whom I met her famous brother Nehru.

The day before I interviewed Nehru in New Delhi, the British High Commissioner, over a leisurely lunch, warned that the Prime Minister was prone to tantrums during which he sometimes became insulting. "You can, of course, walk out if you choose, but if you say nothing he'll get over it in a few minutes."

Sure enough, when, at the beginning of our talk, I mentioned John Foster Dulles, Nehru's handsome face darkened, he pounded on the table, and launched a tirade against Americans, apparently because United States forces were still occupying Japan. "I would," he shouted, "rather see India starve for two centuries than submit to foreign dictation." When I continued to smile, he soon smiled back and for the rest of an hour defended the Chinese communists for "saving" North Korea and "eliminating" class enemies at home.

When finally I asked what India would do if attacked by Red China, he declared the notion too absurd to be considered.

"Intelligent people," I said pleasantly, "can consider any hypothethis."

Nehru relented. "In case of an attack by China, I should call upon the United Nations and the United States for help."

"And in view of your attitude toward the Korean war, do you think many Americans would be eager to help India?"

"You mean you would give us no military aid?"

"Well," I answered slowly, "I feel sure we should send you an ambulance."

One ambulance had been India's contribution to the United Nations action in Korea.

Lilian talked with more people than I did, admiring the energy of the women, yet shuddering in Calcutta at the animal sacrifices in the Temple of Kali Ghat and the sight of people starving to death on the sidewalks.

"Just what," an American agricultural expert in New Delhi asked, "can one do for an insanely proliferating people who permit sacred cows and sacred monkeys to eat up 10 percent of their grain crop?" We left India convinced that without a radical change of attitude— less superstition, caste, international moralizing, and population, and more food—India was heading for unending trouble.

Neither India's misery nor its ruler's fatuity could destroy the profound joy of visiting the Taj Mahal and Fatipur Sikri. The former was almost too perfect, a sort of celestial palace.

The ruined town of Fatipur Sikri fell short of perfection, yet its greater variety fascinated me even more. This was my first experience of the marriage of Moslem and Hindu art and I marveled at its purity.

The Burmese were different, more prosperous, good-humored even while defending themselves against two sorts of internal rebels, the communists and the Karens, who controlled large sections of the country. Prime Minister Nu (each Burmese has a single name) greeted me in his heavily guarded office as an old friend. He explained his friendship: while in Rangoon in 1941, I had predicted that Japan would soon take over his country ("a bull's eye") and he had translated into Burmese, and published, *Germany Puts the Clock Back* ("an eye opener to Burma") without bothering to inform (or pay!) me. These facts made us brothers. Nu struck me as more a devout Buddhist than a politician.

Compared to India, Thailand seemed positively opulent. The people were jolly, hospitable, and fond of good living. The Thai rulers' uncanny ability to rally to victors had enabled them to remain independent.

In independent Java, the town of Batavia, now Jakarta, looked down at the heel, poorer than in 1941, ostentatiously anti-Dutch and anti-American. This in spite of political support and concrete aid by the United States and of the pro-Indonesian attitude of the American member of the United Nations Good Offices Committee, H. Merle Cochran. Communists dominated the labor organization, the SOBSI (which irate American businessmen called "those S.O.B.'s"). Even Moslem Indonesians, like my friend, M. Mohamed Diah, publisher of the newspaper *Merdeka* (Freedom), whose pretty wife had graduated from Columbia University, defended the North Korean and Red Chinese aggressors simply because they were Asians.

So did the Indonesian ruler, Sukarno, to whom I listened for two hours, hearing how he, Bung Karno, had liberated his country single-handedly, why he had been compelled to sell his countrymen as slave labor to the occupying Japanese, and how terrible the Dutch had always been. (Actually Indonesia owed what was left of its former prosperity exclusively to the development of its tin, rubber, and oil by the Dutch.) At the same time, Sukarno invited us to witness a marvelously stylicized performance of Javanese classical drama by its finest actors. If only, I thought, these people would stick to art! But that was the last thing Bung Karno had in mind. Like Nehru's, his joy was in telling off Western imperialists.

Under Sukarno's rule, Indonesia seemed bound to become an international problem.

Britain's Commissioner-General in Singapore, Malcolm MacDonald, and the Sultan of Johore to whom MacDonald introduced me, held that the loss of South Korea to communism would endanger all Southeast Asia. General MacArthur was not the only upholder of the "domino theory."

Both were shocked at Truman's recent summary dismissal of the General. MacArthur had been insubordinate and technically merited removal as commander. But suppose he were right about China—as they thought? Truman's summary action seemed certain to encourage Mao to further aggression.

In Indochina, Ho Chi-Minh and his confederates were nourishing a rebellion that had gone on almost since the French returned to Saigon after the war. Paris' grant of quasi-independence to Vietnam under Emperor Bao Dai made no difference to rebels who wanted their own communist government.

Saigon and Hanoi were, I wrote, "quivering with treason, under armed guard and military law, with military and police, tommy guns in hand, patrolling the streets."

"Safety is restricted to towns, armed convoys and limited country areas. . . . No one in Saigon can ever be quite sure that the European-dressed passerby, the workman repairing the pavement, the elegant Chinese lady in tight white trousers with long black tunic, the merchant behind the counter or the servant in his own house is not a secret agent of Ho Chi-Minh. . . . The local black marketeer who offers you an unusual number of piastres for your foreign currency does so, like as not, to accumulate for his communist friends those dollars which Red China demands for the war material it is supplying to the Vietnamese rebels. . . . If we had not fought in Korea, the Chinese might already have taken Indochina. . . . If the French were forced to yield, the defense of Korea would have been largely in vain."

The American Minister, Donald Heath, Emperor Bao Dai, whom we visited at mountainous Dalat, and the French Governor General, Marshal Jean de Lattre de Tassigny, who had shown his mettle in France in 1944 and 1945, shared this view.

De Lattre had just won a great victory over eighty-four well-equipped communist battalions. He believed that with adequate support, he could stamp out the revolt in spite of the nearby Chinese "sanctuary."

In Berlin, in 1945, Marshal Zhukov had told de Lattre that, having lost twenty-three million Russians in the recent war, the Kremlin would not embark upon a new one until it could count on both China and India to share the expected costs. China was now ready. The West's first task was therefore to prevent a communist takeover of India, toward which that of Indochina was merely a way station. On this account only, he, a Marshal of France, had accepted responsibility for the conduct of the *sale guerre* in Asia. The United States was providing some arms, but he required many more to do the job properly. After all, French losses in Indochina were higher than American losses in Korea. Unless Paris awakened and Washington did more, he expected the worst.

From him we heard the story of Ho's communist past in Paris, of his postwar revolt, and of his tactics—chiefly, the intimidation and torture of unwilling peasants and assassination of enemies. A favorite device was shooting French officers in the back as they sat at a café or restaurant table.

We became great friends with De Lattre, stayed in the Governor's palace in Saigon, and, from Hanoi, inspected the Tonkinese battlefields from two observation planes which he provided.

After a final dinner, we flew to Hong Kong, where British traders were providing Mao Tse-tung with much of what Ho required to keep on fighting.

American officials reported that in China Mao had murdered at least a million and a half "class enemies" in the previous three months.

The American Embassy in Manila was full, but Ambassador Myron Cowen found us shelter in the nearby house of Embassy Secretary Meader. Cowen, a corporation lawyer with a natural gift for international affairs, explained how our hesitancy in Korea had encouraged the Philippine communists, the so-called *Hukbalahap*, to step up subversion and revolt. Fortunately the Huks had found more than their match in President Quirino and his Secretary of Defense, Ramon Magsaysay. With the assistance of an astute American intelligence officer, Colonel Edward G. Lansdale, the Secretary was successful in organizing, protecting, and sometimes resettling the peasants, thus making them proof against the Huks' terrorism and seduction, which they practiced as part of Mao's famous strategy of "swimming among the rural population like fish in the sea." Once the "sea" soured on the "Red fish," the latter had no other place to go. Magsaysay pardoned repentant rebels; the impenitent he hunted down. Whether the system could have worked had the Philippines been adjacent to a Red "sanctuary" nobody could say. There it was a magnificent success.

President Quirino remembered me from 1941 and offered me an interview at Baguio where he insisted on our staying in the presidential villa. He too was disturbed by Truman's failure to win in Korea. "If only he had listened to MacArthur," the President sighed.

Two days later we left for all that remained of the Republic of China.

The city of Taipei offered a curious mixture of old Chinese, Japanese, and Japan-built "Kaiser Wilhelm" architecture. But from Chiang Kai-shek and Mei-ling, who welcomed us as old friends, I heard that on the mainland, communist cruelty had brought about such a revulsion against the regime that the civil war could be revived—if the United States would help. This was confirmed by C. C. Chen, the former Chinese newsman who had rescued Jacques Marcuse and me on the Yellow River in 1938. At an intimate (for China) luncheon (only sixteen people) a guest newly escaped from Shanghai gave us a vivid description of the Chinese people's growing disillusion with Mao and his confederates. This feeling inspired clandestine letters from various parts of the mainland, a large pile of which reached Taipei every day. Moreover, a make-or-break spirit had arisen among the Chinese exiles: Taiwan was the springboard from which they would retake China! In this eventual undertaking Chiang was counting on American support.

Tokyo was uglier and bigger than I had imagined. The people seemed to have lost every scrap of their former pugnacity. Since the Imperial Hotel was bursting with Americans, we found a room in a comfortable Japanese hostel, and came to prefer it.

General MacArthur had unquestionably done a fine administrative job. By a mixture of inflexibility, inaccessibility, and paternalism he had made himself and total disarmament positively popular. Some American diplomats thought he had succeeded too well. Should the Chinese victory in Korea encourage further aggression by Peking, a Japan able and ready to defend itself might be more useful to the world than an impotent Japan. Most educated Japanese were against any rearmament: one defeat was enough. The socialists were publicly yearning for nonalignment. Or was their neutrality in the Korean war just *Schadenfreude* at seeing their Western conquerors humiliated by Chinese fellow Asians?

By pulling every available string, I managed to obtain a noncommittal interview with Prime Minister Shigeru Yoshida and we were both granted an audience by His Imperial Majesty, Emperor Hirohito ("please, no politics"), a charming, diffident man.

In Korea, the fighting no longer warranted a visit to the front. But I interviewed the American civil authorities and had one luncheon with Prime Minister John Myun Chang at Pusan and another with President Syngman Rhee in his villa overlooking the Korea Strait. American liberals were accusing Rhee of being the "reactionary disciple of Woodrow Wilson" because he urged the liberation of *all* of his country. I found him less authoritarian than many of his accusers! At least he knew what the fighting in Asia was about.

Before flying to San Francisco, Lilian and I celebrated in Tokyo the inauguration of the Japanese edition of *Reader's Digest* with DeWitt and Lila Wallace (there for the occasion).

Marvelous as the round-the-world flight had been, I was deeply troubled by what I had seen and heard. Truman was throwing away perhaps the last opportunity to correct his mistake in not preventing Mao's seizure of China. The situation called for a bold new Far Eastern policy.

Instead, Washington was wallowing in domestic turmoil. MacArthur's dismissal had given Republicans the slogans they needed, "Truman's war" and "no substitute for victory." Acheson's claim that the negotiations with the Red Chinese in Korea *were* a victory for the United Nations deceived nobody.

Nor were things going well in Europe. The June election in France had produced a Chamber wherein almost half the Deputies—Communists and Gaullists—were hostile to the Army of Europe, on which Washington was basing its hope of European defense. Britain, according to Churchill, intended to remain the focal point of those three overlapping circles, the Commonwealth, the Anglo-American Alliance, and Western Europe as a poor third. In August the British Labor Party actually campaigned on its success in promoting the disastrous Korean armistice, thus "saving the world from war."

In December, 1951, Abe Ribicoff returned from Europe to report increasing disarray. "The Americans," he said, "believe that Britain and West Europe should unite without the United States; the British, that West Europe should unite without Britain; the French, that West Europe should unite without Germany."

A year later, a devoted French Gaullist, Michel Debré, put his finger on the missing key. "There could," he said, "be no Army of Europe without a Three Power nuclear force." Giving France nuclear weapons was an idea repugnant to Washington and London.

Except in superweapons, the American armed forces were weaker than those of the Soviet Union. Congressman "Scoop" Jackson insisted that our lack of conventional military power had cost us East Europe, China, and North Korea, with further losses in sight. Yet our President saw no immediate reason for recreating the world's most powerful air force and refused to take Yugoslav and Polish refugee volunteers into the American Army. When, in May, some fourteen thousand North Korean prisoners in the hands of South Korea refused to return to Communist China and Syngman Rhee declined to compel them to do so, certain American officials actually advocated our forcing him to repatriate them.

Unmindful of the effect on European unity, Secretary Acheson was trying to get the British out of Egypt, in accordance with the Administration's policy of promoting the "immediate independence, democracy and prosperity of the backward peoples." Truman, like Marx, believed that communism and poverty were Siamese twins. In his 1952 State of the Union Message he insisted that had the rich nations devoted one-third of the cost of the Second World War to feeding the hungry, there would have been no communism. Britain's Barbara Ward, more influential in Washington than in London, argued that the task of the Twentieth Century was to bring a New Deal to the entire world. Yet under existing circumstances any such attempt, I feared, would mean fattening more sheep for Stalin's table.

As the nominating conventions, which we planned to attend, came nearer, both political parties sharpened their political positions. The Republicans charged the Democrats with "corruption, communism and Korea." At their convention in Chicago, Senator McCarthy all but accused the Democratic Administration of treason. Senator Taft, still semi-isolationist at heart, yearned for a return for the good old prewar days. General Eisenhower spoke modestly and moderately—too moderately for my taste.

At the subsequent Democratic convention in the same city, Mrs. Roosevelt told the delegates that we Americans should "win over the Russians by making our hearts pure, our hands clean." (I could hear Stalin's guffaw.) Senator Brian McMahon, an outsider, bid for the presidential nomination by proposing to "wage peace"—as though the United States had not been doing just that since 1945 with no results!

The Democratic platform promised "to free the captive peoples by espousing the contagious liberating influences which are inherent in freedom." Folly (or was it hypocrisy?) could go no further. Only with the acquiescence of at least a part of the armed forces can any people cast off a modern totalitarian dictatorship.

The Democrats' reliance upon "contagious liberating influence" cleared any doubt from my mind: I would support General Eisenhower. To be sure, the General had been partly responsible for our letting the Russians take and keep Berlin. Nobody knew exactly what his foreign policy would be. But it was no secret that if elected he would ask John

Foster Dulles to be his Secretary of State. In his book, *War or Peace,* Dulles had urged the United States to "think in terms of taking the offensive and of *rolling back* the engulfing tide of despotism."

Perhaps it was still not too late to rescue East Europe and China, and thus avoid an atomic war.

Shortly after the conventions, Kenneth Payne, Executive Editor of *Reader's Digest,* proposed I write another article for the magazine. I was reluctant. When I returned from Asia, in accordance with my understanding with DeWitt Wallace, I had offered to write for the *Digest* a piece to be called "Indo China—Next on Moscow's List." Wallace first demurred, then bade me write it, and finally refused to print it as "too far-fetched." Why repeat such an experience?

Ken shrugged off my argument: such fickleness was normal on the part of the *Digest.* Had I not had a free trip around the world? (Actually, I had sold to *Harper's* magazine a "think piece" on what the backward peoples of Asia really wanted: *equality of status.*) Finally I agreed to go to Italy and report on the results of American aid to that country.

On the way to Rome, my wife and I took quick looks at France, Belgium and Germany. In France, I found myself reciting Tennyson's *Lotus Eaters:*

> *Hateful is the deep blue sky*
> *Vaulted over the deep blue sea.*
> *Death is the end of life; oh, why*
> *Should life all labor be?*
> *Let us alone.*

Belgium, however, "never had it so good" and Germany, thanks to four billion dollars from America, was wallowing in an unexpected prosperity that made the people indifferent to politics.

Then, in an inconspicuous Fiat car, during the following four weeks we toured Italy from Calabria to Lombardy, chatting with hundreds of peasants, unemployed workmen, shopkeepers, mechanics, uniformed *carabinieri,* hotel employees, all sorts of citizens, and with American officials. At San Marco Marchesato, in Calabria, we watched a distribution of small farms to the landless. We interviewed the "Red" mayors of Ferrara and Bologna.

By the time we abandoned the car in Milan and flew back to Washington, my bright hopes of any quick economic or politically resurgent Italy had been dashed. According to a courageous and perceptive Italian employed by the American Mutual Security Agency in Rome, Italy's politicians had saddled their country with more social security than it could then afford. In the face of two million unemployed, the State encouraged large families, imposed featherbedding, subsidized public and private monopolies, and maintained a monstrously overstaffed bureaucracy. The list of corporations comprising the State-owned *Industrie Reunite Italiane* (IRI for short) covered twelve typewritten pages. Although total industrial production had increased, individual productivity was a third less than in 1939. All this in spite of some three billion dollars of American aid. American officials had actually encouraged higher consumption at the cost of investment and attached no strings to our assistance. This had been done with the laudable intention of weaning the people from communism. The policy had failed because the communists had succeeded in identifying American aid with a sinister form of imperialism. Even land reform had so far brought no appreciable economic or political results.

Seven years after the end of the war, communism still flourished. In the words of an old Italian friend: "Communism is the little guy's big brother, the little girl's big sister." And because of those American funds, which sifted down to Red administrations, it looked after its own far better than the rival Christian Democracy.

Once back in Washington, I wrote not one but two stories. The first, "Italy in the Red—a Lesson in Foreign Aid," concluded that American aid to Italy was so far largely a failure. What that country needed was an atmosphere of democratic self-reliance wherein communism could not flourish.

The second article, "City Hall Politics in Italy," explained Stalin's hold on the Italian people. It concluded:

"Communism" (in Italy) "has reached the development where it fattens on the very forces that seek to destroy it. It is strong enough and rich enough to reward and protect the faithful but too weak to be held responsible for existing evils like unemployment and poverty or to be expected to fulfill its unlimited promises. *It is a mature parasite that revives with the improving health of the host body.*

"An Italian of modest position has nothing to lose by going along with the Party. If Communism turns out to be the Wave of the Future, he will be riding it when it arrives. If not, his membership will have been a temporary surfboard through rough breakers to a solider future. Nobody is going to penalize an obscure ex-communist.

"Therefore, at this particular stage of its development, communism cannot be bought out of existence (if it ever could). *Rising* living standards produce not *fewer* but *more* communists. The greater the general prosperity, the more the Party can distribute as plums."

The lesson was clear: to "roll back" Tammany-type communism, the Italians would have to smash the Party's political machine. The process could include anything from abandoning proportional representation (always an element of political instability) to *outlawing the Communist Party.*

Ken Payne of *Reader's Digest* was uninterested in my explanation of Italian communism (which I later sold to the *Atlantic Monthly*), but he pounced on Italy in the Red" ("the biggest chunk of economic copy the *Digest* has ever published").

Yet shortly after it appeared in March, 1953, a very disturbed Ken called me from Pleasantville. "Edgar, your article has raised the very devil among Italians. Ambassador Tarchiani in Washington complains it is full of mistakes and our own Ambassador, Clare Luce in Rome, writes that it is grossly unfair both to Italy and to our efforts to help. An Italian magazine, *Produttività,* is preparing a refutation. Should we print a retraction by you?"

"Relax, Ken. Tell Wally that my sources for what I wrote are among the best in Rome. Send me the charges and I'll provide you with a memorandum answering them."

Neither Tarchiani nor Luce was able to show any substantial errors or to refute my main thesis: Italy would have been far better off if American officials had insisted that the Italian government take certain unpopular but salutary measures. Yet for months various Italian publications continued their attacks, doubtless fearing lest the American Administration should take my recommendation to heart and either cease, or put strings upon, further aid. By my frankness I had forfeited the decoration which the Italian government had been about to bestow upon me.

At home, the American people had chosen Eisenhower over Stevenson and the Mowrers relaxed. For even while the new President was emphasizing his love of peace (as any general had to, I supposed), his Secretary of State-designate had committed the Administration to "freeing the victims of aggression at the right time and by the appropriate means."

35

Eisenhower Chooses Discretion

*It is no doubt a good thing to conquer but it
takes greater wisdom and greater skill to make
use of victory.*

—POLYBIUS

ON JANUARY 20, 1953, Lilian and I sat before the East portico of the
Capitol in Washington and heard Dwight D. Eisenhower swear the
oath that made him President of the United States. With us was Paul
Chapman Andrews, formerly of the Cornell University law faculty and
a devoted world federalist. Later at lunch we conjectured about the
new President's foreign policy.

I did not know Eisenhower well. I had met the general briefly
during the war and in 1950 chatted with him at Marnes-la-Coquette
outside Paris. His stubborn amiability had enabled him during the war
to work well with the British, and even with the French when F.D.R.
would let him. In foreign politics, Ike, like Marshall and unlike Mac-
Arthur, had showed himself a rank amateur. Yet in accepting the
Republican nomination, he had promised, if elected, to "lead a crusade
for freedom in America and freedom in the world."

I put more faith in Secretary of State Dulles ("Foster" to his
friends) with whom I had often discussed foreign problems. I admired
his skill in shaping the treaty with Japan. In his book, *War or Peace*
(1950), he had urged "taking the offensive in the world struggle for
freedom and . . . rolling back the engulfing tide of despotism," and,
in *Life* magazine, "striking back against aggression where it hurts by
means of our own choosing."

Andrews reminded me that Dulles would not be in exclusive
charge of foreign policy. Eisenhower had established, while President
of Columbia University, a "chair for peace." During the campaign he
had promised to take no risk of turning the Korean war into a global

395

conflict and since taking office had surrounded himself with passionate economizers like George Humphrey and "Engine Charley" Wilson, neither of whom knew much about world politics. How reconcile a promise of "roll back" and "liberation" with a reduction in military expenses?

Yet not even the President's refusal to repudiate the Yalta agreements nor Dulles' choice of "Yalta boy" Bohlen shook my confidence. Dulles' Assistant Secretary for Public Affairs, an experienced newspaperman, Carl McCardle, assured me that any further appeasement of Stalin was out.

Unhappily for my hopes, the Churchill who had returned to power in 1951 was not the man who had, in 1947, advocated the use of A-bombs to force Stalin out of Eastern Europe. Perhaps the latter's successful test of such a bomb in 1949 had tamed the once indomitable Englishman. Certainly, after Malenkov succeeded Stalin and the U.S.S.R. exploded its first nuclear device nine months after America's, Winston talked like a "Chamberlain-ite" for whom "jaw-jaw" was better than "war-war"—as if that were the choice!

Once Stalin was dead, Churchill favored a nonaggression pact and another of those summit conferences with the Russians that had proved disastrous during the war. In Ottawa, my friend, Lester Pearson, now Foreign Minister, had announced that "in any effort to stop Communism in Asia, the United States would find itself alone." Millions of war-weary Westerners desperately wanted to believe that the Soviet Bear had become a pussy cat, forgetting that Malenkov's purr was more dangerous than Stalin's growls.

Even while the President was giving more aid to the French in tottering Indochina and preparing to defend Formosa if necessary, he was planning to offer an armistice in Korea on the basis of the territorial *status quo* without obtaining the release of American prisoners in Red Chinese hands. Furthermore, he was urging the British to hasten their retreat from Egypt. At home frightened American scientists and some of Ike's close advisers favored offering Msocow "total disarmament."

Was I misjudging the new Administration?

Certainly, I had forgotten that Dulles was a doctrinaire anticolonialist. But if Egypt took the Suez Canal, Panama would surely demand "its" canal, as I warned Majority Leader Knowland at a breakfast in his office. The Senator demurred; he saw no necessary connection between the two situations. . . .

In January, 1954, Secretary Dulles expressed a desire for "a maximum deterrent at a bearable cost." This, in my judgment, led to his strategic choice of "massive retaliation . . . by means and at places of our choosing." A bigger bang for a buck! Yet a failure to produce adequate conventional as well as nuclear forces would handicap any liberation strategy.

Early in 1953, at the request of John B. Adams, a former newsman doing public relations for the Pentagon, I accompanied an Army colonel, a lady diplomat from the State Department, and thirteen distinguished NATO newsmen from ten different countries, on an airplane trip through the eastern part of the United States. Only one of the last had visited America before, and half a dozen spoke no English. Once they became convinced that I was not a Central Intelligence or F.B.I. agent, as they originally suspected, we had long, open discussions during which I realized how much Senator Joe McCarthy's methods of fighting communism had given the United States the reputation of a police state.

These educated Europeans were amazed to find that, in our country, with the exception of the gold bullion in Fort Knox, they could see anything and talk with anyone they pleased! During our trip ordinary American citizens received them at home and answered their probing questions. Only in Washington were top officials and political leaders unaccountably reluctant to talk to such distinguished foreign newsmen, from whom they could have learned much.

Nonetheless, as I could vouch, my colleagues went home convinced that, contrary to beliefs prevailing in their own countries, Senator McCarthy was not America; that the American government was not imperially minded; and that, except in the case of Negroes, American society was basically democratic, without fixed class status for nearly everybody, and with relative abundance and comfort for nearly all.

Their surprise at what they found was so great that when I spoke of it to Ken Payne he asked me to do an article about America's impact. DeWitt Wallace refused the manuscript, but I managed to place a shortened version with *This Week* magazine supplement.

Long years in Europe had convinced me that basically the United States was Occidental civilization in its latest phase. Yet many Americans abroad saw themselves as a nation apart and far from seeking to learn something from the "natives," protected themselves from local contamination, and often from local food, by living together in American ghettos. Many did not even bother to learn the native language or urge their children to do so.

Since our European allies resented this *apartheid* and considered it a symptom of American immaturity, fruitful exchange was difficult. Yet in my eyes the West needed osmosis to survive. Hence I supported the idea of some sort of Atlantic directorate to formulate a common policy, an idea favored not only by Charles de Gaulle but by General Lord Ismay, NATO's Secretary General. To illustrate this view I wrote for the *Saturday Review* an essay on our three-story heritage—human, Western, and American. Awareness of this would facilitate human contacts everywhere.

Impressed by this essay, Paul Smith, now publisher of *Collier's*

Weekly, sent me flying to Paris for a month to "find out what's wrong with France," still my second country.

During four weeks I interviewed French people of varying condition, among them, President Vincent Auriol, Charles de Gaulle, René Pleven, Pierre Mendès-France, Jean Monnet (on the golf course in Luxembourg), Pierre Lazareff of *France Soir,* Hubert Beuve-Mery of *Le Monde,* Communist Party bosses, Paris workers, Burgundy wine growers, and Angevin farmers.

From them all I heard the same: the Fourth French Republic satisfied nobody but those in high office. Ordinary people were bewildered, divided over the war in Indochina and the question of integrating France's armed forces in an Army of Europe that included Germans.

Yet though their aspirations differed widely, the overwhelming majority not only wanted but expected a change. Charles de Gaulle predicted that, having played a star role on the historical stage, the French people would refuse to remain a walk-on. At the recent Radical Party Convention Pierre Mendès-France had warned: "Listen to the rising tumult: we are in 1788"—the year before the Paris mob stormed the Bastille.

The product of the trip I called *France Needs a New Revolution.*

Collier's liked the piece so much that it sent me to the Near East on a new assignment.

Dulles was creating a network of alliances around the communist empire. In the Far East, special agreements with Japan, Korea, the Philippines, the Republic of China, New Zealand, and Australia had been reinforced by the Southeast Asia Treaty Organization. Now he believed that the time had come to fill the gap between Pakistan and Turkey. The necessary negotiations were proceeding steadily. Carl McCardle insisted that I could do both Foster and the United States a service by describing the situation in the countries involved.

Early February, 1954, saw me in New Delhi. Thanks to the efforts of his charming sister, Mrs. Pandit, Jawalharlal Nehru received me and outlined his views more in sorrow than in anger. He and his friend Mao Tse-tung had, he said, determined to keep Southeast Asia a zone of peace based on the five principles (*panch shila*). This peace the United States was disturbing both by arming belligerent Pakistan and by ringing the Soviet Union with a new *cordon sanitaire.* India wanted no part in such provocation. Yet meanwhile, he still saw nothing humiliating in asking for help. In reply I accused him of "seeking peace by incantation" and ignoring Mao Tse-tung's true aims. We agreed to disagree. I left the handsome egoist uncertain in my mind whether he would turn out to be the George Washington or the Eduard Benes of his country.

Next stop, Afghanistan. Since I had never seen the Khyber Pass, perhaps the world's most trodden invasion route, in Peshawar I hired a driver to drive me to Kabul.

The pass was neither beautiful nor spectacular.

Afghanistan, however, fascinated me—"a country where oranges are sour, (some) lemons are sweet and coal mine owners refuse to mine enough to make up for the country's fuel shortage."

At Jalalabad, a young Afghan who spoke English and consented to take a cup of tea with me, opened with the question: "Isn't this a backward, stinking country?"

"Easy, Mr. Police Agent," I thought. "I have met your kind before." Then aloud: "If you think so, why don't you change it?"

"Our government won't let us. We are completely under the thumb of one family. The King, the Prime Minister, the Foreign Minister, ambassadors, all are Duranis."

"And what is your profession?"

"I am in the Ministry of Finance in Kabul, now here on vacation. Most government employees of my age want to modernize Afghanistan. After all, we have a glorious past."

True enough. The examples of Greco-Buddhist art in Kabul left me breathless, as glorious a hybrid as that of Hindu and Islamic architecture in India.

Viewed from a distance, the Afghan capital, like so many Oriental towns, was charming. But the room offered me at the *khan* was so bug-ridden that I gratefully accepted the hospitality of a generous American diplomat.

The only Durani I managed to interview, the Foreign Minister, boasted of playing off the Soviet Union against the United States and obtaining aid simultaneously from both while giving nothing to either, and, with Nehru's support, of demanding that Pakistan hand over its part of divided Pushtunistan. An alliance with America would ruin this game.

"We Afghans," the Foreign Minister remarked modestly, "are the world's cleverest diplomats."

In Pakistan again I renewed contact with old acquaintances, the Prime Minister, the Foreign Minister, and to my delight, General Ayub Khan, all forthright anticommunists who asked nothing better than to join Dulles' planned South Asian alliance. President Iskendar Mirza told me proudly: "If you accept us you will be getting the cream of the former British Army, the finest that this part of the world has known."

Baghdad after sixteen years was as picturesque as ever. The Prime Minister, Fadhil al-Jamali, a thick-set youngish man with an American wife, was flattered when I told him people were already calling Dulles' project the Baghdad Pact. Yet he insisted on the "special difficulties" Iraq would have with other Arab countries if it linked itself to the "imperialistic West." A friend in a foreign embassy explained what he meant.

"King Faisal is ready to accept Dulles' offer. But this country is governed by riot. There are special dealers who organize a five- or ten-thousand-man riot against anything or anybody for so much a head, plus whatever loot the rioters can seize. Those Arab governments that oppose the Dulles proposal may buy a giant riot and overthrow the King. Faisal has to be careful."

Not so the Shah-in-Shah of Iran. General Fazollah Zahedi had, with some American assistance, rescued the country from the weeping Mohammed Mossadegh who, Zahedi told me, had "tried to command the army from under the bed."

Mohammed Reza Shah and Zahedi, now Prime Minister, enthusiastically welcomed Dulles' plan for an alliance. Thanks to former Ambassador Ala, now Court Minister, whom I had known in Washington, the sovereign received me at the ski resort of Abalee near Teheran and offered me a "choice between the real truth, not for publication, or a few perfunctory declarations for your newspapers." When I chose *both*, he grinned and concurred. For two hours this handsome, likable man outlined his plans for the gradual modernization of Iran, a country whose glorious past still lingered in the memory of the millions.

Time was lacking in which to see more of Iran, a country twice the size of Texas. Nonetheless, by a mixture of bribery and flattery, I persuaded the headwaiter at the Teheran hotel to produce a bottle of the finest wine of Shiraz and drank it to the memory of the poets Sa'di and Hafiz, those friends of my student days.

Ankara was new to me. As the guest of Ambassador Avra Warren, I had no difficulty in seeing those I wished to see. Turkish leaders, both in power and in opposition, were already discussing Dulles' proposal with Pakistan, "a people like us."

The spirit of Mustapha Kemal, who had expelled both invading Greeks and Greek inhabitants from Asia Minor, impregnated everything. In the art museum, a young archeologist showed me ancient statues of huge-nosed warriors and commented, "Our ancestors the Hittites." Puzzling: at Ann Arbor, Professor Craig had taught that the Hittites disappeared from history by 1000 B.C. And that they had spoken an Indo-Germanic language. How then could they be the ancestors of Ottoman Turks who arrived in what became Turkey over two thousand years later? When I put this question to a group of young artists and writers, a French-speaking girl winked at the others and answered.

"I'll tell you, sir. The founder of modern Turkey, Kemal Pasha, thought we needed venerable local ancestors and so he invented them for us. However, if early Turkish males were like those of today, and if any female descendants of the Hittites were still around when they arrived, then I am sure we all have Hittite blood." The others guffawed.

In Athens I stayed just long enough to hear from Prime Minister Alexander Papagos that a mid-Eastern defense treaty would "blast

Nehru's monstrous dream of captaining a neutral bloc stretching from India to Egypt and holding the balance of power," and to enjoy another visit to the Acropolis with my all-knowing architect friend, Paul Milonas.

Few things are more to my taste than being well paid for visiting strange places and peoples.

I entitled my article on the new alliance "Secretary Dulles' Master Stroke," to Carl McCardle's, and perhaps, to Foster's, delight.

But even while it was appearing events were undermining the policy of "roll back." In Indochina, General de Lattre's clumsy successor permitted a considerable French force to be surrounded in the relatively remote town of Dien Bien Phu and Paris asked Washington's help in extricating it. Dulles was favorable, even to the extent, if necessary, of ordering American carrier planes to make an atomic strike on the exultant Viet Minh. He was busy putting together a Far Eastern alliance (five years after I first launched the idea!). Eisenhower, however, listened to American generals who told him an air strike alone could not save the beleaguered French, and to Anthony Eden, Britain's Foreign Minister. Without Britain's participation Ike would not move.

The Viet Minh captured Dien Bien Phu and the French survivors, thus achieving a double victory: of communist guerrillas over a regular army, and of Asians over a white nation. This did not disturb the French people. Premier Mendès-France accepted Britain's idea of a peace conference with the Viet Minh at Geneva with—imagine!— Britain, Communist China, and Communist Russia as mediators.

Dulles had wanted to bring NATO into that conference and, being rebuffed, after a brief attendance as an observer, stalked out never to return. Yet even while Eisenhower was serving notice that the United States would be "no party to any treaty that makes anybody a slave," he added that if Indochina *were* divided, there would be "ample time for migration from the relinquished areas of any people who wanted to transfer." (Over a million did.)

Whereupon Mendès-France relinquished the country whose defense had, in seven years, cost the French a hundred and fifty thousand casualties, leaving undefended South Vietnam, Cambodia, and Laos at the mercy of Ho's army. Dulles explained to the Senate Foreign Relations Committee (on June 4, 1954) that if the British could veto American policy, and the Indians veto British policy, and the Chinese veto Indian policy, and the Russians veto Chinese policy, then the Russians held the first veto on anything America wanted to do! Not long thereafter Americans moved as advisers into South Vietnam, and signed a defense treaty with Chiang on Formosa, two essential steps. Even so, Dulles continued to believe that America's relations with Asia should not be influenced by "colonial France and Britain."

Just as our abandonment of Nationalist China had invited Red aggression in Korea and Indochina, so Ho's victory in the North encouraged communist offensives in half a dozen other places.

Red China started building an atomic weapons plant in Sinkiang, launched an attack on Quemoy and Matsu Islands, and was deterred from attacking Formosa only by a demonstration of American sea power and warnings from Washington—and Moscow! Communist rebels stepped up their guerrilla war in the Malay Peninsula. Local Reds all but took over Guatemala. Tito insolently threatened to seize the Italian-held Zone A in Istria.

Within a year that great peace-lover, Nehru, seized Portuguese Goa, Damao, and Diu. Algerian Moslems revolted against pusillanimous France. Misreading the signs, the French Parliament rejected the European Defense Community treaty which would, by providing an integrated army, have almost indissolubly united Western Europe.

An indignant Dulles talked of withdrawing all American troops from there. Scenting danger, Churchill induced France to build a common defense around the Five-Power *Western Union* and grant Germany a national army, the very thing the French had feared most.

By this time my faith in Eisenhower's devotion to liberation was running thin. The American people were already dividing into "hawks" and "doves," with the latter largely in control of the news media.

The specter of appeasement, which I had supposed buried with F.D.R., rose again. Churchill had hailed the death (or murder?) of Stalin and the subsequent replacement of Malenkov by Nikita Khrushchev as sure signs that Soviet communism was losing its malignancy. He had little difficulty in persuading Eisenhower to attend a summit meeting with the new Russian leaders.

After issuing an appeal to Americans to "pray for peace," the President and the Secretary of State flew to what they called the "Geneva Peace Conference." To express my own fear of a new "Yalta" or "Potsdam," I quoted the statement of Soviet intentions publicly uttered in 1930 by Dmitri Manuilsky, then Executive Secretary of the Executive Committee of the Comintern in Moscow:

"To win . . . the bourgeoisie will have to be put to sleep. So we shall begin by organizing the most spectacular peace movement on record. There will be electrifying overtures and unheard-of concessions. The capitalist countries, stupid and decadent, will collapse of their own weight. They will leap at another chance to be friends. As soon as their guard is down, we shall smash them with our clenched fist."

For personal reasons, Lilian and I were happy to be back in the smiling city of dour Jean Calvin. We loved its blue lake and green river, with their dignified swans and greedy, swooping gulls that took crumbs almost from one's hand, and the water spout shooting up hundreds of feet. We treasured the occasional glimpses of mighty Mont Blanc and climbed Mont Salève for the view of the city. We tried to forget the conference, "half church and half circus," at the *Bavaria* and other familiar restaurants. A luncheon with Ernest Cuneo at *Chez le Père Bise* at Talloire lasted from one-thirty to five-fifteen.

Except when they drove through the city, the Russians in an open convertible, Eisenhower in a closed, carefully guarded limousine, we correspondents saw little of the chief participants. The Genevois commented sarcastically on Ike's "timidity" and his affection for Marshall Zhukov, and showed more interest in a revival meeting by Billy Graham.

Once or twice each day, some hundreds of newsmen gathered at the *Maison de la Presse* to be briefed on "the day's progress." At the first briefing, the Russian lady spokesman, in her inimitable English, set the tone:

"President Eisenhower and Marshall Zhukov discovered that they both had grandchildren. This was typical of the friendly atmosphere among the Heads of Governments, one of *joy and respection*."

The peace conference never got beyond grandchildren. The great thaw was a fraud.

The Russians were, in fact, more arrogant than ever. Finding myself one day at a table in the *Maison de la Presse* with the representative of Radio Moscow, I offered him a drink. When he balked at alcohol just before broadcasting, I suggested ginger ale.

"What is ginger?" he demanded suspiciously.

"Ginger is a root and comes, I believe, from India." When the bottle arrived he glanced at it.

"If it comes from India, why does it say Canada on the bottle?" he hissed, and indignantly left the table.

So much for "joy and respection."

At the end of the conference, the Powers issued an optimistic communiqué and the promise of a new conference to clinch the "agreements." American officials publicly emphasized the new "Geneva spirit," while relieved British and French delegates expressed delight that the Russians had calmed down the foolhardy Mr. Dulles. The Russians said nothing.

Lilian and I were happy to leave for Israel, at the invitation of Harry Levine, Israeli Press Attaché in Washington.

She was seeing Palestine for the first time and I had not been back since the war.

The change was startling. A hate-riven British mandate had become a modern society vibrating with the will to survive. Yet half of the country was a wilderness. Most of it lacked adequate water. The frontiers with Jordan, being based on a military armistice, were patently absurd, particularly to the north and south of Jerusalem and in that storied city itself. Arab Jerusalem was taboo not only for Israelis but for all foreigners coming from Israel.

In spite of a common faith, the modern people of Israel were an artificial amalgam—European sophisticates from Vienna, Berlin, Paris, even London; rabbis from Warsaw and Vilna; Sephardic Jews from the Middle East and North Africa, medieval-minded and speaking a different sort of Hebrew.

Old acquaintances, including Teddy Kollek, whom I had left on the collective farm of Ain Gev in 1944, political leaders like Foreign Minister Golda Meir, Milwaukee's gift to Zion, and Prime Minister Ben Gurion, complained that the neighboring Arabs were systematically sending saboteurs and terrorists into Israel. Ben Gurion, a man whose determination stood out like his white hair, told me at Sde Boker that he doubted if the Jews would passively endure such provocations much longer. . . .

To a newsman such a warning was solid gold.

Equally fascinating was the physical Holy Land. Not Tel Aviv or Jewish Jerusalem at whose King David Hotel Jewish terrorists had inadvertently almost blown up my nephew, Richard Mowrer.

What most impressed this Bible-reader was the concentration of so much history in so small an area. Here at the river Kishon, the prophetess Deborah trapped the iron chariots of Sisera. There was the field of Megiddo where the Jews "battled for the Lord." At the Horns of Hittim, Saladin vanquished Richard the Lion-hearted by setting fire to the dry grass, thus anticipating the tactics of American Indians. Every inch of Galilee spoke of Jesus: Nazareth where the Word became flesh, Cana where the water became wine, the Mount of the Sermon. Seated, after a swim, beside the Lake, eating a picnic lunch of fish in honor of Saint Peter, I rejoiced at the sheer weight of so much tradition.

A drive from Tel Aviv to Sodom revealed how, as far south as Beersheba, the Israelis had given life to the desert. Where in 1944 there had been little but cactus, one now saw orange groves and masses of bougainvillea, trumpet vines, and flowering pepper trees. Then the bare Negev—naked hills, mesas covered with low brown bush streaked with deep weathered wadis, baking under a stark blue sky. Around endless curves our car descended to the Dead Sea, 2000 feet below sea level, beyond which the mountains of Moab rose impressively. A last curve and we reached the village from which Lot fled at God's bidding. The temperature was 114 degrees in the shade. Dripping as we were, we thought of a quick swim. But no, the water was intolerably hot with the salt-and-bitter taste of Dead Sea fruit!

On the way back to Tel Aviv we turned westward at Beersheba and drove through more flowers, orange groves, and historic sites: beautiful Ashkelon where blind Samson had pulled down the Philistines' temple and innumerable bathers were now kicking up long buried Roman coins from the shifting sands; tree-grown Ashdod, once the home of a glamor girl called Salome and later bestowed by great Marc Antony upon his erstwhile favorite, one Cleopatra, who happened to be Queen of Egypt. Then back to ultramodern Tel Aviv, our heads swimming with the abrupt historical shift. We would willingly have stayed longer in Israel.

In Rome, Italy's new President, Giovanni Gronchi, a Christian Democratic politician whose leftish inclinations were making Conservatives uneasy, explained his country's difficulties in one sentence:

"Italians are less logical than the French, less pseudo-intellectual than the Germans, less anti-intellectual than the British." Precisely.

There Lilian and I separated, she returning home by way of England and I visiting briefly Munich, Berlin, Bonn, The Hague, Paris, Madrid, and Lisbon.

Among the Germans, the glum *"ohne uns"* atmosphere had given place to an unabashed hedonism. Konrad Adenauer's heroic break with the Nazi past had made possible the reacquisition of full sovereignty. That in turn had made it possible for Ludwig Erhard, classical economics, and hard work, to accomplish what foreigners were calling German's "economic miracle."

West Berlin, at its best in mid-August, was still a fortress, though a disillusioned fortress, of freedom and democracy.

West Berliners had hoped that at the recent conference the Americans would compel the Russians to accept Germany's reunification. Instead, as I learned from Gretel Spitzer, an intelligent young *Berlinerin* who was working for American and English newspapers, when Bulganin and Khrushchev had stopped in Berlin on their way home, they had told Puppet Boss Walter Ulbricht: "We learned in Geneva that we have nothing to fear from President Eisenhower."

Spirit of Geneva, indeed!

Marc von Blankenstein met me with his car at Bonn and the next day we started for The Hague. He confirmed my impression that thanks to Adenauer, the nightmare begun in 1933 was really over.

When I expressed astonishment at the West Germans' lack of political interest, Marc chortled, "I shall show you a prize example."

This was Berthold Beitz, General Director of the Krupp works at Essen. This youngish-looking, tough-minded tycoon expressed his total lack of interest in Germany's reunification.

"Look at me: I have less in common with the Prussians to the east than with the Netherlanders to the west."

"That's the way they all talk," Marc explained as we climbed into his car. For the time being, they mean it."

In The Hague, he took me to the former *Club te Werfe* outside the city, the headquarters of the Royal Dutch Shell Oil Company. There— *mirabile dictu*—we witnessed a volley ball match between Soviet and American diplomats. After losing, the Americans not only proposed a second match with mixed teams, but invited the Russians to eat and drink with them. More "joy and respection."

In Paris, officials were paying far more attention to high prices and to the rebellion in Algeria than to the Soviet threat. A near-fascist movement, led by a bookseller named Pierre Poujade, was making headway. Citizens were grumbling ever more loudly that "things cannot go on like this." General Alfred Gruenther, now Supreme Allied Commander in Europe, was worried about the budding dispute between the champions of "massive retaliation" and those, like Paul Henri Spaak, of "graduated deterrence," in case of an attack from the east.

Madrid was calm, even mephitic in atmosphere, and the Spaniards were profiting to the limit from the American efforts to secure ever broader military rights in that country. Richard Mowrer reproached the American negotiators with being too eager and obtaining far less than they were giving. ("The same wherever we go," I found myself thinking.)

In Lisbon, the Foreign Minister, Paulo Cunha, asked me sarcastically what, at Geneva, had become of Dulles' policy of reuniting Germany.

"Never," as I wrote in an article on the Summit Conference which Norman Cousins had requested, "since the Field of the Cloth of Gold in 1520 has so great a gathering been built upon so small a foundation." This truism was too much for the *Saturday Review*. Norman Cousins sent me a check, but refused to publish my findings.

Many Americans believed that a bear that danced and tried to lick your face, however deceptively, was preferable to one that growled and tried to claw you.

Yet why should they not? Dulles at Chicago had stated that Americans should *not* seek to "cure the injustices" of the division of Germany and the subjugation of the captive peoples by armed force, but instead "bring into play the force . . . of world opinion which, working steadily, will have its way."

Eisenhower, after his severe illness, was campaigning for reelection by "crusading for peace" on a platform of "controlled disarmament" indistinguishable from that of Adlai Stevenson. Rumor insisted he planned to invite fellow grandfather Zhukov to the United States for a friendly visit.

"Engine Charley" Wilson, Secretary of Defense, warned lest the United States become too strong for, if one side became "twice as powerful" as the other, it might "be tempted to impose its wishes on the other side."

Liberating the U.S.S.R.'s captive nations was, of course, precisely what Eisenhower had in 1952 promised to do. On the other hand, Dulles, in an interview with *Life* magazine, boasted that he had "thrice taken the United States to the verge of war in order to avoid war."

Such confusion affected me personally as well as politically. About this time Carl McCardle relayed to me an offer from Dulles to become his special liaison with the *Voice of America,* whose executives were "having difficulty in understanding what the Secretary of State has in mind." If I accepted, I would take orders only from my friends Foster and Carl.

At any time before the Geneva Summit I would have accepted the offer with enthusiasm. For I shared the view expressed in the *Revue de la Defense Nationale* by French General Chassin: "We in NATO are at war and have been so for a long time. If the encirclement foreseen by Mao Tse-tung is ever realized, all will be over." This had been

Foster's original position, and I would have liked nothing so much as to contribute to a policy of liberation. But, however disappointed, to give up my freedom as a columnist in order to promote disguised appeasement was unthinkable. I politely refused the offer and waited for the next crisis.

And come it did, but not, as I expected in Southeast Asia but in Egypt. This venerable country had fallen under the rule of a megalomaniac, Colonel Gamal Abdel Nasser, the author of a book, *Egypt's Liberation*, in which he foresaw the spread of Arab power from Morocco to the Philippines. To achieve this, Nasser's radios were preaching rebellion, arson, and murder throughout Black Africa, his agents were harassing Israel, and he personally was accepting Soviet arms and trying to force the British out of the Suez base. Dulles considered both colonialism and nonalignment immoral. Even while he urged the British to leave Suez as soon as possible, he withdrew his offer to build for Egypt the projected Aswan Dam. Nasser promptly nationalized the Suez Canal, according to a plan upon which he had been working since 1954!

American oil interests looked to Dulles for some sort of satisfactory compromise. As lawyer and anticolonialist, the Secretary sought to maneuver his allies into accepting a face-saving relinquishment of the canal. Apparently he thought he convinced the French and British not to use force.

Instead, the outraged French and British planned to defend their rights by all necessary means, believing that Washington's opposition would remain verbal. Legalisms aside, I felt that we should do nothing to weaken our allies and that Nasser should be compelled to wait until the Suez Company's lease ran out.

Just at this moment the Hungarians revolted against their Soviet masters. Here I saw the long awaited opportunity for a roll back. Yet the timing was against me. Had Britain, France, and Israel postponed their military action against Egypt, and the Hungarians their rebellion until after the American election, Eisenhower's reaction, in spite of Moscow's absurd nuclear threats, might have been different. Dulles, in Eisenhower's name, might not have stated publicly that the United States had no thought of using the liberation of the satellites to Moscow's disadvantage, thereby emboldening Stalin to order his retreating forces to return to Budapest and crush the rebellion. And in the interim the United States might have clinched a victory by dropping paratroopers as a warning to Russia to stay out.

To explain the Administration's passivity, Dulles, now seriously ill, argued that an intervention by limited American forces would have led to their certain defeat and that full-scale intervention by NATO, as advocated by many Europeans, would have led to a major war in which Hungary would have been annihilated. Until a successor government opens the Soviet archives, the world will not know. Yet, neither Eisenhower nor Dulles ever offered a convincing answer to Salvador de Madariaga's blunt question: "Why should the Soviet Union be less afraid than we?"

Personally I cannot without tears remember the final appeal of the Hungarian Freedom Fighters:

"This word may be the last from the last Hungarian freedom station. People of the world, help us, not with advice, not with words, but with action, with soldiers and with arms. . . . People of Europe, whom we defended once against the attacks of Asian barbarians, listen now to the alarm bells ringing from Hungary. Civilized people of the world, in the name of liberty and solidarity, we are asking you to help. Our ship is sinking. The light vanishes. The shadows grow darker from hour to hour. Listen to our cry. Start moving. Extend to us brotherly hands. . . . God be with you and with us."

Having demonstrated that the United States would not lift a finger to liberate the Hungarians, Dulles then stood up in the vast United Nations Assembly Hall, blue with the hopes and golden with the aspirations of mankind, and, however reluctantly, in the Suez affair made common cause with mankind's enemy against his British and French allies as well as against the Israelis who had already defeated Nasser. From this act, the United States' reputation never fully recovered. Not even Eisenhower's subsequent action in Lebanon and the Formosa Strait could conceal the fact that America's President had decided that discretion was the better part of valor. After 1956, "peaceful coexistence" was the opium of the West.

36

A New Start At Sixty-five

Oh say, what have you done, you here
With all your youth?

PAUL VERLAINE

NEVER, during forty odd years of journalism, had I relinquished my claim to be something of a "man of letters." In Germany I had for months played with the idea of writing a new sort of novel illustrating one of my growing convictions. But fiction was not my dish. Personalities interested me less than ideas. What talent I had was expository. I intended my next book to be a collection of mostly nonpolitical essays, to be entitled *A Good Time To Be Alive*.

To achieve greater tranquility, to quench an unquenchable thirst for the great outdoors, and to see more of my poet brother, I had, in 1951, bought a comfortable country house near Paul's in New Hampshire. Wonalancet lies at the southern edge of the Sandwich Mountains in a country of lakes and low picturesque peaks, among them Chocorua, Paugus, Whiteface, Passaconaway and the Sandwich Dome. In summer the region is tourist-ridden, but after Labor Day, when the city folk have left and the maples stage their annual riot of color, it becomes a glory.

Thereafter we spent from one to two months each year at Wonalancet and by 1955 half a dozen essays by me had appeared in various magazines, three had been republished in college textbooks, and the book was well under way.

Yet politics would not let me alone. Harper's was uninterested in my projected book. Duell, Sloan and Pearce would take it only if thereafter I would write another book critical of U.S. foreign policy. The Hungarian rebels, by revealing the vacuity of Eisenhower's promise of "roll back," had reminded me that I still had political promises to keep.

409

And almost a year earlier, fate had tempted me with the chance of a brand new kind of career, political and literary at the same time.

At Bonn, in 1955, a slight, good looking young man had introduced himself as Lucien Radoux, private secretary to Foreign Minister Spaak of Belgium. Over a long breakfast he explained that a number of important Europeans devoted to the North Atlantic Treaty Organization, including Spaak, the influential Dutchman, Paul Rijkens of Unilever Company (a friend of Marc Van Blankenstein), and Emmanuel Monnick of the *Banque de France,* had asked him to assemble the potential staff of a new magazine, in two editions, one in French and one in English, with editors in Paris and in Washington, D.C., respectively. Would I, as a journalist at home on both sides of the Atlantic, consider becoming North American editor? Funds were, unhappily, scarce. My salary would, by American standards, be inadequate. Yet, since the work should require no more than half of my time, perhaps my well-known dedication to the "Atlantic idea" would compensate for the financial inadequacy. How did I feel?

Prudently, I made my acceptance subject to certain conditions: my approval of the other editor, of the format and type of contents of the magazine, and of a contract giving to the North American editor the final authority over contributions from the Western Hemisphere. Otherwise. . . .

Radoux winced but accepted my terms, subject to the approval of his "international advisory board," and invited me to return to Paris to meet the board two months later.

Then, in Paul Winkler's office in Paris, I faced my appraisers, a dozen distinguished newsmen from half a dozen NATO countries, among them young René Dabernat, of *Paris-Presse* and the New York *Times,* already designated as European editor. Apparent on all their faces was doubt concerning the capacity of *any* American to satisfy Europe's "more cultured and sophisticated" reading habits. Would I perhaps give them my ideas of the requirements of an effective Atlantic magazine?

The situation called for self-salesmanship, something I had always abhorred. Yet since I wanted the job, I outlined my notion of such a magazine in as choice French as I could muster. Then feigning to notice for the first time that not all of them understood that language, I repeated my talk successively in Italian, German, and, finally, in English. The Germans, Italians, and Britishers rose to the bait, asking questions each in his own tongue, convinced that this particular American knew his Europe. The advisory board authorized Radoux to engage me as North American editor.

It took the latter a full year, a trip to America by him and another by Paul Rijkens, and two more editorial conferences in Paris, to launch the project. After the editors fended off Radoux's last-minute attempt to switch editorial responsibility to an editorial board of which he would be a member, we agreed on the title, *Western World (Occident* in

French); and on the place of printing, Utrecht; and I acquired a Paris representative, an experienced American newsman, Jan Hasbrouck, to make up the English-language edition.

My tasks in Washington were chiefly two: to obtain official support for the magazine; and to provide each month, for as few dollars as possible, a little less than half of the contents.

The first proved to be easy. The list of American sponsors included, among others, Christian Herter, Adlai Stevenson, "Wild Bill" Donovan, Grayson Kirk, Paul Hoffman, and Jack McCloy. Secretary Dulles vetoed a pending proposal for an official NATO publication in order to give our magazine a free field, and allowed me to circulate two letters in which he expressed his hope for its success.

In other ways, too, I was fortunate. Three pleasant rooms in a former residence on Jefferson Place, near enough to the center of town to be convenient, not too near to be noisy, provided a spacious office. And though the salaries I offered were, like my own, distinctly niggardly, a place on the staff of an international magazine attracted individuals of talent. The assistant editor, Angèle de T. Gingras, of French and French Canadian ancestry, a fiction writer with an M.A. degree in literature, became a "Jill of all work" and carried on the business during my frequent travels.

René and I had already agreed to build each number around a debate, preferably intercontinental, on the most pressing Atlantic issue. But concerning the type of magazine we argued endlessly. He wanted something between *Réalités* and *Newsweek,* with cartoons, photographs a table of the month's events, statistical data, and entertaining aspects of Western life, whether significant or not. In addition he insisted on publishing wordy descriptions of the "working parties" for international discussion, which Radoux organized in London, Paris, and Rome and of multi-voice "forums" and "round tables." Editorials he found *"ennuyeux."*

My preference was for something between *Foreign Affairs* and the *Atlantic Monthly,* combining competence with originality. Editorials were, in my view, essential.

Inevitably we compromised. I resigned myself to Dabernat's "wasted pages" and he to editorials in the form of a monthly Paris-Washington "conversation."

Our differences, we knew, lay partly in our respective ages. In the midst of a hot argument he sometimes muttered, "You are my father." "Working parties, forums, round tables," made him known personally to ever more Europeans.

Most of my life was behind me. My aim was not to entertain but to convince: to fortify Atlantic unity, liberate communism's captive peoples, and hasten the coming of a world under enforceable law.

The first number of *Western World* finally appeared in April, 1957, a month after my sixty-fifth birthday. France's former Premier, Paul Reynaud, and Adlai Stevenson had furnished a superb transatlantic debate. Other contributors were Senator Clinton Anderson, John Knox Jessup, and my philosopher friend, T. V. Smith.

It led off with a five-page explanatory announcement, on which I had worked many months.

"Our magazine," I wrote, "is offering a truly intercontinental forum, a continual two-way conversation, an uninterrupted exchange, plus a readiness to listen. . . ." In its columns Europeans might "freely voice their grievances, complain, sermonize or attack North Americans —and receive as good as they give. Here no legitimate subject of North Atlantic discussion will be tabu. But neither shall it be blown up into a crisis—unless it is a crisis. Even then our writers will seize upon the causes, identify the disruptive elements and in so doing subtract or minimize their explosive force. *Western World* believes that under all foreseeable circumstances, the (Atlantic) Community has a glorious and essential role to fulfill in tomorrow's world. It is by thinking and acting together that the North Atlantic nations can best contribute to whatever world civilization may or may not emerge in coming years."

In spite of some faulty translation and technical errors, *Western World* was an immediate success.

In Washington, at a press reception, the Belgian Ambassador rec-commended the magazine as essential to NATO's future. Robert Valeur of the French Embassy invented, for the occasion, a Western World cocktail. Leading newspapers gave it news and editorial coverage.

Each debate exposed a major political problem confronting the NATO powers: anticolonialism; the future of Africa; the usefulness of the Western alliance; Communist China; the future of the United Nations; the extent of disarmament; the spread of nuclear weapons; a neutralized Germany; Britain and the Common Market; scientists in world politics; U.S. leadership; Europe as a potential Third Force; the struggle for the Middle East; Russo-Chinese relations; and, of course, repeatedly, Western policy toward Moscow. In most debates an American faced a European. Once, three Africans matched words, one of them Kwame Nkrumah, whom I recognized as an incipient tyrant suffering from a bloated ego.

Certain newspapers reprinted these debates regularly. The *Saturday Review* "borrowed" the idea. NBC and other radio chains frequently interviewed one or more contributors. Gradually *Western World* became known from coast to coast in America and throughout Europe. In May, 1959, I heard that the Soviet Union was bringing out in Paris a publication called *Etudes Soviétiques* as a foil to our brainchild.

Other articles were republished in scores of publications, from *Reader's Digest* to the *Army War Library's* reprints.

As literary *hors d'oeuvres*, Dabernat and I invented two fictitious authors who commented deadpan on odd topics, from Europe's women to America's simian artists, Zippy of Long Island and Betsy of Baltimore.

Angèle possessed a gift for eliciting contributions from intellectuals, writers, and politicians and for reducing eight thousand words to three thousand without giving offense. She coaxed badly paid articles out of Joseph Krutch, Russell Lynes, S. L. A. Marshall, J. Donald Adams, David Cort, Rayford Logan, and Monica Dickens; persuaded J. M. Lalley, perhaps the country's finest book critic, to contribute reviews. She even charmed Dick Yardley, of the Baltimore *Sun*, outstanding among American cartoonists, into giving us regular illustrations at a price we could afford. She herself produced several satirical sketches, much to Dabernat's delight. Her brilliant assistant, Mary Chris Parker, could in a pinch do an editorial job.

Thanks to their efficiency, I was able to edit and write editorials for the magazine, as well as turn out my usual four political columns each week, and produce the promised two books. In 1959 *A Good Time To Be Alive* appeared—twelve essays in all.

Once more reviewers approved. One called it "a little book with big ideas." The author was a "thinking men's thinker," in whom "there are new frontiers—the moon, the depths of the oceans, atomic energy, the sun." In him was a "spark of that divine madness with which prophets have always made their contemporaries uncomfortable." August Heckscher, a member of the Liberal Establishment, admitted that my arguments had "persuasiveness they could hardly have had if they were the expression of another pen or of another mind." Adlai Stevenson and Henry Luce wrote enthusiastic letters.

I had to refuse many of the staggering number of TV, radio, and lecture invitations which poured in.

The second promised book, entitled *An End To Make-Believe*, was to be yet another appeal to free men to make victory in the Cold War their immediate purpose, though not to the exclusion of other more distant goals.

Twice before I had written on virtually the same subject. But in *The Nightmare of American Foreign Policy*, 1948, I concentrated on exposing F.D.R.'s fatal misconception of Stalin. *Challenge and Decision*, of 1950, was primarily an argument for a federation of willing peoples.

The second half of the nineteen fifties was making a sterner American policy essential. The Hungarian and Suez crisis had indelibly outlined the disunity within NATO. When I heard of the successful flight of Sputnik, I telephoned Arthur Larson, then a special assistant to the President, and offered a suggestion. Let the President go immediately to the microphone, confess to the American people that he had simultaneously *underestimated* the Soviets' technical capacity and *overestimated* their peaceful intentions, and promise that henceforth he would spare neither effort nor money in reestablishing our military superiority.

Arthur laughed at me. This was the last thing Eisenhower had in mind.

The revolt of the French generals in Algeria not only threatened France, but revealed a dangerous rift in NATO's African policy. Dabernat and I believed in emancipating colonial nations *within* the Western economic sphere. To further this, I approached Eugene Black, head of the World Bank, and proposed that he create a twenty-billion dollar African development fund to help those new states willing to maintain existing economic ties. Nothing came of it. Black believed in basing aid on economic need, not on political attitude.

In November, 1958, Senator Estes Kefauver took me as a consultant to the NATO Parliamentarians' Conference in Paris. I acted as his interpreter and at formal meetings sat directly behind him and passed him notes with suggestions for remarks or rebuttals.

Like the Parliamentarians' previous conferences, this one produced nothing significant. Estes aimed at tightening the alliance, and his premature death a few years later was a national loss.

Charles de Gaulle was finally back in power, thanks to the revolution which I had predicted five years before. From friendly French politicians I learned how close to catastrophe the "generals revolt" had brought the French people. Yet once in the Elysée Palace, Charles was making the most of it. Though I saw him but briefly, from close associates, Louis Joxe and Etienne de Courcel, I learned how deeply he resented Eisenhower's refusal of his request to provide NATO with a three-power executive entrusted with shaping common policy. Washington would not go beyond an "exchange of views." Equally upsetting to this apostle of French greatness was our President's failure to ask Congress to amend the McMahon Act in such a way as to permit American scientists to help France produce an A-bomb, which would have saved that country seven years and two billion dollars. Had we not helped Britain? Such discrimination by America was potential dynamite in the heart of NATO.

In June, 1959, at the invitation of Congressman Brooks Hays, I joined the American Delegation to the NATO Parliamentarians' Atlantic Congress in London. Of the six hundred and fifty delegates from fifteen countries, about a third were Parliamentarians. The others represented international opinion. Almost at once, in committee meetings, at various meals, in long conversations, one felt Europe's revived yen for appeasement. Labor M. P. Dennis Healey went so far as to call NATO "at best irrelevant to the real problem," such as agreement with the Soviets and promoting democracy in liberated colonies.

Why not? Eisenhower was now preaching peace, with Prime Minister Macmillan as his John the Baptist. Our President had *unilaterally* suspended American nuclear tests. In Paris, Chris Herter, who had succeeded Dulles, was offering the Russians concessions if they would call off their threat to West Berlin and ensure that free access to the city to which the three Western countries possessed a legal right. The Germans were properly alarmed. Progress toward disarmament was incompatible with progress toward the reunification of Germany.

In such an atmosphere no conference could accomplish much. Shortly before his recent death, the ever astute Bob Vansittart had written: "Democracies will not see that it is better not to confer when failure is assured. Since the war we have been sated with fiasco."

Under existing circumstances, a Parliamentarians' recommendation of a federated NATO with a single worldwide purpose would be unwelcome to Washington and London. It would be anathema to General de Gaulle. It might irritate Mr. K!

After six days of talk the Atlantic Congress "recommended another convention" and the creation of an Atlantic Institute to give further "scientific study" to pressing problems (as though that was the need!). On everything else the delegates agreed to disagree.

Western leaders, observed Salvador de Madariaga, were confusing peace with "being left in peace."

None of which was lost on Nikita Khrushchev, who came to America in September, 1959, as part of a planned exchange of visits with Eisenhower, to prepare for which the Administration softened the name of *Radio Liberation* to *Radio Liberty*. Hardly had he arrived when he told the National Press Club in Washington that the failure of the revolt in Hungary was still "sticking in American throats like a dead rat," reiterated his threat to West Berlin, and demanded the dissolution of America's military alliances. Studying his little pig's eyes, I concluded that here was an adversary whose false joviality made him a far more formidable adversary than Stalin, whose enmity had always been conspicuous.

A few Americans, such as David Sarnoff, stood up to the Butcher of Budapest, and some Californians actually heckled him. But on the vital issue of Berlin, Eisenhower was far more "flexible" than Charles de Gaulle. The Russian went home convinced that, "like the aging Tolstoy, the West lacks virility." Its peace-minded citizens would force their government to make concessions.

Was this the American President who had twice cowed Red China in the Formosa Strait and saved Lebanon by landing U.S. Marines?

The United States had less reason to fear a nuclear war than did the Soviet Union. From Captain John R. Morse, U.S.N., of the Atomic Energy Commission, I knew that American aviation would for some years be more than a match for Soviet missiles. Our subterranean Strategic Air Command near Omaha disposed of a concentration of power surpassing anything else on earth, as I had seen for myself.

Reassuring too was the understanding of international politics which I had found in the younger military men to whom I lectured on "Divisive Issues Among the Allies" at the Naval War College in Newport, R. I.

Why had Dwight D. Eisenhower been hoodwinked by that "liberal reformer," Fidel Castro? Had nobody in the State Department brought the Cuban situation to his attention? Noting Castro's cunning manner of sidestepping embarrassing questions at the American Editors' Convention in Washington, any shrewd newsman could see that here was another Mao Tse-tung hiding his communism behind systematic misrepresentation. U. S. gullibility had hatched a Red satellite in the Western Hemisphere.

Could it be the effect of our President's illnesses, three within two years? Was it true, as a physician friend insisted, that a severe heart attack rendered its victim incapable of further stern decisions?

During this period, *Western World's* reputation was rising so steadily that by the end of 1959 we had, with the encouragement of the administration, gone some way to preparing a Spanish language edition for Latin America and the Iberian Peninsula. Then Nemesis struck in the shape of an empty purse, something which an experienced publisher would have foreseen from the beginning.

Of money we had never had enough for promotion. Most of our circulation consisted of copies which the various NATO governments purchased and distributed free to deserving citizens. Nor, without promotion, could the magazine acquire more subscribers. The European founders had had no idea of the sum necessary to nourish such a publication as ours, and when they learned, proved unable to provide it.

They had counted on more American advertising and spontaneous contributions to keep the publication afloat. When they finally acquired an American distributor, they kept his remuneration and his activities at a minimum. Never, from the summer of 1956, did Radoux furnish all the money he promised. To launch the magazine, I had had to sell some stock. At one time the magazine owed me almost four thousand dollars, no small sum for a newsman. Several times only a threat to resign produced the overdue check.

To compound my distress, Rijkens and Radoux blamed me for not raising the capital which they were unwilling or unable to collect. On one occasion in New York, when our former Ambassador to Belgium, Myron Cowen, a sturdy supporter of the magazine, gave a lunch for Spaak, at which the latter had promised to appeal for support to the assembled American tycoons, the Belgian forgot to mention the magazine.

For three and a half years I found myself saddled not merely with editing, but with scrounging for gifts.

Yet the fault was not entirely that of the European founders. Had the U.S. Internal Revenue accorded tax immunity to *Western World,* they would have found enough American "angels." Many equally "political" magazines enjoyed tax immunity. But lawyer Ernest Cuneo, well-disposed Senators and Congressmen, and a friend in the State Department pleaded in vain that *Western World* was accomplishing an educational service for the country.

Internal Revenue remained adamant. And *without tax exemption,* as I learned to my sorrow, even the most generous American capitalists were unwilling to contribute the sixty thousand annual dollars upon which, by penny-pinching, *Western World* could in time have built up the circulation requisite to obtaining enough advertisements.

Not even our many friends, Jack McCloy, George Ball, David

Sarnoff, Jack Heinz, Philip Courtney, Chris Herter, Eric Johnston, Floyd Blair, Bob Smallwood, Colonel William Walsh, Jack Speiden of Arizona, even Frank Pace, whose American Council on NATO was a (tax exempt) competitor for funds, could dig enough gold out of the financial hills with a non–tax-exempt shovel.

Nor could *Western World Association,* the tax exempt brainchild of Philip Amram, which counted prominent legislators and socialites among its members, *legally* make up the magazine's regular deficit.

By the end of 1959, I was devoting at least a third of all my time to soliciting gifts. This was a severe strain, but I would not let go.

Sidney Stein of Chicago finally suggested a way of satisfying the Internal Revenue. This was to make the American edition the property of a firm whose partners could legally write off commercial losses. Stein believed it would be possible to find the requisite ten or twelve partners. Malcolm Davis, Jr., was ready to give up a promising public relations job to become business manager. Yet just when the outlook was brightening early in 1960, Rijkens pronounced the death sentence. Radoux owed the Utrecht printer an intolerably large sum. With the issue of March, 1960, *Western World-Occident* ceased to be.

Personally nobody suffered. Radoux had been elected to the Belgian Parliament. Dabernat and Angèle found better paid positions. "Chris," the model assistant, had found a husband. Enough for me that *Western World's* name had become known to millions and was conceivably the most successful failure in the history of magazines.

37

Unfinished Business

Great ills befall the world when the powerful begin to copy the weak.

ERIC HOFFER

OF WORK I still had an abundance.

Unknown to most Americans, Khrushchev was planning to make 1961, to the Chinese the Year of the Mouse, a Year of the Bear. He began in mid-1960 at the Summit Conference in Paris. As a pretext for preventing Eisenhower's planned visit to the Soviet Union, the Russians took the shooting down of an American U-2 intelligence plane over Russian territory for whose presence Eisenhower refused to apologize. To make his position plain, Mr. K. convoked a news conference and to about a thousand newsmen, ranted for an hour, suggesting that somebody "bang Eisenhower's head against the wall." Not since Hitler's outbursts in the Berlin *Sportpalast* had I witnessed and heard anything similar. This was Eisenhower's reward for having, at Camp David, asked Mr. K. to call him friend.

Yet instead of telling the Soviet leader to go to, say, Samarkand and stay there, our President revealed that he had called off further intelligence flights over Soviet territory.

Thus encouraged, Khrushchev at the United Nations Assembly in New York ostentatiously removed a shoe and banged it on the rostrum. The world gasped at his boorishness. Yet a U.S. Assistant Secretary of State was unintentionally responsible. At a diplomatic reception, Andrew Berding, Carl McCardle's successor, had facetiously explained to a Soviet official that unlike Europeans, who *whistled* to show disapproval, Americans *banged on a table with a shoe*. Khrushchev had merely tried to observe the custom of the country.

After the Paris Conference, Charles de Gaulle in the Elysée Palace told me of his total disagreement with my advocacy of further American confrontations with Russia as stated in *A Good Time To Be Alive*. Eisenhower's refusal of the general's suggestion of a Three-Power NATO directorate was bearing bitter fruit. Ike's crusade for peace had made it safe for France to liberate itself from what de Gaulle called American "hegemony." Thenceforth, to be acceptable to him, any united Europe would have to be uniquely "European."

Thirty-five hundred miles to the east, at Rawalpindi in Pakistan, President Ayub Khan echoed the French President's dissatisfaction with the United States. In face of Red China's plan for outflanking and subjugating the Indian Peninsula by seizing Tibet, by infiltrating Laos and by communizing South Viet Nam and Burma, what good to Pakistan, Ayub asked, was a military alliance with an America whose President persisted in encouraging India? I returned to Washington more despondent than ever.

And as Ayub had predicted, a few months later, representatives of eighty-one communist parties agreed at Moscow to widen their struggle for what Khrushchev later called communist domination over "the minds of the majority . . . of the globe."

John F. Kennedy's election to the Presidency faintly raised my hopes. Jack was both literate and likable and had a good, if brief, war record. A year previously, when I had gone to his Senate office to pick up a manuscript which he had promised *Western World,* I found him flushed, disheveled, drooping with campaign fatigue. With an irresistible grin he had confessed that "anyone who seeks the Presidency of the United States must have a screw loose or an overbearing father."

Shortly before the election, he and Senator Hubert Humphrey posed for a picture with me holding a copy of *A Good Time To Be Alive,* which my publisher later reproduced on the jacket of my *End To Make Believe*.

During Kennedy's campaign debates with Nixon he had promised that if elected to the presidency he would "help non-Batista Cubans to liberate their country."

Here was a pledge I had long awaited.

In January 20, 1961, Lilian and I once more sat and shivered before the Capitol while a new President read an ambivalent inaugural address. Beginning with a stirring pledge to "pay any price, meet any hardship, support any friend, oppose any foe, in order to assure the survival and success of liberty," this young Lochinvar from out of South Boston than referred to our foes as "nations which would *make* themselves our adversary." What sort of double-talk was this? A promise never to "negotiate out of fear" was canceled by the subsequent commitment never to "fear to negotiate." Did President Kennedy intend to win the Cold War or was he just a younger Adlai Stevenson?

By March the capital was a-babble. Yuri Gagarin had made his spectacular space flight, with unforeseeable consequences for the United States. Kennedy had sent American troops to threatened Laos, and was talking of sending others to South Vietnam. Something was brewing in Cuba.

At first I accepted the official story that the unknown bombardiers of Cuban airfields were defectors from Castro's air force. Until the truth came out: several hundred Cuban patriots had, with American help, landed at a place called the Bay of Pigs, and were on the point of being annihilated or captured by the Bearded One. Our President had called off the promised second air strike. The invasion was an ignominious failure.

The Administration's "news managers" encouraged journalists to put the blame on the Central Intelligence Agency, which had trained and equipped the Cubans, and on the Joint Chiefs of Staff. But how believe that those same Chiefs who, as field officers, had successfully carried out the amphibious campaign against Japan and the Normandy landing would permit friendly Cubans to undertake a defectively planned assault?

What had happened to J.F.K.'s promises to "put freedom first" and "never to accept a Communist Cuba"?

My friends and I considered the abandonment of the Cuban patriots as disgraceful as F.D.R.'s abandonment of Poland and Ike's passivity toward the revolting Hungarians, and less excusable than either.

Yet two weeks later, a public opinion poll revealed that the President's popularity at home had reached a new high, particularly among young people who had reached the age of indiscretion. Kennedy had saved the peace. What else mattered?

To wise old hands like Charles de Gaulle and Konrad Adenauer, both of whom had brought their war-ravaged countries out of the depths, the Bay of Pigs precedent meant that the new American Administration would hesitate to accept nuclear devastation to save Europe from Russian occupation. Even more disturbing did they find Kennedy's adoption of the "Taylor doctrine" of graduated deterrence in place of "massive retaliation." The Frenchman began looking for a substitute for NATO, the German for a possible auxiliary to that organization.

Among the President's advisers, only Dean Acheson offered me reassurance against another Bay of Pigs, yet Acheson's influence remained limited. Averell Harriman's shrewd diagnoses of Soviet intentions was wasted because of his homeopathic prescriptions for thwarting them.

Dean Rusk, a blander Cordell Hull, whom I had known since the late forties, had, while a Rhodes scholar at Oxford before the war, won a peace prize.

Robert McNamara substituted for political understanding the cocksureness of the typical American technocrat.

Several of the others, comparatively young men with fully developed egos, had been on university faculties, and readily accepted the mumpsimus of the terrified nuclear scientists, namely, that the atom bomb made power politics obsolescent. Ever since my student days I had enjoyed the friendship of professors and appreciated their intellectual and specialized knowledge. Yet with few exceptions, they lacked political insight. Kennedy's academics were no exception. For politics is not a matter of *logic* or of analysis but of knowledge of *people*, something only experience brings. The Rand Corporation and M.I.T. could furnish no end of information concerning an adversary's *capability*, but about Khrushchev's or Mao Tse-tung's *intentions* they and their computers had less to offer than a competent Mata Hari in Moscow or Peking.

Handsome McGeorge Bundy, a Harvard dean and political scientist, owed his start to having ghosted former Secretary Stimson's book, *On Active Service*, which attempted to justify Roosevelt's fixation that he could handle Stalin. Yet McGeorge was now the President's closest adviser on foreign policy!

Walt Rostow, an M.I.T. economist, had written at least one book on foreign policy for the Central Intelligence Agency. With the new special Assistant to the President on Science and Technology, Jerome Wiesner, Rostow had, shortly after Kennedy's election, attended a "Pugwash" disarmament conference in Moscow and swallowed too much peaceful coexistence vodka.

At the age of thirty-five Brother Bobby Kennedy emerged as the "assistant President." He opined that Communists did not *foment* revolts and "little wars of liberation," but merely *exploited* them when they occured from other causes.

Thanks to the influence of such theorists, President Kennedy set about, in the spirit of the Pugwash meetings, to "depolarize" the world. As a start he created a Disarmament and Arms Control Agency, which Dean Acheson labeled a "cruel hoax."

Secretary Rusk began encouraging newly liberated peoples to remain nonaligned rather than to seek a closer tie with the United States. Former Governor G. Mennen Williams of Michigan, an Assistant Secretary of State, toured the young African states peddling an "instant democracy" on which many soon sickened.

In Europe, whither the President went in pursuit of his "dumbbell" Atlantic policy, General de Gaulle told him that the revived Soviet threat to Berlin was either a bluff or a feint to cover some new aggression elsewhere. Yet instead of believing de Gaulle, Kennedy in Vienna assured a blustering Khrushchev of his own readiness to accept the postwar *status quo* (including a divided Germany) and of his lack of any animosity toward Marxist governments that refrained from aggression, and promised to reduce anticommunist propaganda and support to refugee organizations in the United States.

About a month later Senator Fulbright publicly expressed his "surprise" that East Germany, which had lost so many of its better citizens to the West during the previous sixteen years, had not already closed its frontier, *as was its right*!

Why should the Butcher of Budapest not conclude, as he remarked to Robert Frost a little later, that America was "too old" to stand up to "young" Russia and "too generous to fight," and accept Fulbright's suggestion? In mid-August, he ordered the East Germans to close the main refugee leak by erecting a twenty-six-mile wall through the center of Berlin, a flagrant breach of the Four-Power Agreement of New York (May 4, 1949). Only as a prison would East Germany survive. Had the American garrison immediately flattened the Wall with their tanks, neither the Soviet Union nor East Germany would have done more than howl. Yet Kennedy did nothing, excusing himself, as before, by pointing to the danger of a nuclear war. Was this the "vigah" to which he so often alluded? Kennedy, as I commented sarcastically, was trying to reduce the Cold War to a popularity contest while leaving to time and rising prosperity the task of softening up the Kremlin-men.

Perhaps his reluctance to accept the facts of international life was due to his carefully concealed ill health and almost constant pain. As I knew from a friend of his father, John F. Kennedy fulfilled his presidential duties thanks only to regular doses of drugs, three warm daily baths, special exercises, a rocking chair, and a limited diet.

Perhaps for this reason he relied, in moments of crisis, upon what one Republican called "government by bull session." Since his advisers were no more resolute than he, no amount of palaver with them could supply the boldness essential to statesmanship.

I made several attempts to maintain my former rapport with the new President. Over lunch one day, I suggested to Kennedy's press secretary, Pierre Salinger, that any visible eagerness for peace on our part would encourage the communist leaders to further aggression. Might I not perhaps discuss this with the President? Weeks later, having heard nothing, I wrote, reminding Salinger. Still, silence. Kennedy loved newsmen—as a claque. Since I intended to remain "no man's man," I said no more about a private talk with my former acquaintance.

Instead, I studied him at his carefully rehearsed press conferences. Generally he communicated little—but how charmingly! In consequence, these televised seances were his strongest card. The American people had trusted Ike, but he bored them to the point where they welcomed a younger, more colorful, and more articulate successor. John F. Kennedy was neither an egghead nor an aesthete.

Yet now, for the first time since George Washington, America had a royal court instead of a presidential residence, with widely publicized emphasis upon style in the royal dwelling, gourmet food, and a salon where musicians and artists felt at home. Washington society writers became all-important. Certain newsmen purred with pride when the sovereign requested their company or their advice.

Why worry about the weakening of foreign policy?

In September, 1961, Duell, Sloan and Pearce (now part of Meredith Press) brought out *An End to Make-Believe.* "This book," affirmed the publisher, "signals a turning point in world affairs."

Some reviewers agreed. William Henry Chamberlin referred to ours as the "age of make-believe." Charles Poore thanked the author for showing "that the free world can still win."

The *Boston Herald,* the *Christian Science Monitor,* the *Virginia Kirkus Service,* and many others published highly favorable reviews. The *New Yorker* called it "hot-cross punditry by a veteran pundit." Michael Padev in the *Indianapolis Star* suggested that President Kennedy devote thirty minutes of his "fast-reading ability" to "one of the best books within the last decade."

In Paris, Charles de Gaulle, in acknowledging the receipt of a copy, praised the book for "lighting up the past and opening the future," and added: "I read it with even more interest because I know how great is your knowledge of international problems."

But to Liberals, rejoicing in Kennedy's revival of F.D.R.'s attempt to cooperate with the Soviet Union, my assertions of the folly of this policy seemed "unsophisticated." The New Frontiersmen's greatest fear was of nuclear weapons in the hands of . . . Germany! When, shortly thereafter, I wrote an article defending Foster Dulles' policy of brinkmanship as the best guarantee of peace *and* freedom, several previously hospitable editors said no. It finally appeared in the *National Review.*

In 1962, the United States, presented to the United Nations an *Outline of Basic Provisions of a Treaty on General and Complete Disarmament in A Peaceful World,* a document which must have further confirmed the Russians' belief that the American President could be bluffed by a show of force.

That year I accepted an invitation of the German Government to be its guest, visiting successively Bonn, Duesseldorf, Berlin, Hamburg, Munich, and Frankfurt. For the first time since the war I made a thorough *reportage,* talking with hundreds of Germans. I liked what I found. What a superb job Adenauer and Erhard, with the invaluable help of Hans Boeckler of the Federation of Trade Unions, had done! TV and the Common Market had, for the first time since Goethe, brought young Germans fully into the stream of Western Europe.

Yet Berliners resented Kennedy's inaction about the wall. How rely upon an America whose spokesman, Walt Rostow, stated that the United States was not seeking "a victory of the United States over the Soviet Union or of capitalism over Communism." Prince Louis Ferdinand of Prussia, with whom I lunched in Grunewald, was urging his compatriots to offer neutrality to the Russians as the price of reunification.

Brief visits to Geneva, Paris, London, Brussels, and The Hague, convinced me that unless the United States speedily offered full political, military, and scientific cooperation to the Common Market countries, new Europe might one day go its own way, or disintegrate into the prewar jumble of sovereign states.

The autumn missile crisis in Cuba caught the U.S. Administration off base. That master spy, Colonel Oleg Penkovsky, had continually warned the Americans of Mr. K.'s aggressive intentions in Cuba, as well as of Russia's unreadiness for the war with the United States which its military were planning. In his diary he had confided: "I wonder why the West trusts Khrushchev . . . we in the G. R. V., [Military Intelligence] sit around and talk and laugh: 'What fools, they believe us again.'"

Yet for at least a month, the New Frontiersmen made light of refugee reports made public by Senator Kenneth Keating of the arrival in Cuba of Soviet middle-range missiles, presumably with nuclear warheads. They could not believe that the Soviet Union would brazenly defy the United States.

Only when a U.S. plane confirmed their presence did John F. Kennedy for the first and only time in his presidential career go to the verge of war. Here was the opportunity to eliminate Castro once and for all.

After several days of "bull sessions," the President told Moscow to remove its offensive missiles or face dire consequences. The revelation of his ultimatum threw millions of Americans into a panic. This was Armageddon, Doomsday, the end of the human race. . . .

Personally, along with my military and diplomatic friends, including Charles de Gaulle (who immediately offered America full assistance in case of war), I lost no sleep. No Soviet leader would risk the total destruction of the workers' paradise to save communism in Cuba.

As we foresaw, once the Kremlin realized that the White House mean business, Khrushchev, in a rambling letter to the President, offered to withdraw his middle-range missiles in exchange for Kennedy's promise not to invade Cuba. "Fearful of his own courage," the President complied, provided the withdrawal be certified by the United Nations. Yet when Castro refused to permit inspection, Kennedy declared himself satisfied, and congratulated the Russian on his "statesmanlike decision" and contribution to peace. The trembling millions slept once more.

Russian troops and missiles of some sort remained in Cuba. Khrushchev's retreat may have cost him his job, but he had the President's promise not to use force, or permit Cubans to use the United States as a base for using force against Castro. This was revealed in the exchange of letters between him and Kennedy first published in Castro's weekly *Bohemia* on November 2, 1962, and confirmed by Khrushchev in 1967. Shortly thereafter President Kennedy withdrew our missiles from Britain, Italy, Greece, and Turkey and canceled plans for installing others in Portugal, alleging that such weapons were obsolete.

To me our "victory" in the missile crisis painfully recalled Norfolk's remark in Shakespeare's *Henry VIII*:

> ... *Grievingly I think,*
> *The peace between the French and us not values*
> *The cost that did conclude it.* ...

Kennedy's venture in brinkmanship convinced him that a Cold War waged with the threat of nuclear weapons was intolerable. Instead, he accepted the professors' notion that by improving the lot of the communist societies we could hasten their evolution from tyranny to freedom. For a winning policy he tried to substitute disarmament agreements with his pen-pal in the Kremlin.

His schizophrenia became apparent during his visit to Germany in the summer of 1963. To a wildly enthusiastic crowd in Berlin he said:

"Two thousand years ago, the proudest boast was '*civis Romanus sum*.' Today in the world of freedom, the proudest boast is '*ich bin ein Berliner*.'

"There are many people in the world who really don't understand —or say they don't understand—what is the great issue between the free world and the communist world. Let them come to Berlin.

"And there are some who say in Europe and elsewhere, 'We can work with the communists.' Let them come to Berlin.

"And there are even a few who say that it is true that Communism is an evil system but it permits us to make economic progress. Let them come to Berlin."

Yet in subsequent speeches at the Free University of Berlin and again at Frankfurt, he specifically warned the Germans against expecting any immediate reunification: peace was too important to risk! J.F.K. was counting on a relaxation of the nuclear stalemate to bring about what the "Bible of the New Frontier," *Common Action for the Control of Conflict,* called a "substantial, cross-national diffusion of interest and ultimately of power."

That same summer the United States negotiated a nuclear test-ban treaty with the U.S.S.R. that hindered the United States from using its vastly superior financial and technical resources to maintain nuclear preponderance.

In 1963, however, the President finally sent substantial American military forces to South Vietnam, which his policy of pretending to "neutralize" Laos had gravely endangered. There, in a country that had never known democracy, the Catholic nationalist, Ngo Din Diem, was fighting a desperate battle against local communists heavily supported by invaders from North Vietnam.

Vice President Johnson had praised Diem as the "Churchill of Today." Impatient American reformers at home and Liberal correspondents in South Vietnam complained, however, that this "reactionary" Roman Catholic, ignoring the advice of his American allies, repressed militant sabotage by "innocent" Buddhists, some of whom publicly burned themselves to death in protest against his "tyranny." Moreover, Diem opposed any plan of "neutralizing" South Vietnam under a "coalition" government.

In August, 1963, Washington instructed Ambassador Lodge to permit the local military to overthrow the Diem regime. Two months later ambitious Vietnamese generals murdered Diem and his brother Nu.

The murder of an ally filled me with indignation. Whatever Diem's sins against democracy, they remain, compared with Ho Chi-Minh's systematic murders, purely venial. To make matters worse, the two American correspondents most responsible for blackening the Ngo family in the eyes of "progressives" at home received the Pulitzer Prize for their successful defamation. Could I have laid hands on the certificate of my own Pulitzer, I should have returned it to the committee.

Friends explained that the President had not anticipated that the Vietnamese military would go so far. In any case nemesis came swiftly: three weeks after Diem's murder, a neurotic American murdered John Fitzgerald Kennedy.

The Democratic Party made all possible hay out of the tragedy. With what seemed indecent haste, the New Frontiersmen lost no time in putting their remembrances on paper, before accepting lucrative jobs outside the government. During the period of consternation that followed the shocking event, Bobby Kennedy revealed himself, to me at least, as the most ruthlessly ambitious American politician since Aaron Burr.

Thanks to the communications media and the improved techniques of "image building," millions everywhere had relished the "kingly figure" in the White House much as they did movie favorites. "For a time," novelist Norman Mailer sighed, "we thought the country was *ours*. Now it is *theirs*."

Certainly, under the Kennedys, the United States had become less and less my country. Not to bask in power, however glamorous, had my ancestors sailed from royalty-ridden Europe centuries before.

Had President Kennedy's illness paralyzed that *superior coluculus* in his brain to which all animals allegedly owe the will to resist aggression?

Nationally, his impartiality between neutral India and Pakistan cost us the support of a sturdy ally. When India illegally seized Portuguese Goa without consulting the inhabitants, Kennedy never peeped, yet when Red China suddenly turned on its gullible Indian "brother" he immediately promised India unconditional military support.

In the former Belgian Congo, the Administration had aided procommunist Lumumba against prowestern Tshombe; in Southeast Asia it had permitted Ho Chi-Minh to infiltrate troops into "neutral" Laos.

Even more dangerous had been Kennedy's assumption that a

Soviet-American agreement banning the proliferation of nuclear weapons would serve peace.

Finding a spate of unresolved international problems in his lap was not what Lyndon Baines Johnson had expected. Secretary Rusk had assured him that, with the international situation so well under control, he would be free to concentrate on the Great Society.

With some of his proposed domestic reforms I had full sympathy. Constitutional rights for Negroes, Indians, and other minorities were long overdue. The price of social integration was their general acceptance of the prevailing cultural pattern, in this case, of "the American way of life." Some had already made great progress. Given time and real effort, the other minority groups could do the same. My predominantly WASP grandfathers would have found it unthinkable that a half-Jew like Goldwater or a Mormon like Romney could be considered for the presidency. But I did not believe that the Supreme Court could successfully legislate *social integration*. Here I differed with Lyndon B. Johnson.

Moreover, in my view, U.S. assistance to undeveloped countries, except as occasional charity, should be considered a weapon in the Cold War.

The Alliance for Progress would hasten Latin America's economic development only if its application were not coupled with pressure for "reforms" that stimulated further capital flight.

Even while he sought Congress' support of his proposal on domestic reforms President Johnson found himself compelled to escalate American participation in the defense of South Vietnam or see the communists swallow that country. Half a million American soldiers could, in 1946, have saved China and obviated the need for intervention in Korea and Southeast Asia.

In Congress, Lyndon Johnson had supported the containment policy of three successive Administrations. Perhaps, as the son of pioneers and as a Texan who remembered the Alamo and the Indian wars, he would realize the need for victory wherever the United States committed itself and eliminate those of his predecessor's advisers who disagreed. Certainly L.B.J., in Vietnam, as later in the Dominican Republic, rose to the occasion in the teeth of Liberal abuse at home and abroad.

Since I felt sure that the Cold War would be won or lost in Washington, D.C., I overlooked no opportunity of supporting the President's firmer positions. I was at this time serving on the boards of a half dozen anticommunist organizations, notably of *Freedom House,* the *Council Against Communist Aggression and Citizens for Freedom,* and, at the behest of John Fisher of Chicago, as an editorial consultant to the *American Security Council.* For the Council, I wrote a long study, *How We Can Win the Cold War,* embodying my deep conviction that only a common Western policy of *increasing* tensions with communist aggressors could restore peace with freedom.

While receiving a freedom award from the *Assembly of Captive*

Nations, I apologized for our President's effort to "bring all humanity within a single sheepfold, under God," at the expense of the captive nations' freedom and concluded that the "survival chances of a sheepfold that welcomes the wolves and bears while chaining up and muzzling the shepherd dogs are anything but brilliant!"

During three long years I sought in vain to assemble the millions of dollars necessary to create in Washington a new daily newspaper whose foreign policy I could approve. Millionaires who complained bitterly of Washington's weakness and double-talk were unwilling to risk money in order to change things.

Meanwhile, President Johnson followed the advice of Kennedy holdovers who believed that the United States could simultaneously combine resistance with cooperation abroad and attack the "real problems of our time": poverty, hunger, overpopulation, and colonialism (outside the U.S.S.R., of course).

Mao Tse-tung, well on the way to producing nuclear weapons, had expressed his aim in a poem:

> *The four seas are in fury, the clouds and waters rage.*
> *Five continents tremble. All insects must be exterminated.*
> *Not one enemy must remain alive.*

To win the election in 1964, Johnson's supporters stooped to slander. Two motion pictures, *Seven Days in May* and *Dr. Strangelove,* hysterically emphasized the doomsday bomb while, by inference, casting ridicule on the leading Republican candidate for the presidential nomination, Senator Barry Goldwater.

Earlier, foreseeing Goldwater's nomination, Roscoe Drummond and I had lunched with the Senator. We both had the same impression— honesty, unlimited courage, and a disconcerting lack of political tact.

Had he double-talked, Goldwater in my judgment might have won the election. Instead, in an interview with the Berlin *Spiegel,* he suggested using tactical nuclear weapons against the Viet Cong hideouts in Vietnam, a suggestion used by his opponents to brand him as a war-monger.

Once elected, however, L.B.J. extended our bombing to targets in North Vietnam precisely as his defeated and derided adversary had advocated.

Rusk let it be known that Red China "must keep out of South Vietnam or face a war with the United States in the Pacific," but revealed no word of his unwritten agreement with Kosygin and with Mao: you stay out of the war in Vietnam and we shall refrain from invading North Vietnam, blocking Hanoi, or bombing Red China.

Occasionally, fortune smiled upon the Free World. The unforeseen defection of Stalin's daughter, Svetlana, irresistibly refocused the world's attention upon Soviet barbarism. Had the U.S. Administration made the most of it, her repudiation of Soviet society would have a crushing propaganda defeat for the Kremlin. But in Washington, the hope of "cross-national" agreements with the Kremlin prevailed. In Indonesia, Ghana, and Guinea, to mention only the more prominent places, the communists overplayed their hands and lost heavily.

The Sino-Soviet rift revealed an organic disunity in the communist camp. Even more startling, at least to those American "experts" largely responsible for President Truman's abandonment of the Kuomintang in 1946, was the outbreak in China of incipient civil war between "orthodox" Mao Tse-tung and "revisionists" who sought to fashion China along Soviet lines. Mao's nuclear weapons frightened his noncommunist neighbors, but they could not prevent his regime from falling apart. His use of juvenile "Red Guards" (a second "Children's Crusade") revealed to all the world how skin-deep was his faith in his people's conversion to Maoism.

Moreover, Chiang Kai-shek, confounding his disparagers, had, with American help, transformed shabby, long neglected Taiwan into an economically prosperous and militarily almost impregnable island. Given American offensive weapons and logistical support, Chiang's air force could obliterate Red China's nuclear industry in Sinkiang and, at the appropriate moment, foment and exploit an anticommunist insurrection to recover the mainland, thus ending the war in Vietnam and swinging the entire area to our side.

All this became apparent when, in the summer of 1966, Lilian and I visited successively Taiwan, Hong Kong, and Tokyo.

What a fantastic change since our previous visit in 1951! The lack of poverty, the efficiency of the military establishment, and the calm confidence of the Generalissimo, were astounding. Agriculturally, Taiwan was competing with Hawaii on the international market. The underground defenses of Quemoy Island at the nearest point, two thousand yards from the mainland of China, reminded me of a super Maginot Line and, unlike that, offered no gap through which communist forces could outflank the defenders.

In rain-drenched Hong Kong, American and other China watchers testified to Mao's woes.

Foreign observers in auto-infested (no milder phrase describes it) Tokyo, now the world's largest city, dwelt on the perverse pacifism of the Japanese Socialist opposition upon which communists were counting for ultimate victory. Yet even while the Japanese Cabinet remained outwardly unflappable, Japan, an official told me, would be happy to receive defensive anti-missile missiles from America. The promise of American nuclear protection was no longer enough.

One leading anticommunist Deputy reproached anticommunist Americans for not giving financial support to him and his friends. Underneath the prevailing preoccupation with the "economic miracle" lurked in thoughtful Japanese a deep and justified uneasiness concerning their country's future.

We returned home from Asia more than ever mindful of the warning of Founding Father Fisher Ames, namely, that "it is a law of politics as well as of physics, that a body in motion always overcomes a body at rest."

Nowhere was this law so visible as in Europe. Eisenhower's anti-colonialism and his two successors' courtship of the Kremlin had weakened the North Atlantic Treaty Organization. In 1962 I had still been confident that the Common Market countries were moving toward political as well as economic unity and even, given time, toward a genuine Atlantic Community. Yet during a Christmas in France in 1964, I had noted signs of NATO's disintegration.

By the time of our return to Europe in 1967, the New Frontiersmen's carefully fostered myth concerning the fading of the Cold War had been largely accepted by war-weary peoples whom we had more or less forced out of Indochina, Africa, and the Middle East. So long as communist aggression did not threaten Europe, Uncle Sam might worry about it!

Even while Prime Minister Wilson was seeking Britain's admission into the Common Market, a majority of his countrymen, according to a newspaper poll, favored "opting out" of international politics altogether.

General de Gaulle, older and fatter but still friendly, in the course of a forty-minute audience in Paris, predicted twenty years of rivalry between the "two greats." The West European countries led by a nuclearly armed France could remain independent only by keeping the balance between them. Nuclear weapons had rendered conventional weapons useless. So the General believed. Wrongly, I surmised. But if the United States, according to Secretary Rusk, would "never remain the ally of a country with nuclear weapons over whose use we had no control, why should France"?

Going further, Hervé Alphand, now Secretary General of the French foreign office, revealed to me de Gaulle's ambition to reach with the Soviet Union the same sort of special relationship which England maintained with the United States. This would become easier, a member of the French Cabinet explained, owing to the coming political and economic osmosis between Western Europe and the Soviet Union.

Germany was moving slowly in the same direction as I observed during a brief visit to Bonn, Berlin and Munich in March. Eisenhower's refusal of a NATO directorate and to provide our European allies with an independent nuclear force of their own; Kennedy's acceptance of the Taylor strategy of "graduated deterrence and his offer to Europe of a multilateral nuclear force (or "farce," as the French called it)— surface ships with mixed crews carrying nuclear missiles; Johnson's indifference to Germany's unnatural division and his insistence on imposing a nuclear nonproliferation treaty upon his allies—these were causing some German leaders quietly to consider the possibility of a "second Rapallo" whereby, in exchange for Germany's withdrawal from NATO, its permanent disarmament and its economic cooperation with the Soviet Union, the latter would withdraw its opposition to Germany's reunification. As a witness of the "first Rapallo," I shuddered at the prospect. A proliferation of relatively weak European states could be a greater danger than a proliferation of nuclear weapons.

No less an authority that NATO's Secretary General, Manlio Brosio, more or less shared my convictions:

Since 1945, Western fear of nuclear war and wishful thinking concerning the nature and aims of world communism and the Soviet Union had allowed the Red Blight to spread to East Europe and giant China and had brought about our failure to reunite Korea;

Western fear of "escalation" was preventing Nationalist China from obliterating Mao Tse-tung's nuclear plants or from attempting to liberate the Chinese mainland;

Western half-heartedness had allowed Ho Chi Minh to revolutionize North Viet Nam and from there parts of Laos and South Viet Nam, thereby compelling the United States to wage a costly war which it dared not lose yet lacked the will to escalate to success;

American pacifism was depriving us of European support in South Viet Nam, and threatening the existence of the NATO alliance;

Worst of all, perhaps, taken together, these mistakes had sparked a new expansionist drive by the Soviet Union at a time when the United States found itself in financial difficulties, its people riven by pacifism, cynicism, racial revolt and contempt for law and order.

What a picture!

Sometimes, to be sure, I had nagging doubts about the soundness of my judgment. Perhaps Western optimists were right in assuming that the "thaw" of the fifties was genuine and that, "as nationalism," communism was not, or was no longer, a grave threat to human freedom.

Since the end of the Second Great War, the United States had gone further in the pursuit of peace and freedom than any other country, past or present. In spite of major failures in East Europe and China, we had preserved West Europe, Latin America except Cuba, Greece, Turkey, Iran, Thailand, Japan, Formosa, India, and most of Africa.

Even as the Bolsheviks had celebrated half a century of communism, opposition to totalitarian tyranny was rising throughout the communist world. In China, interparty strife could lead to party suicide. The "religious" feud between China and Russia might eventually bring both governments to their senses.

Reviving nationalism and rising expectations might, as Western optimists believed, turn out to be stronger than ideology and, given time, paralyze the urge to aggression. Granted the size of the stake, what was so wrong with Washington's search for a temporary Russo-American dyarchy as the forerunner to a world authority? By what right did I oppose the Kennedy-Johnson policy of seeking peace through patience and a nuclear anti-proliferation treaty? Like Oliver Cromwell to Parliament I warned myself: "Bethink ye by the bowles of Christ that ye may be wrong?" Those whom I considered purblind appeasers were perhaps far-sighted statesmen.

Why not relax and devote my remaining days to my first loves, philosophy and literature?

I could not. Never had the world been in greater disarray, freedom been in greater danger and the American people faced a greater challenge than in the spring of 1968!

I had too long involved in the fight against totalitarianism, black, brown and red, to quit when the struggle was apparently approaching a climax.

My record needed no defending. I had accurately foreseen the intentions of Mussolini, of Hitler, of the Japanese war lords and, since 1939, of Stalin and his successors. At two testimonial dinners, friends had paid tribute not only to the unmanaged newsman but to the foreign political analyst.

My duty was, therefore, to follow my own light and try to share it with others who would carry on the good fight until time or victory made it no longer necessary.

PART EIGHT

Balance Sheet

LORD: *What time is it by de sun and de stars?*
GABRIEL: *Jest half past, Lord.*

MARC CONNELLY
in Green Pastures

38

Harvest

> *Beloved Pan . . . may the outer and the inner*
> *man be at one. . . . May I reckon the wise to*
> *be the wealthy and may I have such a quantity*
> *of gold as a temperate man, and only he, can*
> *bear and carry.*
>
> Socrates' Prayer
> from Plato's Phaedrus

IT HAS BEEN MY FORTUNE to enjoy a ringside seat at many of the crucial events of perhaps the most revealing period in recorded history.

Never before has mankind had such triumphs to celebrate and such dismal failures to bemoan. Never has the future offered such glorious promises and such monstrous perils.

To men and women responsive to the call of adventure, the twentieth century has given satiety. To businessmen and social reformers it has offered unlimited vistas.

Scientists, technologists, and mathematicians have enjoyed two full centuries of unimaginably successful experiment and discovery, culminating in the Electronic Age that points to a future fantastic beyond belief.

Slowly the ocean deeps, the moon, and outer space are yielding their secrets.

One scientist, Victor Weisskopf, even claims to have reduced everything to just two mini-somethings, the baryon (heavy) and the lepton (light). Others postulate the existence of an entire anti-universe consisting of anti-matter.

Nothing seems impossible. "Would you like an education by injection?" Albert Roesenfeld asks: "A larger, more efficient brain? A cure for old age? Parentless babies? Body size and skin color to order? Name it and somebody is seriously proposing it."

In 1938, when no less than twelve million Americans were unemployed, my friend, the Italian poet-merchant, Delfino Cinelli, predicted the evolution of U.S. capitalism into a welfare economy that would not

435

only cover most of mankind's physical needs but ensure its happiness. Sure enough, large sections of the human race have emerged from the economic insecurity that has been man's lot since the caves. Throughout the entire West and parts of the Far East, poverty in the traditional sense of inadequate food, clothing, and shelter, has all but disappeared. Never have so many been preoccupied with alleviating physical suffering. Income differentials within the richer countries have shrunk notably. Barring a nuclear war, mankind may achieve a world-wide integrated economy of enormous productive capacity. For the first time in history, rich countries, led by the United States, have poured massive aid into poor countries.

The trend against legal racial discrimination seems irresistible.

Ever more peoples enjoy nominal independence and at least the promise of self government. Men and women almost everywhere live longer and enjoy better health. Throughout the West, and in postwar Japan, young people are taller, stronger, and handsomer than their forbears.

Yet never anywhere have pessimism and discontent prevailed among the educated and the sensitive. While our society dreams of a more radiant humanity to be created by human reason in the service of human love, its repudiation of, or indifference to, traditional loyalties and convictions is reflected in its permissive attitude toward a hideous renascence of crime, violence, and vice which it obviously lacks the courage to suppress. As early as 1932, the poet Alfred Noyes deplored "the gradual loss of the old simplicity and integrity which went . . . right down to the roots of life."

Twenty-three years later, novelist Thomas Mann accused the previous half century of having produced "a frightening atrophy of culture of the most sinister kind, a loss in education, in decorum, in feeling for law, truth and faith, in simple dependability."

Accompanying, perhaps resulting from this undeniable slump is a generation of young people who unceasingly "protest" while themselves seeking to escape moral responsibility through quietism, indolence, drugs, "pop" art, half-baked Buddhism, and sexual promiscuity or perversion.

Something like this has happened before. About the year 2500 B.C. Egypt's ruler, Ptah Hotep, complained that children no longer wanted to obey their elders. A couple of thousand years later, Socrates complained that "our youths have bad manners . . . contempt for authority, disrespect for elder people. . . ."

But neither Ptah Hotep nor Socrates records such indifference to traditional behavior as that of today's young people. What else should Western society expect when respected professors teach that man has neither consciousness nor free will and that his behavior can be predicted and controlled as surely as a chemical reaction?

Traditionally, leaders of society have inculcated a belief in permanent values and a social and individual purpose. But no longer.

"Change," undefined "progress," and "something for nothing" cannot as social anchors compare with *civis romanus sum,* the God-state of the Middle Ages, the Declaration of Independence, or the Rights of Man.

Even while Asia, Africa, and Latin America tingle with a new hope, the Atlantic Community no longer sees the fixed stars, has lost its compass, and trembles at its own emptiness.

What has gone wrong?

Diagnosticians point to recent horrors and to current military and social threats. Since 1914, they explain, the West, once so confident that mankind had, well, *almost* overcome the scourge of war and of man's inhumanity to man, has experienced two murderous world struggles fought with methods incompatible with what passed for established ethics, witnessed mass massacres which made those of Tamerlane seem almost humane, and now faces the possibility of total destruction.

Why wonder at the growth of cultural relativity even disguised as "structuralism," cynicism, and craving of peace at almost any price?

Conceivably, moreover, nuclear or chemical war is not the only, or perhaps the worst, menace to man's future. Improved diet, hygiene, and medicine, three of our proudest achievements, have visibly furthered a monstrous human proliferation which, unless speedily checked, threatens mass starvation for the many and moral, artistic, and economic loss for everyone. Statisticians foresee, by the year 2000, a world population of some seven billions, six of them in Asia, Africa, and Latin America.

The standardization and depersonalization of individuals through science, technology, and communications are visibly depriving even the richest of that personal freedom of which we still boast, and perhaps of happiness as well.

In some respects, the West's plight and prospects are unique. Yet to those philosophers of history, Oswald Spengler and Arnold Toynbee, our civilization ("culture," to Spengler) is following the inevitable cycle of birth, growth, maturity, decline, and death of all its predecessors. It is entering the period of senescence characterized by a "universal state." Hence, according to this theory, the resemblance of America, the "universal state of modern Faustian civilization," to the early Roman Empire.

By the time of that astute observer, Cicero, the indomitable spirit and stern morality that had characterized Horatius, the Gracchi, and Cato was giving place to uncertainty, to theories, and to superstitions unconcerned with the sense of personal duty and honesty which had made the earlier republic almost unique. Revolts, slave and otherwise, were increasing, along with contempt for the Roman Law which had been the city's pride. The individual Roman no longer put devotion to the state above personal pleasure. Government was passing from the hands of patriotic patricians into those of ambitious adventurers and rootless merchants intent primarily on gain.

How not be reminded of our own society?

Roman stoicism, epicureanism, cynicism, and incipient pacifism have rough approximations in contemporary existentialism, behaviorism, logical analysis, and "hippy quietism." Jean-Paul Sartre's world, like that of Cicero's, smells of a death wish.

Striking, too, in my eyes, is the growing American yearning for a "royal dynasty" which, guided by social scientists, will impose ever more radical "reforms" upon the "stupid" majority. ("When that the poor have cried, Caesar hath wept.")

The American paupers' demand for "welfare" and television sets parallels the Roman mob's insistence on bread (three hundred thousand recipients in the one city) and circuses.

By the time of Juvenal and Marcus Aurelius, imperial Rome, though the undisputed mistress of the Mediterranean world, was losing both its sense of purpose and its physical power, and depending for its defense largely upon foreign mercenaries.

Equally disturbing, to me at least, is Charles de Gaulle's likening of the United States to Carthage. Carthage owed its death overwhelmingly to the pacifism of its ruling merchants. The descendants of the far-wandering Phoenicians, whose Hannibal had all but conquered Rome itself, sank to the point where they paid regular tribute to arrogant Romans and sought to defend themselves only when it was too late: an impressive illustration of Shakespeare's observation (*Love's Labour Lost*):

> Fat paunches make lean pates; and dainty bits
> Make rich the ribs and bankrupt quite the wits.

Happily, certain discrepancies weaken both analogies. As yet, Americans do not share the imperial Romans' readiness to entrust their defense to foreigners or exhibit the falling birth rate and religious revival that, according to Spengler, regularly announce approaching downfall.

Nor, in spite of the "better Red than dead" and "make love, not war" attitude of many, do most citizens as yet appear resigned to a Carthaginian-type submission to Moscow or Peking.

Thus, while recognizing certain American resemblances to both Rome and Carthage, I believe with Toynbee that the West is not "doomed to let history repeat itself": a civilization fades only when it fails to find appropriate responses to its historical challenges.

Where, then, should we seek such responses to ours? Some will answer, in reason: psychology and the social sciences, chiefly economics, offer, they believe, sure keys to improved human contact. This I no longer believe.

Like most Americans of my generation, as a young man I accepted human rationality and progress as axiomatic. Evolution from the amoeba to Leonardo da Vinci had, I felt sure, been continuous and inevitable. It took the First World War, above all the conduct of individual soldiers, friends, and foes alike, once they found themselves free of social constraint and fear of legal punishment, to convince me that moral, like biological evolution, was dismayingly slow.

Plato had noted within each man and woman the existence of "a terrible and lawless brood of desires, which are revealed in sleep." Life, L. L. Whyte noted recently, "must explode and develop latent capacities even at cost of self-annihilation."

From the beginning of recorded time man's emotional nature has remained virtually unchanged. Therefore, as Machiavelli insisted, "Whosoever wishes to see the future must consult the past; for human events ever resemble those of preceding times" (since) "they are produced by men who have ever been, and will be, animated by the same passions."

This applies particularly to the problem of avoiding nuclear war. Before investing vast sums of taxpayers' money in various pseudoscientific institutes to study the path to peace, our statesmen might remember that before Alfred Adler, two modern Italians, Pareto and Umano, each on the basis of historical research, had noted in all human individuals an instinct of *self assertion,* the *libido dominandi* of Saint Augustine, perhaps the élan vital of Bergson, of which sex and greed are aspects. (Whether, as some have recently affirmed, this arises from a basic *sense of property* I cannot say.) Such self assertion varies in individuals from a simple need to be *recognized* by others to the ruthless demand to be obeyed by them. But to some degree it is present in each of us.

This is hard for people taught to consider the past as prologue, to accept. For it would more or less compel them to seek effective responses to today's grave problems not in science but in history.

To be sure, love, group solidarity, or religion can sublimate self-assertiveness in individuals, and satiety, nihilism, fear, or reason moderate its expression. Yet until this occurs simultaneously and equally everywhere, history indicates only one solution to the "problem" of violence and war. This, as Hobbes perceived, is the *rule of law.*

To make their rule profitable to themselves and tolerable to the many, the ruling few impose *law,* and, to make it more acceptable, appeal to whatever group, moral, and religious links exist ("emperor by God's grace," etc.) and, above all, to the need for *internal order.*

Since 1945, fear of the nuclear weapons in the possession of a rival state has prevented *major* war. Even dogmatically aggressive governments hesitate before risking their very existence. Yet the "stalemate of terror" has facilitated armed "conventional" interventions by nuclear powers, and lesser "conventional" struggles among nonnuclear states.

Lasting international peace on all levels must await the emergence either of a truly preponderant state or group of states ready and able to impose a *Pax Romana,* or of a world authority able to *formulate and enforce world law upon all.* So long as neither exists, war, even major war, will remain possible. Such is history's answer to today's most awesome challenge.

Law also offers the most promising remedy to that "prevalence of people" which is overurbanizing mankind, polluting its air and water, and threatening it with wholesale starvation.

To be sure, Sir Charles Darwin, an eminent authority, insists, following Malthus, that there is no remedy, at least not during "the next million years." Man, like all other animals, will, he predicts, proliferate to the edge of famine. Only mass suicide, lemming fashion, or a nuclear war could, temporarily, check this.

Nonetheless, Sir Charles may be wrong: legislation imposing later marriages, sterilization, and taxes increasing with the number of offspring might check overpopulation if governments had the wisdom and courage to apply them.

Other students of history have concluded that, in a world relieved of the need to work by machinery and standardization, the greatest challenge will be the absence of challenge.

This, however, I challenge. Some years ago I "discovered" what I called *Mowrer's Law*. Roughly formulated it reads: *the solution of any human problem automatically creates another, often greater, problem.*

Everybody knows one or more examples.

"The more people share the good things of life, the less attractive these become." (Marya Mannes)

The atomic bomb which made America safe against its acquisition by Nazi Germany provides the Soviet Union the security behind which it safely pursues aggression.

Democratic anti-colonialism has made the liberated peoples susceptible to communist propaganda.

Improved medicine, hygiene, and diet are directly responsible for overpopulation and increasing hunger.

The petroleum deposits which made possible the miracle of modern transportation now threaten to poison humanity.

And so on, indefinitely.

This discovery filled me with a certain pride, until I realized that others had made it before me. Sophocles had written: "And ever this law holds good, nothing vast enters into the life of mortals without a curse." Walt Whitman was more specific: "It is provided in the nature of things that from any fruition of success, no matter what, shall come forth something to make a greater struggle necessary."

An Indian friend further commented: "Of course man will always have cares, more or less the same. If you banish pestilence, you get the A-bomb. We believe that God sends these troubles to man or that man unconsciously creates them for himself. For they are essential to his not getting worse, *or even to his improvement.*"

If my friend's faith be founded, it follows that *today's communist offensive could constitute the challenge in responding to which the West would avoid the eclipse which has overtaken all previous civilizations.*

Provided, of course, that it included reconciliation with those traditional sources of courage and sanity, namely, nature, beauty, and God.

Take nature. Over the last two centuries, proliferating man has consciously carried on a super-Darwinian struggle against other biological species. In so doing he has achieved great, short-run benefits. But at the same time he has upset the natural balance. Only recently have wise ecologists recognized that the further pollution or exhaustion of the soil, the water, and other natural resources will have disastrous consequences. Any exterminated species of plant or animal, even of a microbe or a virus, may in dying exact a fearful revenge. One ecologist, LaMont C. Cole, thinks it may already be too late to save the world. Certainly, the time is approaching when we must recognize our interdependence with all that is and treat it as if it were a single living organism, which, in my judgment, it is.

This is another example of Mowrer's—excuse me—of Sophocles' Law.

A revived solidarity with nature would, moreover, help banish that feeling of alienation which contributes so much to the Age's misery.

Reverence for life is not synonymous with feeding millions of sacred cows and monkeys while human beings go hungry. But it would make scientists think thrice before suppressing other species *or attempting to condition the human mind.* Reconciliation with nature would permit us once more to understand Faust's homage to Spring:

> *The throb of life returns, with pulses beating,*
> *Soft to ethereal dawn. O steadfast earth,*
> *True through the night, you waited for my greeting,*
> *Breathing beneath my feet a glad new birth,*
> *And clothing me afresh in joy of living,*
> *In high resolve that banishes misgiving,*
> *You stir my soul to prove life's utmost worth.*

The Western citizen who can sincerely say this to himself will never find life absurd.

A single definition of beauty is probably impossible, as I realized when, as a philosophy major, I studied aesthetics. Beauty is of many kinds. Man reacts differently to a sunset or a snowcapped mountain than to the Parthenon, Notre Dame de Chartres, the Taj Mahal, or a perfectly proportioned Renaissance façade. A Chinese landscape, a Giotto, or a Rembrandt has another sort of aesthetic appeal than the finest Persian rug. The impact of a Gregorian chant differs in kind from that of *Parsifal,* the *Rosenkavalier,* or *Le Sacré du Printemps.* How remote from the tragic wisdom of Hamlet's soliloquy is Francis Thompson's pure word magic:

> *. . . Spring amid her minstrelsy.*
> *There she sat amid her ladies*
> *Where the shade is*
> *Sheen as Enna mead ere Hades'*
> *Doom fell thwart Persephone.*

Yet what incomparable beauty in both!

It remained for modern America to sacrifice to greed certain supreme beauties of nature (redwoods, for example) and its own rare architectural masterpieces (the Metropolitan Opera House and the Pennsylvania Station in New York!) and to popularize an "international" or "egg-crate" style of architecture, which one German architect calls "brutalism," that reveals the atrophy of good taste. That in nature "function determines form" is no reason to substitute for past masterpieces buildings as repugnant as tree stumps. Or are we to admire human intestines because of the utility of bowel movements? Most modern architects have repudiated not merely all ornament (now an object of contempt) but pleasing proportions as well.

Even greater confusion characterizes today's plastic arts. In seeking to express not his feeling, but the abstraction of his feeling, the modern sculptor reveals only his emptiness or his inarticulate peeves. Modern art, according to Claude Lévi Strauss, presents "the manner in which the artist would execute his picture . . . if by chance he had any to paint." In my view, art either communicates or it remains mere mumbling, as abstract painting demonstrates.

Sculptor Gaudier Brzeska contends, in reply, that modern artists are continuing the tradition of primitive and barbaric peoples "for whom we have sympathy and admiration."

A comparison of genuine primitive art with that of Western imitators explodes this claim. Primitive art is never purely subjective. The primitive artist communicates meaning, aesthetic, emotional, or magical, *in a language which his fellows understand.*

Painting that is successfully produced by chimpanzees and by two-year-old children, or that can find takers when cut up and sold by the yard (as happened in Munich in 1959), has nothing in common with true barbaric art, still less with the representational masterpieces of the cave artists.

Modern music, atonal, serial, electronic, what not, developed along with, if not from, Marinetti's "noisism" (*rumorismo* in Italian) as an expression of *dissent* and of *thirst for novelty at any price.* The search for new forms, combinations, and dissonances has virtually eliminated what Shakespeare called "the true concord of well-tuned sounds, by unions married," the aim of classical composers.

A similar indifference to beauty afflicts much contemporary writing: "new" novels without plot or characters; "anti-plays" depicting "un-people" who manage to make violence and sex tedious; "modern" poetry (mostly unrhythmic prose disguised as verse) lacking in the verbal music, the word magic, and the regularity of rhythm that characterized previous masterpieces. A modern French review of poetry is appropriately entitled *La Délirante.*

Here again the lack of anything important to say and the ensuing craze for novelty are responsible. Pablo Picasso has changed his style of painting almost as often as a couturier his models and, conceivably, for much the same reason. Art in our society has become as much a matter of financial speculation as industrial stocks. Yet in undermining previous aesthetic standards, the Spaniard may, in that field, have done as much harm to the world as Adolf Hitler did in his.

One may, of course, argue that cultural iconoclasts like Picasso are less the cause than the symptoms of decadence. Luca Campiaso, a sixteenth-century Genoese, practiced cubism. The technique found no imitators until three centuries later. The early modern artistic and literary innovators were not so much prophets as symptoms of the coming Armageddons. Critic Jacques Barzun charges, I think with justification, that "the arts in the West for over a hundred years have . . . incited to immorality, revolution and nihilism . . . against everything that under the name of education the government pays for: settled habits, decent thoughts, respect for the family, obedience to law, and adherence to grammar, syntax and democratic ideals."

Unfortunately, as artists like William Butler Yeats, Anton Chekhov, and Igor Stravinsky have pointed out, experimentation is no guarantee of quality.

In any case, a reappearance of artists and writers who, repudiating the current cacophonic dirge, sought to express that beauty which is a chief reason for living would indicate that our civilization was no longer intent on suicide.

Mankind's greatest source of strength has, however, always been the belief that in some mysterious way human life has a meaning beyond all appearances. As Albert Einstein noted, "He . . . who can no longer wonder and stand rapt in awe is as good as dead."

If human beings are but accidental specks of momentary consciousness on an insignificant planet lost in an immensity of quasars and pulsars, why worry about the A-bomb? Not even the prospect of living for thousands of years, like the wilwitchita plant of Southwest Africa, can fill the gap left by unbelief.

Nor can human reason. Science can give no answer to the question put to Cratylus by Plato: if everything "flows" how can man know that which is never in the same state? Like the "men of the last days" described by St. Paul, our scientists are "ever learning and never able to come to the knowledge of the truth."

Their ever-changing postulates seem to indicate that ours is a universe about which much can be *described,* but little *understood* unless by the mixture of faith, intuition, and direct experience which we call religion. It would seem to be no accident that modern nihilism started with Nietzsche's proclamation of God's death. In my student days, Nietzsche had fascinated me. Only later did I discern the pretentious emptiness behind so many of Zarathustra's sayings.

Today I am convinced that nothing would so strengthen the West as a reconciliation with what, in one form or another, all past civilizations have identified as God (or gods). As Goethe put it, "All epochs wherein belief prevails, under what form it will, are splendid."

I am open-mouthed at the resemblance between the Biblical story of creation and the Polynesian poem cited by H. R. Hays in his book, *In the Beginnings*:

> He existed, Taaroa was his name,
>   In the immensity.
> There was no earth, there was no sky;
> There was no sea, there was no man.
>   Above, Taaroa calls.
> Existing alone, he became the universe.

That both accounts reveal a somewhat innocent anthropomorphism does not detract from the impressiveness of the coincidence.

Since my college days I have suspected that no code of morals "without obligation or sanction" can substitute for axiological realism, defined as the belief that human values are somehow *independent* of the people who formulate and pursue them, in short, inherent in something beyond man.

Hence of the three "reconciliations" here suggested that with God is most needed.

Spengler would have dismissed any talk of permanent values as illusion. History, as he saw it, provides no basic "truths" but only blood and "fate." Certainly nowhere is it written that "Faustian" culture will escape the fate of all its predecessors.

Yet against this pessimism stands the fact that almost a hundred years of cultural decay have so far touched only the top and bottom of Western society. The popularity of evangelist Billy Graham and the morale of the American fighting men in Vietnam (perhaps the highest since the Civil War) indicate that most Americans still cherish traditional beliefs. History at all times has been shaped by a few individuals. What we need, as I suggested in an essay in *A Good Time to be Alive*, are leaders equal to every occasion, men like Prince Arjuna of the Bhagavad Gita, who fought without hesitation but without hatred, and Abraham Lincoln, who unleashed a war to save the American Union. A few such might restore discipline and confidence to our badly shaken society and through their example revive in coming generations a saving sense of purpose.

The coming electronic age promises little place for cultural diversity. The cyclical birth and death of separate cultures will, I believe, give way to a worldwide, hopefully stable, civilization. For these and other reasons my faith in our future remains unshaken by the temporary chaos.

I am no mystic. Six years of efforts by an enlightened teacher failed to make me aware of what he called Universal Consciousness, roughly, the state which Romain Rolland called "direct communication with Universal life." One reason may have been that, like many other individualists, I sought to remain myself while achieving union with the "Other," a "marriage" which is impossible.

Yet no longer can I boast, with Descartes, "I think, therefore I am." Instead, with Franz von Baader, I assume that "I am, because *I am thought*" (*cogitur*). *What* thinks in me or how it can be reconciled with my belief in free will and personal responsibility, I cannot say.

Though we sometimes have glimmerings of a collective consciousness, all decisions are individual. No one is or can be his brother's keeper. Hence the final test of any society may be less the height of its civilization than the extent to which it furthers its members' salvation as individuals. Perhaps only a *failing* Roman Empire could have nourished the regenerative fervor of early Christianity. Human life is unsafe at any speed and therein lies much of its fascination.

True or false, this thought would make it easier for me to accept an *Untergang des Abendlandes*, should it occur, as a necessary step in mankind's long pilgrimage to the edge of time.

How could I complain? My own life, though marred by suffering, disappointments, and all too frequent failings, has been a fascinating adventure.

This I owe primarily to the love and encouragement of those nearest to me, my wife, family, and close friends, and to others in fifty lands whom it has been my privilege to know.

I also thank my stars for the good fortune that made me a free citizen of a literate society, and for the chance that, in an age of triumph and turmoil, made me a foreign newspaper correspondent.

To the latter I owe my experience of so many exciting places and, above all, my intimate knowledge of the world's most fascinating cities. At another time and place, say, in classical Greece, in Tang China, or medieval Persia, in Renaissance Italy, in Elizabethan England, in eighteenth-century France, or in Goethe's Weimar, literature in some form would have been my dish. But in our period of cultural waywardness, I should, as a literary critic, have become a common scold. The need to say no to most contemporary writing would have embittered my professional life.

Instead, what I, as a professional observer of the world in a period of unequalled *Sturm und Drang*, have seen and lived, fills me with quiet confidence that somewhere, somehow, some time, men and women will achieve that beauty and wisdom to which the finest among them have always aspired.

Index